APOSTOLIC HISTORY AND THE GOSPEL

FREDERICK FYVIE BRUCE

APOSTOLIC HISTORY AND THE GOSPEL

Biblical and Historical Essays

presented to

F. F. Bruce on his 60th Birthday

edited by

W. Ward Gasque

*Assistant Professor in New Testament, Regent College,
Vancouver, Canada*

and

Ralph P. Martin

*Professor of New Testament, Fuller Theological Seminary
Pasadena, California, U.S.A.*

THE PATERNOSTER PRESS

9

ISBN: 0 85364 098 x

Copyright © 1970 The Paternoster Press

AUSTRALIA:
Emu Book Agencies Pty., Ltd.,
511, Kent Street, Sydney, N.S.W.

CANADA:
Home Evangel Books Ltd.,
25, Hobson Avenue, Toronto, 1

NEW ZEALAND:
G. W. Moore, Ltd.,
3, Campbell Road, P.O. Box 24053,
Royal Oak, Auckland, 6

SOUTH AFRICA:
Oxford University Press,
P.O. Box 1141, Thibault House,
Thibault Square, Cape Town

Made and Printed in Great Britain for
The Paternoster Press Paternoster House
3 Mount Radford Crescent Exeter Devon
by Cox & Wyman Limited Fakenham

CONTENTS

PART II

EDITORS' FOREWORD

THE INTENTION TO MARK THE SIXTIETH BIRTHDAY OF F. F. BRUCE, Rylands Professor of Biblical Criticism and Exegesis in the University of Manchester, was conceived in the year 1967 when the editors were associated with that University, the one as a graduate research student, and the other as a Lecturer in New Testament Studies. *Festschriften* in honour of previous occupants of the Rylands chair and dedicated to Professors C. H. Dodd and the late T. W. Manson showed the wide esteem in which these men were held throughout the world of New Testament scholarship; and initial correspondence with a number of proposed contributors to what is now the present volume encouraged the editors to believe that in the case of the latest Rylands professor this honour would be regarded as equally deserved. This volume, written by those who are linked with F. F. Bruce by ties of scholarly interest and Christian cooperation, is now offered to a larger circle of readers who will wish to join in birthday felicitations to the recipient of this *Festschrift*.

The editors are thankful to have secured the willing assistance of both publishers on the two sides of the Atlantic, and have appreciated the ready consent of a representative team of essayists. It remains only for them to add their personal congratulations to a friendly mentor and distinguished colleague.

In multos annos!

October, 1970

W. WARD GASQUE
RALPH P. MARTIN

TABULA GRATULATORIA

A
Adamson, James B.
Agourides, Saras
Aland, Kurt
Albright, William F.
Allegro, J. M.
Allis, Oswald T.
Andersen, Howard G.
Anderson, A. A.
Anderson, G. W.
Anderson, Hugh
Anderson, J. N. D.
Andrews, John S.
Armerding, Carl E.
Atkinson, James,
Augsburger, M. S.

B
Babbage, Stuart Barton
Baird, J. Arthur
Balchin, John A.
Baldwin, Joyce G.
Barabas, Steven
Barbour, R. S.
Barker, Glenn
Barr, Allan
Barr, James
Barr, O. Sydney
Barrett, C. K.
Beasley-Murray, G. R.
Beasley-Murray, Paul
Beckwith, Roger T.
Belben, H. A. G.
Benoit, Pierre
Berkouwer, G. C.
Best, Ernest
Betz, Hans Dieter
Birdsall, J. N.
Bishop, Eric F. F.
Blackman, E. C.
Blinzler, Josef
Boice, James M.

Boobyer, G. H.
Bovan, François
Bowling, Andrew
Bowman, John
Boyd, Robert L. F.
Boyle, J. A.
Bradnock, Wilfred J.
Brandon, S. G. F.
Braun, F. M.
Bromiley, Geoffrey W.
Brown, Colin
Brown, Harold O. J.
Brown, Raymond E.
Brown, W. Gordon
Buck, Harry M.
Bultmann, R.
Buswell, J. Oliver, Jr.
Butler, B. C.

C
Caird, George B.
Cambier, J.
Cameron, W. J.
Capper, W. M.
Carey, G. L.
Carmignac, Jean
Carrez, Maurice
Catchpole, D. R.
Cave, C. H.
Cawley, F.
Chadwick, H.
Chadwick, W. O.
Clark, Gordon H.
Clements, R. E.
Clifford, Alec
Clines, D. J. A.
Coad, F. Roy
Cole, Alan
Collins, John J.
Colwell, Ernest Cadman
Cooley, Robert E.

Corbishley, Thomas
Cousins, Peter
Cowling, Geoffrey J.
Cranfield, C. E. B.
Cullmann, Oscar
Cunliffe-Jones, Hubert
Curtis, Arthur H.

D
Danker, Frederick W.
Daube, David
Davies, J. G.
Davies, J. H.
Davies, R. E.
de Jonge, M.
de la Potterie, I.
Delling, Gerhard
Denis, Albert-Marie
Descamps, A.
Dodd, C. H.
Douglas, J. D.
Drewery, Benjamin
Driver, G. R.
Duffield, Gervase E.
Dunn, James D. G.

E
Earle, Ralph
Eerdmans, Wm. B., Jr.
Ellis, D. J.
Eltester, W.
Ensworth, George
Enoch, S. Ifor
Epp, Eldon Jay
Evans, Christopher F.
Evans, Owen E.
Ewert, David

F
Farmer, William R.
Farr, George
Fascher, Erich

Feinberg, Charles Lee
Feuillet, André
Fife, J. R.
Fillinger, Robert
Finegan, Jack
Fischer, Bonifatius
Fisher, Fred L.
Fitzmyer, Joseph A.
Flemington, W. F.
Ford, A. R.
Foster, Lewis
France, R. T.
Free, Joseph P.
Friedrich, G.
Friedrichsen, G. W. S.
Friend, J. A.
Fuller, Daniel P.
Fuller, R. H.

G
Garnet, Paul
Garrard, L. A.
Gay, George A.
Geerlings, Jacob
George, A.
Gerstner, John
Geyser, A. S.
Giblin, Charles Homer
Gilmour, S. Maclean
Gingrich, F. Wilbur
Glasswell, M. E.
Goddard, Burton L.
Gooding, D. W.
Goppelt, L.
Gordon, Murdo R.
Grant, Robert M.
Grässer, Erich
Green, E. M. B.
Greenlee, J. Harold
Greeven, Heinrich
Grick, Prospero
Grundmann, Walter
Grogan, G. W.
Gryglewicz, Feliks
Guilding, Aileen
Gurney, O. R.

H
Habinski, Ron. J.
Hadidian, Dikran Y.
Hagner, Donald A.
Hahn, Ferdinand
Hambly, W. F.
Hammer, R. J.
Hanson, A.
Hanson, R. P. C.
Hanton, A.
Harder, Günther
Harpur, George E.
Harris, B. F.
Harris, M. J.
Harris, R. Laird
Harrison, E. F.
Harrison, R. K.
Harrisville, Roy A.
Hegermann, Harald
Helmbold, Andrew K.
Hemer, C. J.
Hengel, Martin
Henry, Carl F. H.
Hiebert, D. Edmond
Hilgert, Earle
Hill, David
Hillyer, Norman
Hironuma, Toshio
Hoehner, Harold W.
Holtz, T.
Hooker, M. D.
Horn, Siegfried H.
Howe, E. M.
Houston, James M.
Hughes, Philip E.
Hubbard, David A.
Hull, J. H. Eric
Hull, William E.
Hunter, A. M.
Hurd, John C., Jr.
Hyland, K. G.

J
Jellicoe, Sidney
Jewett, Paul K.
Job, John B.
Johnson, Aubrey R.

Jones, Edgar
Jones, J. L.

K
Kalland, Lloyd A.
Kaye, Bruce N.
Keck, Leander E.
Keeley, Howard R.
Kerr, William N.
Keylock, Leslie R.
Keller, Walter E.
Kenworthy, F.
Kenyon, Kathleen M.
Kerford, G. B.
Kidner, Derek
King, N. Q.
Kingdon, H. P.
Kirk, J. Andrew
Kitchen, K. A.
Klijn, A. F. J.
Kline, Meredith G.
Knox, John
Kosmala, Hans
Kraft, Robert A.
Krentz, Edgar
Kuerzinger, Josef
Kuiper, G. J.
Külling, S.
Kwiran, Manfred
Knudson, Robert D.

L
Lane, William L.
Langevin, Paul-Emile
LaSor, William Sanford
Leonard, Paul E.
Leaney, A. R. C.
Lejewski, Czeslaw
Léon-Dufour, X.
Lewis, Jack P.
Liefeld, Walter L.
Lilley, J. P. U.
Lindars, Barnabas
Lindeskog, Gösta
Loane, Marcus L.
Longenecker, Richard N.

Love, Richard L.
Lövestam, Evald
Lyonnet, Stanislas

M

McArthur, Harvey K.
McCall, Duke K.
McIntyre, James
McNair, Philip
MacRae, George W.
Manchester University
Library
Mánek, Jindrich
Marchant, G. J. C.
Marsh, John
Massaux, Ed.
Martin, Alvin
Martin, James P.
Martini, Carlo M.
Mastin, B. A.
Mayeda, Goro
Mbiti, J.
Menoud, Philippe–H.
Meye, R. P.
Michaels, J. Ramsey
Michel, Otto
Middleton, D. W.
Mikolaski, Samuel J.
Millard, Margaret L.
Mitton, C. L.
Molitor, Joseph
Montgomery, John
Warwick
Moody, Dale
Motyer, J. A.
Moule, A. W. H.
Moulton, Harold K.
Mudditt, B. Howard
Muliyil, F.
Mussner, Franz

N

Nash, Ronald H.
Neil, William
Nepper–Christensen,
Poul
Neuhäusler, E.
Nicole, Roger

Nineham, Dennis E.
Nixon, R. E.

O

O'Brien, P. T.
Ogg, George
O'Neill, J. C.
Orr, Robert W.
Osborn, E. F.
Oxley, C. A.

P

Packer, J. I.
Padilla, C. René
Pailin, David A.
Parker, Pierson
Paterson, Douglas M.
Paul, Geoffrey
Payne, J. Barton
Peck, John R.
Perkin, J. R. C.
Perry, Michael
Pesch, Michael
Pesch, Wilh.
Pfammatter, Josef
Pickering, Arnold
Pinnock, Clark H.
Piper, Otto A.
Pokorný, Petr
Pollard, N. S.
Pollard, T. E.
Pollitt, Herbert J.
Pollock, John
Porteous, Norman W.
Porter, Laurence E.
Preston, Ronald H.
Proctor, W. C. G.
Putman, Wilbert G.

Q

Quek, Swee Hwa

R

Rack, Henry D.
Ramm, Bernard
Ramsey, A. M.
Rayner, Frank A.
Rengstorf, K. H.

Renowden, C. R.
Reumann, John
Reuss, J.
Reymond, Eve A. E.
Richards, John R.
Richardson, Peter
Ridderbos, H. N.
Rigaux, B.
Robinson, D. W. B.
Robinson, William C.
Robinson, W. Gordon
Rodgers, Brian
Romaniuk, K.
Rossetter, W. F.
Rowdon, Harold H.
Rowley, H. H.
Ruffle, John
Runia, K.
Rupp, E. Gordon
Russell, E. A.
Ryrie, Charles C.

S

Sacon, Y. Herman
Sawyerr, Harry
Scharlemann, Martin
H.
Scheef, Richard L., Jr.
Schippers, R.
Schlier, Heinrich
Schneemelcher, W.
Schubert, Paul
Schwank, Benedikt
Scobie, Charles H. H.
Scott, J. Julius
Scott, Percy
Seitz, O. J. F.
Sharpe, Eric J.
Shedd, Russell P.
Shepherd, Massey H.,
Jr.
Short, Stephen S.
Siotis, Markos A.
Skemp, J. B.
Smalley, Stephen S.
Smith, D. Moody, Jr.
Smith, Terry J.
Smith, Wilbur M.

Snow, Dorothy M. Barter
Southwell, P. J. M.
Sparks, H. F. D.
Spicq, C.
Stalker, David M. G.
Stanton, G. N.
Stefaniak, Ludwik
Stewart, James S.
Stott, John R. W.
Stott, Wilfred
Strecker, Georg
Stunt, T. C. F.
Summers, Ray
Sweet, J. P. M.

T

Tabor, J. T.
Taylor, J. R.
Taylor, John B.
Taylor, Theophilus M.
Tenney, Merrill C.
Thiselton, A. C.
Thomas, D. Winton
Thompson, J. A.

Tinsley, E. J.
Torrance, Thomas F.
Trenchard, Ernest H.
Trilling, Wolfgang
Trites, A. A.
Tyndale, V. S. C.

U

Unger, Merrill F.

V

Vanhoye, Albert
van Unnik, W. C.
Vaughan, P. H.
Vielhauer, Philipp
Vos, Johannes G.

W

Wagner, Günther
Wallace, David H.
Walters, Gwyn
Ward, Arthur Marcus
Ward, R. A.
Warren, P. Derek
Warriner, Thomas C.

Weir, G. A.
Wenham, D.
Wenham, J. W.
White, Wm
Whiteley, D. E. H.
Wilcox, M.
Wilder, Amos N.
Williams, R. R.
Wilson, R. McL.
Wiseman, D. J.
Wood, A. Skevington,
Wood, J. Edwin
Wragg, Joan
Wright, J. Stafford

Y

Yamauchi, Edwin M.
Yates, John E.
Young, Fred Edward
Young, Joy

Z

Zerwick, M.
Zimmermann, Heinrich

FREDERICK FYVIE BRUCE: AN APPRECIATION

G. C. D. HOWLEY

FREDERICK FYVIE BRUCE WAS BORN IN ELGIN, MORAYSHIRE, ON 12TH October 1910. He was educated at Elgin Academy and the Universities of Aberdeen, Cambridge and Vienna. He is a Master of Arts of Aberdeen, Cambridge and Manchester Universities; and in 1957 the honorary degree of Doctor of Divinity was conferred upon him by Aberdeen University. Gold Medallist in Greek and Latin at Aberdeen, he earned several distinctions in those early years. His first post was assistant Lecturer in Greek at Edinburgh University (1935–38). He then moved to Leeds as Lecturer in Greek (1938–47). In 1947 he became Head of the new Department of Biblical History and Literature at Sheffield University, and was appointed Professor in 1955. In 1959 he was invited to accept appointment to the Rylands Chair of Biblical Criticism and Exegesis at Manchester University – in which he followed A. S. Peake, C. H. Dodd and T. W. Manson – which post he has since held.

He has given courses of lectures in the United States and Holland, as well as in Gt. Britain. He is General Editor of *The New International Commentary on the New Testament*, and Convener of the Publications Advisory Committee for the Society for Old Testament Study. He has been Examiner in Biblical studies for several British universities. His wider interests are shown by his presidency of the Yorkshire Society for Celtic Studies (1948–50), the Sheffield Branch of the Classical Association (1955–58), the Victoria Institute (1958–65), the Manchester Egyptian and Oriental Society (1963–65), and the Society for Old Testament Study (1965). He was Editor of *Yorkshire Celtic Studies* during 1945–57, and is currently Editor of the *Evangelical Quarterly* (since 1949), and the *Palestine Exploration Quarterly* (since 1957). His interest in young people is reflected by his membership of the governing bodies of Clarendon School, Abergele, North Wales; Scarisbrick Hall, Ormskirk, Lancs; Cavendish Girls' Grammar School, Buxton; and Chester College of Education.

My first encounter with F. F. Bruce was during a weekend visit I paid to Cambridge shortly after he first went there in 1932. We met at a church service in which he took some part. I had been told of the ability of this young man, and was impressed by the way in which he spoke so plainly, without introducing any "frills" whatever: his talk was within the mental range of every person attending that service. We met a number of times during those Cambridge days, each encounter confirming me in my original impression of the man.

Some years later we met again, this time in the North of England. One occasion stands out in my mind. It was at Shipley, Yorkshire, at a conference in the early days of the war. During the tea interval we had a long chat. From that time I had a strong feeling of some spiritual kinship. I later enjoyed the hospitality of his home, in Leeds and in Sheffield, and was permitted to enter into the atmosphere of the family life of Fred and Betty Bruce, with their children Iain and Sheila. The day began with family devotions after breakfast, a short Bible reading and prayer. It was in those visits that I learned to appreciate the qualities of Betty, his wife, who all through the years has shared with and been the supporter of her husband in his many-sided activities.

The table-talk at home was always stimulating. The informal asides to our table (or armchair) conversation were frequently a revelation, not only of a fertile mind but of one that was also singularly well-informed. Those visits were infrequent, though between them we might meet briefly on different occasions. And all the time one knew of his growing influence and the ever-increasing volume of his literary output, as well as the many causes that he favoured with his presence or help.

Over the years FFB has been a welcome visitor to our home. When our elder son was born, Bruce remarked – speaking as a Nonconformist – that had we been in other ecclesiastical circles, he would probably have been the boy's god-father. His visits to our home have been times that have proved full of interest and mental stimulus. It should be added also, that the Christian character of the man has shone out above the academic (not that this was not always present, it was); and the influence of a Christian scholar has been growingly appreciated in our home circle.

It is profitable to watch the workings of a man's mind. Supposing that some matter were raised over a meal with FFB, we would note that there might be a slight pause, and then, out would come some pearl, whether a piece of information, a story to cap what had been said, or some item that served to enrich the whole conversation. FFB has the scholar's capacity for remembering what he reads or hears. Nothing seems to escape him; he has an almost uncanny ability to root out a matter, and set the whole situation out in a far clearer and more comprehensive manner than we had previously known, or sometimes thought possible. His memory is phenomenal, whether about people or about things. If occasionally he needs to hunt out some reference, this is an encouragement to his weaker brethren who may not possess his special gifts!

His is a warm personality hidden behind a calm Scots exterior. His home in the North of Scotland was in an area where the priorities were right, and people knew what was of truest value in life. They made for those things rather than the more immediate but ephemeral. His parents were of sturdy stock, his father Peter Bruce serving as an evangelist for more than fifty years.

At the time of his father's death in September 1955, FFB wrote me a postcard to inform me; his father had served until the end . . . "He collapsed yesterday while conducting a funeral service", read the postcard. A letter followed in which he paid tribute to his father's influence on his life. "I shall miss him in many ways", he wrote; "I attached great value to his sound judgment, and subconsciously rather than consciously I habitually subjected what I wrote to what I knew his judgment on it would be. We had very much in common, and agreed on most matters. I was still in my teens when he taught me never to accept anything that might be offered as the mind of God unless I saw it clearly for myself in the Scriptures. This was his own policy, and he maintained his intellectual flexibility in accordance with it to the end of his days."

"Intellectual flexibility" is the characteristic of the son as well as the father. One is impressed by the complete intellectual integrity of FFB. He faces the challenges of life and work, comes to terms with them and proceeds quietly and steadfastly towards his goal. This goal is not mere ambition, but the fulfilment of his work, because he regards his career as God's call for his life, and gives himself to his work accordingly. Coupled with integrity is the quality of a genuine humility: a feature of his life of which he is unaware, but which hits those who know him – hard enough at times to challenge them to a like spirit.

His mind has the sometimes rare quality of Christian sanity. There is the balance that can see another point of view. This can be illustrated by a letter he wrote to a correspondent who differed from him on a point of interpretation: "I see that we differ on Acts 20:11 – well, it would be a dull world if we always saw eye to eye, and I have long since learned to say to myself when I differ from one of my brethren: 'The other fellow may be right!'" It is this admixture of independence and deference that helps to make him the lovable person he is. He retains his complete independence, and will not be swayed either by emotional or sentimental judgments; yet there is always a simple deference to the opinions of others, so that there is seldom a clash, even where there are differences of outlook.

This esteem for others reaches right down to the youngest undergraduate or to any youthful member of one of the numerous house-parties for young people at which he and his wife have acted as house-parents. Often I have watched him deep in conversation with some young man who has asked for counsel in some matter. Equally often he could be seen in the part of listener, giving undivided attention to someone unburdening himself of some problem. One cannot begin to imagine the number of authors who have approached him requesting that he read a manuscript they have written. Some of them have been unknown authors, while others have been accomplished scholars. It is all one to FFB. If able to do so, he has accepted the task of going through papers and giving his comments upon them. The forewords he has written are legion, some of them among the best parts of the MSS concerned!

His literary output has been phenomenal. His numerous publications have behind them such a wealth of research; one feels that, whenever necessary, special work has been done for shorter articles in journals, as excellent in quality as the greater amount of work required for some major volume, such as his commentaries on The Acts of the Apostles or the Epistles to the Romans or to the Hebrews. His mastery of the biblical and historical data, not to say scholarly opinion, is widely recognized, and his writings are all models of sound judgment and lucid exposition as well as scholarship. My own experience has been that, time and again over many years, something he has stated or written has opened a new window in the mind, and I have explored the territory thus exposed, to my own lasting profit – and, I hope, the profit of others.

Honours have come his way. The oration delivered by the Promoter in Divinity of Aberdeen University when FFB was made an honorary Doctor of Divinity, stated that, of all its sons who had entered into a similar career, he had brought more honour to his *alma mater* than any other person during the preceding fifty years. There is a different kind of honour, however, that FFB would value more than academic distinctions conferred upon him. It is the honour of trust and confidence that is coupled with affection for someone who is not only an outstanding scholar, but a true man of God, and a true friend. Some men are like rock, in the way they help others towards maturity of mind and stability of character. Bruce is one such; for he has helped more people to such a level of thought and life than his most intimate friends can ever know.

He has been a pioneer in Christian scholarship from whom many have learned and have been set on the road through his encouragement. His influence in the sphere of the Inter-Varsity Fellowship has been far-reaching, and has had the effect of stimulating Evangelical scholarship throughout the world. He has, moreover, been a bridge-builder between people of very different schools of thought. His friendships are most catholic in their nature, embracing scholars, ministers, missionaries and prominent Christian laymen, along with more ordinary individuals.

The letters of FFB are always kept and filed. I have gone over a large number of them ranging over at least twenty-five years, and it has been a rewarding experience to read them again. One that is dated August 24, 1965, begins: "There are some dates that stick in my memory. Today is 50 years precisely since I first went to school (it was a Tuesday as well as being 24th August), and I have been there ever since!" It is often said that the finest teacher is the person who remains a learner; and FFB is ready to learn from all sides, never despising a detail of information that he might hitherto have missed.

His church loyalty has brought him into prominence in his local church.

He has exercised the responsibility of leadership over many years; and his annual series of winter lectures, delivered in the church building, has attracted people of all walks of life and many denominations.

FFB has never owned a car; he is just not interested in driving, though he would like Betty to get one if she so desires. "Our main need for a car", he says, "is when we have visitors, so that we can show them the beautiful scenery that lies so close to Buxton." And that's that. He told me once that he would not mind where he lived, so long as he could pursue his work. He is an example of a person who sits lightly to material things, the things of mind and spirit having first place; and yet, at the same time, the practical requirements of life are never overlooked, as those who have entertained him will know when it comes to washing up after meals! Letters tell of his constant work. Yet he is never too busy to give counsel or information if requested to do so. And letters to him receive a reply with the utmost speed. They never disappoint; answers are always available, and they leave no corner of a matter untouched.

At his sixtieth birthday, and the presentation of this *Festschrift*, his friends join together in conveying to Fred and Betty Bruce every possible good wish for future days. And judging by past years, they will be days of study, exploration into the highways and byways of scholarly research, literary work, travel, lecturing, and the routine matters that come to all, along with his constant ministry of caring for other people, taking an interest in their needs and problems, helping people along the way of life. A good life indeed, for any man or woman.

A Select Bibliography of the Writings of F. F Bruce

Compiled by W. Ward Gasque

1933

"The Early Church in the Roman Empire," *The Bible Student* (Bangalore, India), No. 56 (March–April 1933), pp. 30–32; No. 57 (May–June 1933), pp. 55–58.

1934

"The Chester Beatty Papyri," *The Harvester* 11 (1934), pp. 163, 164.

1935

"The New Gospel," *The Harvester* 12 (1935), pp. 168–70.

1936

"Latin Participles as Slave-Names," *Glotta* 25 (1936), pp. 42–50.

"Early Translations of the Bible," *The Harvester*, a series of essays beginning May 1936 and continuing through November 1938.

1938

"The Earliest Latin Commentary on the Apocalypse," *The Evangelical Quarterly* 10 (1938), pp. 352–66.

"Some Roman Slave-Names," *Proceedings of the Leeds Philosophical Society: Literary and Historical Section* 5 (1938), part I, pp. 44–60.

1939

"The Ascension in the Fourth Gospel," *ExpT* 50 (1938/39), p. 478.

"Old Testament Criticism and Modern Discovery," *The Believer's Magazine* 49 (1939), pp. 242, 243.

1940

"The Date of the Epistle to the Galatians," *ExpT* 51 (1939–40), pp. 396–97.

"The End of the First Gospel," *The Evangelical Quarterly* 12 (1940), pp. 203–14.

1941

"Babylon and Rome," *The Evangelical Quarterly* 13 (1941), pp. 241–61.

1942

"Some Aspects of Gospel Introduction," *The Evangelical Quarterly* 14 (1942), pp. 174–97, 264–80; *ibid.*, 15 (1943), pp. 3–20.

1943

Are the New Testament Documents Reliable? London: The Inter-Varsity Fellowship, 1943. Pp. 118. 2nd ed. 1946. Repr. 1948. 3rd ed. 1950. *The New Testament Documents: Are They Reliable?*) 1960. Pp. 120. Repr. 1961 and 1963 (with bibliography and indices). Pp. 128. Repr. 1965, 1966 and 1968. Grand Rapids: William B. Eerdmans Publishing Company, 1945. Pp. 122. 1960, Pp. 120, 1963, Pp. 128.

German ed. 1953. Spanish ed. 1957. Japanese ed. 1959. Korean ed. 1966. Portuguese ed. 1968. Swedish ed. 1969.

The Speeches in the Acts of the Apostles. (Tyndale New Testament Lecture, 1942.) London: The Tyndale Press, 1943. Pp. 27.

Editor: D. M. McIntyre, *Some Notes on the Gospels.* London: The Inter-Varsity Fellowship, 1943. Pp. 51.

"The Kingdom of God: A Biblical Survey," *The Evangelical Quarterly* 15 (1943), pp. 263–68.

"The Ministry of Women,' *Supplement to the I.V.F. Graduates' Fellowship News-Letter,* No. 9 (April, 1943).

"The Sources of the Gospels," *Journal of the Transactions of the Victoria Institute* 75 (1943), pp. 1–11.

1944

"Aramaic in the Early Church," *Theological Notes* (January 1944), pp. 1–2; "Jesus in the Gospels," *ibid.*, pp. 2–3; "The Church in the New Testament," *ibid.*, pp. 3–4. N.B. *Theological Notes* was published by the Inter-Varsity Fellowship; it was incorporated into *The Tyndale Bulletin* (old series) in 1945, and this, in turn, was incorporated into *The Christian Graduate* in 1948.

"Christology," *Theological Notes* (July and October 1944), pp. 2–3; "Eschatology and Apocalyptic," *ibid.*, pp. 3–5; "True and False Criticism," *ibid.*, pp. 5–7.

"Some Notes on the Fourth Evangelist," *The Evangelical Quarterly* 16 (1944), pp. 101–9.

1945

"Did Jesus Speak Aramaic?" *ExpT* 56 (1944–45), p. 328.

"The End of the Second Gospel," *The Evangelical Quarterly* 17 (1945), pp. 169–81.

"The Gospels and the Apostolic Preaching," *The Bible Expositor* (New Zealand) 1 (1945), pp. 64–69, 115–21, 173–77; 2 (1946), pp. 17–23, 95–104, 142–52; 3 (1947), pp. 42–52, 94–104.

"Review of Some Biblical Studies in 1944," *The Tyndale Bulletin* (old series), (January 1945), pp. 2–7.

1946

"'And the Earth was without form and void' – An Enquiry into the Exact Meaning of Genesis 1, 2," *Journal of the Transactions of the Victoria Institute* 78 (1946), pp. 21–24.

"Marius Victorinus and His Works," *The Evangelical Quarterly* 18 (1946), pp. 132–53.

"Notes on the Aramaic Background of the Gospel Text," *The Tyndale Bulletin* (old series) (January 1946), pp. 5–7; (April 1946), p. 2; (July 1946), p. 5; (January 1947), pp. 1–2; (July 1947), pp. 1–2; (January 1948), pp. 2–4.

"The Second Coming of Christ," *Supplement to the I.V.F. Graduates' Fellowship News-Letter,* No. 17 (January, 1946).

"What do We Mean by Inspiration?," *Journal of the Transactions of the Victoria Institute* 78 (1946), pp. 121–28.

1947

Archaeology and the New Testament. London: Church Book Room Press, 1947. Pp. 24.

"The Four Gospels and Acts," in *The New Bible Handbook,* ed. G. T. Manley (London: The Inter-Varsity Fellowship, 1947), pp. 319–50.

"John Nelson Darby," *The Harvester* 24 (1947), pp. 6, 7.

"The Tyndale Fellowship for Biblical Research," *The Evangelical Quarterly* 19 (1947), pp. 52–61.

1948

The Hittites and the Old Testament. (Tyndale Old Testament Lecture, 1947). London: The Tyndale Press, 1948. Pp. 28.

"Biblical Criticism," *The Christian Graduate* 1 (1948), no. 2, pp. 5–9.

"Bishop Barnes and the Rise of Christianity," *Science and Religion* (April–June 1948).

"The Crooked Serpent," *The Evangelical Quarterly* 20 (1948), pp. 283–88.

"The Origin of the Alphabet," *Journal of the Transactions of the Victoria Institute* 80 (1948), pp. 1–10.

"Studies in Old Testament Introduction," *The Christian Graduate* 1 (1948), no. 1, pp. 15–16; no. 2, pp. 18–19; no. 3, pp. 16–17; no. 4, pp. 21–22; 2 (1949), pp. 53–55, 89–90, 117–20; 3 (1950), pp. 25–26.

1949

"Appendix I. The Geography of Palestine," in *The New Bible Handbook,* 2nd ed. (London: The Inter-Varsity Fellowship, 1949), pp. 425–27.

"Church History and Its Lessons," in *The Church: A symposium,* ed. J. B. Watson (London: Pickering & Inglis Ltd., 1949), pp. 178–95. Also, "Appendix. Note 12. The Council of Jerusalem", *ibid.,* pp. 219–20.

"The Judgment Seat of Christ," *The Bible Expositor* 5 (1949), pp. 66–68.

"The Living Christ," *The Witness* 79 (April 1949), pp. 37–39.

"The Period between the Testaments," *The Bible Student* (January and April, 1949).

1950

The Books and the Parchments: Some Chapters on the Transmission of the Bible. London: Pickering & Inglis Ltd., 1950. Pp. 259+plates. 2nd ed. 1953. 3rd and rev. ed. 1963. Pp. 287+plates. Westwood, N. J.: Fleming H. Revell, 1955. Pp. 259+plates. Rev. ed. 1963. Pp. 287+plates.

The Dawn of Christianity. London: The Paternoster Press, 1950. Pp. 191. Repr. 1954. Japanese ed. 1961. Hindi ed. 1969.

"Daniel's First Verse," *The Christian Graduate* 3 (1950), pp. 81–84.

"The Dead Sea Scrolls," *The Witness* 80 (April 1950), p. 62.

"Recent Discoveries in Biblical Manuscripts," *Journal of the Transactions of the Victoria Institute* 82 (1950), pp. 131–44.

"Recent Literature on the Book of Daniel," *The Bible Expositor* 6 (1950), pp. 46–52.

1951

The Acts of the Apostles: The Greek Text with Introduction and Commentary. London: The Tyndale Press, 1951. Pp. vii+491. 2nd ed. 1952. Pp. xx+491. Repr. 1953,

1956, 1962 and 1965. Grand Rapids: William B. Eerdmans Publishing Company, 1951. Pp. vii + 491. 2nd ed. 1952. Pp. xx + 491.

The Growing Day: The Progress of Christianity from the Fall of Jerusalem to the Accession of Constantine, A.D. 70–313. London: The Paternoster Press, 1951. Pp. 192.

"The Ecclesiastical Writings of the New Testament" [twelve articles], *The Life of Faith* (April–July, 1951).

"Recent Studies in Old Testament Introduction," *The Bible Expositor* 7 (1951/52), pp. 90–98.

"Sir William Mitchell Ramsay: A Centenary Tribute," *The Christian* (9 March, 1951).

"The Wisdom Literature of the Bible," *The Bible Student* (January 1951–October 1952).

"W. E. Vine: The Theologian," in *W. E. Vine: His Life and Ministry*, by P. O. Ruoff (London: Oliphants, 1951), pp. 69–85.

1952

Light in the West: The Progress of Christianity from the Accession of Constantine to the Conversion of the English. London: The Paternoster Press, 1952. Pp. 160.

"Answers to Questions," a monthly feature of *The Harvester*, beginning with volume 31 (July 1952) and continuing to the present.

"Archaeology and the New Testament," *The Bible Expositor* 7 (1951/52), pp. 245–56.

"Interpreting the Bible," *The Senior Teacher's Magazine* 5 (1952), pp. 3–4, 20–1, 35–36, 51–52, 67–68, 83–84, 99–100, 115–16, 132–33, 147–48, 163–64, 179–80.

"Justification by Faith in the Non-Pauline Writings of the New Testament," *The Evangelical Quarterly* 24 (1952), pp. 66–77.

"The Scriptures," in *The Faith: A Symposium*, ed. F. A. Tatford (London: Pickering & Inglis Ltd., 1952), pp. 13–26.

"Sir Frederic George Kenyon . . . 1863–1951," *Journal of the Transactions of the Victoria Institute* 84 (1952), pp. xv–xvii.

1953

The Spreading Flame: The Rise and Progress of Christianity from its First Beginnings to the Conversion of the English. (Vol. 1 of The Advance of Christianity through the Centuries = The Paternoster Church History.) Grand Rapids: William B. Eerdmans Publishing Company, 1953. Pp. 191+192+160. Repr. 1958, 1961, 1964. Rev. Ed. 1966. London: The Paternoster Press, 1958. Pp. 432. Repr. 1961 and 1964. Rev. ed. 1966.

[Replacing *The Dawn of Christianity*, *The Growing Day*, and *Light in the West*.]

"The Apostolic Witness," *The Witness* 83 (December 1953), pp. 209, 212.

"An Expository Study of St. John's Gospel", *The Bible Student* 24 (1953); 25 (1954); 26 (1955); 27 (1956); 28 (1957); 29 (1958); 30 (1959).

"New Bible Translations: A Short Survey," *Inter-Varsity* (Autumn 1953), pp. 15–19.

"The Old Testament in Greek," *The Bible Translator* 4 (1953), pp. 129–35, 156–62. [An excerpt from *The Books and the Parchments*.]

"The Poetry of the Old Testament," "The Wisdom Literature of the Old

Testament" [with F. Davidson], "The Fourfold Gospel," "Judges," "The Acts of the Apostles," "I and II Thessalonians," in *The New Bible Commentary*, ed. F. Davidson (London: The Inter-Varsity Fellowship, 1953; Grand Rapids, 1953. Rev. ed. 1954. Repr. many times.)

1954

Commentary on the Book of the Acts: The English Text with Introduction, Exposition, and Notes. (The New International Commentary on the New Testament – The New London Commentary on the New Testament.) Grand Rapids: William B. Eerdmans Publishing Company, 1954. Pp. 555. London: Marshall, Morgan & Scott, 1954. Pp. 555. Repr. 1956 (twice) and 1962. Japanese ed. 1958.

The Sure Mercies of David: A Study of the Fulfilment of Messianic Prophecy. (The Annual Lecture of The Evangelical Library for 1954.) London: The Evangelical Library, 1954. Pp. 23.

"A British Scholar Looks at the RSV Old Testament," *Eternity* (May 1954).

"The Canon of Scripture," *Inter-Varsity* (Autumn 1954), pp. 19–22.

"Isaiah's Virgin Oracle," *The Reformed Journal* 4 (1954), pp. 5–7.

"Religious Education: Bible Teaching in the Faculty of Arts," *ExpT* 65 (1953/54), pp. 306–7.

"The Victoria Institute and the Bible," *Journal of the Transactions of the Victoria Institute* 86 (1954), pp. 75–81.

1955

The Christian Approach to the Old Testament. London: The Inter-Varsity Fellowship, 1955. Pp. 20. 2nd ed. 1959. Pp. 20.

"The Bible and Evangelism," *The Methodist Recorder* (31 March, 7 and 14 April 1955).

"Census" and "Peter the Apostle," in *Twentieth Century Encyclopedia of Religious Knowledge*, 2 vols., ed. L. A. Loetscher (Grand Rapids: Baker Book House, 1955).

"Exposition of the Epistle of Jude," *Knowing the Scriptures* 11 (1955), pp. 7–9, 20–22, 31–33, 43–45, 55–57, 67–68.

"J. B. Watson: His Writings," *The Witness* 85 (October 1955), p. 199.

"The Planting of Churches," *The Witness* 85 (June 1955), pp. 113–14.

"Qumrân and Early Christianity," *NTS* 2 (1955/56), pp. 176–90.

"Trends in New Testament Interpretation," *Journal of the Transactions of the Victoria Institute* 87 (1955), pp. 37–48.

1956

Second Thoughts on the Dead Sea Scrolls. London: The Paternoster Press, 1956. Pp. 144. 2nd ed. 1961. Pp. 160. 3rd ed. 1966. Pp. 160. Grand Rapids: William B. Eerdmans Publishing Company, 1956. Pp. 144.
German ed. 1957.

"The Bible: Book of the Month: The Acts of the Apostles," *Christianity Today* 1, 5 (December 1956), pp. 18–19.

"Exposition of the Epistle to the Ephesians," *Knowing the Scriptures* 11 (1955/57), pp. 81–83, 91–93, 104–6, 116–19, 129–32, 140–43, 151–3, 152–5, 176–9, 189–92; continued after *Knowing the Scriptures* ceased publication in *The Believer's Magazine* 68 (1958)–69 (1959).

"The Greek Language and the Christian Ministry," *Clifton Theological College Magazine* (Trinity Term 1956), pp. 5–10.
"Modern Scribes on the Judean Scrolls," *Christianity Today* 1, 11 (4 March 1956), pp. 5–7.
"A Second Look at the Dead Sea Scrolls," *Eternity* (October 1956).
"Some Implications of the Dead Sea Scrolls," *The Christian Graduate* 9 (1956), pp. 127–8.
"Textual Criticism," *The Christian Graduate* 6 (1956), pp. 135–9.

1957

Commentary on the Epistles to the Ephesians and the Colossians. With E. K. Simpson. [Bruce writes on Colossians.] (The New International Commentary on the New Testament – The New London Commentary on the New Testament.) Grand Rapids: William B. Eerdmans Publishing Company, 1957. Pp. 159–328. London: Marshall, Morgan & Scott, 1957.
New Horizons in Biblical Studies. (Inaugural Lecture, 27 February 1957.) Sheffield: The University of Sheffield, 1957. Pp. 18.
The Teacher of Righteousness in the Qumran Texts. (Tyndale Lecture in Biblical Archaeology, 1956.) London: The Tyndale Press, 1957. Pp. 36.
"The Apocrypha, Revised and Introduced," *Eternity* (November 1957).
"Biblical Jerusalem," *University of Leeds Review* 5 (1957), pp. 290–99.
"Chronicle: Recent Literature on Qumran," *Terminal Letter of the Theological Students' Fellowship* (Summer 1957), pp. 6–8.
"Minister of the Word of God [Harold St. John]," *The Witness* 82 (July 1957), pp. 143–4.

1958

"Archaeological Confirmation of the New Testament," in *Revelation and the Bible*, ed. C. F. H. Henry (Grand Rapids: Baker Book House, 1958; London: The Tyndale Press, 1959), pp. 317–31.
"The Dead Sea Habakkuk Scroll," *The Annual of Leeds University Oriental Society* 1 (1958/59), pp. 5–24.
"Eschatology," *London Quarterly and Holborn Review* (1958), pp. 99–103.
"The Fourth Gospel in Recent Interpretation," *Terminal Letter of the TSF* (Spring 1958), pp. 2–6. Also contained in *A Symposium from Past Terminal Letters* (1960), pp. 11–14.
"George Henry Lang: Author and Teacher, 1874–1958," *The Witness* 88 (December 1958), pp. 253–4.
"Qumran and the New Testament," *Faith and Thought* 90 (1958), pp. 92–102.

1959

Antichrist in the Early Church. Blackburn: Durham & Sons Ltd., 1959. Pp. 27.
Biblical Exegesis in the Qumran Texts. (*Exegetica* 3, 1.) The Hague: van Keulen, 1959. Pp. 84. Rev. ed., Grand Rapids: William B. Eerdmans Publishing Company, 1959. Pp. 88. London: The Tyndale Press, 1960. Pp. 88.
The Defence of the Gospel in the New Testament. (Calvin Foundation Lectures, 1958.) Grand Rapids: William B. Eerdmans Publishing Company, 1959. Pp. 105. Repr. 1965 and 1968.
Published in the U.K. under the title: *The Apostolic Defence of the Gospel: Christian*

Apologetic in the New Testament. London: The Inter-Varsity Fellowship, 1959. Pp. 96. Repr. 1961. 2nd ed. 1967. Pp. 96. Spanish ed. 1961.

"A Century of Conservative Criticism," *The Christian,* Centenary Commemoration Issue (July 1959).

"Bible Book of the Month: Jude," *Christianity Today* 3, 17 (25 May 1959), pp. 34–35.

"Biblical Archaeology," in *The Bible Companion,* ed. by W. Neil (London: Skeffington & Son Ltd., 1959), pp. 29–49.

"Erich Sauer," *The Witness* 89 (April 1959), p. 79.

"Qumran and the Old Testament," *Faith and Thought* 91 (1959), pp. 9–27.

"The True Apostolic Succession: Recent Study of the Book of Acts," *Interp* 13 (1959), pp. 131–43.

1960

"As Originally Given," *Terminal Letter of the TSF* (Spring 1956), pp. 2–3. Also contained in *A Symposium from Past Terminal Letters* (1960), pp. 7–8.

"Criticism and Faith," *Christianity Today* 5 (1960/61), pp. 145–8.

"Dead Sea Scrolls," "Eschatology," "Form Criticism," "Fulness," "Interpretation (Biblical)", "Will-worship," in *Baker's Dictionary of Theology,* ed. E. F. Harrison (Grand Rapids: Baker Book House, 1960).

"The Gospels," in *The Biblical Expositor,* ed. C. F. H. Henry (Philadelphia: A. J. Holman Company, 1960) 3, pp. 15–22.

"Recent New Testament Studies," *Christianity Today* 4 (1959/60), pp. 397–400.

"The Scottish Reformation, 1560–1960," *The Witness* 90 (October 1960), pp. 366–7.

"The Son of Man Came," *The Harvester* 39 (April 1960), pp. 54–55.

1961

The English Bible: A History of Translations. London: Lutterworth Press, 1961. Pp. xiv+234. New York: Oxford University Press, 1961. Pp. xiv+234. Repr. London: Methuen/University Paperbacks, 1963. Rev. ed. 1970.

The Epistle to the Ephesians: A Verse-by-Verse Exposition. London: Pickering & Inglis Ltd., 1961. Pp. 140. 2nd ed. 1968. Pp. 140. Westwood, N. J.: Fleming H. Revell, 1962. Pp. 140. 2nd ed. 1968. Pp. 140.

"The Authorized Version and Others," *The International Review of Missions* 50 (1961), pp. 409–16.

"The Book of Zechariah and the Passion Narrative," *BJRL* 43 (1960/61), pp. 336–53. [*Note:* All of Bruce's Rylands Lectures were also printed in booklet form.]

"The Dead Sea Scrolls," *The Modern Churchman* N.S. 4 (1961), pp. 45–54.

"The Gospel of Thomas," *Faith and Thought* 92 (1961), pp. 3–23.

"New Testament Studies in 1960," *Christianity Today* 5 (1960/61), pp. 388–90.

"The New English Bible," *Christianity Today* 5 (1960/61), pp. 493–96.

"The New English Bible," *Faith and Thought* 92 (1961), pp. 47–53.

"The Person of Christ: Incarnation and Virgin Birth," *Christianity Today* 6 (1961/62), pp. 30–31. Also contained in *Basic Christian Doctrines,* ed. C. F. H. Henry (New York: Holt, Rinehardt & Winston, 1962), pp. 124–30.

"The Transfiguration," *Inter-Varsity* (Summer 1961), pp. 19–21.

"Who are the brethren?" *The Witness* 91 (November 1961), pp. 406–7. [Repr. as pamphlet by Pickering & Inglis Ltd.]

1962

Paul and His Converts: 1 and 2 Thessalonians, 1 and 2 Corinthians. (Bible Guides, 17.) London: Lutterworth Press, 1962. Pp. 87. Repr. 1965. Nashville and New York: Abingdon Press, 1962. Pp. 87.

"Abilene," "Acts," "Ananias," "Araunah," "Areopagus," "Asiarch," "Assassins," "Babylon (N.T.)," "Barak," "Bar-Jesus," "Beast (Apocalyptic)," "Bible," "Biblical Criticism," "Book of Life," "Calendar (sections 2 and 3)," "Cananaean," "Census," "Chamberlain," "Chenoboskion," "Claudius Lysias," "Coelesyria," "Cornelius," "Corruption," "Council (Jerusalem)," "Covenant (Book of)," "Dalmanutha," "Dan," "Dead Sea Scrolls," "Deborah," "Deputy," "Derbe," "Easter," "Egyptian," "Epaphras," "Essenes," "Galatians," "Genealogy of Jesus Christ," "Gospels," "Hebron," "Herod," Herodias," "Hittites," "Hour," "Interpretation (Biblical)," "Israel," "Israel of God," "Jerahmeel," "John the Baptist," "Josephus," "Jude (Epistle of)," "Kiriath-arba,""Lycaonia,""Lysanias,""Machaerus,""Mamre," "Melchizedek," "Mene Mene Tekel Upharsin," "Meroz," "Messiah in New Testament," "Proconsul," "Procurator," "Rahab," "Rufus," "Salt, City of," "Sapphira," "Suburb," "Synagogues," "Tahtim-hodshi," "Theophilus," "Thessalonians (Epistles to)," "Theudas," "Unknown God," "Zadok," "Zealot," in *The New Bible Dictionary*, ed. J. D. Douglas *et al.* (London: The Inter-Varsity Fellowship, 1962; Grand Rapids: William B. Eerdmans Publishing Company, 1962). [Bruce was one of four Consulting Editors.]

"Acceptance," "Access," "Comfort," "Consolation," "Conversation," "Corruption," "Deny," "Gift, Giving," "Mark (Goal, Sign)," "New, Newness," "Seeing," "Tribulation," "Trinity," "Vain," in *The Interpreter's Dictionary of the Bible*, 4 vols., ed. G. A. Buttrick *et al.* (New York and Nashville: Abingdon Press, 1962).

"Aeneas," "Ägypter," "Damaris," "Dionysius," "Eutychus," in *Biblisch-Historisches Handwörterbuch* 1, ed. Bo Reicke and Leonhard Rost (Göttingen: Vanden- & Ruprecht, 1962).

"Christianity under Claudius," *BJRL* 44 (1961/62), pp. 309–26.

"Diversity of Gifts," *The Student World* 55 (1962), pp. 19–28.

"The Epistles of Paul" and "Hebrews" (commentary), in *Peake's Commentary on the Bible*, rev. ed., ed. M. Black and H. H. Rowley (London: Thomas Nelson & Sons Ltd., 1962).

"The Gospels and Some Recent Discoveries," *Faith and Thought* 92 (1962), pp. 149–67. [The First Rendle Short Memorial Lecture. Delivered in the University of Bristol on 2 March 1962.]

"New Light from the Dead Sea Scrolls," *Holman Study Bible* [RSV] (Philadelphia: A. J. Holman Company, 1962), pp. 1171–83.

"New Testament Studies in 1961," *Christianity Today* 6 (1961/62), pp. 406–8.

"Preparation in the Wilderness: At Qumran and in the New Testament," *Interp* 16 (1962), pp. 280–91.

1963

The Epistle of Paul to the Romans: An Introduction and Commentary. (Tyndale New Testament Commentaries.) London: The Tyndale Press, 1963. Pp. 288. Repr. 1963, 1966 and 1967. Grand Rapids: William B. Eerdmans Publishing Company, 1963. Pp. 288.

Israel and the Nations from the Exodus to the Fall of the Second Temple. Exeter: The

Paternoster Press, 1963. Pp. 254. Repr. 1965 and 1968. Illus. ed. 1969. Pp. 254+
Plates I-XIII and 3 maps. Grand Rapids: William B. Eerdmans Publishing Company, 1963. Pp. 254. Dutch ed. 1967.
Editor: *Promise and Fulfilment*. (Essays presented to Professor S. H. Hooke.) Edinburgh: T. & T. Clark, 1963. Pp. vii+217.
"Altar," "Ashdod," "Ashkelon," "Azekah," "Carmel," "Dog," "Dragon," "Dreams," "Ethics," "Gezer," "Hittites," "Idolatry," "Image," "Makkedah," "Shittim," "Siddim, Vale of," "Tabor, Mount," in *Dictionary of the Bible*, ed. James Hastings, rev. ed., ed. F. C. Grant and H. H. Rowley (Edinburgh: T. & T. Clark, 1963; New York: Charles Scribner's Sons, 1963). [Some articles only slightly revised; others re-written.]
"Bible [a survey of biblical studies 1962]," *Eternity* (January 1963).
"The History and Doctrine of the Apostolic Age," in *A Companion to the Bible*, rev. ed., ed. H. H. Rowley (Edinburgh: T. & T. Clark, 1963), pp. 495–522.
"New Testament," in *Zondervan Pictorial Bible Dictionary*, ed. M. C. Tenney (Grand Rapids: Zondervan Publishing House, 1963).
"'Our God and Saviour': A Recurring Biblical Pattern," in *The Saviour God* (Essays presented to Professor E. O. James), ed. S. G. F. Brandon (Manchester: Manchester University Press, 1963), pp. 51–66.
"Promise and Fulfilment in Paul's Presentation of Jesus," in *Promise and Fulfilment*, ed. F. F. Bruce (Edinburgh: T. & T. Clark, 1963), pp. 36–50.
"Recent Studies in the Epistle to the Romans," *TSF Bulletin* 35 (Spring 1963), pp. 8–10.
"Survey of New Testament Literature," *Christianity Today* 7 (1962/63), pp. 412–14.
"'To the Hebrews' or 'To the Essenes'?" *NTS* 9 (1962/63), pp. 217–32.
"When is a Gospel not a Gospel?" *BJRL* 45 (1962/63), pp. 319–39.

1964

Commentary on the Epistle to the Hebrews. (New International Commentary on the New Testament—New London Commentary on the New Testament.) Grand Rapids: William B. Eerdmans Publishing Company, 1964. Pp. lxiv+447. London: Marshall, Morgan & Scott, 1964. Pp. lxiv+447.
"The Baptism of the Spirit," *Calling* (Vancouver, B.C., Canada) (Fall 1964), pp. 7–9; also contained in *The Witness* 95 (July 1965), pp. 247–9.
"The Church of Jerusalem," *The Journal of the Christian Brethren Research Fellowship* 4 (April 1964), pp. 5–14.
"The Easter Event," *Christianity Today* 8 (1963/64), pp. 578–80.
"History and the Gospel," *Faith and Thought* 93 (1964), pp. 121–45; rev. ed. in *Jesus of Nazareth: Saviour and Lord*, ed. C. F. H. Henry (Grand Rapids: William B. Eerdmans Publishing Company, 1966; London: The Tyndale Press, 1966), pp. 89–107.
"Julius" and "Lasäa," in *Biblisch-Historisches Handwörterbuch* 2.
"New Testament Studies: 1963," *Christianity Today* 8 (1963/64), pp. 439–41.
"One Faith," in *Christian Unity* (Bristol: Evangelical Christian Literature, 1964), pp. 47–57.
"St. Paul in Rome," *BJRL* 46 (1963/64), pp. 326–45.

1965

Expanded Paraphrase of the Epistles of Paul. Exeter: The Paternoster Press, 1965. Pp. 323. American edition: *The Epistles of Paul: An Expanded Paraphrase.* Grand Rapids: William B. Eerdmans Publishing Company, 1965. Pp. 323. [Appeared originally in *The Evangelical Quarterly*, 1957–1964.]

"Herod Antipas, Tetrarch of Galilee and Peraea," *The Annual of Leeds University Oriental Society* 5 (1963/65), pp. 6–23.

"John the Forerunner," *Faith and Thought* 94 (1965), pp. 182–90.

"Josephus and Daniel," *Annual of the Swedish Theological Institute* 4 (1965), pp. 148–62. [Presidential address to the Society for Old Testament Study, London, January 1965.]

"New Testament Studies in 1964," *Christianity Today* 9 (1964/65), pp. 485–87.

"St. Paul in Rome: 2. The Epistle to Philemon," *BJRL* 48 (1965/66), pp. 81–97.

"Tribute to the Rev. Professor A. Guillaume," *The Annual of Leeds University Oriental Society* 5 (1963/65), pp. 4–5.

"Unity in the New Testament," *Northern Baptist College Magazine* 1 (1965), pp. 28–31.

1966

"Agrapha," "American Standard Version," "Annunciation, The," "Ascension, The", "Beatitudes, The", "Bible", "Biblical Criticism," "Bishops' Bible," "Codex," "Crucifixion," "Douay Bible," "Epiphany, The", "Exegesis", "Golden Rule, The," "Great Bible," "Gutenberg or Mazarin Bible," "Higher Criticism," "King James Version," "Last Supper, The," "Lord's Prayer," "New English Bible," "Parables of Jesus, The," "Polyglot Bibles," "Pseudepigrapha," "Resurrection of Christ, The," "Revised Standard Version," "Revised Version," "Sermon on the Mount," "Synoptic Gospels," "Textual Criticism or Lower Criticism," "Transfiguration, The," "Widow's Mite, The," in *Encyclopedia International*, 20 vols. (New York: Grolier, 1966).

"Charles Harold Dodd," in *Creative Minds in Modern Theology*, ed. P. E. Hughes (Grand Rapids: William B. Eerdmans Publishing Company, 1966), pp. 239–69.

"The Dead Sea Scrolls and Early Christianity," *BJRL* 49 (1966/67), pp. 69–90.

"Jesus and Paul," *TSF Bulletin* 46 (Autumn 1966), pp. 21–26.

"Johannine Studies since Westcott's Day," in new ed. of B. F. Westcott, *The Epistles of John* (Abingdon, Berkshire: The Marcham Manor Press, 1966), pp. lvii–lxxvi.

"Myth and the New Testament," *TSF Bulletin* 44 (Spring 1966), pp. 10–15.

"New Testament Studies in 1965," *Christianity Today* 10 (1965/66), pp. 445–7.

"The Pattern of Poetry," in G. S. Gunn, *Singers of Israel* (Bible Guides 10) (London: Lutterworth Press, 1966; Nashville and New York: Abingdon Press, 1966), pp. 32–36.

"Prätorium," "Rhode," "Tertullus," "Theudas," "Urbanus," in *Biblisch-Historisches Handwörterbuch* 3.

"Recent Literature on the Epistle to the Hebrews," *Themelios* (Lausanne) 3 (1966), pp. 31–36.

"St. Paul in Rome: 3. The Epistle to the Colossians," *BJRL* 48 (1965/66), pp. 268–85.

"The Story of the Bible," in *The Bible* [RSV] (London: Lutterworth Press, 1966), pp. 1–7 [separately paged].

1967

"The Epistles of John," *The Witness* 97–98 (January 1967 – December 1968). [A verse-by-verse exposition of the three epistles.]
Introduction to William Tyndale's Five Books of Moses called the Pentateuch, ed. J. I. Mombert (1884), repr. in "Centaur Classics" (Fontwell, Sussex: Centaur Press, 1967), pp. cxlvii–cliv.
"The Last Thirty Years," additional chapter to F. G. Kenyon, *The Story of the Bible*, ed. F. F. Bruce (Grand Rapids: William B. Eerdmans Publishing Company, 1967), pp. 114–46.
"Literature and Theology to Gregory the Great," *Journal of Ecclesiastical History* 18 (1967), pp. 227–31.
"Noteworthy Advances in the New Testament Field," *Christianity Today* 11 (1966/67), pp. 433–6.
"Plymouth Brethren," *Chambers's Encyclopaedia* 10 (1967), pp. 821–22.
"Plymouth Brethren," *The Encyclopaedia Britannica* 18 (1967), pp. 75–76. [N.B., Bruce should not be held responsible for the inaccuracies concerning the Plymouth Brethren in North America. These statistics were added by the editor.]
"St. Paul in Rome: 4. The Epistle to the Ephesians," *BJRL* 49 (1966/67), pp. 303–22.
"The Society for Old Testament Study, 1917-67," *ExpT* 78 (1966/67), pp. 147–8.
"Tell el-Amarna," in *Archaeology and Old Testament Study*, ed. D. Winton Thomas (Oxford: The Clarendon Press, 1967), pp. 3–20.
"Understanding the Bible," *The Harvester*, a series of essays on hermeneutical principles, beginning June 1967 and continuing through January 1969.

1968

This is That: The New Testament Development of Some Old Testament Themes. (The Payton Lectures, Fuller Theological Seminary, 1968.) Exeter: The Paternoster Press, 1968. Pp. 122. American edition: *The New Testament Development of Old Testament Themes*. Grand Rapids: William B. Eerdmans Publishing Company, 1969. Pp. 128.
Co-editor (with E. Gordon Rupp): *Holy Book and Holy Tradition*. (International Colloquium held in the Faculty of Theology of the University of Manchester, 1966). Manchester: Manchester University Press, 1968. Pp. viii+244.
"Alan Rowe," *PEQ* 100 (1968), pp. 76–77.
"Jesus is Lord," *Soli Deo Gloria: New Testament Essays in Honor[sic] of William Childs Robinson*, ed. J. McDowell Richards (Richmond, Va.: John Knox Press, 1968), pp. 23–36.
"The Literary Background of the New Testament," *Faith and Thought* 97 (1968), pp. 15–40.
"Paul and Jerusalem," *Tyndale Bulletin* 19 (1968), pp. 3–25.
"St. Paul in Rome: 5. Concluding Observations," *BJRL* 50 (1967/68), pp. 262–79.
"Samuel Henry Hooke," *PEQ* 100 (1968), pp. 77–78.
"Samuel Henry Hooke (1874–1968)," *The Witness* 98 (March 1968), pp. 101, 107.
"Scripture and Tradition in the New Testament," in *Holy Book and Holy Tradition*, ed. Bruce and Rupp (Manchester: Manchester University Press, 1968), pp. 68–93.

1969

New Testament History. London: Thomas Nelson & Son Ltd., 1969. Pp. xiv+434.
"The Book of Daniel and the Qumran Community," in *Neotestamentica et Semitica*
(*Festschrift* for Matthew Black), ed. E. E. Ellis and M. Wilcox (Edinburgh: T. & T.
Clark, 1969), pp. 221–35.
"The Fourfold Gospel," "The General Letters," and "Revelation" (commentary),
in *A New Testament Commentary*, ed. G. C. D. Howley (London: Pickering &
Inglis, Ltd., 1969. [Bruce served as one of two Consulting Editors.]
"Galatian Problems: 1. Autobiographical Data," *BJRL* 51 (1968/69), pp. 292–309.
"Harold Henry Rowley," *PEQ* 101 (1969), p. 134.
"Hebrews in Recent Study," *ExpT* 80 (1968/69), pp. 260–64.
"Holy Spirit in the Qumran Texts," *Annual of Leeds University Oriental Society* 6
(1966/68), pp. 292–309.
"Jesus and the Gospels in the Light of the Scrolls," *The Scrolls and Christianity*
(S.P.C.K. Theological Collections 11), ed. M. Black (London: S.P.C.K., 1969), pp.
70–82.
"The Kerygma of Hebrews," *Interp* 23 (1969), pp. 3–19.
"The Palestine of the Gospels: The Ministry of Christ" and "The Archaeology of
the New Testament," in *Zondervan Pictorial Bible Atlas*, ed. E. M. Blaiklock (Grand
Rapids: Zondervan Publishing House, 1969).
"The Qumran Discoveries and the Bible," *Ekklesiastikos Pharos* (Alexandria,
Egypt) 51 (1952–69), pp. 49–59.
"Thoughts from my Study," *Calling* (Summer 1969), pp. 14–16. [The first essay
of a continuing feature.]
"Thoughts from my Study: Tradition Good and Bad," *Calling* (Fall 1969), pp.
12–14.

Forthcoming

Tradition Old and New (Exeter: The Paternoster Press), 1970.
The Epistles of John. London: Pickering & Inglis Ltd., 1970.
1 and 2 Corinthians. (The Century Bible, new edition.) London: Oliphants Ltd.
1970.
Matthew. (Scripture Union Bible Study Books.) London: Scripture Union, 1970.
"Acts of the Apostles," "Age," "Colossians, Epistle to the," "Criticism," "Hittites,"
"Paul, the Apostle," in *The International Standard Bible Encyclopaedia*, rev. ed., ed.
G. W. Bromiley *et al.* (Grand Rapids: William B. Eerdmans Publishing Company.)
"Aquila," "Barjesus," "Barnabas," "Elymas," "John the Baptist," "Priscilla,"
"Stephen," in *Wycliffe Bible Encyclopedia*, ed. C. F. Pfeiffer (Chicago: Moody
Press).
"Between the Testaments" (new article), in addition to the revision of original
articles and commentaries, in *The New Bible Commentary*, rev. ed. (London: The
Inter-Varsity Fellowship).
"The Christ of the Scriptures," in *The Bible in the World* (London: British and
Foreign Bible Society). Autumn, 1970.
"Copper Scroll," "Dead Sea Scrolls," "En Feshkha," "Kittim," "Lies, Man of,"
"Lies, Prophet of," "Lion of Wrath," "Murabba'at," "Pesher," "Qumran,"
"Seekers after Smooth Things", "Serekh," "Shapira Fragments," "Sons of
Light," "Teacher of Righteousness," "War Scroll," "Wicked Priest," "Yahad,"

"Zadokite Work," in *Encyclopedia Judaica*, ed. C. Roth *et al.* (Jerusalem, Israel). [Bruce is Departmental Editor for Dead Sea Scrolls.]

"Corinthians, First Epistle to the," "Form Criticism," "Hebrews, Epistle to the," "Parable," "Romans, Epistle to the," in *Zondervan Pictorial Encyclopedia of the Bible*, ed. M. C. Tenney (Grand Rapids: Zondervan Publishing House).

"Corinthians, Second Epistle to the," in *Encyclopedia of Christianity* 3 (Marshallton, Delaware: National Foundation for Christian Education).

"Dead Sea Scrolls," in *Man, Myth and Magic*, ed. R. Cavendish (London: B. P. C. Publishing Company, 1970. Serial publication from January 1970), No. 22, June 18, 1970.

"Exiles in an Alien World" (The Theology of the Catholic Epistles, Hebrews, and the Apocalypse), in Scripture volume (title undecided), ed. J. Bradley (Gastonia, N.C.: Good Will Press).

"Galatian Problems: 2. North or South Galatians?," *BJRL* 52 (1969/70), pp. 243–246.

"Inter-Testamental Literature," in *The Study of Theology: An Introduction*, ed. F. G. Healey (London: Lutterworth Press).

"The Message of the New Testament," Volume on Scripture (title undecided), ed. D. J. Ellis (London: Pickering & Inglis Ltd.).

"The New English Bible Old Testament," *Christianity Today* 14 (January 30, 1970).

"New Light from the Dead Sea Scrolls" (revision) and "The Early Manuscripts of the Bible" (new article), in *Holman Study Bible*, rev. ed., ed. S. B. Babbage (Philadelphia: A. J. Holman Company).

"New Testament Background," essay in RSV Study Bible to be published by Thomas Nelson & Sons Ltd.

"The Origins of 'The Witness'," *The Witness* 100 (January 1970).

"Qumran," in *Dictionary of Comparative Religion*, ed. S. G. F. Brandon (London: Weidenfeld & Nicolson, 1970).

"Plymouth Brethren" and related articles, in *A Dictionary of Liturgy and Worship*, ed. J. G. Davies (London: SCM Press).

"The Letter to the Ephesians" in *Universal Bible*, Vol. 7, ed. J. Marsh and J. S. Bosch (Oxford: Religious Education Press).

"Septuagint and Other Greek Versions," "Old Testament in Apocrypha and Pseudepigrapha" and "Exegesis of the Dead Sea Scrolls," in *A History of Jewish Biblical Exegesis*, ed. R. Loewe (Cambridge: Cambridge University Press).

"Bible", in Biographical Dictionary of English Literature, ed. A. Pollard (London: Sphere Books).

NOTE: A Supplementary Bibliography of the Writings of F. F. Bruce will be published in *The Journal of the Christian Brethren Research Fellowship* in the autumn of 1970. Copies of this issue of the Journal may be obtained from the publications office of the C.B.R.F. (34 Tewkesbury Avenue, Pinner, Middlesex, England).

EDITORSHIPS

Associate Editor, *The Evangelical Quarterly* (1942).
Assistant Editor, *The Evangelical Quarterly* (1943–49).
Editor, *The Evangelical Quarterly* (1950——).
Editor, *Yorkshire Celtic Studies* (1945–57).

Editor, *Journal of the Transactions of the Victoria Institute* (1949–57).
Contributing Editor, *Christianity Today* (1956——).
Editor, *Palestine Exploration Quarterly* (1957——).
General Editor, *The Paternoster Church History = The Advance of Christianity through the Ages* (1961——).
Consulting Editor, *Eternity* (1961——).
General Editor (with William Barclay), *Bible Guides*, 22 vols. (1961–66).
General Editor, *The New International Commentary on the New Testament ⇒ The New London Commentary on the New Testament* (1963——).
Editorial Co-operator, *Erasmus* (1970——).

ABBREVIATIONS

AJP – *American Journal of Philology.*

AnLov – *Analecta Lovaniensia Biblica et Orientalia.*

Arndt – Arndt-Gingrich-Bauer, *A Greek–English Lexicon of the New Testament* (1957).

ATR – *Anglican Theological Review.*

BC – *The Beginnings of Christianity*, ed. Foakes-Jackson and Lake (5 vols., 1920–33).

Blass-Debrunner – *A Greek Grammar of the New Testament*, E.T. (1961).

Bib – *Biblica.*

BHH – *Biblish-historisches Handwörterbuch*, 3 vols. (1962–66).

BJRL – *Bulletin of the John Rylands Library.*

BNTC – *Black's New Testament Commentaries* (=*Harper's*).

BZ – *Biblische Zeitschrift.*

BZNW – *Beihefte zur Zeitschrift für die neutestamentliche Wissenschaft.*

CBQ – *Catholic Biblical Quarterly.*

CIG – *Corpus Inscriptionum Graecarum*

CIL – *Corpus Inscriptionum Latinarum.*

CNT – *Commentaire du Nouveau Testament.*

DSS – Dead Sea Scrolls.

EGT – *Expositor's Greek Testament.*

EQ – *The Evangelical Quarterly.*

EvTh – *Evangelische Theologie.*

Exp – *The Expositor.*

ExpT – *The Expository Times.*

FRLANT (NF) – *Forschungen zur Religion und Literatur des Alten und Neuen Testaments*, Neue Folge.

HJ – *Hibbert Journal.*

HERE – Hastings' Encyclopaedia of Religion and Ethics, 13 vols. (1908–26).

HNT – Lietzmann, *Handbuch zum Neuen Testament.*

HTR – *Harvard Theological Review.*

IB – *The Interpreter's Bible.*

IDB – *Interpreter's Dictionary of the Bible*, 4 vols (1962).

IEJ – *Israel Exploration Journal.*

IF – *Indogermanische Forschungen.*

Jnterp – *Interpretation.*

IBL – *Journal of Biblical Literature.*

JerB – *Jerusalem Bible.*
JNES – *Journal of Near Eastern Studies.*
JQR – *Jewish Quarterly Review.*
JRS – *Journal of Roman Studies.*
JSS – *Journal of Semitic Studies.*
JTS – *Journal of Theological Studies.*
JTVI – *Journal of the Transactions of the Victoria Institute.*
KD – *Kerygma und Dogma.*
Loeb – Loeb Classical Library.
LSJ – Liddell, Scott, and Jones, *Greek–English Lexicon* (1940).
LXX – The Septuagint.
Meyer – Meyer, *Kommentar über das Neue Testament.*
MNTC – Moffatt's *New Testament Commentary.*
NIC (=NLC) – *New International Commentary* (=*New London Commentary*).
NovTest – *Novum Testamentum.*
NRT – *Nouvelle Revue théologique.*
NTD – *Das Neue Testament Deutsch.*
NTS – *New Testament Studies.*
OCD – *Oxford Classical Dictionary.*
Peake[2] – *Peake's Commentary on the Bible,* rev. ed. (1962).
PEQ – *Palestine Exploration Quarterly.*
PG – Migne, *Patrologia Graeca.*
PW – Pauly-Wissowa, *Real-encyklopädie der klassischen Altertumswissenschaft.*
RAC – *Reallexikon für die Antike und Christentum.*
RB – *Revue Biblique.*
RechSR – *Recherches de Science Religieuse.*
RGG – *Die Religion in Geschichte und Gegenwart.*
RHPR – *Revue d'Histoire et de Philosophie religieuses.*
RNT – *Regensburger Neues Testament.*
RSR – *Revue des Sciences Religieuses.*
RSV – Revised Standard Version.
RV – Revised Version.
SBU – *Symbolae Biblicae Upsalienses.*
SNTS – *Studiorum Novi Testamenti Societas.*
Strack-Billerbeck – Strack and Billerbeck, *Kommentar zum NT aus Talmud und Midrasch* (1922–8).
StTh – *Studia Theologica.*
TDNT – *Theological Dictionary of the New Testament* (E.T. of TWNT).
ThB – *Theologische Blätter.*
ThLZ – *Theologische Literaturzeitung.*
ThZ – *Theologische Zeitschrift.*
TNTC – *Tyndale New Testament Commentaries.*

TR – Textus Receptus.

TU – *Texte und Untersuchungen zur Geschichte der altchristlichen Literatur* (3 series), ed. Harnack et al. (1883–).

TWNT – Kittel-Friedrich, *Theologisches Wörterbuch zum NT.*

VC – *Vigiliae Christianae.*

VT – *Vetus Testamentum.*

WMANT – *Wissenschaftliche Monographien zum Alten und Neuen Testament.*

ZATW – *Zeitschrift für die alttestamentliche Wissenschaft.*

ZKT – *Zeitschrift für katholische Theologie.*

ZNTW – *Zeitschrift für die neutestamentliche Wissenschaft.*

ZThK – *Zeitschrift für Theologie und Kirche.*

Editions – indicated by superior figures, e.g. RGG[3]

PART ONE

PART ONE

CHAPTER I

THE ACTS OF THE APOSTLES AS A DOCUMENT OF FIRST CENTURY HISTORY

E. M. BLAIKLOCK

THE GENERAL RELUCTANCE OF HISTORIANS TO RECOGNIZE THE VALUE OF the Acts of the Apostles as a document of life and society in the mid-first century is a curious phenomenon to be explained only by some deep-seated suspicion of a biblical text. The book begins with the emergence of the Christian Church in Palestine, and traces one movement of its expansion through important tracts of the Empire. The central figure in this historic process was a citizen of Rome, a Jew by birth and heritage, a rabbi by education, a Greek by virtue of his Tarsian environment . . . in a word the first recorded person to combine in himself the three elements of Western European culture. The organization which he shaped and fashioned was destined to confront and ultimately overcome the political power of Rome, and to modify the whole course of history. To weigh the worth of such a genesis and such consequent biography would seem to be an obvious duty of research. To recognize that pages of the record are written with a vigour and a realism hardly to be matched in extant contemporary literature, prescribes no attitude towards the Christian faith. It demands no more than the acceptance of its ancient presence and significance.

Consider in illustration the article on Tarsus in the *Oxford Classical Dictionary*, by no less a scholar than A. H. M. Jones. In something like one hundred and eighty words the eminent historian outlines the story of Tarsus from its legendary founders to the end of the first century of the Christian era, concluding: "During the first century B.C. Tarsus was the seat of a celebrated philosophic school." Why did Professor Jones not claim two hundred words, and use the final score to say: "Tarsus was the birthplace of Paul who wrote a large part of the New Testament and founded the Gentile Church"?

The same scholar's monumental work on the cities of the eastern provinces[1] betrays a similar hesitation. Paul, the Church, Christianity are not listed in the index. In both the dictionary and his book, Jones describes the Syrian Antioch without mentioning its role as the second capital of the group which was to overrun the Empire. He writes with knowledge and in

[1] A. H. M. Jones, *Cities of the Eastern Roman Provinces* (Oxford, 1937).

detail of the ecclesiastical organization of the later Roman world, and the eastern bishoprics command four lines of references in his index. The faith which all bishoprics presuppose lacks description. The same odd reticence marks a fine chapter on Syria. The fourth century is in view when suddenly Professor Jones notes that "Hadrian's attempt to paganize Galilee ultimately failed. It remained a stronghold of Judaism long after Judaea had become Christian, and in the fourth century Tiberias and Diocaesarea were so completely controlled by Jews that no pagan, Samaritan or Christian was allowed to set foot in them." Failing wider knowledge, the reader might search text and notes in vain to discover who these Christians might be. It should in fairness, but hardly in elucidation, be added that Jones' bibliography does full justice to the books and articles of W. M. Ramsay.

The conspiracy of silence is broken here and there with some timidity. Writing on Ephesus in the OCD, W. M. Calder notes the vivid light thrown on the story of the city by Acts 19, a theme more generously developed by Charles Seltman in 1957.[1] Writing on Corinth, P. N. Ure manages to confine Christian reference to one word. The city, he says, after its restoration in 44 B.C., was "visited by apostles, emperors . . . Gallic hordes and earthquakes". So much for Gallio on his judgment seat, and the light shed on the cosmopolitan port by the Corinthian epistles. Max Cary, who writes on Philippi, does mention that the colony was "the first city in Europe to hear a Christian missionary".

This almost studied disregard for the evidence of the New Testament by authorities on ancient history, has recently met a strong and refreshing challenge in the Sarum Lectures of 1960–61 by A. N. Sherwin-White.[2] This historian, writing with all the care, indeed with the distrust of unsupported evidence proper to his profession, is yet prompted to chide the unbalanced scepticism and fanciful theorizing of the New Testament "form critics". His restrained amazement at their gloomy conclusion that "the historical Christ is unknowable and the history of his mission cannot be written", while historians pursue with convincing optimism the truth about the motives and person of Christ's "best-known contemporary", Tiberius Caesar, is a sobering comment on New Testament criticism, both healthy and overdue.[3] This of the Gospels, while, says the same authority, "for Acts the confirmation of historicity is overwhelming".

Neglect of the New Testament documents has been the more reprehensible in view of the paucity of alternative sources. In Nero's day no Cicero wrote a running commentary in letters to friends and relatives which sombre fate preserved from tendentious editing. No provincial Pliny consulted a patient Trajan on affairs of local interest and preserved the mutual letter file. It is interesting, in fact, to survey the contemporary

[1] C. Seltman, *Riot in Ephesus* (London, 1958), pp. 25–86.
[2] A. N. Sherwin-White, *Roman Society and Roman Law in the New Testament* (Oxford, 1963).
[3] *Op. cit.*, pp. 187, 188.

literary scene, and to set Luke's narrative in its context. If the book was written in the early sixties of the first century, and this date may be reasonably accepted, there is little surviving of literary or historical significance to rival it. Curiously, the bulk of such surviving work came from Spaniards, a foretaste of what Spain was to contribute to Roman life. A host of senators, a dozen writers, and three emperors, including Trajan and Hadrian, were to come from the Iberian peninsula, a hint perhaps of Paul's foresight when he included a visit to Rome's western bastion in his strategic plan.[1]

To list them is no protracted task, if enumeration is confined to those active in Nero's day. Caught like Paul in that evil confluence, and destined like Nero's Christian scapegoats for death, were an uncle and a nephew, both from Spain. Lucius Annaeus Seneca, the most considerable literary figure since Augustus' principate, was born in Corduba about the time of the Nativity, in 5 B.C. He came to Rome as a child, achieved a senatorial career and accumulated wealth, neither of which worldly successes he judged inconsistent with the profession and practice of an austere philosophy. Banished to Corsica in Claudius' day, Seneca endured eight years' exile with scant stoicism, and returned to Rome in A.D. 49 to be the youthful Nero's tutor, a thankless task shared with Burrus, the commandant of the Praetorian Guard. Together they managed the Empire well, and "Nero's Five Years" became a proverb in the provinces for sound government. A discreditable lampoon by which Seneca avenged himself on the dead Claudius can hardly be called literature, but in the early sixties, horrified by Nero's mounting lawlessness, Seneca retired to write his philosophical treatises and "moral letters", works of noble and enduring worth. There is a reference to the Campanian earthquake of 63, and to the great fire at Lyons of 64, and these give some indication of the date of composition. Seneca died in Nero's Terror of 65. He was a tormented man, easy unsympathetically to charge with inconsistency, one who, in happier circumstances, might have been a good man. His life and writing, says E. P. Barker in a hostile assessment, "present a fairly clear-cut picture of neurosis".[2] Such damage was difficult to escape for those entangled in that troubled and sinister environment. The story of the dialogue between Paul and Seneca is a legend whose invention pays a compliment to the ill-starred Spanish-Roman, for it finds in his sinewy Latin a mind which the apostle would have been glad to explore.

Seneca's nephew, who also died in the aftermath of Calpurnius Piso's clumsy conspiracy of A.D. 65, was Marcus Annaeus Lucanus, the poet. Lucan, as he is familiarly called, was only twenty-six years old, but a precocious writer whose epic on the civil war between Julius Caesar and Pompey survives. It is a considerable monument of Silver Latin,

[1] Rom. 15:24, 28.
[2] OCD, p. 827.

competent, epigrammatic verse which provoked Nero's artistic jealousy. It needed no more to earn a death sentence from that vulgar tyrant, although there is no reason to doubt that Lucan was involved in Piso's plot. The pity is that so salutary a project failed to find better leadership.

Yet another Spaniard was Lucius Junius Columella, who published his book on agriculture about A.D. 60. Columella was born at Gades, and in A.D. 36, the year of Pilate's recall, when the nascent Church was finding its second home in Antioch, he was serving as a tribune with the Sixth Legion in Syria and Cilicia. Retired and middle-aged, a practical farmer at Ardea in Latium, he turned his thoughtful mind to agriculture. While Nero was moving from Seneca's tutelage to youthful tyranny, and events in Britain were heating to the explosion of Boudicca's revolt, Columella was studying the agricultural treatises of Cato, Varro and Vergil, and deploring the importation of foreign corn, absentee landlords, and the decline of Italian farming. His book is brief, dim light on a quieter Italy, and an industrious countryside hardly aware of the tense and dark events in the crowded city.

There was one writer who survived the holocaust which followed the collapse of Piso's conspiracy[1] only to fall a victim, twelve months later, to the crimes of Ofonius Tigellinus, Nero's notorious commander of the household troops. This considerable literary figure and personality was Gaius Petronius, nicknamed Arbiter from his Beau Nash vocation as dictator of elegance in Nero's court. Tacitus devotes two chapters to this voluptary, an aristocrat not unknown to the modern world from Henryk Sienkiewicz's brilliant portrait in his novel, *Quo Vadis*. Petronius once governed Bithynia with energy and efficiency, but nothing is known of this more reputable activity. He is rather known as the indolent director of the young Nero's pleasures, and as the author of the *Satiricon*, a picaresque novel unlike anything else in Latin Literature. Large fragments survive. They tell of the disreputable doings of three Greek scamps on the Campanian coast. Oddly enough, if a comparison between works so disparate may be hazarded, Petronius' satire, Columella's *De Re Rustica*, and the *Acts of the Apostles* must be bracketed as the only surviving publications of Nero's principate which consistently give some indication of a section of society outside the capital and its dominant minority. Apart from being a storehouse of popular Latin, Petronius' novel shows the common life of that age of money-making and vulgarity, of low crime and shattered morality, among the poor and the undeservedly rich, in the market-place and the slum. The reader becomes aware of the Roman proletariat, of a populace about its petty business and varied carnality, remote from the Palatine and aristocratic voice. It is a world glimpsed briefly in the Pompeian graffiti, or here and there in the Gospel parables. It is also visible in the story which Paul's physician-friend was writing at

[1] The story is told by Tacitus in *Annals* 15:48sqq.

the very time when the Arbiter Elegantiarum was amusing himself with the tale of his trio of rascals, of uncultured parvenus, and the underworld of the Italian coast.

Little more can be said in this survey of Luke's contemporaries. Two or three names might, for completeness, be mentioned. The satirist Aulus Persius died in A.D. 62 at the age of twenty-eight years. Over six hundred of his laboured and academic hexameters survive. His satire lacks contact with life. It is imitative and trite. Persius may have been acquainted with Nero, who may be the popular young Alcibiades whom the satirist addresses in his fourth poem, exhorting him to search his soul and scorn the crowd's acclaim.

It was also under Nero that Gaius Plinius Secundus wrote. This diligent man, called the Elder Pliny to distinguish him from the letter writer and future governor of Bithynia, who was his nephew, returned from his soldiering in Germany in A.D. 57. Shrewdly observing the perils of public life, he set about the harmless task of writing a history of Germany, unfortunately lost, and collecting the thousands of facts and fancies which survive in the thirty-six books of his *Natural History*. He had no style, and his work, built out of an industry equal to that of Isaac D'Israeli, tells nothing of life at large. Pliny survived Nero, returned to public life, and became an admiral. He died of cardiac failure and asthma, the victim of his scientific curiosity, when Vesuvius erupted in August A.D. 79. Quintus Asconius Pedianus, who became blind in A.D. 64, and some fragments of whose commentaries on Cicero precariously survive, may have been writing at the same time as Luke. Perhaps Quintus Curtius Rufus was busy on his account of Alexander the Great. The dates are quite uncertain. Silius Italicus, middle-aged at the time, elected to postpone his writing of the longest surviving epic in Latin until he was old. Flavius Josephus, still a priest in Palestine, could foresee neither his Latin name nor literary career in turgid Greek.

Such were Luke's contemporaries of the pen. The closing years of the decade saw the deaths of Paul, Luke and Nero himself, a squalid suicide in suburban Rome. The year 69 saw the ends of the earth march on Rome, and four claimants striving for imperial power. The Beast was "wounded to death", but, to the world's wonder, "healed of its deadly wound".[1] Rome was indeed doomed, slow though the deadly bleeding was, for the legions had the "secret of empire". It was the fatal fact that "an emperor could be made elsewhere than in Rome".[5]

It is a vital period fraught with the issues of the future. Tacitus, his account bisected by the lamentable gap of three years between the surviving books of his *Annals* and his *Histories*, tells the story of Nero's principate in powerful Latin. Tacitus is one of the great stylists of all literature, and

[1] Rev. 13:3–4.
[2] Tacitus, *Histories* 1:4.

Ronald Syme has brilliantly succeeded in establishing his accuracy and worth as an historian. Nothing, however, can replace the casual and contemporary record, especially the document which reveals the realities of life and society without immediately seeking to do so. Tacitus wrote half a century after the events. So did Suetonius, whose gossiping biography is of much less value. Other surviving history is inconsiderable. And all was Rome-centred, little concerned with provincial or proletarian life. For any touch of common humanity the very dust of history must be sifted, coins scrutinized, tattered papyri pieced together, inscriptions interpreted, and the fragments of the archaeologist's digging considered and assessed. Caesar's household, caught in one New Testament phrase, reveals, for one example, a few facets of its activity in the funerary inscriptions which have survived to find a modern listing.[1]

It should therefore be with some sense of excitement and interest that the student of Roman history turns to Acts. If he can do so unimpeded by the perverse speculations of those who have expended too much sceptical ingenuity over the document; if he can come encouraged by some such assurance of the historical competence of the writer as that which, at the beginning of the century, converted W. M. Ramsay from sceptic to champion, he will realize with delight how illuminating a story lies in his hands.

A. N. Sherwin-White has written some enthusiastic pages on the theme.[2] He stresses the exactitude of the historical framework, the precision of detail of time and place, the feel and tone of provincial city life, seen, not through the eyes of Strabo or Dio of Prusa, but through those of an alert Hellenistic Jew. "Acts," he writes, "takes us on a conducted tour of the Greek and Roman world with detail and narrative so interwoven as to be inseparable." Detail need not here detain us. Since Ramsay's well-known demonstration, Luke's fastidious regard for exactitude in nomenclature, and his sure handling of elusive fact, is sufficiently accepted. "I may fairly claim," wrote Ramsay seventy years ago,

> to have entered on this investigation without prejudice in favour of the conclusion which I shall now seek to justify to the reader. On the contrary, I began with a mind unfavourable to it, for the ingenuity and apparent completeness of the Tübingen theory had at one time quite convinced me. It did not then lie in my line of life to investigate the subject minutely; but more recently I found myself brought in contact with the book of Acts as an authority for the topography, antiquities and society of Asia Minor. It was gradually borne in upon me that in various details the narrative showed marvellous truth. In fact, beginning with a fixed idea that the work was essentially a second century composition, and never relying on its evidence as trustworthy for first century conditions, I gradually came to find it a useful ally in some obscure and difficult investigations.[3]

[1] *CIL* 6; M. P. Charlesworth lists others.
[2] *Op. cit.,* pp. 120-22.
[3] W. M. Ramsay, *St. Paul the Traveller and the Roman Citizen* (London, 1898), pp. 7-8.

The whole of the chapter is worth reading. Historical criticism has obviously travelled far from the days when F. C. Baur could speak of statements in Acts as "intentional deviations from historical truth". Has any collection of ancient documents been subjected to such emotional denigration as those which form the New Testament?

Ramsay first gave expression to his testimony in the Morgan Lectures of 1894, and the Mansfield College Lectures of 1895.[1] A. N. Sherwin-White's confidence in the book was set forth in the Sarum Lectures of 1960–61. The men of Tübingen would have been horrified to turn the pages. There are classical historians who might open wider eyes . . .

> The narrative in fact shows remarkable familiarity with the provincial and juridical situation in the last years of Claudius. An author familiar with the later situation in Cilicia, and the final form of the judicial custom of *forum delicti*, would have avoided the question of Paul's *patria*, or place of origin.
> The scene belongs unmistakably to an era which did not survive the age of the Antonines . . . The evidence in Acts not only agrees in general with the civic situation in Asia Minor in the first and early second centuries A.D., but falls into place in the earlier rather than the later phase of the development.

> The author of Acts is very well informed about the finer points of municipal institutions at Ephesus.[2]

The random quotations reveal the drift of the modern historian's conclusions.

There is no need here to list or to review evidence for the reliability and historical significance of Acts which the two scholars quoted, sixty-five years apart, have set out and developed with such careful competence. Luke's detail bears investigation. It may, however, be of some interest to take a wider view, to survey the canvas, as it were, and not, as Ruskin once said might so profitably be done with Turner's oils, examine the quality of the brushwork. We shall look quickly at the picture of life and events at large, as one might do who came fresh to the narrative with some knowledge of the mid-first century, and in quest of closer intimacy.

Glance first at Palestine, where one of the great traumatic events of that century was taking shape. The Great Rebellion, Rome's cruel Vietnam, ranks with the civil war of A.D. 69 as one of the darker experiences of early imperial history. Tacitus has told of the grim struggle in some vivid chapters. Josephus' awkward Greek cannot obscure its horror. But how vivid are the scenes from a tense and heated Palestine, where the coming clash, so precariously avoided in the mad Caligula's day, and inevitable a few years later, is in full and ugly view. One can almost hear the orders in the briefing-room at Caesarea before the alert Lysias marched his cohort up to Jerusalem. Swift, sharp action by his trained riot-squad snatches their

[1] *Op. cit.*, Introduction.
[2] *Op. cit.*, pp. 57, 85, 87.

victim from the mob's lynching. And, a sinister revelation in a dozen words, the havoc cry which set the crowd roaring, came from Asian Jews who had seen an Ephesian with Paul in the temple. Only a few weeks before Paul had been forced to change his travel plans because of a plot against him hatched by the Achaean Jews. The coherence of international Jewry, expressed and evident in more than one eastern Mediterranean city in the uprisings of both A.D. 66 and 132, is visible in both incidents. A man who openly declared a Roman citizenship was marked down as a renegade, and faced mortal peril all through the cities where Jews were settled, and tides of national consciousness were flowing. Claudius' expulsion of the whole Roman colony in A.D. 49 may have had some valid and weighty reasons in the mind of the ruler who wrote so sternly to the Alexandrian Jews in 42.[1]

By the date of Paul's last ill-advised visit to Jerusalem the situation had deteriorated alarmingly. In Palestine itself, order in parts of the countryside must have practically collapsed, when it required an escort of four hundred and seventy men to slip one prisoner by night out of the turbulent city. The seventy cavalrymen included in this task-force were no doubt the guard detailed to convey Paul down the exposed and guerrilla-haunted road to the coastal plain. It runs under boulder-strewn slopes, where today the rust-proofed ruin of Israeli jeeps and trucks lies as a reminder of the changeless ways of human strife. The clash between the Jerusalem mob and the garrison which sparked the ghastly war was still six or seven years away, but the darkening stage was clearly set.

The Romans, who were doing all in their power to avoid a confrontation, must by this time have been practically confined to their strongpoints and garrison towns. Success in dealing with rural banditry, such as that which Tertullus, no doubt with some justice, mentions in his preamble before Felix, can have been little more than a temporary alleviation of a gravely deteriorating situation. Festus' care to honour a puppet-king, whose selfless efforts to avert disaster were to be demonstrated a few years later, is also a pointer to the anxiety which was mounting in Caesarea. The Romans did too little and too late. It was a fundamental error of frontier and provincial strategy to endeavour to hold so restless and difficult an area with a garrison at Caesarea of only 3,000 men, and the limited authority of procurators. The legate of Syria, who disposed of the nearest legionary force, was too remote for the swift intervention which a crisis might at any time require. Rome's reliance on the able Herod family, who served Rome well for a century, is evident all through Acts and was perhaps an element in the great miscalculation. Perhaps the Empire overestimated the strength and hold of collaborating elements. It was always a policy to use available instruments of order, and to this end the Romans were prepared to overlook some abuse of authority. Stephen was

[1] London Papyri 1912.

riotously stoned. Saul, with the Sanhedrin behind him, was permitted to arrest and persecute as far as Damascus. All such activity was presumptuous under the rule of those who reserved and sequestered the power of capital punishment. Usurpation was being overlooked, provided that illegal violence was channelled and directed against a proletarian minority on whose goodwill no issue of security depended. Rome could act, as her able officer Lysias demonstrated, with vigour and decisiveness, when a critical situation demanded, and halt the action short of the provocation which precipitated disaster in A.D. 66.

The similarly illuminating Ephesian riot has attracted the attention of both Sherwin-White[1] and Seltman.[2] Ramsay[3] regarded it as a most revealing chapter,

> the most instructive picture of society in an ancient city which has come down to us. . . . We are taken direct into the artisan life of Ephesus, and all is so true to common life, and so unlike what would occur to anyone writing at a distance, that the conclusion is inevitable: we have here a picture drawn from nature.

The terse account[4] reads, says Charles Seltman, who had no sympathy for Paul's puritanical and Christian invasion of the Asian city, "like a modern press report".[5] It runs, if some attempt be made so to render it, thus:

> At this juncture a considerable disturbance arose about Christianity. One Demetrius, a silversmith who made souvenir shrines of Artemis, provided plenty of work for his craftsmen. He gathered them together along with workmen in associated trades, and, addressing them, said: "Men, you are aware that our prosperity depends upon this business, and you see and hear that not only in Ephesus but through almost all of the province, this Paul, by his preaching, has turned away a great host of people telling them, as he does, that you cannot manufacture goods. Not only is our trade in danger of falling into disrepute, but the temple of the great goddess Artemis will cease to be respected, and her majesty, whom all Asia and the civilised world worships, will be heading for destruction." When they heard these words they were filled with rage, and shouted: "Great is Artemis of the Ephesians." The whole city was a scene of confusion. They surged with one accord to the theatre. The Macedonians, Gaius and Aristarchus, who had come with Paul, were caught in the moving crowd. Paul wished to face the mob, but the Christians would not allow him; and some of the Asiarchs, who were well-disposed towards him, sent and urged him not to risk an appearance in the theatre. All this time some were shouting one thing, and some another, for the assembly was in confusion, and most of them had no idea why they were all there. Some of the crowd explained it to Alexander, and the Jews put him forward. Alexander, waving his hand for silence, tried to make a speech; but when he was seen to

---

[1] *Op. cit.*, pp. 83–88.
[2] *Op. cit.*, pp. 73–86.
[3] *Op. cit.*, pp. 277–78.
[4] Acts 19:23–32.
[5] *Op. cit.*, p. 83. Arnold Toynbee's striking testimony to the vividness of the passage is found in *The Study of History*, X, pp. 138, 139.

D

be a Jew, all voices merged in a chant which they kept up for two hours: "Great is Artemis of the Ephesians." When the city-clerk had quietened the crowd, he addressed them: "Ephesians, what human being is there who does not know that the city of Ephesus is temple-warden of the great Artemis, and the Thing Which Fell from Zeus? These facts are beyond dispute, and it befits you to show restraint and not act recklessly. I say this for you have brought forward these men who are guilty neither in act nor speech of offensive behaviour towards our goddess. If therefore Demetrius and his fellow-tradesmen have a complaint against anyone, courts are set up and there are proconsuls. Let those concerned go to law. If you have any other matters to enquire about, they will be aired in the regular city-meeting. In fact we risk being called to account for today's civil disturbance, there being no valid reason we can give for this uproar." With such words he broke up the assembly.

The facets of life and history which glint in this plain and well-told story are worth examination. The characters stand out – the two Macedonians, recognized as friends of Paul, and hustled down the street on the wave of the moving horde; Paul, cool as ever in a crisis; the provincial custodians of the Caesar-cult, not sorry to see some damage to the religion of Artemis; Alexander, probably a Hellenistic Jew anxious not to be exposed to unpopularity or pogrom because of the conduct of a splinter-sect. . . . Observe, too, the germs of coming conflict with the proletariat, which Tacitus and Pliny note in their first secular accounts of Christianity. The metrical chant is almost audible, as it takes the place of reason in the collective mind of an eastern mob, which Luke describes with a phrase of classic irony.

Note, too, the sure touch of Luke's plural,[1] which slips like a remembered phrase into his report of the city-official's politic speech. "There are proconsuls," he reminds the promoters of the tumult. See this in the context of the speaker's anxiety over the privileged standing of his city with the watchful imperial authorities, and another of those small convincing marks of historicity emerges. The plural could grammatically be "generalizing"; but it is much more likely to convey a touch of obsequious respect for the two imperial stewards, who, having murdered the proconsul of Asia, M. Junius Silanus, the great-grandson of Augustus, must have been left with the administration of the province on their hands pending the appointment of a successor. The crime was of Agrippina's devising, shortly after Nero's accession in the autumn of A.D. 54. Tacitus takes occasion to make a bald account of it the preamble to his vivid narrative of Nero's principate. The tactful plural in the official's speech could be evidence in a syllable of the aftermath of political assassination.

Ephesus was a sensitive point in the imperial network. There were other corners of the Empire where Rome could afford to overlook some measure of disorder, especially where local and responsible diagnosis could judge its

---

[1] *Loc. cit.,* v. 38.

incidence as harmless or salutary. Hence the significance of the story of Gallio, Seneca's genial and polished brother, and his judging of the Jewish tumult in Corinth. In that cosmopolitan city the Jewish minority presented no Alexandrian peril, and a magistrate could afford an exhibition of Rome's liberal disregard of other laws than her own. Claudius' edict of expulsion was also a recent memory, and the ghetto, swollen by immigrant malcontents, may have been due for a rebuke. With a breath of anti-semitism in the air, Gallio judged it wise to allow a brief outlet for emotion, as long as it was in full view and under remote control. Corinth was an important centre on a crossroads of commerce, and it required a cool man, sure of support from Rome, to manage a riotous occasion with such skill. Sherwin-White has dealt with the point of legal procedure which the incident illustrates. Its more interesting significance is its demonstration of Rome in action. Her government was a rough-hewn art, at this time, not a science based on text-book rules. The varied incidence of persecution, even in later and more rigidly centralized eras of government, illustrates the survival of some measure of this juridical independence.

Lystra is another illustration of the Empire's working. Popular superstition, based on a local legend of a theophany of Zeus and Hermes, led to an attack on two visitors by a disappointed rout of native Lycaonians. There was no riot-squad to rescue the victims, no city-clerk voiced concern in a popular assembly. No proconsul noted the outbreak of lawlessness with nicely calculated inaction. It was a remote edge of the Empire, a border town with highland territory beyond, where pacification was marked rather by the absence of armed turbulence than by Romanized or Hellenized living. Cicero in Cicilia a century before, Quirinius on the central plateau, half a century earlier, had dealt with back-country banditry by force of arms. "Perils of robbers" formed a traveller's hazard in the rugged peninsula, and it seems clear that Rome did not expect to police its remoter borderlands as effectively as she policed Italy. Edmund Burke once expounded that principle of rule when he urged colonial restraint upon an obdurate and unheeding English government. He said:

> Three thousand miles of ocean lie between you and the colonies. No contrivance can prevent the effect of this distance in weakening government. Seas roll, and months pass, between the order and the execution; and the want of a speedy explanation of a single point is enough to defeat a whole system. You have, indeed, winged ministers of vengeance, who carry your bolts in their pounces to the remotest verge of the sea. But there a power steps in that limits the arrogance of raging passions and furious elements, and says 'So far shalt thou go and no farther.' Who are you that should fret and rage, and bite the chains of nature? Nothing worse happens to you than does to all nations who have extensive empire. The Turk cannot govern Egypt and Arabia and Kurdistan as he governs Thrace; nor has he the same dominion in Caria and Algiers.[1]

[1] *Causes of Disobedience in the Colonies.*

Rome had discovered that principle of imperial government a millennium and a half before the Turk became a power on the rim of the Inland Sea. Gaston Boissier expounded it in a perceptive book published over sixty years ago:

> When Roman rule under the Empire is mentioned, everyone has the notion of an overwhelming despotism, and a suffocating centralisation. Times and places are, in fact, confused. Despotism prevailed only in Rome; centralisation came only later. When Rome had subdued the world she treated it less harshly than is supposed. Pitiless during the struggle, she became merciful after victory, whenever she could without danger. She had too much political sense than to take pleasure in useless severity. In general she asked of conquered peoples no more than the sacrifices necessary to secure her conquest. She left them their customs and religion and played on their vanity – last consolation of the defeated.[1]

Acts shows how inventively Rome was able thus to adapt, conform, and accommodate. She accepted the local customs and patterns of power, she used the terminology of time and place. The "politarchs" of Thessalonica, the "praetors" of Philippi, the "first" of Malta, all demonstrations of Luke's careful reporting, are also an indication of governmental adaptability and indigenous rule. The intelligent use of the Herods, the role of the Asiarchs, the functioning of the Areopagus, are severally illustrations of the same multilateral state craft. Add the procurators and the "free city" leaders in varied action.

The Areopagus merits a final word. Here is a prime example of the statecraft which Boissier noted – "she played on their vanity". The story of Athens, and Paul's appearance before the philosophers, is another example of Luke's superb reporting. The picture of the great Greek city is utterly convincing, the Athens of the afternoon, her glory shorn to a self-conscious preoccupation with the past. The speech, which may be read in exquisite lettering on a bronze plaque fixed to the flank of the Areopagus rock under the magnificence of the temple-crowned Acropolis, contains less than two hundred Greek words. In such brevity Luke caught the feeling of a great oration, the pattern of its argument, its allusive reference and quotation, the form and nature of its subtle persuasiveness, and the uncompromising point of its challenge. The whole report contains only three hundred and seventy words but reveals the city in a flash as a disapproving and ironical eye saw it, and yet the eye of one who had a way of moving to the centre of the stage. Like Socrates, and donning the manner of the Attic Greek, he argued in the market-place. He dismissed the Parthenon with a hand's sweep, an exhibition as theologically absurd as Ephesus' Fallen Thing. Hadrian and Herodes Atticus were soon to see the city with differerent eyes. It required the Christian to see what Thucydides and

[1] G. Boissier, *L'Opposition sous les Césars* (Paris, 1913), p. 29.

Demosthenes would undoubtedly have seen, could they have but returned, the fading glory, fastidious decadence, effete culture.

The story is found in the seventeenth chapter of the Acts of the Apostles. Simply translated, it runs thus:

> While Paul was waiting for his friends in Athens, he was deeply stirred to see the city given over to idols. And so in the synagogue he debated with the Jews and their adherents, and in the market-place every day with any he chanced to meet. Some of the Epicurean and Stoic philosophers met him, and some of them said: "What is the purpose of this picker-up of oddments?" And others said: "He appears to be a preacher of foreign deities" – for Paul was preaching Jesus and the Resurrection. So they brought him urgently to the Hill of Ares, saying: "May we know this new teaching of which you speak? For you bring to our hearing matters quite strange to us. And so we want to know what these things mean." (All the Athenians and the strangers residing there spent their leisure in nothing else but talking and hearing about the latest novelty) . . . Paul stood in the middle of the Hill of Ares and said: "Athenians, I observe that in every way you are uncommonly religious, for going about and looking at the objects of your worship, I even found an altar on which was inscribed TO THE UNKNOWN GOD! That which you worship, therefore, in ignorance, I am making known to you. God who made the universe and all that it contains, He, the Lord from all time of the heavens and the earth, does not dwell in temples which hands have made, nor is He served by human hands, as though He needed something, giving, as He does to all, life, and breath, and everything. And He made of one blood every race of men, causing them to dwell upon all the face of the earth, marking out for them their boundaries in time, and their place of habitation, and prompting them to seek God, if perhaps they might grope for Him and discover Him, though He is not far from any one of us. For in Him we live, and move, and indeed, exist, as some of your own Stoic poets have said: 'For we are also His offspring.' Being therefore, by the nature of things, God's offspring, we ought not to think that the Divine is like gold, or silver, or stone, carved work of man's devising. Well, then, the times of ignorance God overlooked; but now calls on all men everywhere to repent, because He has set a day in which He purposes to judge the world in righteousness, by the Man Whom He has appointed, giving assurance to all men by raising Him from the dead." On hearing of a resurrection of the dead, some scoffed. Others said: "We shall hear you again about this." So Paul came out from their company. But some men remained with him and believed. Among whom was Dionysius a member of the Court of the Hill of Ares, a woman named Damaris, and others along with them.[1]

A glimpse so vivid of the great Greek city could be matched only here and there in the writings of Demosthenes and Plato, already four centuries old.

But perhaps it is too easy for the classical historian, preoccupied with the picture of Athens in the early afternoon of Rome, to miss the true historical significance of the remarkable story. Surely the abiding meaning of the

[1] Acts 17:16–34.

chapter, and of all the second half of Acts, is found in the person of a man. Paul was no figure of the afternoon. He was the representative of a world unborn, the prototype of a Europe yet to be.

The strains and stresses which were to destroy the ancient world tug and bend around him – in Jerusalem, where the symbolic shout for Barabbas was moving to sanguinary conclusion; in Ephesus, where the spectre of proletarian persecution was taking a shape soon to walk more widely; in Athens, world-weary and too proud for violence in her rejection; in Corinth where a cultured Roman disdained a moment of history.

The choice which was to confront the Empire was becoming clear, along with the first shadow of the Empire's disastrous mistake, that move to repression and persecution, not commonly her policy, which was to weaken and divide her body when weakness and division were most likely to harm and enervate. Paul had seen the vision of a wider Rome, one which Julius and Vergil had fleetingly apprehended, and he tried to implant in the moribund system the seeds of a new life. With varied inventiveness and supreme audacity, he sought to conquer Rome for Christ.

And failed, yet in that failure demonstrated what could be. He was the first citizen of Europe, if the true European is one who carries in his culture, character and outlook, the threefold heritage of the ancient world. The rabbi of Jerusalem, the Greek of Tarsus, the citizen of Rome; trilingual, participant in three civilizations, interpreter of East to West; Paul, the apostle of Christ, emerges from the record more real than any other personality known to us from his generation. To know him and to understand him is to understand the next nineteen centuries. So meaningful is Acts.

CHAPTER II

THE ROLE OF THE CHRISTIAN PROPHET IN ACTS

E. EARLE ELLIS

IN SEVERAL PASSAGES IN ACTS, THE PHENOMENON OF PROPHECY IS ASCRIBED to Christian disciples generally. Thus, the Pentecostal experience of tongues, which is identified as prophecy,[1] is manifested by the whole Christian community. Likewise, the Ephesian disciples "began to speak with tongues and prophesy" (Acts 19:6) upon their reception of the Holy Spirit. Ananias, who received a prophetic revelation concerning Paul, also is designated simply as "a certain disciple" (Acts 9:10). Alongside these texts is the equally significant fact that Luke restricts the term or title προφήτης, as it is used of his contemporaries, to a select number of "leading men" (cf. Acts 15:22) who exercise considerable influence in the Christian community.[2] Among them are a group from the Jerusalem church visiting Antioch, including Agabus (Acts 11:27 f.; cf. 21:10); a group resident in Antioch, including Barnabas and Paul (Acts 13:1);[3] and the two prophets who accompanied the Jerusalem Decree to Antioch, Judas Barsabbas and Silas (Acts 15:22, 32). Peter also, who is not called προφήτης, nevertheless has the marks of a prophet, for example, in the knowledge of men's hearts (Acts 5:3; 8:21 ff.; cf. Luke 7:39) and in the experience and proclamation of revelations in visions and dreams.[4] Among such leaders

---

[1] Acts 2:4, 11, 17 f. Probably the equation of the proclamation in tongues with prophecy arises because the various tongues are, in fact, the native, understood languages of the respective hearers. Similarly, the "prophecy" in Acts 19:6 probably is an interpretation of the preceding strange "tongues" (cf. Acts 10:46; 1 Cor. 14:13). This appears to be preferable to an identification of the two phenomena although that cannot be ruled out (cf. H. Conzelmann, *Die Apostelgeschichte* [Göttingen, 1963], p. 27). In 1 Cor. 14:5, 39. Paul also desires that the whole congregation should prophesy.

[2] Apart from references to Old Testament prophets cf. Lk. 4:24; 7:16, 39; 9:8, 19; 13:33; 24:19; Acts 3:22 f.; cf. Acts 7:37 (of Jesus) and Acts 11:27; 13:1; 15:32; 21:10; cf. Lk. 11:49 (of Christians). Cf. Lk. 1:76; 7:26; 20:6 (of the Baptist). The verb form always in Acts refers to Christians: Acts 2:17 f.; 19:6; 21:9.

[3] It is probable *pace* J. Lindblom that both "prophets and teachers" describe the whole group. See below, p. 62.

[4] Acts 10:10; cf. 9:10; 16:9; 18:9; 22:17 ff.; 27:23. Visions and dreams (Joel 3:1 = Acts 2:17) are specific manifestations of prophecy. Cf. Num. 12:6; J. Lindblom, *Prophecy in Ancient Israel* (Oxford, 1962), pp. 147 f., 201. Apparently miracles were not necessarily or even usually associated with a prophet (*ibid.*, pp. 201 f., 217; cf. Jn. 10:41 with Lk. 7:26 par.). In Lk. 7:16 the disciples and the crowd make an explicit connexion between them; but Lk. 7:20 ff. better expresses the Evangelist's view of the significance of miracles. Acts (2:17 f., 43; 5:12-16; 10:34, 40; 19:11 f.) distinguishes prophecy from miracle working and, like Paul (2 Cor. 12:12; cf. Rom. 15:19), associates signs and miracles with the "apostle", but not exclusively so (Acts 6:8; 8:6 f., 13; 1 Cor. 12:28 f.; 14:22).

perhaps should be included the four daughters of Philip "who prophesied".[1]

In summary, Christian prophecy in Acts is represented as an eschatological power of the Holy Spirit from God (Acts 2:17) or from the risen Jesus (Acts 1:8; 2:17, 33; cf. Psa. 68:19 (18); Eph. 4:8). Although prophecy is a possibility for any Christian, it is primarily identified with certain leaders who exercise it as a ministry (see below). The specific "prophetic" functions of these persons is more difficult to establish. That is, which of their activities are specifically a manifestation of their role as προφήτης? What is the relationship of prophecy to other ministries in Acts? To identify the role of the Christian prophet it is necessary to discover Luke's understanding of what constitutes and what distinguishes prophecy.

I

Certain functions of the Christian προφήτης are clearly reminiscent of the role of the prophet in the Old Testament. In addition to the marks of the prophet mentioned above, these include the prediction of future events (Acts 11:28; 20:23, 25; 27:22), the declaration of divine judgments (Acts 13:11; 28:25–28), and the employment of symbolic actions (Acts 21:11). The prophets in Acts also expound the Scriptures and "exhort" and "strengthen" the disciples. Whether these activities also represent for Luke a distinctly prophetic function requires a closer look.

Luke's use of παρακαλέω/παράκλησις with reference to Christian prophets is relatively frequent. The verb is used to describe the proclamation of the Baptist[2] as well as the ministry of those in Acts who are designated prophets.[3] As a description of Peter's preaching, it may be one of the prophetic traits that characterize Luke's presentation of the apostle's ministry.[4] In Acts 15:32 the phrase παρακαλέω καὶ ἐπιστηρίζω ("exhort and strengthen") is specifically connected to the fact that Judas and Silas are prophets.[5] It is found elsewhere in the New Testament only

---

[1] Acts 21:9. The patristic references (Eusebius, *Ecclesiastical History* 3, 31, 4; 3, 37, 1) suggest that their activity was not an occasional phenomenon but was a distinguished and long-remembered ministry. So, J. Lindblom, *Gesichte und Offenbarungen* (Lund, 1968), p. 179, who distinguishes them as persons who have the prophetic charism as "a continuing possession". Cf. Lk. 2:36 where Anna is called a prophetess; Rev. 2:20.

[2] Lk. 3:18; cf. 7:26.

[3] Barnabas (Acts 11:23), Paul and Silas (Acts 16:40), Paul (Acts 20:2). It is noteworthy, however, that the term is not used to describe the ministry of Jesus.

[4] Acts 2:40 (διαμαρτύρομαι καὶ παρακαλέω); cf. 1 Thes. 2:12; above, p. 55, n. 4. On μαρτυρέω cf. also Acts 10:42 f.; 18:5; 20:21 ff.; Eph. 4:17. It appears at times to be virtually a *terminus technicus* for an utterance in the Spirit, i.e., prophecy.

[5] F. J. F. Jackson and K. Lake, *BC*, 4, p. 182, noting the parallelism between Acts 15:27 and Acts 15:32, translate "Judas and Silas themselves, being prophets . . ." and reject the reading, "who also were themselves prophets", with its allusion to Acts 13:1 f.

in Acts 14:22, used of the prophets Paul and Barnabas, and (with the cognate στηρίζω) in the Thessalonian letters.[1] The noun παράκλησις, which occurs in the New Testament only in Luke–Acts, Paul and Hebrews, is associated by Luke with the activity of the Holy Spirit.[2] Furthermore, the written παράκλησις of the Jerusalem Decree is set in parallel with the verbal "exhortation" of the prophets Judas and Silas, and the term "son of παράκλησις", applied to Barnabas in Acts 4:36, possibly represents "son of prophecy".[3] The understanding of παράκλησις as the specific ministry of a prophet is supported in the Pauline literature by 1 Corinthians 14:2 f. There the prophets' ministry of "edification" is accomplished by means of παράκλησις and παραμυθία[4] which are, in the words of G. Stählin, "a part of the work of prophesying".[5] A similar impression is given in Romans 15:4 f., where the Scripture or God gives παράκλησις and in 2 Corinthians 5:20 where God "exhorts" through Paul and Timothy.[6] It is true that in Paul παράκλησις is not always explicitly identified as a Spirit-mediated, eschatological reality and, even as a charism, it can be listed alongside of and distinct from προφητεία (Rom. 12:8). Nevertheless, it probably has a special connexion with Christian prophecy, even when that connexion is not explicitly expressed.

To return to Acts 15:32, in the light of the above considerations it is very likely that the fact that Judas and Silas are prophets is the basis of their ministry of παράκλησις.[7] The clause should then be translated, "since they themselves also were prophets". It compares their verbal exhortation with the written, and also prophetic, παράκλησις of the Jerusalem Decree.[8]

---

[1] 1 Thes. 3:2; 2 Thes. 2:17. The former describes the task given to Timothy, their "fellow-worker", by Paul and Silas.

[2] The church walks "in the παράκλησις of the Holy Spirit" (Acts 9:31); the prophets Paul and Barnabas are invited to give a "word of παράκλησις", i.e., an exposition of Scripture (Acts 13:15); the Jerusalem Decree, which is given through the Holy Spirit, is termed a παράκλησις (Acts 15:28, 31). Cf. O. Schmitz, TDNT 5 (1954–1968), pp. 794–96.

[3] Bar-ne bû'āh or bar-nebiyyā, assuming that παράκλησις in Acts 4:36 means "exhortation". So, already commonly a century ago, J. A. Alexander, The Acts of the Apostles (New York, 1884 [1857], 1, p. 183; cf. H. J. Holtzmann (Die Apostelgeschichte, Tübingen), 1901, p. 45; Jackson and Lake, op. cit., 4, p. 49; F. F. Bruce (The Acts of the Apostles, London, ²1952), pp. 130 f. If this interpretation is correct, his Christian name like Peter's (Matt. 16:18) describes what his distinctive ministry or function in the Christian community was or was to be (cf. Matt. 1:21; Acts 13:1). The clause, "called Barnabas by the apostles", makes improbable the suggestion that Barnabas was a family designation or surname.

[4] That is, paraklēsis and paramuthia show or define the nature of the oikodomē. Similarly, H. D. Wendland, Die Briefe an die Korinther (Göttingen, 1965 [1936]), p. 109; H. Conzelmann, Der erste Brief an die Korinther (Göttingen, 1969), p. 277; otherwise: A. Robertson and A. Plummer (The First Epistle of St. Paul to the Corinthians, Edinburgh, 1914),p. 206. Cf. 1 Thess. 2:12; Phil. 2:1 where these two terms are joined to describe respectively the ministries of Paul, Silas and Timothy and, more generally, the effects of the Holy Spirit in the congregation.

[5] G. Stählin, TDNT 5 (1954–1968), p. 82. Cf. 1 Cor. 14:31.

[6] Cf. also 2 Thes. 2:16 f.

[7] So, E. Haenchen, Die Apostelgeschichte (Göttingen, ⁶1968), p. 395.

[8] Acts 15:27 f., 31. E. Käsemann (New Testament Questions of Today [London, 1969], p. 74) has called attention to the parallel between Acts 15:28 and the edict of the Spirit reflected in 1 Cor. 14:37. See below, p. 61.

In Luke's thought παράκλησις is one way in which the Christian prophets exercise their ministry and, in this context, is a form of prophecy.

The interpretation of Scripture, usually in the synagogues, is a key feature of the missions of the prophets Paul and Barnabas, Paul and Silas, as well as of Peter and other Christian leaders.[1] This manner of teaching is elaborated in Acts 13:16–41 in the form of a synagogue homily. It may or may not be significant that the "prophets" in question also are "teachers". (The exposition of Scripture is ascribed to Barnabas [Acts 13:5; 14:1] but not to Silas.) Also this activity in Acts is not described as "prophecy" nor limited to "prophets". In what degree then can it be regarded as "prophetic" activity?

The interpretation of Scripture as an activity of a prophet was not unknown in the first century since it was explicitly ascribed to Daniel (9:2, 24). It may be inferred also from other Old Testament texts in which the prophet uses and reapplies older biblical phraseology and ideas.[2] These phenomena support the views of S. Krauss and others who connect the prophets with the origins of the synagogue and regard them as the first to dispense religious teachings in such assemblies.[3] The rabbinic tradition, reflects a similar picture. According to the Targum to Judges 5:9, Deborah, under prophetic inspiration, "did not cease to give exposition of the Torah."[4] The rabbis, moreover, regarded themselves, as the teachers of Israel, to be the successors of the prophets: they sat "in Moses' seat".[5]

With respect to the interpretation of Scripture, then, there was not a

---

[1] E.g., Acts 2:14–36; 3:12–26; 4:8–12 (Peter); 6:9–11; 7:2–53 (Stephen); 8:30–35 (Philip); 9:20–22; 13:5, 16–41; 17:2, 10 f., 17 (22–31); 18:4; 19:8; 26:22 f.; 28:23 (Paul); 18:24–28 (Apollos).

[2] For example, cf. Jer. 48:45 with Num. 21:28; 24:17; Jer. 50–51 with Isa. 13–14; Zeph. 2:15 (zō't = αὔτη) with Isa. 47:8. On Dan. 11:30 as a reinterpretation of Num. 24:24 see F. F. Bruce, "The Book of Daniel and the Qumran Community", *Neotestamentica et Semitica*, ed. E. E. Ellis and M. Wilcox (Edinburgh, 1969), p. 233. See also my article in the same volume, p. 61. Cf. 2 Chr. 13:22.

[3] Cf. L. Zunz, *Die gottesdienstlichen Vorträge der Juden* (Hildesheim, 1966 [1892]), pp. 37 f.: Already in the Old Testament period older Scriptures were interpreted and in a certain sense changed. Ezra and the Levites appear as interpreters of the laws; the Chronicler makes use of midrash; Daniel is the interpreter of Jeremiah. The schools of the prophets become assemblies of the wise. S. Krauss (*Synagogale Altertümer* [Hildesheim, 1966 (1922)], p. 54) sees the incipient synagogue reflected in the "house of the people" (Jer. 39:8) = "house of assembly" (Ps. 74:8), which began as assemblies in the temple area. I. Elbogen (*Der jüdische Gottesdienst* [Hildesheim, 1967 (1931)], p. 235), on the other hand, finds the origin of the synagogue in assemblies in the Exile in which prophets "strengthened the religious consciousness of the people by readings from the Scriptures followed by teachings of exhortation and consolation". Cf. *SB* 4, p. 115. For a different view cf. B. Reicke, *The New Testament Era* (Philadelphia, 1968), pp. 119 f.

[4] *SB* 4, p. 116. Cf. R. Meyer, *TDNT* 6 (1959–1969), p. 817: According to the rabbis the prophets are "the oldest expositors of the Law ..."

[5] Matt. 23:2; R. Meyer, *op. cit.*, 6, pp. 818 f. "Since the temple was destroyed prophecy has been taken from the prophets and given to the wise" (Baba Bathra 12a). Haggai, Zechariah and Malachi were viewed as the first members of the chain of rabbinic tradition (Krauss, *op. cit.*, pp. 47 f.). "Moses received ... and delivered to Joshua, and Joshua to the elders, and the elders to the prophets, and the prophets to the men of the great synagogue" (Aboth 1:1). See also J. Jeremias(*Jerusalem in the Time of Jesus*, London, 1969), pp. 233–245.

sharp division between the prophet and the teacher. This is perhaps to be most clearly observed in the Qumran community's "teacher" (*mōreh*) and the wider number functioning as "instructors" (*maśkīlīm*). In a perceptive essay Professor Bruce has compared the wisdom possessed by "Daniel the prophet"[1] and by the "wise" (*maśkīlīm*) in Daniel 11, 12 with that of the "wise" at Qumran. "The *maśkīl* here, as in Daniel, is one who, having received from God understanding in his hidden purpose, is thus in a position to impart that understanding to others".[2] Without identifying themselves as prophets, the teachers at Qumran engage in an interpretation of Scripture that has as its model the activity of Daniel the prophet. This becomes more significant for the present essay when one observes the similarities between the method of biblical interpretation at Qumran and that in Acts 13:16–41.[3] In Acts, however, the interpreter is given the title "prophet" as well as "teacher".

Both terms also are applied to Jesus. It is clear from Luke 7:39 f. that they are not mutually exclusive: the one who is addressed as teacher may also be (the eschatological) prophet. Also, Jesus' teaching "in their synagogues"[4] often must have included *ipso facto* a midrash or exposition of Scripture.[5] It is less clear, however, to what degree such teaching is the cause of, or attached to, the conviction that Jesus is a prophet.

Two passages that bear upon this question are Mark 1:21 (cf. Lk. 4:31)

---

[1] So identified in 4Qflor 2:3. Cf. Dan. 9:22, 25.

[2] Bruce, "Daniel and Qumran", pp. 228 f. Cf. 1QS 9: 17–19: the *maśkīl* is to conceal the teaching of the Law from the men of falsehood but to instruct the Community "in the mysteries (*rāzēy*) of wonder and truth"; 1QH 12:11 f.: "as a *maśkīl* have I come to know thee, my God, through the spirit that thou hast given me, and by thy Holy Spirit I have faithfully listened to thy marvellous secret counsel (*sôdh*)." Similarly, of the Teacher of Righteousness, "to whom God made known all the mysteries (*rāzēy*) of the words of his servants the prophets' (1Qp Hab. 7:4 f.).

[3] Cf. E. E. Ellis, "Midrashic Features in the Speeches of Acts," *Hommage au Professeur B. Rigaux* (Gembloux, 1970), pp. 306 f.

[4] For example, Lk. 6:6; 13:10; Jn. 6:59; 18:20; cf. Mk. 1:39 parr. In Matt. (4:23; 9:35) it is included in the editorial summaries of Jesus' ministry. Some of the "teaching in the temple" (ἱερόν; Mk. 12:35), which is primarily concerned with the exposition of Scripture, may have its historical setting in a synagogue in the temple enclosure. On the existence and services of such a synagogue compare Elbogen, *op. cit.*, p. 236; Krauss, *op. cit.*, pp. 66–72, 95; and I. Levy, *The Synagogue* (London, 1963), pp. 15 ff. Cf. Yoma 7:1; Sotah 7:7. One of the temple episodes, Mk. 12:1–12 parr. (= Isa. 5:1f. + parable + Ps. 118:22 + Dan. 2:34 f., 44 f.) has the form of an ancient synagogue homily. Cf. *SB* 4, pp. 173 f.: In the oldest form (pre-second century) "the speaker more or less reproduced the Scripture lesson or parts of it, thereby pointing to the exhortation, warning or consolation included in this or that word in it. Or he illumined the Scripture lesson by means of a parable and strengthened the words that he himself had added by a further Scripture text" (p. 173). For a different approach to Jesus' teaching cf. M. Hengel, *Nachfolge und Charisma* (Berlin, 1968).

[5] Cf. Lk. 4:16–28; Acts 13:14–43; Philo, *Quod Omnis Probus Liber* 81 f.; E. Schürer, *A History of the Jewish People* (Edinburgh, c. 1890), 2, 2, pp. 54 f., 76, 82; Elbogen, *op. cit.*, pp. 194 f.; *SB* 4, p. 171. A Greek inscription in a first century Jerusalem synagogue states that it was built "for the reading of the law and the teaching (διδαχή) of the commandments" (E. L. Sukenik, *Ancient Synagogues in Palestine and Greece* [London, 1934], p. 70). *lmdh* (=διδάσκω) and its derivatives are used in the oldest rabbinic exegetical literature to couple the text to its exposition (cf. W. Bacher, *Die exegetische Terminologie der judischen Traditionsliteratur* [Darmstadt, 1965 (1899)], 1, pp. 94 ff.).

and Mark 6:2 (cf. Lk. 4:16; Matt. 13:54). In the former text Jesus' exposition, in contrast to that of the Jewish theologians, is characterized by ἐξουσία. Although some commentators interpret ἐξουσία as pointing to the prophetic character of Jesus' teaching,[1] this is not as clear as one might wish. For the word is seldom if ever used elsewhere to describe a prophet's teaching[2] although it may, in the New Testament, represent his personal rights in the congregation or his miraculous powers.[3] The prophetic character of Jesus' exposition may perhaps be inferred, however, from its connexion with his miraculous powers, which also are described as a "teaching" (Mark 1:27).[4]

In Mark 6:1–6 also both Jesus' synagogue teaching and his miraculous powers are the cause of the people's astonishment. Nevertheless, there are two significant differences: his teaching is here described as σοφία, and Jesus compares or identifies his role with that of a prophet.[5] The "wisdom" (σοφία) that is "given" to Jesus is recognized by his audience to be an extraordinary pneumatic power; the question is whether it has a divine or demonic origin. In an instructive essay on the concept of σοφία U. Wilckens writes that Mark uses his received picture of Jesus as a Scripture teacher to present him as the archetype of Christian charismatics.[6] Whether such a broad inference may be drawn from this text or not, it is true in any case that Jesus is so regarded in the primitive church.[7] Furthermore, probably no strong dichotomy should be made between the rabbinic "wisdom" of being learned in the Scriptures – the ordained rabbi[8] – and the "wisdom" of the knowledge of God's mysteries that is present in the prophets and teachers of Jewish apocalyptic, especially in Daniel and

[1] V. Taylor, *The Gospel according to St. Mark* (London, 1959), pp. 173, 470; C. E. B. Cranfield, *The Gospel according to St. Mark* (Cambridge, 1959), p. 74; J. Schniewind, *Das Evangelium nach Markus* (Göttingen, 1960 [1936]), p. 18.

[2] Cf. C. K. Barrett, *The Holy Spirit and the Gospel Tradition* (London, 1947), p. 96; G. Friedrich, *TDNT* 6 (1959–1969), p. 843.

[3] 2 Thes. 3:9: Paul and Silas (cf. Didache 13); Rev. 11:6.

[4] Cf. E. Schweizer, *Das Evangelium nach Markus* (Göttingen, 1967), p. 27.

[5] Cf. Lk. 13:33. C. K. Barrett (*op. cit.*, p. 97) objects to taking the proverbial expression, "a prophet is not without honour except in his own country" (Mk. 6:4), as representing Jesus' literal estimate of his ministry. But even if Jesus is only referring to an (admittedly) common view of himself, "by not merely adopting the view but also preparing to exemplify it, Jesus numbers himself among the prophets" (Friedrich, *op. cit.*, p. 841; cf. pp. 843 f.). Of course, for both Jesus (cf. Lk. 7:26) and the Evangelist "prophet" is not a category exclusive of any other, higher role. Cf. O. Cullmann, *The Christology of the New Testament* (Philadelphia, 1959), p. 44.

[6] U. Wilckens, *TWNT* 7 (1964), p. 515; cf. P. Bonnard, *L'évangile selon S. Matthieu* (Neuchâtel, 1963), p. 213. The accusations that Jesus was demonically inspired concern not only his miraculous powers (Mark 3:22 parr) but also his teaching (Jn. 8:48, 52; 10:19 f.; Mk. 3:21; cf. D. E. Nineham, *The Gospel of St. Mark* [Harmondsworth, 1963], p. 123). Also, according to the rabbinic tradition Jesus was condemned because he practised sorcery and enticed Israel to apostasy. The latter charge is couched in the words of Deut. 13:8 f., the condemnation of a false prophet (Sanh. 43a). Cf. Justin, Dial. 69; J. L. Martyn, *History and Theology in the Fourth Gospel* (New York, 1968), pp. 64–68.

[7] Cf. E. Schweizer, *Church Order in the New Testament* (London, 1961), pp. 189 f. (23b). See above, p. 258.

[8] Wilckens, *op. cit.*, 7, pp. 505 f. Daube (*op. cit.*, pp. 207, 216) thinks that the passage represents Jesus to be teaching as though he were an ordained rabbi.

Qumran.[1] The context of the wisdom, that is, the biblical revelation, is the same. The difference in the case of Jesus, however, is not just that he, an unordained person, manifests the bearing and biblical knowledge of an ordained rabbi (so Daube). There is also a qualitative distinction. Like the synagogue teaching of his later follower Stephen, no one "could withstand the wisdom and the spirit" with which Jesus expounded the Scriptures.[2]

While the limited amount of evidence does not allow certainty in the matter, it is probable that not only the miracle-working context but also the manner of Jesus' exposition of Scripture in the synagogue contributed to the conviction that he was a prophet. And it could do so because such exposition was regarded as the proper activity of a prophet. Very likely Luke, at least, views the same kind of exposition of "prophets and teachers", e.g., in Acts 13 also to be an exercise of a prophetic gift.[3] It is true that this conclusion depends in some measure on Luke's understanding of the relationship of "teacher" and "prophet" (see below). But it is supported as well by the mention given to Judas and Silas in connexion with the Jerusalem Decree.

E. Käsemann has noted the similarity of the words in the Decree, "it seemed good to the Holy Spirit and to us" (Acts 15:28), to the promulgation of eschatological law elsewhere in the New Testament. He thinks that the latter is the work of Christian prophets, and that often "holy Scripture provided the primitive Christian prophets with the stylistic form in which to clothe their sentences of holy law".[4] Indeed, the formula λέγει κύριος in Acts 15:16–18 reflects something more: the *exposition* of Christian prophets.[5] In addition, the theme of the citation, the inclusion of the Gentiles, is specifically the "mystery" that according to Paul "has now been revealed to (Christ's) holy apostles and prophets by the Spirit".[6]

---

[1] See above, p. 59 Cf. Wilckens, *op. cit.*, 7, pp. 503 ff.

[2] Acts 6:9 f.; cf. 6:8 (δύναμις); Lk. 2:46 f., 52. Although he did not follow out its implications for the synagogue teaching of Jesus, C. H. Dodd rightly called attention to this distinction as an important clue for understanding "Jesus as Teacher and Prophet" (*Mysterium Christi*, ed. G. K. A. Bell and A. Deissmann [London, 1930], pp. 56 ff.).

[3] The eschatological interpretation of Scripture in Acts 2, Acts 7, and elsewhere is no different even when προφήτης is not used and the location is not the synagogue (but cf. Acts 6:9). Cf. Lk. 4:22 with Acts 4:13.

[4] E. Käsemann, "Sentences of Holy Law in the New Testament", *New Testament Questions of Today* (London, 1969), p. 77; cf. pp. 74, 76 ff. The content and style of the Decree itself are admittedly quite different from Käsemann's "Sentences of Holy Law".

[5] Like the texts that Käsemann adduces, the λέγει κύριος quotations also sometimes include the theme of *jus talionis* (Rom. 12:19; 14:11; 1 Cor. 14:21; Heb. 10:30). And they form a distinct class of quotations that are most likely the product of Christian prophets. Cf. E. E. Ellis, *Paul's Use of the Old Testament* (Edinburgh, 1957), pp. 107–12, 146 f.; Lindblom, *Gesichte*, p. 188. It is also worth noting that Acts 15:14, 15 ff. follows a recognizable midrashic style, Current Event→Scripture (cf. Ellis, "Speeches", pp. 308 f.; B. Gerhardsson, *Memory and Manuscript* [Uppsala, 1961], pp. 252, 260) and that traces of a midrashic literary form are evident elsewhere in James' speech (Acts 15:14–21; cf. J. W. Bowker, *NTS* 14 [1967–68], 107 ff.).

[6] Eph. 3:3–5; cf. Rom. 16:25. Note the use of γνωρίζω and (in Acts) γνωστός.

This theme is, in turn, directly related to the "new temple", a major motif in the λέγει κύριος quotations.[1] Taken together, these facts strongly suggest that the prophets Judas and Silas were not chosen incidentally to accompany the Decree. Probably they were chosen because they had already exercised an influential role in establishing (or proclaiming) the biblical rationale upon which the provisions of the Decree were justified.[2]

The foregoing discussion enables us to return to the question raised earlier and to answer it with some measure of confidence. The interpretation of Scripture was indeed regarded, under certain conditions, as prophetic activity.[3] And it is likely that Luke does so regard it, even in such persons as Peter and Stephen who are not given the explicit appellation προφήτης.

II

The persons in Acts named προφῆται exercise a rather widespread ministry and they do so in a varied fashion – singly or in groups, travelling or in settled congregations. The content of their activity also is varied – prediction (Acts 11:28; 20:23, 25, 29 f.; 21:11), specific direction of the community in its decisions (Acts 13:1 f.; 15:27) and teaching by exhortation and biblical exposition.[4] Yet, as was noted at the outset, persons who are not termed "prophets" exercise some of the same functions. This fact raises two questions that must be answered if the role of the prophet in Acts is to be placed in clearer perspective. First, in view of the breadth of the prophetic function, why is the term relatively so restricted? Furthermore, what is the relationship of the prophet to other designated ministries in Acts, specifically the apostle, the teacher, and the elder?

Long ago H. B. Swete distinguished between those in the primitive Church who on occasion prophesied and a relatively small number who were known as οἱ προφῆται, "forming a charismatic order to which a recognized position was given in the Church".[5] In a recent study J. Lindblom reaches a similar conclusion, apparently independently, and enumerates as such "berufsmässige Propheten" Agabus and his companions (Acts 11:27 f.), the Antioch circle (Acts 13:1 ff.), Judas and Silas (Acts 15:32), and the daughters of Philip (Acts 21:9).[6] This kind of distinction, which is supported by several texts in Paul and in Revelation, may be the best

---

[1] Eph. 2:20; cf. Acts 7:48 ff.; 2 Cor. 6:16 ff. On Heb. 8:8–12 cf. Ellis, *Testament*, p. 108.

[2] Similarly, Lindblom, *Gesichte*, p. 185 n. Significant also is the fact that the Decree is termed a παράκλησις (see above, pp. 57 f.).

[3] Cf. E. G. Selwyn, *The First Epistle of St. Peter* (London, 1946), p. 134: "In the case of Christian prophets . . . the searching of the Scriptures . . . was an important part of their task . . ."

[4] Lindblom, *Gesichte*, pp. 180–88.

[5] H. B. Swete, *The Holy Spirit in the New Testament* (London, 1910), p. 377.

[6] Lindblom, *Gesichte*, p. 179; see above, p. 56.

explanation of the matter.[1] E. Schweizer rightly cautions against making a sharp distinction in the earliest period between official or "ordained" and unordained ministries, and the *caveat* applies to Luke's own time as well.[2] Nevertheless, a special recognition and authoritative status appear to be conferred upon the *persons* of those who have manifested certain charisms in a prominent and/or continuing manner.[3]

Except for the twelve apostles (Acts 1:22, 6:2, 6) Luke shows little interest in defining the ministries that he names. Even in that case it is "the twelve" whose ministry is (partly) explained by apostleship, not apostleship by the twelve. This is clear from the fact that Luke can also call them "disciples" and name other persons apostles.[4] The latter instance presents a further complexity in that "the apostles Barnabas and Paul" are previously named "prophets and teachers". Thus, the triad of gifts in 1 Corinthians 12:28 are clustered around and apparently applied to the same persons in Acts.[5] Also, in Acts 20:17, 28 the editorial "elders" is equivalent to the term "bishops" in the speech of Paul that follows (cf. Phil. 1:1). In part the ambiguous nature of the specified ministries in Acts is traceable to the differing terminology in Luke's sources, terminology that he is unconcerned to conform to a consistent pattern. But the lack of concern itself suggests that for Luke no less than for his traditions there is a certain ambiguity and fluidity in the designation of ministries. On the one hand, the Spirit is itself the gift and to be "full of the Spirit" implies the empowerment to manifest a variety of gifts (Acts 2:33; 6:3, 8 ff.). On the other hand, certain persons may be so identified with a specific gift as to be recognized and set apart in the community on that basis. For Paul also certain persons are set apart in terms of a specific charism (1 Cor. 12:28).[6] At the same time one person may manifest a multiplicity of charisms (1

---

[1] There is an apparently recognized group of prophets (in Corinth) whom God "appointed (τίθημι) in the Church" (1 Cor. 12:28; cf. 14:29 ff.; Acts 20:28) and who "have prophecy" (1 Cor. 13:2). Similarly, Rev. 22:9.

[2] Schweizer, *Church Order*, pp. 102 f., 184-87 (5i, 7m, 22efg). See below, p. 66.

[3] For example, in the case of apostleship cf. 1 Cor. 9:1 ff.; 12:28 f.; 15:9; 2 Cor. 1:1; 12:11 f.; Gal. 1:1, 17 ff. Further, H. Greeven, "Propheten, Lehrer, Vorsteher bei Paulus," *ZNTW* 44 (1952-53), 1-43: "by προφῆται (1 Cor. 14:29) specific, known persons appear to be meant . . ." (pp. 4 f.); teaching also is designated not just as an activity (Rom. 12:7) but also with reference to specific persons (pp. 16 f.). [See R. Schnackenburg's essay in the present volume, pp. 287-303. Edd.]

[4] Lk. 9:12, 16 (22:14, 30, 39); Acts 14:4, 14; 15:6, 13 (?James); cf. Acts 1:25 f.; Gal 1:19; Lk. 11:49. Otherwise, Gerhardsson, *op. cit.*, p. 220.

[5] M. Goguel (*The Primitive Church* [London, 1964 (1947)], p. 111) shows that the triad of gifts in 1 Cor. 12:28 are embodied in Paul. A fourth-century work, which may reflect a much earlier textual tradition of Acts 13:1 ff., identifies Barnabas and Paul as "prophets and teachers", the others as "prophets". The text is given in Bruce, *Acts*, p. 253; cf. T. Zahn, *Introduction to the New Testament* (Grand Rapids, 1953 [1909]), 3, p. 28. On the basis of τε instead of καί before Manaen and Saul (Acts 13:1) W. M. Ramsay (*Saint Paul the Traveller* [London, 1896], p. 65) concluded that they were teachers and the others were prophets. But this is a slight basis for distinguishing the functions (so Haenchen, *op. cit.*, p. 338). Probably both titles apply to all. Cf. Fascher, *op. cit.*, p. 185; Zahn, *op. cit.*, 1, p. 116; Schweizer, *Church Order*, pp. 72, 183 (5k, 22c). Otherwise, Lindblom, *Gesichte*, p. 176 n.

[6] See above.

Cor. 12:31; 14:1; 2 Tim. 1:11), and (some) charisms and charismatics may be grouped in an undifferentiated manner as πνευματικά and πνευματικοί (1 Cor. 14:1, 37; 3:1).

In this context it is not always easy to distinguish the role of the prophet from that of other ministries. Seeking to do so, G. Friedrich concludes that "teachers expound Scripture, cherish the tradition about Jesus and explain the fundamentals of the catechism, the prophets . . . speak to the congregation on the basis of revelations . . ."[1] While this distinction may be true as far as it goes, it does not give sufficient weight to the teaching role of the early Christian prophet. Predictive prophecy, of course, presents no problem. But as the above discussion has shown, there is no clear division in Judaism or the primitive church between the teaching of a prophet and of a teacher. Likewise, the false prophets in the church teach (1 Jn. 2:22, 26 f.; 4:1 ff.), and the false teachers in the church correspond to the false prophets of the Old Covenant (2 Pet. 2:1). As H. Greeven rightly recognizes, both the prophet and the teacher expound the Scriptures and the sayings of the Lord, and in this area the transition from teaching to prophecy is "gewiss fliessend".[2] For Paul prophecy apparently is a formal term embracing various kinds of inspired teaching.[3] The teaching of the prophet apparently overlaps that of the teacher and can be distinguished from it only by the manner in which it is given or by the recognized status as "prophet" of the one who is teaching. In Acts also various kinds of teaching are present in the activities of the prophets. Probably the same relationship between the prophet and the teacher is assumed. But one cannot speak with assurance, especially since διδάσκαλος occurs only in Acts 13:1.

There also is an overlapping of the roles of apostle and prophet. Indeed, E. C. Selwyn argued that "apostles" were "prophets on circuit" in contrast to "prophets in session".[4] That is, an apostle is simply a prophet who is sent (ἀποστέλλω) as a missionary. In support he cites Didache 11: 3-5.

> But concerning the apostles and prophets (τῶν ἀποστόλων καὶ προφητῶν do according to the ordinance of the gospel. Every apostle who comes to you receive as the Lord . . . But if he remains three days he is a false prophet.

The usage is remarkable, and it is one possible explanation why Barnabas and Paul on tour are called apostles (Acts 14:4, 14) but are named prophets only while resident in Antioch (Acts 13:1). However, it is more likely that

---

[1] Friedrich, op. cit., 6, p. 854; cf. Gal. 1:12.
[2] Greeven, op. cit., p. 29; cf. Fascher, op. cit., p. 185.
[3] Goguel, op. cit., p. 265. Neither προφητεία nor διδασκαλία occurs in Luke-Acts; in Acts διδάσκαλος appears only at 13:1.
[4] Cf. E. C. Selwyn, The Christian Prophets (London, 1900), pp. 24 f.; Saint Luke the Prophet (London, 1901), pp. 35, 27-32. So also, Fascher, op. cit., p. 185. Selwyn's works contain considerable information and some good insights, but they are marred by an erratic style and by unsupported and extravagant assertions.

the shift in terminology reflects Luke's use of a different tradition. In any case the explanation hardly accords with the use of the terms elsewhere in Acts where "apostles" reside in Jerusalem and "prophets" travel.

To pose the question differently, is there any activity ascribed to the Christian prophet that is not also true of those named apostle? Apparently there is none. The example of the apostle Peter, mentioned above, illustrates that every activity of the prophet – including prediction, exhortation and biblical exposition – can also be ascribed by Luke to the apostle.[1] On the other hand, unlike the prophets the apostles do "many wonders and signs" (2:43), witness to the resurrection of Jesus (1:22; 13:31; cf. 26:16), exercise an authority in the congregations, and impart the Holy Spirit (8:15 ff.; cf. 19:6). It may be significant that it is in connexion with one of these activities, miracle-working, that Barnabas and Paul are named apostles.[2] Likewise, in the Pauline literature the mark of an apostle includes "signs and wonders and mighty works" (2 Cor. 12: 12; cf. 1 Cor. 9: 1). In summary, the ministries of the apostle and the prophet in Acts may be compared to two concentric circles, in which the circle of the prophet's activity is somewhat smaller.

Christian "elders" ($\pi\rho\epsilon\sigma\beta\acute{\upsilon}\tau\epsilon\rho\omicron\iota$) appear in Acts as a leadership group in the congregations of Jerusalem (11:30; 21:18), Galatia (14:23), and Ephesus (20:17). Their function is "to shepherd" ($\pi\omicron\iota\mu\alpha\acute{\iota}\nu\epsilon\iota\nu$) the church of God (20:28), a term whose cognate $\pi\omicron\iota\mu\acute{\eta}\nu$ is listed in Ephesians 4:11 among the spiritual gifts. In Acts the elders also are given their task by the Holy Spirit (20:28) even though they may be appointed by a prophet or apostle (14:23).[3] The description of the prophets Judas and Silas as "leading men" apparently sets them apart from the "apostles and elders" in Acts 15:22 (so Haenchen). However, several facts suggest that the elder, like the prophet, had a teaching function in addition to his responsibilities of general oversight of the community.

The Christian use of the term $\pi\rho\epsilon\sigma\beta\acute{\upsilon}\tau\epsilon\rho\omicron\varsigma$ is clearly derived from Judaism where it was used of a group in the Sanhedrin and of the community and/or synagogue leaders.[4] Traditionally the elders in Judaism were a "lay nobility", heads of ancient patrician families. In the first

---

[1] See above, p. 64. Cf. Friedrich, op. cit., 6, p. 850.

[2] Acts 14:3 f., 10, 14. Their authority over the congregations is indicated in the same chapter (14:23) but its description is perhaps more reminiscent of Acts 13:1 ff. than, for example, of Acts 6:6. It should be added that miraculous signs also are ascribed to Stephen and Philip, persons who are called neither apostles nor prophets. Cf. Acts 6:8; 8:6 f.; Schweizer, Church Order, pp. 196 f. (24b).

[3] Ibid., pp. 183 f., 186 (22df). Cf. 1 Pet. 5:1 f. The term $\pi\rho\epsilon\sigma\beta\acute{\upsilon}\tau\epsilon\rho\omicron\varsigma$ does not appear in the Pauline literature outside the Pastoral Epistles where, like Acts 20:17, 28, it is equated with $\dot{\epsilon}\pi\acute{\iota}\sigma\kappa\omicron\pi\omicron\varsigma$ (Tit. 1:5, 7; cf. Phil. 1:1).

[4] According to G. Bornkamm, TDNT 6 (1959–1969), pp. 662 f., the elders in Acts 11:30; 21:18 resemble a synagogue council; the "apostles and elders" in Acts 15 reflect a different tradition and, patterned after the Sanhedrin, function "as a supreme court and normative teaching office for the whole Church". Similarly, Gerhardsson, op. cit., p. 251. But does this give sufficient weight to the charismatic and prophetic nature of the assembly's actions?

E

century, however, persons who also had been trained as scribes were preferred when community or synagogue leaders were chosen. That is, one who was selected to be elder was likely to be a theologian.[1] For the early Christian community this would correspond to a charismatic person, e.g., a teacher, even though he may have been titled πρεσβύτερος (in conformity with the Jewish custom) or ἐπίσκοπος within the organizational structure.

This view of the matter accords with a number of New Testament texts. (1) As they do in Judaism, the elders in Acts 15 and Acts 20 function as guardians of the tradition, although the similarity is qualified by the role of the Spirit among the Christians.[2] (2) The Christian elder may exercise a specific ministry of teaching (1 Tim. 5:17; 2, 3 Jn. 1).[3] However, the same kind of ministry may be exercised without reference to any name or title.[4] Although in Acts the elder is a part of the organized expression of the church, he is very likely selected on the basis of certain spiritual gifts.[5] And his ministry itself is doubtless viewed as a manifestation of a charism. Therefore, the role of the prophet may overlap that of the elder as it does that of the apostle and the teacher, especially in certain teaching functions. But unlike the prophet the apostle (in Jerusalem at least) and the elder or "shepherd" are incorporated into the organizational structure.

III

At a number of places in Acts the early Christian mission is viewed as a continuation of Jesus' mission and as a contest between conflicting spirit-powers. The former is expressed most clearly as the immediate action of the exalted Lord himself (Acts 1:1 ("began"); 9:5; 10:13; 16:7; 22:18; 23:11). The contest is explicit in the encounter of Peter with Simon Magus (8:9-24) and the encounter of Paul with the false prophet Barjesus (13:6ff.)

---

[1] Jeremias, op. cit., pp. 236 f. The Sadducees obtained their scribes from within this lay nobility, i.e., the "elders", who thus functioned as interpreters and guardians of the tradition (p. 231).

[2] Cf. also, 1 Pet. 5:1 ff.; Schweizer, Church Order, p. 200 (24i).

[3] Concerning 2, 3 John cf. Bornkamm, op. cit., 6, p. 671. The elder also may be expected to exercise gifts of healing (Jam. 5:14). According to Didache 15 the bishops and deacons "also perform the service of the prophets and teachers". "Bishop" (ἐπίσκοπος) is here equivalent to πρεσβύτερος.

[4] Cf. 1 Cor. 16:16; 1 Thes. 5:12 with 1 Tim. 5:17.

[5] Cf. Acts 6:3; Schweizer, Church Order, p. 184 (22e). The absence of the term in Paul (outside the Pastorals) is remarkable and its use possibly "represents a later assimilation to Jewish forms" (ibid., p. 200). But in view of the early necessity of structure (Acts 6) and the Church's identification of itself as the true Israel it is more likely that in some Jewish–Christian communities the term was used in an official way from the beginning. Cf. B. Reicke, "The Constitution of the Primitive Church," The Scrolls and the New Testament (New York, 1957), pp. 143–56. A comparison of Acts 1:20b, 25 (ἐπισκοπή, ἀποστολή) with Acts 20:17, 28 (πρεσβύτερος, ἐπίσκοπος) suggests that for Luke the apostle may be a special kind of elder just as the Twelve are a special kind of apostle (cf. 1 Tim. 3:1; see above, p. 65). This would place Acts 15 in a different light and clarify both its relation to Acts 11:30; 21:18 and the readings of Codex Bezae at Acts 15:5, 12, 41 ("elders.").

and the medium in Philippi (16:16). The same kind of conflict may be inferred from the episode of the Jewish exorcists (19:13–20). The role of the Christian prophet is related to both of these Lukan themes. The prophet is the Lord's instrument, one among several means by which Jesus leads his church. As one who makes known (γνωστός) the meaning of the Scriptures, exhorts and strengthens the congregation, and instructs the community by revelations of the future, the Christian prophet manifests in the power of the Spirit the character of his Lord, who is the Prophet of the end-time (3:22).

CHAPTER III

THE JOURNEY MOTIF IN LUKE-ACTS

FLOYD V. FILSON

I

THE JOURNEY NARRATIVE SO STRIKINGLY USED IN LUKE-ACTS IS ONE OF the dominant literary patterns of the Biblical story. This pattern is prominent in the Book of Genesis, which tells of the nomadic wanderings of the patriarchs from Ur to Haran and then southward to the land of Canaan and even down to Egypt. These journeys are followed by the Exodus and the forty years in the wilderness before Joshua leads Israel into the promised land.[1] The period of the Judges still saw no fixed centre of worship and government. The prophet Samuel carried on a rather itinerant ministry in which Mizpah, Bethel, Gilgal, and Ramah were centres of limited role (1 Sam. 7).

Not until David captured "the stronghold of Zion" (2 Sam. 5:7) did the ark, the portable journeying focus of the worship of Israel, find a stable resting place. Plans were developed by David for a temple as the fixed centre of the religious life of God's people. But the building of the temple by Solomon did not provide a satisfying and spiritually worthy focus of worship; the apparently stable religious life of Israel was in fact often linked with polytheistic and syncretistic practices, particularly forms of Baal worship; and the Biblical writers consider the exile, first of the northern kingdom and then of the Jerusalem leaders, to be the well-deserved result of the largely unworthy royal, priestly, and popular life of Israel. The return from exile sounded again the journey motif of a people restlessly seeking the satisfaction of their spiritual hunger in a homeland and way of life truly loyal to their God (Isa. 40:3).

Likewise in the New Testament we find a detachment from the more stable institutions of the day. The Qumran sect had dramatized this withdrawal from existing religions. This sect withdrew from the Jerusalem-centred Jewish worship and in the wilderness awaited a true priesthood and worship which could command its loyalty. John the Baptist, though of priestly descent, withdraws to the wilderness and preaches there to those who come to hear him. Jesus responds to the wilderness preaching of John and soon returns to Galilee to carry on an itinerant ministry, which probably was interrupted more than once by a brief visit to Jerusalem and

[1] See the use of this motif in Ernst Käsemann, *Das wandernde Gottesvolk*[2] (Göttingen, 1957). Cf. the journey as a quest for heavenly rest in the letter to the Hebrews.

finally was followed by a climactic journey to Jerusalem, a journey noted in all four Gospels (least clearly in the Gospel of John) and accented especially in Luke, and undertaken by Jesus to give a final challenge to his people and especially to its leaders, challenging them to respond to his last appeal for repentance and obedience to God. After his death and resurrection his followers carried on a witnessing ministry outwardly centred in Jerusalem and its temple but essentially outside of the formal structure of the religious life of his people and without any clearly planned programme to shape the expansion of the developing Christian church. (Acts 1:8 is not a systematic programme for the Christian mission.) But characteristic of the informally developing pattern of Christian mission was the continual travel which began at Jerusalem and spread out over a large portion of the eastern Mediterranean area. (No journey to Mesopotamia or to Egypt is mentioned but note a possible hint in Acts 2:9, 10 and the story of the Ethiopian eunuch in Acts 8:26-40.) Both the ministry of Jesus and the preaching of the Apostles and other Christian leaders were marked by itineration and continual journeying rather than by stable authoritative resident leadership. James the brother of Jesus was essentially of the latter kind (but see I Cor. 9:5). The future of the church, however, was not with him, as we shall see.

In both the Old and the New Testament Jerusalem most nearly provides a stable and organizing centre of the worship and life of God's people. But it rarely if ever proved the fully worthy centre for which dedicated men looked. Most of the kings were unworthy; they "did what was evil in the sight of the Lord." (In 1 and 2 Ki. this familiar formula occurs over thirty times.) This condemnation is applied especially to the kings of Israel but also to many of the kings of Judah. The priesthood was often corrupt. The lay leaders of Jerusalem were repeatedly unjust and greedy. In the New Testament the Roman overlords and the Jewish priests and social leaders were no better. Jerusalem was a promise never really fulfilled. The sensitive and loyal among God's people had to sit loose to the standards, the rulers, the priests, and the economic and social leaders of Jerusalem. As a result many of the devout men of Israel, such as the Qumran sect and John the Baptist, had to make the reverse journey, not to the promised land and its central city, but away into the wilderness from which Israel had entered the promised land. Jerusalem and its institutions were not really built upon the solid and durable foundations for which the faithful people of God looked. Life continued to be a restless journey, a constant quest for the divine gift which Israel's existing life failed to give them. This is why the itinerant ministry of John the Baptist and Jesus evoked so great a response; it promised the blessings and the rest which the journeying people of God had so long been seeking.

II

Both the Gospel of Luke and the Book of The Acts share this general Biblical pattern of the journey. The wilderness sojourn and later the preaching of John the Baptist (Lk. 1:80; 3:1–20), the journey of Joseph and Mary to Bethlehem and Jerusalem at the time of Jesus' birth (Lk. 2:4, 22), their journey to Jerusalem with him when he was twelve years old (Lk. 2:42), his itinerant preaching travels culminating in the decisive journey to Jerusalem to challenge the religious leaders there (Lk. 4:14; 9:51), and the continual journeys in Acts, chapters 8–28, mark the journey motif as consistently characteristic of the New Testament period and movement. It is not surprising, though it is significant, that Luke, whom I take to be the author of Luke–Acts, gives great prominence to this common Biblical journey motif.

Our concern, however, is with the fact that Luke makes his own distinctive use of this recurring journey motif. He does this not merely or mainly by including the journeys of Luke 1 and 2 and by extending the story of "the things of which" Theophilus had "been informed" (Lk. 1:1–4) to include not only the itinerant ministry of Jesus but also the developments of the Apostolic Age. All of these "things" are important. He does it even more strikingly by including two great travel sections, one in the middle of the Gospel of Luke (9:51–19:44) and one forming the last third of the Book of The Acts (19:21–28:31). In each case the *extended* journey narrative indicates that special meaning attaches to the journey reported.

We must first note the characteristics of each of these two substantial blocks of material. We then must consider what meaning Luke wished to convey by so arranging his material as to throw such emphasis on the journey pattern. Each of these two travel sections has its own peculiar features and can tell us something of the thinking that lay behind Luke's literary use of the journey motif.

III

The great travel section of the Gospel of Luke (9:51–19:44) tells of the decisive journey of Jesus from Galilee to Jerusalem, a section which takes up nearly 40 per cent of this Gospel. It fills ten of the twenty-four chapters of the Gospel of Luke. For comparison, note that in Matthew this journey occupies only two chapters (19 and 20) and in Mark but one (ch. 10). The place where this section begins in Luke is clear; it is plainly marked by the explicit statement of 9:51: "When the days drew near for him to be received up, he set his face to go to Jerusalem." The Galilean ministry is ended; Jesus sets out for Jerusalem. There is some difference of opinion as to where the travel narrative ends. This may be due, in part at least, to a tendency of some scholars to end the travel section where Luke resumes parallelism with Mark (Lk. 18:15). The logical end of the travel section, however, is where Jesus arrives at Jerusalem. This means that the special Lucan travel section begins with 9:51 and ends with 19:44.

The effect of making this middle section of the Gospel of Luke into a long travel narrative is, first of all, to eliminate one journey found in Matthew and Mark, the journey into the district of Tyre and Sidon (Matt. 15:21–28; Mk. 7:24–30; for Luke the gospel is to go from Galilee to Jerusalem and from Jerusalem out into the world). The effect in the second place is to reduce the role which Galilee plays in this gospel. Whereas in Matthew the Galilean ministry occupies the space from 4:12 to 18:35 (fourteen and one-half chapters), and in Mark from 1:14 to 9:50 (eight and two-thirds chapters), in Luke it is compressed into the much shorter section beginning at 4:14 and ending at 9:50 (about five and one-half chapters). This is only partly explained by Luke's lack of any parallel to Mark 6:45–8:26. In his concern to make the significance of Jesus' journey to Jerusalem stand out, Luke deliberately shortens the Galilean ministry and builds up the travel section, in part with material which in Matthew and Mark is located during the Galilean ministry. Luke knows that it was at Jerusalem that the final decision concerning Jesus' ministry and appeal had to be made. He therefore so structures his gospel as to build attention and suspense directed towards that final crisis and decision at Jerusalem.

An intriguing feature of Luke's literary procedure is his cautious introduction of references to Samaria and Samaritans. The Gospel of Matthew in its one mention of the Samaritans (10:5) limits itself to saying that the disciples should "enter no town of the Samaritans". The Gospel of Mark simply ignores Samaria and the Samaritans. The Gospel of John in 4:1–42 reports Jesus' encounter with the Samaritan woman and his brief ministry in her city. Luke proceeds in his own way. Luke 9:52 and 17:11 locate the travelling Jesus on the border between Galilee and Samaria, and at least one of the ten lepers whom Jesus heals in 17:11–16 was a (grateful) Samaritan. Moreover, it is the humane Samaritan who is the praiseworthy figure in the famous parable in Luke 10:25–37. So Luke has an interest in Samaria and Samaritans. Luke's interest in Samaria is further shown by his attention to the early spread of the gospel to Samaria in Acts 1:8; 8:5–25; 9:31. But it must be noted that Luke does not know and makes no specific claim to know of any actual ministry by Jesus in the region of Samaria. He merely pictures Jesus travelling on the border between Galilee and Samaria. The incidents he reports in his extended travel section have as a whole the atmosphere of Jewish life. This conclusion that Luke really knows of no Samaritan ministry by Jesus is supported by the use in his travel section of Jewish oriented material from "Q" and "L". It seems to have its setting in Jesus' ministry not to the Samaritans but to the Jews.

His travel section in his gospel (Lk. 9: 51–19:44) prepares for but does not begin the ministry to the Samaritans.

IV

The other great travel section of Luke–Acts is the final third of the Book of The Acts (19:21–28:31). At 19:21 Luke clearly begins a new section. He has told of the crucial beginnings of the church at Jerusalem (1:1–6:7); he then has reported the ministry of the Seven, the martyrdom of Stephen, the outreach to Samaria, and Saul's conversion (6:8–9:31); the next section tells of Peter's ministry on the Palestinian coastal plain, the extension of the church northward to Antioch in Syria, and Peter's imprisonment, release, and departure from Jerusalem (9:32–12:24); the fourth section tells of the missionary preaching of Barnabas and Paul in Cyprus and south-central Asia Minor, and the agreement that Gentiles may become Christians without prior conversion to Judaism (12:25–16:5); and then the fifth section reports Paul's independent mission to Macedonia, Achaia, and Asia (16:6–19:20). Up to this point the story of The Acts has dealt with the basic beginnings of the church and its missionary outreach, especially through Paul, and each of the five sections has closed with a summary which attests that Luke has a definite outline in mind as he writes.[1]

The rest of The Acts has its own clear objective. It is announced in 19:21 "Now after these events Paul resolved in the Spirit to pass through Macedonia and Achaia and go to Jerusalem, saying, 'After I have been there, I must also see Rome.'" The days of Paul's independent mission in the eastern half of the Mediterranean world have ended. His thoughts and plans now look westward. He is at Ephesus. He will not forget the churches he has founded. He must first visit and strengthen those churches in Macedonia and Achaia. But that done, he will go to Jerusalem (to take the collection his churches have been raising for the Jewish Christians at Jerusalem, although Luke only hints at that errand in Acts 24:17). Then from Jerusalem he intends to go to Rome, a visit he has long desired to make and one which he has conceived as a step on the way to Spain for new missionary work (we learn of his purpose in Rom. 1:10–15; 15:23–29). Luke, however, does not mention the plan to go on to Spain. It is the journey to Rome that holds all his attention. He tells the story in great detail. In Luke's view there obviously was special importance in the going of Paul to Rome to preach.

The fact that Acts 19:21–28:31 constitutes a unit and is the longest section of the book of Acts is often overlooked. This neglect seems due mainly to a mistaken emphasis on the so-called three missionary journeys

[1] On this question, see my *Three Crucial Decades* (Richmond, Va., 1963), chapter one.

of Paul, the first to Cyprus and southern Galatia (Acts, chs. 13–14), the second to southern Galatia, Troas, Macedonia, and Achaia (15:40–18:22), and the third to southern Galatia, Ephesus, Macedonia, and Achaia, ending with a journey to Jerusalem (18:23–21:17). This thinking in terms of three missionary journeys gives no real place to Paul's decision to go to Rome; the Roman destination in this view becomes vital only as the result of Paul's appeal to Caesar (25:11); this view gives no place to the clear statement of Acts 19:21 that while at Ephesus Paul determined to revisit his churches and Jerusalem and then go to Rome, so that Paul's determination to go to Rome dominates the last third of Acts.

For Luke the journey to Rome is planned at Ephesus. That journey is prepared for by a circuit of the Aegean Sea to revisit the churches Paul had founded on his independent mission in Macedonia and Achaia. The journey to Rome for Paul would be possible only after he had again visited Jerusalem, doubtless to take the collection which his Gentile churches are to send to Jerusalem to show their oneness with the Jewish Christians there (24:17 – this is what seems to be in mind). It is wrong to ignore the clear indication of 19:21 that the entire section of The Acts from 19:21 to 28:31 is a unit. Paul's plan to visit Rome is so important that Luke feels justified in giving the final and climactic section of The Acts, one-third of his entire account of the Apostolic Church, to the story of how Paul determined to go to Rome and finally did so.

Professor F. F. Bruce gives to the section 19:21–28:31 the heading: "Paul plans to visit Rome via Jerusalem and achieves his aim in an unexpected way."[1] He says of 19:21: "This verse summarizes the remainder of Acts." This view of Bruce is a faithful reflection of the data of The Acts.

V

What observations can we make which will throw light on the question: Why did Luke think Paul's journey to Rome so important that he devoted to it one full third, the climactic final third, of the Book of The Acts?

It is no real answer to this question to say that this journey narrative shows, as do other parts of the Biblical narrative, that God's purpose may be realized in ways that man has not planned or expected. This final third of The Acts does illustrate that point. Paul had planned to go to Rome as a free traveller, but he went as a prisoner; and he had thought to preach in Rome as a free Roman citizen, but he had to preach while chained to a Roman guard. It does not sound to modern ears like a success story; Paul was maligned, plotted against, imprisoned, and shipwrecked, but he reached Rome and preached there, even if he did not do so as he had

[1] *The Acts of the Apostles* (London, 2nd ed., 1952), p. 360.

intended. We modern Christians tend to see mainly frustration in what Paul had to endure, but Paul himself and Luke saw in it the providence of God.

This point is instructive, but it is no reason why Luke should give the entire final third of The Acts to the travel narrative of Paul's journey to Rome. The point could have been made by a much briefer narrative. There must be a more adequate and distinctive reason why Luke devoted a full third, the final climactic third, of his story of the Apostolic Age to the journey which brought Paul to Rome.

It comes nearer to the truth to say that in this final narrative of The Acts Jerusalem and its spiritual leaders lose their opportunity to be the focus and centre of the Christian movement. To put it in other words, these closing chapters of The Acts attest both the potential continuing import-ance and the actual dispensability of Jerusalem and its temple for the Christian church. Up to this point in The Acts, Jerusalem has been the central city of the story. It has been mentioned far more often than any other city, and it has remained thus far the dominant city of the church. Antioch in Syria, Corinth, and Ephesus have been prominent, Antioch especially as a missionary centre founded by Hellenistic Jewish disciples but soon reaching out in a Gentile mission; but none of them has thus far rivalled Jerusalem in importance. Even Paul, the Apostle to the Gentiles, has recognized the importance of Jerusalem. He had lived there for a time; he has visited it more than once (9:26; 11:30; 15:2–4; 18:22). That he should feel bound to go to Jerusalem again before going to Rome is a witness to the importance Jerusalem had for him. To be sure, he has a special reason to take this final trip thither; he goes with "alms" (24:17), collected for the poor Christians of Jerusalem by the Gentile Christians in other cities,[1] but this specific errand does not exhaust the significance of his going to Jerusalem at the risk of his life before he sets out for Rome. As was true in the ministry of Jesus, Jerusalem cannot be ignored; the gospel must be preached there; if it is ready to accept its opportunity and respon-sibility, it will continue to be the centre and focus of the Christian church; the gospel will continue to go out from there; it will lose its primacy only by its own decision, and particularly the decision of its leaders, not to accept the gospel.

Yet if Jerusalem fails to meet its opportunity, that will not be the end of the church. As in the Old Testament, the purposes of God can go forward even if the city does not accept its divinely given role and opportunity. Just as in the Old Testament the fall of Jerusalem was not the end of God's purpose nor the substantial defeat of his will, so also in this new situation the divine purpose can go forward in spite of the rejection of the gospel

---

[1] In Acts the fact that this collection was for the poor Christians of Jerusalem is not clearly stated; Luke does not mean to deny this, but he sees the gift as in a real sense a gift Paul was bringing to his people.

and in spite of the aggressive hostility to Paul on the part of the Jewish leaders of the temple and the city.

It is the repeated emphasis of the closing chapters (and indeed of the earlier chapters) of The Acts that the gospel is the fulfilment of God's promises to Israel as found in the Old Testament; the church is the divinely given continuation of the life of Israel and so the church is the true Israel. Jerusalem could have continued to be the focal geographical and spiritual centre of that new and true Israel. But it failed to avail itself of its privilege. With the mob attack on Paul in the temple and the active attempt of the Jewish leaders to put Paul out of the way, Luke sees the failure of Jerusalem to accept and fulfil its role; and so Luke in this final third of The Acts is presenting the lost opportunity which Jerusalem had and the essential transfer of the centre of the church from Jerusalem to Rome.

The fact is that Luke sees theological meaning in the geography of his story. He thinks in terms of centres of the life of God's people. He saw no possibility that Galilee could serve as the dominant centre of the church. As we have seen, he reduces greatly the proportion of his gospel which deals with Jesus' Galilean ministry. His outline of the gospel gives much more attention to the journey from Galilee to Jerusalem than it does to the entire ministry in Galilee. And when Jesus leaves Galilee for Jerusalem, he takes final leave of the Galilean scene. He never comes back. The disciples stay in Jerusalem after the crucifixion, and in the Gospel of Luke none of the resurrection appearances is located in Galilee. In the entire Book of The Acts there is no word of preaching in Galilee (it is even omitted in 1:8). Only the one bare brief mention of the church in Galilee in 9:31 breaks this curious silence about Galilee. Luke's attention focuses on other regions.

VI

It would capture the essential geographical outlook of Luke to entitle the Gospel of Luke "From Galilee to Jerusalem", and the Book of The Acts "From Jerusalem to Rome". Jerusalem was the goal of the ministry of Jesus; it could have been the focus and centre of the ongoing church; because it rejected its privilege and opportunity, the centre moves to Rome; Paul executes and symbolizes that transfer. It may be objected that there were already Christians at Rome – indeed, there was a widely known and noteworthy church there – before Paul arrived (Acts 28:14–15; Rom. 1:8 f.). This is true. But for Luke the coming of Paul to Rome signals and symbolizes the entrance of Rome into the role of focal centre of the church and missionary home base of its gospel outreach. The centre of the church is no longer Jerusalem; it now moves to Rome.

Another way to see the significance of Acts 19:21–28:31 is to think back to Acts 1:8. In that programmatic verse at the beginning of The Acts the disciples are charged to take the gospel to Jerusalem, Judea, Samaria, and "to the end of the earth". The narrative of The Acts tells how that charge was carried out. But how can Paul's going to Rome and his preaching there fulfil Acts 1:8, which commands the disciples to take the gospel to "the end of the earth"? We can understand this only if we think, as Luke and Paul both did, from the Roman point of view. To a Roman the city of Rome was the centre of the world; from the golden milestone in the Forum at Rome roads went out in all directions to all parts of the Empire. So when The Acts ends with Paul in Rome preaching the gospel, Luke must mean that now from the centre of the world the gospel is beginning to go out in all directions to all parts of the Empire. For Luke, Paul's preaching in Rome is not just a local evangelistic programme; it is or at least symbolizes and sets in motion the broad Empire-wide fulfilment of Acts 1:8. The gospel centre has come from Jerusalem to Rome and is beginning to spread out from there in all directions.

It is noteworthy that Luke centres attention on Paul's *preaching* in Rome. This is the emphasis of the closing words of The Acts in 28:30-31. The personal fortunes of Paul are not Luke's focus of interest. The focus is rather on the gospel, and the preaching of the gospel by the one who is representing his Lord in the capital city of the Empire. It is curious that through the centuries Christians have discussed the later traditions about the coming of Peter to Rome and his preaching and leadership there, but in all this discussion have tended to ignore almost entirely the fact that in The Acts Peter is not the founder of the Roman church or the apostolic guarantor of the gospel preached there. The Acts gives no hint that Peter ever visited Rome. For Luke, Paul is the Apostle who came to Rome and became the sponsor and guarantor of that church's message. There is no hint in The Acts (or in anything Paul wrote) that Peter brought the gospel to Rome or was the founder or sponsor of the church there.[1] This distinction as apostolic sponsor Luke gives to Paul.

VII

For Luke Paul is the outstanding figure of the Apostolic Church. He receives far more space and attention than Peter. And he is the one apostolic sponsor of the church at Rome and is the apostolic guarantor of its gospel.

The later one dates The Acts, the more remarkable this ignoring of Peter at Rome becomes and the more striking is the basic role given Paul there. There was a church at Rome before Paul arrived there, but Peter did not found it or lead it before Paul's arrival; that Peter came there a little later,

[1] For a careful study of the career of Peter and his death in Rome see Oscar Cullmann, *Peter: Disciple, Apostle, Martyr*,[2] trans. by F. V. Filson (Philadelphia, 1962).

near the end of his career, is probably true, but this does not change the fact that for Luke Peter had no role at Rome, and instead Paul was the apostolic sponsor and guarantor of the gospel at the centre of the Roman Empire.

The fact that Paul is the apostolic guarantor of the gospel at Rome and the representative of the church's outgoing mission there helps us to see why The Acts ends as it does. Christians usually end their reading of The Acts with questions about the personal fortunes of Paul. Was he tried and condemned? Was he executed? Was he released after a trial? Was he released by default after two years of waiting in vain for a hearing or trial? Did he do further preaching in Spain and/or in eastern Roman provinces where he had previously preached the gospel? A rather good case can be made out that he *was* released and did further travel and preaching. But the point is that The Acts says nothing on these matters. Luke was not writing a biography of Paul.

The term "the Way" (Acts 9:2; 19:9, 23; 22:4; 24:22), which is used in Acts five times as a designation for the Christian faith and group, is another indication that Luke and the apostolic church found journey language congenial.

That Paul reached Rome, that he was the apostolic sponsor of the gospel there and so of the Roman church, that he preached there and represented the world outreach of the gospel at the centre of the Roman Empire – this is what Luke has to say. This is the goal of the journey which is reported in the climactic final third of the Book of The Acts.

CHAPTER IV

THE PREFACE TO LUKE AND THE KERYGMA IN ACTS

A. J. B. HIGGINS

ACCORDING TO ANCIENT TRADITION LUKE WROTE BOTH THE GOSPEL and the Acts.[1] While the identity of "Luke" is disputed, unity of authorship, including the "we" sections of Acts in their present form, is widely accepted on the basis of style and language.[2] The Lukan writings also form a distinct theological unit within the New Testament, so that we can speak of "the theology of Luke".[3] The most notable attempt to disprove unity of authorship on linguistic grounds was that of A. C. Clark,[4] who tried to demonstrate that the linguistic differences between Luke and Acts are much more important than the resemblances; that they cannot be explained, as Hawkins thought, by the supposition that Acts was written considerably later than the gospel; and that they point, in fact, to different authors. But the complete unsoundness of Clark's arguments was proved by W. L. Knox.[5] The common authorship of the two Lukan writings may be regarded as established.

I

Does the Lukan preface (Luke 1:1–4) refer only to the gospel, or to both the gospel and Acts?[6] The former view is supported by H. Conzelmann[7] and E. Haenchen.[8]

---

[1] Muratorian Canon; Anti-Marcionite Prologue; Irenaeus, *Haer.* iii. 1.1; etc.

[2] This was established by A. Harnack, *Luke the Physician* (London, 1907), and J. C. Hawkins, *Horae Synopticae*[2] (Oxford, 1909), pp. 174–93.

[3] H. Conzelmann, *The Theology of Saint Luke* (London, 1960).

[4] *The Acts of the Apostles* (Oxford, 1933), pp. 393–405.

[5] *The Acts of the Apostles* (Cambridge, 1948), pp. 2–15, 100–109; cf. É. Trocmé, *Le "Livre des Actes" et l'histoire* (Paris, 1957), pp. 38–41.

[6] It has even been suggested (by J. L. Moreau, see R. H. Fuller, *The New Testament in Current Study* [London, 1963], p. 103) that the preface was originally prefixed to Acts, which was published by a different author subsequently to the gospel, and that when the two works were combined, it was transferred to the beginning of the gospel and replaced by a new introduction to Acts. But it is impossible to imagine how a preface which certainly alludes, at least in its first part, to the gospel, could originally have been intended only for Acts.

[7] *The Theology of Saint Luke*, p. 15, n. 1.

[8] *Die Apostelgeschichte*[12] (Göttingen, 1959), p. 105, n. 3; "Das 'Wir' in der Apostelgeschichte und das Itinerar", *ZThK* 58 (1961), pp. 362–66 (Eng. trans., "'We' in Acts and the Itinerary," *Journal for Theology and the Church* 1 [1965], pp. 95–99).

In 1953 R. Koh[1] and C. S. C. Williams[2] suggested independently of one another that the πρῶτος λόγος in Acts 1:1 is not our third gospel, but a sort of Proto-Luke. The present Lukan gospel was written after Acts. If so, the Lukan preface must have been prefixed to the former after the completion of both works. Doubtless the author intended his writings to be read in the correct chronological order: the ministry of Jesus recorded in his gospel, and the life of the church recorded in Acts. The preface could then have been planned to refer to both writings, although they had been composed in the reverse order. The case for the priority of Acts, however, is not strong, and πρῶτος λόγος in Acts 1:1 seems a more apt description of the gospel of Luke than of a hypothetical first draft of it.

The majority view is, in fact, that Luke 1:1-4 is a preface to both gospel and Acts as two parts of a single work.[3] This accords with the practice in antiquity of dividing a work into volumes (especially when it would not all go on a single papyrus roll), with a preface prefixed to the whole, and with secondary prefaces introducing later volumes and summarizing briefly the contents of the preceding volume.[4] An excellent example of this practice, including the renewed address to his patron Epaphroditus, is to be found in the two parts of the work of Josephus Against Apion.[5] The striking similarities to the beginnings of Luke and Acts not only show that these too are really two parts of a single work, but also suggest that the Lukan preface is intended also for Acts. The difficulties arise when it comes to actual interpretation of the preface. Although this refers to Acts as well as to the gospel, it is not to be expected that all its phraseology applies equally to both. The author himself says in Acts 1:1 that his πρῶτος λόγος concerns the earthly ministry of Jesus. Acts itself does not.

The crux in the preface is undoubtedly the phrase κἀμοὶ παρηκολουθηκότι ἄνωθεν πᾶσιν ἀκριβῶς. According to Cadbury, παρακολουθέω does not mean follow in the sense of investigate or inquire into, for which (he claims) there is no lexical support, but to observe, to be in close touch with,

---

[1] The Writings of St. Luke (Hongkong).
[2] "The Date of Luke-Acts," ExpT 64, pp. 283 f.; Cf. The Acts of the Apostles (London, 1957), pp. 12 f.; also H. G. Russell, "Which was written first, Luke or Acts?" HTR 48 (1955), pp. 167-74, and P. Parker, "The 'Former Treatise' and the Date of Acts," JBL 84 (1965), pp. 52-58.
[3] So recently E. E. Ellis, The Gospel of Luke (London, 1966), p. 62.
[4] Cf. E. Norden, Agnostos Theos (Leipzig/Berlin, 1929 = 1913), pp. 311-13; H. J. Cadbury, BC 2 (1922), p. 491.
[5] Apion I.1, κράτιστε ἀνδρῶν Ἐπαφρόδιτε (cf. Lk. 1:3, κράτιστε Θεόφιλε); I. 1 (3), ᾠήθην δεῖν γράψαι (Loeb edn., pp. 162 f.; cf. Lk. 1:3, ἔδοξε κἀμοὶ . . . γράψαι); Apion II. 1, διὰ μὲν οὖν τοῦ προτέρου βιβλίου, τιμιώτατέ μοι Ἐπαφρόδιτε (Loeb edn., pp. 292 f.; cf. Acts 1:1, τὸν μὲν πρῶτον λόγον ἐποιησάμην περὶ πάντων, ὦ Θεόφιλε); F. F. Bruce, The Acts of the Apostles: the Greek Text, etc.[2] (London, 1962), p. 66.

or to participate in events.[1] As an example he cites Josephus, *Apion* I. 10 (53).[2]

δεῖ τὸν ἄλλοις παράδοσιν πράξεων ἀληθινῶν ὑπισχνούμενον αὐτὸν ἐπίστασθαι ταύτας πρότερον ἀκριβῶς, ἢ παρηκολουθηκότα τοῖς γεγονόσιν ἤ παρὰ τῶν εἰδότων πυνθανόμενον.

"It is the duty of one who promises to present his readers with actual facts first to obtain an exact knowledge of them himself, either through having been in close touch with the events, or by inquiry from those who knew them."[3]

By using παρηκολουθηκότα Josephus refers to his first-hand experience of events in the war with the Romans, contrasted with inquiry from others. Similarly in Luke 1:3 the author, in employing this word in conjunction with the first person pronoun, is drawing a distinction between reports about Jesus which had reached him by tradition, and his personal knowledge of or participation in subsequent events, and in the latter case is referring to the second part of Acts, in which the "we" passages occur. Cadbury does, however, allow that Acts as a whole could be meant. [4]

A different interpretation is offered by Haenchen in the latter part of his article cited above.[5] Luke 1:1 makes it clear "that the prologue is intended only for the gospel: there were several gospels . . . but not acts of the apostles."[6] The use in the main sentence (verse 3) of ἀκριβῶς with παρηκολουθηκότι shows that, although the verb *can* denote first-hand knowledge, in the sense of participation in events, the context does not favour that meaning here. What is meant is investigation from the beginning,[7] and ἄνωθεν is equivalent to ἀπ' ἀρχῆς in verse 2. If Cadbury were correct in supposing that Luke meant that he had closely followed everything for some considerable time past, and that he was referring to the second part of Acts, "then the whole thing would be senseless; Luke in his foreword to the Third Gospel would only be indicating his qualification as a writer of history in the second half of Acts but would be saying nothing about his qualification as writer of the *historia Jesu*."[8] Haenchen, then, judges that Luke claims to be qualified to write a gospel, because he has accurately

---

[1] *BC* 2 (1922), pp. 501 f.; *The Making of Luke-Acts*[2] (London, 1958), pp. 345–47; "'We' and 'I' Passages in Luke-Acts," *NTS* 3 (1956–57), pp. 128–32. In his full study of the word ("The Knowledge Claimed in Luke's Preface," *Exp* 8th series, 24 (1922), pp. 401–20) Cadbury wrote (p. 408) of the former meaning, "For a century this semasiological impostor appears to have held practically absolute sway," but pointed out that Hug in 1808 defended the same thesis as himself. He found an enthusiastic follower in J. H. Ropes, *JTS* 25 (1924), pp. 70 f., and *The Synoptic Gospels*[2] (1960), pp. 63 f.

[2] *BC* 2 (1922), p. 502; cf. *Exp* 24 (1922), p. 404; *NTS* 3 (1956–57), p. 130.

[3] Loeb edn., pp. 184 f.

[4] *NTS* 3 (1956–57), p. 131: "Acts as a whole or its later part."

[5] The page numbers are those of the English translation, followed by those of the German original in parentheses: pp. 95–99 (pp. 362–66).

[6] *Op. cit.*, p. 96 (p. 363).

[7] *Op. cit.*, p. 97 (pp. 364 f.); cf. W. Bauer, *Griechisch–Deutsches Wörterbuch*[3] (1963), 1227 = Arndt, p. 624.

[8] *Op. cit.*, p. 98 (p. 365).

investigated the matter in detail right from the beginning of the story of Jesus in the infancy narratives (ἄνωθεν πᾶσιν).[1]

In his valuable study of the "we" and "they" passages,[2] J. Dupont refuses to follow Haenchen in excluding all allusion to Acts from the Lukan preface, since an ancient preface applied to a work as a whole, "even if certain of its expressions apply only to a part."[3] On the other hand, he agrees with Haenchen against Cadbury that "the things which have been accomplished among us" can hardly be events in Acts and especially in the second part of Acts, but must be the events affecting all Christians ("us"), and forming the material of earlier attempts at producing gospel narratives. Dupont's remark, "What the eyewitnesses transmitted by their ministry of the word is to be found in the Gospel; Acts seek [sic] to show rather how they transmitted it,"[4] is a pointer towards a correct understanding of the implications of the Lukan preface.

The preface, then, does not refer solely to the gospel but, like other ancient prefaces, to the whole work. The question is, which of its statements refer to which parts of this work?

The first two verses refer to the gospel alone, and not at all to Acts. This might be expected from mere considerations of chronological order, but it is confirmed by examination of content and language. First are mentioned the things fulfilled among "us", that is, all Christians. And what has happened is the gospel story of salvation in the life, ministry, death, resurrection and exaltation of Jesus (cf. Acts 1:1 f.), of which many, i.e., several,[5] predecessors of Luke have endeavoured to draw up a narrative. There is no evidence, on the other hand, that Acts was preceded by any attempts to record systematically the activities of the early churches and their leaders, nor could παρέδοσαν and the following words bear any such meaning. Verse 2 alludes to the transmission of the tradition about Jesus by those (in particular, we may suppose, the Twelve) who had been eyewitnesses of his ministry, and after the resurrection "servants of the Gospel" (NEB). Although the writer distinguishes himself from these primary authorities, and includes himself among the recipients of the tradition ("us" in verse 2 perhaps denoting especially himself and his predecessors in gospel writing), it does not follow that he lived so much later (near the end of the first century) that he might not have been Luke, the companion

---

[1] Cf. W. G. Kümmel, *Introduction to the New Testament* (London, 1966), p. 127, siding with Haenchen against Cadbury and Dupont, and not recognizing in the "I" of the preface any preparation for the "we" passages in Acts 16 ff.

[2] Chapter VI of *The Sources of Acts* (London, 1964).

[3] P. 110, n. 52.

[4] *Ibid.*, p. 110, n. 53.

[5] Perhaps only three? Cf. J. Bauer, "ΠΟΛΛΟΙ, Luk.i:1," *NovTest* 4 (1960), pp. 263–66 (p. 266). Less plausibly B. P. W. Stather Hunt, *Primitive Gospel Sources* (London, 1951), pp. 44 ff., suggested that Luke refers to a single document, a primitive testimony book of proof-texts and their fulfilment in Jesus, to the compilation of which many had contributed, and undertakes to improve its chronological arrangement.

F

of Paul. παρέδοσαν does not necessarily signify a prolonged process of transmission of tradition, as is clear from 1 Cor. 11:2, 23; 15:3.

We now come to the disputed passage in verse 3a: ἔδοξε κἀμοὶ παρηκολουθηκότι ἄνωθεν πᾶσιν ἀκριβῶς καθεξῆς σοι γράψαι. As we have seen, there is a tendency to adopt one of two meanings for παρηκολουθηκότι, either investigation,[1] or close acquaintance with, and even personal involvement and participation in, events. In the latter case the events can only be those in Acts and especially, as Cadbury maintains, in the second part of Acts, in particular the passages punctuated by the intrusion of "we". In fact, however, verse 3 refers to both the Lukan writings. It is unnecessary to expect that, because verses 1 f. refer only to the gospel, the next statement refers only, or even primarily, to Acts. Reference to the gospel is guaranteed by the fact that this is the apodosis of a sentence which begins by speaking about predecessors in gospel writing. "I also decided to write a gospel narrative as others before me have done." But if verse 3 refers to both the gospel and Acts, the need for a firm choice of one of the two possible meanings of the verb παρηκολουθηκότι disappears. In regard to the gospel material Luke has "investigated" matters in detail. He has done the same thing for Acts, but with the advantage that he has more immediate knowledge of more recent events, and has actually participated in some of them himself. And Cadbury sees in the "I" in the Lukan preface a preparation for the reader's encounter with "we" in the second part of Acts.[2]

The words ἄνωθεν πᾶσιν mean that the whole narrative, although divided into two parts, is a unity. It starts from the beginning of the story in the nativity narratives of John the Baptist and Jesus, and recounts all the acts of God manifested first in Galilee, Samaria and Jerusalem, and then in the spread of the gospel from Jerusalem as far as Rome.[3] The preface concludes by saying to Theophilus that he now has at his disposal, in this orderly and connected narrative (καθεξῆς), full confirmation of the reliability of the matters of which he had been informed.[4] Since by this we are to understand the truth of the tradition about Jesus' deeds and teaching, the reference is in the first instance to Luke's gospel. If, however, the record of Acts is included in what is said in verse 3, it must be intended here as well. That is, Acts is an essential part of the confirmation Luke is able to provide, because so much of it, and not only in the *preaching* of the church leaders, is a witnessing to the truth of the *historia Jesu* which

---

[1] Cf. E. E. Ellis, *op. cit.*, p. 63.

[2] Whether the author, on the assumption that he was the Luke of tradition, utilized a personal diary of his own, cannot be proved. That he used the diary or notes of someone else who had been a companion of Paul on some of his journeys (and could, therefore, have belonged to a later period), is less likely, if only because the occurrence of "we" is so slight and sporadic.

[3] Cf. W. Grundmann, *Das Evangelium nach Lukas* (Berlin, 1961), p. 44.

[4] Whether as already a Christian is uncertain.

Theophilus had learned and which is now recorded afresh in the "former treatise".

II

This former treatise records "all" that Jesus "did and taught".[1] Acts, in its turn, as part two of a single work, records both the post-resurrection proclamation of the good news of Jesus Christ by leading personalities, and also their deeds. The kerygmatic speeches in Acts 2–5, 10, and 13 have been held by many, following C. H. Dodd, to represent "the *kerygma* of the Church at Jerusalem at an early period".[2] Others, however, see in them a reflection, not of the earliest preaching, but of the church's preaching in the author's own day. According to Dibelius, all these speeches are Lukan compositions echoing the pattern of preaching current when Luke wrote Acts about A.D. 90.[3] A basically common outlook is shared by Haenchen, Conzelmann, and Wilckens. The last named calls Luke the theologian of the post-apostolic period. The common pattern of the kerygmatic speeches summarizes Lukan theology at the end of the first century, and preserves no ancient tradition.[4] In Britain C. F. Evans has reached similar conclusions.[5]

This more recent approach, however, should not necessarily be accepted without question or modification as a new orthodoxy, completely supplanting the findings of Dodd and his followers. It may well be that Dibelius and others have attributed too much construction of speeches to the author of Acts.[6] But analysis confirms that the kerygmatic speeches are of basically identical structure, while at the same time they appear to use older material in the christological parts.[7] The question is, how old is this material? M. Wilcox maintains that the relative absence of "semitized" material from the kerygmatic (or "credal") elements, "suggests that it is less probably a statement of the primitive preaching of the Apostles than a traditional liturgical or apologetical summary of the cardinal elements of the gospel."[8] At any rate, the contacts between the early speeches in Acts, and the Pauline epistles and other parts of the New Testament, particularly

---

[1] Cf. Haenchen, *Die Apostelgeschichte*, p. 106, and H. Conzelmann, *Die Apostelgeschichte* (Tübingen, 1963), p. 20, on why the rendering "*began* to do and teach" (as in RSV) is probably incorrect; *per contra* F. F. Bruce, *op. cit.*, p. 66, taking ἤρξατο as emphatic.

[2] C. H. Dodd, *The Apostolic Preaching and its Developments* (London, 1936), p. 37.

[3] M. Dibelius, *Studies in the Acts of the Apostles*, ed. H. Greeven (London, 1956), especially essay 9, "The Speeches in Acts and Ancient Historiography." Dibelius, however, allowed for occasional use of old kerygmatic or liturgical formulae, cf. p. 3.

[4] U. Wilckens, *Die Missionsreden der Apostelgeschichte* (Neukirchen, 1961), pp. 186, 193.

[5] "The Kerygma," *JTS* N.S. 7 (1956), pp. 25–41.

[6] Cf. A. Ehrhardt, "The Construction and Purpose of the Acts of the Apostles," *The Framework of the New Testament Stories* (Manchester, 1964), pp. 86–88.

[7] Cf. E. Schweizer, "Concerning the Speeches in Acts," *Studies in Luke–Acts* [in honour of Paul Schubert], ed. L. E. Keck and J. L. Martyn (New York, 1966), pp. 208–16.

[8] *The Semitisms of Acts* (Oxford, 1965), p. 182.

in the use of *testimonia* from the Old Testament, are less probably due to mere imitation on the part of Luke, than to parallel, although possibly rather later, use of firmly established features of the primitive preaching. Granted that Acts and the Gospel of Luke have a distinctive theology, the author of Acts reveals himself in other aspects of his work (e.g., in his knowledge of Roman institutions), as one who was hardly likely to have been ignorant of what that preaching was like.[1]

We go on to the importance for the author of Acts of prominent figures in the early church as proclaiming, or witnessing to, the good news of Jesus Christ both in words and in deeds.

The idea of witnessing is included in five of the six kerygmatic speeches in Acts 2-5, 10, and 13. The preacher claims that he and his associates are μάρτυρες.

In the following passages the apostles are witnesses of the resurrection of Jesus.

2:32, "This Jesus God raised up, and of that we all are witnesses" (Peter).

3:15, ".... whom God raised from the dead. To this we are witnesses" (Peter).

5:32, "And we are witnesses to these things," the resurrection and exaltation of Jesus (Peter and the apostles).

13:30 f., "But God raised him from the dead; and for many days he appeared to those who came up with him from Galilee to Jerusalem, who are now his witnesses to the people" (Paul).

In 10:39-41 Peter says the apostles are both witnesses to Jesus' ministry, and chosen by God as witnesses of his resurrection.

The idea of the apostles as witnesses also occurs a number of times elsewhere in Acts, in non-kerygmatic settings. In 22:15 Paul relates how he had been told by Ananias that he would be a witness of the risen Lord who had recently appeared to him on the way to Damascus. In the same address Paul calls Stephen the μάρτυς of Jesus (22:20). The word here (and in Rev. 2:13 (Antipas)), while still meaning a witness, is on the way to the meaning of martyr (Rev. 17:6), through its association with the death of the witness. In his account of his conversion addressed to Festus and Agrippa, Paul says the risen Jesus appeared to him in order to appoint[2] him as his servant and witness (ὑπηρέτην καὶ μάρτυρα). See also, in addition to the passages in the last footnote, Acts 4:33: "And with great power the apostles gave their testimony (μαρτύριον) to the resurrection of the

---

[1] Cf. R. P. C. Hanson, *The Acts* (Oxford, 1967), pp. 35-39.

[2] προχειρίσασθαι, 26:16. The same verb is used, and again in close connection with μάρτυς, in Paul's first version of his conversion. Ananias informed him that God had appointed him to see and hear the Just One, "for you will be a witness for him to all men of what you have seen and heard" (22:14 f.). This points to witnessing as a Lukan idea (see below), which has also been imported into the christological kerygma; cf. especially 10:41, μάρτυσιν τοῖς προκεχειροτονημένοις ὑπὸ τοῦ θεοῦ, ἡμῖν. To the vocabulary of witnessing belong also μαρτύρομαι (26:22 f.) and διαμαρτύρομαι (2:40; 8:25; 10:42; 18:5; 20:21, 24; 23:11; 28:23).

Lord Jesus"; and 22:18 (μαρτυρίαν), 23:11 (μαρτυρῆσαι), both referring to Paul.

Is this idea of the apostles as witnesses a part of the traditional kerygma? T. F. Glasson[1] has claimed that it is. He does not mention, however, the absence of this feature from Peter's speech in 4:8–12, which has other primitive traits, in particular the proof-text Psalms 118:22. This weakens his contention that the mention of witnesses was an integral part of the apostolic preaching, notwithstanding his appeal to 1 Corinthians 15:5–8, 15.

μάρτυς is not used in kerygmatic contexts outside Acts.[2] The use of the term in the kerygmatic speeches in Acts is prepared for by the author in Luke 24:48, in the words of the risen Jesus to the apostles, "You are witnesses of these things"; in Acts 1:8, "You shall be my witnesses in Jerusalem and in all Judaea and Samaria and to the end of the earth"; and finally in 1:22, where the man to be chosen as successor to Judas must be a witness of the resurrection of Jesus. There is little room for doubt that the concept of witnessing did not belong to the traditional kerygma, but has been introduced by Luke himself.[3] The purpose of this procedure, it is suggested, is to focus attention on the speakers as the fully accredited witnesses appointed by the risen Jesus in person, and charged by him with the preaching of the kerygma.

Here it may be noted that two of the kerygmatic speeches which include the idea of witnessing are occasioned by, and closely associated with, incidents in which the speaker has been involved. Peter's address in Solomon's porch (3:12–16) is the immediate sequel to the healing of the lame man (3:1–11). The next speech, delivered before the Sanhedrin (4:8–12), also refers back to this healing (vv. 9 f.). Peter's speech in 10:34–43 links Cornelius's report of how he came to summon him with the descent of the Holy Spirit. The concept of witnessing in Acts transcends the vocabulary, for the church leaders bear their testimony not only in words, but in actions.

III

In thus emphasizing the importance of leading personalities, does the author of Acts depend on earlier information and interest? Was there anything much of this kind available to him? The first and broader aspect of this question is whether first-century Christians were conditioned for a biographical interest in their great leaders by the climate of the times in which they lived. The Graeco-Roman world certainly did not lack interest in prominent figures. Outstanding among biographical works are, on

---

[1] "The Kerygma: is our version correct?" HJ 51 (1952–53), pp. 129–32.
[2] In 1 Pet. 5:1, Peter is a witness, but of the *sufferings* of Christ.
[3] See also above, p. 84, n.2.

the Latin side, the *Agricola* of Tacitus and Suetonius's *Lives of the Twelve Caesars*, and on the Greek side, Plutarch's *Lives* and the *Life of Apollonius of Tyana* by Philostratus. It would, therefore, hardly be surprising if converts to Christianity in the empire beyond Palestine showed an interest in the lives of the apostles and other pioneers – not to mention that which does not concern us here, the life of Jesus himself. Nor is it necessary to suppose that biographical interest was first aroused in the church outside Palestine, and was therefore a secondary development. The Old Testament, inherited and claimed by the church as its own possession, is a rich storehouse of traditions concerning the patriarchs, prophets, and kings of Israelite history. Biographical interest must have been firmly rooted in the earliest, Palestinian churches, and this was fostered with the spread of the missionary enterprise farther afield. At a later stage we encounter the fabrications of the apocryphal writings, produced in response to a growing curiosity in the lives of Jesus and his apostles, which the canonical books failed to satisfy.

The second and more immediate aspect of the matter involves the related questions of whether in fact, and not according to probability alone, however strong, there existed traditions about the apostles and other prominent leaders, from which the author of Acts could have drawn, and whether his work can be subjected to form-critical analysis.

In his famous essay of 1923, "Style Criticism of the Book of Acts,"[1] Dibelius turned from the search for literary sources to style analysis, and maintained that Luke wrote Acts in a very different way from his gospel. Yet he conceded that he did use traditional material, for example, the travel diary, and such narratives as that of Peter's release from prison (12:5–17), which he described as "preserved by Luke, almost ungarnished, in the form in which, as an isolated story, it was current among Christians."[2] But Luke's creative activity, Dibelius held, is such that, generally speaking, he is much more an author where Acts is concerned, than a transmitter of tradition. If this is pressed, however, form-critical analysis is going to be much less successful than in the case of Luke's gospel. Himself a pioneer of the application of the form-critical method to the gospels, Dibelius reached far less fruitful results in extending it to Acts. Perhaps his clearest statement appears in his essay on the form-critical study of the New Testament outside the gospels, namely, that one searches in vain for paradigms in Acts, because there was no preaching about the apostles in the early church.[3] In Acts the situation is quite different from that in the

---

[1] *Studies in the Acts of the Apostles*, pp. 1–25.
[2] *Ibid.*, p. 21.
[3] "Zur Formgeschichte des Neuen Testaments (ausserhalb der Evangelien)," *Theologische Rundschau*, N. F. 3 (1931), pp. 207–42 (pp. 233–41 on Acts): "Die für die Predigt bestimmten Beispiele [of paradigms] sucht man in der Apostelgeschichte natürlich überhaupt vergeblich, denn von den Aposteln gepredigt hat man in der Urkirche noch nicht" (p. 236).

gospels, in which everything revolves round the central figure of Jesus, and the stories about him are adapted for use in preaching.

Haenchen[1] in his commentary represents the culmination of this estimate of Acts, in association with Conzelmann's interpretation of Lukan theology. Whereas the early church expected an early parousia, and so had no interest in preserving traditions about the apostles, Luke views the present as the time of the church and its mission until the end of the world. This new epoch is the continuation of the gospel. Luke had no predecessors; neither had he any successors, because the apocryphal Acts are in quite a different category. To Luke the link between the life of Jesus and the time after the ascension is the preaching to all peoples of the message of forgiveness of sins and salvation through faith in Jesus. The description of this mission in itself serves to awaken faith, and so to lead to the attainment of salvation. For this purpose Luke allows full play to his powers as a creative author, and from such material as was available constructs stories about its leaders for the church's edification.

J. Jervell has shown, however, from a study of the Pauline letters as the earliest extant Christian writings, that a tradition about the apostles co-existed with the tradition about Jesus from an early date.[2] I give a few of his examples, and his conclusions. In Romans 1:8 Paul thanks God that the faith of the Roman Christians is proclaimed in all the world. Since the word he uses ($\kappa\alpha\tau\alpha\gamma\gamma\acute{\epsilon}\lambda\lambda\epsilon\iota\nu$) is kerygmatic (cf. 1 Cor. 2.1; 9:14; 11:26; Phil. 1:17; Acts 4:2; 17:23), the faith of the church itself is what is proclaimed. Similarly, in 1 Thessalonians 1:8 ff. the word of the Lord is the faith of the Thessalonians. The message consists (1) of the entry of the apostles among the Thessalonians and its results, and (2) of the content of their faith. Thus in the early tradition the activities of the apostles and the faith of the churches naturally belong together. The apostles themselves can act as an exhortation. They are examples to be imitated (1 Cor. 4:17; 11:1; Phil. 3:17; 4:9; 2 Thess. 3:7 ff.). Such exhortations, in which the apostle presents himself as an example to the churches, must have formed part of the regular instruction, and could only have been effective if a church was well informed about the apostle's life and activities. Moreover, the tradition about Jesus itself included tradition about the apostles and the church. The appearance of the risen Lord to Peter and the Twelve in 1 Corinthians 15:3 ff. is striking evidence of this. What Paul had received and in turn handed down, is the preaching of the primitive church, which is at the same time a preaching *about* the primitive church.[3]

In answer to Dibelius and Haenchen, then, Jervell produces strong

---

[1] *Die Apostelgeschichte*, especially pp. 87 f., and his essay "The Book of Acts as Source Material for the History of Early Christianity", *Studies in Luke–Acts* [in honour of Paul Schubert], pp. 258–78.

[2] "Zur Frage der Traditionsgrundlage der Apostelgeschichte," *StTh* 16 (1962), pp. 25–41. This article is summarized in part by the late Professor Johannes Munck on pp. XXXIX–XLI of his commentary on Acts (*Anchor Bible*, vol. 31, New York, 1967).

[3] "Eine Verkündigung über die Urgemeinde," Jervell, p. 39.

evidence that, so far from conditions being unfavourable to the formation of a tradition of the apostolic period, accounts of the apostles and of the faith of the communities had their place in the preaching from the beginning. If this is so, the presumption is that the author of Acts has built upon a *Traditionsgrundlage*.

In Part I it has been argued that the preface to Luke was intended by the author to refer to both parts of his work. The first two verses concern the gospel alone, but the next two refer to both the gospel and Acts. That is, Luke has investigated in detail both the tradition about Jesus and, as we perhaps may now say, the coexistent tradition about the apostles and other leaders and the churches with which they were associated. If the whole narrative of Luke–Acts is fundamentally a unity, from the beginning of the story of Jesus to the arrival of Paul with his gospel in Rome, it would be rather surprising, to say the least, to find the author, in his preface, describing only his use of tradition and sources in the *gospel*. When Luke came to write Acts, he found he had the advantage of more immediate and, at certain points, even personal knowledge of events – a fact reflected in his choice of the word παρηκολουθηκότι to cover something more than historical investigation; on the completion of his gospel and Acts, he prefixed to the former the preface as an introduction to both parts of his work.

In a study which has not received adequate attention, S. E. Johnson[1] attempted to show that from the form-critical point of view the difference between Luke and Acts is one of degree rather than of kind. "Although Luke undoubtedly did allow himself more freedom in Acts, nevertheless he was dealing with traditional material much of which can be subsumed under the standard categories employed by form-critics." In this Johnson is much more positive than Dibelius who, while admitting the presence in Acts both of *Novellen* (e.g., the healing of the lame man at the Beautiful Gate, 3:1–10) and of numerous legends (e.g., Peter's release from prison, 12:5–19), says there are no paradigms there, because the subject of the early preaching was Jesus alone, with nothing about the apostles.[2] Johnson, however, begins his own investigation with seven stories "which bear a certain resemblance to the paradigms of the gospels", namely, 1:4–8; 1:23–26; 2:37–39; 4:5–12; 4:13–20; 5:26–32; 6:9–14, all of which "could be useful for preaching purposes".[3] He goes on to list *Novellen* (miracle stories) and "legends" (or "stories").[4] The former include five centred upon Peter (3:1–10; 5:15; 5:17–23; 9:32–35; 9:36–43), of which the healing miracles resemble those in the gospels. This is especially true

---

[1] "A Proposed Form-critical Treatment of Acts," *ATR* 21 (1939), pp. 22–31.
[2] Johnson, it may be noted, does not mention Dibelius's essay in *Theologische Rundschau*, cited above.
[3] Johnson, p. 23.
[4] Cf. the "stories about Jesus," V. Taylor, *The Formation of the Gospel Tradition* (London, 1933), pp. 142 ff.

of the last (the raising of Tabitha or Dorcas), which has affinities with the raising of the young man at Nain (Lk. 7:11–17). Johnson then lists eleven stories about Paul approaching closely the *Novellen* type, including four miraculous healings (16:16–18, the girl with a spirit of divination; 19:11 f., "healing by relics of Paul"; 28:1–6, Paul unharmed by a viper; 28:7–10, healing of the father of Publius), and twenty stories of the *Legende* category.

However, there remains more in Acts than in the gospels which cannot easily, or in some cases at all, be classified on form-critical principles. It is also true that while, as a comparison with Matthew and Mark shows, Luke impresses his own literary and theological stamp on much of the Markan and Q material, in Acts he uses with greater freedom whatever sources and traditions were available to him. Perhaps the knowledge that he had no predecessors in the field of "church history", as he had in gospel writing, was a contributory factor. Possible imitation of gospel pericopae in Acts is another factor to be borne in mind, and one which could materially reduce the validity of form-critical analysis of the book. Nevertheless, despite legitimate uncertainties as to when the author is accurately transmitting earlier material, and when he is imitating the gospel tradition, embellishing, or even inventing, much recent scepticism as to his reliability is insufficiently based. Acts may be taken to preserve a rich storehouse of tradition from the expanding missionary first-century church, much of it centred upon the apostles Peter and Paul, but also including other prominent leaders like Ananias of Damascus, Apollos, Barnabas, James of Jerusalem, Judas Barsabbas, Philip, Silas, and Stephen.

To sum up. Since Acts, like the gospels, is susceptible of form-critical analysis, much of its content must have reached its present form along somewhat similar lines to the gospel material. Before Acts was written, there existed a living apostolic tradition alongside the Jesus tradition. This was used in instruction and exhortation; the activities of prominent leaders were remembered and repeated as part and parcel of the Christian message. In this connexion the work of Jervell on the Pauline letters is important, and has a direct bearing on Acts. This viewpoint is supported by the interpretation of the preface to Luke given above.

IV

It has been maintained earlier in this paper that witnessing did not form part of the primitive kerygma, but is Lukan, and that the purpose of its introduction by Luke is to focus attention on the pioneers of the church as bearing testimony to the gospel both in their preaching and in their deeds. This concept of witnessing, however, is securely based on information derived from reliable tradition about its leaders current in the church. The acceptance of Luke's substantial integrity as a historian in his use of tradition, not only in his gospel, but also in Acts, is not inconsistent with the recognition of a considerable degree of interpretative elaboration of traditional material for edifying and theological purposes.

Doubtless Luke regarded himself also as a witness in the writing of his two-part work. Above all, however, it is the Holy Spirit who is the witness, the supreme witness. He alone enables the apostles to be witnesses.

"You are witnesses of these things. And behold, I send the promise of my Father upon you; but stay in the city, until you are clothed with power from on high" (Lk. 24:48 f.).

". . . he charged them not to depart from Jerusalem, but to wait for the promise of the Father, which, he said, 'you heard from me, for John baptized with water, but before many days you shall be baptized with the Holy Spirit'" (Acts 1:4 f.).

"But you shall receive power when the Holy Spirit has come upon you; and you shall be my witnesses in Jerusalem and in all Judaea and Samaria and to the end of the earth" (Acts 1:8).

"And we are witnesses to these things, and so is the Holy Spirit whom God has given to those who obey him" (Acts 5:32).[1] This gift of the Spirit is not confined to the first sermon at Pentecost and to the first wonders and signs wrought through the apostles (Acts 2:43), but pervades the whole of Acts.

Luke regards the witness of the apostles in the preaching of repentance and forgiveness of sins to all the nations in the name of Jesus as part of the fulfilment of scripture.

"Thus it is written, that the Christ should suffer and on the third day rise from the dead, and that repentance and forgiveness of sins should be preached in his name to all nations" (Lk. 24:46 f.).

But in Acts he will show that the works of the Christian leaders are also part of their testimony, and therefore, we may suppose, are also part of the fulfilment of the gospel foretold in scripture. The ministry of Jesus in works and words (Acts 1:1) is continued in the ministry of his witnesses. This is the link between the Gospel of Luke and the book of Acts (Lk. 24:46–48).

The witnessing, both in (a) words and (b) works, leads to faith in Jesus on the part of the hearers or the onlookers. For (a) see Acts 4:4 (Peter); 8:12 f. (Philip); 11:20 f. (men of Cyprus and Cyrene); 13:48 (Paul and Barnabas); 14:1 (Paul and Barnabas); 16:31–34 (Paul and Silas); 17:12 (Paul and Silas); 17:34 (Paul); 18:8 (Paul). For (b) there are the following narratives. In 5:12–16 the working of signs and wonders by the apostles resulted in some people thinking that even Peter's shadow would be sufficient for the working of a cure. Of Paul it is said that his miracles were so extraordinary, "that handkerchiefs or aprons were carried away from his body to the sick, and diseases left them and the evil spirits came out of

[1] Cf. J. H. E. Hull, *The Holy Spirit in the Acts of the Apostles* (London, 1967), pp. 46 f.

them" (19:11 f.).[1] Only in the former of these passages is there explicit mention of faith (5:14). Peter's healing of Aeneas led all the inhabitants of Lydda and Sharon to turn to the Lord (9:34 f.), and many believed in the Lord after his raising of Tabitha from the dead (9:42). The proconsul Sergius Paulus "believed" when he saw the effect of Paul's stern rebuke of Elymas the magician (13:12). To these are to be added the occasions when the name of Jesus is invoked in a healing miracle: 3:6 (cf. 3:16, with probable reference also to the healed man's faith); 16:18; and especially 9:34, where Peter says to Aeneas, "Jesus Christ heals you".[2]

The kerygma in Acts, then, is not confined to the missionary preaching. Through the power of the Holy Spirit the apostles show the reality of the gospel they proclaim by their miracles performed in the name of Jesus, as Jesus himself demonstrated the reality of his proclamation of the coming kingdom of God through mighty acts already in the present. The author of Acts interprets the kerygma in this extended sense as the bearing of witness to Jesus. It is to this kerygma in Acts, as well as to the *historia Jesu* in his gospel, that Luke, in the second part of the preface to the gospel, refers Theophilus, "so that your Excellency may learn how well founded the teaching is that you have received."[3]

---

[1] These two passages foreshadow the later cult of the saints, and especially the veneration of Peter and Paul.

[2] Cf. also the following additions to the text: 6:8 + διὰ τοῦ ὀνόματος (ἐν τῷ ὀνόματι E) κυρίου Ἰησοῦ Χριστοῦ D (E 33) 614 *al* it sa; 9:40 Ταβειθα, ἀνάστηθι+ in nomine domini nostri Iesu Christi g m p vg(D) syh (sa Cypr) Ambr; 14:10 φωνῇ + σοὶ λέγω ἐν τῷ ὀνόματι τοῦ κυρίου Ἰησοῦ Χριστοῦ CD (E) 614 *al* it syh(mg) sa bo(pc) Ir Ambr.

[3] JerB. Although he studies Lk. 1:1–4 from a completely different angle (and interprets the passage also as referring only to the gospel), H. Schürmann's recently republished essay of 1962 may be mentioned here for its characteristically thorough discussion of the exegetical problems: "Evangelienschrift und kirchliche Unterweisung. Die repräsentative Funktion der Schrift nach Lk. 1:1–4," *Traditionsgeschichtliche Untersuchungen zu den synoptischen Evangelien* (Düsseldorf, 1968), pp. 251–71.

CHAPTER V

THE RESURRECTION IN THE ACTS OF THE APOSTLES

I. Howard Marshall

ACCORDING TO THE THEOLOGY EXPRESSED IN THE ACTS OF THE APOSTLES the fundamental place in salvation history is to be assigned to the resurrection of Jesus Christ. Although the opening chapter of Acts makes a chronological separation between the resurrection of Jesus and his farewell appearance to his disciples forty days later, it is one saving event, including resurrection, ascension and exaltation, which is in mind.

In affording this central place to the resurrection, Luke was fully in line with the thought of the early church as expressed elsewhere in the New Testament.[1] It is, therefore, surprising that no detailed attempt has been made to expound his theology of the resurrection, as reflected in Acts, and to inquire how far it is dependent upon tradition and how far it is peculiar to himself. Much attention has indeed been devoted to the wider problem of tradition and interpretation in the writings of Luke, but in the main our theme has been given only incidental treatment in such discussions.

Since most of the teaching in Acts about the resurrection occurs in the speech material, which is at present often regarded as a *Musterbeispiel* of Lucan creative activity, it may seem hopeless to expect to find primitive tradition about the resurrection. We must briefly examine this question before coming to grips with our subject.

I

Among the earliest contributions to New Testament study by the distinguished scholar in whose honour this volume is published was a slim monograph entitled *The Speeches in the Acts of the Apostles*, which initiated the series of Tyndale New Testament Lectures (1942). The essay was notable for the conservative estimate which it reached regarding the historical verisimilitude of the speeches in Acts. The author concluded:

> Reason has been shown to conclude that the speeches recorded by Luke are at least faithful epitomes, giving the gist of the arguments used. Even in summarizing the speeches, Luke would naturally introduce more or less of his

---

[1] For the resurrection as the central theme of NT theology see W. Künneth, *The Theology of the Resurrection* (London, 1965). Less *konsequent* is F. V. Filson, *Jesus Christ the Risen Lord* (Nashville, 1956).

own style; but in point of fact it frequently seems to be less, not more. Taken all in all, each speech suits the speaker, the audience and the circumstances of delivery; and this, along with the other points we have considered, gives good ground, in my judgment, for believing these speeches to be, not inventions of the historian, but condensed accounts of speeches actually made, and therefore valuable and independent sources for the history and theology of the primitive Church.[1]

These conclusions were certainly not based on ignorance of the powerful arguments which have been urged against the primitive nature of the speeches. It is noteworthy that Professor Bruce choose as a representative statement of the opposite point of view not the well-known essay by H. J. Cadbury[2] but rather (with prophetic insight) the available writings of M. Dibelius;[3] he was thus able to refer to *Paulus auf dem Areopag* (Heidelberg, 1939), although it was not until 1949 that the celebrated essay on "The Speeches in Acts and Ancient Historiography" (completed in 1944) was available to scholars.[4]

Since 1942 the prevailing tide of opinion has been strongly against the point of view adopted by Bruce.[5] The arguments which have had most weight in the minds of subsequent scholars have been as follows:

(*i*) The analogy of ancient historiography suggests that Luke placed on the lips of his principal characters those sentiments which he considered most appropriate. He used the speeches primarily for literary purposes, and moulded them carefully to fit into their contexts.

(*ii*) The speeches uniformly bear the marks of Lucan style in vocabulary, style and composition; so thoroughly has Luke worked over any sources which he may have employed that it is virtually impossible to uncover them.

(*iii*) The speeches are based upon a common pattern and they supplement one another in filling out its various aspects. They contain a unified theology, and this theology is shown to be Luke's own by its occurrence elsewhere in his writings. Moreover, Luke's theology is not the theology of the early church but rather reflects the outlook of his own time. His purpose was not to give accurate historical reports of the primitive church but rather to give an interpretation in accordance with the needs of his own era. The speeches may be based on fragmentary traditions, but primarily they are sources for Luke's own theology.

Within the scope of the present article this case cannot be fully

---

[1] *Op. cit.*, p. 27.
[2] "The Speeches in Acts", *BC* V, pp. 402–27; cf. F. F. Bruce, *op. cit.*, p. 13.
[3] M. Dibelius, *A Fresh Approach to the New Testament and Early Christian Literature* (London, 1937); cf. F. F. Bruce, *op. cit.*, p. 6.
[4] The essay, originally published in 1949, reappeared in M. Dibelius, *Aufsätze zur Apostelgeschichte* (ed. H. Greeven, Göttingen, 1951); English translation: *Studies in the Acts of the Apostles* (London, 1956).
[5] The research is chronicled in U. Wilckens, *Die Missionsreden der Apostelgeschichte* (Neukirchen-Vluyn, 1963²), pp. 7–31.

considered, but the following points may be briefly noted as indicating that the evidence is not all on one side.

(i) The problem of the analogy with other ancient historians was already taken up by Bruce in 1942; he observed that Thucydides' practice was one of "adhering as closely as possible to the general sense of what they really said". Thucydides, therefore, cannot be quoted as an example of intentional free composition.[1] The real question, therefore, is how far Luke shared the attitude of Hellenistic historians like Josephus rather than the Thucydidean approach of Polybius.[2] It is easy to exaggerate the unconcern of the Hellenistic historians about factual accuracy in the depiction of *Historie*.[3] Luke's work must be considered on its own merits.

(ii) There is no doubt that Luke has thoroughly rewritten his sources in his own vocabulary and style.[4] This means, on the one hand, that the presence of Lucan characteristics in a passage is in itself no proof that sources are not being used.

On the other hand, it means that the search for such primitive features as residual Semitisms is not very likely to be successful. This is in fact the case. The thorough study of M. Wilcox, *The Semitisms of Acts* (Oxford, 1965), did not produce a very impressive harvest of linguistic material. But this should not surprise us. One speech in Acts, that of Paul in ch. 22, is explicitly stated to have been delivered Ἑβραΐδι διαλέκτῳ, and it is not characterized by Semitisms. If this speech is authentic, Luke has thoroughly removed the evidence of its Semitic origin from his translation or source; if it is his own composition, he has not striven for verisimilitude by imposing a Semitizing style appropriate to the situation. In either case, the search for Semitisms as a mark of primitive tradition is not likely to be fruitful elsewhere in Acts.[5]

But is it necessary to find Semitisms in order to trace primitive material? The evidence continues to accumulate that Greek was one of the languages spoken in Palestine, and spoken by Jews.[6] It may well be that some of the speeches in Acts to Jewish audiences were originally spoken in Greek. In particular, the familiar argument from use of the LXX in the speeches to inauthenticity loses much of its force.

(iii) There is evidence that at least some of the speech material in Acts is based on tradition. Thus U. Wilckens admits that a traditional pattern,

[1] T. F. Glasson, "The Speeches in Acts and Thucydides", *ExpT* 76 (1964–65), p. 165; R. M. Grant, *A Historical Introduction to the New Testament* (London, 1963), p. 141.

[2] W. Barclay, "Great Themes of the New Testament IV. Acts 2:14–40" *ExpT* 70 (1958–59), pp. 196–99.

[3] A. W. Mosley, "Historical Reporting in the Ancient World", *NTS* 12 (1965–66), pp. 10–26; H. Weiss, "History and a Gospel", *NovTest* 10 (1968), pp. 81–94; G. W. Barker, W. L. Lane and J. R. Michaels, *The New Testament Speaks* (New York, 1969), p. 306.

[4] B. M. F. van Iersel, *"Der Sohn" in den synoptischen Jesusworten* (Leiden, 1964²), pp. 32–51.

[5] Compare the lack of Semitisms in Josephus, *Bellum Judaicum*, which was originally composed in Aramaic.

[6] R. H. Gundry, *The Use of the Old Testament in St. Matthew's Gospel* (Leiden, 1967), pp. 174–78; J. N. Sevenster, *Do you know Greek?* (Leiden, 1968).

attested elsewhere in the New Testament, is to be found in the speeches to Gentile audiences in Acts 14 and 17.[1] He also argues, however, that the different form of speech found earlier in Acts and addressed to Jewish audiences cannot be shown to be traditional by comparison with other New Testament evidence, and holds that in this case the *argumentum e silentio* is a convincing one.

One critic at least has not been persuaded by Wilckens' reasoning about the earlier speeches,[2] and there is certainly a good case against it. The fact that Luke did use traditional material in Acts 14 and 17 would suggest that he also used similar material in other parts of Acts. In fact the pattern of the earlier speeches is very like that of the later ones,[3] and suggests that Luke was drawing on traditional material throughout.

At one point the search for traditional material has been particularly rewarding. This concerns the use of the Old Testament in the speeches in Acts. There is sufficient evidence for claiming that the patterns of exegesis found in the speeches are often of a primitive nature.[4]

One speech is not discussed at all by Wilckens, that by Stephen in Acts 7. Because of what he calls "its special character" he leaves it aside.[5] It is, however, precisely this "special character" which makes it the Achilles' heel of his theory, for there is good reason to believe that a rather specialized tradition has been utilized in the composition of this speech.[6]

These various pieces of evidence all suggest that the search for primitive tradition in the speeches in Acts may well be more fruitful than is generally assumed. Although the analogy between the Gospel of Luke and Acts should be used with caution, the evidence of the Gospel confirms our tentative conclusion that Luke was making use of existing sources rather than freely inventing material.[7] We have, therefore, some incentive for reconsidering the particular question of the place of the resurrection in the speeches in Acts in order to see how far the theology of Luke is based on tradition.

---

[1] U. Wilckens, *op. cit.*, pp. 72–91.

[2] J. Dupont, *Etudes sur les Actes des Apôtres* (Paris, 1967), pp. 133–55 (originally published in *RB* 69 (1962), pp. 37–60). See also J. Rohde, *Rediscovering the Teaching of the Evangelists* (London, 1969), pp. 215–17.

[3] Among the many synopses and discussions see especially E. Schweizer, "Concerning the Speeches in Acts", in L. E. Keck and J. L. Martyn (ed.), *Studies in Luke–Acts* (Nashville, 1966), pp. 208–16; also published in German in *Theologische Zeitschrift* 13 (1957), pp. 1–11, and in E. Schweizer, *Neotestamentica* (Zürich, 1963), pp. 418–28.

[4] J. W. Doeve, *Jewish Hermeneutics in the Synoptic Gospels and Acts* (Assen, 1953); E. Lövestam, *Son and Saviour* (Lund, 1961); M. Wilcox, *op. cit.*; J. de Waard, *A Comparative Study of the Old Testament Text in the Dead Sea Scrolls and in the New Testament* (Leiden, 1965); J. W. Bowker, "Speeches in Acts: A Study in Proem and Yelammedenu Form", *NTS* 14 (1967–68), pp. 96–111. A forthcoming publication by G. Stanton will give evidence for a pre-Lucan tradition in Acts 10:36–43.

[5] U. Wilckens, *op. cit.*, p. 30, n. 5; for an attempt to fit the speech into Luke's theology see J. C. O'Neill, *The Theology of Acts* (London, 1961), ch. 3.

[6] Cf. M. Scharlemann, *Stephen: A Singular Saint* (Rome, 1968).

[7] I. H. Marshall, "Tradition and Theology in Luke," *Tyndale Bulletin* 20 (1969), pp. 56–75.

II

The first question which must be raised concerns the centrality of the resurrection in the preaching and apologetic in Acts.

In two main passages Luke relates that the early church laid stress on the resurrection in debate with the Jews. Acts 23:7 f. refers to the well-known dispute between the Pharisees and the Sadducees, the former accepting the fact of the general resurrection and the latter denying it. According to Luke the question of the resurrection of Jesus could be regarded as a particular aspect of the general question of the resurrection of the dead. As he puts it elsewhere, the apostles preached "in Jesus the resurrection from the dead" (Acts 4:2). The main opposition came from the Sadducees (Acts 4:1 f.), but the Pharisees (or some of them) were less ready to condemn the Christians unheard (Acts 5:33 ff.). Representatives of both parties, however, were converted to the faith (Acts 6:7; 15:5). In a second main passage the issue is put by attributing to Paul the claim that both he and the Jews shared a belief in "a resurrection of both the just and the unjust" (Acts 24:15, 21).

The description of this method of apologetic is often regarded as historically inaccurate and motivated by Lucan theological considerations. "What Paul says about his faith is in keeping with the Lucan conception; the general resurrection is the link between (real) Judaism and Christianity. The Jews must consequently see that their faith comes to fulfilment in Christianity."[1] It follows that the Sadducees are not real Jews. Luke misrepresents their position by claiming that they were pure sceptics, whereas in fact their denial of the resurrection was the result of their restriction of religious authority to the Torah.

This estimate of Luke's narrative is very hard to accept. The existence of the dispute between the Pharisees and Sadducees over the resurrection is amply attested,[2] and Luke correctly records it.[3] That the resurrection of both the righteous and the unrighteous to stand before the judgment seat of God was a common Christian belief is also certain.[4] The situation with

[1] H. Conzelmann, *Die Apostelgeschichte* (HNT, Tübingen, 1963), p. 129; cf. p. 133; E Haenchen, *Die Apostelgeschichte* (Meyer, Göttingen, 1959¹²), pp. 570 f.

[2] Josephus, *Ant.* 18. 1. 3 f.; *Bel.* 2. 8. 14; Aboth R. Nathan 5; Sanhedrin 90b; Tanchuma 3a; Berakhoth 9. 5; cf. Sanhedrin 10. 1; see Strack-Billerbeck I, pp. 885 f.; 893 f.; IV 1, p. 344; *TWNT* VII pp. 46 f. (R. Meyer).

[3] Note, however, that Luke's statement that the Sadducees denied the existence of angels and spirits has been challenged. It is not confirmed by Jewish sources, and E. Haenchen (*op. cit.*, p. 567 n. 1) observes that the Torah refers to angels. R. Meyer (*TWNT* VII, p. 54) suggests that the Sadducees and early Christians may have rejected popular superstitious demonology.

[4] All men will face the future judgment: Jn. 5:28 f.; Rev. 20:12–15; cf. Rom. 2:5–16; 2 Cor. 5:10; 2 Tim. 4:1. For the raising up of the unrighteous see Lk. 10:12–15 (=Matt. 10:15; 11:20–24); Lk. 11:31 f. (=Matt. 12:41 f.). The phrase "the resurrection of the just" (Lk. 14:14) refers to resurrection into the life of the world to come (Lk. 20:35; cf. Jn. 5:29) and does not exclude the thought of the resurrection of the unrighteous for judgment.

regard to Judaism is less certain because the discussions do not always make it clear whether the reference is to the raising up of the dead to face judgment or to the raising up of the righteous to eternal life. But development of belief in a final judgment was incompatible with the maintenance of the view that the unrighteous would simply be left to perish in Sheol or Gehenna, and consequently it is probable that Christian belief about the general resurrection reflected Jewish belief.[1] E. Haenchen's view that the Pharisees did not believe in the resurrection of the unrighteous[2] rests upon the testimony of Josephus, but P. Billerbeck has shown that this testimony is of doubtful value.[3]

The argument which is attributed to Paul in this context is quite fitting. In the early Jewish Christian church a person might become a Christian and remain a Pharisee, but a Sadducee would need to change his whole theological position.[4] There was, therefore, nothing inconsistent about a claim that Christian belief was in effect the fulfilment of Judaism (Acts 28: 20).[5] Moreover, the link between the general resurrection and the resurrection of Jesus is one which Paul certainly made in another context, namely in 1 Corinthians 15, where he argued both that denial of the general resurrection logically involves denial of the resurrection of Christ and hence of the whole Christian faith, and also (conversely) that the historical fact of the resurrection of Christ establishes the fact of the general resurrection

So far as the representation of the attitudes of the Pharisees and Sadducees, is concerned, there is no reason to question Luke's account. The support given by the Pharisees to the Christians is paralleled by the way in which the Pharisees appear among both the supporters and the opponents of Jesus in the Gospel, both in Luke's sources and in the final redaction. The Gospel also makes it clear that Luke was well aware of the reason for the scepticism of the Sadducees (Lk. 20:27-40, especially 37), and has not misrepresented their position.

Finally, the later Acts is dated, the less likely it becomes that Luke should have invented this motif. For after A.D. 70 the Sadducees ceased to be of any importance in Jewish politics and theology,[6] and it is most unlikely that

---

[1] For the resurrection of both the righteous and the unrighteous see Dan. 12:2; 1 Enoch 22; 51; T. Benjamin 10; 2 Esd. 7:32, 37; 2 Baruch 42:7; 50:2; Sibylline Oracles 4:180-92; Apocalypse of Moses 41 (Strack-Billerbeck IV 2, pp. 1167-72). In the Rabbinic evidence note especially P. Aboth 4:22 and T. Sanhedrin 13:3 f. The conclusion of W. Bousset and H. Gressmann (*Die Religion des Judentums* [Tübingen, 1966⁴], pp. 269-74) that belief in the resurrection only of the righteous was more common does not take the Rabbinic evidence into account. See Strack-Billerbeck IV 2, pp. 1172-98.

[2] E. Haenchen, *op. cit.,* p. 583 n. 1.

[3] Strack-Billerbeck IV 2, pp. 1172 ff., 1188 f. Cf. G. F. Moore, *Judaism* (Cambridge, Mass., 1932), II, pp. 317 f.

[4] F. F. Bruce, *The Acts of the Apostles* (London, 1951), p. 411; *The Book of the Acts* (London, 1954), pp. 452 f. According to C. K. Barrett, "Paul remained in many respects not merely a Jew but a Pharisee and a Rabbi;" nevertheless, he "had in fact ceased to be a practising Jew" (*The First Epistle to the Corinthians* [London, 1968], pp. 211, 240).

[5] See, for example, F. F. Bruce, *The Apostolic Defence of the Gospel* (London, 1959), ch. 1.

[6] Strack-Billerbeck IV 2, pp. 343 f.; *TWNT* VII, pp. 45 f. (R. Meyer).

G

Luke would have deliberately bothered to draw attention to a group which was irrelevant to Christian–Jewish relationships. The indications are that in stressing the importance of the resurrection Luke was reflecting the actualities of debate with the Jews in the early church.

III

According to Luke Paul's missionary preaching could be summed up as "explaining and proving that it was necessary for the Christ to suffer and to rise from the dead, and saying, 'This Jesus, whom I proclaim to you, is the Christ'" (Acts 17:3). This indicates that one main purpose of the preaching of the resurrection was to make the apologetic points that the Messiah expected by the Jews would do certain things prophesied in the Old Testament, that Jesus had done these things, and that therefore he was the Christ. It has, however, been maintained that this type of argument was possible only at a later date. According to J. C. O'Neill "Luke's usage consistently implies that Χριστός was a Jewish title with a fixed and definite meaning, and that it was possible to conduct an argument with Jews as to whether Jesus did or did not meet the specified requirements." But, he holds, the development of a fixed concept of the "Messiah" belongs to a later date; consequently Luke is reading back a post-70 type of argument into the earlier period.[1]

"Messiah" is admittedly not an Old Testament title, but there was an expectation of a future deliverer whom the Jews believed to be prophesied in various ways in the Old Testament. Further, there is not a great deal of evidence in Judaism for the use of the title "Messiah" to designate the coming deliverer.[2] Christians at a later date could and did misrepresent Jewish beliefs on this matter.[3] However, there is sufficient evidence of interest in Messianic prophecy and of the use of the title in the period which concerns us.[4]

What is of greater importance is that the argument attributed by Luke to Paul must have developed much earlier in the church than O'Neill allows. In 1 Corinthians 15:3 ff. Paul quotes an early piece of tradition concerning the death, burial and resurrection of Christ.[5] The interesting point is that the statements in this passage are made about *Christ*, not about

---

[1] J. C. O'Neill, *op. cit.*, pp. 119–29; quotation from p. 122.
[2] O'Neill cites G. F. Moore in BC I, pp. 346–62. For more recent surveys see F. Hahn, *Christologische Hoheitstitel* (Göttingen, 1964²), pp. 133–58; M. de Jonge, "The use of the word 'anointed' in the time of Jesus," *NovTest* 8 (1966), pp. 132–48; A. J. B. Higgins, "The Priestly Messiah," *NTS* 13 (1966–67). pp. 211–39.
[3] A. J. B. Higgins, "Jewish Messianic Belief in Justin Martyr's *Dialogue with Trypho*," *NovTest* 9 (1967), pp. 298–305.
[4] F. Hahn, *ibid.*
[5] My attention was drawn to the relevance of this passage (and of 1 Pet. 1:11) to the present problem by F. F. Bruce, *The Acts of the Apostles*, p. 325.

Jesus. The statement thus *assumes* that Jesus is the Christ, and therefore predicates of him various experiences which are regarded as being in accordance with the Scriptures. In other words, this piece of tradition presupposes that at an earlier stage the identification of Jesus with the Christ had been made, so that in 1 Corinthians 15:3 ff. it was possible to assume the equation of Jesus with the Christ.[1] Hence 1 Corinthians 15 presupposes the argument set out in Acts 17:3. Since "Christ" is very probably an original part of this tradition and not a Pauline addition,[2] the identification must have been made at a very early stage. Whether by accident or design, Luke has correctly reflected this early stage in Christian theology.[3] The formulation of the message is Luke's own,[4] but the essential content of it is primitive.[5]

It thus emerges that the process of applying the title of "Messiah" to the expected eschatological deliverer took place earlier than O'Neill allows. It is likely that the decisive steps in this direction were made by the Christians themselves, and that it was their use of the title of "Messiah" of Jesus which forced the Jews into defining their own ideas and adopting the title as one with a fixed content.

IV

But what about the actual Old Testament proofs used to show that the Messiah must rise from the dead? In his comprehensive study U. Wilckens allows that the use of Scripture in this way is primitive, but holds that some of the texts actually used in Acts do not necessarily reflect primitive usage. Thus the use of Psalms 2:7 and 118:22 is traditional, but the use of Psalm 16:8-11 and Isaiah 55:3 is not attested in the early tradition.[6]

The key stone in Wilcken's argument is obviously the use of Psalm 16, since this *testimonium* plays a major part in both Acts 2:25-31 and Acts 13:35-37. In an interesting argument B. Lindars has submitted that the wording of Psalm 16 has affected the whole structure of Acts 2:24-36 and that Luke himself was unaware of this fact; consequently we have here

---

[1] It is not certain whether $X\rho\iota\sigma\tau\acute{o}s$ is here a name or a title (for the latter see F. Hahn, *op. cit.*, pp. 207-14).

[2] W. Kramer, *Christ, Lord, Son of God* (London, 1966), pp. 38-44 (8a-g).

[3] The same argument is presupposed in 1 Pet. 1:11 where it is stated that the prophets predicted the sufferings of Christ and the consequent glory; it is not clear whether the word "Christ" here means "the Messiah" or simply "Jesus", but in any case the identification of Jesus as the Messiah is presupposed.

[4] The verse is full of Lucanisms: $\delta\iota\alpha\nu o\acute{\iota}\gamma\omega$, $\pi\alpha\rho\alpha\tau\acute{\iota}\theta\eta\mu\iota$, $\delta\epsilon\hat{\iota}$, $\grave{\alpha}\nu\acute{\iota}\sigma\tau\eta\mu\iota$, $\kappa\alpha\tau\alpha\gamma\gamma\acute{\epsilon}\lambda\lambda\omega$. For the mixture of indirect and direct speech see I. H. Marshall, "Luke xvi. 8 – Who commended the Unjust Steward?", *JTS* N.S. 19 (1968), pp. 617-19.

[5] The use of $\delta\epsilon\hat{\iota}$ is found in the Son of man sayings, and is equivalent to the appeal to Scripture in other texts (cf. F. Hahn, *op. cit.*, p. 216 n. 3); $\pi\alpha\theta\epsilon\hat{\iota}\nu$, though common in Luke is not a Lucanism (F. Hahn, *op. cit.*, p. 217 n. 1). On the use of $\grave{\alpha}\nu\acute{\iota}\sigma\tau\eta\mu\iota$ see below.

[6] U. Wilckens, *op. cit.*, pp. 140-42.

"the survival of a very primitive argument for the Messiahship of Jesus".[1] Lindars makes the following points:

(i) Psalm 16:8–11, when taken literally, must apply to the Messiah, since it could not apply to David himself. Since, however, Jesus rose from the dead, thus fulfilling literally the wording of the Psalm, it follows that he must be the Messiah (Acts 2:25–36). What is interesting, according to Lindars, is that no reference is made to the Davidic descent of Jesus as a proof that he is the Messiah. This is said to be a primitive form of argument.

(ii) The odd phrase "loosing the pangs of death" in Acts 2:24 is said to be due to the speaker's understanding of Psalm 18:4 ("The cords of death encompassed me") in terms of Psalm 16:6 ("The lines have fallen for me in pleasant places"). Luke himself did not realize that Psalm 16:6 was here being used as a commentary on Psalm 18, since the exegetical link was made on the basis of the Hebrew text.

(iii) The reference to the exaltation of Jesus in the speech (Acts 2:33) is usually understood to be based on Psalm 110:1, which is quoted in the succeeding verse. Lindars suggests, however, that the author started from "the pleasures at God's right hand" of Psalm 16:11 and annotated this phrase by means of Psalm 110:1 and Psalm 68:19 to refer to the exaltation of Jesus and the pouring out of the Spirit.

Although this exegesis gives a remarkable unity to the passage, it is doubtful whether it can be sustained throughout. In particular, the explanation of Acts 2:24 is not convincing. In effect Lindars is here offering an explanation of the use of ὠδῖνας. But the real crux in the verse is rather the use of λύσας, and the correct solution of it is to be found in F. Field's translation as "to bring to an end". Further, there is a similar use of the Psalm in 1QH 3:28.[2] This suggests a different reason for anchoring this part of the speech in early tradition.

That Luke has taken over the use of Psalm 16 from tradition is also maintained by T. Holtz, who holds that, although the quotation in Acts 2:25–28 is from Luke himself, the allusion in verse 31 which (according to Holtz) has a different textual form comes from primitive material.[3] More weight, however, should probably be attached to the exegetical links of Psalm 16 with other Old Testament material in Acts 13, a fact which suggests that Luke is here making use of tradition.[4] The use of Isaiah 55:3 (the other *testimonium* attributed by Wilckens to Luke) in this latter passage falls within this same circle of ideas, and its meaning in this context is sufficiently obscure to make it likely that it is a primitive testimony taken over by Luke rather than his own contribution to the

---

[1] B. Lindars, *New Testament Apologetic* (London, 1961), pp. 38–45.
[2] For details see M. Wilcox, *The Semitisms of Acts*, pp. 46–48.
[3] T. Holtz, *Untersuchungen über die alttestamentlichen Zitate bei Lukas* (TU 104. Berlin, 1968), pp. 48–51.
[4] T. Holtz, *op. cit.*, pp. 145–53.

argument.[1] The case, therefore, for seeing tradition here rather than Lucan theology, is not strong, but it is adequate.[2]

V

If the place of the resurrection and the use of Scripture to interpret it in Acts are primitive, the same is also true of the christology which is related to it. To be sure, this is not generally acknowledged. A brief but influential article by H. Braun advocated the thesis that the resurrection of Jesus is presented in a distinctly subordinationist manner in Acts compared with the earlier material in the New Testament.[3] This thesis was taken up by U. Wilckens who argued that Luke speaks of Jesus being raised from the dead by God (*Auferweckung*), but in the "passion summaries" the Son of man rises from the dead (*Auferstehung*) by his own power. Luke prefers the active form ἐγείρω to express the initiative of God, and in his rendering of the passion summaries he understands the action to be that of God rather than of the Son of man.[4] This thesis falls down when examined in detail.

(*i*) It is not the case that Luke has a predilection for ἐγείρω instead of ἀνίστημι. He uses ἐγείρω 18 times in the Gospel and 12 times in Acts. Of these 3 uses in Luke (active form) and 6 uses in Acts (passive form) refer to Jesus.[5] The verb ἀνίστημι is used intransitively of the resurrection of Jesus 4 times in Luke and twice in Acts, and transitively (with God as subject) 5 times in Acts.[6] There is no preference for ἐγείρω here.[7]

(*ii*) In any case, the use of ἐγείρω with reference to Jesus is firmly planted in early usage, both in the active and passive forms.[8] The intransitive

---

[1] E. Lövestam, *Son and Saviour*; J. Dupont, *Etudes sur les Actes des Apôtres*, pp. 337–59 (originally in *RB* 68 [1961], pp. 91–114); T. Holtz, *op. cit.*, pp. 137–45.

[2] H. Conzelmann (*Die Mitte der Zeit* [Tübingen, 1964⁵], pp. 188 f.) and others regard the 'stress' on σάρξ in Acts 2:31 as a Hellenistic motif due to Luke (cf. Lk. 24:39 f.). But since Luke here avoids the dualism of soul and flesh which Ps. 16:9 f. might have suggested, by *not* taking up ψυχή from the quotation (verse 27), it is more likely perhaps that σάρξ is here simply a designation of the whole person (cf. E. Schweizer, *TWNT* VII, p. 124).

[3] H. Braun, "Zur Terminologie der Acta von der Auferstehung Jesu," *ThLZ* 77 (1952), cols. 533–36.

[4] U. Wilckens, *op. cit.*, pp. 137–40. For the terminological distinction see E. Lohmeyer, *Das Evangelium des Markus* (Meyer, Göttingen, 1959¹⁵), p. 167.

[5] ἐγείρω is used (1) of raising men from the dead: Lk. 7:14, 22; 8:54; 9:7; (2) of the final resurrection: Lk. 20:37; Acts 26:8; (3) (active) of Jesus: Acts 3:15; 4:10; 5:30; 10:40; 13:30, 37; (4) (passive) of Jesus: Lk. 9:22; 24:6, 34.

[6] ἀνίστημι is used (1) transitively, of Jesus: Acts 2:24, 32; 13:33, 34; 17:31 (*not* Acts 3:26; Acts 9:41 also does not refer to resurrection); (2) intransitively, of men being raised from the dead: Lk. 8:55; 9:8, 19; Acts 9:40; (3) intransitively, of the final resurrection: Lk. 11:32; (4) intransitively, of Jesus: Lk. 16:31; 18:33; 24:7, 46; Acts 10:41; 17:3.

[7] Only at Lk. 9:22 has Luke altered an original ἀνίστημι to ἐγείρω (cf. Matt. 16:21). B. Lindars, *op. cit.*, p. 65, speaks of Luke's preference for the root ἀνίστημι.

[8] Active: Rom. 4:24; 8:11 *bis*; 10:9; 1 Cor. 6:14; 15:15 *bis*; 2 Cor. 1:9; 4:14; Gal. 1:1; Eph. 1:20; Col. 2.12; 1 Thes. 1:10; 1 Pet. 1:21; Passive: Matt. 16:21 (=Lk. 9:22); 17:9, 23; 20:19; 26:32 (= Mk. 14:28); 27:63, 64; 28:6, 7 (=Mk. 16:6=Lk. 24:6); Lk. 24:34; Jn. 2:22; 21:14; Rom. 4:25; 6:4, 9; 7:4; 8:34; 1 Cor. 15:4, 12, 13, 14, 16, 17, 20; 2 Cor. 5:15; 2 Tim. 2:8.

use of ἀνίστημι is also traditional.[1] The new feature, which does require explanation, is the use of the active form ἀνίστημι in Acts.

(iii) Since Wilckens has not shown that Luke *prefers* ἐγείρω, there is no need to ask with him why Luke continued to use ἀνίστημι as well. Nevertheless, his argument must be followed through. He holds that Luke took over ἀνίστημι from the passion summaries, where the intransitive form was used to describe the *self-raising* of the Son of man, in contrast to the general view of the early church that the resurrection was *God's* act.[2] But this theory cannot be upheld.[3]

In Mark itself the intransitive form which is found in the passion summaries is also used of persons raised from the dead by Jesus[4] and of persons raised by God at the final resurrection;[5] the same is true throughout the New Testament.[6] Similarly, the noun ἀνάστασις can be used indifferently of the resurrection of men and of Jesus.[7] Now there is never any suggestion that men can raise themselves from the dead. In Jewish thought it is God who raises the dead.[8] Since the same intransitive form of the verb is used of men and of Jesus, it follows that the choice of this verb in the passion summaries is no ground for supposing that these texts regard the Son of man as raising himself from the dead. Only in the Johannine tradition is Jesus said to have power to lay down his life and to take it up again – and this power is the gift of the Father.[9] The fact that Paul can use both types of formulation is not, as Wilckens holds, a sign of tension in his thinking, but rather a further indication that the thesis is false.

It might be argued against our view of the passion summaries that their phraseology is influenced by Hosea 6:2 (LXX) which speaks of "rising up" on the third day. But here there is no suggestion that the people rise up by their own power; the context makes it clear that an act of God is meant, and the MT in fact has "he will raise us up".

In fact we should expect the passion summaries to speak of God raising up the Son of man. C. F. D. Moule has drawn attention to the situation of the Son of man as one who is vindicated by God,[10] and this fact should warn us against the tendency to ascribe too great a degree of independent authority to the Son of man.

[1] Mk. 8:31; 9:9, 10, 31; 10:34 (=Lk. 18:33); Lk. 16:31; 24:7, 46; Jn. 20:9; 1 Thes. 4:14.

[2] Cf. F. Hahn, *Christologische Hoheitstitel*, p. 49; H. E. Tödt, *The Son of Man in the Synoptic Tradition* (London, 1965), pp. 185 f.

[3] Cf. H. Conzelmann, *RGG*[3] I, cols. 698 f.; G. Delling in C. F. D. Moule (ed.), *The Significance of the Message of the Resurrection for Faith in Jesus Christ* (London, 1968), p. 90. n. 33.

[4] Mk. 5:42 (=Lk. 8:55); cf. Acts 9:40; Eph. 5:14 (metaphorical).

[5] Mk. 12:23, 25 (note τὴν δύναμιν τοῦ θεοῦ); Matt. 12:41 (=Lk. 11:32); cf. Lk. 9:8, 19; Jn. 11:23 f.; 1 Thes. 4:16.

[6] See the references in the two previous notes.

[7] A. Oepke, *TWNT* I, p. 372. (The translation in *TDNT* I, p. 372, needs correction.)

[8] E.g. Shemoneh Esreh 2.

[9] A. Oepke, *TDNT* I, pp. 370 f.; II, p. 335 (Jn. 2:19, 21; 10:17 f.).

[10] C. F. D. Moule, "From Defendant to Judge – and Deliverer," in *The Phenomenon of the New Testament* (London, 1967), pp. 82–99, especially pp. 87–90. (Originally in *Bulletin of the Studiorum Novi Testamenti Societas* 3 [1952], pp. 40–53).

Our argument is confirmed, finally, by the editorial work of Matthew and Luke. Wilckens draws attention to the way in which Matthew substitutes the passive of ἐγείρω for Mark's ἀνίστημι (Matt. 16:21; 17:9, 23; 20:19), but draws the wrong inference from it. Study of Matthew's usage reveals that he dislikes ἀνίστημι and avoids it.[1] He is not therefore changing the meaning of the passion summaries, as Wilckens holds, but expressing them in his own vocabulary, and possibly clarifying them. As for Luke, the fact that he does not alter the verb used in Mark 10:34 (Luke 18:33) shows that he regarded the two types of expression as synonyms.

(iv) We conclude that Luke's stress in Acts on the raising of Jesus by God is fully consistent with the teaching of the rest of the early church. The only new feature is the active use of ἀνίστημι with God as subject, and there does not seem to be any other motive for this use than a desire for literary variation. There is certainly no reason to suppose that its use reflects an especially subordinationist tendency on the part of Luke compared with the rest of the early church; on the contrary the belief that it was God who raised Christ was well nigh universal in the early church.[2] Consequently, at this point also Acts faithfully mirrors the teaching of the early church.

VI

It is well known that Luke does not make particularly strong links between the death of Jesus and the offer of salvation in the preaching of the gospel. "The death of Jesus has no saving significance, and consequently Luke's christology completely lacks any soteriological content."[3] If this verdict is justified, there would be a decisive difference between the theology of Luke and that of the primitive church.

For Luke the blessings of salvation consist in the reception of forgiveness and the gift of the Holy Spirit (Acts 2:38). The latter gift is dependent upon the fact that Jesus has been exalted (Acts 2:33), and the former is offered "through his name" (Acts 10:43). Both blessings are thus dependent upon the fact of the resurrection.

This description of salvation is primitive in content. The phrase "forgiveness of sins" (ἄφεσις ἁμαρτιῶν) is especially characteristic of Luke and, by contrast, is rare in Paul (Eph. 1:7; Col. 1:14). But the appearance of a contrast is somewhat deceptive, since other equivalent phrases were in use; "justification" is the Pauline synonym.[4]

---

[1] Matthew uses the verb only 4 times (compare Mark: 17 times; Luke: 26 times). In 9:9 and 26:62 the verb is taken over from Mark, in 12:41 from Q, and in 22:24 from the LXX; elsewhere Matthew does not take over the word from his sources.

[2] Luke does not imply that Jesus was "adopted" as Messiah by means of the resurrection.

[3] U. Wilckens, op. cit., pp. 216 f.

[4] For ἄφεσις ἁμαρτιῶν see Matt. 26:28; Mk. 1:4; cf. Heb. 9:22; 10:18; for ἀφίημι see Rom. 4:7; 1 Jn. 1:9; 2:12. Note Paul's use of πάρεσις (Rom. 3:25) and χαρίζομαι (Eph 4:32; Col. 2:13; 3:13).

Luke's "theory" of the objective means of salvation is found in Acts 10:43: "To him all the prophets bear witness that everyone who believes in him receives forgiveness of sins through his name." At first sight this is a strange statement. Prophecies of forgiveness by the Messiah are hard to find, and the allusion to "*all* the prophets" seems highly exaggerated (cf. Lk. 24:27). The solution to the problem lies in two statements. First, in the Old Testament forgiveness is associated with the name of Yahweh, "the Lord". It is the prerogative of God; those who seek the Lord find that he will abundantly pardon them (Isa. 55:6 f.).[1] Second, the effect of the resurrection is that Jesus is exalted and receives the title of Lord (Acts 2:36). The conclusion is obvious: by virtue of his exaltation Jesus has received the prerogative of God the Lord to dispense forgiveness of sins (cf. perhaps Stephen's prayer, Acts 7:60). What is asserted of God in "all the prophets" can now be asserted of the exalted Jesus.[2]

The soteriological theory of Acts, according to which Jesus as the exalted Lord offers salvation, is not peculiar to Luke. It is to be found in Paul in Romans 10:9–13 and perhaps 4:24 f., both of which probably contain pre-Pauline material. We may perhaps also trace it in the pre-Pauline "hymn" in Philippians 2:6–11, where there is the same silence regarding the atoning character of the death of Jesus and the same stress on his exaltation to be the Lord. Of a similar character is the brief "hymn" in 1 Timothy 3:16.[3] Although there is no explicit mention of forgiveness in these passages, they undoubtedly testify to the exaltation of Jesus to be the Lord who bestows salvation on men; it is possible that they reflect the worship of the church rather than its evangelistic message.[4] What the hymns implicitly affirm is expressed openly in Acts: the exaltation of Jesus is the means of forgiveness.

What, then, is the place of the death of Jesus in the thought of Luke? Luke, to be sure, does not use the Suffering Servant concept (with which he is familiar) to express the character of the death of Jesus as a vicarious atonement. The same, however, is true of Paul who makes little use of this category of interpretation. What must be stressed is that there is no reason to suppose that Luke has deliberately suppressed references to the atonement which he found in his sources.[5] Such passages as Luke 22:19–20 (the

---

[1] Cf. Isa. 33:24; Jer. 31:34; 36:3 (negatively, 18:23); Ezek. 36:25; Dan. 9:19; Amos 7:2; also Exod. 34:7; Num. 14:18; 1 Ki. 8:34; *et al.* The fact of Yahweh's forgiveness is thus to be found in "all the prophets" and indeed throughout the Old Testament.

[2] Even before his exaltation Jesus had authority to forgive sins (Lk. 5:17–26 = Mk. 2:1–12; Lk. 7:36–50); it is in keeping with this fact that Luke calls Jesus ὁ Κύριος in his Gospel narrative.

[3] Cf. E. Schweizer, "Two New Testament Creeds compared. 1 Cor. 15:3–5 and 1 Tim. 3: 16," in W. Klassen and G. F. Snyder, *Current Issues in New Testament Interpretation* (London, 1962), pp. 166–77. [Compare R. H. Gundry's essay in the present volume pp. 203–222, Ed.]

[4] I. H. Marshall, "The Christ-Hymn in Philippians 2:5–11," *Tyndale Bulletin* 19 (1968), pp. 104–27, especially pp. 124 f.

[5] Luke's omission of Mk. 10:45 is due to his following another source in the parallel passage (Lk. 22:27); see especially H. Schürmann, "Lk. 22, 19b–20 als ursprüngliche Textüberlieferung". *Bib* 32 (1951), pp. 366–92, 522–41, especially p. 523.

longer text), Acts 20:28 and the references to Jesus "hanging on a tree" (Acts 5:30; 10:40; cf. 13:29) are sufficient proof that Luke accepted the theory of Jesus' death as a means of atonement.[1] Luke is quite clear that the death of Jesus took place by the deliberate plan of God – it was not a human "accident" which God then turned to good account – and sees that it occupied a vital place in the divine plan of salvation. Nevertheless, he does not go out of his way to emphasize its soteriological character.

The question therefore arises whether Luke is in fact preserving a strand of primitive teaching in which salvation and forgiveness were closely linked with the person of Jesus as the exalted Lord who had been given divine authority to save men.[2] At an early stage in the tradition it would have been natural to see the resurrection as the divine legitimation of Jesus and his establishment as Lord with authority to save men. The earliest Christian confession was "Jesus is Lord", and his position was based upon his resurrection (Rom. 1:3 f.; cf. Rom. 10:9; 1 Thess. 1:9 f.). The gospel tradition also shows plainly that the saving activity of Jesus and his authority to forgive existed before his death on the cross. It is tempting to see in Acts a further testimony to a time when the resurrection itself was seen as the saving event. From an early date, however, the death of Jesus was closely associated with his resurrection as the saving event (Rom. 4:25; 1 Cor. 15:3–5). It is highly improbable that Luke should have "advanced" beyond this synthesis by denying or playing down the significance of the cross, and it is much more likely that he reflects an earlier stage when especial stress was laid on the resurrection. Thus Acts provides a further example of the "humiliation and exaltation" pattern found throughout early church theology.[3]

VII

So important an event as the resurrection must rest on firm historical attestation. This is supplied in Acts by the witnesses who claimed to have seen the risen Jesus. But is Luke's view of the witnesses taken over from tradition or is it his own creation? We do not need to spend time in debate with H. Braun who holds that Luke has substituted for the earlier accounts of appearances to individual witnesses a set of generalizing statements about the appearances to the Twelve.[4] In reality, the "form" of a resurrection story is peculiar to the gospels. Apart from the special case of the appearance to Paul (not one of the Twelve!), the New Testament contains no narratives of resurrection appearances outside the Gospels; they belonged to the special category of "Gospel tradition" which is not handled

[1] L. Morris, *The Cross in the New Testament* (Exeter, n.d.), ch. 3.
[2] Cf. the view of L. Cerfaux mentioned by U. Wilckens, *op. cit.*, pp. 77, n. 3.
[3] E. Schweizer, *Lordship and Discipleship* (London, 1960); H.-T. Wrege, *Die Uberlieferungsgeschichte der Bergpredigt* (Tübingen, 1968), pp. 179 f.
[4] H. Braun, *op. cit.* (see p. 101 above).

outside the Gospels.[1] Having recorded the appearances to individuals in his Gospel, Luke confined himself to general references in Acts (cf. Paul's procedure in 1 Cor. 15).

U. Wilckens goes further and urges that Luke had a special theory of the witnesses: the men to whom Jesus appeared and gave a special commission were those who had accompanied him from Galilee to Jerusalem, in particular the Twelve, and they had the special *heilsgeschichtlich* function of handing down the message of salvation to the people.[2]

This theory is an exaggeration of the facts. In reality the Lucan concept is close to that of Paul. For Paul, an apostle is one who has seen the risen Lord, who has had a special call from God to preach, and whose ministry is attested by the fact of his converts (1 Cor. 9:1 f.; Gal. 1:15 f.). But these are precisely the qualifications listed by Luke (Acts 10:41 f.; 13:31), with the one addition that Luke is said to hold that the witnesses must have been companions of Jesus from the time of his work in Galilee.

Much has been made of this extra qualification, according to which Paul is said to be denied the status of an apostle. Paul, however, distinguishes between the Twelve and the larger, inclusive group of "all the apostles" (1 Cor. 15:5, 7), and does not reckon himself among the former. It is also significant that he distinguishes between the Jewish mission carried on by Peter and the Jerusalem church and the Gentile mission carried on by himself and his companions.[3]

In Acts Paul is not one of the Twelve, but he and Barnabas are called apostles in Acts 14:14, and it is too easy a solution of the difficulty to say that Luke has here taken over a source, perhaps absentmindedly. Further, a broad distinction can be made between the mission of the Twelve and their associates to "the people", i.e. Israel (Acts 13:24, 31), and that of Paul to the Gentiles (Acts 9:15; 22:21; 26:17). Thus the picture is similar to that in Paul's own writings.

The lines, however, must not be drawn too sharply. W. Schmithals undoubtedly exaggerates when he claims that Paul did not preach to the Jews. Paul's own evidence[4] is supplemented by the evidence of Acts (26:22 f.; cf. 9:27–29; 24:21; 26:17, 20), where he is a *witness* to the Jews. This leads H. Strathmann to assert that Luke is inconsistent in his use of the word, since Paul was not a witness in the sense of Acts 1:22;[5] but it is rather the case that Strathmann has overstressed the importance for Luke of the necessity of witness to the earthly ministry of Jesus. The centre of the gospel was rather the resurrection, and Paul was a witness to this.

[1] We accept in part the suggestion of H. Riesenfeld (*The Gospel Tradition and its Beginnings* [London, 1957]) that the Gospel tradition was a "holy Word", handed down in particular forms and channels.

[2] U. Wilckens, *op. cit.*, pp. 145–50.

[3] Cf. W. Schmithals, *Paul and James* (London, 1965).

[4] See C. K. Barrett, *The First Epistle to the Corinthians*, p. 211.

[5] H. Strathmann, *TDNT* IV, pp. 474–514, especially pp. 492–94.

Luke and Paul, then, are in basic agreement. Two differences, however, must be observed. The first is that the word "witness" is characteristic of Acts; Paul uses the verb of his own preaching only in 1 Corinthians 15:15, and he does not describe himself as a μάρτυς.[1] The difference is largely one of terminology. The second difference lies in Luke's stress on "from Galilee", which is unknown to Paul. It seems probable that for Luke witness to "the people" had to be carried on by those who could testify both to the earthly ministry of Jesus and to his resurrection; since Paul was primarily concerned with preaching outside Palestine where there was less stress on the earthly life of Jesus in the preaching, Luke's narrower concept of witness did not concern him.

Luke, therefore, in reality is close to Paul in his concept of apostleship and witness. For both writers testimony to the resurrection by those who were witnesses to the risen Jesus was an essential ingredient in the preaching of the early church.[2] It may fairly be claimed that Luke is here following tradition.

VIII

The result of our study is to show that Luke's presentation of the resurrection in Acts is firmly based on tradition. Our task has been the modest one of finding evidence for tradition. It has not extended to inquiring in any detail how far Luke may have modified that tradition. But sufficient has been said to show that Luke's dependence on tradition is greater than is sometimes asserted. The main lines of his presentation of the resurrection can all be attested as dependent on primitive theology, and consequently some limits can be set to his redactional activity. It has become clear that *Redaktionsgeschichte* must not be carried on independently of source criticism and *Traditionsgeschichte*, lest one be tempted to exaggerate the claims of either partner.

Theologically, we have established the important place of the resurrection in the early church as the decisive act whereby in accordance with prophecy God exalted his Son to be the Lord and revealed him to chosen witnesses in order that they might preach the good news of forgiveness in his name.

---

[1] See also 1 Cor. 1:6; 2:1; 2 Thess. 1:10.
[2] T. F. Glasson, "The Kerygma: Is our Version Correct?", *HJ* 51 (1952–53), pp. 129–32.

CHAPTER VI

THE PURPOSE OF ACTS: SCHNECKENBURGER
RECONSIDERED

A. J. MATTILL, JR.

I

PROFESSOR BRUCE IN HIS COMMENTARY ON ACTS REFERS BRIEFLY, BUT with approval, to Schneckenburger's view that the Petrine-Pauline parallels of Acts are intended to defend Paul's apostolic claims.[1] The time is ripe to reconsider Schneckenburger's position.

Matthias Schneckenburger's *Ueber den Zweck der Apostelgeschichte*[2] was the first elaborate investigation of the purpose of Acts. Although Schneckenburger defended Luke's general reliability, he treated Acts as a *Tendenzschrift*, thus laying the foundation of all later comprehensions of Acts as having a non-historical purpose. He contended that Acts is directed towards Jewish Christians in Rome and has a twofold apologetic purpose: (1) to defend the Apostle Paul in his apostolic dignity, in his personal and apostolic behaviour, especially in the matter of the Gentiles, against all attacks of the Judaizers, the same charges against which Paul defended himself in his Epistles; (2) to demonstrate to these same Jewish Christians the political legitimacy of Paul, for they opposed preaching to Gentiles not only because of their particularistic pride but also because of their fear of the Roman government, which, though it recognized the legitimacy of their Judaism, prohibited the proselytizing of Gentiles. Luke, by recounting Paul's acquittals in other cities, assures the Jewish Christians of Rome that their security will not be endangered by Pauline universalism. Schneckenburger found that the following features of Acts can be explained only by Luke's tendentious purpose:

(1) Luke reports Paul's Jewish practices: Paul circumcizes Timothy (16:3); after living with Aquila the Jew for eighteen months, Paul permits Aquila's hair to be shorn (18:18); he rejects an invitation to preach in Ephesus in order to travel to Jerusalem to observe the next feast (18:21); he interrupts his journey to celebrate the feast of unleavened bread in Philippi (20:6); he sails by the Ephesian church so as to be in Jerusalem at Pentecost (20:16), and purifies himself in the Temple (21:17-27).

These additions to our knowledge of Paul based upon his Epistles are

---

[1] F. F. Bruce, *The Acts of the Apostles* (Grand Rapids, 1951), pp. 33–34.

[2] Bern, 1841. Also "Beiträge zur Erklärung und Kritik der Apostelgeschichte . . .," *Theologische Studien und Kritiken*, 28 (1855), pp. 498–570.

accounted for by Luke's apologetic tendency to picture Paul as a Jewish Christian living according to the Law. Luke's reference to Aquila's vow is an indirect defence of Paul against the charge that he induced Jewish Christians to renounce the Law (21:21). Paul's rite of purification harmonizes with Luke's design to defend Paul against the charges of Judaizers, for what better could serve that purpose than to show that these charges when raised in Jerusalem were refuted by Paul, through the performance of a rite, to the satisfaction of the Judaizers?

(2) Luke omits every trace of Paul's renunciation of the Law, and such events as Paul's "painful" visit to Corinth, and makes only a vague reference to Paul's third visit to Corinth (20:1-3). He omits Paul's refusal to circumcize Titus; Paul's dispute with Peter at Antioch; Paul's conflicts with the Corinthians and Galatians; the collection (except 24:17); the cool relations between Paul and the church in Rome, where Paul lives in his own dwelling and not with the church (cf. Phil. 1:17; 2 Tim. 4:16); Paul's work in Phrygia and Galatia, where he deviated from the practice depicted in Acts and preached only to Gentiles; and many of Paul's sufferings, which his opponents regarded as inconsistent with Paul's apostolic dignity. Luke largely overlooks the work of other Apostles, who recede behind Peter and Paul, and neglects the origin of numerous churches.

Such omissions occur because Luke did not want to awaken memories of Paul's collisions with judaizing opponents. Particularly in Luke's portrayal of Paul's activity in Rome do we see the pragmatism of Acts, for here Luke seeks to justify Paul against the same criticism as Paul himself refutes in Romans 10:14-21; 11:8-11. A mere historical purpose cannot explain why Luke, who was in Rome, devotes only one verse (28:15) to Paul's visit with the church there, and yet stresses Paul's meeting with Jews. Moreover, Luke does not end his narrative in Rome simply because he desired to describe the geographic spread of Christianity from the centre of Judaism to the centre of heathenism, but because he now wants to represent Paul (whom he had previously pictured as predominantly sympathetic towards the Jews and only incidentally as serving the Gentiles) as permanently rejected by the Jews themselves and predominantly sent to the Gentiles, thus fulfilling Jesus' own command (1:8). This final hardening of the Jews against Paul's gospel is prefigured in the first part of Acts by Jewish opposition to the original apostolic preaching. Luke's omissions in respect to the work of other Apostles and the founding of other churches is also explained by Luke's tendency, for if Luke had been writing straight history he would have had to include such information.

(3) Luke emphasizes that Paul is on friendly terms with the primitive church, which he portrays in the glory of the Jerusalem tradition. Ananias, a pious man according to the Law (22:12) and a witness of Paul's direct call from Christ, introduces Paul to the Christians. Paul's good relations are conspicuous at his first meeting with the Apostles. Luke's portrayal of

Barnabas is for the purpose of letting Paul appear in harmony with the Jerusalem church. The John Mark who in 12:25 joins Paul is shown in 12:12 to be on intimate terms with the Apostles. Even James' demand (21:17 ff.) is a sign of confidence, not suspicion. Not even the problem of Gentile converts disrupts this harmony. Long before Paul, Gentiles had been baptized, by Peter himself. The question of admission of Gentiles had been decided by Peter's vision, by the primitive church, and by the elder Apostles (cf. 8:14–17), in whose steps Paul merely followed. The principles expressed by these early Christians concerning Jews and Gentiles, Law and faith, are the same as those developed in Romans (Acts 2:38 f.; 3:19, 26; 4:12; 7:53; 10:15; 11:18; 15:9–11, 14–18). In Acts I (chaps. 1–12) Pauline ideas are as clearly expressed as in the second, Pauline part (chaps. 13–28) they are concealed. The universal destination of Christianity is placed at the beginning of Acts as a command of Jesus (1:8), which is symbolically confirmed at Pentecost, and carried out by Paul. The geographical notice of 1:12 has the apologetic purpose of reminding Jewish Christians that the Sabbath was not violated in connexion with the Ascension.

In contrast to Paul's independence of the primitive Apostles in Galatians, Luke subordinates Paul to the Twelve, especially in 9:17–30 (which attempts to show that Paul was legitimized by the Apostles), at the Council (15:1–35), where the Apostles agree with Paul, and as executor of the Decree (16:4), which was a formal legitimation of Paul's activities.

Paul gives due respect not only to the Apostles but also to the Jews, to whom he first preaches the gospel, and from whom he turns to the Gentiles only when rejected by the Jews (13:46; 17:5; 18:6; 19:9; 22:21; 28:28). Paul began to preach in Jerusalem and wished to remain there to win the Jews, but their obstinacy and Christ's command compelled him to go to the Gentiles (9:28 f.; 22:17–21; 26:20).

Luke's presentation of Paul's peaceful, but subordinate, relationships with the primitive church is also a result of Luke's apologetic purpose to stamp the Jerusalem church's seal of legitimacy upon Paul's criticized activity. The unity of Acts consists in its tendency to represent the difference between Peter and Paul as insignificant. And when Pauline ideas, which Paul expounded in Romans against Jewish accusations, are expressed in the first part of Acts by the Jewish–Christian Apostles, whereas in the second part Paul is made to speak and act in conformity with Jewish demands, the judgment is confirmed that the apologetic purpose for Paul lies at the basis of all of Acts. And the emphasis upon Paul's preaching in synagogues, even when little detail is otherwise given of Paul's activities, shows that so long as there was hope for his people, Paul went to them first.

(4) Luke records parallel miracles, visions, sufferings, and speeches of Peter and Paul. There is no degree of miracle told of Peter without its

Pauline analogy: healing of a man lame from birth (3:1–10; 14:8–14); healing of Aeneas and of Publius' father (9:33–35; 28:8); healings by Peter's shadow and Paul's handkerchiefs and aprons (5:15; 19:12); victories by Peter over Magus and by Paul over Elymas, the pythoness, and Ephesian magic (8:7–13; 13:6–12; 16:16–18; 19:13–19); punishment of Ananias and Sapphira, and Elymas (5:1–11; 13:6–12); raisings of Dorcas and Eutychus (9:36–42; 20:9–12); veneration of Apostles (5:13; 10:25 f.; 14:15; 28:7); gift of the Spirit by laying on of hands (8:17; 19:6); release from prison (5:19–21; 12:6–11; 16:23–34); Pharisaic defence (5:34; 23:9); and interlocking visions (chaps. 9–10).

Paul's speech in Acts 13 is only an echo of the discourses of Peter and Stephen (chaps. 2; 3; 7). Apart from 17:31, the author of Paul's Lystran and Athenian discourses could have been a liberal Jew. Outside of 20:28, the speech at Miletus contains no reference to Pauline doctrine. This paucity of Pauline doctrinal matter is the more evident in comparison with the abundance of Paul's self-vindication. Moreover, Paul's mildness in Acts both towards Jews and the antithesis between faith and Law is extraordinary. If Paul always so preached, how could the charges of 21:21 have arisen?

The purpose of these parallels is to make Paul equal to Peter. Peter's vision and its acknowledgment by the primitive church is an indirect legitimation of Paul's visions, for the Judaizing opponents of Paul did not want to let Paul's visions be regarded as proof of his apostleship. One cannot accept Peter's vision, nor those of Ananias and Cornelius, and reject Paul's. Luke, by omitting Paul's sufferings and narrating Peter's, conforms Paul to Peter; and by showing that the sufferings are conducive to Paul's glory, Luke refutes those who asserted that Paul's fate was unworthy of an Apostle. Paul's speeches show him to be a pious Israelite and no apostate from the Law. The speeches of defence (chaps. 22–26) demonstrate not only Paul's Jewish piety but also his full legitimation as the Apostle of the Gentiles, for Christ directly commissions him (22:21; 26:17 f.). So too Acts gives three accounts of Paul's conversion to answer those Corinthians and Galatians who denied Paul's apostleship. This one-sided picture of Paul and his activity, which does not altogether conform to Paul's self-portrait in his Epistles, could not have been sketched by a Paulinist unless he had an apologetic purpose. When we consider all of the connexions and parallels between Acts I and Acts II, we see that I is an introduction to II. There is no part of the primitive history (I) which is not connected with the Pauline history (II). The choice of Matthias is a prototype of Paul's call; Stephen's speech is a preparation for 28:25–28; and the deaths of Stephen and James are prototypes of Paul's unmentioned death. The accounts of I have their purpose in Paul.

(5) Luke's complex interweaving of his narratives also reveals his pragmatic purpose. Historically, those who had been dispersed because of the

Jerusalem persecution were the first to preach to Gentiles: Philip evangelized the Samaritans (who were regarded by the Jews as little better than Gentiles) and the eunuch (the first Gentile to receive baptism). Others of the dispersed preached to Gentiles at Antioch, and conceivably Paul did likewise in Arabia and Cilicia. Peter and Paul, during their first visit, may have discussed the conversion of Gentiles, and then Peter's reservations about work among Gentiles stimulated his vision (chap. 10).

But according to Acts, Peter first preached to Gentiles, followed by the dispersed and Paul. Therefore Luke omits Paul's activity in Arabia and attributes no importance to the eunuch. The dispersed appear first in 8:4–40 as preachers and not again until 11:19 ff., in order that the precedent of Peter and his recognition by Jerusalem may first be narrated. Chronologically, Peter's journey to Lydda, Joppa, and Caesarea occurred after 8:40. But Luke inserted the narrative of Paul's conversion between 8:40 and 9:32, where Luke could make it plain, on the one hand, that Paul was prepared to enter at once upon the Gentile mission at Antioch, and, on the other hand, that when Paul first worked among Gentiles he did so under the glow of legitimation established in the case of Cornelius.

(6) Finally, Schneckenburger found that his thesis illumines the later fortunes of Acts. The fact that Acts was less well known than other N.T. writings is more easily understood if Acts had a limited apologetic purpose. Moreover, the varying positions of Acts in the manuscripts suggest that the usual concept of Acts as a church history continuing the gospel history was not the decisive one. Further, both the extreme antipaulinists and the extreme Paulinists rejected Acts as having an unacceptable portrait of Paul.

II

F. C. Baur at once reviewed Schneckenburger's "much desired publication", commending Schneckenburger for having proved the apologetic character of Acts, but contending that Schneckenburger's study could not "remain at the point at which he left it. We must either go backward from the aim stated by the author or go forward beyond that aim to further investigations of the historical character of Acts."[1] The Tübingen School went forward.

Both Schneckenburger and the Tübingen School regarded Acts as a *Tendenzschrift*. Schneckenburger's "irenic, apologetic tendency", however, must not be confused with the Tübingen "conciliatory tendency." For Schneckenburger, Acts was written exclusively for Jewish Christians from the Pauline side with a predominantly personal interest (an apology for Paul by his friend Luke), before A.D. 70, at the very beginning of the schism when the basic harmony of the church was disturbed only by Judaizing extremists, so that the credibility of the book was not seriously

[1] *Jahrbücher für wissenschaftliche Kritik*, Nos. 46, 47, 48 (1841), cols. 361–68, 369–75, 377–81.

affected by the author's tendency. For the Tübingen School, Acts was written for both Jewish and Gentile Christians (and possibly pagan authorities) from a mediating position in a primarily partisan interest (the reconciliation of the two hostile parties by a Pauline unionist who made concessions to both sides), in the second century at the threshold of the Old Catholic Church, with the result that the reliability of the book was undermined. In short, Schneckenburger neither shared the Tübingen theory of the development of early Christianity nor the Tübingen interpretation of Acts as a document of the mediating party in the church of the second century.

Today the Tübingen attempt to go beyond Schneckenburger is generally rejected for various reasons: (1) Since Jewish Christianity lost its power after A.D. 70, it could not have played the role in the second century ascribed to it by the Tübingen theory. (2) Peter and Paul were in basic agreement, not two hostile Apostles heading two hostile parties preaching two hostile gospels in two hostile missions. (3) Early church history cannot be fitted into the Hegelian categories of thesis (Petrine Christianity), antithesis (Pauline Christianity), and synthesis (Old Catholic Church). (4) Nor did Luke deliberately falsify positively his narrative in the interests of a tendency.

III

After the Tübingen attempt to go forward on Schneckenburger's road, the Conservative School of the nineteenth century preferred, on the whole, to go back to Acts as a pure historical writing.[1] They contended that Acts gives the impression of being a pure history, that the historical purpose of the book could not be more clearly expressed than in Luke 1:1-4, and that even if Luke 1:1-4 did not originally apply to Acts (as Schneckenburger had argued), Acts is nevertheless the continuation of the Gospel and follows no other object than indicated in the Gospel prologue. The Conservative School generally thought that Acts either had to be straightforward history or unhistorical; they felt that historicity and tendency do not naturally go together.

The Conservative School over-reacted to the Tübingen equation of tendency with fiction by rejecting all tendency lest Acts become a fabrication. Now that we are more than a century removed from the Tübingen excesses we can see that an apologetic purpose is not necessarily incompatible with historical contents and that the apologetic aim of Acts grows out of its historical foundation. We recognize today that a work can be an account of historical events and yet be a theologized history, an apologetic history, a dramatic history, or a typological history. All N.T. books have a

[1] See my dissertation, *Luke as a Historian in Criticism since 1840* (Ann Arbor: University Microfilms, 1959), pp. 85-167, 415-20.

H

non-historical purpose, a theological purpose, for they were written "from faith to faith" (Rom. 1:17; Jn. 20:31; 2 Tim. 3:15). The fact that a Gospel precedes Acts as the first volume of a two-volume work suggests a non-historical purpose. An apologetic purpose is recognizable even in Luke's prologue, where it appears that Luke wished to correct misunderstandings about Christianity and Paul.[1] Furthermore, Luke had more than one purpose in writing and need not have expressed them all in his prologue. Schneckenburger, however, was wrong in holding that Luke and Acts are not a unit. We shall see that it is this unity manifested in the parallel structure of Luke-Acts which strongly supports Schneckenburger's view of Acts as a Pauline apology.

IV

We have seen that the Tübingen School was unsuccessful in its attempt to go beyond Schneckenburger's apologetic tendency to a conciliatory tendency, and that the Conservative School likewise failed when it sought to retreat from Schneckenburger's tendentious purpose to a historical purpose. Now we note the unwitting support which Schneckenburger received from Rackham's commentary on Acts.[2]

Rackham, without mentioning Schneckenburger, and without accepting a Pauline apologetic purpose, goes beyond Schneckenburger in finding parallelisms between Acts I and Acts II, and between Peter and Paul.

But Rackham gave even greater support to Schneckenburger's concept of Acts. We have noted Schneckenburger's failure to see the unity of Luke-Acts, for he thought that Acts could not be a Pauline apology if it were really one with the Gospel, which he believed followed a historical and didactic purpose. Rackham, however, again unwittingly, corrects Schneckenburger at this point, and in doing so supplies conclusive proof that Acts is a Pauline apology. Rackham finds numerous intentional parallels between Luke's Gospel and Acts, of which we mention only a few.

The active ministries of Jesus and Paul are concluded by narratives of passion and resurrection, each occupying seemingly disproportionate space. There is a remarkable correspondence between the journeys of Jesus and of Paul to Jerusalem (Lk. 17:11–19:48; Acts 20:1–21:17), which shows that while Luke is describing Paul's victory over the temptation to abandon his purpose (Acts 21:11–14), he has in mind the Lord's last journey to Jerusalem and his passion there.

Luke 22–24 parallels Acts 21:18–28:31, where the history of the Lord's passion seems to be repeating itself: Paul is carried before the Sanhedrin and smitten on the mouth; the multitude cries "Away with him," and he is

---

[1] Henry J. Cadbury, *The Making of Luke-Acts* (New York, 1927), p. 315.
[2] Richard B. Rackham, *The Acts of the Apostles* (London, 1901), pp. xlvii f.

delivered into the hands of the Gentiles. Breaking bread, darkness, plunging into the deep, and three months' rest are followed by entrance into new life.

Here, then, we have Luke's highest apology for Paul. He shows Paul so conformed to the life of the Lord that even his sufferings and deliverance are parallel.

V

Building upon the insights of Schneckenburger, Rackham, and subsequent criticism,[1] I shall now attempt to rehabilitate Schneckenburger and at the same time suggest what may be a new concept of the occasion of Acts.

As Paul's party travelled towards Jerusalem, Luke accepted with gratitude the kindness of their host Philip, but he noted that Philip was a Hellenist, possibly the first to see that Stephen's principles required the admission of all men to the church apart from the Law. Luke naturally supposed that in Jerusalem Paul could count upon the hospitality of friends. Instead, Paul stayed with a stranger, Mnason, a liberal, and possibly one of the earliest preachers to Gentiles (11:20). Luke saw that Caesarea, the last Hellenistic church along the route to Jerusalem, was the last congregation which was receptive to Paul. Luke may have perceived that Agabus' prophecy (21:10–12) was based upon the fear that Paul could not rely on any help from Jewish Christians in Jerusalem. Agabus no doubt told Paul of the Jewish–Christian conviction that Paul was teaching apostasy from the Law (21:21), for Agabus had come straight from Jerusalem; and Agabus, like Philip and Mnason, had also been connected with the early Gentile church and gratefully recalled Paul's generous response to his famine prophecy (11:27–30). But Paul had also been warned by the disciples of Tyre (21:4), and no doubt by Philip's prophesying daughters (21:9), not to set foot in Jerusalem because of the anti-Pauline mood prevailing there.

In Jerusalem Paul's party was received with gladness by the brethren in Mnason's house (21:17). Luke soon discovered how carefully and falsely Judaizing teachers had "catechized" the Jewish Christians about Paul (21:21); that is, the Judaizers had literally dinned their teachings into their ears by incessant repetition. Luke noted the dilemma in which Paul was placed by James and the elders when James ordered Paul to perform a rite of purification (21:22–25). If Paul did submit, he would be compromised in the eyes of his Gentile converts; and if he did not, he would alienate the thousands of Jewish Christians zealous for the Law.

As Luke watched the riot in the Temple, the suspicion dawned upon

---

[1] Etienne Trocmé, Le 'livre des Actes' et l'histoire (Paris, 1957), supports Schneckenburger, as do others in varying degrees.

him that Judaizers had drawn Paul into an ambush by luring him into the Temple. Luke also learned that the mother church had now decided against Paul in the question concerning Paul's attitude towards the Law, thus reversing their previous action (15:1–35; 21:25). But the biggest shock to Luke was the refusal of the Jerusalem church to accept Paul's collection, thereby symbolizing their break with the Pauline mission.[1]

Possibly the collection was so small it reflected lack of Gentile interest in the mother church, thus offending Jewish Christians. And in addition to the ever-increasing Jewish-Christian coolness towards Paul's "antinomianism", Luke could also feel the pressure of the Jews upon the Jewish Christians to break with Paul. The Jerusalem church knew that if it declared its solidarity with Paul by accepting the collection and approving his position in respect to the Law, it would destroy the possibility of its own mission among Jews, indeed, would risk its own destruction at the hands of Jews who could not tolerate any preaching of freedom from the Law, and who resented Paul's diversion of annual dues from the Temple to the collection for the Jerusalem church, money which would have come to the Temple if Paul had compelled Gentiles to become proselytes to Judaism and thus obligated to pay the Temple tax.

In the midst of this charged atmosphere Luke kept recalling the anxiety Paul had frequently expressed about his journey to Jerusalem and his fear that the collection would be refused (Rom. 15:30 f.). Paul too had told Luke that Jewish and Jewish–Christian opposition had dashed his hopes of successful work in the East and therefore he was planning to visit Rome and Spain (Rom. 15:23–33). Luke too had realized that the Jewish plot which forced Paul to change his route (Acts 20:3) was an ominous beginning for an errand of reconciliation. Luke and Paul were going up to Jerusalem, prepared for the worst. Luke knew that a lesser spirit than Paul might have regarded the contractual agreement of Galatians 2:10 as broken by the Jewish-Christian hostility since the Council.

Luke saw that Paul was never nearer to death than when the mob tried to beat Paul to death on the spot (Acts 21:30–32). The sight of Paul being borne above the heads of soldiers made an indelible impression upon Luke, for this was a mode of conveyance as undignified as being let down from a wall in a basket (9:25). But where were the Jewish Christians? They could have helped because of their faithfulness to the Law and Temple, but they sat idly by. And the many Jewish Christians on hand from Judea and Galilee may have been even more zealous for the Law than those of Jerusalem and even less subject to whatever control the leadership of the Jerusalem church may have wished to exercise. Everything had gone wrong.

[1] Cf. Oscar Cullmann, "Dissensions Within the Early Church," *Union Seminary Quarterly Review*, 22 (1967), pp. 83–92.

Luke had been gathering material for a narrative of the early church from persons such as Philip and Mnason. But when he saw the indifference and hostility of the Jewish Christians in Jerusalem towards Paul, Luke decided that his narrative must be a defence of Paul against the charges and attitudes of Jewish Christians. Three times Judaizers had attacked those who preached to Gentiles (11:1–18; 15:1–35; 21:20–25). There could yet be time to appeal successfully to the more moderate Jewish Christians. Luke began at once to shape his narrative according to this apologetic purpose.

Acts 21, thus understood, supplies us with the occasion of Acts. Acts 21, which ranks next to Acts 15 in the study of Luke as a historian, now becomes the key to the composition of Luke–Acts, for it was in this situation that Luke found the thread with which to tie his mixture of materials together. This was the great day when Luke perceived the *dominant* purpose of his work, the purpose which shaped the form and content of Luke–Acts.

With this purpose in mind, Luke listened to Paul's defences in Jerusalem and Caesarea, with the result that the next five chapters of Acts are chiefly concerned to refute the charge that Paul was an apostate from the Law who encouraged others to apostatize. Here Luke stresses Paul's fidelity to his ancestral religion to show that the Jerusalem church erred in condemning Paul, and that Christianity is true Judaism. To be a Christian is to hold to the Jewish faith, especially belief in the resurrection.

Luke, while in Caesarea, travelled to Jerusalem several times to visit the church there. During these visits he came to realize that to reach Jewish Christians he must stress Paul's good relationship with the primitive church and portray this church in the glory of its own tradition. Thus Jerusalem became "the centre of Luke's theological universe"[1] and the frame of Paul's ministry. From the infancy narratives, where Luke dwells on the connexion of John the Baptist and Jesus with the Temple, on through his Jerusalem tradition of the resurrection appearances to his idealization of the Jerusalem church and Apostles and their control of missions, Luke had the Jerusalem church constantly in mind. Twice the Risen Christ commands a Gentile mission, beginning at Jerusalem (Lk. 24:47; Acts 1:8). Significantly, the only distances recorded in Luke–Acts are the two which indicate the proximity to Jerusalem of the resurrection appearances (Lk. 24:13; Acts 1:12). Luke of course did not know it, but his Gospel would be the only one to begin and end in the Temple. Luke even changed the order of the Temptations so as to create an artistic frame of four Temple scenes (Lk. 1:5 ff.; 2:25 ff.; 2:41 ff.; 4:9 ff.). And after an extensive travel narrative focused on Jerusalem (9:51–19:44) Luke placed a Jerusalem scene framed by two Temple scenes (19:45–24:53). Luke–Acts is an alternation of Jerusalem scenes (Lk. 1:5–4:13; 19:45–24:53; Acts 1:4–7:60;

[1] M. D. Goulder, *Type and History in Acts* (London, 1964), p. 69.

21:18–26:32) and travel narratives (Lk. 4:14–19:44; Acts 8:1–21:17; 27:1–28:31).[1]

So too Luke determined to stress the Jewish features and practices of Paul and to select incidents which would play up the parallel between Paul and Peter, the Jerusalem Apostle *par excellence* and leader of the Jewish–Christian mission. Luke would not, of course, create an absolute similarity between Peter and Paul, but he would insist upon the undeniable essential similarity of the two. In Acts 1–20 Luke created a balance between Peter and Paul by devoting sixty verses to the speeches of Peter and fifty-nine to those of Paul. By the Pauline speeches of chaps. 22–28 Luke clinches "the unexcelled significance of Paul."[2] Luke's summaries liken the results of Paul's work to those of Peter (2:47; 4:4; 6:7; 9:31; 13:49; 16:5; 19:20). Luke felt that by recording Paul's vision in the Temple (22:17–21) he could best refute the charge that Paul had defiled the Temple and also tell Paul's opponents that the God of the Temple is the God of the Gentile mission. He hoped that by pointing out the large numbers of Jewish Christians (2:41, 47; 4:4; 6:1, 7; 9:31; 21:20) and by giving no precise indication of the strength of Gentile Christians he could allay the fear of Jewish Christians that they would be swallowed up by Gentiles.

Likewise Luke would accentuate Peter's precedent in preaching to Gentiles and would refer three times to Cornelius' Jewish piety (10:2, 22, 30–32) and point out that the God who gave the Law also revealed the purification of the Gentiles (chap. 10). He shows that the Cornelius incident is a fulfilment of Jesus' words at Nazareth (Lk. 4:25–27) and of the Elijah-widow and Elisha-Naaman prophecies.[3]

Luke would omit or tone down conflicts between Paul and Jewish Christians. At the Council (15:1–35) the church supports Paul, and 15:4 f. is parallel with 11:1–3, showing that Peter faced similar opposition. In 15:36–41 Luke glosses over the deeper reason for the estrangement between Paul and Barnabas (cf. Gal. 2:11 ff.), but records the incident to show that Paul is not merely an agent of the Jerusalem church but stands pre-eminent as the Apostle of the Gentiles, corresponding to Peter at Jerusalem. In chapter 21 Paul does attempt to satisfy the Jewish Christians, and Luke, by making no clear reference to Paul's collection, softens the bitterness of Paul's last visit to Jerusalem. At 18:22 Luke omits the main reason for Paul's journey to Jerusalem at that time, namely, to discuss with the church his plans for the collection. Luke also says nothing about the colleague appointed at this time by the churches of Judaea at Paul's

---

[1] Robert Morgenthaler, *Die lukanische Geschichtsschreibung als Zeugnis* (Zürich, 1948), 1. Teil, pp. 163–72.

[2] Paul Schubert, "The Final Cycle of Speeches in the Book of Acts," *JBL*, 87 (1968), pp. 1–16.

[3] Larrimore C. Crockett, "Luke 4:25–27 and Jewish-Gentile Relations in Luke–Acts," *JBL*, 88 (1969), pp. 177–83.

request to help him with the collection (cf. 2 Cor. 8:18–24) and to avoid suspicion of dishonesty and lack of enthusiasm on Paul's part.[1] So too at 20:4–5 Luke names the seven delegates of the churches, but omits the fact that their mission was to deliver the collection. Luke's omissions in respect to the collection are also part of his defence of Paul's apostolic authority, in that he would refute the contention that Paul was only a collector for Jerusalem.

Again with Jewish–Christian readers in mind, Luke would portray Jesus as the antitype of Moses (Acts 3:22; 7:20–43), but not as the New Lawgiver (Matt. 5–7; hence Luke relegates the Sermon on the Mount to the background and makes it a Sermon on the Plain), but as the One who, on the Day of Pentecost, pours out the Spirit (Acts 2:33) upon all flesh, thereby establishing the New Covenant and restoring both the unity of God's people and the unity of language, even as Moses gave the Law as the basis of the Old Covenant, commemorated on Pentecost, when a voice announced the commandments to all nations in the seventy languages of the world. Possibly there is some connexion between this seventy and the seventy disciples of Luke 10.

After two years in Caesarea, Luke accompanied Paul on the perilous voyage to Rome. During the three months on Malta Luke had time to reflect upon the theological significance of the wreck and deliverance, and as he did so the parallel between Paul and the Lord began to impress itself more and more upon Luke's mind and upon the structure of his narrative. In Rome, during Paul's imprisonment, the striking parallel between Paul and the Lord became a dominant feature of Luke's writing, so that to a remarkable degree Gospel and Acts correspond.

In his Nazareth pericope (Lk. 4:16–30), Luke lets the Lord's dramatic appearance anticipate the life and work of Paul in a number of respects: Paul's Gentile mission (cf. also Lk. 24:46 f.); Paul's famine visit to Jerusalem and his promotion of table fellowship between Jews and Gentiles (Lk. 4:25 f.; Acts 11:25–30; 15:1–35; 27:33–38); Paul's preaching in synagogues in the manner of his Lord (Acts 13:14 ff., etc.); the Jews' infuriation at the extension of blessings to the Gentiles (13:46, 50), to the extent of seeking to kill Paul (22:21 f.), and even by stoning, as in the case of Jesus (Lk. 4:29. Acts 14:5, 19); and the Jews' rejection of the gospel, Jesus himself preparing readers at the beginning of Luke–Acts for Paul's statement at its end (28:28).

Luke records that like the Lord Paul healed a lame man (Lk. 5:17–26; Acts 14:8–14), a possessed person (Lk. 8:26–39; Acts 16:16–18), and many sick (Lk. 4:40; Acts 28:9), cured a fever (Lk. 4:38–39; Acts 28:8), and raised a young man (Lk. 7:11–17; Acts 20:9–12).

At Luke 8:10 Luke minimizes Mark's (4:12) predestined Isaianic rejection of the Jews so that the Jews might have every chance to accept the gospel before Paul, quoting fully Isaiah 6:9 f., rejects them as a whole (Acts 28:26–28). But before this action, Luke takes care to show that Paul, against great opposition, so loved his people that he went to them first, and that even at the last Paul had no complaint against his people (28:19). And to make this rejection as inoffensive as possible to Jewish Christians, Paul quotes a Jewish prophet, as all four gospels were to do. Jewish Christians could hardly deny that this prophecy was fulfilled by those Jews who rejected the teaching of the Law and prophets concerning Jesus. In turning to the Gentiles, Paul was fulfilling not only Isaiah's prophecy but also Jesus' command (Acts 1:8).

Luke points out (Lk. 11:30) that Jonah's importance lay in his preaching to Gentiles, thus foreshadowing Paul's Gentile mission, especially his journey to the greatest Nineveh and his going down into the deep (Jon. 1:5, 9; Acts 27:18, 23).

At Luke 21:12–19 Luke recasts Mark 13:9–13 to anticipate Paul: "they shall lay their hands upon you" (Lk. 21:12; Acts 21:27); prisons (Lk. 21:12; Acts 16:23, etc.); kings and governors (Lk. 21:12; Acts 24:10–25; 25:6–12; 26:1–23); apologies (Lk. 21:14; Acts 22–26); and physical safety (Lk. 21:18; Acts 27:34).

Luke also relates that Paul, like his Master, had four trials (Jesus: Sanhedrin, Pilate, Herod Antipas, and Pilate; Paul: Sanhedrin, Felix, Festus, and Herod Agrippa).[1]

Luke concludes the active ministries of Jesus and Paul with narratives of journeys to Jerusalem, passions, and resurrections occupying a seeming disproportionate space. By thus accentuating the parallels between Paul and the Lord, Luke created his most effective apology for Paul.

Luke knew that Vol. I required Vol. II and vice versa, for the parallels could not be complete without both volumes. Luke–Acts is one well-planned work in two volumes; Acts was no afterthought. Luke knew that in these two volumes he would focus upon key personalities rather than present a well-rounded account of the institutional development of the church. He would tell, not how the gospel, but how Paul came to Rome. He would literally allow his narrative to bog down in the details of Paul's career. Yet he would not write a history of the Pauline mission, but deal with that only in part (chaps. 13–18). Certainly he would omit much information which would be included were he writing a biography of Paul.

But what was the origin of Luke's portrayal of the parallels between Paul and Jesus? This portrayal originated, not with Luke, but with Paul himself. That Paul conceived of himself as God's suffering servant after the pattern of the Lord and of the Servant Songs of Isaiah is indicated by the allusions to these songs in the accounts of Paul's call in Galatians and Acts, by the connexions between 2 Timothy 4:16–18 and Psalm 22, and by

[1] Goulder, op. cit., pp. 176 f., 114–17, 40 f.

the self-emptying of Christ and Paul described in Philippians 2:1–3:14. Luke had heard Paul reciting, like the Master, Passion Psalm 22, and he had listened to Paul tell of his determination to follow in Christ's footsteps to death and victory.[1] Luke knew too that in a suffering servant song (Isa. 52:15) Paul had found the guiding principle of his missionary work (Rom. 15:21).

From Paul Luke had also learned the Semitic imagery of death, according to which "going down in a storm was the metaphor *par excellence* in scripture for death, and being saved from one resurrection" (2 Cor. 1:8–10; 11:23). Possibly too Paul had likened his own conversion to the Lord's resurrection ("Saul was raised up from the earth," Acts 9:8), and had spoken of his baptism as dying and rising with Christ.[2]

Again under Paul's influence Luke stresses the universal appeal of the gospel (Lk. 2:10, 30–32; 3:6, 34–38; 10:29–37; 13:29; 17:11–19; 19:1–10; 24:47) and omits statements which might be regarded as hostile to Gentiles, such as Matthew 7:6; 10:5 f., 15:24; and Mark 7:24–30. With Paul's attitude towards the Law in mind, Luke's Sermon on the Plain does not mention or quote the Law, omitting especially Matthew 5:17 –20.

By including the parable of justification (Lk. 18:9–14), Luke anticipates the Pauline note of Acts 13:39, thereby linking Paul's controversial teaching with that of the Lord (cf. Lk. 7:50 and Acts 16:31). "The God who justifies the ungodly" (Rom. 4:5) could be written over all the parables of grace (Lk. 7:41–43; 14:7–11, 16–24; 15:1–32). Small wonder that the Gospel of Luke was later called "the Gospel of Paul", and Paul's references to "my gospel" (Rom. 2:16; 16:25; 2 Tim. 2:8) were taken to mean the Third Gospel.

In Rome, Luke was to learn much more of Jewish–Christian intransigence and to see more clearly the urgency of rehabilitating Paul. At first Luke was surprised by the unexpected kindness with which Paul was welcomed to Rome and recorded this reception as an example of how Paul should be received by the churches (28:15). Luke found that in the Roman church were substantial numbers of Jewish Christians, who probably controlled the church there. It was a church founded by the Jewish–Christian mission of Jerusalem, and there were some 60,000 Jews in Rome.

Luke once again saw Paul becoming a victim of Jewish–Christian jealousy (Phil. 1:15–17; cf. 1 Clem. 5–6). There were few in the Roman church whom Paul could trust (Phil. 2:20–22). The Epistle to the Romans may have been occasioned by Roman prejudice against Paul based upon Jewish–Christian misrepresentations. Romans 1:13 suggests that Paul was hindered in coming to Rome by Jewish Christians who were saying that

---

[1] Johannes Munck, *Paul and the Salvation of Mankind*, trans. Frank Clarke (Richmond, 1959), pp. 24–33, 331–34; T. E. Pollard, "The Integrity of Philippians," *NTS*, 13 (1966–67), pp. 57–66.

[2] Goulder, *op. cit.*, pp. 39, 94 f.

Paul dared not come to Rome with his gospel. Hence Paul affirms that he is not ashamed of his gospel (1:16).

Yet with all of its Jewish–Christian orientation the Epistle to the Romans had failed to win the Jewish Christians of Rome to Paul's gospel. At Paul's first hearing in court, every one of the Roman Christians deserted him (2 Tim. 4:16). Luke observed the cool relations between Paul and the Roman church – Paul was even staying in his own hired dwelling and not with the church. If Luke needed any additional assurance of the necessity of an apology for Paul, he found it in this Roman coolness.

But Luke was also keenly aware that the Jewish Christians of Rome opposed Paul because they suspected his political legitimacy. Luke decided that the best way he could defend Paul was by relating Paul's acquittals in other cities (16:38 f.; 17:9; 18:14 f.; 19:37–40; 23:29; 24:27; 25:25; 26:31 f.). Even though Paul had spent years in Corinth and Ephesus, Luke would tell his readers little of Paul's activities there except his official exculpations. And he would reveal in his account of Paul before the Sanhedrin that within Judaism there existed greater differences than between Christians and Pharisees. Christianity as the true Israel was faithful to the synagogue, Temple, and Scriptures (Lk. 1–2; 3:8; 4:16–30; 19:45–47) and was respectful of Roman citizens and law (Lk. 3:13 f.; 4:5–8; 5:27–32; 7:2–9; 20:20–26; 22:50–53; 23:1–4, 15, 20–24, 47). Luke would also make plain Paul's Roman citizenship (Acts 16:37; 21:39; 22:25–28), and point out that Cornelius was a Roman citizen and officer (10:1). In this fashion Luke shaped his narrative to allay suspicion of Paul, even as Paul himself had sought to do so by insisting upon obedience to authority (Rom. 13:1–7).

In view of the crying need for a defence of his master, Luke must hasten to publish his two volumes while the conflict was intense, even before Paul's two-year imprisonment was ended. Luke soon had his work ready, and he appropriately dedicated each volume to his God-loving patron, Theophilus, a name in common use among both Jews and Greeks, and thus an appropriate person to whom to dedicate a defence of the Apostle of the Gentiles against Jewish–Christian charges originating chiefly in Jerusalem and Rome.

CHAPTER VII

ANCIENT ASTROLOGICAL GEOGRAPHY AND
ACTS 2:9-11

BRUCE M. METZGER

ACCORDING TO THE BOOK OF ACTS, ON THE DAY OF PENTECOST AFTER the Holy Spirit had come upon the disciples and they began to speak in other tongues, the multitude of the Jewish pilgrims in Jerusalem were amazed and wondered, saying, "Are not all these who are speaking Galileans? And how is it that we hear, each of us in his own native language? Parthians and Medes and Elamites and residents of Mesopotamia, Judea and Cappadocia, Pontus and Asia, Phrygia and Pamphylia, Egypt and the parts of Libya belonging to Cyrene, and visitors from Rome, both Jews and proselytes, Cretans and Arabians, we hear them telling in our own tongues the mighty works of God" (2:7-11). This passage has given rise to several questions that have perplexed commentators. Why, for example, are these and no other countries specified? And if these countries, why are they cited in the order in which they now stand?

In 1948 more or less satisfactory answers to both these questions seemed to be supplied in a brief article by Stefan Weinstock published in a British journal of the classics, in which the author drew attention to a somewhat similar list of names of countries in an astrological treatise compiled by Paulus Alexandrinus, who lived in the latter part of the fourth Christian century.[1] In this treatise Paulus assigns to the several signs of the zodiac a dozen or more lands and nations, whose similarity to the list in Acts struck Winstock as remarkable. Consequently Weinstock concluded that the author of Acts, "however strange his list is, meant in fact to say 'the whole world' . . . [i.e.] all nations who live under the twelve signs of the

---

[1] "The Geographical Catalogue in Acts II, 9-11," *JRS*, 38 (1948), pp. 43-46. Weinstock indicates that his attention was drawn to the similarity between the lists when he came upon F. C. Burkitt's copy of an off-print of Franz Cumont's article, "La plus ancienne géographie astrologique" (*Klio* 9 [1909], pp. 263-73), in the margin of which Burkitt had pencilled the names of the countries and lands of Acts 2:9-11 opposite the text of Paulus. Burkitt himself expressed no opinion concerning the relationship between the two lists.

Actually Weinstock was not the first to publish a discussion concerning the similarity between the list of countries in Paulus Alexandrinus and in Acts 2; at the beginning of the twentieth century Joseph Halévy included a brief discussion of the data in his little-known article entitled "Nouvelles considérations sur le cycle turc des animaux", published in the journal *T'oung Pao*, sér. II, 7 (1906), pp. 270-95, especially 279 ff. Halévy argues that the priority belongs to the list in Acts, which was excerpted later by a Christian astrologer (a view rejected by Boll, see below).

zodiac received the gift to understand [the apostles'] preaching immediately."

Soon Weinstock's article began to be quoted by commentators on Acts: one of the first to do so was Professor F. F. Bruce, whose interest and competence in the classics are well known. After presenting a brief summary of Weinstock's argument, Bruce concluded, "Whatever may be the literary affinities of Luke's catalogue, we take leave to doubt the presence of astrological considerations in his mind."[1]

It seems to be appropriate in a *Festschrift* in honour of Professor Bruce to give renewed attention to the comparison between Acts 2:9–11 and Paulus; first, because there is now available a critically established text of the astrological treatise of Paulus Alexandrinus, based on forty-eight manuscripts[2] (the only previous edition is the sixteenth-century *editio princeps* prepared by Andrew Schato,[3] based upon a single manuscript); and, secondly, because several recent commentators on Acts have made rather extravagant statements concerning the degree of similarity thought to exist between the list in Acts and the list in Paulus[4] – statements that tend to mislead those who have no ready access to the text of Paulus Alexandrinus.

I

Before we consider Paulus's assignment of countries and lands to the signs of the zodiac, it will be useful to mention several details concerning Paulus and other ancient astrologers.[5]

---

[1] *Commentary on the Book of the Acts; the English text with Introduction, Exposition and Notes* London, 1959), p. 61, note 20.

[2] Παύλου ᾿Αλεξανδρέως Εἰσαγωγικά, *Pauli Alexandrini Elementa Apotelesmatica*, edidit Æ[milie] Boer, Interpretationes astronomicas addidit O. Neugebauer (Bibliotheca Scriptorum Graecorum et Romanorum Teubneriana; Leipzig, 1958).

[3] Pauli Alexandrini, *Rudimenta, in doctrinam de praedictis natalitiis* (Wittenberg, 1586; second, corrected ed., 1588). Nothing is known of Schato beyond the fact that he produced the first printed edition of Paulus's Greek text, accompanied by a Latin translation; in fact, it is not altogether certain how his name should be spelled, whether Schato, Schaton, or Schatus.

[4] E.g., C. S. C. Williams implies that eleven-twelfths of the names of the countries in the list in Acts agree with those in Paulus Alexandrinus (*Commentary on the Acts of the Apostles* [London and New York, 1957], p. 64); G. W. H. Lampe finds that Paulus's list "strikingly resembles Luke's list in order and content" (in *Peake's Commentary on the Bible*, ed. by M. Black and H. H. Rowley [London and New York, 1962], p. 888); and R. P. C. Hanson declares the list in Acts to be "almost exactly the same as an astrological list, known from other writers, in which each land corresponded to a sign of the Zodiac (only *Judea* is out of place; it was not, after all, a foreign land; Luke may have made it replace another name)" (*The Acts in the Revised Standard Version, with Introduction and Commentary* [Oxford, 1967], p. 64). Likewise J. A. Brinkman, S. J., in his article "The Literary Background of the 'Catalogue of the Nations' (Acts 2:9–11)," *CBQ* 25 (1963), pp. 418–27, thinks that "the two lists are too similar in both contents and sequence not to have come from the same tradition" (p. 423).

[5] For a conveniently arranged list of almost a score of ancient astrological authors and anonymous treatises, see Hans Georg Gundel, *Weltbilde und Astrologie in den griechischen Zauberpapyri* (=*Münchener Beiträge zur Papyrusforschung und antike Rechtsgeschichte*, 53) (Munich, 1968), pp. 74–78.

It is appropriate to mention at this point that the present writer is deeply indebted to Prof.

Of Paulus Alexandrinus very little is known other than that which can be gleaned from his *Rudiments of Astrology*.[1] He is reasonably called Alexandrinus because many of his astronomical data fit the latitude of Alexandria only; and this is supported by his use of the Egyptian names of the months and the four-year Egyptian period with an intercalary day. That he flourished in the second half of the fourth century of the Christian era seems to be a fair deduction from his reference in chap. 20, where to illustrate an argument he uses the 20th day of the month Mecheir in the 94th year of the Diocletian era (i.e. Feb. 20, A.D. 378).[2] Paulus was not a Christian, for he believed the planets to be the abode of gods.[3]

Paulus's *Rudiments* found early and general acceptance, and became the subject of a commentary, written, as it has been thought, by a certain Heliodorus,[4] who had been a pupil of Proclus in Athens and who made astronomical observations at Alexandria between 498 and 509.[5] Considerably shorter than the celebrated *Tetrabiblos* of Claudius Ptolemy,[6] who

[1] The title of the work varies in the manuscripts; some read Εἰσαγωγικά (which is adopted by Boer); others read Εἰσαγωγικαὶ μέθοδοι, which is expanded in still others by the addition of εἰς τὴν ἀποτελεσματικὴν ἐπιστήμην.

[2] Cf. Franz Cumont in *Catalogus Codicum Astrologorum Graecorum* 1 (Brussels, 1898), p. 57, n. 1, and 5 (1904), pp. 194 ff.

[3] Cf. e.g. the title of chap. 20, Περὶ τοῦ γνῶναι ἑκάστην ἡμέραν, τίνος τῶν θεῶν ἐστιν, and other passages mentioned by Wilhelm Gundel in his article on Paulus in *PW*, XVIII, 4 (1949), col. 2377. Several of the manuscripts of Paulus occasionally reflect modifications presumably introduced by Christian scribes in the interest of removing polytheistic expressions.

[4] The text of the Commentary, which has been transmitted in two forms, has been edited by Miss Æ. Boer in the Teubner series under the title, *Εἰς τὸν Παῦλον <'Ηλιοδώρου>, Heliodori, ut dicitur, in Paulum Alexandrinum Commentarium*, Interpretationes astronomicas addiderunt O. Neugebauer et D. Pingree (Leipzig, 1962). The authorship of the commentary remains doubtful; the name "Heliodorus" is properly attested by only the later of the two groups of manuscripts. The editor considers the name to be a Byzantine expansion, but thinks it may have been added on good authority, and so retains it, though with an expression of some doubt. On the Heliodorus whose astronomical observations between 498 and 509 are extant, see Boll in *Byzantinische Zeitschrift* 8 (1899), p. 525, Anm. 1, and in *PW* VIII, 1 (1912), cols. 18-19, and also Praechter, *ibid.*, col. 1305. On the other hand, for what can be said against the identification, see G. J. Toomer in *Gnomon* 35 (1963), p. 270.

According to information kindly supplied by Prof. Pingree, in an article to be published in *Byzantinische Zeitschrift*. L. G. Westerink argues that "the commentary consists of notes taken by a student at a course of lectures delivered by Olympiodorus in the spring and summer of A.D. 565".

[5] The statement made by Wilhelm Gundel and Hans Georg Gundel (*Astrologumena; die astrologische Literatur in der Antike und ihre Geschichte* [*Sudhoffs Archiv; Vierteljahrsschrift für Geschichte der Medizin und der Naturwissenschaften und der Pharmazie und der Mathematik*, Beiheft 6] [Wiesbaden, 1966], p. 239), that Paulus's influence extended even to India and that the *Pauliśasiddhânta*, which is no longer extant, was a commentary on his *Rudiments*, is apparently without foundation, resting upon a misapprehension; see David Pingree in *Isis* 54 (1963), p. 237, n. 63; cf. also *Gnomon* 40 (1968), p. 277.

[6] Edited and translated into English by F. E. Robbins in the Loeb Classical Library (London, 1940).

David Pingree of the Oriental Institute of the University of Chicago, with whom he discussed the first draft of this paper. Besides confirming the general point of the paper, Prof. Pingree saved me from making more than one egregious blunder concerning the intricacies of ancient astrological lore.

flourished about the middle of the second Christian century, Paulus's work appears to be a synopsis of elements of ancient astrology. It opens with a summary of the properties of the twelve signs of the zodiac, explains terms and techniques employed by astrologers,[1] and then discusses horoscopes and climacterics.[2]

A horoscope depicting the character of a person and prophesying (or describing) events in his life is made by preparing a diagram representing the heavens at the time of his birth, and showing the positions of the heavenly bodies with relation to one another and to the horizon. As a typical example among the nearly two hundred Greek horoscopes of individuals that have been preserved from antiquity, the following may be quoted:

> Sun (and) Saturn in Capricorn, moon in Scorpio, Jupiter in Leo, Mars in Pisces, Venus (and) Mercury in Aquarius, Horoscopos in Virgo, the Lot of Fortune in Scorpio, the Daimon in Cancer. Then in opposition to the Daimon, which forecasts the intellectual and the spiritual, was Saturn, and he was in dominant aspect to the (preceding) full moon (in Cancer) and to the phase at that time, and the ruler of the Lot of Fortune (♂) was in opposition to the Horoscopos. Thus this person had in the fated places injury and tender feet and most of all he was lunatic.[3]

One aspect of ancient astrology treats of astrological geography,[4] or the placing of lands and regions of the earth under the dominion of heavenly bodies. Although some scholars have argued that astrological geography originated in Meopotamia, perhaps as long ago as Sumerian times,[5] the

[1] For an invaluable glossary of the technical terms used by ancient astrologers, see O. Neugebauer and H. B. Van Hoesen, *Greek Horoscopes* (=*Memoirs of the American Philosophical Society*, 48) (Philadelphia, 1959), pp. 191 ff. For a general introduction to what is commonly called judicial astrology (which deals with the supposed influences of the heavenly bodies upon the fortunes of men and nations), see Felix von Oefele, "Sun, Moon, and Stars (Introductory)" in *HERE* 12 (Edinburgh, 1922), pp. 48–62. The notes and commentary of H. W. Garrod on book II of Manilius's *Astronomicon* (Oxford, 1911) can be consulted with profit concerning ancient astronomy in general.

[2] According to astrological lore the climacteric years, or critical periods of a person's life, are the years ending the third, fifth, seventh, and ninth period of seven years, to which some add the eighty-first year. The sixty-third year was called the *grand* or *great climacteric*. It was believed that each of these periods is attended by some remarkable change in respect of health, life, or fortune.

[3] Preserved by Vettius Valens in his *Anthologiarum libri*, II, 36 (ed. Wilhelm Kroll, p. 113, lines 3–10). According to the computations of Neugebauer and Van Hoesen, whose English translation is given here, the horoscope leads to A.D. 106, January 16, about 10 p.m. (*op. cit.*, p. 103).

[4] Instead of "geography", Auguste Bouché-Leclercq prefers the expression "chorography"; cf. his contribution "Chorographie astrologique", in *Mélanges Graux; Recueil de travaux d'érudition classique dédié à la mémoire de Charles Graux* (Paris, 1884), pp. 341–51, and his magisterial monograph, *L'Astrologie grecque* (Paris, 1899; reprinted, Brussels, 1963), pp. 328 ff.

[5] Cf. B. L. van der Waerden, "History of the Zodiac", *Archiv für Orientforschung* 16 (1952–53), pp. 216–30, and Eckhard Unger, "Fata Morgana als geisteswissenschaftliches Phänomen im alten Orient", *Rivista degli studi orientali* 33 (1958), pp. 1–51, especially pp. 4 ff.

differences between Paulus and the Mesopotamian traditions are both numerous and decisive. For those who were acquainted with the Septuagint, the idea of the correlation of nations with heavenly bodies seemed to be countenanced by Deuteronomy 4:19.[1]

During the centuries various systems of astrological geography were developed, as more and more countries and lands came to be assigned to the several signs of the zodiac. Furthermore, differences among the lists arose not merely for, so to speak, numerical reasons, but also as the result of an effort to show that the assignment of countries was not aimless or arbitrary, and that reasons exist, at least in certain cases, for the association of land and sign. Among the several systems, that preserved by Paulus Alexandrinus is the simplest, and for this reason has been regarded by some scholars as the oldest (although this view can be disputed). According to Housman, "it was devised when the world was small and nothing mattered much beyond the eastern Mediterranean and the west of Asia. The west and north of Europe are unknown to it; there is no Scythia nor even any Ethiopia or Arabia; the only far distant land which enters its circle is India."[2]

More complicated lists are those of (a) Dorotheus Sidonius (third quarter of first century A.D.), who assigns some thirty countries to the twelve signs of the zodiac, (b) Manilius (end of first century B.C. and beginning of first century A.D.), who has close to fifty to dispose of, and (c) Ptolemy (second century A.D.), who, with more than seventy countries, follows Eratosthenes of Cyrene (who, in the second century B.C., computed with remarkable accuracy the circumference of the earth) and divides the inhabited earth into four quadrants by drawing lines from west to east and from north to south roughly corresponding to the parallel and meridian of Rhodes. The lands within each quadrant are assigned to a zodiacal trigon (i.e. three signs); furthermore, lands situated at the inner angle of a quadrant have affinity with the trigon ruling the quadrant diametrically opposite.[3] Still other systems were devised, accommodated to the progress of history, by which countries are allotted not to signs but to portions of signs and to planets.[4]

---

[1] In the Septuagint Dt. 4:19 reads ἰδὼν τὸν ἥλιον καὶ τὴν σελήνην καὶ τοὺς ἀστέρας. . . . ., ἃ ἀπένειμεν κύριος ὁ θεός σου αὐτὰ πᾶσιν τοῖς ἔθνεσιν τοῖς ὑποκάτω τοῦ οὐρανοῦ (cf. Boll in PW Suppl. IV [1929], col. 654 Anm.).

[2] A. E. Housman, M. Manilii Astronomicon, liber quartus (London, 1920), p. xiii.

[3] For a list of the seventy-two (or seventy-three) countries that Ptolemy assigned to the twelve signs of the zodiac, see his Tetrabiblos II, 3 (73).

[4] For an account of these various schemes, see Bouché-Leclercq, L'Astrologie grecque, pp. 332 ff.; Housman, op. cit., pp. xiii ff.; and, more briefly, Boll in PW Suppl. IV (1929), col. 656 Anm. For a convenient collection of the Greek texts relating to astrological geography, drawn from Ptolemy, Paulus, Dorotheus, Valens, and other ancient writers, see Arthur Ludwich, Maximus et Ammonis Carminum de actionum auspiciis reliquiae (Leipzig, 1877), "Anecdota astrologica," Αἱ χῶραι συνοικειούμεναι τοῖς ιβ ζῳδίοις, pp. 112–19.

II

Turning now to Paulus Alexandrinus and his *Rudiments*, one observes that the subject of astrological geography occupies only a marginal part of his attention. At the beginning of his compendium the reader finds a compact statement concerning the astrological powers and the significance of each of the twelve signs of the zodiac. After giving brief and succinct accounts of the twelve signs Paulus provides summaries of information arranged according to topic; for example, all of the signs that are regarded as male are gathered in one group, and all that are female in another group. Among such summarizing paragraphs is one that deals with astrological geography. It is as follows:[1]

Προσπαθεῖ δὲ ταῖς χώραις τὰ ζῴδια· ὁ μὲν Κριὸς τῇ Περσίδι, ὁ δὲ Ταῦρος τῇ Βαβυλῶνι, οἱ δε Δίδυμοι τῇ Καππαδοκίᾳ, ὁ δὲ Καρκίνος τῇ Ἀρμενίᾳ, ὁ δὲ Λέων τῇ Ἀσίᾳ, ἡ δὲ Παρθένος τῇ Ἑλλάδι, ὁ δὲ Ζυγὸς τῇ Λιβύῃ, ὁ δὲ Σκορπίος τῇ Ἰταλίᾳ, ὁ δὲ Τοξότης τῇ Κρήτῃ, τοῦ Αἰγοκέρωτος τῇ Συρίᾳ ἀπονενεμημένου, τοῦ Ὑδροχόου τὴν Αἴγυπτον λαχόντος, τῶν Ἰχθύων τὴν Ἰνδικὴν χώραν προσῳκειωμένων.

When the items in this paragraph (called hereafter Paulus II) are compared with the variety of specifications that Paulus had assigned earlier in his treatise to each zodiacal sign, four differences are apparent, all of them involving slightly fuller descriptions of geographical areas that are assigned to the individual signs (called hereafter Paulus I). Thus, to Virgo are allotted Greece *and Ionia*; to Libra, Libya *and Cyrene*; to Sagittarius, *Cilicia and* Crete; to Pisces, *the Red Sea and* the land of India. Let us now examine the two lists from Paulus set side by side with the list from Acts 2:9–11 (see the table on p. 129).

III

The problem raised by an examination of these lists is whether the degree of similarity or dissimilarity between the list in Acts and one or the other list derived from Paulus is such as to make it probable (*a*) that Paulus drew upon the book of Acts; or (*b*) that Paulus reproduced a much older list, pre-Christian in origin, upon which Luke also was somehow dependent for his list in Acts; or (*c*) that there is, in fact, no discernible relation between Acts and the sources used by Paulus.

The view of Halévy (see p. 123 footnote 1) that Paulus depended, directly or indirectly, on the list in Acts, is altogether improbable.[2] Not

---

[1] Chap. 2 *fin.* (p. 10, lines 1–8, ed. Boer).
[2] Cf. Franz Boll in *T'oung Pao*, sér. II, 13 (1912), p. 715.

	PAULUS I	PAULUS II	ACTS 2 : 9–11	
1.	Περσίσ	Περσίσ	Πάρθοι καὶ Μῆδοι καὶ Ἐλαμῖται,	Aries (♈), the Ram
2.	Βαβυλών	Βαβυλών	καὶ οἱ κατοικοῦντεσ τὴν Μεσοποταμίαν,	Taurus (♉), the Bull
3.	Καππαδοκία	Καππαδοκία	Ἰουδαίαν τε καὶ Καππαδοκίαν,	Gemini (♊), the Twins
4.	Ἀρμενία	Ἀρμενία	Πόντον	Cancer (♋), the Crab
5.	Ἀσία	Ἀσία	καὶ τὴν Ἀσίαν,	Leo (♌), the Lion
6.	Ἑλλάσ καὶ Ἰωνία	Ἑλλάσ	Φρυγίαν τε καὶ Παμφυλίαν,	Virgo (♍), the Virgin
7.	Λιβύη καὶ Κυρήνη	Λιβύη	Αἴγυπτον καὶ τὰ μέρη τῆσ Λιβύησ τῆσ κατὰ Κυρήνην	Libra (♎), the Balance
8.	Ἰταλία	Ἰταλία	καὶ οἱ ἐπιδημοῦντεσ Ῥωμαῖοι, Ἰουδαῖοί τε καὶ προσήλυτοι	Scorpio (♏), the Scorpion
9.	Κιλικία καὶ Κρήτη	Κρήτη	Κρῆτεσ	Sagittarius (♐), the Archer
10.	Συρία	Συρία		Capricorn (♑), the Goat
11.	Αἴγυπτοσ	Αἴγυπτοσ		Aquarius (♒), the Water Bearer
12.	Ἐρυθρὰ θάλασσα καὶ Ἰνδικὴ χώρα	Ἰνδικὴ χώρα καὶ Ἄραβεσ		Pisces (♓), the Fishes

only does Paulus show no (other) acquaintance with the New Testament, but the way in which he incorporates the geographical data one by one in his series of paragraphs describing the powers of the twelve signs, as well as the differences between the two lists, stands firmly against such a supposition.

Cumont attempted to carry the prototype of Paulus's list back to the time of the Persian Empire, pointing out that (a) the list is headed by Persia and (b) each of the three pairs of countries (included in Paulus I) involves a free country and a satrapy.[1] It is open to question, however, whether these facts have any significant bearing on the date of the composition of the list.

Boll suggested that Paulus's list was known to Teucros the Babylonian, who flourished about 10 B.C.[2] Since, however, Teucros survives only in the writings of a sixth-century editor, Rhetorius the Egyptian, who was familiar also with Paulus's treatise, it is possible that Rhetorius took over the material from Paulus rather than Teucros.[3]

Those who attempt to trace the ancestry of Paulus' astrological geography to a pre-Christian date usually assume that because Paulus mentions fewer countries than those included in lists compiled by other authors, his material represents an earlier stage than theirs. This assumption must be challenged. Apart from the question whether it is likely that a fourth-century astrologer would have wished to preserve what was, on this theory, an archaic astrological list, it is more to the point to observe that Paulus is not concerned to provide fully consistent lists of countries assigned to the signs of the zodiac. The fact that Paulus does not include in his summary tabulation (ch. 2 *fin.*) more than one country for each zodiacal sign, whereas in previous paragraphs he includes a pair of regions under each of four of the twelve signs, gives us a hint that his intention was to provide an epitome of astrological lore. This hint becomes even more significant when one observes how numerous are the countries listed by such writers as Hipparchus, Dorotheus, Vettius Valens, Ptolemy, and other

---

[1] Franz Cumont, "La plus ancienne géographie astrologique," *Klio* 9 (1909), pp. 263–73. Cumont also reports (p. 273) a suggestion communicated to him by F. C. Burkitt, to the effect that an early date is supported by the circumstance that in Dan. 8:20 f. a ram, representing the king of the Medes and Persians, is attacked by a he-goat (=Capricorn), representing the king of the Greeks, and thus the author or redactor of the book of Daniel must have been familiar with the list. According to Paulus, however, the Capricorn is assigned to Syria, not Greece, and it is precarious to argue, as Cumont attempts to do, that this assignment merely shows that the motif was earlier than the Seleucids, and thus the nucleus of the list may still belong to the Persian period of the fourth century B.C.

One may also compare Cicero's comment in *de Divinitate* I, 121 (53): "[The Divine Will] sends us signs, of which history has preserved numerous examples. We find the following ones recorded: When just before sunrise the moon was eclipsed in the sign of Leo, this indicated that Darius and the Persians would be overcome in battle by the Macedonians under Alexander, and that Darius would die..." (Loeb ed., trans. by William A. Falconer).

[2] Cf. Franz Boll, *Sphaera; neue griechische Texte und Untersuchungen zur Geschichte der Sternbilder* (Leipzig, 1903), pp. 5 ff., and Weinstock, *op. cit.*

[3] Cf. Cumont, *op. cit.*, pp. 264 f., and Brinkman, *op. cit.* p. 423, note 14.

ancient astrologers, some of whom would have been known to Paulus.[1] For example, under the second zodiacal sign, that of Taurus the Bull, Hipparchus lists Media, Scythia, Armenia, Cyprus; Dorotheus lists Media, Arabia, Egypt; Vettius Valens lists Media, Babylonia, Scythia, Cyprus, Arabia, Persia, Caucasus, Ethiopia, Elymais, Carchedonia, Armenia, India, Germany; and Ptolemy lists Parthia, Media, Persis, Cyclades, Cyprus, Asia Minor; – while Paulus gives merely Babylonia.[2] In view of such data as these it seems to be both hopeless and meaningless to debate, as Weinstock, Brinkman, and others do, in which respects Luke or Paulus preserves more accurately the "original" assignment of an individual land or country to a given zodiacal sign.

IV

At this point it is appropriate to raise the fundamental issue that most scholars have taken for granted: are, in fact, the similarities between the list in Acts and those in Paulus significant enough to warrant tracing both back to a common origin? Or, are the two lists no closer than would be expected if two ancient authors independently drew up lists comprising a dozen or fifteen representative countries and peoples?

In any attempt to analyse the points of contact between Luke and Paulus, it is obviously not licit to rearrange the order of the list in Acts (as Weinstock and, following him, Brinkman have done) by moving Egypt from the seventh to the eleventh place, thus increasing the similarity between the two lists. Not only does the position of Egypt differ in the two lists, but the generally accepted text of Acts has nothing corresponding to Syria in Paulus's list (on this point see the Textual Addendum below). Furthermore, it seems impossible, despite many ingenious and sometimes farfetched arguments, to correlate Paulus's Greece and Ionia with Luke's Phrygia and Pamphylia, or Paulus's Armenia with Luke's Pontus.

In the light of such obvious differences one is struck also by the paucity of actual similarities between the lists. When one seeks for precise equivalents between Acts and either one of Paulus's lists, the results are meagre enough. Of sixteen names of countries or peoples in Acts, only five are identical with those in Paulus: namely, Cappadocia, Asia, Libya, Crete, and Egypt. Certainly it is misleading in the extreme to represent the lists as "almost exactly the same" (see p. 124, footnote 4). In fact, all that can be said without distorting the picture is that both Luke and Paulus start from countries or peoples in the upper part of the Fertile Crescent and then move generally westward, turning eventually south and finally

---

[1] Professor Pingree has given me permission to say that, in his view, Paulus drew upon a fuller stock of astrological lore, but that it is "meaningless to take [his list] as a document earlier than the fourth century A.D."

[2] Cf. Ludwich, *op. cit.*, pp. 113 f., supplemented by information from Hipparchus.

south-eastward – though each list departs more than once from a strict sequence.[1] That there are, out of the sixteen countries or peoples mentioned in the list in Acts, five which are mentioned also by Paulus, is perhaps not so remarkable after all.[2]

V

The main point of this paper has been made, namely to assess the degree of similarity between the lists of countries in Acts and in Paulus, a similarity that appears to be far less striking than has sometimes been thought. A much more constructive approach to the list in Acts, as it seems to the present writer, will be the analysis of the sequence of names in terms of the inner dynamic of the catalogue itself. As has been pointed out recently by an author in *Theologische Zeitschrift*,[3] the sequence of names in Acts 2 exhibits a lively and spontaneous form of expression[4] with its own rhythm and structure, disclosed partly by the author's use of connectives (καί and τε καί). Even the "coda" at the close, "Cretans and Arabians,"[5] which at first sight seems to be merely an afterthought, has many parallels in other examples of what can be called the catalogue-form. How far Luke may have been influenced in his choice of countries that he included in the list by following a list kept by leaders of the church in Antioch of lands to which Christian missions had been sent prior to about the year A.D. 50 is an interesting speculation proposed by Reicke,[6] but which need not be pursued here. Enough has been said, it is hoped, to set in more sober perspective the very dubious connexion thought by Weinstock and others

---

[1] Pingree has kindly called to my attention the *Dimensuratio provinciarum* of pseudo-Jerome (in *Geographi latini minores*, ed. Alexander Reise [Heilbronn, 1878], pp. 9–14), which follows a pattern of listing areas of Asia Major, Europe, and Africa, though again with a few exceptions of countries that stand outside this sequence (e.g. the list closes with Britannia). In comparison with such a scheme one thinks of Eusebius's account of the work of the Apostles who evangelized the whole world, from Persia to Britain (*Dem. Evang.* III, 5 [=Migne, *PG* XXII, col. 204A]).

[2] It cannot be denied that in antiquity there may well have been some remote connexion between geography and astrology, revealed perhaps in the custom of beginning to enumerate a list of lands and countries starting in the East (at the rising of the sun). At the same time, however, it is doubtful whether the average cultured Greek and Roman writers were any more conscious of such a connexion than the modern Englishman is aware of the astrological matrix from which the word "disaster" arose.

[3] Johannes Thomas, "Formgesetze des Begriffs-Katalogs im N.T.," *Theologische Zeitschrift* 24 (1968), pp. 15–28.

[4] It goes without saying that what is referred to is Luke's form of expression, not that of the speakers whose words he is professedly reporting.

[5] On this pair of names, see Otto Eissfeldt, "Kreter und Araber," *ThLZ* 72 (1947), cols. 207–12.

[6] Bo Reicke, *Glaube und Leben der Urgemeinde. Bemerkungen zu Apg. 1–7* (=*Abhandlungen zur Theologie des Alten und Neuen Testaments*, 32) (Zürich, 1957), pp. 32–37. Although Reicke supposes that the list in the Antiochian church was originally drawn up with one eye, so to speak, on an assumed prototype of Paulus's astrological geography, this hypothesis is not a necessary part of his main speculation. For a negative reaction to Reicke, see E. Haenchen's remarks in his *Apostelgeschichte*[5] (Göttingen, 1965), pp. 133 f., Anm. 3.

to exist between the list in Acts 2 and the astrological speculations eventually incorporated in Paulus of Alexandria's *Rudiments of Astrology*.

Textual Addendum to Acts 2:9

The problem that confronts the textual critic at Acts 2:9 is the almost total unanimity of external evidence supporting the traditional reading 'Ιουδαίαν over against a variety of internal difficulties – difficulties which various scholars have sought to remove by emendation. The inclusion of 'Ιουδαίαν in a catalogue of Diaspora Jews has seemed to many commentators to be altogether inappropriate in the following respects: (a) the word stands in an unusual sequence in the list (between Mesopotamia in the east and Cappadocia in the north); (b) it is properly an adjective and therefore when used substantively (as in Acts 2:9) it ought to be preceded by the definite article;[1] and (c) it involves the curious anomaly that inhabitants of Judea should be amazed to hear the apostles speak their own language (Acts 2:6).

In view of such difficulties, the names of other countries have been proposed. Thus, Tertullian and Augustine (once) substitute *Armeniam*, Jerome substitutes (*habitantes in*) *Syria*, and Chrysostom 'Ινδίαν. Modern scholars have suggested a wide variety of conjectures in place of 'Ιουδαίαν including Idumaea (Caspar, Spitta, Lagercranz), Ionia (Cheyne), Bithynia (Hemsterhuis, Valckenaer), Cilicia (Mangey), Lydia (Bentley, Bryant), India ([following Chrysostom] Erasmus, Schmid), Gordyaea (Greve, Burkitt), Yaudi (Gunkel), Adiabene (Eberhard Nestle), and Aramaea (Hatch).[2] Others, including Eusebius, von Harnack, and C. S. C. Williams, omit 'Ιουδαίαν altogether, considering it a scribal gloss. Perhaps the least violent conjecture is the proposal made by Hilgenfeld[3] to omit τε following 'Ιουδαίαν, thus allowing the latter to serve as adjective qualifying Μεσοποταμίαν (though why Mesopotamia should deserve to be called "Judean" is not easily explained).[4]

Amid such diversity among proposed conjectures, no one of which has gained general approval, probably the least unsatisfactory solution to an admittedly difficult problem is to accept the reading attested by the overwhelming weight of witnesses.

---

[1] According to Blass-Debrunner "anarthrous 'Ιουδαίαν is certainly corrupt" (§ 261, 4).
[2] For discussions of the last two proposals, see Eberhard Nestle, *ZNTW* 9 (1908), pp. 253 f., and W. H. P. Hatch, *ibid.*, pp. 255 f. (the latter cites most of the conjectures that are mentioned above).
[3] Adolf Hilgenfeld, *Acta Apostolorum, graece et latine* (Berlin, 1899), pp. 260, n. 1.
[4] For an attempt to explain the collocation, see Ernst von Dobschütz ("Zu der Volkerliste Act. 2, 9–11," *Zeitschrift für wissenschaftliche Theologie* 45 [1902], pp. 407–10), who adduces several somewhat similar expressions in rabbinical sources.

CHAPTER VIII

SEMITISMS IN THE BOOK OF ACTS

D. F. PAYNE

I

PALESTINE, AND INDEED THE WHOLE LEVANT, HAS OFTEN BEEN ACKNOW-
ledged as the place where East and West meet. Two millennia ago,
those who met there were respectively speakers of Aramaic and
Greek – unrelated languages, the former Semitic, the latter Indo-European.
The New Testament, as a result, presents us with a very interesting phenomenon, in that the writers were nearly all Semites, Aramaic speakers and of
Jewish descent, heirs of a long non-Greek culture (not in total isolation
from Greek thought, to be sure) who nevertheless all chose to pass on
their priceless message in the Greek language.

It is no surprise that their command of Greek varied considerably from
one writer to another; it is perhaps somewhat surprising, on the other
hand, that they all showed such proficiency in handling Greek as they did.
At any rate, the good Greek of James and 1 Peter has often served as one
reason for doubting the traditional authorship of both epistles. It is
interesting to note that *The Jerusalem Bible* states of 1 Peter that the "Greek
is too accurate and unforced for a fisherman from Galilee";[1] yet when
discussing the Epistle of James it makes the more appropriate observation
that "no accurate estimate . . . can be made as to how competent first-
century Palestinians were in writing Greek"![2]

The author of the third gospel and of Acts, however, was no Palestinian,
if the traditional authorship is to be accepted; the anti-Marcionite Prologue
to the third gospel indicates that the author of both books was Luke, "an
Antiochian of Syria, a physician by profession". That he was a Gentile is
often deduced from Colossians 4:10–14, where Paul distinguishes him
from "men of the circumcision". From these early data it might reasonably be inferred that the writer of Acts lacked both the Hebraic background and the knowledge of the Aramaic language which characterized
the great majority of the New Testament writers. One might therefore
have expected to find that Luke and Acts stood apart from all the rest of
the New Testament documents, by presenting "pure" Greek, free of all
trace of Semitism. But this is in fact far from being the case; the Semitisms

[1] *The Jerusalem Bible* (London, 1966), New Testament, p. 393.
[2] *Ibid.*, p. 391.

of Acts alone have recently necessitated a book of 200 pages for an adequate discussion of them.[1]

How, then, are the clear evidences of Semitic influence to be explained? An immediate possibility is that Luke was not after all a Gentile, but a Hellenistic Jew; Colossians 4 is not really the strongest evidence, particularly in view of the fact that the phrase "of the circumcision" is of uncertain meaning.[2] For the present writer, Colossians 4 most probably does make Luke a Gentile; but in any case, the decision as to the background of the author of Luke–Acts must depend on a thorough examination of those books; Colossians 4:11 cannot be said to settle the issue. Gentile or not, as an Antiochian Luke could well have been bilingual, for Aramaic as well as Greek was spoken in Syrian Antioch and its environs. But then we cannot be sure of the accuracy of the Antiochian tradition, and again we are forced to study the Semitisms themselves.

If there is uncertainty about Luke's own cultural and linguistic background, it is at least clear that much of his subject-matter relates to Palestine and a Jewish milieu. The whole of his gospel, and the first half (and more) of the Book of Acts, are staged against such a Semitic backdrop; and patently his sources (whether oral or written) for three-quarters of his work will have been inevitably to some extent Semitic. But there is no *a priori* reason why later sections of Acts, set in a Gentile environment, should exhibit any Semitic colouring at all.[3] Hence the general attractiveness of C. C. Torrey's hypothesis that in Acts 1–15 Luke has translated an Aramaic document for his readers.[4] In fact, many of Torrey's arguments have been virtually overthrown; criticisms of his hypothesis have been many and various, but not least among them is the very fact of the quantity of Semitisms to be found in Acts 16–28, where a theory involving an Aramaic source would have little plausibility.

A thorough linguistic examination of the Book of Acts is, therefore, indispensable for any clear understanding of the author of the book and of the sources he utilized. It also has a bearing on the question of the historicity of Acts. If it could be established, for instance, that the speeches of Acts are of so Semitic a character that they must derive from Aramaic sources, then the probability of Luke's historical reliability would be considerably enhanced.

But if the importance of the question is undeniable, the difficulties inherent in such a study are equally beyond dispute. In the first place, how is a "Semitism" to be defined? The term is usually applied to linguistic

[1] M. Wilcox, *The Semitisms of Acts* (Oxford, 1965).

[2] That the third evangelist was Jewish has been held by A. Schlatter, E. C. Selwyn, B. S. Easton, A. H. McNeile, B. Reicke, W. F. Albright, and E. E. Ellis. [See E. E. Ellis, "'Those of the Circumcision' and the Early Christian Mission," in *Studia Evangelica* 5 (*TU* 102; Berlin, 1968), pp. 390–99 Edd.].

[3] The scene reverts to Palestine in 15; 21:7 – 27:3, although for the most part Paul's company in the later chapters was non-Jewish.

[4] C. C. Torrey, *The Composition and Date of Acts* (Cambridge, Mass., 1916).

elements (whether words, expressions, idioms, syntax, grammar or style) which are alien to Greek and which owe their origin to either Aramaic or Hebrew. But as C. F. D. Moule has written,

> It is not always possible to determine where to draw the line between a clear, alien "Semitism" and a term or idiom which is indeed reminiscent of a characteristically Semitic equivalent but which is none the less good or tolerable Greek, and may, therefore, owe little or nothing to Semitic influence. Sometimes it is only the frequency of its occurrence, and not its actual existence, that a term or phrase owes to the alien influence.
>
> Obviously, too, this problem is complicated by the question of how far the generally understood, secular κοινή had unconsciously absorbed and, so to speak, naturalized what were originally alien elements from Semitic populations.[1]

Generally speaking, one would require a reasonable quantity of Semitisms before deciding that a particular passage was clearly influenced by or translated from a Semitic language. All too often, features of New Testament Greek which appeal to one scholar as clear Semitisms tend to be disallowed by the next scholar.[2]

A second difficulty is occasioned by the very vagueness of the term Semitism. In theory, the New Testament documents and manuscripts might have been influenced by classical Hebrew, by contemporary spoken Hebrew, or by several contemporary dialects of Aramaic – Judaean, Galilean, Antiochian among them. Strictly speaking, therefore, one ought to look for Hebraisms, Aramaisms, and Syriacisms, and then subdivide these categories still further; but in practice relatively few acknowledged Semitisms can be neatly pigeon-holed in such a fashion. The dialects of Aramaic did not differ too radically from one another; and Hebrew, though a different language, is very closely akin to Aramaic. Moreover, our materials for distinguishing distinct Aramaic dialects are still much scantier than we could wish, despite recent discoveries of importance.[3]

A further complication is caused by New Testament textual variations. As is well known, the text of Acts preserved in Codex Bezae (D) is almost an *editio altera* of the book, as compared with the TR or the Westcott and Hort text. Both in the Synoptic Gospels and Acts, moreover, the D text exhibits far more Semitisms than can be found in other textual traditions. A good case can be made for viewing many of these additional Semitisms as original; it is rather more likely that in the course of transmission some

---

[1] C. F. D. Moule, *An Idiom-book of New Testament Greek*[2] (Cambridge, 1959), p. 171. Moule's chapter on "Semitisms" [pp. 177–91] is a useful introduction to the subject in general.

[2] See especially M. Black, *An Aramaic Approach to the Gospels and Acts*[3] (Oxford, 1967), chapter 1, for examples. Wilcox's recent list of significant Semitisms, for all his cautious treatment, would be reduced by J. A. Emerton (cf. his review of Wilcox in *JSS* 13 [1968], pp. 282–97). For a critical appraisal of Black's work, see J. A. Fitzmyer's review of the 3rd ed. in *CBQ* 30 (1968), pp. 417–28.

[3] Cf. Black, *op. cit.*, chapter 3.

alien elements in Greek were removed than that Aramaic-speaking scribes deliberately or unconsciously recast the Greek which they were copying into a more Semitic mould. Even so, some caution must be observed. Wilcox very properly stresses the importance of the "eclectic" method of textual criticism, and adds that "textual criticism and judgment on Semitism must proceed hand in hand".[1] The simple view that the Western text gives us more or less the original text of Acts[2] is now even less likely than it was, since E. J. Epp has demonstrated the scope and extent of theological reinterpretations in D.[3] Some of the Semitisms of D may well be secondary; but Epp's most convincing examples are those where there is variation in vocabulary, and it would not be easy to find theological motives for mere syntactical and grammatical variations, which in no way affect the general sense of the passages concerned.

In the scrutiny of the Semitisms of Acts, then, difficulties abound on every hand; but the greatest of them all is to assign the source of the individual Semitisms. If source-criticism of documents has been characterized as "guess-work", how much more so the source-criticism of single words and phrases! A wide variety of possibilities has to be taken into account. First, there are "naturalized" Semitisms, that is to say, local Aramaisms which had long since affected the Greek spoken in any bilingual area (such as Antioch). Koine Greek in general shares some features with Semitic languages which would not have been tolerated in classical Greek, and it may safely be assumed that in bilingual areas the local Greek dialect will have had an Aramaic colouring over and above such common features. Secondly, there are "Biblicisms", or Semitisms due ultimately to the influence of the Old Testament. These might take the form of direct quotations from the Scriptures, or of allusions to the Old Testament, or simply of a style and phraseology borrowed from it. Thirdly, we find a certain ecclesiastical vocabulary owing more to the Palestinian and Jewish environment in which the church was born than to the Greek world into which it moved so rapidly. Fourthly, there may be a residue of Semitisms most naturally attributed to sources, written or oral, which were available to Luke. The Semitisms of Acts, accordingly, require to be analysed and distributed between these various categories. The importance of this analysis is evident in the observation that Hebraisms will time and time again belong to the category of Biblicisms, whereas Syriacisms would probably derive either from the "naturalized" Semitisms of the Antioch region or else from documents or living traditions of this same area.

[1] Op. cit., p. 185.
[2] Cf. A. C. Clark, The Acts of the Apostles (Oxford, 1933).
[3] E. J. Epp, The Theological Tendency of Codex Bezae Cantabrigiensis in Acts (SNTS monograph 3. Cambridge, 1966).

II

Academic study of the Semitisms of Acts (as indeed of the Gospels too) may be said to have proceeded in three phases: observation, conjecture, and analysis. Observation and amassing of appropriate material obviously must be the first step towards a scholarly discussion of the phenomena; and this process still continues. The second stage, that of conjecture, has been traced back by Wilcox as far as 1857, when a particularly interesting variant reading (in Acts 3:14) was discussed by W. W. Harvey in the light of a possible Semitic background.[1] Harvey's discussion may be termed conjectural in one respect; he guessed at the Semitic (specifically, Syriac) verbs which he thought to underlie the two Greek verbs, ἠρνήσασθε and the variant ἐβαρύνατε. But it was not long before much greater conjectures were being built upon such foundations; in 1893, for example, F. H. Chase utilized this conjecture of Harvey's, among others, to argue for a strong influence by Syriac versions upon D (which reads ἐβαρύνατε).[2]

In the case of Torrey in particular, we find a sweeping conjecture (i.e., of a literally-translated document behind Acts 1–15) based largely upon conjectural evidence. The type of Semitism which most appealed to Torrey was what might be termed "hidden" Semitisms; that is to say, instances where the Greek does not immediately strike the reader as owing something to a Semitic language, but which on investigation suggest that the best explanation of the Greek is nevertheless some Semitic *Vorlage*, either because the Greek does not appear to say what one would expect, or because of textual variants difficult to explain on the basis of corruption or deliberate alteration of the Greek. In a number of cases of this sort, Torrey sought and found (to his own satisfaction, at least) Aramaic words which might have been mistranslated or misread.

Two such "hidden" Semitisms discovered by Torrey in the Gospel of Luke may be mentioned briefly. In Luke 1:39 a strangely vague expression occurs, εἰς πόλιν Ἰούδα, "to a city of Judah". The form Ἰούδα rather than the more usual Ἰουδαία in itself suggests a Semitic source here; and Torrey plausibly conjectured that the Greek πόλις here represented an ambiguous Semitic word, the Hebrew mᵉdînāh or its Aramaic equivalent, which Luke ought to have translated "province".[3] An example of a misreading rather than a simple mistranslation could be the οἰκοδομεῖτε, "you build", of Luke 11:48 as opposed to the υἱοί ἐστε, "you are sons", of Matthew 23:31; the Aramaic word for "builders" is bānîn, for "sons" bᵉnîn, and the two words would be indistinguishable in an unvocalized

[1] W. W. Harvey, *Sancti Irenaei . . . adversus Haereses* (Cambridge, 1857), vol. 2, p. 55. Cf. Wilcox, *op. cit.*, pp. 1 f.

[2] F. H. Chase, *The Old Syriac Element in the Text of Codex Bezae* (London, 1893).

[3] C. C. Torrey, *HTR* 17 (1924), pp. 83–89.

document.[1] These two examples have Black's strong support; indeed, he describes them as "brilliant" discoveries by Torrey.[2] Similar examples from the Book of Acts tend to be more controversial; one or two are discussed below.

Some of Torrey's alleged mistranslations in Acts may survive criticism, and it must be admitted that no type of Semitism is quite so convincing as an apparent mistranslation; it is perhaps the only convincing evidence of a Semitic source document. But the fact remains that *all* such evidence is conjectural; we do not know what sources Luke used, far less do we know the precise wording of those sources.

The conjectural approach to the whole question reached its high watermark with Torrey. Not only was his methodology questionable, but even more so his attempt to force all the Semitisms he found in Acts into a single category, the pigeon-hole of "Aramaisms" due to a source document. Torrey's critics were from the first able to point out defects in his methods and conclusions, and in doing so they were obliged to be more thoroughly analytical than he.[3] Thus study of the Semitisms of Acts progressed into the analytical stage; the important article of H. F. D. Sparks, "The Semitisms of the Acts,"[4] deserves special mention in this connexion, for its careful and persuasive critique of Torrey's work on the subject. Torrey's alleged "mistranslations" were shown to lack cogency in many cases; he had sadly neglected the influence of the LXX, in Acts 1–15 and indeed the later chapters too; he had paid even less attention to the Semitisms in Acts 16–28; and finally he had failed to account satisfactorily for the "incontestable unity of Acts".[5]

All of these criticisms by Sparks were legitimate and remain valid. Nevertheless, he too showed a tendency to look for a single pigeon-hole, in his case the "Biblicism". While allowing for some influence on Luke by Aramaic and "Semitic-Greek *patois*" speakers, he opined that "most [Semitisms] . . . are his own 'septuagintalisms'".[6] He concluded his article by depicting Luke as an artist and a dramatist, and asked "What more appropriate language . . . than the language of the Bible could anyone possibly choose as the main medium through which to present the manifestation of the Mystery?"[7] Thus with Sparks too the element of conjecture is present, alongside his analytical work.[8]

But four years before the publication of Sparks's article, there had already appeared a major, thoroughly analytical, treatment of the whole subject, in Matthew Black's book, *An Aramaic Approach to the Gospels and*

[1] C. C. Torrey, *Our Translated Gospels* (London, n.d.), pp. 103 f.
[2] Cf. Black, *op. cit.*, pp. 12 f.
[3] A notable example (by J. de Zwaan) appears in *BC*, vol. 2, pp. 44–64.
[4] In *JTS* N.S.1 (1950), pp. 16–28.
[5] *Ibid.*, p. 21.
[6] *Ibid.*, p. 26.
[7] *Ibid.*, p. 27.
[8] He analysed with some care three specimen passages, Acts 4:23–31; 7:54–8:1; 9:36–43.

Acts.[1] As the title indicates, the author was careful not to isolate Acts from the other relevant New Testament documents, and this feature in itself adds to the weight and validity of his analysis. On the other hand, the work is not too easily used by the student who is interested solely in the Book of Acts; moreover, as the title again shows, Black's purpose was to examine Aramaism as such, not Semitism in general. Hence the need for and value of the recent book by Max Wilcox, *The Semitisms of Acts*.[2]

Black felt the need to re-examine the Semitisms of the gospels and Acts in a thorough, scientific and impartial fashion, eschewing pure conjecture as far as possible, and also to remedy the deficiencies of earlier study in two respects, namely linguistic and textual. In the first place, Aramaic words had been confidently placed on the lips of Jesus with very scant regard for the fundamental question, which dialect of Aramaic did Jesus in fact speak? Dalman had not overlooked the importance of this question, to be sure, but he had probably been wrong in the answer he gave to it.[3] There is considerably more information on Aramaic dialects available today than there was when Dalman wrote. Black's work is probably most important, therefore, when it relates to the *ipsissima verba* of Jesus; but similar questions must be asked and answered about any postulated Aramaic source documents, for the gospels or Acts. As for the textual question, Black stressed the need to scrutinize all the text-types, and particularly that exemplified in Codex Bezae, rather than to rely exclusively on one text (in practice, usually that of Westcott and Hort); the relevance of this issue to the Book of Acts needs no arguing. In fine, Black's work exhibits a breadth and depth of treatment which are essential to a study of the subject if it is not to lead to facile and mistaken conclusions. He has, moreover, kept his work fully up-to-date, with a carefully revised third edition in 1967.

One important point which emerges from the history of the study of Semitism in Acts is that, for all the detailed work that is obviously requisite, broad perspectives must always be kept in view; successive critics of Torrey and his predecessors have constantly opened up fresh perspectives. The work began, of course, by locating and collating possible examples of Semitism to be found in Acts – a task within the powers of any Semitist able to read Greek. But the alleged Semitisms required analysis; and it demands a competent Hellenistic Greek scholar to isolate "Septuagintalisms" and special *koine* usages which are shared with some Semitic language, and a very well equipped Semitist to distinguish dialectal variations within Aramaic. The distribution of the Semitisms was important too.

---

[1] First edition 1946. It had its precursors, e.g., W. F. Howard's appendix on "Semitisms in the New Testament" in J. H. Moulton and W. F. Howard, *A Grammar of New Testament Greek*, vol. 2 (Edinburgh, 1929). Howard's treatment offers relatively little material relating directly to Acts, however.

[2] Oxford, 1965.

[3] See discussion in Black, *op. cit.*, pp. 6, 18–28.

Sparks demonstrates, in a scrutiny of three specimen passages from Acts, how Semitisms and typical Lucanisms are interwoven – a serious embarrassment for the literal-translation hypothesis. Here the New Testament expert plays his part. Then Black drew fresh attention to the relevance of New Testament textual criticism; so also has Epp, more recently, if in a rather different way. Wilcox has shown that Old Testament textual criticism is also relevant; and further, he pays some attention to "liturgical and apologetic factors" and brings patristic evidence to bear on the subject. Recent work on the topic has also shown the value of statistical analysis.[1]

III

The complexity of the whole question may now be shown by some examples. Two cases of alleged mistranslation, first isolated last century, are still allowed by Black to possess "a high degree of plausibility". They appear in Acts 2:47 and 3:14 respectively.[2] In the former passage we read that the early church at Jerusalem was held in favour by all the "people" (λαόν); but Codex Bezae reads "world" (κόσμον). The two Greek words are obviously quite dissimilar, but in the Semitic languages the differences are slight, "world" having just one extra letter.[3] E. Nestle accordingly maintained long ago that here was one clear trace of a Semitic original lying behind the early part of Acts.[4] Torrey agreed and found a further Semitism in the verse (the phrase ἐπὶ τὸ αὐτό, to which we shall return later). Black noted that a theological motive might equally explain the D text, which might represent the attempt of a scribe "to magnify the impression made by these early converts on the 'whole world'".[5] Epp goes further, firmly rejecting the Nestle/Torrey hypothesis; he has shown that many of the peculiar readings of Codex Bezae are attributable to an anti-Judaic motive, and Acts 2:47 is no exception. The word λαός in Acts regularly refers to Israel specifically, and was therefore deliberately eschewed by the anti-Jewish editor and reviser of the text at this point.[6]

The other example of which Black concedes the plausibility is far more complex; it is the textual variant of Acts 3:14 to which Harvey first drew attention. Peter accused his hearers in the temple courts of "denying" Jesus in the presence of Pilate, according to most MSS (ἠρνήσασθε); but Codex Bezae reads "oppressed" (ἐβαρύνατε). Harvey, as we have seen, found the solution in Syriac; he conjectured that the majority reading was

[1] Cf. K. Beyer, *Semitische Syntax im Neuen Testament*,[2] Bd. 1, Teil 1 (Göttingen, 1968); R. A. Martin, "Syntactical Evidence of Aramaic Sources in Acts I-XV," *NTS* 11 (1964–65), pp. 38–59.
[2] Black, *op. cit.*, pp. 13 f.
[3] In Hebrew, "people" is '*m*, "world" '*lm*. The Aramaic is comparable.
[4] E. Nestle, "Some Observations on the Codex Bezae", *Exp.*, series 5, 2 (1895), pp. 235–40.
[5] *Op. cit.*, p. 13.
[6] Epp, *op. cit.*, p. 77.

a translation of *k-p-r*, while the Bezan variant rendered *k-b-d*. Nestle argued for Hebrew rather than Syriac.[1] Torrey preferred an Aramaic solution, his conjectural roots being *k-d-b* and *k-b-d* respectively.[2] But it is unfortunate for all three hypotheses that the Semitic root *k-b-d* appears to denote irritation rather than oppression.[3] Rendel Harris and Ropes inclined to think that the Latin New Testament supplied the clue to the variants;[4] if either was right, Semitisms are ruled out here. Epp once again points out that the Bezan text is patently more anti-Judaic than the majority reading, and again views it as a deliberate theological reinterpretation, owing nothing to underlying Semitisms.[5] A simpler suggestion is that the D reading is merely a stylistic improvement, which avoids repetition of the Greek word ἠρνήσασθε.[6]

The other alleged Semitism in Acts 2:47, the phrase ἐπὶ τὸ αὐτό, raises quite different questions. There is not the same problem of variant readings; it is simply a question of what the phrase means.[7] (It looks as if Codex Bezae reinterpreted it, by appending the phrase ἐν τῇ ἐκκλησίᾳ Torrey noted that the Greek phrase ought to mean "together" or "in the same place", and proceeded to emphasize the inappropriateness of such a sense in Acts 2:47. He accordingly seized upon an underlying Aramaic *laḥdâ* as the explanation. Etymologically this meant "into one" (hence the Greek rendering), but in contemporary Judaean Aramaic in fact meant "greatly". Luke should therefore have said, "The Lord added *greatly* day by day to the saved".[8] But was Luke, *ex hypothesi*, such an incompetent translator? As W. F. Howard pointed out tersely, "Such a blunder is not likely on the part of one who could give the right rendering in 6:7".[9] Black went on to challenge the Aramaic basis of Torrey's contentions; the Greek phrase would be the equivalent (if Torrey were right) of *kaḥdâ*, not *laḥdâ*.[10] Equally damaging to Torrey's case is the fact that nowhere else in Acts could the phrase mean "greatly".

The immediate alternative explanation would appear to be that we have here a Septuagintalism; the LXX frequently renders Hebrew *yaḥad* or *yaḥdāw* ("together", "with one accord") by ἐπὶ τὸ αὐτό. But as has been suggested above, the "Biblicisms" category of Semitisms is as liable to misuse as any other. Thorough examination of New Testament and patristic documents reveals that the Greek phrase regularly means more

---

[1] In his article, *op. cit.*
[2] *Documents of the Primitive Church* (New York and London, 1941), p. 145.
[3] Cf. Wilcox, *op. cit.*, pp. 140 f.; Black, *op. cit.*, pp. 13 f.
[4] Cf. Wilcox, *op. cit.*, pp. 139 f. for details and references.
[5] Epp, *op. cit.*, pp. 51–53.
[6] Cf. F. F. Bruce, *Commentary on the Book of the Acts* (*NIC*; Grand Rapids, 1954), p. 86 n.
[7] There are a number of variant readings, but they all seem to be attempts to clarify the sense; cf. Wilcox, *op. cit.*, p. 93 n.
[8] Torrey, *The Composition and Date of Acts*, pp. 10–14.
[9] In Moulton and Howard, *A Grammar of New Testament Greek*, vol. 2, p. 473. The Greek word in Acts 6:7 is σφόδρα.
[10] *Op. cit.*, p. 10.

than merely "together" or "with one accord"; it is almost a technical term, denoting "in church (fellowship)";[1] but such a sense does not arise directly from Old Testament or LXX usage. Qumran studies have almost certainly cleared up the difficulty: the Qumran documents often use the Hebrew term *yaḥaḏ* to denote the (Qumran) community, and the Lucan phrase προστιθέναι ἐπὶ τὸ αὐτό seems to be a literal rendering of a Hebrew expression, *h'sp lyḥd*.[2] By whatever route, the Greek phrase owes its origin to a living Hebrew tradition.[3]

IV

Few of Torrey's alleged mistranslations have escaped criticism. The instance he himself felt to be most weighty was 2:47, where, as we have seen, his view has proved untenable. The two instances Black selected as particularly plausible have been rendered more dubious by Epp's researches.[4] Even so, there may still survive one or two mistranslations. To decide the plausibility or probability of them is a very subjective matter, and different scholars will come to different conclusions. F. F. Bruce, for example, finds two of Torrey's cases persuasive, and allows the possibility of several more.[5] Wilcox seems to concede the possibility of eighteen instances, though all of them he describes as "weak".[6] A distinction has to be made between mistranslation of a Semitic document and a debt to Semitic phraseology; the discussion above of ἐπὶ τὸ αὐτό sufficiently shows this, for while Torrey's view of a mistranslation is untenable, the phrase is nevertheless based on Semitic usage. Wilcox is dubious about the presence of actual mistranslations in Acts, but he is far from denying Semitism altogether. Black, for his part, is inclined to find instances of mistranslation of the ubiquitous Aramaic particle *dᵉ* at least twice in Acts.[7]

What of the Biblicisms category? Wilcox has demonstrated that this has been overpressed in one or two ways. In the first place, the simple fact that a Semitic idiom in the Greek text of Acts can be paralleled, exactly or approximately, from the LXX does not automatically make the usage a Biblicism; much depends on the frequency or significance of the LXX parallel. For instance, the over-literal rendering of the Hebrew expression *bāḥar bᵉ* ("to choose") by ἐκλέγεσθαι ἐν is rare in the LXX, the correct Greek idiom (ἐκλέγεσθαι + accusative) being far more common; for that reason, we ought not to class it as a Septuagintalism

---

[1] The AV rendering is thus justified, and seems preferable to that of RSV or NEB.
[2] 1QS v. 7. Cf. Black, *op. cit.*, p. 10 n.
[3] See full discussion of Acts 2:47 in Wilcox, *op. cit.*, pp. 93–100.
[4] I.e., Acts 2:47 (the κόσμον-λαόν variation) and 3:14. Both are discussed *supra*.
[5] Acts 3:16; 4:25. Cf. Bruce, *The Acts of the Apostles*[2] (London, 1952), *ad loc.*
[6] *Op. cit.*, pp. 153 f.
[7] 1:17; 7:39. Cf. Black, *op. cit.*, p. 92.

when we meet the phrase in Acts 15:7.[1] As for Septuagintal parallels bearing a different connotation from the Acts usage, exemplified by ἐπὶ τὸ αὐτό, they are plainly irrelevant. There are also, on the other hand, a number of genuine Septuagintalisms in Acts which seem to have been mediated to Luke through church usage. Wilcox instances the phrase τιθέναι ἐν τῇ καρδίᾳ (Acts 5:4), a Semitism, but one which is only thrice found in the LXX; the explanation of its use by Luke may well be the importance to the early church of the story of David and the bread of the Presence,[2] a narrative which in the LXX contains this same Greek expression at 1 Reigns 21:13.[3]

In the second place, the undeniable fact of the use of the LXX made by Luke in Acts must be balanced by other evidence. It is remarkable that of the actual citations from the Old Testament by Luke, a significant number do not seem to be drawn verbatim from the LXX, as one might have expected, if Luke depended so heavily on the LXX. Wilcox has found citations having affinities with the MT or with other textual traditions, as against the LXX. Thus in Acts 7:16 παρὰ τῶν υἱῶν Ἐμμώρ is closer to the MT of Joshua 24:32 than is the παρὰ τῶν Ἀμορραίων of LXX;[4] while the ἡγούμενον of 7:10 is not represented in MT or LXX of Genesis 41:41 ff., but is the equivalent of the s-r-k-n of Targum Pseudo-Jonathan.[5] Even more interesting, if inconclusive, is the case of 15:16 ff., where James is depicted as citing Amos 9:11 f. Sparks makes great play of this passage, emphasizing that it presents the LXX text, which here "not merely diverges from but contradicts the Hebrew in the interests of universalism".[6] The divergence from the MT is beyond dispute – "the rest of men" is patently not the same thing as "the remnant of Edom" – but contradiction seems too strong a word.[7] One can also set the LXX against the Targum and the Peshitta. But even so, it may not be without significance that the first few words of the citation in Acts 15:16 are totally different from the LXX:

Acts: μετὰ ταῦτα ἀναστρέψω καὶ ἀνοικοδομήσω τὴν σκηνήν....
LXX: ἐν τῇ ἡμέρᾳ ἐκείνῃ ἀναστήσω τὴν σκηνήν....

If one looks for anything akin to the Acts reading, the nearest text is the partial quotation of Amos 9:11 found twice in the Qumran literature; it begins with the Hebrew whqymwty, "and I will raise up", which seems to require a preceding verb.[8] To this small piece of evidence Wilcox can add only one point: both of the Qumranic citations, like Acts, prefix the words of the prophet with the introductory formula "as it is written."

---

[1] Cf. Wilcox, op. cit., pp. 62 f.
[2] 1 Sam. 21; cf. Mk. 2:25 f.; Matt. 12:3 f.; Lk. 6:3 f.
[3] Cf. Wilcox, op. cit., pp. 62 f.
[4] Ibid., p. 31.
[5] Ibid., p. 27 f.
[6] Op. cit., p. 20.
[7] Cf. Bruce, op. cit., p. 298.
[8] CD vii. 16; 4QFlo 1.30. Cf. Wilcox, op. cit., p. 49.

This point, at first sight insignificant, is well taken. J. A. Fitzmyer has listed no fewer than seventeen introductory formulae used in Acts to prefix Old Testament citations, and has found parallels for the great majority of them in the Qumran texts.[1] It is at least clear that for the first part of this particular citation Acts does not follow the LXX, and that in general it would be a mistake to lean too heavily on the LXX or to neglect the Qumran literature in any linguistic scrutiny of the Book of Acts. One may reasonably expect that the Dead Sea Scrolls will shed more light on the diction of Acts as research progresses. Fitzmyer opines that "the influence of Qumran literature on Acts is not so marked as it is in other New Testament writings (e.g. John, Paul, Matthew, Hebrews)".[2] Nevertheless he has drawn attention in his article to three idioms or technical terms common to the Qumran scrolls and to Acts, namely, "the Way" (used absolutely),[3] "the fellowship",[4] and "the congregation".[5] If these terms had not precisely identical connotations for the two communities, the Qumran sect and the infant Christian church, nevertheless the usage is similar enough to warrant our viewing the expressions as Semitisms in Acts.

A salutary warning against over-pressing Septuagintal influence on Luke is also to be found in the statistical count of K. Beyer.[6] Most of his investigations to date are concerned with conditional constructions, and it may be that further research will produce different results; but he has shown that the syntactical usages so far examined reveal over twice as many typically Semitic constructions in Acts as there are comparable Septuagintal constructions. The third gospel exhibits an even greater preponderance of Semitic constructions – 422 examples as against 23 "Septuagintalisms". In fact, both Luke and Acts have a considerably higher ratio of Semitic as against Hellenistic Greek constructions than any other New Testament book except Matthew (which has the highest proportionate quantity of Semitisms of all).[7] It is a pity, however, that Beyer's statistics relate to books as a whole, and so make no differentiation between different sections or subsections of Acts.

R. A. Martin has endeavoured to remedy this deficiency in Beyer's statistics by sampling three specific aspects of the syntactical data of Acts 1–15, and weighing one section against another. He concludes that at least thirteen passages are based on Aramaic sources, since they reveal syntactical marks of translation Greek as opposed to those of original

---

[1] Cf. J. A. Fitzmyer, "Jewish Christianity in Acts in the Light of the Qumran Scrolls", in L. E. Keck and J. L. Martyn (eds.), *Studies in Luke–Acts* (New York and Nashville, 1966; London, 1968), pp. 233–57.

[2] *Ibid.*, p. 253.

[3] Hebrew *drk*, Greek ὁδός.

[4] Hebrew *yḥd*, Greek κοινωνία.

[5] Hebrew *hrbym*, Greek τὸ πλῆθος.

[6] In his *Semitische Syntax im Neuen Testament*.

[7] See the table in Beyer, *op. cit.*, p. 298.

Greek works.[1] The possibility exists that other passages too owe much to Aramaic sources; but if so, the Semitic elements in them have been more thoroughly eliminated in translation and editing.

V

That there are Semitisms in Acts is in the last resort undeniable, whatever their origins and sources. Wilcox has isolated a number of what he calls "hard-core" Semitisms, that is to say, words and expressions in Acts which cannot be explained on the basis of *koine* Greek or of textual corruption. Luke's indebtedness to the LXX was profound, but it was by no means his only influence. Other Old Testament textual traditions were known to him; Semitic idioms common in the contemporary church (or what Wilcox calls "liturgical and apologetical factors") affected his diction; and there is no good reason to doubt that he had access to traditions or documents couched in, or translated from, a Semitic language. The resulting Semitisms can be seen here and there in the vocabulary, word-order, grammar, syntax and idioms of Acts – whatever may be said of mistranslations. However, such Semitic elements in Luke's writing must not be pressed to support conclusions which they will not bear. Sparks emphasizes, after analysis of his specimen passages, that Lucanisms surround the Semitisms. Wilcox too, on the basis of his more full analysis, asserts that his survey shows that "in almost every case the material in which they ["hard-core" Semitisms] are embedded has a strongly Lucan stamp".[2] This fact is probably fatal to such a theory as Torrey's, although it could perhaps be argued that the presence of Lucanisms merely serves to show that Luke himself translated and recast the hypothetical source document(s).[3]

Of special interest is the question of the distribution of Semitisms in Acts. Torrey's view that they were scattered liberally throughout Acts 1–15 but were so rare as to be negligible in the remaining chapters, was exaggerated in both respects, though it has to be admitted that the preponderance of Semitisms is in the first half of the book. (This fact is not surprising, in view of the subject matter and locale, if Acts has the slightest claim to historical accuracy.) What is now evident is that time and again the Semitisms are to be found in the speeches of Acts. Black, for instance, finds examples of *casus pendens* – confined to the speeches;[4] some examples of asyndeton in the D text – many of them in the speeches;[5] two instances

---

[1] *Art. cit.* The passages are: 1:15–26; 2:1–4; 4:5–12, 23–31; 5:17–42; 7:1–53; 9:10–19a, 19b–30, 31–43; 10:26–43; 11:1–18; 12:1–25; 13:16–41.

[2] *Op. cit.*, p. 177.

[3] A translator, after all, is bound to utilize his own favourite vocabulary so far as his material permits; and his selection from the documents would be determined by the relevance of their contents to his own themes and purposes.

[4] *Op. cit.*, pp. 53 ff.

[5] *Ibid.*, p. 59.

of mistranslation of Aramaic d^e – both in speeches;[1] a few cases of the use of a proleptic pronoun, especially in the D text – mainly in speeches;[2] several examples of the indefinite use of ἄνθρωπος (=τις) – nearly always in direct speech;[3] and two instances of a Semitic prepositional idiom – both in speech.[4] Wilcox's investigations have a similar result, and he concludes, "Luke used, or rather seems to have used, some kind of source-material for certain parts at least of the speeches in Acts."[5] Fitzmyer's list of seventeen introductory formulae are without exception located in direct speech; even if the distribution of this feature is not surprising (since citations of Scripture are more natural in speech than in narrative), one must still ask where they came from. Finally, of R. A. Martin's thirteen subsections of Acts 1–15 which show indebtedness to Semitic source material, eight consist, in their entirety or almost so, of direct speech.

Recent study of the language of the Book of Acts, therefore, has done little to undermine the arguments set forth in F. F. Bruce's monograph, *The Speeches in the Acts of the Apostles*,[6] where considerable emphasis was laid on the Aramaic substratum of the speeches. Summing up, he wrote, "We need not suppose that the speeches in Acts are verbatim reports. . . . But I suggest that . . . the speeches reported by Luke are at least faithful epitomes."[7] The Lucanisms and Septuagintal diction must of course be taken into account too, but the Semitic substratum is not to be discounted.[8] The argument that Luke used a Semitic type of Greek where he considered it to be appropriate sounds very reasonable; but the obstinate fact remains that where we are in a position to check his stylistic policy, i.e., where he has utilized and adapted Marcan material, he has tended to eliminate Semitisms (while admittedly leaving many untouched); he has certainly not created many. It is not at all clear why Luke should think "Semitic" Greek appropriate for the speakers in Luke 1 f. and in Acts, but feel otherwise about the words and deeds of Jesus.[9]

Outside the speeches of Acts, some narrative sections appear to contain a greater Semitic element than others, and Wilcox draws attention to the fact that in general they are passages having a close connexion of some sort with Antioch.[10] So far as the linguistic evidence goes, it thus tends to support the tradition that Luke was an Antiochene, and also the general historical reliability of these sections.

[1] *Ibid.*, p. 92. [2] *Ibid.*, pp. 99 f.
[3] *Ibid.*, p. 106. [4] *Ibid.*, p. 117.
[5] *Op. cit.*, p. 177. [6] London, 1944.
[7] p. 27.
[8] As it would appear to be in the article "Concerning the Speeches in Acts" by E. Schweizer in Keck and Martyn, *op. cit.*, pp. 208–16.
[9] Cf. E. E. Ellis, *The Gospel of Luke* (Century Bible, new ed. London, 1966), p. 3.
[10] *Op. cit.*, pp. 178 f.

VI

We may be sure that research into the Semitisms of Acts will continue, and that Wilcox's contribution will not close the topic. Without doubt, other scholars will reject some of his Semitisms or add to their number. But it will be interesting to see what new avenues of exploration will yet be opened up. It seems to the present writer that an important need is a quantitative and qualitative analysis of New Testament Semitisms, balancing one writer against another, and also paying close attention to the *total* diction of each individual author. As it is, Dr Wilcox's book cannot provide these wider perspectives. There are of course older works, such as de Zwaan's useful chapter in *The Beginnings of Christianity*, entitled "The use of the Greek language in Acts,"[1] taken in conjunction with Lowther Clarke's "The use of the Septuagint in Acts";[2] but there is now an urgent need to up-date these treatments. Beyer's *Semitische Syntax im Neuen Testament* represents an important first step in this direction.

It is all too often assumed that outside influences upon an author have only positive effects; but possible negative effects, if fewer in number and more difficult to pin down, may be equally important. Fitzmyer's article draws attention to the relevance of this mode of inquiry to our topic: he suggests that in at least two respects in the book of Acts Luke may have deliberately avoided Semitic, specifically Qumranic, terminology. The "poor" of Jerusalem, so much a matter of concern to Paul, are nowhere in Acts described as $\pi\tau\omega\chi o i$ – the obvious word for them, one would have thought. More remarkable, the term $\epsilon\pi i\sigma\kappa o\pi o s$ appears but once in the whole book; the sole occurrence of it is in 20:28, on Paul's lips, when he addressed church leaders far from Palestinian soil. Fitzmyer thinks it not irrelevant that the Hebrew equivalents of these nouns, respectively *'bywnym* and *mbqr*, were common technical terms among the Dead Sea sect. Did Luke feel that such terms, even in Greek, might have unfortunate connotations for his readers? Or was it his sources which avoided such terminology? There is clearly room for further inquiry of this sort.

If it could be demonstrated that Luke was indeed sensitive to the possible connotations of words like $\pi\tau\omega\chi o s$ and $\epsilon\pi i\sigma\kappa o\pi o s$, then this fact would tend to militate against the view that he knew nothing but Greek.[3] There is no obvious reason why a writer ignorant of Hebrew and of Palestinian Judaism should avoid such terminology.

While one swallow does not make a summer, nor two missing swallows a winter, this suggestion of Fitzmyer does point us in a new direction,

---

[1] *BC* vol. 2, pp. 3–65.
[2] *Ibid.*, pp. 66–105.
[3] Cf. Moule, *op. cit.*, p. 171.

namely that of semantics. To what extent, we may ask, does the vocabulary of Acts consist of Greek words carrying Semitic overtones? Here is a question scarcely touched on by Black or Wilcox. Their treatment of Semitisms in vocabulary is almost entirely restricted to transliterations of Semitic words (e.g. Ἀκελδαμαχ) and to idioms (e.g. ἐκλέγεσθαι ἐν). The only interesting word, from a semantic point of view, discussed by Wilcox is the ἰδιώτης of Acts 4:13; he suggests that this noun has its "rabbinical" rather than its native Greek connotation.[1]

It is not my purpose here to enter into the debate which was raised by J. Barr in his important book *The Semantics of Biblical Language*,[2] and to which D. Hill's recent *Greek Words and Hebrew Meanings*[3] made a contribution of no little value. Both writers would agree, at least, that the New Testament documents in general do betray thought-forms and concepts alien to the Greek world, and owing much to the Septuagint. The question whether the distinctive ideas lie chiefly in the vocabulary itself or in the sentence structure and in the actual statements made is not particularly relevant to our present purpose. The latter writer, however, has usefully reminded us that words like "righteousness", "life" and "spirit" tended to be employed in different ways in the Hebraic world and in the Greek one, and that the Greek terms used first in the LXX and subsequently in the New Testament inevitably reflect Hebraic rather than Greek usage. That being so, we may well ask how far Luke's handling of vocabulary reveals a Hellenistic, and how far a Semitic, background. If he were a Gentile and made little use of source material, we might expect to find a much less Semitic cast of thought and expression than if he were a bilingual Jew making great use of Semitic source documents (to talk in terms of extreme positions). Such a study might conceivably show merely that Luke (whoever he was and whatever documents were available to him) was deeply influenced by the language of the LXX, as indeed he was; but different results might reveal themselves. We noted earlier that the phrase ἐπὶ τὸ αὐτό in Acts had more affinity with Qumran vocabulary than with either Hellenistic Greek or LXX usage; similar results might possibly emerge from a thorough semantic investigation of the vocabulary of Luke/Acts.

So far as Acts is concerned, Dr. Hill's study sheds relatively little light on this problem. In any case, soteriological terms (to which Hill's attention is restricted in his monograph) will have been common currency in the early church, in quasi-technical senses, drawn from and based on the LXX; therefore, no early Christian is likely to have used them in a purely

---

[1] I.e., "an ordinary person" rather than "private person"; cf. Wilcox, *op. cit.*, p. 101. Cf. also Bruce, *Commentary on the Book of the Acts*, p. 102 n. This case may be a special one, however, for the equivalent Semitic word (both Hebrew and Aramaic) is *hdywṭ*, itself a loan-word from the Greek. In bilingual areas it is scarcely likely that ἰδιώτης and *hdywṭ* would have borne subtly different connotations.

[2] London, 1961.

[3] SNTS monograph 5. Cambridge, 1967.

Hellenistic sense.[1] It is intriguing, nevertheless, that of the terms examined by Hill, ἱλάσκομαι and cognates never occur in Acts, λύτρον and cognates only once, ζωὴ (αἰώνιος) rarely, δίκαιος and δικαιοσύνη seldom; and that all of them are found only in direct speech,[2] and may therefore derive from Luke's sources. By contrast, πνεῦμα is of course ubiquitous in Acts. The rarity of the other terms may mean anything or nothing. The Book of Acts is largely narrative in character, and thus would have little use for abstract and theological terminology except in the speeches; the Spirit, on the other hand, was no abstract, passive Being in Luke's view of the matter!

Modern linguistic science might suggest another method of approach to the vocabulary of the New Testament, namely the study of "semantic fields". This approach has been pioneered for Old Testament Hebrew by T. Donald, in an article where he examined the implications of the various Hebrew words associated with folly in the Wisdom literature of the Old Testament, assessing in particular the overtones of culpability carried by the differing terms.[3] It is conceivable that comparisons of semantic fields in Hebrew or Aramaic with their counterparts in Greek would throw some light on Luke's use of vocabulary. But a great deal of basic research would need to be done before any effective comparative work became possible.

It is a privilege and an honour for me to have the opportunity of offering this slim tribute to Professor Bruce, who first introduced me to the Greek text of Acts, who first taught me three of the Semitic languages, and whose friendship and guidance I value increasingly with the passing years.

---

[1] This applies to other common terms too, such as ἐκκλησία. It is difficult to accept the view of E. M. Blaiklock that in Acts 7:38 ἐκκλησία "bears its Greek connotation" and "views Israel through the eyes of Greek city organization" (*The Acts of the Apostles*, TNTC, London, 1959, *ad loc.*). In the LXX, ἐκκλησία commonly renders Hebrew qāhāl, and this is surely the background here. The previous verse cites Dt. 18:15; and Dt. 18:16 immediately goes on to refer to "the day of the assembly" (LXX ἐκκλησία).

[2] The sole exception is the occurrence of δικαιοσύνη in 24:25; but here too the word is probably so to speak between quotation marks.

[3] Cf. T. Donald, "The Semantic Field of 'Folly' in Proverbs, Job, Psalms and Ecclesiastes," *VT* 13 (1963), pp. 285–92.

CHAPTER IX

SOME ARCHAEOLOGICAL OBSERVATIONS ON PAUL'S FIRST MISSIONARY JOURNEY

BASTIAAN VAN ELDEREN

IN THE AREA OF NEW TESTAMENT STUDIES, PROFESSOR F. F. BRUCE'S MAJOR contribution has been in his commentaries on the Book of Acts and his special studies in first-century Christianity. To his brilliant and expansive scholarship not only we of the present generation but those of generations to come will be debtors. It is a great pleasure to participate in the publication of this volume in honour of one who is a stellar example of Christian scholarship, genuine devotion, and loyal stewardship.

In the preface to the first edition of his commentary on the Greek text of the Acts of the Apostles (published in 1951), Prof. Bruce acknowledges with appreciation the contributions of Sir W. M. Ramsay when he writes: "I am particularly indebted to the works of W. M. Ramsay."[1] He reaffirms this in the preface to the second edition in these words: "My debt to the writings of Sir William Ramsay is evident throughout the book, and I am repeatedly amazed by modern writers who deal with areas of New Testament scholarship to which Ramsay made contributions of peculiar value, with hardly so much as a hint that such a person ever lived."[2] As one interested in New Testament and Early Christian Archaeology (and especially in Asia Minor where Ramsay worked so extensively), I share Bruce's appreciation of Ramsay's contribution and his dismay that it has had so little impact in New Testament studies. Ramsay's pioneer work must be continued and intensified[3] and this essay will attempt to present some new light in one area of Ramsay's and Bruce's interests.

I

Sergius Paulus of Acts 13:7

Luke reports (Acts 13:7-12) that on the first missionary journey, when Barnabas and Saul (Paul) reached Paphos on the island of Cyprus, they

---

[1] *The Acts of the Apostles* (London, 1951), p. vii.

[2] *The Acts of the Apostles* (London, 1952), p. viii. I experienced a similar amazement upon discovering that C. K. Barrett's *Luke the Historian in Recent Study* (London, 1961) contains no reference to or citation from Ramsay's works. Bruce's appreciation of Ramsay is also expressed in the Foreword of W. Ward Gasque's *Sir William Ramsay: Archaeologist and New Testament Scholar* (Grand Rapids, 1966), pp. 7-9.

[3] This need was also voiced in my article "New Perspectives in Biblical Research," *Calvin Theological Journal* 1 (1966), pp. 180 f.

had a conference with the proconsul Sergius Paulus. Observing Paul's encounter with Elymas, the proconsul "believed . . . for he was astonished at the teaching of the Lord" (Acts 13:12). The nature of his faith has been a subject for debate.

Attempts to identify Sergius Paulus in non-Biblical sources have centred around two inscriptions. These and a third inscription, also relevant to this discussion, are described and discussed below.

The full name of a Roman citizen consisted of three names: *praenomen, nomen, cognomen.* Luke has only given us the *nomen* and *cognomen* of the proconsul under discussion. The names Sergius Paul(l)us were not un-common in the Roman world.[1] A further complication in this identifica-tion is that the list of proconsuls of first-century Cyprus is very defective-in fact, almost non-existent. Consequently, the little relevant epigraphic evidence is often cited and frequently over-extended for the sake of some parallelism or identification. Such an identification could throw some light on the strange episode recorded in Acts 13. In addition, a firm date for such a proconsul would provide a much-needed item in the chronology of the Apostle Paul. The Gallio Inscription provides a date in the second missionary journey, but for events immediately before and after the early fifties there are no fixed dates upon which to structure a chronology. Unfortunately, the present discussion is not able to provide such data.[2] Scholars usually place the first missionary journey of Paul between A.D. 46 and 49.

The numbering and publication data of the inscriptions in this discussion are:

Inscription 1 – *Inscriptiones Graecae ad res Romanas pertinentes* III.930. Corrected reading in T. B. Mitford, *Annual of British School at Athens* 42 (1947), pp. 201–06.

Inscription 2 – *CIL* VI.31545.

Inscription 3 – *Inscriptiones Graecae ad res Romanas pertinentes* III.935. Corrected reading in John L. Myers, *Handbook of the Cesnola Collection of Antiquities from Cyprus* (New York: Metropolitan Museum of Art, 1914), p. 319 (no. 1903) and p. 548 (no. 1903).

Inscription 1

This Greek inscription, found at Soli on the north coast of Cyprus, gives a date-line ἐπὶ Παύλου [ἀνθυ]πάτου. The date-line also contains an era date, although the numeral is difficult to read. Mitford reads the numeral

---

[1] The Greek spelling of the name is Παῦλος and the Latin spelling is Paullus.
[2] Haenchen's observation regrettably is still valid: "Die Hoffnung, sein [Sergius Paulus] Amtsjahr in einer Inschrift zu finden, blieb unerfüllt" (*Die Apostelgeschichte* [Göttingen, 1965], p. 57).

as 10 and, since his study of Cypriot inscriptions indicates that dating in the first century was by regnal year, he calculates that regnal year 10 = A.D. 50 (if reign of Claudius).[1] However, the date-line appears to be a later addition to the inscription (irregular lineation, variant script, and possible later terminology), and Mitford therefore concludes: ". . . on epigraphic grounds this inscription, while it cannot be earlier, is in all probability considerably later."[2]

Earlier discussions of this inscription sought to identify the proconsul with Sergius Paulus in Acts 13. D. G. Hogarth, although having difficulty with the year numeral, made this identification.[3] However, since Kirsopp Lake's discussion[4] of this inscription, few commentators are inclined to make this identification.[5] Furthermore, Mitford with his reading and interpretation of the date-line has closed the discussion of this inscription and Sergius Paulus of Acts 13. Even granting the earliest possible date suggested by Mitford (A.D. 50) places the consulship too late in the chronology of Paul since on the basis of the Gallio inscription he was in Corinth (Acts 18) during the second missionary journey in A.D. 51.

Inscription 2

This Latin inscription lists a Lucius Sergius Paullus as one of the curators of the Tiber (*curatores riparum et alvei tiberis*) under Claudius. No date is given in the inscription, but it is surmised that this person went to Cyprus following this position in Italy.[6] Hence, numerous commentators identify this Lucius Sergius Paullus with the Sergius Paulus of Acts 13:7.

Ramsay has carried this identification and discussion a step farther. At the turn of the century he suggested that the Paulus of the inscription from Soli (our Inscription 1) "probably is the same governor" that is mentioned in Acts 13[7]. In a later discussion about Sergius Paulus of Acts 13, he does not cite this evidence,[8] but builds an ingenious and intriguing theory on a few other inscriptions. One of these, discovered by Ramsay and J. G. C. Anderson near Pisidian Antioch in 1912, mentions a "L(ucius) Sergius Paullus the younger, son of L(ucius)."[9] Ramsay confidently

---

[1] *Op. cit.*, p. 205.

[2] *Ibid.*

[3] *Devia Cypria* (1889), p. 114, no. 36.

[4] *BC* V, pp. 455-59.

[5] Nevertheless, the identification persists in some writings; e.g., Merrill F. Unger affirmed as recently as 1960 that this inscription "without any reasonable doubt refers to the Sergius Paulus whom Paul introduced to Christianity" (*Bibliotheca Sacra* 117 [1960], p. 233).

[6] Lake (*op. cit.*, p. 458): "The date would fit admirably if he went to Cyprus soon after being one of the curators of the Tiber." Similarly, Bruce (*op. cit.*, p. 256): "If he went to Cyprus after this curatorship, the date would fit with his appearance in Ac."

[7] *St. Paul the Traveller and the Roman Citizen* (London, 1903), p. 74.

[8] In a chapter entitled "Sergius Paullus and his Relation to Christian Faith," in *The Bearing of Recent Discovery on the Trustworthiness of the New Testament* (London, 1920), pp. 150–72.

[9] *Ibid.*, p. 151.

identifies the elder Lucius Sergius Paullus as the proconsul of Acts 13. The Lucius Sergius Paullus who was consul in A.D. 152 and 168 Ramsay identifies as the great-grandson of the proconsul of Cyprus.[1] Ramsay's discovery in 1913 of the full name Sergia Paulla on an inscription in Antioch allowed him to make further identifications and deductions.[2] This woman, identified on the stone as the daughter of Lucius and the wife of Gaius Caristanius Fronto, Ramsay considers to be the daughter of the elder Lucius, the proconsul of Cyprus. He further calculates that the younger Lucius was governor of Galatia about A.D. 72–4 and the marriage of his sister and Caristanius took place about the same time.[3] It was their son who erected the inscription. His use of Greek and his subsequent disappearance from the records of Antioch (a kind of *argumentum e silentio*) led Ramsay to conclude that he was a Christian, influenced by his mother, Sergia Paulla, who in turn was influenced by her father, the proconsul of Cyprus.[4]

Admittedly, Ramsay has built an interesting theory from the scattered data at his disposal. However, some of his assumptions simply demand too much imagination to be convincing.[5] Nevertheless, the crucial issue is the identification of Lucius Sergius Paullus with Sergius Paulus of Acts 13. It must be observed and emphasized that there is presently no evidence linking Lucius Sergius Paullus with Cyprus. This is a serious weakness in Ramsay's theory and in the proposal to identify L. Sergius Paullus of our Inscription 2 with the proconsul of Cyprus. That the curator of the Tiber mentioned in Inscription 2 later went to Cyprus is assumed, not directly attested. The absence of the *praenomen* in Acts 13:7 makes the name too indefinite to identify it simply with someone who has the same *nomen* and *cognomen*.

A further difficulty with Inscription 2 is its possible date. It is placed in the reign of Claudius (*ex auctoritate Ti. Claudi Caesaris Aug. Germanici*) – A.D. 41 to 54. Mommsen suggests that possibly the year of this inscription was A.D. 47/48.[6] At best, this is an inference but certainly presents a difficulty with the Pauline chronology. If Mommsen is correct and Lucius Sergius Paullus was the proconsul of Cyprus, the *terminus a quo* for this proconsulship is A.D. 48[7] – a rather late date for most Pauline chronologies.[8] One can hardly avoid reckoning A.D. 48 as the *terminus ad quem* for

---

[1] *Ibid.*, p. 152.   [2] *Ibid.*, p. 153.

[3] *Ibid.*, p. 157.

[4] *Ibid.*, pp. 157–64. This argument is repeated and conclusion accepted by Stephen L. Caiger (*Archaeology and the New Testament* [London, 1939], pp. 142–44) and Egbert C. Hudson ("The Principal Family at Pisidian Antioch", *JNES* 15 [1956], pp. 104–06). Bruce (*op. cit.*, p. 256) cites the argument without evaluation or judgment.

[5] Lake's evaluation seems correct when he describes Ramsay's theory as "marvellously ingenious, but not very convincing combinations" (*op. cit.*, p. 458).

[6] *ZNTW* 2 (1901), p. 83, footnote 3.

[7] Suggested by A. Wikenhauser, *Die Apostelgeschichte und ihr Geschichtswert* (Münster, 1921), p. 339.

[8] For example, Bruce (*op. cit.*, p. 55) dates the first missionary journey c. 47–48.

the first missionary journey. On the other hand, Groag has concluded that the date must be before A.D. 47, the supposed date of Claudius' censorship, which title would be included if the inscription were cut after the censorship.[1] However, Arthur Gordon has shown that this cannot be a criterion for dating the inscription since the absence of the title does not necessarily mean he was not censor at the time and furthermore the exact date of his censorship is not known.[2] In the light of so many unknown factors regarding this inscription and this period of Paul's ministry, no definite conclusions can be drawn about this chronology.

In conclusion, Inscription 2 cannot be confidently cited as a solution to the identification of Sergius Paulus. Perhaps even Bruce's cautious judgment says too much: "He may be the Lucius Sergius Paullus referred to in *CIL* vi 31545 [our Inscription 2]."[3] Furthermore, the evidence of our Inscription 3 introduces another possible identification which in many respects is more convincing than either of the above attempts.

Inscription 3

This Greek inscription, found at Kytheria on Cyprus and now housed in the Metropolitan Museum of Art in New York, contains a decree regulating sacrifices and offerings. The date-line at the end of the inscription is not complete, but the following reconstruction by Myers is very attractive:[4]

9   Κλαυδ]ίου Καίσαρος Σεβαστοῦ καὶ
10   ἐπὶ Κ]οίντου Σεργ-
11   [ίου Παύλου ἀνθυπάτου]

Palaeographically, the inscription belongs to the first century – e.g., the four-bar sigma and early omega. The preserved portions of line 9 indicate that the emperor is from the Julio-Claudian line. Hence, the restoration [Κλαυδ ίου is very plausible.[5] Likewise, the reading [Κ]οίντου Σεργ[ίου] in lines 10 and 11 is virtually certain. Mitford considers Myers' restoration in line 11 of Παύλου ἀνθυπάτου "at least plausible."[6]

However, Myers does not want to identify Quintus Sergius (Paullus) with the Sergius Paulus of Acts 13.[7] Mitford is somewhat more inclined to the identification,[8] and Emilio Gabba virtually makes the identification.[9]

[1] *PW*, II A, col. 1717, no. 34.
[2] *Album of Dated Latin Inscriptions*, Vol. I: *Text* (Berkeley, 1958), p. 97.
[3] *Op. cit.*, p. 256.
[4] *Op. cit.*, p. 548.
[5] The other possibility might be Tiberius, but this may be too early and perhaps require more titles.
[6] *Op. cit.*, p. 206, footnote 21.
[7] *Op. cit.*, p. 319. Elsewhere, he states that an inscription "exists of that Sergius Paulus who was proconsul in A.D. 46 when the island was visited by St. Paul" (*ibid.*, p. xli). He does not further specify – apparently he is alluding to either Inscription 1 or 2 above.
[8] *Op. cit.*, p. 206.
[9] *Iscrizioni Greche e Latine per lo Studio della Bibba* (Torino, 1958), pp. 71–73.

What is the status with regard to the identification of Sergius Paulus in non-Biblical sources? In summary, it must be noted that Inscription 1 cannot be associated with him. Inscription 2 can hardly be used to identify Sergius Paulus, and surely Ramsay's conjectured family of Sergii Paulli and their Christianity must be rejected. It may be that in Inscription 3 there is a probable identification. This most attractive possibility of the three discussed above is here presented with a measure of reservation. Conclusive proof is not available at this time. Perhaps continued epigraphical studies and the current excavations at New Paphos by a Polish archaeological team eventually will solve this problem and throw some light on the chronology of the first missionary journey.

II

The New Site for Derbe

In Luke's account of Paul's first missionary journey it is reported that Paul and Barnabas went from Iconium to Lystra and Derbe, cities of Lycaonia (Acts 14:6). Only a brief account of Paul's activities in Derbe is recorded – ". . . and on the next day he went on with Barnabas to Derbe. When they had preached the gospel to that city and had made many disciples, they returned to Lystra . . ." (Acts 14:20, 21). Paul re-visited Derbe on his second missionary journey (Acts 16:1). It is possible that he also visited Derbe at the beginning of his third missionary journey (Acts 18:23). A disciple and companion of Paul from Derbe is mentioned in Acts 20:4.[1]

1. Location suggested by Ramsay

Until about the end of the nineteenth century, no convincing site for ancient Derbe had been advanced. Prof. J. R. Sitlington Sterrett was the first to suggest locating Derbe in the neighbourhood of the large mound of Gudelisin.[2] Shortly after that, Ramsay advanced the theory that the mound of Gudelisin is the site of Derbe.[3] On and near this mound he found "plain traces of an ancient city of moderate extent."[4] Later he wrote: "Gudelisin is the only site in this district where a city of the style of Derbe, the stronghold of the 'robber Antipater', could be situated."[5] It should be noted that this location is not based on any epigraphical or extensive archaeological evidence. In fact, surface exploration and a very limited

---

[1] Manuscript D has Δουβ[έ]ριος instead of Δερβαῖος.

[2] *Wolfe Expedition to Asia Minor*, p. 22. Actually Sterrett suggested that the twin cities of Bosala and Zosta (Losta) in ancient times were one city – namely, Derbe.

[3] *The Cities of St. Paul* (New York, 1907), pp. 393–97. Ramsay identified what Sterrett called Derbe as ancient Possala, and located Derbe about four miles west at Gudelisin.

[4] *Ibid.*, p. 395.

[5] *The Church in the Roman Empire Before A.D. 170* (New York, 1912), p. 55.

excavation for a day yielded no convincing evidence.[1] Hence, in 1912 Ramsay could write that "the site of Derbe is not established on such certain evidence as that of Lystra"[2] – the evidence for Lystra being the inscription found on the mound near Hatunsaray.

This location for Derbe has been the more or less accepted one since Ramsay's suggestion.[3] Gudelisin is located about sixty miles south of Konya in the Taurus foothills. It is the location given in practically all the maps describing Paul's missionary journeys. However, subsequent to Ramsay, no further evidence has been advanced to confirm this location. On the other hand, in recent years a new site has been suggested for the location of Derbe. The evidence for this new site will be reviewed and evaluated below.

2. New Site suggested by M. Ballance

In 1956 M. Ballance discovered an inscribed white limestone block which mentions the people of Derbe.[4] This block was found at Kerti Hüyük, lying on the gently sloping skirt of the mound. The size of the stone is 105 cm. high, 69 cm. wide, and 68 cm. thick. Ballance thinks that it probably formed the shaft of a large statue-base. Because of its size and weight (about a ton), he believes that it could hardly have been moved very far, if at all, prior to its discovery. The inscription is a dedication by the council and people of Derbe and can be dated in A.D. 157. Lines 9 and 10 read:

$$\nu, \ K\lambda\alpha\nu\delta\iota o]\delta\epsilon\rho\beta\acute{\eta}\tau\omega\nu \ \acute{\eta} \ \beta o\upsilon\lambda\grave{\eta} \ \kappa-$$
$$\alpha\grave{\iota} \ \acute{o} \ \delta]\hat{\eta}\mu o\varsigma \ \acute{\epsilon}\pi\grave{\iota} \ K o\rho\nu\eta\lambda\acute{\iota} o-$$

The stone has been moved to Konya and is housed in the new museum for Classical Antiquities at Konya. Presently it stands next to the Lystra inscription in the courtyard of this attractive museum.

Kerti Hüyük is a sizeable, although not prominent, mound located about fifteen miles north-northeast of Karaman (ancient Laranda). Karaman is about sixty-five miles southeast of Konya (ancient Iconium). Between 1962 and 1968 I visited this area seven times to conduct epigraphic surveys and surface explorations of mounds in the vicinity of Kerti Hüyük and the Thousand and One Churches (to be described below). Surface sherds on Kerti Hüyük indicate extensive occupation during the Roman and Hellenistic period with possibly some earlier

---

[1] *The Cities of St. Paul*, pp. 395 f.

[2] *The Church in the Roman Empire*, p. 54.

[3] E. Kraeling reflects the hesitation of most writers in the following statement: "Derbe has not been located with absolute certainty to this day; but it is believed that it lay about three miles northwest of the present Zosta, where there is a large mound of an ancient city, the surface remains of which are late Roman" (*Rand McNally Bible Atlas* [New York, 1956], p. 434).

[4] *Anatolian Studies* 7 (1957), pp. 147-51.

evidence.[1] Byzantine evidence, although scanty on Kerti Hüyük, can be definitely identified on nearby mounds. The building ruins scattered about the area around Kerti Hüyük and the provenance of tombstones described below indicate that the city of Derbe may have been extensive, rather than concentrated, in Byzantine times.

3. *Further Evidence for the New Site*

In June 1962 I was shown an inscription in a small house in Suduraya, a village near Kerti Hüyük.[2] Later that summer the inscription was moved to a storeroom in Karaman where it was still located in 1968. The marble slab fragment is the upper right-hand corner of a tombstone. The measurements of the fragment are: top: 65 cm; bottom: 56 cm; left side: 70 cm; right side: 50 cm; thickness: c. 9 cm. There is a narrow recessed border on the top and right side of the stone. The major part of the stone is covered with an inscription of six lines within five concentric circles. In the upper right-hand corner is a small circle in which are inscribed two lines of four and three letters, respectively.

The text in the larger circle mentions "the most God-loving Michael, bishop of Derbe" – ὁ θεοφιλέστατος Μιχαὶλ ἐπίσκοπος Δερβίς. The date-line is found in both circles: June 8, Indiction 14. This does not allow for precise dating, since the 14th year of indiction would occur every 15 years (in the fifth century: 401, 416, 431, 446, 461, 476, 491). Palaeographically,[3] a late fourth to fifth century date is possible.

In 1962 the natives of Sudaraya maintained that the inscription had been found on Kerti Hüyük. Ballance reports that the stone was found at Devri Şehri, about two and a half miles south-southeast of Kertie Hüyük.[4] Hence, he now proposes this site as the location of Derbe. In view of the inconclusive nature of surface sherding (hardly exclusive and at best inclusive) and the indefiniteness regarding the provenance of the Michael inscription, Kerti Hüyük cannot be so quickly eliminated as the site of ancient Derbe.

Additional evidence of early Christianity has been found in the immediate vicinity of Kerti Hüyük. In 1965 a blue marble slab was found in one of the villages. It is a fragment of a beautifully inscribed tombstone of a

[1] The surface of the mound is rather irregular and ravined; hence, surface evidence at best must be considered tentative. Further conclusions must await careful stratigraphic excavation.

[2] I was informed about the inscription by Mr. Önder, then the Director of Museums in Konya, who gave me the publication rights of this inscription. In December 1963 I reported on this inscription in a paper, entitled "Further Confirmation of the New Site for Derbe," presented at the annual meeting of the Society of Biblical Literature held in New York. M. Ballance presents a short report on this inscription in *Anatolian Studies* 14 (1964), pages 139–40. He reports that he saw the inscription in 1958.

[3] The square *sigma* and *epsilon*, the *upsilon* as a Roman V, the broken cross-bar *alpha* and small looped *rho* and *beta* occur in dated fourth-century inscriptions and are well-attested in the early fifth century (cf. *Monumenta Asiae Minoris Antiqua* 7, pp. xxxvi-xliii).

[4] *Op. cit.*, p. 139. Also accepted by Bruce, *New Testament History* (1969) p. 259.

presbyteros (elder) of a Christian church.[1] Some Christian inscriptions in the storeroom at Karaman are reported to have come from the area around Kerti Hüyük.

In conclusion, the epigraphic evidence clearly indicates that previous attempts to locate Derbe have been erroneous. The territory of Derbe must be located about thirty miles east of the area suggested by Ramsay. It must be located in the vicinity of Kerti Hüyük, and in all probability on Kerti Hüyük itself. This new location places Derbe more in the centre of Lycaonia, but has little bearing on the problem of the boundary between Phrygia and Lycaonia raised by some first-century writers and Acts 14:6.

4. Significance of the New Site

In the light of this new evidence it is now possible to speak with confidence regarding the general location of Derbe.[2] It also indicates that Acts 14:20 must be translated: "On the next day he set out with Barnabas towards (or for) Derbe." The Greek text of the passage does not necessarily imply that they made the trip in one day.[3]

In Acts 14:6 Luke writes that Paul fled to the cities of Lycaonia – Lystra and Derbe – and the surrounding country. Ramsay has interpreted this passage and other evidence to indicate that Derbe and Lystra were in the Roman province of Galatia. One of Ramsay's presuppositions regarding this is that Paul restricted his work to the limit of the Roman territory. George Ogg has shown the weakness of this presupposition since Paul obviously passed through and ministered in non-Roman territory at the beginning of both the second and the third missionary journeys.[4] On the other hand, this new location for Derbe agrees better with the data in Strabo. Strabo describes the territory of Lycaonia and Cappadocia as separated from Cilicia Tracheia on the south by the Taurus Mountain (p. 568). The boundary between Lycaonia and Cappadocia lies between Garsaüra and Coropassus, located northeast of this new site for Derbe. Strabo indicates that Derbe lies especially close to Cappadocia and that it with Laranda was under Antipater Derbetes, but later was held by Amyntas. The above data would surely suggest that Derbe was as far east as Laranda, if not farther east.

In his description of the administrative divisions of Cappadocia just prior to A.D. 17 and the death of King Archelaus, Strabo (p. 535) describes an eleventh prefecture formed by the Romans as including the country round Castabala and Cybistra in Cilicia and extending westward to Derbe.

---

[1] This and other inscriptions will be published in a forthcoming collection of epigraphic evidence of early Christianity in this area.
[2] More specific data must await a systematic excavation of the mound or soundings in various locations in the vicinity.
[3] Jack Finegan, *Light from the Ancient Past* (Princeton, 1959), p. 343, footnote 35a.
[4] *NTS* 9 (1963), p. 368.

Derbe and Laranda do not seem to be included in this division. However, Ptolemy (V. 6:6) places them with Olbasa and Mousbanda in the prefecture of Antiochus. The date to which Ptolemy refers is in dispute. Numismatic evidence indicates that Laranda belonged to Antiochus IV of Commagene from A.D. 41 on.[1] That this may also be true of Derbe is suggested by its new location slightly east of Laranda. Hence, the question of the location of the eastern border of the province of Galatia and Derbe's inclusion in that province is raised anew. George Ogg has shown that Ramsay's argumentation (whereby he places Derbe in the province of Galatia) no longer is valid[2] and hence concludes that "no compelling reasons have thus far been given for the inclusion of Derbe in the Province of Galatia in St. Paul's time, and consequently that at present it is an open question whether it was then inside or outside it".[3] A related question is whether Derbe is one of the Galatian churches who are the recipients of the Epistle to the Galatians, according to the South Galatian theory.[4] In view of the fluctuating political conditions in this part of Asia Minor during the first century and the present incomplete data, no conclusive judgment is possible at this time.

This new inscription provides evidence regarding the Christian church at Derbe. We have here a reference to a bishop of Derbe from possibly the late fourth or fifth century. The name of another bishop of Derbe is also known – Daphnus, who was present at the Council of Constantinople in A.D. 381. This provides another interesting piece of evidence regarding Christianity in central Asia Minor in this period.

Furthermore, this new location for Derbe places it in close proximity to, and possible relation with, the area designated as "The Thousand and One Churches". This area lies in the vicinity of Kara Dağ (Black Mountain). Modern villages in this area are Madenşehir and Deyle. In his investigations of this area with Gertrude Bell, Ramsay identified the ruins of almost fifty churches.[5] Recent investigations have located additional ruins – although some of those described by Ramsay are hard to locate because local natives have been removing some of the dressed stones for modern building purposes. Most of the ruins are dated between the sixth and eleventh centuries. Our location of Derbe about nine or ten miles from this concentration of churches suggests the possibility of relationship. Possibly the Christianity represented by the ruins of "The Thousand and One Churches" has its origins in the church established by Paul at Derbe in the first century. In any case, in spite of relatively meagre references in the

[1] Ogg, loc. cit., p. 369.

[2] Ibid., pp. 367–70.

[3] Ibid., p. 367. According to the provincial boundaries set by Ramsay in the map included in the back cover of The Church in the Roman Empire, the new location for Derbe places it outside the Provincia Galatia and in the Regnum Antiochi.

[4] A position maintained by Bruce in his commentary (op. cit., p. 38) and assumed in a recent lecture (BJRL 51 [1969], p. 292).

[5] Ramsay and Gertrude L. Bell, The Thousand and One Churches (London, 1909).

literary sources to this area of ancient Christendom, much has been learned about it through archaeological surveys and studies in recent decades.[1]

III

In spite of Ramsay's pioneer work in the early part of this century, nearly all the studies on the Acts of the Apostles have doubted or ignored its historical reliability. Ward Gasque in a recent paper has carefully documented and rightly lamented this sceptical tradition.[2] As archaeological and historical studies uncover more and more about the eastern Mediterranean world, the historical reliability of New Testament authors becomes more and more impressive – and Luke in Acts is no exception. On the other hand, mere affirmation of this characteristic of Lucan writings will not be the answer to current scholarship nor do justice to the message of Luke. Luke obviously is not merely writing history. He has a purpose, an apologetic interest, an argument, an objective – a theology.

The primary concern of this essay with some historical problems in the Acts of the Apostles is not intended to overlook the theological dimension necessary for a balanced study of this book. To understand Luke (and any New Testament author) requires an integration of historical and theological studies. In recent decades we have come to know Luke as a theologian – it is now time to recognize and appreciate him as a theologian-historian. Bruce himself has fittingly expressed this thought in these words: "I see no incompatibility between theology and history: in fact I am tempted, in face of a strong contemporary trend, to say that – within the Jewish and Christian tradition, at least – a man cannot be a good theologian unless he is a good historian."[3]

[1] The British Institute of Archaeology at Ankara under the direction of Dr Michael Gough has been excavating the ruins of at least three impressive fifth-century churches about twenty-five miles south of Karaman. Although their relationship with Derbe is questionable, these churches nevertheless give evidence in sculpture and architecture of a creative and imaginative Christianity in this area. Preliminary reports of these excavations can be found in *Anatolian Studies* 12 (1962), pp. 173–84; 13 (1963), pp. 105–15; 14 (1964), pp. 185–90; 17 (1967), pp. 37–47; 18 (1968), pp. 159–67.

[2] *EQ* 14 (1969), pp. 68–88. Blaiklock's essay in this present volume establishes the setting of Acts squarely in the first-century Graeco-Roman world.

[3] *BJRL* 51 (1969), p. 294.

PART II

PART II

CHAPTER X

A COMPARISON OF PAUL'S MISSIONARY PREACHING AND PREACHING TO THE CHURCH

WILLIAM BARCLAY

MOST PREACHERS PREACH TO THE HOME CHURCH OR TO THE MISSION field, but not to both. Generally speaking a preacher will preach either to the converted or the unconverted. He will be either an itinerant missionary with no settled sphere of work, or he will be the pastor of a settled community in one place. But Paul had to play both roles. He was the missionary preacher who preached to men who had never heard the name of Jesus Christ, and he was the pastor who had to deal with all the problems of congregational life. In the New Testament we have specimens of Paul's preaching in both spheres, for in the recorded sermons of Acts we see Paul preaching as a missionary, and in the Letters we see him acting as a pastor. Within the limits of an essay such as this we shall try to look at him in both areas of his work.

I

First, we look at Paul as a missionary preacher. Two things at once stand out about his missionary preaching.

i. He had the gift of beginning where his hearers were. We possess records of three of Paul's missionary sermons. There is the sermon preached in the synagogue in Antioch in Pisidia (Acts 13:16–41); the sermon preached in Athens (Acts 17:22–31); the sermon preached in Lystra (Acts 14:15–17). We must note here and now – the fact will become very relevant later – that these can be only the briefest notes of what Paul said. The longest of them, as it stands in Acts, the sermon at Antioch in Pisidia, would in its present form take no more than three minutes to deliver. These are not verbatim reports; they are the merest summaries of what was originally said.

The significant fact is that in the three sermons the approach, at least on the surface, is completely different. In Antioch in Pisidia Paul was preaching in a synagogue to Jews, to proselytes and to God-fearers. He therefore began in Jewish history, and used the Old Testament as an arsenal of proof-texts to prove his case. He knew that he could do this for he knew that his audience was steeped in Jewish history and in the scriptures. In Athens he began from local religious worship, and he quoted from the Greek poets (Acts 17:28). He never mentions Jewish history and he makes no quotation from the scriptures. He knew that it would be futile to talk about a history which no one knew and to quote from a book which no one had read, and the authority of which no one would accept. In Lystra Paul used still another method. In Lystra he was out in the wilds. Certainly no one there would know anything about Jewish history or Jewish scriptures. Lystra had not the widely disseminated culture of Athens, and there was no point in quoting the Greek poets. He therefore started straight from nature, from the sun and the wind and the rain and the growing things. In his missionary approach Paul had no set scheme and formula; his approach was completely flexible. He began where his audience was.

  ii. The second thing which stands out very clearly is that for Paul missionary preaching was not a monologue but a dialogue. True, it was proclamation, but it was not take-it-or-leave-it proclamation. It was proclamation plus explanation and defence. The characteristic word of Paul's missionary preaching in the synagogue is the word *argued*. In Damascus, in Thessalonica, in Athens, in Corinth, in Ephesus Paul argued in the synagogue (Acts 9:22; 17:2, 17; 18:4; 19:8). The faith was proclaimed and defended at the same time. Acceptance of it was not given on a wave of emotion; from the beginning the mind had to be satisfied as well as the heart.

  Let us then look at the pattern of Paul's missionary preaching. First, let us look at the sermon preached in Antioch in Pisidia (Acts 13:16-41). It begins with a survey of Jewish history (verses 16-23). It moves on to the immediate preparation for Jesus by John the Baptist (verses 24, 25). It proceeds to the narrative of Jesus' rejection, death and resurrection (verses 26-29). It claims that all these events were foretold in prophecy (verses 23-27), and quotes the appropriate prophecies. It ends with a warning to those who still reject the offer of God in Jesus Christ (verses 40, 41).

  Let us now look at the sermon at Athens. The strange thing about it is that, on the face of it, it looks very different, but when we begin to examine it, the pattern is almost exactly the same. It begins with history, only this time the history is not the history of the Jewish people, but the history of the search of the soul for God (Acts 17:23-28). It presents the coming of Jesus Christ as God's decisive event (verse 30). It proclaims the fact of the resurrection and the threat of judgment (verse 31). With the exception of the reference to John the Baptist – who would have been irrelevant to an Athenian audience – the elements of the sermon in Antioch reappear in the sermon at Athens.

  The sermon at Lystra (Acts 14:15-17) is so very short that it would seem to have little to contribute, but that is not so. History is still there, for there is stressed the continuing activity of God (verses 15, 17). And, short as it is, it reproduces one of the essential ideas of the sermon at Athens. In the sermon at Athens Paul said:

> The times of ignorance God overlooked, but now he commands all men everywhere to repent (Acts 17:30).

And in the sermon at Lystra Paul said:

> In past generations he (God) allowed all the nations to walk in their own ways (Acts 14:16).

This is to say that in both sermons the coming of Jesus Christ is presented as the decisive event of history, and from the brief sermon at Lystra it may well be held that, when it was possible to say very little, this was the one thing that Paul was determined to say.

We are now in a position to reconstruct the main elements in Paul's missionary preaching.

i. History is a preparation for the coming of Jesus Christ, whether that history be a series of events in the life of the Jewish nation, or the search for God among the Gentiles.

ii. In this time of preparation God was not detached from men, like someone who set a process going and then stood back to watch it. He is not far (Acts 17:27, 28); he was active in the unfolding of history (Acts 13:16–23; 17:26); he was caring and providing for men in the processes of nature (Acts 14:17).

iii. In Jesus Christ God acted decisively. After Jesus' coming life can never be the same again. There has been a confrontation in which God entered the human situation. There has been a revelation of God, which has laid man under a new obligation, and which has confronted him with a situation in which he must accept or reject (Acts 14:16; 17:30).

iv. The aim of this confrontation was solely the good of man. It is good news which is brought. It is a message of salvation that the preacher preaches. It is a Saviour whom he proclaims. It is forgiveness and freedom, otherwise unobtainable, which are offered (Acts 13:23, 32, 38, 39).

v. In spite of this, this offer was rejected by the Jews. Jesus was treated as a criminal. Pilate was persuaded into ordering his death. He was rejected, crucified and buried (Acts 13:27–29).

vi. But this was not the end. The rejection was followed by the resurrection. The resurrection was foretold in the scriptures (Acts 13:34–37), and the apostles were witnesses of it (Acts 13:31) – a double proof that it really happened.

vii. The resurrection has given Jesus the right of judgment (Acts 17:31), and men must now beware that they do not bring judgment and destruction upon themselves by rejecting the revelation and the offer of God (Acts 13:34–37, 40, 41).

When we look at this survey of Paul's missionary preaching, one thing is bound to strike us. There does not on the surface seem to be in it any-thing about the actual historical life of Jesus of Nazareth. From this it has been argued that Paul knew little or nothing about the earthly life of Jesus, and that he was indifferent to it. All that mattered to him, so it has been claimed, is the risen Christ. But if we examine this preaching material of Paul more closely, we will find that this is a view which is quite untenable.

Let us go back to the sermon in the synagogue in Antioch in Pisidia (Acts 13:16–41). In verse 23 the name of Jesus is suddenly introduced. In verses 24 and 25 John the Baptist appears equally suddenly on the scene. It is quite incredible that any audience would not ask: "Who is this Jesus? Who is this John?" This is so on quite general grounds. A name has no more meaning than the symbol X unless it is filled out with some informa-tion about the person who bears it. A name by itself is meaningless. It must raise a picture of a person or it means nothing at all. Further, on particular grounds, practically every religion in the ancient world had its cult story, in which the candidate was given careful instruction before he could become an initiate. Anyone in the ancient world would expect, if not demand, the cult story. And, if the cult involved, and was even based on, the idea of the incarnation of God, then the cult story becomes a first essential.

These are perfectly general considerations, but when we go further with the sermon (verses 27–31) we come on this passage which is central to the sermon:

> For those who live in Jerusalem and their rulers, because they did not recognize him nor understand the utterances of the prophets which are read every sabbath, fulfilled those by condemning him. Though they could charge him with nothing deserving death, yet they asked Pilate to have him killed. And when they had fulfilled all that was written of him, they took him down from the tree, and laid him in a tomb. But God raised him from the dead; and for many days he appeared to those who came up with him from Galilee to Jerusalem, who are now his witnesses to the people.

Suppose ourselves to be listening to this for the first time – who and what is Pilate? Here is a name out of the blue. The plain fact about a passage like this is that *it is intelligible to us only because we already know the story*. It is intelligible as a summary of that which is already known; it is not intellig-ible, at least it is not meaningful, to those who are hearing it for the first time without very considerable expansion. It implies the whole story of the life, the trial and the death of Jesus. It implies the story of the death and of the resurrection of Jesus. Without that, it would be tantalizing rather than appealing. As a summary of that which is known, it is effective; as a statement of that which is unknown, it is merely bewildering.

From this it would seem that it is a fair deduction that in the missionary preaching there must have been instruction in the actual historical life of

Jesus. There is a phrase in one of Paul's letters which makes this to all intents and purposes certain. In appealing to the Corinthians Paul writes: "I, Paul, myself entreat you, by the meekness and gentleness of Christ" (2 Cor. 10:1). It is perfectly plain that such an appeal is meaningless unless the Corinthians were aware of actual incidents and events in the life of Jesus in which this meekness and gentleness were demonstrated. This appeal would be totally ineffective unless it was made to people who knew that life in which the meekness and gentleness were clear for all to see. It appears that Paul's whole method of preaching involves a background knowledge of the life of Jesus.

This would also emerge from the basic method of early Christian preaching. The great claim of the Christian preachers, including Paul, was that the proof of Jesus' Messiahship was the fulfilment of prophecy in his life and in the events of his life. That is an argument which is ineffective and indeed unusable, unless there was a record of the events which were claimed to be fulfilments. The argument from prophecy implies a knowledge of the events of Jesus' life.

Where did this knowledge come from? There are in the New Testament a body of men who are mentioned high in the lists of Christian workers, but whose precise duties are never described. These were the teachers (Rom. 12:7; 1 Cor. 12:28; Eph. 4:11). It would be very natural for the man whose interest had been aroused to be handed over to the teachers for instruction in the story of the life of Jesus. The teachers would be the living books in which the material which became our gospels was contained. It may well have been these teachers who were responsible for the "forms" which lie behind the finished versions of the gospels.

But another interesting possibility arises. When Paul and Barnabas set out on the first missionary journey, they took John Mark with them. "They had also John to their minister," as the AV puts it (Acts 13:5). The RSV reproduces the Greek less literally: "And they had John to assist them." The Greek is: εἶχον δὲ καὶ Ἰωάννην ὑπηρέτην. If this means that they had John as their assistant, we should have expected that either ὑπηρέτην would have come at the beginning of the sentence, or that it would have been preceded by ὡς. A long time ago now F. H. Chase in his article on John Mark in Hastings' *Dictionary of the Bible* (vol. iii), made the suggestion that ὑπηρέτης was not a description of the work which John Mark was to do with Paul and Barnabas, but that it was a title, that John Mark was John the ὑπηρέτης. What would this mean? It would mean that John Mark was the synagogue official known in Hebrew as the *ḥazzan*, and in Greek as the ὑπηρέτης, and an important part of the duties of that official was that he was the synagogue teacher, responsible for the education of children, and, of course, in Judaism education was education in the faith. F. H. Chase finds some support for this in the fact that in the Acts passage the synagogue is mentioned in the same verse (Acts 13:5). If

Chase's suggestion could be accepted, it would mean that Paul and Barnabas went out with, so to speak, a teacher on their staff to give the very instruction which is implied. But it is not necessary to accept Chase's suggestion regarding John Mark to hold that the early missionary preaching included instruction in the life of Jesus. That instruction is implied in Paul's preaching by itself.

II

Let us now turn to Paul's preaching in the church, his preaching to the converted, to those who had already accepted Jesus Christ. This preaching we will find in his letters. Paul's letters are sermons far more than they are theological treatises. It is with immediate situations that they deal. They are sermons even in the sense that they were spoken rather than written. They were not carefully written out by someone sitting at a desk; they were poured out by someone striding up and down a room as he dictated, seeing all the time in his mind's eye the people to whom they were to be sent. Their torrential style, their cataract of thought, their involved sentences all bear the mark of the spoken rather than of the written word.

They have two main aims – to tell men what they must believe and how they must act, now that they are Christians. Their aim is to produce and to preserve right belief and right conduct. Their purpose is to preserve in their purity the Christian theology and the Christian ethic. Right belief and right action are the twin subjects of Paul's preaching within the church. That is why Paul's preaching is characteristically corrective and prophylactic. It is designed either to deal with some threatening situation which has arisen, or to take steps to see to it that such a situation does not arise.

Behind Paul's letters there lie three theological dangers, which are permanent threats to the new convert to the faith. In the space at our disposal we can deal with them only in the broadest outline.

i. There is the danger of *relapse*. Paul's converts did not have centuries of Christian tradition behind them; they were so short a distance from the life which they had once lived. They did not live in a society permeated by Christian ideals and ideas, even when it has abandoned Christian belief. They were, as it has been put, a little island of Christianity surrounded by a sea of paganism. We can identify two of the relapses into which Paul's converts were liable to fall.

(a) There was, for the Jews especially, the relapse into legalism. If a man had been brought up in a faith into the very substance of which were woven rules and regulations and rites and observances, a faith in which life was law and law was life, a religion of faith alone was so new that at times it seemed an impossibility. If a man had been trained to believe that circumcision was the very mark of God, it was very difficult of him to think of circumcision as something which was of no importance. The result is that he was always in danger of a relapse into legalism (Gal. 2:16; 3:2–5). The man who all his life has been intent on earning salvation finds it difficult to believe that he must accept salvation. He will be very apt, even, so to speak, for safety's sake, to add the old law to the new faith, and thereby by implication to deny the total adequacy of Jesus Christ.

(b) There was the danger of the relapse into astralism. It was an age when men were "servile to all the skyey influences" (S. Angus, *The Religious Quests of the Graeco-Roman World*, p. 254). Men were convinced of the power of the stars to settle their life and destiny. Astrology was "a learned superstition, which up to modern times has exercised over Asia and Europe a wider dominion than any religion has ever achieved" (F. Cumont, *Astrology and Religion*, p. xv). S. Angus begins the first of his chapters on Astralism (*op. cit.*, p. 254) by quoting Romans 8:39 in the form: "I am persuaded that neither the ascension of the stars nor their declinations shall be able to separate us from the love of God." It would be very difficult for a first-century man to break away from this background of thought. It is at least possible that it is to this that Paul refers when he says that the Galatians had once been slaves to the elemental spirits (Gal. 4:3), and when he tells the Colossians that with Christ they had died to these same spirits (Col. 2:20). When we remember the influence that astrology has on even the people of the twentieth century, we can understand its pull on the mind of the new converts of the first century.

Paul had to take steps to see that his converts did not relapse into legalism or astralism.

ii. The second danger was the danger of *syncretism*. Christianity entered the world in an intensely syncretistic age. It had been the avowed aim of Alexander the Great "to marry the East to the West". On the famous occasion at Susa he himself had married Statira, the eastern queen; a hundred of his officers, and ten thousand of his soldiers had married eastern brides (Arrian, *Anabasis* 7:4). The East was being literally married to the West. So the eastern religions came flooding into the West. Men could not believe that there was only one way to so great a goal, or only one possessor of so great a secret. Exclusiveness was something in religion which the ancient world, with the exception of the Jews, could not understand.

Further, there was a way of equating gods and goddesses with corresponding deities in other religions and in other countries. So Apuleius (*Metamorphoses* 11:5) hears Isis say:

> Parent of nature, mistress of all the elements, the first-born of the ages . . . whom the Phrygians adore as the Pessinuntian Mother of the gods, the Athenians as Minerva, the Cyprians as Venus, the Cretans as Dictynian Diana, the Sicilians as Proserpina, the Eleusinians as Demeter, others as Juno, or Bellona, others as Hecate or Rhamnusia, while the Egyptians and others honour me with my proper name of Queen Isis.

In a religious atmosphere like this it was not difficult to get a hearing for the story of Jesus. It was not even difficult to gain for him a place among the many saviour gods. But it was very difficult for people to think of him as the one and only Saviour. The necessary intolerance of Christianity was a difficult concept.

The echoes of this syncretistic controversy sound in the letter to the Colossians, with its insistence that Jesus is the very image of God, that in him there is the fulness of the godhead in bodily form (Col. 1:15–20; 2:9). That whole letter is taken up with the all-sufficiency of Jesus Christ. He is not one of many; he is the only one. He is not to be identified with anyone else; he is himself. It was impossible to play safe by adding him to the pantheon, so, as it were, not to miss a chance. Commitment to him meant the abandonment of all others.

In a syncretistic age Paul had to defend the uniqueness of Christ.

iii. The third danger was the danger of *the perversion of the faith.* A religion and ethic of legalism will not normally run into the danger of immorality. But there is a certain inherent danger in a religion of grace. A doctrine of grace can be perverted into an excuse, and even a reason, for sinning, and this happened in some of Paul's churches.

It is this perversion of grace which is in the background of Romans 6. That chapter is a kind of summary conversation between Paul and those who wished to misinterpret and misuse the conception of grace. The argument runs somewhat as follows. "So, then," they said to Paul, "you argue that grace is the greatest thing in the world?" "Most certainly," Paul answered. "You also argue that the grace of God is wide enough to forgive and cover every sin?" "Most certainly," Paul answered. "If that is so," they said, "let us go on sinning, for the more we sin, the more chances this wonderful grace of God will have to operate. Sin is a good thing, for the effect of sin is to produce more and more grace." "God will forgive," as Heine said. "It is his trade."

This is an argument which has emerged again and again in the history of the church, and it is an argument which has unconsciously or consciously affected many a man's life and action. Human nature being such as it is, it is an attractive argument. But in this argument, as Paul points out, two things have been forgotten. First, the obligation of grace has been forgotten. Any gift brings its obligation and the gift of grace does supremely so. Second, it has been forgotten that grace has a future as well as a past reference, that it has not only a forgiving power, but also a transforming power. Truly to experience grace is not only to experience forgiveness for the past, but also transformation for the future. The obligation and the transformation of grace are the answer to the perversion of grace.

So, then, in the protection of right belief Paul had within the church to take steps in his preaching to guard against the dangers of relapse, of syncretism and of perversion of the faith.

We began the section on Paul's preaching within the church by saying that it had two aims – to preserve right belief and right conduct, to maintain a true theology and a true ethic. We have looked at his preaching as it affects belief; we now turn to look at it as it affects conduct. We may say that Paul's teaching about right conduct falls into two sections – the conduct of the Christian within the church, and the conduct of the Christian outside the church.

First, then, we turn to Paul's ethical demands on those inside the church. They may be summed up under three heads.

(*a*) There is the demand for *unity*. This comes out most clearly in I Corinthians 11 and 12. The discussion emerges from the wrong way in which the Corinthians are treating the Christian common meal. That which should have been an experience and a demonstration of unity had become a thing of cliques and socially separated groups. The Christians should have been the body of Christ, and the body has been disintegrated and dismembered. Not to discern the body (1 Cor. 11:29) is to eat and drink in an unworthy way, and to lose the blessing of the sacrament. It is to be noted that the correct reading here is not, "not discerning the Lord's body," but, "not discerning the body." And the meaning is that, unless Christians discern their unity in Christ, they are not fit to approach the Lord's Table at all. Christians are a body; more, they are the body of Christ, and not to discern that unity is the most serious of sins.

(*b*) Closely allied with this is the demand that this unity must issue in *co-operation in service* (Rom. 12:4–8; 1 Cor. 12:27–30). Whatever gift a man has, he has received from God, and he must use it in the service of God and in the service of man. One man's gift will not be another man's gift. A man must accept himself as he is, and consent to use himself, and to be used. Only thus will the body of which he is a part function correctly.

(*c*) The third demand is also a closely allied demand; it is the demand for the awareness of *mutual responsibility*. This emerges most clearly in that enterprise which was most dear to the heart of Paul, the collection for the church at Jerusalem (2 Cor. 8 and 9). Here was a visible demonstration of the responsibility of the comfortable for the poor, of the Gentile for the Jew, of the new-comer for the veteran. Congregationalism in the narrower sense of the term was far from the mind of Paul. For him, not only the congregation, but also the whole church was one body, no part of which dare neglect the need of any other part.

The conception of the church as the body of Christ, the demand for unity, the demand for awareness of mutual responsibility, the demand for cooperation in service are for Paul the basis of right living within the church.

Second, we turn to Paul's demand for right living on the Christian in his life outside the church.

In every area of life the demand is the demand for *holiness*, but it is important to see what this holiness means and implies. The standard title for the Christians is "the saints" (cf. 1 Cor. 1:2; 2 Cor. 1:1; Eph. 1:1). The word is *hagios*, of which the basic meaning is *different*. That which is *hagios* is different. The temple was *hagios* because it was different from other buildings; the Bible is *hagios* because it is different from other books; God is *hagios* supremely because he is "the wholly other". So, then, the first demand, and the basic demand, is the demand for difference. But it has always to be remembered that that difference is to be expressed and worked out, not by withdrawal from the world, but by involvement in the world. Again and again it is the demand of Paul that the Christian should have a chastity and a charity and an honesty which are not to be found in the world in which he lived. Transformation not conformation, was the Pauline watchword (Rom. 12:2). There are few more difficult demands that can be made upon a man than the demand to be different, but this was Paul's basic demand on the Christian within the world.

We now turn to Paul's ethical teaching to the Christian in his life outside the church. Here there are three main areas, and we may take Paul's teaching regarding two of them together, because the principles are the same in both areas. These two areas are the family and work (Eph. 5:21–6:9; Col. 3:18–4:1). In these two areas three things may be said about Paul's ethical demand.

(*a*) In each case the ethic which Paul teaches and preaches is what can only be called a reciprocal ethic. That is to say, he never lays down a claim without at the same time laying down a duty. So the husband must receive the obedience and the respect of the wife, but he must give his love and care and consideration to the wife. The child must give the parent obedience and respect, but the parent must treat the child in such a way that the child will not be depressed and discouraged. The servant must give the master his best work, but the master must give the servant just and generous treatment. Always a privilege brings a responsibility. Always to have a claim on a person is to have that person have claim on us. Reciprocity is the key-word to this ethic of family and industry.

(*b*) Always Paul's ethical teaching is based on the recognition and acceptance of just and legitimate authority. It is built into the human situation that the husband exercises authority over the wife, the parent over the child, and the master over the workman. Paul sees life in terms of what might be called natural authorities. But it must be remembered that that authority gives no right to dominate and to tyrannize. It is, as we have seen, an authority the obverse of which is duty.

(*c*) It is always to be remembered that there is an eschatological element in the ethic which Paul teaches. The master must remember that he has a Master. All alike must do everything as if it were done for Christ. And at the end of the day there is judgment for every man (Rom. 14:10;

2 Cor. 5:10). There is a sanction which is more than an earthly sanction. There is destiny as well as there is life.

The third area on which Paul has instruction to give to his converts is with regard to the state (Rom. 13:1–7). Here again there enters into the matter the idea of subjection to a just and lawful and even divine authority. Paul makes it clear that Christianity and good citizenship go together. Only the bad man has any reason to fear the just magistrate.

There is one other thing which not only Paul but the whole New Testament preaches in regard to the duty of the Christian outside the church. Again and again it is laid down that the best propaganda for Christianity and the best sermon is the witness and the evidence of a Christian life (Col. 4:5, 6).

Paul's preaching to those outside the church was for commitment in faith to Jesus Christ, and his preaching inside the church was designed to maintain right belief and right action, which are the sign and the proof of that commitment.

CHAPTER XI

THE CONVERSION OF PAUL, AND ITS INFLUENCE ON HIS UNDERSTANDING OF SALVATION BY FAITH

JACQUES DUPONT, O.S.B.

This study was presented during a colloquium held at Rome, at the monastery of St. Paul-outside-the-Walls in April, 1968. The French text is due to appear in the series *Analecta Biblica*, published by the Biblical Institute of Rome. (The English translation was made by Ralph P. Martin).

THE TITLE OF MY ESSAY WILL RECALL THAT OF THE EXCELLENT STUDY, published in 1953, by Ph.-H. Menoud: "Révélation et tradition, L'influence de la conversion de Paul sur sa théologie."[1] In that article. as in the one which appeared in 1964 in the *Festschrift* for E. Haenchen,[2] Menoud thought that Paul's aberration while he was still a Pharisee and a persecutor of the church was to be found precisely in his messianic belief.[3] Paul was furious at seeing Christians identify the Messiah promised by God with an individual who was put to death on the cross as a man accursed by God. On the road to Damascus he then received the revelation that Jesus was indeed the Messiah who was promised to Israel; it is, therefore, a truly messianic revelation which led to his conversion. Beginning from that fact, Paul saw what was needful to reinterpret the shameful death of Jesus: in his office as Christ, he bore the curse which rested on sinners; his death was the price for human redemption. These explanations locate Paul's conversion in a change of mind which he underwent in regard to the Messiah. After he had passionately denied that a crucified man could be the Messiah, he came to grant that Jesus was indeed the Messiah and, as a consequence, re-thought all his messianic ideas.

The way in which Menoud thinks of Paul's conversion is found in other writers. It is very similar to the interpretation which M. Goguel had already proposed.[4] But it is not the only one to be considered.

---

[1] In *Verbum Caro* 7 (1953), pp. 2–10 = "Revelation and Tradition. The Influence of Paul's Conversion on his Theology", in *Interp* 7 (1953), pp. 131–41.

[2] "Le sens du verbe πορθεῖν. Gal. 1, 13, 23; Acts 9, 21" in *Apophoreta. Festschrift für Ernst Haenchen* (BZNW 30) (Berlin 1964), pp. 178–86.

[3] "When Paul speaks of his past life, he does not describe his conduct as a moral or spiritual failure but as an aberration concerning the Messiah," *loc. cit.*, p. 4 (ET, p. 134).

[4] M. Goguel, *Introduction au Nouveau Testament*, IV, 1 (Paris, 1925), pp. 183 f. *La naissance du christianisme*, Paris, 1946, pp. 99 ff. (ET *The Birth of Christianity* [London, 1953], pp. 81 ff.). Cf. A. D. Nock, *St. Paul* (London, 1938), p. 74; H. G. Wood, "The Conversion of St. Paul: Its Nature, Antecedents and Consequences," *NTS* 1 (1954–55), 276–282 (278).

Instead of being placed as an afterthought and regarded as a consequence, the transformation of Paul's soteriology can be set at the beginning and can become the immediate occasion of the revelation at Damascus. It is the Christian understanding of salvation by Christ which Paul had to deal with before his conversion, and the appearance at Damascus would have convinced him not only that Jesus was the Messiah but more precisely that he is the one on whom the salvation of all men depends.

The article published in 1959 (in *ZThK*) by U. Wilckens under the title "Die Bekehrung des Paulus als religionsgeschichtliches Problem"[1] follows this line. The author emphasizes that, according to Paul's own witness, it was his devotion to the Jewish law which turned him into a persecutor of Christians. The Jews' offence because of the Christian message is connected less with the affirmation of Jesus' messiahship than with the attributing to Jesus of a saving role which robbed the law of all its value in the purpose of salvation. Violently hostile to the Christian faith because of the importance which he attached to the law as a way of salvation, Paul was converted on the road to Damascus. He recognized in Christ the only principle of salvation to the exclusion of the law. Both before and after his conversion, faith in Christ seemed to him incompatible with faith in the law. The choice had to be made: Christ or the law. There could be no compromise. The dilemma presented itself in an essentially soteriological perspective. It was a question of knowing whether salvation came to men by Christ or by the law.

In brief, these are the two different views on Paul's conversion and the orientation which each gives to his theological thought. The title given to my paper indicates sufficiently the way in which, in my view, the matter should be tackled, as stated with succinctness by Wilckens.[2] I shall not deal further with the state of the debate, which has been comprehensively surveyed up to 1962 by B. Rigaux.[3]

I

My study relies on the witness of the epistles: in effect, 1 Corinthians, Galatians and Philippians. In view of the method to be followed, the

---

[1] *ZThK* 56 (1959), pp. 273–93. Cf. W. Pesch, "Die Bekehrung des Apostels Paulus nach dem Zeugnis seiner Briefe" in *Bibel und Kirche* 16 (1961), pp. 36–38.

[2] Wilckens adopts the thesis of D. Rössler according to which the apocalyptic circles would have had an understanding of the law which was different from that of the Pharisees and the rabbinical tradition. Paul would have shared the apocalyptic view. We must be satisfied to refer on this matter to the criticisms brought by A. Nissen, "Tora und Geschichte im Spätjudentum. Zu Thesen Dietrich Rösslers," *NovTest* 9 (1967), pp. 241–77.

[3] B. Rigaux, *Saint Paul et ses lettres* (Studia Neotest., Subsidia, 2) (Paris-Bruges, 1962), pp. 63–97.

M

refusal to summon the witness of Acts[1] and of 1 Timothy 1:12–14[2] need not be justified. It is preferable not to run together references from different backgrounds.

The texts to which appeal is made are often short and not very explicit. Two, however, are more developed, and I shall have to refer to them often in the course of my treatment. It will be useful to go over at once what these are.

1. In the opening of the epistle to the Galatians,[3] Paul is anxious to stress his apostolic authority; he, therefore, insists upon the divine origin of the mission with which he has been entrusted (1:1), and then he insists upon the divine origin of the gospel he preaches and proclaims to the Gentiles. This gospel had not come to him from men but as a revelation of Jesus Christ (verse 12). Verses 13–16 specify the circumstances of this revelation. Paul begins by recalling his manner of life as a Jew (verses 13–14);[4] he persecuted to the utmost God's church and laid it waste;[5] he was more advanced[6] in the Jewish faith than most of his contemporary fellow-Jews, being possessed of an outstanding zeal for the ancestral traditions. Taken together, these two verses lead us to suppose that there was a connexion between the violent animosity of Saul directed against the Christians and the fervour of his zeal for the traditions of Judaism.

Verses 15–16 speak of the change which then followed. The profound cause of this must be sought in the divine "good pleasure" ($\epsilon\dot{v}\delta o\kappa\acute{\iota}a$). Out of this wholly gracious goodwill, God had chosen Paul; he had set him apart from before his birth. This election resulted in a call. The one whom God had chosen was called by his grace.[7] The call was presented to Paul in the form of a manifestation of God's Son, as a "revelation"[8] which to a certain degree anticipated the glorious manifestation of the end-time. For Paul the revelation of the glory of God's Son was a call from God, a summons. It was granted to him with a view to a mission: "that I might proclaim him among the Gentiles." While the

---

[1] There is an excellent recent study by G. Lohfink, *Paulus vor Damaskus. Arbeitsweisen der neueren Bibelwissenschaft dargestellt an den Texten Apg 9, 1–19; 22, 3–21; 26, 9–18* (Stuttgarter Bibelstudien, 1) (Stuttgart, 1965) = *La conversion de saint Paul. Demonstration de la méthode récente des sciences bibliques à propos des textes (Actes, 9, 1–19; 22, 3–21; 26, 9–18) (Lire la Bible, 11)* (Paris, 1967).

[2] There is an analysis of this witness in G. Klein's *Die zwölf Apostel. Ursprung und Gehalt einer Idee* (FRLANT 77) (Göttingen, 1961), pp. 133–39.

[3] In addition to the commentaries (especially that of H. Schlier), we may mention the study we have made of Galatians 1–2, "Saint-Paul, témoin de la collégialité apostolique et de la primauté de saint Pierre" in *La Collégialité épiscopale. Histoire et Théologie* (Unam Sanctam, 52) (Paris, 1965), pp. 11–39.

[4] Cf. G. Klein, *Die zwölf Apostel*, pp. 128–32.

[5] On this verb, see the article by Ph.-H. Menoud cited on p. 176.

[6] On this verb, see G. Klein, *Die zwölf Apostel*, p. 130, n. 632.

[7] Paul was a recipient of "mercy": 1 Cor. 7:25; 2 Cor. 4:1.

[8] Cf. A.-M. Denis, "L'investiture de la fonction apostolique par 'apocalypse'. Etude thématique de Gal. 1, 16," *RB* 64 (1957), pp. 335–62 and 492–515, in addition to our observations on this article: "La révélation du Fils de Dieu en faveur de Pierre (Mt. 16, 17) et de Paul (Gal. 1, 16) " *RSR* 52 (1964), pp. 411–20.

text does not specify the thought, yet we may believe that insofar as he became the apostle of the Gentiles Paul found himself inevitably in conflict with the Jewish tradition which up to then had been so precious to him.

The sequel which developed emphasizes Paul's independence of those who were apostles before him. Although his gospel had not originated with them, they recognized its authenticity and confirmed by their sanction the message entrusted to Paul for the sake of the Gentiles.

2. Chapter 3 of the letter to the Philippians is marked by a controversial tack. I will avoid entering into those discussions which have plagued the interpretation of this section and, in particular, the precise identity of the enemies Paul deals with.[1]

The opening verses of the chapter indicate that these people wanted to induce the Philippian Christians to be circumcized.[2] In verse 3 Paul replies: "It is we Christians who are the circumcision; we have worship inspired by God's Spirit, and it is we who exult in Christ Jesus instead of reposing our trust in the flesh." In order to make his thought clear the apostle offers himself as an example. Because of the Philippians' affection for him the personal argument would no doubt be one which would surely appeal to them.

He begins by remarking that he possessed, before his conversion, all the advantages which his opponents were claiming in order to place their confidence in the flesh. Verses 5 and 6 list these advantages which fall into two groups. First, those which he owed to his birth.[3] He had been circumcized on the eighth day; he belonged to the nation of Israel, the tribe of Benjamin; he was a Hebrew, the son of a Hebrew father. Then, there are those advantages which arose from his personal conduct. In regard to the law, he was a Pharisee; in respect of zeal, a persecutor of the church; in regard to the righteousness demanded by the law, he showed himself beyond reproach.

Set against these advantages from a Jewish point of view, there is the "revolution" (in verses 7–11) which happened at the time of his conversion.[4] All that he attributes to his "active" life becomes sharply a "passive"; all that to him was "gain" or "profit" is seen as a "loss" according to the new set of values which had been revealed to him at that moment. Various

[1] This matter has recently been investigated with great care by J. Gnilka, "Die antipaulinische Mission in Philippi," *BZ* 9 (1965), pp. 258–76. We also may note W. Schmithals, "Die Irrlehrer des Philipperbriefes," *ZThK* 54 (1957), pp. 297–341; H. Koester, "The Purpose of the Polemic of a Pauline Fragment (Philippians III)," *NTS* 8 (1961–62), pp. 317–32; (P. Feine, J. Behm) W. G. Kümmel, *Einleitung in das neue Testament* (Heidelberg, 1963), pp. 239–41 (ET *Introduction to the New Testament* [London, 1966], pp. 235–7); V. P. Furnish, "The Place and Purpose of Philippians III," *NTS* 10 (1963–64), pp. 80–88; A. F. J. Klijn, "Paul's opponents in Philippians III," *NovTest* 7 (1964), pp. 278–84.
[2] J. Gnilka, *art. cit.*, p. 261.
[3] Cf. 2 Cor. 11:22. See Gnilka, pp. 262 ff.
[4] See Gnilka, *art. cit.*, pp. 264–73.

expressions describe this set of values which finds its highest boon in the knowledge of Jesus Christ,[1] or in gaining Christ, or being found in him as the possessor of a righteousness which is not gained by the practice of the law but which comes from God through faith in Christ. And, finally (vv. 10–11) it means "to know Christ and the power of his resurrection" which implies "fellowship in his sufferings,[2] being conformed to his death" with an eye to attaining the "resurrection of the dead". This is the new perspective which came to Paul and which caused him to treat as "filth" all that he had previously boasted of as a Jew.

It should be observed that, in this explanation, contrary to that given in the epistle to the Galatians, Paul does not view the Damascus event in relation to his apostolic mission. He describes it as a discovery of that which contains the pith of Christianity and is therefore true for every Christian. This viewpoint was evidently dictated to him by the teaching he wishes to give to the Philippians; they must realise that the place held by Christ in the Christian faith transforms into its opposite that which seemed advantageous from the Jewish point of view.

Verses 12–14 add a third consideration to the two antithetical statements of verses 4–6 and 7–11. The movement of thought[3] matches very well that in the epistle to the Romans, where chapter 5 complements the antithetic statements of 1:18–3:20 and 3:21–4:25; and the last part of chapter 8 (vv. 18–39) comes after the antithesis which sets the administration of the law (7:7–25) against that of the Spirit (8:1–17).[4] The Christian's state is defined not only by contrast with the state of man under the law's regime. It must be understood equally and so essentially as a "not yet"; it is the state of expectation and hope in the face of eschatological fulfilment. The Christian finds himself in a state of tension set up between what he has already received and what remains the object of his hope. To explain this, verses 12–14 appeal to the athletic imagery of running a race. The verbs λαμβάνω and καταλαμβάνω quite naturally favour the imagery, having to do with "receiving a prize" and "laying hold on a trophy".[5] τελειοῦμαι should be taken in this context as "reaching the winning-post".[6] So we can translate verse 12: "Not that I have already carried off

---

[1] We may call attention to J. T. Forestell, "Christian Perfection and Gnosis in Phil. 3, 7–16," *CBQ* 18 (1956), pp. 123–36.

[2] See B. M. Ahern, "The Fellowship of his Sufferings (Phil. 3, 10)," *CBQ* 22 (1960), pp. 1–32.

[3] Cf. G. Bouwman, *De brief van Paulus aan de Filippiërs* (Het N.T.) (Roermond-Maaseik, 1965), pp. 81 f.

[4] Cf. J. Dupont, "Le problème de la structure littéraire de l'Epître aux Romains," *RB* 62 (1955), pp. 365–97.

[5] After καταλαμβάνω there is no occasion to supply δικαιοσύνην as Klijn has proposed, *NovTest* (1964), p. 281.

[6] Cf. J. Huby, *Saint Paul. Les Epîtres de la Captivité* (Verbum Salutis, VIII), 14th ed. (Paris, 1947), p. 351; J. Dupont, *Le Discours de Milet, testament pastoral de saint Paul* (Actes 20, 18–36) (Lectio divina 32) (Paris, 1962), pp. 98–101; G. Delling, art. τελειόω *TWNT* VIII (fasc. 2. 1965), p. 85; F. W. Danker, "Romans V. 12: Sin under the Law," *NTS* 14 (1967–68), pp.

the prize or yet reached the winning-line, but I am pressing on, endeavouring to lay hold on the prize, since I have myself been laid hold on by Christ Jesus." The goal to which Paul bends his efforts is that described in the previous verses: to know Christ and the power of his resurrection. to arrive at (through suffering and death) the resurrection of the dead, which is a sharing in the glorious state of the risen Christ. Paul's path to this goal starts from a being "laid hold on" by Christ: Christ seized him as an athlete lays hold on the prize of his victory.[1] If Paul is now on the race track, as he describes it in verses 13-14, he has to thank this "start" which came with the Damascus event.

We can pass on more quickly to the rest of the chapter. At verse 17, Paul invites the Philippians to find their example in him in contrast to the people who preach circumcision and behave as enemies of the cross of Christ (vv. 18-19). Verses 20-21 return to the Christian hope. Christians are awaiting their salvation in the glorious coming of their Saviour, the Lord Jesus Christ who will transform our lowly bodies and conform them to his body of glory.[2] We must ask whether it is not necessary here, as in verse 12, to have in mind the revelation of the Damascus road. The salvation spoken of in verse 20 matches that which Paul had seen realistically when God showed his Son to him.

This is the text on which I rely, along with Galatians 1, in seeking to pinpoint the theological thought of Paul before his conversion and the revolution which Christ's appearance occasioned for him.

II

Martin Dibelius, I should agree, is correct when he says that, if one is to gain a true meaning of Paul's experience on the Damascus road, it is necessary right away to understand the motive which made him, according to his own witness, a persecutor of Christians.[3] That my essay is devoted particularly to what Paul tells about his attitude before his conversion need then occasion no surprise. First of all, we are struck by the way Paul describes his spiritual state when he was a Pharisee; then, he speaks of "zeal" which made him a persecutor of the church. We shall inquire, next, whether his way of speaking of the scandal of the cross throws light on his past life as a Jew. We conclude with an attempt to see how his

[1] Cf. J. Huby, *Les Epîtres de la Captivité*, p. 352.
[2] Like Phil. 2:6-11; cf. N. Flanagan, "A Note on Philippians 3, 20-21," *CBQ* 18 (1956), pp. 8-9.
[3] M. Dibelius-W. G. Kümmel, *Paulus* (Sammlung Göschen, 1160) (Berlin, 1951), p. 46 (ET *Paul* [London, 1953], p. 46).

424-39 (433). In making the sporting metaphor begin with v. 12 we are in agreement with K. Barth, *Erklärung des Philipperbriefes* 6th ed. (Zürich, 1947), p. 106 (ET *The Epistle to the Philippians* [London, 1962], p. 106) against V. C. Pfitzner, *Paul and the Agon Motive. Traditional Athletic Imagery in the Pauline Literature* (Suppl. NovTest XVI) (Leiden, 1967), pp. 139-53, who makes the metaphor begin at v. 13.

account of the Damascus experience throws light on what were the consequences of the event for his theological thought.

A. Saul, the Pharisee

A number of features of Pharisaic theology provided Paul with reasons for being satisfied with himself.

1. He emphasizes, at the start, the pride which membership of the elect race gave him: "of the race of Israel, of the tribe of Benjamin, a Hebrew son of Hebrew parents" (Phil. 3:5; cf. 2 Cor. 11:22 and Rom. 11:1). The description of Galatians 2:15 is even more to the point: "We who are Jews by birth and not these Gentile sinners." While Gentiles, by their state, are sinners and "children of wrath" (Eph. 2:3), Jews, because of the election and thanks to the fathers, are loved by God (Rom. 11:28). And later, when he had become a Christian and apostle to the Gentiles, Paul would remain deeply convinced of Israel's prerogatives: "To them belong the filial adoption, the glory, the covenants, the law-code, the cult, the promises; to them also belong the fathers, and it was from them, in natural descent, that the Christ was born" (Rom. 9:4-5). These verses are evidence of the beliefs in which Paul was schooled, his pride as an Israelite, and the confidence he drew from them in God's presence.[1]

2. Within the elect nation Paul was aware of belonging to a spiritual élite: he was a Pharisee. "Concerning the matters of the law, a Pharisee" (Phil. 3:5), i.e. adhering to the most strict and rigorous obedience (cf. Acts 22:3; 26:5; likewise 23:6) and most firmly attached not only to the letter of the law but to the ancestral traditions (cf. Gal. 1:14) which spelled out the meaning of the law and protected its observance as though by a hedge of complementary prescriptions.[2]

3. That was not all. Paul was a fanatic among fanatics. Without wishing to compare himself with the great teachers, he notes with satisfaction that he was "more advanced in the Jewish religion than many of his fellow contemporaries" (Gal. 1:14). He stood out from others by an exceptional zeal ($\pi\epsilon\rho\iota\sigma\sigma\sigma\tau\acute{\epsilon}\rho\omega\varsigma$).

4. Philippians 3:6 gives the last word: "concerning the righteousness according to the law, found to be beyond reproach" ($\kappa\alpha\tau\grave{\alpha}\ \delta\iota\kappa\alpha\iota\sigma\sigma\acute{\nu}\nu\eta\nu$ $\tau\grave{\eta}\nu\ \dot{\epsilon}\nu\ \nu\acute{\omega}\mu\wp\ \gamma\epsilon\nu\acute{\omega}\mu\epsilon\nu\sigma\varsigma\ \ddot{\alpha}\mu\epsilon\mu\pi\tau\sigma\varsigma$).[3] The exertion with which he observed scrupulously the law's prescriptions, interpreted in their most

---

[1] Cf. K. H. Schelkle, "Paulus vor Damaskus" in *Bibel und Leben* 8 (1967), pp. 153-7 (154).

[2] On the connection between law and tradition in the Judaism of the first century, see W. G. Kümmel, "Jesus und der jüdische Traditionsgedanke", *ZNTW* 33 (1934), pp. 105-30 (116-18) =*Heilsgeschehen und Geschichte. Gesammelte Aufsätze 1933-1964* (Marburger theologische Studien, 3) (Marburg, 1965), pp. 15-35 (24 ff.).

[3] Cf. M. Goguel, "$\kappa\alpha\tau\grave{\alpha}\ \delta\iota\kappa\alpha\iota\sigma\sigma\acute{\nu}\nu\eta\nu\ \tau\grave{\eta}\nu\ \dot{\epsilon}\nu\ \nu\acute{\omega}\mu\wp\ \gamma\epsilon\nu\acute{\omega}\mu\epsilon\nu\sigma\varsigma\ \ddot{\alpha}\mu\epsilon\mu\pi\tau\sigma\varsigma$ (Phil. 3, 6). Remarques sur un aspect de la conversion de Paul", *JBL* 53, (1934), pp. 257-67. See too W. Grundmann, art. $\mu\acute{\epsilon}\mu\phi\omega\mu\alpha\iota$, *TWNT* IV (1942), pp. 576-78 (ET *TDNT* IV, 1967, pp. 573-4).

rigid sense, led him to attain a perfection which was without lapse or defect.

In all the evidence none is found which expresses a recollection of his being restless, tortured by an unattainable ideal. As he saw himself, Paul was, at the eve of his conversion, a man well satisfied, contented with his membership of the elect race and of an élite group of his people, and confident of attaining by his religious observance an ideal of righteousness which would make him beyond reproach in the eyes of God, men and his own conscience.

It does not seem necessary to comment on the fact that one cannot succeed in opposing against this perfectly clear witness the description which Romans 7 gives of the wretched state of a sinful man under the law's regime. It is admitted, since the dissertation which W. G. Kümmel published in 1929,[1] that we should not look for, in this passage, the reverberation of an experience Paul underwent in Judaism. It is rather the reflection of a Christian theologian who is meditating on the mystery of sin with the experience of redemption as his starting-point. I am glad on this point to refer to the works of Fr. Lyonnet[2] and to a recent article by J. Blank.[3]

B. The Zeal of the Persecutor

1. Paul associates the violence with which he had persecuted the church with the "zeal" which motivated him at that time. There is a link between his passion to keep the law in an irreproachable way and the ardour with which he opposed primitive Christianity. In Philippians 3:6, after he has given his rank as a Pharisee to prove his attachment to the law ("concerning the law, a Pharisee") he adds: "concerning zeal, persecuting the church" (κατὰ ζῆλος, διώκων τὴν ἐκκλησίαν). One can see in his activity as persecutor the display and proof of his "zeal". Galatians 1:13–14 says the same thing. In persecuting murderously and working havoc on the church of God, Paul showed to what remarkable degree he was ζηλωτής, full of zeal for the tradition which he inherited from his ancestors. We see here that the zeal found its real objective in "the traditions of the ancestors" which, on the understanding of the Pharisees, formed the whole of the religious scheme of Judaism with the law as the basis but

---

[1] W. G. Kümmel, *Römer 7 und die Bekehrung des Paulus* (Untersuchungen zum *NT*, 17) (Leipzig, 1929). Cf. R. Bultmann, *Theologie des Neuen Testaments* (Neue theologische Grundrisse), (Tübingen, 1953), p. 185 (ET *Theology of the New Testament*, vol. 1 [London, 1952], p. 188). For the different interpretations given to this chapter, see the excursus "Zur Geschichte der Auslegung von Röm 7, 7–25" in O. Kuss, *Der Römerbrief* II (Ratisbon, 1959), pp. 462–85.

[2] S. Lyonnet in J. Huby-S. Lyonnet, *Saint Paul. Epître aux Romains* (Verbum Salutis, X), 2nd ed. (Paris, 1957), pp. 601–04; "L'histoire du salut selon le chapitre VII de l'Epître aux Romains" in *Bib* 43 (1962), pp. 117–51.

[3] J. Blank, "Der gespaltene Mensch. Zur Exegese von Röm 7:7–25" in *Bibel und Leben*, 9 (1968), pp. 10–20. See too P. Grelot, "Péché originel et rédemption dans l'Epître aux Romains", *NRT* 90 (1968), pp. 449–62.

inseparable from the traditions which interpreted and complemented it.[1] So one can appreciate that it was Paul's devotion to the law in its entirety which made him a persecutor hostile to the Christian church.

It is not without interest to observe how the same mode of expression is found in Acts 22:3-4 in the speech of Paul to the inhabitants of Jerusalem when they gathered against him: "At the feet of Gamaliel I was trained in the punctilious observance of the law of our fathers and was full of *zeal for God*, just like all of you today: I persecuted this Way [Christianity] to death, binding and casting into prison both men and women." What made Paul a persecutor was his zeal for God,[2] his ardent devotion to the law given to the fathers and observed with "exactitude" by the Pharisees.

2. To throw light on what Paul says of his "zeal"[3] in relation to his activities as a persecutor, it is helpful to turn to 1 Maccabees 2. Messengers of Antiochus Epiphanes have been sent to the small town of Modin to organize an idolatrous sacrifice and to compel the people to commit apostasy. Mattathias proudly declares that he will not obey the king's commands: "As for me, my sons and my brothers, we will stand by the covenant of our fathers. God will save us from surrendering the law and the ordinances" (vv. 20, 21). But not everyone shows the same determination: a Jew approaches the altar to make sacrifice: "When Mattathias saw it, he burned with zeal and his heart was stirred. He gave vent to righteous anger; he ran and killed him upon the altar. At the same time he killed the king's officer who was forcing them to sacrifice, and he tore down the altar. Thus he burned with zeal for the law, as Phinehas did against Zimri the son of Salu. Then Mattathias cried out in the city with a loud voice, saying: 'Let every one who is zealous for the law and supports the covenant come out with me!' And he and his sons fled to the hills and left all that they had in the city. Then many who were seeking righteousness and justice went down to the wilderness to dwell there" (1 Macc. 2. 24-29, RSV).

This scene is characteristic. The attitude of Mattathias himself is inspired by his fervent devotion to the law. His zeal for the law becomes devastating wrath when he sees an Israelite committing an act of apostasy. In commending Mattathias' exploit, the narrator does not shirk from comparing it to that of Phinehas who, in the Bible, is the prototype of zeal. Phinehas was the priest who, at Shittim, killed with a thrust of a spear the Israelite and the Midianite woman who were indulging in sacred prostitution. This outstanding proof of zeal secured for him the promise of a priesthood which could never be lost to him or his descendants. (Cf. Num. 25:1-18; Ps. 106:31; Ecclus. 45:23; 1 Macc. 2:26,54; 4 Macc. 18:12.)

---

[1] See W. G. Kümmel in the work quoted on p. 182.

[2] In Rom. 10:2 Paul recognizes that the Jews have a zeal for God, but it is an unenlightened zeal. They are concerned simply to establish their own righteousness.

[3] Full survey of these texts in A. Stumpff's article, ζῆλος *TWNT* II (1935), pp. 879-90 (ET *TDNT* II, 1964, pp. 878-88). This article should be complemented by the evidence drawn from the *Testament of the Twelve Patriarchs* and the Qumran texts.

We should observe that alongside Phinehas the Bible quotes other examples of zeal. The prophet Elijah gave evidence of zeal when at Horeb he called for vengeance on the enemies of God (1 Ki. 19:10, 14; Ecclus. 48:2; 1 Macc 2:58); king Jehu, when he slaughtered all the family of the ungodly Ahab (2 Ki. 10:16); and the patriarch Simeon himself, who showed his zeal in slaughtering the inhabitants of Shechem (Jud. 9:4).

The close of chapter 2 in 1 Maccabees contains the speech of Mattathias to his sons before his death. It is above all an exhortation to give proof of "zeal": "Be zealous for the law, my children, and give your lives for the covenant of our fathers" (v. 50). He recalls the great examples of the past, in particular of those to do with zeal, examples of Phinehas (v. 54) and Elijah (v. 58).[1]

This chapter of Maccabees enables us to understand better the nature of Paul's religious zeal in regard to the law and the ancestral traditions. At the same time it enables us to grasp the reason for the zeal which made him a persecutor of Christianity. His conduct makes it clear that Christianity seemed to him to be apostasy in regard to the law, and the Christian faith to be a denial of his ideal of the strict observance of the law's requirements. He sought to uproot Christ's religion because he had a conviction that it was incompatible with the religion of the law and with the place he accorded to the law in the plan of salvation.

To judge by Acts 21:20-21, the reaction of Saul the Pharisee to Christianity would therefore seem similar enough to the reaction of Jewish Christians of Jerusalem to Paul's teaching. James forewarned Paul, on his arrival at Jerusalem, of the danger he was running. There were in the city myriads of Jews who had become believers, but they continued zealous for the law (ζηλωταὶ τοῦ νόμου). Moreover, they had heard it said that Paul induced the Jews of the Dispersion to defect from Moses, no longer to have their children circumcized and no longer to follow the traditional customs. If Paul had not found a way of quashing these rumours, the fanaticism of Jewish Christians would have turned upon him just as his own fanaticism at an earlier time had led to his persecuting the Christians. Their faith had seemed to him to be at odds with fidelity to the law.

3. An objection must be considered here.[2] It does not seem, in fact, that the early Christians had so soon reached a conviction concerning the radical disparity between their faith in Christ and the attachment which they continued to show to the law. The disparity did not show itself until much later, thanks to the penetration of Paul's teaching itself. The notions which the believers had originally cannot have been very different from those of

---

[1] We may observe too *Test. Asher* 4:5 where it is the good people who give the impression of being fierce, "but in everything they are pure because they are inspired by a zeal for the Lord in abstaining from the things which God hates and are forbidden by the commandments"; 1QH 14:14: "I am full of zeal against all the workers of iniquity and the men of deceit."

[2] Cf. U. Wilckens, *Die Bekehrung*, pp. 278-81.

the Jewish Christians mentioned by James to Paul on the occasion of the latter's final visit to the holy city. It is thus a weak explanation that Paul's zeal for the law made him a persecutor of Christians at a time when there were those who did not think that their faith in Christ should call in question their fidelity to Judaism. If we grant that Paul was able in those earlier years to imagine the conflict which was certain to be produced in the later time, does this not credit him with an unlikely prescience?

To avoid this difficulty while doing justice to Paul's witness, Wilckens proposes that Paul had a conception of the law which was different from that of rabbinic theology and which had links with the theological tradition of apocalyptic. Other solutions, less hazardous,[1] have been proposed. I will content myself with three observations on this matter:

(a) We should not forget that Paul wrote twenty years after the events. It would be normal for these ideas to be more precise than they were at the time of which he speaks.

(b) As far back as we can trace, the Christian faith attributed a redeeming value to Jesus' death. Wilckens has no difficulty in granting that Paul would know an interpretation which considered the death and resurrection as acts of God "for us," for men's salvation.[2] This salvation, available by grace, is therefore independent of the law.

(c) Wilckens does not take account of a fact on which several authors, Bultmann especially,[3] insist, namely, the fact that Paul was brought into contact with the Christian faith through the mediation of the Hellenistic community. What exactly do we know of the thought of "Hellenistic-Christians"? It would not perhaps be wise to evaluate them solely by Stephen's speech in Acts 7. In any case, one matter is not in doubt: they were Christians who founded the church at Antioch at a date which must be close to that of Paul's conversion. The community at Antioch was very quickly distinguished by the

---

[1] See above, p. 127.

[2] Wilckens observes, to begin with (p. 280): "Since then the synoptic tradition in its entirety, and more especially Luke and John in their particular way, see the real scandal of the Jews in regard to Jesus in his messianic pretension as such, and consequently proclaim the recognition of Jesus' messiahship as the decisive factor in the conversion to Christianity, Paul made *the* scandal of the Jews when faced with the gospel the fact that the law had lost its worth in salvation history; and consequently he proclaimed, as the pith of what messiahship means, the death and resurrection of Jesus seen as a saving action of God ὑπὲρ ἡμῶν, i.e. for all men, both Jews and Gentiles."

Guided by a remark of G. Bornkamm (in *Das Ende des Gesetzes*, 2nd. ed. [Munich, 1958], p. 40), Wilckens adds this significant comment: "The title of Messiah/Christ does not at all in Paul mean the messiahship of Jesus as such. Nearly always he uses the term Χριστός in the kerygmatic formulae which show the death and resurrection of the Messiah in their saving significance – i.e. where the sense is always determined by this ὑπὲρ ὑμῶν which points to salvation history" (*ibid.*). The point at issue is to discover the perspective characteristic of Paul. Wilckens has shown himself ready to follow the idea that "ancient kerygmatic formulae were already speaking, often by reference to Isa. 53, of the death of Christ 'for us' " (p. 281). But, before Paul, no one had drawn the conclusions which followed in regard to the law. The first Christians had not forged a link between their christology and the question of the law.

[3] *Theologie des neuen Testaments*, pp. 184 ff. (ET *Theology of the New Testament*, pp. 187 ff.).

presence of Christians who were Gentiles by extraction and untouched by either circumcision or Jewish observances. It would not be rash to conclude that the Hellenistic Christians from whom Paul had known the Christian message had ideas on the subject of the law less orthodox from a Jewish point of view. Otherwise, how would they have been able to arrive at the conviction that faith in Christ was enough to make a person a member of the community of salvation, without it being necessary to maintain the practice of the law? Surely this aids our understanding of the devoted attachment of Paul to the law which turned him into a persecutor of Christianity.

C. The Stumbling-Block of the Cross

The conclusion we have so far reached may seem negative enough: before his conversion Paul thought of Christianity as incompatible with the religion devoted to the law. One would like to know more directly the estimate he passed on the Christian message. That estimate will be clarified when we see what he wrote on the matter of the stumbling-block of the cross.

The texts to be examined fall into two groups. First of all, there are those which locate the scandal of the cross in the difficulty which it made for the belief that Jesus was the Messiah. Menoud depends on these texts in his presentation of the conversion of Paul as a commitment to the teaching concerning Jesus' messiahship. There are also other texts in which the cross of Christ appears as a scandal for the Jews in its antithesis to circumcision, that is to say, insofar as the cross rendered useless both circumcision and the observance of the law as a way of salvation. In these texts the cross is seen in its saving significance. We shall examine these texts and inquire which have most to teach us on the conviction of Paul before his conversion.

1. The first group is represented by two very important passages: Galatians 3:10-14 and 1 Corinthians 1:17-24.

I cannot do better than quote Menoud who explains the Galatians passage thus:

> Saul was dominated by a zeal for God when he persecuted those who believed in Jesus. For him Christians were simply impostors, because Jesus could not be the Messiah. In Paul's view and in the eyes of every Jew, a crucified Messiah was a stumbling-block, a contradiction in terms. According to the prevailing expectation, Messiah would appear suddenly in power and glory to wind up the present age and establish the kingdom of God. But Jesus had been condemned not only by the highest authorities within Judaism but even by God himself who had allowed

him to suffer a most shameful death and to fall under the sentence of the law: "Cursed is anyone who hangs on the tree" (Deut. 21:23, quoted in Gal. 3:13).[1]

My problem concerns the use of this text to arrive at an understanding of Paul's thought when he was still an adherent of Judaism. Galatians 3:10 is used as a warning. If the Galatians accept circumcision, they must then observe all the requirements of the law[2] – or else they will bring down on themselves the curse imposed by the law on those who do not observe it in its entirety. This way of regarding the law as an agency of curse puts it in a perspective which is not exactly the same as that which Paul has in mind when he refers to his convictions before his conversion. Verses 11 and 12 set the "law" against "faith", the life which the law brings to those who observe it and the life which is promised by faith without regard to all observance. It is clear that Paul is here referring to the Christian concept of "faith". Verse 13 goes on: "Christ has redeemed us from the law's curse by becoming himself a curse for us." The belief that Christ has taken on himself the curse of the law is not to be divorced from the way in which verse 10 presents the law as an agency of curse in contrast to verse 14 which speaks of the blessing which comes from the promise made to Abraham.[3]

It seems to me, therefore, that these verses in Galatians must be understood as the reflections of a Christian theologian. It would not be wise to seek in them an evidence of how Paul thought when he was once a Pharisee and zealous for the law.

The other text to consider is 1 Corinthians 1:17–24, the *locus classicus* on the scandal of the cross. At verse 17 Paul remarks that his mission is to proclaim the gospel and to do it without reliance on the σοφία λόγου – the wisdom of speech – which reduced the cross of Christ to nothing. Verses 18–21 underscore the fact that the message of the cross appears as folly, i.e. since the world was not able to know God by its wisdom, God was pleased (in his own wisdom) to save those who believe, and to save them by the folly of the message (of the cross). Up to verse 21, we should note, it is only a matter of the *message* of the cross, set over against the wis-

---

[1] *Révélation et tradition* p. 4 (ET "Revelation and Tradition", p. 133).

[2] Cf. Gal. 5:3.

[3] The interpretation of Gal. 3:10–14 must obviously take account of the full exposition to which these verses belong. First, verses 6–14 form a unity and set the blessing linked with Abraham's faith over against the curse linked with the law. On a broader scale, in chapter 3 as a whole, Paul wants to show that righteousness is given not by the law but by faith (vv. 1–5 argue from the absurd; vv. 6–14 argue from the Scripture; vv. 15–29 argue on legal grounds, drawing upon arrangements under a will and testament). The same attention to the full explanation is needed in Rom. 4.

Nothing stands in the way of the view, supported by G. Jeremias, *Der Lehrer der Gerechtigkeit* (Studien zur Umwelt des NT, 2) [Göttingen, 1963], pp. 133–35 on the basis of 4 QpNah 7–8 that the exegesis of Deut. 21:23 in Gal. 3:13 is inspired by an interpretation adopted from Jewish circles. But it should not be forgotten that this feature is part of a theological argument completely foreign to Judaistic thought.

dom of men; verses 22–24 graft on the idea of the *stumbling-block* of the cross. While the Jews ask for signs – striking manifestations of God's power – and the Greeks seek for wisdom, we proclaim a Christ who is crucified, a scandal for the Jews and folly for the Greeks, but for those who are called, Jews and Greeks, the power of God and the wisdom of God.

Paul then speaks of the stumbling-block of the Jews over against the message of a crucified Christ. To imagine that this scandal arose simply from the contrast between this message and the Jewish hope of a Messiah whose coming would be attended by an impressive show of divine power would surely lead us to think that Paul was making appeal here to his personal experience and to convictions which inspired him before his conversion; but we cannot grant that the passage has any autobiographical character or that the portrayal of the Jew scandalized by the cross of Christ gives the impression of being patterned on the description of the Greek who regarded the message of the cross as folly. It would be difficult to look to this development of detailed teaching for the state of Paul's mind before his conversion.

2. Three other texts on the interpretation of the scandal of the cross point in a different direction. The scandal arises from the saving significance of the cross as a substitute in place of the law as a way of salvation.

We begin with Galatians 5:11: "As for me, brethren, if I am still preaching circumcision why am I still being persecuted? What has then become of the scandal of the cross?" Paul is exposed to persecution because he did not preach circumcision. He accepted the scandal of the cross, which was a scandal in the eyes of his persecutors because it stood over against circumcision, because it did away with the entire need of circumcision and, most of all, the requirements of the law.[1] The element in Paul's preaching which offended his enemies was not specifically that a crucified man was presented as the Messiah, but the statement that righteousness and salvation depended on that death of Christ on the cross, and that for righteousness and salvation a person could not turn to the observance of the law. For this reason Christianity seemed to them to strike a blow at the basic tenet of Judaism. In the motives which Paul attributes to his persecutors, he is clearly recognizing the same motives as those which had turned him into a persecutor of the church.

The conclusion of the letter, Galatians 6:12–16, strikes the same note. Verse 12 describes the attitude of those who wanted to win over the Galatians to this practice of circumcision. They hoped thereby to avoid being persecuted for the sake of the cross of Christ. The Jews, therefore, persecuted the Christians because of the cross of Christ; specifically because the

---

[1] "Περιτομή und σταυρός stehen sich für ihn als einander ausschliessende Mittel und Zeichen des Heiles entgegen, wobei die περιτομή natürlich der Inbegriff des Gesetzes und also der heilswirksamen gesetzlichen Leistung und des gesetzlich erworbenen Vorzuges ist": H. Schlier, *Der Brief an die Galater*[10] (Meyer, VI) (Göttingen, 1949), p. 173 [12th ed., pp. 239–40, Edd.].

cross of Christ led Christians no longer to place a value on circumcision (and legal observances as a whole). Verse 13 remarks that Paul's enemies were not really concerned about the law. They did not fulfil it themselves; they wanted simply to make a good appearance to the Jews in order to deflect their hatred. At verse 14 Paul explicitly repudiates this tactic for he wants to boast only in the cross of our Lord Jesus Christ. He goes on (vv. 15–16): circumcision counts for nothing, uncircumcision counts for nothing: what matters is being a new creature and being a member of the Israel of God. This passage shows again that the Jewish persecutors found fault with the cross because it was at odds not with their Messianic teaching but with circumcision. The cross made circumcision useless. There was a radical opposition between the Christian faith centering in the redeeming mystery of the cross and the Jewish teaching of the necessity of circumcision and the practice of the law for salvation. It should be noted that what Paul here says of the motive which turned the Jews into persecutors of Christianity harmonizes remarkably with what he says of zeal for the law as the motive of his hostility to the church before his conversion.

I conclude by reverting to Philippians 3. At verse 3 Paul has stated that we Christians are the true circumcision and we find our confidence in Christ Jesus instead of putting our confidence in the flesh. Verses 18–19 bring a charge which is aimed at people who "behave as enemies of the cross of Christ" and "who find their confidence in their shame". We recall the contrast in the Epistle to the Galatians between the Jewish (or Judaizing) practice of boasting in circumcision and the Christian position, which establishes its pride solely upon Christ and Christ's cross. They who preach circumcision act as "enemies of the cross of Christ"; they make out that Christ's cross is not enough to save. Before his conversion, Paul belonged to these "enemies of the cross of Christ", undoubtedly because he had already concluded that the value placed by Christians on the cross was at odds with the role which Judaism accorded to circumcision and the observance of the law for the securing of righteousness and salvation.

We can conclude by stating that these last texts relating to the Jews' scandal when faced with the cross agree well enough with other verses in which Paul speaks of his own "zeal" in persecuting the church. Judaism rested entirely on the conviction that the observance of the law by itself could secure salvation. The Christian faith destroyed this foundation by the saving interpretation it gave to the mystery of Christ's cross. To judge from the epistles, it is exactly in this interpretation that the motive of Paul's hostility to early Christianity is to be sought.

We may note yet again that Paul's foresight is perhaps surprising. At the time when he persecuted the Christians, most of them did not appear to have understood the fatal blow which their theology of the cross would strike at Judaism. It must at least be conceded that the Christian church was already in possession of this teaching. It is sufficient to recall here the studies of Jeremias and Lohse[1] on the ancient confession of faith in 1 Corinthians 15 which affirmed that Christ "died for our sins according to the scriptures" (v. 3) and to recall also the traditional liturgical form of 1 Corinthians 11:24 which related how, at the Last Supper, Jesus had apprised his disciples that he would be delivered up for them: ὑπὲρ ὑμῶν, "for you".

In attaching a redemptive meaning to the sacrifice of the cross, Christianity was unable to avoid entering into conflict with the Jewish soteriology, based on the law. We can by this explain the fury with which Paul at the start reacted against the Christian faith in the name of his devotion to the law.

D. The Appearance at Damascus

After having investigated at length the question of the reason why Paul persecuted the church before his conversion, I can now deal quickly with the information which he rather summarily gives us about the event which transformed his life and made him an apostle of Jesus Christ. It seems to me that four observations should be made.

1. The first remark is that Paul confesses to *having seen* Jesus, our Lord (1 Cor. 9:1). Christ appeared to him (1 Cor. 15:8).[2] He ranks this appearance after those which Jesus made after his resurrection to those persons who had been his disciples during his earthly ministry. He thus regards himself as belonging to the group of witnesses to the resurrection of Christ.[3]

The Acts of the Apostles tells what happened when he came near Damascus. Paul was surrounded by a light from heaven (9:3; 22:6); he saw this light brighter than the sun, shining around him and his travel companions (26:13). Falling to the ground, he then heard a voice (9:4; 22:7; 26:14). But the three accounts apparently suggest that Paul did not see who it was who spoke to him. This Lukan picture cannot silence the witness, both clear and unmistakable, which Paul himself gives that he had really seen Jesus.

2. We must next observe that the Christ who showed himself to Paul did so in an *irresistible way*. This fact is already clear in the figure of speech in

---

[1] Cf. J. Jeremias, *Die Abendmahlsworte Jesu*[3] (Göttingen, 1960), pp. 95–97, 160 ff., 188, 218–23 (ET *The Eucharistic Words of Jesus*, second ed. [London, 1966], pp. 101–03, 166 ff., 195, 225–31); *TWNT* V (1959), pp. 703 f. and 707 (ET *TDNT* V, 1967, pp. 703 f., 706); E. Lohse, *Märtyrer und Gottesknecht. Untersuchungen zur urchristlichen Verkündigung von Sühntod Jesu Christi* (FRLANT 64) (Göttingen, 1955), pp. 113–16, 131–35, 147 ff.

[2] Cf. U. Wilckens, *Die Bekehrung*, p. 274. It is unnecessary to discuss here the psychologizing interpretations which have recently been offered by W. Prentice, "St. Paul's Journey to Damascus," *ZNTW* 46 (1955), pp. 250–55, and W. Prokulski, "The Conversion of St. Paul", *CBQ* 19 (1957), 453–73. See on this subject the pertinent comments of B. Rigaux, *Saint Paul et ses lettres*, pp. 68 ff. and 78 ff.

[3] He belonged to this group, albeit as the last member and in spite of his unworthiness because he had persecuted the church of God (vv. 8–9). See too Eph. 3:8.

Philippians 3:12: Christ laid hold on Paul just like the runner who gains the prize of his victory. I Corinthians 9:16–17 is more explicit. The apostles have the right to make a living from the gospel but Paul holds that, in his case, the right is not so evident since, though he does proclaim the gospel, he does not do it from choice. The appearance of Christ has charged him with a mission which is for him a necessity. Paul has not given himself to Christ; he has the consciousness that it is Christ who laid hands upon him all at once without giving him the chance to break free. From this point of view, the occurrence on the Damascus road hardly resembles what we normally call a "conversion".

3. In the third place, Paul saw *Christ in his glory*. In this respect the Damascus appearance is plainly different from the Easter appearances which are recorded in the gospels.

In Galatians 1:12, 16 Paul speaks of this appearance as an "apocalypse",[1] a glorious manifestation in which Christ revealed himself to Paul in his state as Son of God, such as will be his appearance at the end-time.

2 Corinthians 4:4, 6 alludes to Paul's conversion. God had caused light to shine in his heart in order that he might see and then shed abroad the knowledge of God's glory which shone in the face of Christ, the perfect image of God.[2] The inner illumination is connected with a manifestation of the glory of God beaming from the person of Christ.

Here again, so it seems, Philippians 3 is most significant. At the moment of his meeting with Christ, Paul reckons with the only thing which henceforth will count with him: "to know Christ and the power of his resurrection" (v. 10). He has begun then a course at the end of which is a "prize", he knows, the divine call and the resurrection of the dead (cf. vv. 11, 14).[3] Verses 20, 21 make this clear: "We are citizens of heaven, from where we await as Saviour the Lord Jesus Christ who will change our lowly bodies and make them like his body of glory, by the power which gives him the ability to subdue all things to himself." The glory in which Paul saw Christ is at the same time powerful. Thanks to that, Christ makes the elect share in the glory which he has since his resurrection. Put otherwise, the glorious Christ, who appeared to Paul, stands for – in Paul's mind – salvation already achieved. He could now think of salvation only as a sharing in the glory of the risen Christ. Salvation which meant becoming like him was effected by the power that he possessed; and therefore, salvation depended on him and on him alone.

4. A final datum must be taken into consideration to explain Paul's experience on the Damascus road. Paul links the appearance of Christ with his *mission as apostle to the Gentiles*.[4] Paul often alludes to the mission with

---

[1] See A.-M. Denis, *RB* (1957) (cited on p. 178).

[2] Cf. J. Dupont, *Gnosis. La connaissance religieuse dans les épîtres de saint Paul* (Univ. Cath. Lov., Diss. ad gradum magistri in Fac. Theol., II, 40) (Louvain-Paris, 1949=1960), pp. 37 ff.

[3] Cf. G. Bouwman, *De brief van Paulus aan de Filippiërs*, p. 87.

[4] Cf. Rom. 1:5, 13; 11:13; 15:16, 18; Gal. 2:2, 8–9.

which he knows himself to be charged and which defines his particular place in the apostolic church. It devolved upon him to proclaim the gospel to the Gentiles. He traces back this calling to the Damascus event. God "revealed his Son to me so that I should proclaim him among the Gentiles" (Gal. 1:16).[1] He did not claim that Christ had given him the command to evangelize the Gentiles and there is nothing to allow us to imagine that this injunction was given him explicitly at this time.[2] But he was none the less convinced that his call to the apostleship of the Gentiles was bound up with the experience of Damascus. Implicit in such a call is that this experience could not consist only in the discovery of Jesus' messiahship. The attitude of the first Christians at Jerusalem shows sufficiently that it was one thing to recognize in Jesus the promised Messiah and another to have an immediate understanding of the necessity of proclaiming the gospel to the Gentiles. Paul's conviction is far better explained as a recognition of the glorious Christ as the Lord on whom depended exclusively the salvation of all men, whether Jews or Gentiles.

The apostleship of the Gentiles has, therefore, been entrusted precisely to this Pharisee who was filled with destructive zeal for the law, to this Pharisee who saw religion, righteousness and salvation only in the observance of the law. Christ's appearance has made him the herald of salvation exactly for those who are ignorant of the law and who are not troubled about it. For Christ is sufficient. Salvation comes only by him and by faith in him, without the works of the law.

The mission with which Paul knew himself charged for the sake of the Gentiles since the Damascus appearance implied a soteriology wholly suspended on Christ. It could not be adequately explained as arising from belief in the messiahship of Jesus. Its basis could only be located in the faith of the saving, universal and exclusive role of the risen Christ. As Saviour of all men, he must play a beneficent role for Gentiles as well as Jews. As a unique Saviour, he takes away all significance from the law as a principle of righteousness and salvation. Paul writes in Romans 10:4: τέλος γὰρ νόμου Χριστός, which seems to state that Christ has brought an end to the law.[3] Now there is both righteousness and salvation for anyone who believes in Christ. But the Jews do not understand this, since verse 2 attributes to them a true but ill-informed zeal. Paul himself had opposed, from

[1] Cf. U. Wilckens, *Die Bekehrung*, pp. 274-7.

[3] According to Acts, it is Ananias who received a revelation concerning the mission awaiting Paul (9:15) and who gave him news of it as the party concerned (22:14-15). One can understand why Paul did not wish to mention this indirect call.

[3] The *Traduction oecuménique de la Bible* (Paris, 1967), p. 78, notes: "The term in Greek which we translate as 'end' (*fin*) (*telos*) expresses at the same time the idea of purpose, conclusion and fulfilment." The meaning "end" (*fin*) is adopted notably by U. Wilckens, *Die Bekehrung*, p. 276; G. Delling, *TWNT* VIII, 57; J. A. Fitzmyer, "Saint Paul and the Law" in *The Jurist*, 27 (1967), pp. 18-36 (22 and 27).

It is rejected in favour of the idea of "goal" (*but*) by R. Bring, "Das Gesetz und die Gerechtigkeit Gottes. Eine Studie zur Frage nach der Bedeutung des Ausdruckes τέλος νόμου in Röm. 10, 4" in *StTh* 20 (1966), pp. 1-36.

N

the very first and with all his strength, this Christ who had put an end to
the role of the law. The vision at Damascus persuaded him that the role of
the law was truly finished and the time had come to proclaim to the
Gentiles salvation by faith in Christ.

III

The study of Paul's conversion from the point of view of the repercus-
sions which it had on his theological thought has inevitably led us to problems of soteriology. We have found ourselves faced by the resultant conflict between the Pharisaic soteriology of Paul before his conversion, a
soteriology based on the observance of the law, and the Christian soteriology wholly centered in Christ, in Christ's cross, in faith in Christ and in the
redemptive worth of his death on the cross. We have seen how decisively
and suddenly Paul passed from one soteriology to the other at the time
when the glorious Christ appeared to him, effecting in his person the
salvation which was Paul's object of hope in the world to come.

We have encountered what might be called the three fundamental presuppositions of Pauline soteriology:

1. First of all, there is *the personal experience* which came to Paul at Damascus. He then received the revelation, not of a doctrine of salvation but of
the practical realization of salvation in the person of the risen Christ.[1] More
than that, he recognized in the Christ who appeared to him the author of
salvation and one who possessed by his resurrection the power to grant to
believers in him a share in his glory.

2. This revelation led Paul to take over *the interpretation which the primitive
church gave to the death of Jesus on the cross.* Christ died for us, for our sins,
for human salvation. His death has, therefore, a redemptive worth. The
Hellenists were not slow to seize the practical consequence of this teaching
in welcoming Gentiles to the Antiochene community. It was not necessary to be a Jew and to submit to the prescriptions of the law to have
a share in the salvation granted to men by Christ.

3. It is needful likewise to take account of the *Pharisaic soteriology* which at
the first Paul set against the Christian faith and against which he later
reacted with the utmost vigour.[2] In rejecting entirely and without reserve
the notion of a righteousness and a salvation which may be secured by observance of the law, he came to grasp with greater penetration and to express with greater clarity what it was that constituted the novelty and
originality of the Christian soteriology, viz. that salvation is given only by
and in Christ to those who are joined to him by faith.

---

[1] We are glad to avail ourselves, in this way, of the expression used by H. G. Wood,
"Paul was converted to Christ rather than to Christianity" (*NTS* [1954–55], p. 279).

[2] Cf. H. G. Wood, *NTS* (1954–55), p. 280.

CHAPTER XII

PAUL AND THE LAW – "ALL THINGS TO ALL MEN"

H. L. Ellison

"I am no man's slave, but I have made myself a slave to all, in order to win the more for Christ. To the Jews I have made myself as a Jew, in order to win Jews; to those who live under the law I have come as one under the law, in order to win those who are under the law – not that I myself am under the the law. To those who live without the law I have come as one without the law, in order to win those who are without the law – not that I am really under no law in relation to God, for I am bound by the law of Christ. To those who are weak I have made myself weak, so as to win the weak; in fact, I have become all things to all people, in order that, one way or another, I may rescue some of them. But I do it all for the sake of the gospel, so that I may share its blessings with others" (1 Cor. 9:19–23, Bruce, *Expanded Paraphrase*).

I

For those unfamiliar with Paul the words "all things to all men" suggest an unprincipled, chameleon-like attitude, an adapting of one's words and actions to one's surroundings without any reference to one's real thoughts and principles. For those familiar with their original setting they often suggest the key to successful missionary activity and the secret of the church's advance among the diverse nations and cultures of the world.

G. Bornkamm in a recent study[1] makes it clear enough that Paul is not concerned merely with a missionary technique or with a modification of the changeless gospel. As he puts it, "To speak as if Paul Judaized it in one place and paganized it in another is wholly inaccurate" (*op. cit.* p. 197). He sees rather a change of "stance" according to his hearers – not the gospel, but its presentation and the explanation of it are changed. It is subsidiary to his interpretation that since he finds no trace of this change of "stance" in the sermons reported in Acts, he queries the validity of Luke's picture.

This judgment hardly does justice to the outline sermons presented by Luke. There may not be the change of "stance" demanded by Bornkamm, but there are indubitably interesting and remarkable differences in approach in the addresses given in Pisidian Antioch (Acts 13:16–41), Derbe (Acts 14:15–17) and Athens (Acts 17:22–31). In addition, it may well be

---

[1] "The Missionary Stance of Paul in 1 Corinthians and in Acts" in *Studies in Luke-Acts*, edited by L. E. Keck and J. L. Martyn (Nashville, 1966), pp. 194–207.

questioned whether this alleged change of "stance" has left many traces in the Pauline Epistles.

More important, it is also questionable whether this interpretation really does justice to Paul himself. Quite apart from our interpretation of this passage in 1 Corinthians, it seems clear that Paul regarded his attitude and actions as both exceptional and demanding. It seems obvious that his words are in some way linked with his refusal to receive any payment for his activity, even though he is entitled to it. Were it relevant, a strong case could be made out for thinking that this refusal was particularly connected with Corinth; in part, at any rate, it may be seen as his method of refusing to let himself be identified with any of the diverse factions there. In his letter he passes on to the athlete and his training, thereby suggesting, at the very least, that being all things to all men did not come naturally to him or to others. We may question whether the mental and spiritual agility demanded by Bornkamm really satisfies the claim made by Paul.

A closer investigation of the passage will show that Paul is thinking of a relatively narrow area, though its effects may be very far-reaching. He is clearly concerned with the Law and with its claims and effects on four groups of persons: the Jew, those under the law – it must not be too readily assumed that these two groups are completely synonymous – those outside the law, the weak.

The last named, the weak (cf. 1 Cor. 8:11; Rom. 14:2), seem clearly enough to be converts who adopted a rigorist attitude, even though they did not accept the Mosaic Law as a whole. It is quite likely that some of them had been sincere "God-fearers" before their conversion to Christianity; if so, they will have observed the Noachic commandments[1] carefully, while they were on the fringe of the Synagogue. If that is so, those "under the law", looked on as a class alongside the Jew, may well represent those Gentiles who had not become proselytes – in which case they would have been regarded as Jews – but who tried to keep the law, not confining themselves to the Noachic commandments; after their acceptance of Jesus as Messiah they will have adopted the views of the Judaizers.

II

When the Christian is faced by a Jew today, he is seeking contact with an unknown. Beyond the fact that he is presumably of Jewish birth, the name Jew means nothing definite. Not even in the State of Israel have the law-makers been able to define who is a Jew. In the days of Paul, however, for a man to be known as a Jew meant that he kept the law. However widely Jews differed they all kept the law. The various sects

[1] The Noachic commandments were the minimum expected of Gentiles, if they were to have social contacts with Jews, or, at least in theory, live in Jewish settlements. They were the prohibition of (i) blasphemy (ii) idolatry, (iii) sexual immorality, (iv) murder, (v) robbery, (vi) eating part of a living animal; and finally there was (vii) the injunction to do justice.

within it varied in their interpretation of certain commandments, but in their actions they were remarkably alike.

We hear today repeatedly about our "permissive" society and of the problems it creates. For this we must in large measure thank the journalist who can judge contemporary behaviour only in a contemporary frame of reference. Although it was adumbrated by Alexander the Great and his Hellenistic successors, the concept of a unitary society was created by "the Great Church", when it had risen to a position of power. It was developed and probably perverted by humanism. Today the concept is collapsing, with the result that we are returning to the permissive society which existed before Catholic Christianity, and which in many parts of the world had never ceased. The great difference is the wide spread fragmentation and individualization of society which lessens the demand for group conformity.

In the Mediterranean world in which Paul lived, subject to the all-overriding interests of the Roman state, each ethnic and cultic group was permitted and even expected to live according to its traditions. It was not only the Jew who lived so far as possible in his own quarter or municipal district. Today it is not our new permissive society but rather the age-old one of India which will best convey the true flavour of the society of which Paul formed part. The rules and customs of one's ethnic and cultic group could be as determinative as one's caste loyalty in modern India.

The principle that the commandments had been given that men might *live*[1] by the doing of them led to a wide relaxation of rules of dress, etc. for Jewish travellers journeying through hostile areas. Once, however, they had arrived where there was a Jewish community, they were expected to revert to the accepted norms. That Paul was readily permitted to speak in a strange synagogue and even invited to do so (Acts 13:15) suggests that Paul proclaimed his Jewishness and even his rabbinic standing by his dress.[2]

If in Corinth Paul moved to the house of Titius Justus, a God-fearer, next door to the synagogue (Acts 18:7), it is not likely to have been intended as a deliberate challenge to those who had refused to accept his message. It is far more likely that the God-fearers, who were from then on to be the main target for Paul's words, found that their semi-Judaism was rendered easier, if they lived in or near the Jewish district of the town. This easily comprehensible centripetal force was powerfully reinforced by the wish to avoid seeing idol-figures, whenever they went out of doors, and to be able to avoid continual insult, when they observed the Sabbath. We cannot affirm it with certainty, but in a large commercial and industrial centre like Corinth it is highly probable that the tentmaker's business of "Aquila & Paul" was in the Jewish quarter.

---

[1] Cf. Lev. 18:5; Sifra 86b; Abodah Zarah 27b, etc.

[2] The average Jew in the Diaspora dressed very much like his neighbours, but he was marked out by his wearing tassels or fringes (*ṣîṣīt*) on his outer garments, cf. Num. 15:38 ff., Deut. 22:12, Matt. 9:20. See Strack-Billerbeck, IV, 1, Excursus 12.

All this adds up to the certainty that most of Paul's activity in Corinth, and indeed in any other larger centre of population, was carried out in close proximity to the local Jewish community, and was more often than not watched closely by Jewish critics and enemies. For him the antinomy so often observable in Jewish missions today was not possible. Even in Israel no contradiction is felt, if the Christian worker has bacon for his breakfast, while seeing to it that the food placed before his guests at other meals meets normal Jewish dietary requirements. There were really only two possibilities open to Paul. Either he did not observe the law at all, or he was strict in its observance at all times. A casual example of the latter is his keeping of the Day of Atonement under conditions when it might not have been expected. Yet Luke reports it in such a way as to show that he saw nothing remarkable in it (Acts 27:9).[1] Incidentally, if Acts were really from the end of the first or even from the first half of the second century, would this have been taken for granted? Indeed, would it have even been understood in churches which had become mainly Gentile?

III

It would be interesting, if we could discover the real religious outlook of the Jewish Hellenizers who helped to precipitate Judea into a life and death struggle in the time of Antiochus IV Epiphanes. Certainly they will not have been simply the worldly apostates presented to us in 1 Maccabees. Fundamentally they may well have been descendants of those who did not accept Ezra's basic concepts.

Be that as it may, they lost the day and their views perished with them. Long before Paul's day being a Jew, as has already been said, had become synonymous with keeping the Law. Sadducee and Pharisee, Qumran Covenanter and Zealot varied widely in their interpretation of how this or that commandment was to be carried out, but they all agreed that the law was supreme and had to be rigorously applied. In fact, so wide was the area of agreement, that the outsider might have failed for a long time to notice the disagreements. It follows that if Paul wished to be accepted by Jews as a Jew, he was hedged in by a multitude of things which he had either to observe or avoid. Two outstanding matters will have been the observance of the Sabbath and the dietary laws, though in neither would the Pharisaic exaggerations have been considered binding on him; he may, however, have let himself be so bound, for by upbringing he was a Pharisee and a descendant of Pharisees.

The account of Paul's arrest in Jerusalem and his appearance before tribunals both Jewish and non-Jewish is instructive. The original charge by Jews from Asia (Acts 21:28) was that Paul taught against the people, i.e.

---

[1] Cf. Strack-Billerbeck, *ad loc.*, F. F. Bruce, *The Acts of the Apostles* (London, 1951), *ad loc.*; W. M. Ramsay, *St. Paul the Traveller and Roman Citizen* (London, 1895), p. 322.

the Jews, the law and the temple, and that he had brought a Gentile into the Temple. Before Felix the last point was pressed, but the former were summed up in the accusation that he was a ringleader of the Nazarenes (Acts 24:5 f.). In other words, he was accused of an offence against a specific law, which was also accepted by the Romans as valid, and of views against which at the time there was no authoritative ruling by the Jewish authorities. This was not made until the rabbinic meeting in Yabneh (Jamnia) about A.D. 90.[1] The farce before the Sanhedrin (Acts 23:6–10) was possible only because Paul's accusers had no specific charge against him; for the Pharisees in it he might be a bad Pharisee, but a Pharisee he still was.

In Acts 26:5 the RSV is probably correct in translating the aorist ἔζησα by "I have lived", instead of by the past tense as in AV, RV, NEB. Not merely would there have been little point in stressing to King Agrippa what he had done, if he no longer did it, but in addition it hardly brings out the force of the καὶ νῦν that follows, which implies not a contradiction but rather an intensification. So we are justified in thinking that throughout his missionary activity Paul lived in a way that would have called for no adverse comment from a Pharisee who might have met him however much he would have rejected his teaching.

This is borne out, even if negatively and indirectly, by Jewish tradition. Elisha ben Abuyah (c. A.D. 90–150) was one of the great rabbis of his time, and he has left his name in *Pirqe Aboth* 4.20. He was excommunicated and is almost always referred to as *Aḥer* (The Other One). There was never any danger in tradition's keeping his memory green, for it told also of how he had deliberately profaned the Sabbath. In other words, his false teaching had been sterilized and rendered harmless, not so much by his excommunication but rather by his notorious breach of the law. With Paul, however, his memory had to be forgotten, for there were no stories that could be told about him that would neutralize his teaching. As Joseph Klausner has put it:

> From all that has been said above in the chapters treating the teaching of Paul and its consequences, the fact has become clear that the Jews could not have taken any attitude towards Paul and his teaching except a negative one. So in his time, and so after his time, up to the present day.
> The Jews also rejected Jesus; yet he is mentioned a number of times in Talmud and Midrash – and not always unfavourably. But Paul is mentioned clearly not even once in either of the two Talmuds or any early Midrash. Only hints about him can be found in the Talmud.[2]

If this is so, and there are very few authorities today that would doubt it, then Paul's being all things to all men can have no reference to any

[1] See the articles *Birkat ha-Minim* and *Minim* in *The Encyclopedia of the Jewish Religion* (edd. R. J. Zwi Werblowsky and G. Wigoder, London, 1967).
[2] J. Klausner, *From Jesus to Paul* (London, 1942), p. 600.

modifications of outward living as he moved in different circles. Above all, it cannot suggest any compromises with the customs he found in the various centres in which he founded churches. Equally obviously, however, a varying "stance" towards the law can hardly be intended. For the Jew a man's "stance" over against the law was of little or no interest. Either he kept it or he did not. The only excuse for failing to keep it was, as has been indicated earlier, danger to life. Failure to accept the standards of the Pharisees or of Qumran might place a barrier in the way of full social fellowship, but the relative laxity of the lax was not taken seriously, so long as there was no intention of not keeping the commandment in question.

The diaspora Jews of Paul's day were, in fact, little interested in what his converts did. They considered that if they were Jews they were under obligation to keep the law; if they were Gentiles, then they were not. Indeed they expected no more of the latter than that they should keep the Noachic commandments – so did Paul, but not because the Synagogue had formulated them in this way. If the converts wanted to do more, they should become Jews, take on themselves "the yoke of the Torah" and so do the thing properly. Their objection was that Paul placed the Gentile believer in the Messiah on the same level as the Jewish believer in him and higher than the Jew who did not believe, in spite of the fact that he was not asking him to accept the obligations that came on the Jew in virtue of Sinai.

IV

There is little point in asking what Paul's attitude towards the modern convert from Judaism would be. We can hardly believe that he would condemn the orthodox Jew for continuing in his orthodox practices after he had found his Messiah. After all, the orthodox Jew keeps the Torah less because he hopes for salvation thereby and more because he considers it his obligation inherited from his ancestors from Sinai on. It is most unlikely that he would demand from the one who has never known orthodoxy that he seek it because he has found the God of his fathers through Jesus. But in the historical setting of the first century to deny the law in practice was to deny that one was a Jew. As has always been the case within Jewry, not one's theory about the Torah but one's practical relationship to it was the important point. So out of no soteriological theory, but from the sheer logic of historic fact Paul continued to live as he always had, only with a new power and motive behind his living. When he told a Jew that he had found the long-promised Messiah, he appeared to his hearer as a Jew telling of a Jewish discovery. If it were not for the centuries' old church prejudice which demands that a Jewish convert must renounce all that smacks of Judaism, there would be no difficulty here.

But what happened when Paul met Gentiles, no matter whether they were attracted to the law, or whether they kept the Noachic commandments as a sort of entrance fee for attendance at synagogue worship, or whether they were uninterested in the whole Jewish way of life? Let us remember here that we constantly influence others more by our lives than by our doctrines. How could a man who carefully kept the law in its externals fail to influence others in favour of its being kept?

We have earlier seen that there is probably some link between Paul's unwillingness to receive financial help from the Corinthians and his attitude towards those he wished to win. Paul had to feel free to react to each person and group empirically, one might almost say existentially. His hearers were to react neither to his outward manner of life nor to his followers' customs, but to the proclamation that God's King and Saviour had come. If they accepted it, then the power of Christ's Spirit would enable them to analyse and appreciate Paul's manner of life aright. He was not presenting himself to them as an example, though that might come later, e.g. 1 Corinthians 4:16, but as a herald. But on the other hand, there had to be something in the quality of Paul's life that would suggest to his hearer that here he was seeing the actualization of his own dreams and best aspirations.

While we shall probably agree that Paul was correct in not trying to create pale patterns of himself among his converts, we may not realize how difficult it is to achieve this goal, until we remember how outstanding Christian leaders have at all times been copied and imitated. Paul knew that if he was to achieve his desired end, it would call for the strictest self-discipline of every part of his personality to create the harmony of the whole that was needed. We shall understand this best, if we ponder on the impact made on us by Christians whom we come to know. Some impress us by their harmonious unity which makes agreement and understanding so easy, and causes our points of difference to fade into insignificance. Others strike us by their salient points, and these are all too often matters on which we disagree. When their names are mentioned, we think at once of their peculiarities; when they are discussed, it is normally the points in which they differ from the majority that become the subject of conversation.

Over many centuries the church has appealed to the memory of Paul and has laid on the convert from Judaism the yoke of refraining from keeping the traditional law. When he has not conformed completely to his Gentile environment, he has been suspected of Judaizing, or of merely nominal conformity to the dominant religion. Yet the facts of Paul's continuing conformity to the practices of traditional Judaism are there plainly on the face of Scripture, for those willing to find them. The contortions of many commentators faced with Paul's acceptance of the suggestion made by James that he should associate himself with the men who had taken a Nazirite vow (Acts 21:23, 24) would be ludicrous, if they were not often tragic. Let a recent example suffice: "It is an extraordinary action for the Paul of the Epistles to perform; but it is not wholly incredible (cf. 1 Cor. 8:19 f.), if his reception by James, and probably the acceptance of the offerings of the Gentile churches, depended on it."[1]

Why is it that so many have been blind to the true facts for so long? The obvious answer seems to be that Paul's principle, as laid down by himself, has seldom been taken very seriously, above all as it is displayed in his letters and in the account by his friend and companion Luke.

Paul's personal practices derived from his Jewish background had so little importance for him, that if he referred to them at all, it was almost by accident. For Luke these matters were as incidental as the clothes the apostle might be wearing at any given moment. Paul so fits into the scenes in which we find him, that he seems to act as though they had always been familiar to him.

When Jesus the Messiah introduces himself to men, he always comes with the shock of the unexpected. He is never quite what we have been led to expect, and he always challenges our conceptions of what he should be like. Yet there is also something familiar about him. He is the second man, the true man, the one we always felt ought to be possible. When Paul says, "I have become all things to all men," he is really saying that he is so at Christ's disposal that there is nothing in his own peculiarities and practices that could be used to erect a barrier between his Lord and those to whom he would reveal himself. When all is said and done, how many, when they first hear of Jesus of Nazareth, are really conscious that they are being introduced to an observant Jew from Palestine? Even so Paul claims that his life has taken on the pattern willed by his Lord for *him*. Because this pattern was not forced on him from outside but moulded him from within, his own peculiarities ceased to impose themselves on others when he spoke to them about his Lord.

[1] G. W. H. Lampe in Peake's *Commentary on the Bible*²(ed. by H. H. Rowley and M. Black, London, 1962) *ad loc.*

CHAPTER XIII

THE FORM, MEANING AND BACKGROUND OF THE HYMN QUOTED IN 1 TIMOTHY 3:16

ROBERT H. GUNDRY

I

BY COMMON CONSENT 1 TIMOTHY 3:16 CONTAINS A QUOTATION FROM an early Christian hymn:

Line 1: ὃς ἐφανερώθη ἐν σαρκί

Line 2: ἐδικαιώθη ἐν πνεύματι,

Line 3: ὤφθη ἀγγέλοις,

Line 4: ἐκηρύχθη ἐν ἔθνεσιν

Line 5: ἐπιστεύθη ἐν κόσμῳ,

Line 6: ἀνελήμφθη ἐν δόξῃ[1]

The hymnic quotation is notorious for the different schematizations and consequently varying interpretations laid upon it by modern commentators. Some see a more or less chronological progression throughout the six lines. Each line then receives somewhat independent treatment without emphasis on the parallelism of couplets or triplets. Others discern two strophes of three lines each (or two lines with a refrain). The currently prevalent viewpoint divides the hymnic quotation into a triplet of couplets. An examination of some representative treatments will lead into a re-examination of the form, content, and background of the passage.

Typical of those who treat the six lines somewhat separately but in chronological progression are H. Alford and C. K. Barrett.[2] For Alford, line 1 refers to the birth of Jesus. Line 2 refers to his baptism, when he received the Holy Spirit, and to his temptation, when the Spirit led and empowered him (Mark 1:12; Matt. 4:1; Luke 4:1). Thus the righteousness of Jesus was both approved at his baptism and proved by his resistance of temptation. Line 3 refers to the ministry of angels to Jesus after his temptation (Mark 1:13; Matt. 4:11). Line 4 refers to the apostolic preaching *which began during Jesus' ministry*. Alford must add the italicized qualification in order to keep peace between his insistence on chronological

---

[1] Whether the hymn was a baptismal hymn "to Christ as to a god" (Pliny the Younger, *Epp.* x. 96, 97), a "song of the redeemer" of the type G. Schille thinks he has isolated (*Frühchristliche Hymnen* [Berlin, 1962], p. 38), or another kind remains uncertain.

[2] H. Alford, *The Greek Testament* (London, 1865) III, p. 334; C. K. Barrett, *The Pastoral Epistles* (Oxford, 1963), pp. 65 f.

progression and his understanding of line 6 as a reference to the ascension. This forces him to maintain an initial, if not primary, reference to the Jews in ἔθνεσιν; for the pre-ascension ministry of the apostles was restricted to the Jews (Matt. 10:5 f.). Line 5 refers to the faith of the *first* disciples – again to avoid a post-ascension reference. And line 6 refers to the ascension.

To Alford it is clear that lines 1 and 6 refer to Jesus' birth and ascension respectively and that everything in between must therefore be chronological in order to form a résumé of Jesus' earthly ministry from beginning to end. This view has obvious faults. It forces very unnatural meanings upon the proclaiming of Christ to the nations and the believing on him throughout the world – surely references to the extensive and successful Christian mission beyond Palestine and Jewry, and therefore after the ascension. Also, Jesus' baptism and temptation and especially the angelic ministry to Jesus after his temptation appear to be unlikely points of emphasis for a hymnic précis of Jesus' ministry. Besides, angels appeared to Jesus throughout his earthly ministry, not he to them.

Instead of squeezing the contents of the hymnic quotation into the period from Jesus' birth to ascension, C. K. Barrett postpones line 6 to the final victory of Christ at his Parousia (cf. 1 Cor. 15:25; Phil. 2:10 f.). Thus, "who was manifested in flesh" refers to the incarnation, "vindicated in spirit" to the resurrection, "seen by angels" to the ascension, "proclaimed among nations" to the mission of the church, "believed on in [the] world" to the success of that mission, and "taken up in glory" to Jesus' final exaltation. The chief flaw here is that "taken up in glory" most naturally refers to the ascension rather than the consummation. Indeed, ἀναλαμβάνω describes the ascension in Acts 1:2, 11, 22 [and Mark 16:19],[1] and in view of these parallels the noun ἀνάλημψις almost certainly refers to the ascension in Luke 9:51 (cf. 24:51).[2]

Those who see in the hymnic quotation two strophes of three lines each tend also to follow a chronological approach, but with somewhat less emphasis than those who treat the lines singly. For W. Lock, the first strophe describes the life of the incarnate Lord as seen on earth ("who was manifested in flesh, vindicated by the Spirit") and as watched in

---

[1] In 4 Kg. 2:11 LXX of Elijah's translation and in Sir. 49:14 of Enoch's translation.

[2] Without the parallels in Acts, ἀνάλημψις in Luke might well be taken as a reference to Jesus' decease. To circumvent the difficulty of line 6 for the chronological interpretation, W. B. Wallis argues that "taken up in glory" is not limited to the ascension but includes all subsequent exhibition of glory ("I Timothy", *The Wycliffe Bible Commentary*, ed. C. F. Pfeiffer and E. F. Harrison [Chicago, 1962], p. 1376). But since "taken up" must at least include the ascension, the chronological difficulty remains. R. A. Knox admits the chronological inconsistency, but only as a deliberate accentuation of the paradox that the ascended Christ is more influential in the world than he was in the days of his flesh (*A New Testament Commentary for English Readers* [London, 1958], vol. III, p. 11). The paradox is doubtful, however, for one half of it – viz., lack of influence during the earthly ministry – receives no mention in the passage.

heaven ("seen by angels"). The second strophe describes the life of the ascended Lord as preached on earth ("proclaimed among nations, believed on in [the] world") and as lived in heaven ("taken up in glory").[1] It would have been much better for Lock's view had line 6, "taken up in glory", introduced the second strophe and thereby marked the shift from incarnate to ascended life. As it is, the supposed second strophe lacks a leading statement to balance the leading statement, "who was manifested in flesh", in the first strophe. Nor is it certain, or even probable, that "seen by angels" refers to angelic observation of our Lord's earthly ministry.[2] Finally, the second of the three antitheses "flesh/spirit", "angels/nations", and "world/glory" breaks down any strict division into two strophes by bridging the supposed boundary between them.[3]

This last consideration likewise militates against H. von Soden's view that lines 1–3 depict the developing stages in Jesus' personal career and lines 4–6, the results on earth through the church. To maintain an earthly locale for line 6, von Soden interprets the taking up of Christ to mean a taking up *by men*, presumably through the appropriation of faith.[4] But that idea has already been stated in line 5. Δόξῃ appears to *contrast* with κόσμῳ. Ἀνελήμφθη is technical for the ascension. And in the parallels adduced by von Soden, ἀναλαμβάνω has the sense of metaphorical appropriation only with impersonal objects (Acts 7:43; Eph. 6:13, 16) and carries a purely physical sense (inappropriate to von Soden's view of line 6) when a personal object is in view (Acts 20:13 f.; 23:31).

E. F. Scott also identifies two strophes, but limits them to two lines each (lines 1–2 and 4–5) and adds a refrain to each strophe. The first strophe – "who was manifested in flesh, vindicated in spirit" – describes the life of Christ on earth (cf. Lock's interpretation). The refrain "seen by angels" celebrates the triumph of his ascension. The second strophe – "proclaimed among nations, believed on in [the] world" – describes the larger life of Christ in the church. The refrain "taken up in glory" again celebrates his triumph, but this time the *final* glory after the Parousia and last judgment.[5] But the antithesis "angels/nations" still ties lines 3 and 4 together and thus leaves no room for the interruption necessary to the beginning of a new strophe in line 4. Furthermore, the antithesis "world/glory" ties lines 5 and 6 together and rules out separation of line 6 as a

[1] W. Lock, *The Pastoral Epistles* (Edinburgh, 1924), p. 45.
[2] See below, pp. 214 ff.
[3] Cf. B. Weiss' admission of chronological inconsistency in line 6 and explanation that lines 5 and 6 were reversed so that line 5 ("believed on in [the] world") might naturally follow line 4 ("proclaimed among nations") – even though lines 4 and 5 belong to different couplets in Weiss' view (*Die Briefe Pauli an Timotheus und Titus*[5] [Göttingen, 1902], p. 159).
[4] H. von Soden, *Kolosser, Epheser, Philemon, Pastoralbriefe*[2] (Tübingen, 1893), p. 237. Cf. the somewhat similar view of M. Albertz, *Die Botschaft des Neuen Testaments* (Zollikon-Zürich, 1952), vol. I/2, p. 132, who correlates lines 1 and 4, 2 and 5, 3 and 6 with reference to Christ and the church respectively in each pair.
[5] E. F. Scott, *The Pastoral Epistles* (New York, n.d.), pp. 41 ff.; followed by B. S. Easton, *The Pastoral Epistles* (New York, 1947), p. 136.

refrain. And again, ἀνελήμφθη in line 6 must refer to the ascension, not to final glory.[1] Sir Robert Falconer draws parallels between the respective lines of each of two strophes. The first lines of each strophe (1 and 4) present Christ as manifested and proclaimed. The second lines (2 and 5) present him as vindicated and acknowledged. The third lines (3 and 6) present him as receiving homage from and in the heavenly world.[2] Once again, however, the pairs of antitheses at the ends of the lines do not receive enough attention. Indeed, Falconer's scheme would link "(Christ's) flesh" and "nations", "spirit" and "world", and "angels" and "glory". All except the last are unlikely combinations, especially when the antitheses "flesh/spirit", "angels/nations", and "world/glory" are ready to hand.

The majority of current commentators favour division of our hymnic quotation into three couplets.[3] J. N. D. Kelly puts this interpretation in its simplest form. He notes three couplets with the antitheses flesh/spirit, angels/Gentiles, and world/glory. The first couplet indicates Christ's incarnation at birth and vindication at resurrection. The second couplet indicates the appearance of Christ to angels and the proclamation of him to mankind. The third couplet indicates the acceptance of Christ both in the world and in heaven.[4]

M. Dibelius, H. Conzelmann, J. Jeremias, C. Spicq, and especially E. Schweizer have considerably expanded the interpretation in which three couplets are identified. Each of the couplets contrasts the heavenly and earthly spheres of existence. Furthermore, these contrasts exhibit the threefold chiastic pattern a/b, b/a, a/b:

a earthly – "flesh" (line 1)
b heavenly – "spirit" (line 2)
b heavenly – "angels" (line 3)

---

[1] The view of W. J. Dalton is essentially that of Scott except that for Dalton the refrain of line 6 *repeats* the reference to ascension in the refrain of line 3 rather than progresses to and beyond the Parousia (W. J. Dalton, *Christ's Proclamation to the Spirits* [Rome, 1965], p. 90, n. 19). Overlooking the sets of antitheses which combine lines 1–2, 3–4, and 5–6, Dalton simply asserts incompatibility between lines 3 and 4 and between lines 5 and 6 and therefore opts for two strophes. J. N. D. Kelly similarly makes the suggestion, only to reject it, that lines 1–3 delineate the successive phases in Christ's exaltation – incarnation, resurrection, and ascension through the sphere of angelic powers – and that lines 4–6 celebrate the universality of Christ's reign – among the Gentiles (or all men), in the whole world (or the entire universe), and in heaven itself (J. N. D. Kelly, *The Pastoral Epistles* [New York, 1963], p. 92).

[2] R. Falconer, *The Pastoral Epistles* (Oxford, 1937), p. 138.

[3] The view itself, however, is not new. For example, A. R. Fausset identified three couplets with antitheses between earth and heaven and also noted the a-b-b-a-a-b-arrangement (in R. Jamieson, A. R. Fausset, and D. Brown, *A Commentary Critical and Explanatory on the Whole Bible*, first published in 1877, re-edited and reprinted several times since). See also B. Weiss, *loc. cit.*

[4] Kelly, *loc. cit.* A. Descamps argues that abandonment of chronological consistency for poetic lyricism indicates a hymn rather than a confession (*Les Justes et la Justice dans les évangiles et le christianisme primitif hormis la doctrine proprement paulinienne* [Gembloux, 1950], p. 84). Thus, R. Deichgräber even rejects the designation "*credal hymn*" (*Gotteshymnus und Christushymnus in der frühen Christenhei* [Göttingen, 1967], p. 133, n. 3).

a earthly – "nations" (line 4)
a earthly – "world" (line 5)
b heavenly – "glory" (line 6)

The movement of thought is spatial rather than chronological because the one important point is that the Saviour has reunited heaven and earth. Lines 1 and 2 summarize his work of salvation as a whole. By incarnation he was "manifested in flesh", the sphere of divine epiphany, and by resurrection "justified in spirit", that is, made to enter into the divine sphere of exaltation. Lines 3 and 4 lead on to the thought that the accomplishment of salvation must be, and has been, proclaimed to both angels and men. And in lines 5 and 6 the singing church praises the victory of Christ. The theme of vindicative exaltation also receives prominence. Jesus rises from the dead (line 2) and triumphantly ascends through the celestial regions as the angelic powers worship him (line 3). He becomes the subject of proclamation throughout the nations (line 4) and the object of faith among men (line 5). Climactically, he arrives in the immediate presence of God (line 6).[1]

Jeremias and Spicq add a history-of-religions dimension by suggesting that in form the hymnic quotation is patterned, perhaps unknowingly, after the enthronement ceremony in ancient Egypt. The first stage is exaltation: the new king receives divine attributes (lines 1 and 2). The second stage is presentation: the deified king is presented to the gods (lines 3 and 4, here to angels and men). The third stage is enthronement: the king receives his rulership (lines 5 and 6).[2] Kelly thinks the resemblance is superficial and coincidental.[3] Indeed, there are difficulties in working out the parallels. Manifestation in *flesh*, with the connotation of human weakness and limitation, does not tally with exaltation unless it be claimed that line 1 merely sets the stage for the exaltation in line 2. Even then, "taken up in glory" at the *end* (line 6) sounds closer to the elevation which comes *first* in the Egyptian ceremony as reconstructed by Spicq and Jeremias.[4] Also, although "seen by angels" may be comparable to presentation to the

---

[1] M. Dibelius – H. Conzelmann, *Die Pastoralbriefe*[3] (Tübingen, 1955), pp. 50 ff.; J. Jeremias, "Die Briefe an Timotheus und Titus", *NTD*[5], Teilband 9 (Göttingen, 1949), pp. 21 f.; C. Spicq, *Les Épîtres pastorales* (Paris, 1947), p. 108; E. Schweizer, *Lordship and Discipleship* (London, 1960), pp. 64 ff.; idem, "Two New Testament Creeds Compared", *Current Issues in New Testament Interpretation: Essays in Honor of Otto A. Piper*, ed. W. Klassen and G. F. Snyder (New York, 1962), pp. 168 ff.; idem, *Erniedrigung und Erhöhung bei Jesus und seinen Nachfolgern* (Zürich, 1955), pp. 62 ff.; cf. H. Flender, *St. Luke: Theologian of Redemptive History* (Philadelphia, 1967), pp. 37–39. Noting that line 6 would have followed line 2 or 3 in a chronological scheme, Spicq sees a pastoral concern in the last position of line 6: Christ is left in heaven whence Christians look for his return (*op. cit.*, p. 110).

[2] See Jeremias, *loc. cit.*, who claims that the three stages became a stylistic convention which outlived the ceremony itself; Spicq, *op. cit.*, pp. 108 f. R. Deichgräber has recently reiterated the hypothesis (*op. cit.*, pp. 133–7). Spicq also suggests that the hymnic quotation is a Christian answer to "Great is Diana [or Artemis] of the Ephesians" (Acts 19:28, 34, and inscriptional evidence cited by Spicq concerning hymns to Diana; *ibid.*, pp. 107 f.).

[3] Kelly, *op. cit.*, pp. 92 f.

[4] Cf. C. F. D. Moule, *The Birth of the New Testament* (New York, 1962), p. 24.

gods, proclamation to the nations on earth is doubtfully similar. And although the enthronement of Christ in the hearts of believers is a fine devotional thought, it is again doubtful that "believed on in [the] world" parallels the final stage in the Egyptian ceremony, viz., enthronement. Furthermore, E. Schweizer has pointed out that in the Egyptian ceremony the order and content were somewhat different from the reconstruction of Spicq and Jeremias. First came a hymn of the heavenly beings (missing here), then guidance (lines 3–5?), then surrender to the judgment (line 2), and finally deification and access to God (line 6).[1]

With due appreciation for these recent opinions, we may proceed further. It must first of all be acknowledged that the datival nouns at the ends of the lines fall into three *antithetically* parallel pairs along the a/b, b/a, a/b pattern. On the other hand, the meanings within each pair of lines considered as wholes denote roughly *synonymous* ideas. Manifestation by incarnation (line 1) and vindication by the *Descensus ad Inferos* or the resurrection (line 2) both emphasize revelatory action. Similarly, the being seen by angels (line 3) and preached among nations (line 4) both denote publication or announcement of the news concerning Christ. In the same fashion again, the being believed on (line 5) and taken up (line 6) indicate the welcome reception on earth and in heaven of the proclaimed Christ. Thus, the three roughly synonymous couplets successively indicate the revelation, proclamation, and reception of Christ; the pairs of antithetic nouns indicate contrasting spheres in which each of the three basic actions takes place.

But there is a danger that the clear antitheses at the ends of the lines and the rough similarities of the whole lines as pairs blind us to yet further relationships between lines which do not belong to the same couplet when paired 1/2, 3/4, and 5/6. It should be quite apparent, for example, that lines 4 and 5 form a couplet characterized by *synthetic* parallelism: the proclamation among the nations results in belief throughout the world.[2] Both take place in the realm visible to men. Likewise, lines 2 and 3 form a couplet with synthetic parallelism: the vindication in spirit leads on to the appearance of Christ to angels. Both take place in the realm invisible to men. Lines 1 and 6 will then form a couplet which appropriately frames the whole verse[3] – again with synthetic parallelism: the appearance in flesh culminates in the ascension to heaven. This couplet begins in the visible realm and passes into the invisible. In other words, the recognition of the

---

[1] E. Schweizer, *Lordship and Discipleship*, pp. 65 f., and *idem, Erniedrigung*, p. 65, with citation of the material in A. J. Festugière, *La révélation d'Hermès Trismégiste* (Paris, 1953) III, pp. 149–52. Kelly, *loc. cit.*, also objects that the Egyptian parallel destroys the point of the antitheses flesh/spirit, angels/nations, and world/glory. But I do not see why, for the exaltation, presentation, and enthronement could take place in the two halves of the cosmos in parallel fashion.

[2] Cf. Rom. 10:14.

[3] Cf. Ps. 15:2–5b, bracketed by 1 and 5c; 6:8b–9, bracketed by 8a and 10; 11:5b–7a, bracketed by 5a and 7b, etc., especially in the strophic arrangement of the Jerusalem Bible; and see M. Dahood, *Psalms II, 51–100* (Garden City, 1968), p. XXII.

parallelism between lines 1 and 6, 2 and 3, and 4 and 5 takes advantage of the synthetic pairs of datival nouns flesh/glory, spirit/angels, and nations/world – and the synthetic pairs of verbs – manifested/taken up, vindicated/seen, and proclaimed/believed on – which receive no attention when our gaze fixes exclusively on the antithetic pairs of datival nouns.

II

Before an assessment of the theological background of the hymnic quotation, it is necessary to examine the meanings of each line. "Manifested in flesh" has traditionally been taken as a reference to the incarnation. Support derives from the similar phraseology, "Who was descended from David according to the flesh", in the credal quotation of Romans 1:3, 4, where reference to the incarnation is indubitable. Further support comes from the use of φανερόω elsewhere for the incarnate ministry of Jesus (Jn. 1:31; Heb. 9:26; 1 Pet. 1:20; 1 Jn. 1:2; 3:5, 8) and from the use of σάρξ elsewhere for the humanity of Jesus (Jn. 1:14; 6:51 ff.; Rom. 8:3; 10:5; Eph. 2:14; Col. 1:22; Heb. 5:7; 10:20; 1 Pet. 3:18; 4:1; 1 Jn. 4:2; 2 Jn. 7; cf. Lk. 24:39), not to delineate the very common uses of "flesh" for humanity in general and for human life on this earth. In view of several considerations, "manifested in flesh" probably refers to the entire earthly career of Jesus right up to the ascension, not to his birth alone: (1) the use of σάρξ for human lifetime (Gal. 2:20; Phil. 1:22, 24; and especially Heb. 5:7, "in the days of his flesh"); (2) the generality of the verb "manifested", as opposed to a more specific verb (say, "born"); and (3) the synthetic relationship to "taken up in glory" (line 6). Ἐφανερώθη then becomes a constative aorist.

The considerations in the preceding paragraph undercut D. M. Stanley's argument that because σάρξ in contrast to πνεῦμα means human nature in its weakness, creatureliness, and sinfulness, line 1 refers not to the incarnation, but to the crucifixion. It is true that Paul connects the σάρξ and death of Christ in Colossians 1:22 and 2:14 (but not Rom. 8:3, where God's sending his son in the likeness of sinful flesh is more general).[1] However, the references cited by Stanley show that the connexion between Christ's σάρξ and death is incidental to the incarnation as a whole. And Stanley's argument from the sinfulness of σάρξ would work equally against his own view that line 1 refers to Jesus' death (see 2 Cor. 5:21: "who knew no

---

[1] D. M. Stanley, *Christ's Resurrection in Pauline Soteriology* (Rome, 1961), p. 237; *idem*, "The Divinity of Christ in New Testament Hymns", *Studies in Salvation History*, ed. C. L. Salm (Englewood Cliffs, N.J., 1964), p. 193. R. P. Martin's argument against Stanley that the hymnic quotation presents the baptizand with his liberation from the hostile cosmic powers through Christ's victory rather than with Christ's death and resurrection takes for granted the very point at issue. After all, Jesus' death and resurrection have some relationship to baptism and the defeat of hostile powers (see, e.g., Rom. 6. 1 ff.; Col. 2:10-15; R. P. Martin, "Aspects of Worship in the New Testament Church", *Vox Evangelica*, II [London, 1963], p. 26). Like Stanley, A. R. C. Leaney interprets line 1 in terms of the crucifixion, but his parallels are even further afield (Lk. 24:26, 46; Jn. 3:14; 8:28; 12:32, 34; Rom. 6:7; Phil. 2:8-11; Col. 2:15; A. R. C. Leaney, *The Epistles to Timothy, Titus and Philemon* [London, 1960], p. 61).

sin"). That view would seem to require "suffered", "crucified", or "put to death", as in 1 Peter 3:18. Anyway, σάρξ does not always or even usually carry the connotation of sinfulness. Consequently, Descamps, J. Dupont, and B. Schneider take the opposite tack by seeing line 1 as a summary of Christ's post-resurrection appearances in corporeal form (ἐν σαρκί), with support from Luke 24:39; Titus 2:11; 3:4; and especially 2 Timothy 1:10 where it is claimed that the first of Christ's two great appearances consists in the post-resurrection appearances (as a group), not the incarnation.[1] But the appearance of God's grace and kindness in Titus 2:11 and 3:4 is not tied specifically or exclusively to the resurrection of Jesus. And in 2 Timothy 1:9, 10 the clause "who abolished death" simply modifies "our Saviour Christ Jesus" without restricting to the resurrection his "appearing" by which God's "purpose and grace" have been revealed. Only in Luke 24:39 is the resurrection mentioned in connexion with Christ's flesh (and bones), but there neither φανερόω nor the similar ἐπιφαίνω occurs so that the parallel is doubtful. It remains preferable, therefore, to see in line 1 a reference to the earthly career of the incarnate Christ.

The meaning of "vindicated in spirit" (line 2) lies in doubt. For ἐδικαιώθη Dibelius suggested the Hellenistic meaning "divinized". But that sense is absent in the rest of the New Testament, and the extra-Biblical evidence for it post-dates the first century. Even the earliest example, Ignatius' Epistle to the Philadelphians 8:2, could be disputed.[2] Recognizing the problem, Schweizer thinks that the more Hebraic "declared righteous, vindicated, validated" comes to about the same meaning as the Hellenistic "divinized", for both refer to entry into the divine sphere. But Schweizer's parallel references from the New Testament period and before – Romans 3:4 (=Ps. 51:6); Psalms of Solomon 2:16; 3:5; 4:9; 8:7 – carry only the meaning of vindication, not entry into the divine sphere.[3]

Nevertheless, it is commonly thought, even by those who fail to see anything approaching a Hellenistic meaning in ἐδικαιώθη, that ἐν πνεύματι carries the somewhat abstract meaning, "in the spiritual or

---

[1] Descamps, op. cit., pp. 84–87; J. Dupont, ΣΥΝ ΧΡΙΣΤΩΙ. L'Union avec le Christ suivant saint Paul (Paris, 1952), pp. 108–10; B. Schneider, "Κατὰ Πνεῦμα Ἁγιωσύνης (Rom. 1, 4)" Biblica 48 (1967), pp. 367, 384 f. Thus, to Dupont, 1 Tim. 3:16 is a paschal hymn which celebrates exclusively the risen, glorified Christ, not including the earthly Christ. Dupont classifies the Johannine uses of φανερόω for Jesus' earthly ministry as unique and overlooks the others, which are cited above.

[2] That is, it is questionable that Ignatius thought of attaining full discipleship, justification, and Jesus Christ at martyrdom in terms of divinization. See M. Dibelius, Die Pastoralbriefe[2] (Tübingen, 1931), p. 39, and Schweizer, Erniedrigung, p. 64, for references in later literature.

[3] Schweizer, Lordship, p. 65; idem, Erniedrigung, p. 64. On the basis of the connexion between justice and glory in the Old Testament, Descamps thinks that "justified" = "glorified", a view similar to Schweizer's and subject to the same criticism (op. cit., pp. 87–89). For δικαιόω as vindication, see Matt. 11:19; Lk. 7:29, 35; 10:29; Rom. 3:4 (=Ps. 51:6); cf. Ps. 19:10; TDNT, II, 214 f. Knox, loc. cit., notes that in Rom. 3:26 justness and justifyingness are closely related.

heavenly sphere", so that by contrast ἐν σαρκί means "in the fleshly, corporeal, or earthly sphere". Thus the two ἐν's are both locative as they must be, it is argued, because of parallelism.[1] But although ἐν πνεύματι and ἐν σαρκί may denote contrasting realms of being, it is doubtful that they do so apart from very particular and individualistic references in context. For confirmation, one need only check a concordance for the phrases ἐν (τῇ) σαρκί and ἐν (τῷ) πνεύματι. In 1 Timothy 3:16, just as ἐν σαρκί surely denotes the individual physical manifestation of Christ as well as the general sphere in which his manifestation took place, so also ἐν πνεύματι denotes the individual human spirit of Christ as well as the general sphere in which his vindication took place.[2] So also in 1 Peter 3:18, the phrase θανατωθεὶς μὲν σαρκί contains a dative of reference (or locative) concerning the physical death of Christ, so that the parallel ζῳοποιηθεὶς δὲ πνεύματι must likewise contain a dative of reference (or locative) concerning his human spirit rather than an instrumental dative concerning the Holy Spirit (cf. 1 Pet. 4:1, 6).[3] In neither 1 Peter nor 1 Timothy does the anarthrousness of the nouns limit them to general or abstract meanings. It stems simply from the condensed nature of these formulary expressions.

Some would treat ἐν πνεύματι in 1 Timothy 3:16 as an instrumental dative with reference to the Holy Spirit (cf. Rom. 1:4; 8:11). However, in the absence of a qualifier such as ἁγίῳ with πνεύματι (contrast Rom. 1:4; 8:1-11) the conjunction with the flesh of Christ favours a reference to his human spirit. Also against the interpretation, "Vindicated by the [Holy] Spirit", the parallel ἐν σαρκί can be taken instrumentally only with

[1] See Schweizer et al., Spirit of God (London, 1960), p. 57; idem, "Two New Testament Creeds Compared", p. 169; idem, Lordship, pp. 59 f.

[2] Cf. LSJ, ἐν s.v., "I. Of Place, . . . 10 . . . in the form of . . ."; E. DeWitt Burton, Spirit, Soul, and Flesh (Chicago, 1918), p. 198. Only an exaggerated view of the unitary nature of man will rule out a dual reference here to Christ's flesh and spirit. Within the Biblical understanding of man there is a subdued dualism, or rather, duality.

[3] See E. G. Selwyn, The First Epistle of St. Peter (London, 1958), pp. 325, 277. Selwyn suggests that 1 Pet. 3:18-22 rests on the hymn quoted in 1 Tim. 3:16. Cf. the same suggestion made earlier by N. J. D. White, EGT, vol. IV, p. 118, and carried out also by M.-E. Boismard, Quatre hymnes baptismales dans la première épître de Pierre (Paris, 1961), pp. 60 f., 65 f. Selwyn supports the hypothesis by drawing parallels between manifestation in flesh and death as to flesh, vindication in spirit and being made alive in spirit, appearance to angels and preaching to the spirits in prison with subjugation of cosmic powers, proclamation among nations/belief throughout the world and baptism as the pledge of a good conscience towards God, and translation in glory and ascension into heaven to a position at God's right hand. The parallels are sometimes impressive, but one demurs because of the phraseological differences (even though there may be relationships) between manifestation and death, vindication and being made alive, and proclamation/belief and baptism. Following Spicq, Stanley, "The Divinity of Christ", p. 191; idem, Christ's Resurrection, pp. 236 f., thinks that 1 Tim. 3:16 continues the hymn quoted in Eph. 5:14. Lock, loc. cit., had made the same suggestion. The ὅς with which the quotation in 1 Tim. 3:16 begins would then pick up the last word of the quotation in Eph. 5:14, viz., Χριστός. Spicq adds some unimpressive parallels to Mk. 16:9-19 (op. cit., p. cxlv). H. A. Blair, A Creed Before the Creeds (London, 1955), sees the hymn in 1 Tim. 3:16 behind many passages in the New Testament; but his views seem fanciful, as also his theory that the hymn expands the primitive homologia, Jesus (lines 1 and 2) Christ (lines 2 and 3) is Lord (lines 4 and 5).

awkwardness ("manifested by means of flesh") and all the other ἐν's are locative.[1] Alone, these arguments are admittedly indecisive, for Romans 1:4 contains a contrast between Jesus' flesh and the Holy Spirit. Again, in 1 Timothy 3:16 the simple dative ἀγγέλοις in line 3 interrupts the parallel ἐν's so that the parallelism is neither perfect nor complete. The string of ἐν's may come from the desire for similar sound without the requirement of identical sense. It has even been questioned whether early Christians distinguished Christ's human spirit from the Holy Spirit.[2] (But see Mark 2:8; 8:12; 15:37; Matthew 27:50; Luke 23:46; John 11:33; 13:21; 19:30.) Taken together, nevertheless, the unlikelihood of an instrumental ἐν in the hymnic quotation and the greater naturalness in the pairing of Jesus' own flesh and spirit tip the scales against a reference to the Holy Spirit.

But what constituted the vindication of Christ in spirit? All those views which see references to his anointing with the Spirit at baptism and to his miracles, exorcisms, preaching, and spotless life through the Holy Spirit[3] stumble against the foregoing arguments that ἐν πνεύματι is not instrumental but locative and does not refer to the Holy Spirit but to the human spirit of Christ. So also does the common view which sees a reference to Jesus' resurrection (perhaps with inclusion of the ascension) by the (Holy) Spirit. Other passages do, of course, associate the resurrection with the Holy Spirit (notably the parallel credal quotation Rom. 1:4; cf. 8:9, 11; Jn. 6:63). But here a reference to the Holy Spirit as the agent of the resurrection would require an awkward instrumental ἐν (resurrection "in the Spirit" hardly makes sense) against the locative ἐν's in parallel lines. It would also require a reference to the Holy Spirit against the more natural pairing with Jesus' human spirit (so also in the parallel 1 Peter 3:18, closer than Romans 1:4 where πνεῦμα is modified by ἁγιωσύνης). These same objections to treating ἐν πνεύματι instrumentally concerning the Holy Spirit militate also against interpreting line 2 as a reference to the vindication of Christ by the outpouring of the Spirit on the Day of Pentecost.[4]

A reference to the resurrection of Jesus may still be seen in line 2, not by the operation of the Holy Spirit, but in the realm of spirit with reference to the spiritual nature of Christ's glorified body. If the ascension be included as a concomitant, there is an added reference to the vindication of Christ as he passed through the spiritual realm (intermediate heaven) of the cosmic powers on his way from earth to God's right hand (cf. line 3, "seen

---

[1] *Pace* Deichgräber, *op. cit.*, p. 136, n. 3.

[2] Kelly, *op. cit.*, pp. 90 f.

[3] Matt. 12:18, 28; Lk. 4:18 f.; Acts 10:38. Falconer, *loc. cit.*, cites Lk. 3:22; 9:35; 10:21-24; Jn. 16:14.

[4] The view of A. Schlatter, *Die Briefe an die Thessalonicher, Philipper, Timotheus und Titus* (Stuttgart, 1950), p. 160; somewhat differently in *Die Kirche der Griechen im Urteil des Paulus*[2] (Stuttgart, 1958), p. 114.

by angels"). Thus, the phrase "in spirit" does not deny the corporeality of the risen, ascending Christ; it rather affirms the spiritual nature of his body (cf. 1 Cor. 15:35 ff., esp. 44 f.).[1] If line 2 does refer to vindication by resurrection/ascension, this understanding of "in spirit" is probably correct. One hesitates, however, because the locative ἐν πνεύματι is surely an awkward way to express the spiritual nature of a body. Place, rather than quality, seems to be in view. And "the spiritual realm" appears to be somewhat too abstract and impersonal a meaning, particularly when standing in contrast to Christ's appearance in flesh, the flesh of his human body.

We need then to consider the view that line 2 refers to the vindication of Christ during and by the *Descensus ad Inferos* in spirit-form between death and resurrection (cf. 1 Pet. 3:18 ff.). This presupposes, of course, that Dalton is wrong in maintaining that 1 Peter 3:18 ff. refers to Christ's preaching to the cosmic powers imprisoned in the lower heavens during an ascension right after his resurrection.[2] Perhaps the strongest argument for Dalton's view and against the traditional understanding is that ζῳοποιηθείς, which *precedes* the preaching, must refer to the resurrection as the word usually does elsewhere (Jn. 5:21; Rom. 4:17; 8:11; 1 Cor. 15:22, 36, 45). But the argument loses some of its cogency because of the spiritual sense (συν)ζῳοποιέω bears in John 6:63; 2 Corinthians 3:6; Galatians 3:21; Colossians 2:13; and especially Ephesians 2:5, where it stands in contrast to (συν)ἤγειρεν and indicates a vivification distinct from and prior to resurrection and exaltation. Other considerations favour retention of the traditional understanding: (1) the subterranean implication of ταρτρώσας in the parallel 2 Peter 2:4; (2) the apparent distinction between vivification and resurrection with placement between the two of the proclamation to the spirits, as seen in the progression "died/put to death" – "vivified" – "having gone and preached to the spirits in prison" – "resurrection of Jesus Christ" – "at the right hand of God, having gone into heaven"; (3) the repetition of πορευθείς so that "having gone into heaven [at God's right hand]" stands in sharp contrast to "having gone and preached . . . in prison", i.e., the preaching in prison contrasts with the ascension to heaven whereas Dalton wishes to identify them;[3] (4) the consistency (despite Dalton's pleas to the contrary) with which the prison of the fallen Watchers in 1 Enoch appears to be a bottomless abyss in the far west of the earth. 1 Peter then means that upon his expiration Jesus came alive again in spirit through renewed fellowship with the Father ("Father, into your hands I commit my spirit," Luke 23:46), went to the abyss in spirit-form to proclaim his triumph, and thus enjoyed vindication before the hostile spirits there. By the same token, line 2 in 1 Timothy

[1] F. D. Gealey, *IB*, vol. XI, p. 422; W. J. Dalton, *op. cit.*, pp. 130 f.; cf. Schneider, *op. cit.*, pp. 367 f.
[2] Dalton, *op. cit.*
[3] Cf. M. Scharlemann's review of Dalton's book in *JBL* 84 (1965), pp. 470–72.

3:16 most likely refers to that vindication in spirit prior to the resurrection.[1]

According to line 3, Christ "appeared to angels". But when and to what angels? Surely not to angels in the sense of human, apostolic messengers who had witnessed the risen Christ. For although ὤφθη occurs prominently in connexion with the post-resurrection appearances (Lk. 24:34; Acts 9:17; 13:31; 1 Cor. 15:5-8; cf. Acts 26:16), the word commonly occurs in other connexions, too, and the meaning "angel" for ἄγγελος predominates throughout the New Testament (see the concordance).[2] Because support is lacking, we may also dismiss the passing suggestion of W. Barclay that angels may have seen Jesus before his incarnation.[3]

Others refer line 3 to angelic observation of the whole incarnational revelation of Christ (1 Pet. 1:12; Eph. 3:10; Lk. 2:9-15; Mk. 1:13; 16:5-8; Matt. 4:11; 28.2-7; Lk. 24:4-7 [?]; John 20:12 f.; Acts 1:10 f. [?])[4] or to the resurrection alone.[5] However, in none of the references cited does Christ appear to angels. If there is an appearance at all, *they* appear. This difficulty for the view is aggravated by the fact that ὤφθη nearly always means the *self*-exhibition of the subject, "appeared or showed himself (to)", so that what follows is a true dative rather than an instrumental of agent. Technically, then, "was seen by angels" is a wrong and misleading translation.[6] (It is used above solely to capture the feel of the passive verbal forms in parallel construction.)[7]

The most common view is that line 3 refers to the exaltation of Christ over all angelic powers at his ascension and installation at God's right hand (cf. 1 Pet. 3:22; Col. 2:15; Phil. 2:9-11; Heb. 1:3, 4; Rev. 5:8-14; Polycarp to the Philippians 2:1).[8] If the angels to whom Christ appeared

---

[1] See above, p. 211, note 2, in answer to the objection that this view is too dichotomous of human nature. Cf. 2 Cor. 12:2, 3.

[2] It is invalid, however, to argue against the meaning "messengers" from the anarthrousness of ἀγγέλοις (as do Schweizer, *Erniedrigung*, p. 64, and B. Weiss, *loc. cit.*), for that may be due to the parallelism of lines.

[3] W. Barclay, *The Letters to Timothy, Titus and Philemon*[2] (Philadelphia, 1961), pp. 104 f. Barclay does not commit himself to this view.

[4] So especially J. H. Bernard, *The Pastoral Epistles* (Cambridge, 1899), p. 63.

[5] W. Hendriksen, *New Testament Commentary, Exposition of the Pastoral Epistles* (Grand Rapids, 1957), pp. 140 ff.; Knox, *loc. cit.*; Wallis, *op. cit.*, pp. 1375 f., includes the ascension with the resurrection (cf. 1 Pet. 3:22).

[6] See A. T. Robertson, *A Grammar of the Greek New Testament in the Light of Historical Research*[3] (Nashville, 1934), p. 534; M. R. Vincent, *Word Studies in the New Testament* (New York, 1900), vol. IV, p. 241; Arndt, s.v.

[7] The difficulty in referring "seen by angels" to angelic observation of Christ's earthly ministry upsets the view of H. Schlier (*Religionsgeschichtliche Untersuchungen zu den Ignatiusbriefen* [Giessen, 1929], pp. 171 f.) that lines 3 and 4 carry out line 1 regarding the incarnation, and that lines 5 and 6 carry out line 2 regarding the glorification of Christ.

[8] See esp. R. Bultmann, *Theology of the New Testament* (New York, 1955) II, p. 153, who adds other references not entirely parallel: 1 Cor. 2:6-8, which refers to the crucifixion; 15:24-26, which refers to the future τέλος; Ignatius to the Trallians 9:1, which refers to the crucifixion; and Ignatius to the Eph. 19, which refers to the nativity. But cf. also the Ascension of Isa. 11:23 ff.; and Heb. 1:6, understood in terms of already accomplished exaltation (A. Vanhoye, "L'οἰκουμένη dans l'épître aux Hébreux", *Bib* 45 [1964], pp. 248-

are actually or potentially hostile powers in the lower heavens through which he ascended, line 3 indicates his triumph over them. But unless lines 2 and 3 are synthetically parallel (see below), that would repeat too closely the thought of vindication in line 2; and ὤφθη in line 3 does not by itself suggest triumph. If the angels to whom Christ appeared are the good angels around the divine throne, line 3 may carry more the note of adoration at the sight of his exaltation (cf. especially Rev. 5:11 f.). It might be objected that by making line 3 parallel to "taken up in glory" in line 6, this interpretation introduces an unlikely redundancy. However, line 6 refers to the ascension as such; line 3 would refer to angelic observation of it. And there is a similar and indubitable parallelism (or redundancy) between "proclaimed among [the] nations" (line 4) and "believed on in [the] world" (line 5) where the event is the same but the emphasis different.

The synthetic parallelism between lines 4 and 5, however, raises the probability that the true parallel to line 3 is not the distant line 6, but line 2 immediately preceding (see above, pp. 208 f.). If so, and if line 2 refers to vindication through descent into hades (see above, pp. 212 f.), "seen by angels" in line 3 refers to the sight of the vivified Christ in spirit-form by the "spirits in prison" (cf. the use of ἄγγελος for these imprisoned spirits in Jude 6). Then "seen by angels" does carry the note of triumph – through association with ἐδικαιώθη in the foregoing line.[1]

The only serious question in line 4 is whether ἔθνεσιν means "nations" or "Gentiles". Fausset and Bernard chose "Gentiles", those farthest from God, as a contrast to "angels", those nearest to God.[2] But line 3 probably refers to fallen angels, indeed, to those specially wicked spirits now imprisoned because of their nefarious activity just before the Deluge. Knox also preferred "Gentiles" as a characteristically Pauline touch.[3] Chary of a Pauline origin for the hymnic quotation, Barrett prefers "Gentiles" as an allusion to the work of Paul (cf. 2:7).[4] But the antithesis ἀγγέλοις/ἔθνεσιν appears not to contrast Jews and Gentiles or angels and Gentiles,

---

[1] W. M. L. de Wette, *Kurzgefasstes exegetisches Handbuch zum Neuen Testament* (Leipzig, 1847), vol. II, p. 86, interpreted line 3 in terms of the *Descensus*. C. J. Ellicott, *A Critical and Grammatical Commentary on the Pastoral Epistles*[2] (London, 1861), p. 53, opposed any reference to evil angels on the ground that the parallel angels/nations militates against such a restrictive connotation. But if the nations to whom proclamation is made are non-Christian, why may not the angels to whom Christ appears be hostile?

[2] Fausset, *op. cit.*, p. 412; Bernard, *loc. cit.*

[3] Knox, *loc. cit.* But see Lock, *op. cit.*, pp. 44 f., against attributing the hymn to the author of the pastorals.

[4] Barrett, *loc. cit*

---

53). L. Cerfaux stresses the parallel in the Ascension of Isaiah (*Christ in the Theology of St. Paul* [New York, 1959], pp. 372–74). Stanley draws the exaltation of Christ above angels into relationship with the outpouring of the Holy Spirit at Pentecost as proof of that exaltation (cf. Acts 2:33) and notes that preaching to the nations in line 4 follows naturally after enduement with the Spirit (*Christ's Resurrection*, pp. 238 f.). Schlatter comments that since the ascension, Christ is no longer visible to men but is visible to angels (*Die Briefe*, p. 160; *Die Kirche*, p. 114).

but superhuman and human beings. "Nations" therefore is to be preferred.[1]

"Believed on in [the] world" (line 5) denotes by synthetic parallelism the result of "preached among nations" (line 4) and by antithetic parallelism with "taken up in glory" (line 6) a contrast in the two spheres of Christ's reception, the world and (by implication from "taken up") heaven. The contrast with "taken up in glory" restricts κόσμῳ to *this* world, despite Selwyn's argument that κόσμῳ must mean the whole universe because in a restricted sense it would merely repeat the thought of ἔθνεσιν in line 4.[2]

We have already determined that "taken up in glory" refers to the ascension rather than to the final glory of Christ at his Parousia. The verb "was taken up" suggests that ἐν might be tinged with the meaning of εἰς, "into",[3] as well as its own proper meaning "in" with reference to attendant circumstance. If so, the prepositional phrase would mean both "into glory"[4] and "in the cloud of glory" in which Jesus ascended (and in which he will return).[5] However, ἐν in the sense of εἰς is unusual. That sense would deviate from the usage of ἐν in the parallel lines, and the consistency with which ἐν δόξῃ elsewhere denotes accompanying circumstance[6] favours that meaning here – all to the exclusion of the sense "into glory".

III

From what kind of theological milieu in the early church did the hymnic quotation in 1 Timothy 3:16 come? Gnosticism will not be a convincing answer until confirmation that the myth of a descending and ascending redeemer dates from before or during the rise of Christianity.[7] Even then, the hymn's universalistic emphasis would seem to go against rather than derive from gnosticism.

Schweizer thinks of the Hellenistic wing of the church.[8] His main argument is that the hymnic quotation prominently exhibits a spatial contrast between upper and lower spheres which would arise from and appeal to the Hellenistic mind in contrast to the temporally oriented Jewish mind.

In the first place, however, we now know from the Dead Sea Scrolls, other archaeological discoveries in Palestine, and the work of scholars

[1] Selwyn, *op. cit.*, p. 326, n. 3.

[2] Schweizer, *Lordship*, pp. 59 f.; *idem, TWNT*, VII, p. 138; cf. Martin, *loc. cit.*, pp. 25 ff.

[3] This is not to deny pre-Christian speculation about Adam and Primal Man.

[4] Mk. 8:38; 10:37; Matt. 6:29; 16:27; 25:31; Lk. 9:26, 31; 12:27; 1 Cor. 15:34; 2 Cor. 3:7, 8, 11; Col. 3:4.

[5] Mk. 8:38; 13:26; Matt. 16:27; 24:30; Lk. 9:26; 21:27; Acts 1:11; 1 Thes. 4:17; Rev. 1:7 (cf. 11:12); 14:14–16. Cf. Exod. 16:10 LXX: καὶ ἡ δόξα κυρίου ὤφθη ἐν νεφέλῃ.

[6] But "glory" appears *not* to mean heaven; it refers to a condition rather than a place and thus is not a spatial concept. See the lexica and concordances to the New Testament and LXX.

[7] Cf. Lk. 24:26; Arndt, *ἐν s.v.*

[8] Cullmann's suggestion that ἔθνεσιν may refer to the dead requires further qualification of ἔθνεσιν in the text or supportive parallel passages, so far lacking (*The Earliest Christian Confessions* [London, 1949], p. 60). By that interpretation Cullmann thinks he has put everything before the ascension (line 6), but he still has to reckon with line 5, "believed on in [the] world". Parry (*loc. cit.*) thinks that ἔθνεσιν instead of, say, ἀνθρώποις emphasizes wide range.

such as S. Lieberman, W. L. Knox, J. N. Sevenster, and J. P. Mahaffy[1] that Hellenism had invaded Palestine of the New Testament era more pervasively than used to be thought. Semitic literary features and Hellenistic concepts went together. The religious ideas and expressions of first-century Palestine were a mixed bag. Therefore, to say "Hellenistic" or even "Jewish Hellenistic" is to be ambiguous. The crucial question is: Palestinian, Jewish, and early, or extra-Palestinian, Gentile, and late?

In the second place, Schweizer himself has supplied ample evidence that the contrast between upper and lower spheres is not distinctively "Hellenistic" at all, but appears in the Old Testament, grows in the LXX and Jewish apocryphal and pseudepigraphal literature, and receives expression in rabbinical literature.[2] For example, God comes down to view the Tower of Babel and descends upon Mount Sinai. Enoch and Elisha are taken up at their translations. The Lord's Prayer, which could hardly be more un-"Hellenistic" and Semitic, carries the contrast "as in heaven, so on earth", as also the prayer of Rabbi Eliezer (c. A. D. 90), "Do thy will in heaven above and give quietness of spirit to them who fear thee in the earth" (Tract. Berak. 3:7), and Psalms 135:6, "Whatever the Lord pleases he does, in heaven and on earth." Whatever spatial contrast may be in 1 Timothy 3:16, then, it is no more than could have come from Palestine at the very beginning of the church.

In the third place, the spatial contrast in the hymnic quotation is not nearly so strong as Schweizer thinks. Even where it looks most apparent – viz., in lines 5 and 6, "believed on in [the] world, taken up in glory" – it is subdued; for "glory" does not refer to a place, heaven, but to a condition, the accompanying circumstance of the shekinah-cloud at the ascension (see above pp. 216). The only spatial contrast comes from the verb "was taken up" in relation to the preceding phrase, "in the world". But that is no more "Hellenistic" than the description of Elijah's translation: "And Elijah went up by a whirlwind into heaven; καὶ ἀνελήμφθη Ἠλίου ἐν συσσεισμῷ ὡς εἰς τόν οὐρανόν" (4 Kg. 2:11, LXX).

Nor does the antithesis flesh/spirit in lines 1 and 2 favour "Hellenistic" origin. The same duality appears in the Dead Sea Scrolls;[3] and that duality

[1] S. Lieberman, Hellenism in Jewish Palestine (New York, 1950); W. L. Knox, Some Hellenistic Elements in Primitive Christianity (London, 1944); J. N. Sevenster, Do You Know Greek? (Leiden, 1968); J. P. Mahaffy, The Progress of Hellenism in Alexander's Empire (Chicago, 1905); see also R. H. Gundry, "The Language Milieu of First-Century Palestine", JBL 83 (1964), pp. 404–08.

[2] Schweizer, "Röm. 1, 3 f. und der Gegensatz von Fleisch und Geist vor und bei Paulus", Evangelische Theologie 15 (1955), p. 568; idem, Spirit of God, p. 58; idem, TWNT, vol. VII, 108 ff. Sample references are Gen. 11:5, 7; 18:21; Exod. 3:8; 19:11–20; 34:5; 1 Enoch 15. Cf. the designation of God as the Most High ('Elyon), the Mesopotamian distinction between the supernal Igigi and the infernal Anunnaki, and the Hittite "upper" and "l ower" gods (šarrazēs and katterēš). I owe the last two references to T. H. Gaster, "Angels", IDB, vol. A–D, p. 131.

[3] 1QH xvii. 25; xiii. 13; iv. 20. See the summary in H. Ringgren, The Faith of Qumran (Philadelphia, 1963), pp. 97 ff., and the well-known literature cited there. See also a passage like Isa. 31:3. I do not imply that such passages in Jewish literature are fully dualistic in the Greek sense; but neither do lines 1 and 2 of 1 Tim. 3 : 16 have to be.

is not spatial, i.e., earthly versus heavenly. It is possible for a person living on earth to be either ἐν σαρκί or ἐν πνεύματι (Rom. 8); and the author of IQH xvii. 25; xiii. 13 calls himself a "spirit of flesh". Besides, as noted above, "flesh" and "spirit" do not refer to earthly and heavenly spheres of being so much as to the specific flesh and spirit of Christ in his physical incarnation and spiritual vivification (or resurrection) respectively (cf. I Pet. 3:18). The contrast lies not in spatial differentiation, but in bodily versus bodiless (or spiritual) modes of being. If "vindicated in spirit" has to do with the *Descensus*, the spatial implication (but only an implication, not a point of emphasis) has to do with the underworld, the prison of the specially evil spirits from antediluvian times. And that concept was native to first-century Palestinian thinking as we know from its presence in I Enoch combined with the discovery of Enochian fragments (except for the Similitudes) at Qumran. Or if (doubtfully) "vindicated in spirit" refers to the resurrection of Christ in a spiritual body (cf. I Cor. 15:35 ff., esp. 44 f.), the locale is earthly, not heavenly. The resurrection did not take place in heaven. Even though it be insisted that at first the resurrection included the exaltation and vice versa, in Christian thought the process of raising began *on earth* as the very use of the terms ἐγείρω, ἀνίστημι, and cognates for Christ's resurrection-exaltation imply. Only by making πνεύματι a synonym for heaven (and σαρκί for earth) and applying line 2 to an exclusively celestial event such as the installation at God's right hand could lines 1 and 2 support a spatial antithesis between earth and heaven. But the usage of πνεῦμα and σάρξ elsewhere will not bear the weight of such definitely spatial understandings here.

The contrast between angels and nations in lines 3 and 4 is equally weak to support distinction between heaven and earth as the basic backdrop behind the hymnic quotation. For the angels may well be those imprisoned below rather than those active above. Spatial progression receives clear statement only in lines 5 and 6, " ... in [the] world, taken up ...," so that only by reading the verse backwards could one gain the impression of strong spatial contrasts. In lines 1–4 spatial ideas occur only by silent implication, and then with probable reference to the underworld as well as to earth and heaven:

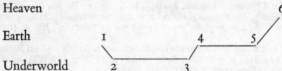

Above all, there is nothing distinctively "Hellenistic" in the sense of extra-Palestinian, Gentile, and late.

It is also argued for Hellenistic origin that its message announces deliverance from the fatalism which gloomed the Hellenistic world. A Palestinian theology of the cross is entirely missing. In its place is a theology of cosmic triumph over the "angels", who contrast with the earthly nations and make up the astral powers to whom Christ appeared during his ascent through the lower heavens to God above.[1] Even so, the angelology of first-century Palestinian Judaism suffices to handle that category of celestial beings.[2] But a reference to powers in the lower heavens is not at all certain, or probable. The angels may be the adoring angels around the throne of God also well known in first-century Palestinian Judaism.[3] Most likely, however, "seen by angels" constitutes a second reference to the *Descensus* synthetically parallel to "vindicated in spirit" (see above, pp. 213 f.). Here again the Enochian literature found at Qumran vitiates the theory of Hellenistic origin. Concerning the failure of a reference to the death of Christ, we should keep in mind that the lack of an antecedent for ὅς may mean that we have only part of the hymn.[4] Argument from silence is especially weak here. Who knows whether an unquoted part may have contained a theology of the cross? What inferences might be drawn if Paul had quoted only what is contained in Philippians 2:9–11 of the hymn he begins to quote in verse 6? Although Stanley has not succeeded in delimiting manifestation in flesh to the crucifixion, his references to the use of σάρξ in connexion with Christ's death (Col. 1:22; Eph. 2:14) do show that manifestation in flesh *includes* the crucifixion.[5] And if lines 2 and 3 in 1 Timothy 3:16 have to do with the *Descensus*, as argued above, they at least imply the death of Christ. In any case, the emphasis on vindication implies the humiliation of his suffering and death. And the note of triumph sustained throughout the hymnic quotation is sufficiently accounted for by the desire of early Christians for vindication in the face of persecution (not necessarily including frequent martyrdom) and their expectation of that vindication after the pattern of Christ (cf. 1 Pet. 1:3–12; 3:18 - 4:6,

[1] Cf. R. P. Martin, *Carmen Christi* (Cambridge, 1967), pp. 307 ff. On p. 298, Martin argues that the hymn in Phil. 2:6–11 does not come from the mother church in Jerusalem because of the absence of the following items known from Acts to be characteristic of her Christology: (1) Davidic origin of Jesus; (2) fulfilment of Messianic prophecy; (3) Jesus' mission to the Jews; (4) the public ministry of Jesus; (5) the crucifixion; (6) the resurrection; (7) the Parousia. The same argument might apply to 1 Tim. 3:16. However, it would overlook that passages in Acts exhibit Christology in relation to gospel-preaching, whereas 1 Tim. 3:16 exhibits Christology in relation to the experience of Christians under persecution (see below, p. 221). Christologies differ for situational as well as geographical and religio-ethnic reasons.

[2] See the discussion and numerous references, especially those to the apocrypha and pseudepigrapha, by T. H. Gaster, *op. cit.*, pp. 132 ff., and by C. D. Morrison, *The Powers That Be* (London, 1960), *passim*. Samples are 1 Enoch 19:1 ff.; 41:3–9; 60:11 ff.; 61:10; 72:1; 74:1, 2; 75:3; 1QH 1:10, 11.

[3] See, e.g., J. Strugnell, "The Angelic Liturgy at Qumran – 4Q Sérek Sîrôt 'ôlat Haššabbāt", *VT Suppl.* 7 (1960), pp. 318–45; 1 Enoch 40:1 ff.; 61:12. Cf. the often-mentioned "angels of the presence".

[4] H. Duensing's suggestion (relayed by J. Jeremias, *The Eucharistic Words of Jesus*[2] [London, 1966], p. 132) that ὅς is intentionally obscure because of esoteric Christology stumbles against the meaning of mystery as an *open* secret now to be proclaimed and against the note of public triumph throughout the verse, but esp. in line 4. It remains possible that ὅς was a conventional way in which Christians opened their hymns to Christ. Cf. Deichgräber's argument that 1 Tim. 3:16 is too well-rounded to be considered only a fragment (*op. cit.*, p. 134, n. 1).

[5] See above, p. 209 f.

13; Acts 4:23–30). This desire and expectation along the lines of the Old Testament (especially Job) obviates the need to import Hellenistic ideas of fate and meaninglessness into the background of the hymn. Besides, were such ideas behind the hymn, the proclamation of Christ among the nations and belief on him in the world (lines 4 and 5) become irrelevant. For Christians concerned with rejection by society at large, however, those are signs of divine approval and ultimate victory.

Building upon D. Georgi's thesis concerning 2 Corinthians, R. H. Fuller has pressed for a Hellenistic milieu behind 1 Timothy 3:16 by arguing that "manifested in flesh" exhibits a Christology of epiphany based on the Hellenistic concept of a θεῖος ἀνήρ.[1] In particular, Fuller contrasts the emptying or hiding of divine glory in the hymn quoted in Philippians 2:6 ff. and the manifestation of divine glory in 1 Timothy 3:16. By drawing such a contrast, however, Fuller has overstated what 1 Timothy 3:16 actually says. Divine glory receives mention not until the reference to ascension in line 6. Furthermore, the reference to vindication right after line 1 may imply rejection of the manifestation just because it was inglorious. Nor is the use of φανερόω in line 1 distinctively Hellenistic, for (to take but one example) it occurs in 1 Peter 1:20 concerning Christ's first advent in a context very Hebraic in style and content.[2] The verb also occurs in connexions other than with the incarnation, so that we should not regard it as a telltale catchword of Hellenistic Christology. "Manifested in flesh", then, fails to constitute a clue to a Hellenistic milieu.

It is not only that we are not bound to see necessarily Hellenistic features in 1 Timothy 3:16; a number of features positively favour an early Palestinian Jewish matrix rather than a "Hellenistic" one.[3] E. Norden long ago noted that the only true isocolon is the contrast between flesh and spirit, but even here μὲν—δέ is missing. Moreover, ἐν is missing in line 3; and Greeks tended not to put verbs first, whereas Jews did (as in the hymn quoted in Eph. 5:14 and in the Lord's Prayer; also, Isa. 37:17; Sir. 36; Wis. 10:15 ff.). For word-order and contrast a Greek would probably have written,

ἐν κόσμῳ μὲν ἐπιστεύθη,
ἐν δόξῃ δ' ἀνελήμφθη.

Perhaps most impressive of all is the characteristically Semitic passive form of the verbs in all six lines. For this phenomenon the passives in the Lord's Prayer are apt parallels.[4] Here are additional evidences for a Semitic

---

[1] R. H. Fuller, *The Foundations of New Testament Christology* (New York, 1965), pp. 217 f., 227 f.

[2] The passage alludes to Lev. 11:44; 19:2; 20:7; Ps. 89:26; Isa. 40:6–8; 52:3; 53:7; Jer. 3:19. Τὰς ψυχάς appears as a reflexive pronoun. We read phrases such as "fear [of the Lord]" and "children of obedience".

[3] The following is also against Stanley, "The Divinity of Christ", p. 194, who sees behind the hymn a Gentile church, perhaps the Ephesian.

[4] E. Norden, *Agnostos Theos* (Leipzig, 1913), pp. 254 ff.; followed by Spicq, *op. cit.*, p. 108.

matrix: (1) the similarity of the implied pre-existence of Christ in line 1[1] to Jewish ideas concerning the pre-existence of the Torah, the tabernacle, the Messiah, and so on, (2) the similarity of Christ's manifestation in line 1 to Old Testament theophanies,[2] (3) the Semitic flavour of ἐδικαιώθη in the sense of vindication,[3] (4) the use of ὤφθη (line 2) in a way reminiscent of its frequent use in the LXX for nir'ah concerning divine appearances, (5) the correspondence of the simple dative (rather than ὑπό with the genitive) to 'el in the same Old Testament texts,[4] (6) the similarity of lines 2 and 3 (if they refer to the Descensus) to the Enochian world of thought, and (7) the similarity of line 6 to the ascensions of Enoch and Elijah and to the concept of the shekinah glory.[5]

One feature of the hymn relevant to establishing its origin, a feature sometimes used to argue for Hellenistic origin, has so far remained unmentioned. It is that the universalistic note, particularly the preaching among nations and belief within the world in lines 4 and 5, points to a community concerned with widespread evangelism and to a time when that had already started and gained some success.[6] The community in which this hymn originated, then, had to be (a) universalistic in outlook, to account for the preaching among nations throughout the world; (b) Jewish at least initially, to account for the Semitic as opposed to "Hellenistic" features of the hymn; and (c) persecuted, to account for the motif of triumphant vindication.[7] A group of Christians who qualify in all three respects are those early Jewish Christians who migrated from Palestine to Syrian Antioch because of the persecution starting with Stephen's martyrdom, began to evangelize the Gentiles in Antioch with great success,[8] and sent Paul and his companions on their missionary journeys (Acts 11:19-26; 13:1 ff.).[9]

---

[1] "Who was manifested" does not necessarily imply pre-existence, but within a Christian context probably does in the opinion of most commentators. Cf. 2 Tim. 1:9.

[2] Of course, Gentiles who heard and learned the hymn may have thought in terms of appearances of the gods (cf. Acts 14:8-18).

[3] See G. Schrenk on δικαιόω in TDNT, vol. II, pp. 212 ff.; D. Hill, Greek Words and Hebrew Meanings (Cambridge, 1967), pp. 82 ff.; C. H. Dodd, The Bible and the Greeks (London, 1935), pp. 50-59.

[4] Cf. J. Jeremias, The Eucharistic Words of Jesus² (London, 1966), p. 103.

[5] I am not inclined to posit an Aramaic or Hebrew Vorlage, mainly because a putative Aramaic or Hebrew form cannot match the series of Greek verbal endings in -θη, which seem to be original to the hymn. Also, κόσμῳ lacks a sufficient equivalent. Nevertheless, a Greek original does not necessarily imply Hellenistic origin. See above, p. 217, n. 1.

[6] Conceivably, one might restrict lines 4 and 5 to preaching and believing among the Diaspora. But since evangelization of Gentiles accompanied evangelization of the Diaspora, the restriction would not be valid.

[7] Cf. the argument of O. R. B. Wilson, "A Study of the Early Christian Credal Hymn of I Timothy 3:16" (unpublished doctoral thesis, Southern Baptist Theological Seminary, Louisville, Ky., 1954), pp. 38-43, that ὁμολογουμένως in the introduction reflects persecution since confession of Jesus as Lord occasioned it.

[8] Regardless of the textual critical question in Acts 11:20, the contrast with "Jews alone" in verse 19 requires the sense "Gentiles" in verse 20. To be sure, those who first began preaching to Gentiles were Cyprians and Cyrenians, but like Barnabas the Cyprian (Acts 4:36) they had been living in Palestine and only recently had emigrated.

[9] Cf. Martin's association of the hymn with a Hellenistic Jewish Christian community

If the hymn originated in that group, the significance of a very high Christology among first-generation Christians from Palestine should not escape notice. Paul may have learned the hymn in Antioch and late in life recorded it here in 1 Timothy 3:16.[1] If so, Paul takes a Jewish Christian hymn which grew out of persecution and exulted in the success of Christ and the gospel and reapplies that hymn to the rising threat of incipient gnosticism, described in 4:1 ff. (cf. the Colossian heresy). The stress on incarnation, which originated in the Jewish idea of theophany,[2] now counteracts gnostic docetism and asceticism. The stress on universalism, which originated in the persecuted Christians' feeling of vindication by means of divinely ordered success in evangelism, now contradicts gnostic esotericism.

[1] The suggestion holds even though Pauline authorship of the Pastorals be denied, for the Pauline disciple could have learned the hymn in Antioch or from Paul himself who had learned it there. Did Peter also learn the hymn in Antioch and reflect it in 1 Pet. 3:18 ff.? See above, p. 211, n. 3.

[2] But the incarnation was no casual theophany.

possibly having connexion with Stephen "Aspects of Worship", p. 26; cf. *idem, Carmen Christi*, pp. 304 f.).

CHAPTER XIV

REVELATION AND TRADITION IN PAUL

G. E. LADD

THE KERYGMA OR PROCLAMATION OF THE APOSTLES AND PREACHERS OF New Testament times confronts us with a difficult problem in understanding the relationship between tradition and revelation. This *kerygma* consisted primarily of the heralding of certain recent events in history: Jesus' death and resurrection. It included, along with the events themselves, the proclamation of the redemptive meaning of these events. At the same time, Paul claims that the *kerygma* is a revelation from God, purposed through all ages, but now disclosed to men through the apostles and prophets (Rom. 16:25-26; Eph. 3 : 5). Reflection on these statements could easily lead to the conclusion that revelation is concerned only with the redemptive meaning of these historical events, not with the events themselves. This could, in turn, lead logically to the further conclusion that revelation did not take place in past historical events, but only in the proclamation of the meaning of these events, i.e., in the preaching of the gospel. Only in the proclamation of the word does God confront man and reveal himself.

This conclusion has been drawn by modern existentialist theologians who see the event of revelation and salvation as "nowhere present except in the proclaiming, accosting, demanding, and promising word of preaching".[1] In Bultmann's view this salvation occurrence took place in the proclaimed word of the apostles, and continues to take place in the word as it is proclaimed today. From this point of view, the gospel is not the recital of past events; it is a present event. Revelation is not the disclosure of truths about God, the communication of knowledge; revelation is the confrontation with God which occurs in the proclaimed word.[2]

This view finds apparent support in the fact that there are sayings in Paul in which revelation seems to occur in the *kerygma* (preaching) and in the *euangelion* (gospel) rather than in past events. Romans 16:25-26 appears to equate the gospel and the *kerygma* of Jesus Christ with the revelation of the mystery kept secret for long ages but now disclosed and made known to all nations. Furthermore, the gospel is the power of God unto salvation (Rom. 1:16). The gospel itself is "mystery" (Eph. 6:19), i.e., a secret

---

[1] R. Bultmann, *Theology of the New Testament* (New York, 1951), I, p. 302.
[2] R. Bultmann, "Revelation in the NT," *Existence and Faith*, S. M. Ogden ed. (New York, 1960), pp. 58 ff.

purpose of God now made known to men. The gospel is not only of divine origin;[1] it is a divine activity performed for the benefit of men.[2] The gospel does not merely bear witness to salvation history; it is itself salvation history,[3] for it is only in the preaching of the gospel that salvation is accomplished. Bultmann is right, therefore, when he underlines the "existential" character of the gospel.[4]

However, the *kerygma* and the gospel cannot be limited to the activity of preaching; they designate also the message itself, the *content* of preaching. God's purpose to save men through the "foolishness of preaching" (1 Cor. 1:21, AV) does not refer to the activity but the content of preaching[5], and this content is "Christ crucified" – an event in history which is offensive and foolishness to all but believers (1 Cor. 1:23). Thus the gospel includes the proclamation of facts in history: the death of Christ, his resurrection, his appearances to his disciples (1 Cor. 15:3 ff.).[6] However, it is not the proclamation of mere events, but of events meaningfully understood. Christ died *for our sins*. The gospel is both historical event and meaning; and the meaning of the event is that God was acting in history for man's salvation. The historical facts must be interpreted to be understood for what they are: the redeeming, revealing act of God; and in the gospel, this redemptive event is proclaimed.

There exists a dynamic unity between the event and the proclamation of the event, for the proclamation is itself a part of the event. It is impossible to place primary emphasis upon events as past history, or as present proclamation; the two are inseparably bound together, for two reasons. Apart from proclamation (*kerygma, euangelion*), the events in history cannot be understood for what they are: the redeeming acts of God. Furthermore, apart from proclamation, the events are mere events in past history; but in proclamation, they become present redeeming events. The past lives in the present through proclamation. This is why Paul can speak of the gospel as itself the power of God unto salvation.

This tension between the past and the present is confirmed by the concept of tradition in Paul.[7] Paul frequently refers to his preaching and

---

[1] Rom. 1:1, I Thes. 2:2. "The gospel of God" is subjective genitive.

[2] O. Piper, "Gospel", *IDB*, II, p. 414.

[3] G. Friedrich, *TDNT*, II, p. 731

[4] O. Piper, *loc. cit.*

[5] See G. Friedrich, *TDNT*, III, p. 716; C. H. Dodd, *The Apostolic Preaching* (London, 1936), p. 3; C. T. Craig, *IB*, 10, p. 30; F. W. Grosheide, *First Corinthians* (Grand Rapids, 1953),p. 47.

[6] Bultmann's one-sided emphasis upon the *kerygma* as proclamation and not content requires him arbitrarily to exclude 1 Cor. 15:3-8 from the *kerygma*. See *Kerygma and Myth*, H. W. Bartsch, ed.. (New York, 1953) I, p. 112.

[7] For literature, see A. M. Hunter, *Paul and His Predecessors*[2] (London, 1961), ch. 2; Oscar Cullmann, "The Tradition", in *The Early Church*, A. J. B. Higgins ed. (London, 1956), ch. 4; B. Gerhardsson, *Memory and Manuscript* (Uppsala, 1961), pp. 288–321; H. N. Ridderbos, *Paul and Jesus* (Philadelphia, 1958), pp. 46–53; L. Goppelt, "Tradition nach Paulus", *KD*, 4 (1958), pp. 213–33; R. P. C. Hanson, *Tradition in the Early Church* (Philadelphia, 1962), Ch. 1. [Cf. also P. Fannon, "The Influence of Tradition in St. Paul." *Studia Evangelica* IV (*TU* 102, Berlin, 1968) pp. 292-307. Edd.].

teaching in the same terms which are used of the Jewish oral traditions: to deliver (παραδίδοναι) and to receive (παραλαμβάνειν) tradition (παράδοσις). Jesus had contrasted the Jewish traditions with the word of God (Matt. 15:6 and forbade his disciples to imitate the rabbis (Matt. 23:8–10), and yet Paul commends the Corinthians for maintaining the traditions which he had delivered to them (1 Cor. 11:2) and exhorts the Thessalonians to hold to the traditions which they had been taught (2 Thess. 2:15) and to shun those who ignored the tradition they had received from him (2 Thess. 3:6). This idiom establishes a distinct similarity between Jewish rabbinic tradition and Christian tradition; for the terms are the same,[1] and they are used at times quite synonymously with preaching the gospel. The Corinthians received the gospel (παρελάβετε) which Paul had preached to them (1 Cor. 15:1). The gospel which the Galatians received (παρελάβετε) is normative; there can be no other gospel (Gal. 1:9). The Thessalonians received (παραλαβόντες) as the word of God the message which they heard from Paul, recognizing in Paul's words something more than human tradition – the word of God itself (1 Thess. 2:13). In all of these passages, the idiom reflects the handing on and receiving of an oral tradition with a fixed content.

This tradition embodied the apostolic *kerygma* or *euangelion*. Paul delivered (παρέδωκα) to the Corinthians the gospel which he also received (παρέλαβον), that Christ died for our sins, that he was buried, that he rose on the third day, that he appeared to his disciples (1 Cor. 15:1–5). It is[2] generally accepted that verses 3b–5 embody a primitive piece of pre-Pauline *kerygma* which Paul has received as a tradition from those who were apostles before him.[3]

The same idiom of oral tradition appears in connexion with the preservation of a piece of tradition from Jesus' life, viz., the Lord's Supper. Paul received "from the Lord" the account which he delivered to the Corinthians of the institution of the Eucharist (1 Cor. 11:23). Some scholars understand the expression "from the Lord" to mean that Paul received his knowledge of the Lord's Supper by direct illumination from the exalted Lord, as he received knowledge that Jesus was the Messiah on the Damascus road.[4] However, in view of the language and the content of the tradition, this is highly unlikely. Most commentators think Paul means to assert that this tradition which he received from other apostles had its historical origin with Jesus. Paul says he received ἀπό, not παρά the Lord. The latter would suggest reception directly from the Lord, whereas the

[1] See O. Cullmann, *op. cit.*, pp. 63 ff.
[2] Probably the appearances mentioned in vv. 6–8 were added by Paul to the tradition he received.
[3] See J. Jeremias, *The Eucharistic Words of Jesus* (Oxford, 1955), pp. 129–130.
[4] See F. Godet, *First Corinthians* (Edinburgh, 1890) II, p. 149. C. T. Craig thinks Paul may be asserting that his interpretation of the Lord's Supper was received from the risen Lord (*IB*, 10, p. 136).

P

former indicates ultimate source.[1] In any case, the words mean at least this: that the chain of historical tradition which Paul received goes back unbroken to the words of Jesus himself.[2] Thus Paul includes two things in the tradition handed down orally from earlier apostles: the good news of salvation in Christ, and at least one piece of tradition from Jesus' life which found its way also into the gospels.

While the oral gospel tradition is in some ways similar to Jewish oral tradition, in one all-important respect it is quite different. To receive the gospel tradition does not mean merely to accept the truthfulness of a report about certain historical facts, nor does it mean simply to receive instruction and intellectual enlightenment. To receive the tradition means to receive ($\pi\alpha\rho\epsilon\lambda\acute{\alpha}\beta\epsilon\tau\epsilon$) Christ Jesus as Lord (Col. 2:6). In the voice of the tradition, the voice of God himself is heard; and through this word, God himself is present and active in the church (1 Thes. 2:13). Thus the Christian tradition is not mere instruction passed on like Jewish oral tradition from one teacher to another. The tradition handed on is in the form of preaching ($\epsilon\mathring{v}\eta\gamma$-$\gamma\epsilon\lambda\iota\sigma\acute{\alpha}\mu\eta\nu$, 1 Cor. 15:1), and the reception of the message involves a response of faith ($\mathring{\epsilon}\pi\iota\sigma\tau\epsilon\acute{v}\sigma\alpha\tau\epsilon$, 1 Cor. 15:2). The tradition about the resurrection of Jesus must be believed in the heart and confessed with the mouth (Rom. 10:8, 9), and issues in salvation. Such confession is possible only through the Holy Spirit (1 Cor. 12:3).

Thus the tradition has a two-fold character: it is *both* historical tradition *and* kerygmatic-pneumatic tradition at one and the same time. It is historical because it is tied to events in history and the tradition preserves the report of these events. It is kerygmatic because it can be perpetuated only as kerygma and received as a confession of faith. It is pneumatic because it can be received and preserved only by the enabling of the Spirit.[3]

A recognition of the kerygmatic-pneumatic character of the tradition provides the background for understanding Paul's statement that he received the tradition of the Lord's Supper "from the Lord" (1 Cor. 11:23). The "Lord" designates the Jesus of history who is now the exalted Lord. The tradition had its origin with Jesus himself; but as the exalted Lord, Christ now stands behind the tradition and speaks to the church through it. The tradition which Paul received from men both comes from Jesus and is also the word of the exalted Lord to Paul. The tradition of the Lord's Supper also bears the dual character of being both historical and pneumatic at the same time.[4]

---

[1] See J. Héring, *First Corinthians* (London, 1962), pp. 114 f.; F. W. Grosheide, *First Corinthians* (Grand Rapids, 1953), p. 269.

[2] J. Jeremias, *op. cit.*, p. 129.

[3] This has been best expounded by L. Goppelt, *op. cit.*, pp. 216–17.

[4] L. Goppelt, *op. cit.*, p. 223. Cullmann finds even more in this passage. He believes that for Paul, the exalted Lord is both the author and the content of the tradition, and that the Lord and tradition are practically identical. "There can be only one legitimate tradition, that which

The kerygmatic-pneumatic character of the tradition is reflected most vividly in the fact that although it is the words of men mediated through the act of preaching, it is also the word of God (I Thes. 2:13). This word of God, which is received as tradition, is also the gospel (Eph. 1:13; Col. 1:5), the *kerygma* (1 Cor. 1:18, 21), the mystery (Col. 1:25), which is proclaimed not only by the apostles but sounded forth from the churches unto all the surrounding region (1 Thess. 1:8). While it is a word which can be taught and learned (Gal 6:6), it is also a divine trust committed to men (2 Cor. 5:19). While it is dependent upon human utterance for its propagation (Phil. 1:14), it is God's word which cannot be fettered (2 Tim. 2:9) and must speed on to triumph (2 Thess. 3:1). The word of God is a word about a crucifixion (1 Cor. 1:18); but the cross seen not as an isolated event in history but understood as the disclosure of the age-long redemptive purpose of God (Col. 1:25-6). The word is the subject of preaching, (2 Tim. 2:19) which is to be received by its hearers (1 Thess. 1:6) and to indwell them (Col. 3:16), bringing salvation (Eph. 1:13; Phil. 2:16).

Neither the historical nor the kerygmatic aspects of the word of God can be emphasized to the neglect of the other. Existentialist theologians emphasize the kerygmatic aspect of the word at the expense of its historical dimension, and the redemptive event becomes God's acting in the *kerygma*, not in events in history. Bultmann recognizes that the historical Jesus is the origin of the word of God, but he says, "we must speak of God as acting only in the sense that he acts with me here and now."[1] This is contrary to the New Testament, which sees the acting of God to have occurred in the historical Jesus. However, the gospel is both past event and present proclamation. When the kerygmatic aspect is neglected, the kerygma becomes a recital of facts and events lying in the past and thereby loses its character as salvation event. Both aspects must be retained. "Since the revelation occurred in history, the gospel involves a report of historical events, yet the proclamation of the gospel is itself a powerful event."[2]

As the word of God, the gospel is indeed a divine communication; and it includes facts, truths, doctrines. However, if the gospel does no more than communicate facts and doctrines, it has been reduced to the level of human tradition. In the word, God communicates not only facts about redemption and truths about himself; God communicates himself, salvation, eternal life. The word of God is both the report about a redemptive

---

[1] R. Bultmann, *Jesus Christ and Mythology* (New York, 1958), p. 78. See G. E. Ladd, "What does Bultmann Understand by the Acts of God?" *Bulletin of the Evangelical Theological Society*, 5 (1962), pp. 91-97.

[2] William Baird, "What is the Kerygma?" *JBL* 76 (1957), p. 191. Baird studies the historical and the kerygmatic aspects of the gospel in C. H. Dodd and R. Bultmann and concludes that the Pauline gospel includes both.

---

is transmitted by the apostles, and is designated as *Kyrios*" (O. Cullmann, *op. cit.*, p. 75). This appears to go further than the evidence allows. It has, however, been accepted by A. M. Hunter. See *Paul and His Predecessors* (London, 1961), p. 118.

event, and is itself a redemptive event, for in the word of the cross, the Crucified himself confronts men to communicate to them the benefits of his redeeming death.

We may now draw certain conclusions about the Pauline concept of revelation. The focus of revelation is Jesus Christ. In the event in history of Jesus' life, death, resurrection, and exaltation, God has revealed himself redemptively to men. The revelation which occurred in the cross and resurrection is not complete; there yet awaits the revelation of the glory and salvation (Rom. 13:11) of God at the Parousia of Christ, when faith will be exchanged for sight and we shall see face to face (2 Cor. 5:7; 1 Cor. 13:12). Both the redemptive meaning of what God had done in the cross and resurrection, and the disclosure of what God will yet do at the consummation (1 Cor. 3:10) is revealed in the *kerygma*, the gospel, the word of God which exists in the form of a historical kerygmatic-pneumatic tradition. This tradition is a complex of several streams including traditions from the life of Jesus (1 Cor. 11:23), a summary of the Christian message expressed as a formula of faith and uniting facts of the life of Jesus and their theological interpretation (1 Cor. 15:3 f.), and also regulations or rules for practical Christian conduct (1 Cor. 11:2; 2 Thess. 3:6).[1] The tradition had its origin with Jesus himself (1 Cor. 11:23) and with the apostolic eye-witnesses (1 Cor. 15:1 ff., 8). Among the primary apostolic functions is not only the propagation of the tradition, but also its preservation from corruption with human traditions (Col. 2:8), and from distortion by false apostles who preach a Jesus who is different from the Jesus of the apostolic tradition (2 Cor. 11:3-5). The tradition is both a fixed and growing tradition; that is, the tradition cannot be changed, but it can be enlarged. That the gospel embodies a core of fixed tradition committed to the apostles is the explanation for Paul's passionate rejection of any message which diverges from the accepted tradition, even if it is propagated by an apostle himself (Gal. 1:8-9). On the other hand, the Spirit can add to the tradition by granting through the apostles and prophets an unfolding and outworking of the redemptive purpose of God which is already implicit in the redemptive work of Christ. This is seen in Paul's use of the term, μυστήριον, or revealed secret. The "mystery" is the total meaning of God's redemptive purpose which he has accomplished in Christ (Rom. 16:25-26). Particular disclosures of God's secret purpose revealed through the apostles include the fact of Christ as the embodiment of all wisdom and knowledge (Col. 2:2), the indwelling of Christ in the hearts of his people (Col. 1:27), the abolishing of the distinction between Jew and Gentile in the body of Christ, the church (Eph. 3:3-6), the intimacy established between Christ and his church (Eph. 6:19), the present rejection of the gospel by Israel, the salvation of the Gentiles, which will lead to the future salvation of Israel (Rom. 11:25-26), the translation of living saints into

[1] See O. Cullmann, *op. cit.*, p. 64.

resurrection life at the Parousia (1 Cor. 15:51), and the final restoration of divine order in Christ to a disordered universe (Eph. 1:9-10). While all of these facets of the mystery of God's redemptive purpose embody new understandings and disclosures, they are all implicit in what God has done in the death, resurrection and exaltation of Christ. Revelation is thus seen as an event which includes both deeds and words. The meaning of the events in history and their implications for Christian life are given in a historical tradition through which the exalted Christ himself speaks, and in direct disclosures by the Holy Spirit through the apostles and prophets.

In his letter to the Galatians, Paul seems to reject the role of tradition in revelation and to claim that revelation occurs only by direct illumination by the Holy Spirit. He appears to declare his complete independence from the Primitive Church. He asserts that he did not receive his gospel from men, that it did not come to him by tradition (παρέλαβον) nor by instruction, but by direct revelation of Jesus Christ (Gal. 1:12). He declares his independence from the Jerusalem apostles. After his conversion, he did not go up to Jerusalem to receive the approval of the apostles but withdrew to Arabia. When he did go to Jerusalem three years later, it was not to establish an abiding relationship, but only to make a short visit to get acquainted with Peter and James (Gal. 1:17-19). Taken out of context, the assertions in this passage seem to contradict the statements of 1 Corinthians 11 and 15 that Paul handed on what he had received by tradition.

Various solutions to this apparent contradiction have been offered. Some have suggested that in Corinthians Paul refers only to the facts about Jesus which he learned from other Christians, while the meaning of these facts, i.e., their true interpretation came to him not from men but only by the direct revelation of the exalted Lord.[1] This is, of course, true. Unquestionably, as Machen points out, Paul was familiar with many of the facts about Jesus' life and death, as well as the Christian claims for him as the Messiah, when he was still in Judaism. In fact, it was his Jewish understanding of the facts that made Saul a persecutor; what he gained on the Damascus Road was a new and correct understanding of the facts, viz., that Jesus was the Messiah. However, the tradition in 1 Corinthians 15 includes interpretation: "Christ died *for our sins*"; and it includes also a fact which undoubtedly Paul as a Jew did not accept, viz., that Jesus was raised from the dead and appeared to his disciples.

Others have maintained that Paul received the form of his proclamation from men but its essential content he received not from men but from the Lord. In its form, the Pauline *kerygma* was essentially the same as the tradition of the Jerusalem church; but in its essential dynamic nature, his gospel could not be transmitted by men but only communicated by direct revelation.[2] This solution is not satisfactory, for it contradicts the kerygmatic

[1] J. G. Machen, *The Origin of Paul's Religion* (New York, 1928), pp. 144 ff.
[2] William Baird, "What is the Kerygma?" *JBL* (1957), pp. 190 f.

nature of the tradition and views it as though it were only a human tradition.

The apparent contradiction is due to the different purposes involved in the two passages. In Corinthians, Paul is thinking of particular aspects of the substance of his gospel: the Lord's Supper, the saving death, the resurrection and the appearances of Jesus. These include both facts and at least something of the meaning of the facts. In the substance of his gospel, Paul stands in agreement with earlier Christians, and indeed, he received information from them as to the gospel itself. However, in Galatians, Paul is dealing with his apostolic authority and with the one central fact of the gospel, viz., that Jesus was the resurrected and exalted Messiah. This he did not learn from other men, even though it was later corroborated by what he did learn from them. Paul was not converted by Christian preaching but by an immediate confrontation by the exalted Christ.[1] Neither did Paul receive his apostolic office from men. Both – his gospel and his apostolic office – came to him directly from the Lord, unmediated by men. The fact that subsequent to his conversion Paul consulted with Peter[2] and James and received from them both facts about Jesus and the gospel and their interpretation of it would in no way weaken his claim to complete independence in his reception of the gospel. The purpose of the passage is to argue that Paul enjoys the same apostolic authority as those who were apostles before him (Gal. 1:17), because he, like them, received his commission and his gospel directly from the Lord.

[1] Here is an overlooked weakness in Bultmann's reconstruction of the *kerygma*, for Paul was not brought into "authentic existence" by the kerygma or Christian proclamation as Bultmann's interpretation requires. See "Paul" in *Existence and Faith* (New York, 1960), p. 115.

[2] G. D. Kilpatrick thinks that ἱστορῆσαι Κηφᾶν (Gal. 1:18) means "to get information from Peter". See *New Testament Essays*, A. J. B. Higgins, ed. (Manchester, 1959), pp. 144–9. But see F. Büchsel in *TDNT*, III, pp. 395–6. [Cf. the essay by R. Schnackenburg, p. 290 in the present volume, Edd.]

CHAPTER XV

I CORINTHIANS 11:2-16: AN INTERPRETATION

WILLIAM J. MARTIN

I

MANY AND VARIOUS ARE THE INTERPRETATIONS THAT HAVE BEEN put upon this passage in Paul's writings, and not all have been complimentary to Paul's logic or his lucidity. That this passage is difficult no one would deny. The source of the difficulty is two-fold: the infrequency of occurrences in the *koine* in general of some of the terms used, and our usual inability to reconstruct with any degree of certainty the contemporary background to the actual situation within and without the church. No one familiar with the literary remains of Paul would lightly assume that he would be guilty of either inconsistencies or illogicalities. It would, therefore, be an unaccountable lapse in the light of his extraordinary linguistic gifts and his avowed principles if there occurred here any evident contradiction to statements elsewhere in this letter or even in any other of his writings.

The passage (11:2-16) occurs within a framework of a discussion on the significance and observance of the Lord's Supper and its place as the central theme in the act of worship.

The first thing to note about this passage is that it is an "approving" passage ("Now I praise you" etc. v. 2), whereas the next section beginning at verse 17 is a "disapproving" section ("I praise you not" etc.). Any wrong or undesirable practices, therefore, referred to in the first section would be *ipso facto* only in a hypothetical sense. True, Paul's commendation would embrace a great deal more than the custody of articles of association with regard to a worship formula, but in the context it is primarily applicable to the matter in hand.

Having expressed his approbation of their steadfastness in what was committed, he now proceeds to announce the theme of the section, namely, The Headship of Christ. ("I will that you recognize that the head of every man is Christ" v. 3). His purpose here is not to teach the principles of public prayer and edifying instruction, or to enunciate the rules for their practice, but to deal with the significancy of the Headship of Christ, and only what is relevant to this theme would be in place here. Whether or not Paul was influenced by the metaphorical extension of the semantic field of the word for head either in Hebrew (*rōš*) or in Aramaic (*rēš*) must remain an open question. Examples of parallel development in the linguistic field are far from rare,[1] and *rōš* and *κεφαλή* are a case in point.

---

[1] Cf. *qaqqadu* and *rēšu* in Akkadian, and *tp* in Egyptian (A. Erman and H. Graspow, *Wörterbuch der ägyptischen Sprache* V, p. 265).

Hebrew usage affords interesting linguistic evidence for the way in which such extensions take place and in this particular instance with significant limitations. While the semantic field of the words for "hand", "arm", "eye" and "face" is extended to a degree where these words in certain contexts are no more than worn-out metaphors, the word "head" seems to be subject to analogical restraint. For instance, while any one of the former anthropomorphic terms may be used freely to describe the activities of God, "head" is never found in this connexion. A better understanding of linguistics has taught us that "anthropomorphic" terms are not confined to a primitive stage in communication but are found at all levels of culture and are in fact an integral part of all linguistic communication.[1] The literal meaning of rōš (head of an animate creature) was apparently early extended to include the description of inanimate objects (Gen. 8:5 "the head of the mountains appeared"; Gen. 11:4 "a tower whose head will be in the heavens"). Then it is extended to rank (Num. 1:4 "a man who is head of the house of his fathers"; 1 Sam. 15:17 "head of the tribes of Israel"); it is used to express totality (Num. 31:26 "Take the sum of the plunder"). It is used to describe the seat of responsibility (2 Sam. 1:16 "thy blood be upon thy head; 1 Ki. 2:44 "God will return your evil on your head"). It is not expressly used as a linguistic term for the "seat" of thought, but its use to describe the activity of the wise man (Eccl. 2:14 "the eyes of the wise man are in his head") is clearly metaphorical and must refer to his rational faculty. There is, too, the reference in Daniel 4:2 (E.V. verse 5) to "visions" of the head. In Hebrew, however, thought is predominantly associated with the heart, in a psychological, not, of course, in an anatomical sense. The passages that could have influenced Paul in the selection of the word are those in which it is applied by transference to rank, and particularly those where it is used specifically of God or the Messiah, such as 1 Chronicles 29:11 ("the One exalted as head above all") or in Psalm 118:22 ("the stone . . . . has become the head of the corner"), or even those passages in which a diminutive form of rōš (rīšōn) is used (Isa. 44:6, 48:12). The fact that Paul had a word in Greek with the right semantic field ready to hand, does not necessarily exclude the possibility of Paul's being influenced by the semantic field of the word in Hebrew, or of his availing himself of what could have been for him virtually a loan-translation.[2]

Paul proceeds to explain the respective rôles of the man and the woman ἐν ἐκκλησίᾳ that is, in a church worship-meeting convened for the specific purpose of commemorating the Lord's Supper. These rôles reflect the relationship that exists with Christ as Head of every man, using the word generically and with the limitations imposed on it by the character of the addressee, namely a Christian church. Man is to appear

[1] H. Güntert and A. Scherer, Grundfragen der Sprachwissenschaft (1956), pp. 63 ff.
[2] E. Richter, Fremdwortkunde (1919), pp. 84 ff.

with uncovered head for he is the glorious image of God (v. 7), whom he represents and in a sense personates in the worship of the true Head. The woman, on the other hand, acts the part of the church. Now, if a distinction is to be made between the man and the woman in the worship-meeting, this requires an explanation. If the woman here is to behave differently or to be treated differently from the man, it would be the only instance where the requirements incumbent upon them were not identical. As they received forgiveness in the same way, were baptized in the same way, they should surely worship in the same way. Any distinction would have seemed a clear contradiction of the great truth that in Christ there is neither male nor female (Gal. 3:28).

For her rôle as representing the church, the woman is required to conform with certain conditions. As the man's uncovered head betokens the supremacy of the true Head, whom he represents, so it is necessary for the woman as the symbol of the church to acknowledge by her 'covered' head the Headship of Christ. Several indications show beyond reasonable doubt that Paul is using the term "covered" to refer to long hair.[1] First, he uses it in contradistinction to the state of the man who is debarred from "having the (hair) hanging down"[2] (v. 4). To make the wearing of a head-covering the opposite of short hair would be a false antithesis. It would have been pharisaical casuistry, and sheer quibbling to say that wearing a head-covering compensated for being shorn. To annul the state of being shorn you must be the opposite. To be transparently honest Paul would have had to say there is only one way, one simple, plain, unambiguous, right way to efface the shame of being shorn and that is to have long hair; and that is surely what Paul is saying. Second, nowhere in the passage is any word ever used for a material veil or head-dress. Third, as the forms of the verb κατακαλύπτω (to cover) found here (vv. 6 and 7) are not construed with an indirect object, it is best to take them as passive. Fourth, in v. 15 Paul states unequivocally that a woman's long hair takes the place of an item of dress.[3] Besides, one would expect Paul to use some more explicit term for "unveiled", such as γυμνοκέφαλος "bare-headed" (cf. γυμνόπους "bare-footed").

There was evidently something undesirable and even disreputable associated with shorn hair. What it was we can no longer say with certainty.[4] Shorn hair among the Jews was a sign of mourning. (Job. 1:20; Jer. 7:29;

---

[1] On the possibility of a woman's dressed hair meeting Jewish requirements, see Strack-Billerbeck III, pp. 428 f. The uncertainty in dating Rabbinical material, however, deprives any deductions made from it of much of their cogency.

[2] Chrysostom took this to refer to long hair

[3] "Coiffure" has developed in the reverse direction, from "coif" a close-fitting cap.

[4] There does not seem to be enough evidence in the works of secular writers to suggest that "shorn hair" was the mark of a prostitute. At a former period Corinth was a by-word for immorality and great hordes of prostitutes were associated with the temple of Aphrodite (H. L. Jones, *The Geography of Strabo*, Loeb, IV, pp. 190 f.). It is unlikely that the resuscitation of the city by the Romans led to any marked improvement in its moral habits.

Mic. 1:16). The use of the definite article in ἡ ἐξυρημένη "the shorn woman" (v. 5) would seem to point to the existence of a specific class to whom this designation could be applied. Paul in any case would have disapproved of the practice because of its association with heathen superstition. The practice of cutting off the hair among the Greeks as a religious rite is well attested. The Vestal virgins and all Greek girls did it on reaching puberty. The earliest form of the custom appears to have been the vow or dedication of hair to a river, to be fulfilled at puberty or at some crisis, or after deliverance from danger.[1] Some of the Hellenized Jewesses may well have copied their Greek neighbours.

The next verse (6) (in the A.V. "For if a woman is not covered, let her be shorn: but if it is shame for a woman to be shorn or shaven, let her be covered"), although evidently only of a parenthetical nature, presents some difficulty, and a right understanding of it is indispensable to the meaning of the whole passage.

The first point that strikes one in attempting to understand it is the use of οὐ "not", which is almost invariably used with the "real" indicative, that is, something actually existing or happening, and not contrary to fact.[2] Thus this state of things was actually occurring.

Second, an explanation for the use of two forms of the imperative, aorist and present, must be sought. This change in "aspect"[3] by a writer of Paul's syntactical precision is unlikely to be merely whimsical. What then was the distinction in function of these two verbal forms?

II

A vast literature[4] has grown up around the problem of the character of

W. H. D. Rouse, *Greek Votive Offerings* (1902), p. 240; I owe this reference to Mr R. W. Hutchinson.

[2] A. T. Robertson, *A Grammar of New Testament Greek in the Light of Historical Research* (New York and London, 1914), p. 1011; Blass-Debrunner, 428.

[3] It is probably best to take "aspect" as subjective, and *Aktionsart* ("mode of action") as objective: see W. Wundt, *Völkerpsychologie* I, part 2 (1906), pp. 190 f.

[4] On "aspect" in general: G. Guillaume, *Temps et Verbe: Théorie des Aspects, des Modes et des Temps* (1929); a systematic piece of work with helpful diagrammatic representations. E. Koschmieder, *Zeitbezug und Sprache*; stimulating, but his postulate of "Zeitrichtungsbezug" (relation of direction in time) strikes one as a little *verkünstelt*; for a criticism of the work, see the review by A. Debrunner in *IF* 48 (1930), pp. 89 ff.; also E. Hermann, "Aspekt und Aktionsart", *Nachrichten der Gesellschaft der Wissenschaften zu Göttingen, Phil. Hist. Kl.* (1933), Heft 4, pp. 470 ff.; for Koschmieder's reply to these criticisms, see *IF* 53 (1935), pp. 280 ff. W. Streitberg, "Die Benennung der Aktionsarten", *IF* 22 (1907/8), Anzeiger, pp. 72 ff.; F. Hartmann, "Aorist und Imperfektum", *Kuhn's Zeitschrift* 48 (1918), pp. 1 ff., and *idem* 49 (1920), pp. 1 ff.; G. O. Curme, *Grammar of the German Language* (1922), § 164; E. Hermann, "Objektive und Subjektive Aktionsart", *IF* 45 (1927), pp. 207 ff.

On "aspect" in Greek: G. Curtius, *Erläuterungen zu meiner griechischen Schulgrammatik* (1863), pp. 171 ff.; E. D. Burton, *Syntax of the Moods and Tenses in New Testament Greek*[3] (1898); W. W. Goodwin, *Syntax of the Moods and Tenses of the Greek Verb* (1897); H. Meltzer, "Zur Lehre von den Aktionen besonders im Griechsichen", *IF* 17 (1905), pp. 186 ff.; B. Romano, "Il significato fondamentale dell'aoristo greco", *Rivista di filologia* 50 (1922), pp. 197

the aorist in general and the Greek aorist in particular. While the Greeks themselves recognized that the tense-forms combined time-relation and "aspect" in their meaning, they referred to the future and aorist simply as indeterminate forms of the verb outside the tenses proper.[1] It is, doubtless, easier for those whose speech habits by accident of birth are acquired from a language in which "aspect" is operative and who, as it were, have assimilated "aspect", to grasp the nature of its genius. Some writers on the subject ascribe to "aspect" an exaggerated complexity or a too ingenious subtlety, presupposing a quality of mental juggling beyond the capabilities of most men.

In the New Testament usage the distinction between the present imperative[2] and that of the aorist is broadly speaking that of universal and particular. While the present imperative is used to denote an action of unlimited extension or habitual occurrence, of which the bounds, if such exist, have no relevant practical significance, the aorist describes a specific action, limited in duration.[3] The action may be egressive (effective), or terminative. Where the stress may be on the ingressive character of the action, it is still defined with a perfectly specific delimitation. The term "punctiliar", often used of the aorist, could be misleading, since the chief function of the aorist is not to denote the initial or the final point of the action. A segment of time is involved and it is the nature of this segment as a whole and its particularistic character that evokes the use of the aorist. The kind of action with which it deals could often best be described as "cessative".

One must bear in mind the fact that the action of a verb by its very nature may comprise a "tense-aspect", say, durative, and thus have, as it were, a "built-in" tense-aspect. Again, some present imperatives are forms of weak semantic content or have become stereotype. Verbs of motion, in particular, seem highly susceptible to this kind of deflation,[4] but it is not necessarily or invariably so. Again, the negative seems to act on occasion as an aspectual catalyst.[5] This can be clearly seen in Hebrew, for example,

---

[1] R. H. Robins, *Ancient and Mediaeval Grammatical Theory in Europe* (1951), pp. 36 f.
[2] On the nature of the imperative in general, see *Rivista degli Studi Orientali* 32 (1957), pp. 315 ff.
[3] For the view of Apollonius Dyscolus, see J. Wackernagel, *Vorlesungen über Syntax* I 1926), p. 150.
[4] Matt. 9:6 (cf. Lk. 5:24); Mk. 1:44; Jn. 4:16; 7:3; 9:7.
[5] Wackernagel, *op. cit.*, I, pp. 214 f.

---

and 335; J. H. Moulton, *A Grammar of New Testament Greek* I (Edinburgh, 1908), II (1929) and III (1963), pp. 74 f.; A. T. Robertson, *op cit.*, pp. 855 f.; J. E. Harrison, *Aspects, Aorist and the Classical Tripos* (Cambridge, 1919); C. W. Peppler, "Durative and Aoristic", *AJP* 54 (1933), pp. 47 ff.; E. Schwyzer and A. Debrunner, *Griechische Grammatik* (1950) II, pp. 246 ff.; Blass-Debrunner, *op. cit.*, § 335-37; C. Grassi, "Imperativo presente e aoristo nelle preghiere agli dei", *Studi Italiani di Filologia Classica* 35 (1963), pp. 186 ff.; W. F. Bakker, *The Greek Imperative* (1966).

by the modification made in the aspect of the action of the verb by the presence of *bᵉterem* "not yet" in any construction.

The New Testament abounds in examples illustrating the universal character of the present imperative and the particularizing function of the aorist imperative. Take for instance, the passage in Acts 12:8: "And the angel said to him 'Dress yourself and put on your sandals'. And he did so. And he said to him, 'Wrap your mantle around you and follow me.'" There are here three aorist imperatives followed by one present. The aorists all refer to specific actions of limited duration (ζῶσαι "wrap yourself", ὑπόδησαι "tie on', περιβαλοῦ "dress") and could be described as egressive, but for the action of unspecified duration the present is used (ἀκολούθει "follow"). Compare with this the use of this same verb in an aorist imperative in Luke 22:10 (ἀκολουθήσατε "follow") to express an egressive action on a particular occasion with the end-point explicitly given (εἰς τὴν οἰκίαν "into the house"). Again, in Luke 3:11, where a specific article (one coat) is in question we find the aorist (μεταδότω "let him share"), but for a recurring action in a possible everyday situation, the present imperative (ποιείτω "let him do") is used. Again, in the parable of the good Samaritan (Luke 10:30–35), the limited extent of the inn-keeper's liability is brought out by the aorist with the end-point expressed – "my return": ἐπιμελήθητι "take care of him" (verse 35), while the universal obligation for such actions is expressed by present imperatives: πορεύου "go", ποίει "do" (verse 37). Again, in Luke 11:5 the aorist brings out the temporariness of the request and the specified quantity (3 loaves), its limitation: χρῆσόν "lend to tide me over", whereas in verse 9 actions for universal performance are expressed by present imperatives: αἰτεῖτε "ask", ζητεῖτε "seek", κρούετε "knock", In Luke 17:8 the aorist imperative implies a particular occasion: ἑτοίμασον "make ready now", but the present brings out the fact of the permanent relationship between master and servant, inherent in the word δοῦλος; the duty is habitual: διακόνει "serve" (as always). The soliloquy of the rich man (Luke 12:19) shows with what effect the various forms can be used: ἀναπαύου "take your ease" (present – time's unlimited!), φάγε, πίε "eat, drink" (aorists, off and on; special times of feasting?), εὐφραίνου "be glad" (present, on and on, without end or break). The contrast can be clearly seen in a passage like Matthew 8:21. The speaker uses an aorist imperative where a specific task is involved, the burial of his father: ἐπίτρεψόν "suffer me"; but for a demand without limitations Christ uses the present: ἀκολούθει "follow me", while the next imperative reverts to an aorist, as it refers to a particular instance: ἄφες "leave" (this burial to those who put such things first). Similarly, in Matthew 16:24 the aorists: ἀπαρνησάσθω "let him deny himself", ἀράτω "let him take up", are egressive and ingressive respectively, but the present ἀκολουθείτω "let him follow", is a command that implies total acquiescence. Even in

John 7:24 the variation in the forms is unlikely to be accidental: the present is universal: μὴ κρίνετε κατ' ὄψιν "never judge according to the appearance"; the aorist is particular κρίνατε "judge" (in this case). In John 5:8 following two aorist imperatives ἔγειρε "stand up", ἆρον "take up", there follows a present imperative, περιπάτει "walk". An aorist with its limitative associations would have implied a limit in distance or in time, and would have been totally incongruous here. The present is instinct with assurance and promise that the cure was permanent.

No one with a sense for "aspect" could fail to note the deep significance on occasion of Christ's use of one or other of these forms. In the parable of "The Great Supper" (Luke 14:16–24), the present imperative of the first invitation stands in significant contrast to the aorists that come later. The present: ἔρχεσθε "come" (verse 17) points to the unlimited extent of the invitation and the unbounded generosity of the host, but those that follow are couched in aoristic form and with expressed limitations ἔξελθε "go out" (places specified), εἰσάγαγε "bring in" (particular people) (v.21). In verse 23 even greater restrictions are imposed. Again, in his discourse on the judgment of the nations in Matthew 25 none could have missed the reason for the forms of the imperatives used. In contrast with the aorist (v. 34) κληρονομήσατε "inherit" with its consummative force giving it a note of glorious attainment, there is the fateful present imperative used to the lost (v. 41) πορεύεσθε "go (for ever)", the irrevocable sentence of endless separation and limitless despair.

That Paul does not deviate in his usage from this pattern can be seen from many examples scattered throughout his letters. In 1 Corinthians 15:58 the present imperative γίνεσθε "be ye" is used for an action of universal character, re-inforced by πάντοτε in the immediate context, while in chap. 16:1 the aorist imperative ποιήσατε "do" is used of a particular situation terminating in Paul's arrival. Similarly in 2 Corinthians 6:17 aorists are used for cessative actions: ἐξέλθετε "come out", ἀφορίσθητε "be ye separated" (note the passive), but for the settled pattern of conduct a present imperative is used: ἅπτεσθε "touch not (at all)". Paul's effective use of these two forms is well illustrated in Colossians 3 where present imperatives are used in (v. 1) ζητεῖτε "seek" – a constant attitude, (v. 2) φρονεῖτε "set your mind upon" (habitual), (v. 15) βραβευέτω "let (peace) be a (permanent) arbitrator", (v. 16) ἐνοικείτω "let (the word of Christ) make its home (in you)". But aorist imperatives are also used: (v. 5) νεκρώσατε "put to death" (egressive), (v. 8) ἀπόθεσθε "put away" (a defined list), (v. 12) ἐνδύσασθε "put on" (particular things). A similar state of affairs obtains in Ephesians 6:1 ff., where Paul uses present imperatives when he enjoins actions of a universal and unrestricted character (verses 1, 2, 4, 5 and 9) but aorists where the actions are patently limited (verses 11, 13, 14 and 17). For those who have ears to hear, there is a striking display of Paul's masterly skill and delicate touch in Phm. 17. How easy and light the particular burden is that he is seeking to impose on Philemon, he brings out by using, as his Master did before him (Matt. 11:29), the aorist: προσλαβοῦ "receive" (a specific and known charge).[1] In contrast with this is the unlimited liability that he imposes on himself, latent in the present imperative: ἐμοὶ ἐλλόγα "debit it to me" (here's an open cheque, and the sky's the limit!). The incomparable tact and the utter graciousness of it all reveal the instincts and the fine feelings of the perfect Christian gentleman.

Of particular interest for the matter in hand are the forms found in 1 Corinthians 7:9 f. The aorist imperative (v. 9) γαμησάτωσαν "let them marry", refers clearly to a cessative action, the present imperative (v. 11) μενέτω "let her remain" (unmarried), envisages no end-point, the aorist in the same verse καταλλαγήτω "let her effect a reconciliation "again denotes a cessative action in that it would bring to an end the separation from her husband.[2]

III

What then is being said in 1 Corinthians 11 verse 6, that would induce Paul to employ an aorist imperative and a present imperative in adjacent clauses? The kind of situation that was likely to arise was one that has been common to all true revivals of religion that impenetrate a total cross-section of the community, often drawing in a disproportionate number of converts from among the social outcasts and outsiders. It would be unthinkable that among Paul's many converts there were not women of the "shorn woman" class. What then was to be done about their inability to conform with the requirement of having long hair? Were they to be excluded until such time as nature would remedy their lack? Certainly not. It would have been monstrous to exclude any believer from the immediate enjoyment of the privileges of church fellowship. Did not the father receive the prodigal just as he was, minus the external trappings of sonship? The problem of such converts could be the situation dealt with here, in what is, in all probability, a parenthesis. Thus, (v. 6) – εἰ γὰρ οὐ κατακαλύπτεται γυνή, καὶ κειράσθω· εἰ δὲ αἰσχρὸν γυναικὶ τὸ κείρασθαι ἢ ξυρᾶσθαι, κατακαλυπτέσθω. "For if a woman is not covered'

---

[1] This modest and moderating quality of the aorist may be the factor that accounts for the popularity and prevalence of the form in prayers. On that prevalence, see E. Kieckers, "Zum Gebrauch des Imperativus Aoristi und Praesentis", IF 24 (1909), pp. 10 ff. (The conjecture on pp. 16 f. betrays great ingenuity, but is almost certainly wide of the mark).

[2] The number of passages that present difficulty or show an apparent deviation from this usage is remarkably small: 1 Cor. 7:21, χρῆσαι "make use of it" (in this particular instance, in contrast to the preceding general injunctions in the present imperative), 2 Cor. 13:12, ἀσπάσασθε "greet" (a specific group – the bearers of the letters?). Other occurrences of the form could possibly be explained in the same way. 1 Pet. 2:17, τιμήσατε, should probably be taken with the preceding clause, thus: "But all such as are servants of God, honour."

(has not long hair)[1] then let her remain cropped (for the time being; κειράσθω,[2] aorist imperative with cessative force, referring to a particular situation), but since it is a shame for a woman to be cropped or shorn let her become 'covered'" – (i.e. let her hair grow again; κατακαλυπτέσθω (present imperative for a non-terminative, inchoative action).

The positive reason for Paul's direction with regard to the woman's hair seems amply clear. The woman in worship had a vital part to play and to fit her for this it was essential that she should retain the visually distinctive mark of womanhood – the glory of her hair, for she plays the part of the Bride, the church. This involved a gesture of subordination. Is the part of the man then superior to that of the woman? It would be as meaningless to ask if the bread is superior to the wine. The man is no more superior to her than God is to the Son. Subordination does not for one moment imply inferiority, as Paul is quick to point out (verses 11 and 12). The gesture required of her and which apparently differentiated her from the man is one with which:

(a) she should comply – otherwise she would dishonour her Head (verse 5);

(b) she could comply – far from making any impossible demands on her, by conforming she avoids bringing shame on her womanhood (verse 6);

(c) she would comply – because it would be non-natural not to (verse 13 ff.).

This last is one of the most gracious tributes in all literature to womanhood, for putting it at its lowest, nature, God's own creative laws, teaches her that she should (v. 14). Of all the lovely things in this world of beauty, the loveliest of all is a woman. In a world of beautiful things which proclaim God's love of beauty, she is the crown. The best works of the greatest artists and sculptors confirm it. God would never expect a woman to mutilate the glory of his greatest masterpiece.

How much more appropriate the symbolism of the hair given to her (v. 15, and Paul must mean in the purpose of God) than any material object that could have been chosen by human agency.[3] It would have been strange, surely, if Paul had introduced into the service of worship an object, such as a veil, for which there was no authority from Christ. The New Testament church had escaped with one bound from the fetters of ritualism, that pictographic stage where the models and methods of the

---

[1] The difficulty of defining similar variable terms, e.g. "middle-aged", is discussed by W. P. Alston, *Philosophy of Language* (1964), pp. 84 ff. Alston seems a little too ready to admit defeat. For practical purposes the requirement here would be unambiguous contrast with that of the man.

[2] Because of the nature of the action of the verb described by κείρω, it can be either active or passive, but not reflexive.

[3] While the logical conclusion to be drawn from the foregoing is that it is not necessary for women to wear a hat or other head-covering, Christian women, nevertheless, in their dress and behaviour will always comply with accepted conventions consistent with decorum.

kindergarten were legitimately used, a prior but not a more primitive stage. The believer was now occupied in worship, not with visual objects as such, but with conceptual entities and spiritual realities. Sacredness or holiness was no longer attributed to material things.[1]

These reasons given above, one would have thought, were of such importance, that it would not be necessary to seek any other. Nevertheless, another has been adduced and often assigned an importance far and away greater than any of these, namely, that the purpose of remaining "covered" was to enable the woman to participate audibly in the service.[2] This involves the assumption that the converse "it is seemly to pray unto God covered" can be read into the passage, although, in fact, it is nowhere stated. One so well versed in the ways of logical thinking, as Paul evidently was, could not have been unaware of the fact that since a converse is not necessarily true, it must, therefore, if valid, not be left unexpressed[3] Calvin on 1 Corinthians 7:1 remarked that the statement "it is a good thing for a man not to touch a woman" did not imply "it is a bad thing to do so". All this might seem to savour of sophistry, were it not for the fact that minutes later (some 15 minutes, reading at a speed of 120 words a minute) Paul makes a statement that shows that the converse was not in his mind; it is the unambiguous statement: "let the women keep silence in the churches, for it is not permitted to them to speak" (I Cor. 14:34).

Paul may also have seen in the woman's silence yet another symbolic act in her rôle of representing the church. The church had made no positive contribution to her salvation; it was solely the work of her Head. Here then would be a significant gesture, silently proclaiming her negative part in the work of redemption.

Paul refers also to the order and purpose of the creation of man[4] (vv. 8 and 9), possibly seeing in it a reflection of the relationship between Christ and his church. The woman was created for the man as was the church for Christ. The man had priority in creation,[5] the woman the initiative in transgression. A wound was the price the man had to pay for his helpmeet; a deeper and a deadly wound was the price paid for the church.

Thus like a great master musician who superimposes on the basic theme

---

[1] Even as late as the third century, to consecrate an earthly house was considered a pagan practice; see F. W. Deichmann, *Früchristliche Kirchen im Rom* (Basel, 1948), pp. 9 ff.

[2] Praying was evidently not necessarily an audible exercise or one for general participation (cf. Acts 3:1; 16:13; 1 Cor. 14:15). The noun seems also to be used on occasion as an elliptical term for worship (Matt. 21:13).

[3] For example, if in this passage it does not say that a woman should wear a head-covering, it would not follow that she should not wear one. But it would not be thought necessary in the ordinary course of events to state that this converse does not hold good.

[4] The so-called "second account" of creation can be taken as complementary to that in Gen. 1. On descriptive technique in general, see "Dischronologized Narrative in the Old Testament", *VT* (Rome Congress volume, 1969), pp. 179ff.

[5] For interesting comments by a medical authority, see D. M. Blair, *The Beginning of Wisdom* (London, 1946), pp. 30 f. and 90.

another melody, God has superimposed on the central theme of worship a glorious counterpoint of heavenly chords, the near echo of things eternal. Under all that Paul writes lies the substance of destiny. It cannot be detected merely by the mechanics of insensate scholarship. How at times one covets the skill and the insight which *die Stillen im Lande*[1] have possessed in such rich measure.[2] Between their skill and ours is often the difference between that of the mannequin-maker with his measuring tapes and calipers, and that of the surgeon moving with unerring skill among the living tissues.

To one who possesses an ideal combination of skills these fallen ψιχία picked up by a mere Hebraist from under the master's table, are a small γενέθλιος δόσις offered as a token of affectionate esteem.

[1] Psa. 35:20 (Luther).

[2] E.g., F. W. Robertson, *Expository Lectures on St. Paul's Epistles to the Corinthians* (London, 1872).

Q

CHAPTER XVI

COVENANT AND COMMUNION IN FIRST CORINTHIANS

A. R. MILLARD

WHILE THE CURRENTS OF NEW TESTAMENT INQUIRIES ARE REFLECTED frequently in studies of the Old Testament, the streams of Old Testament research are followed into the New Testament less often. This is a natural situation in view of the New Testament's claim to fulfil the Old, a claim which Professor Bruce has helped to elucidate.[1] An attempt is made here, with temerity, to approach one of Paul's epistles in the light of a fashionable Old Testament theme.

At present the Covenant concept is being investigated by form criticism on the basis of knowledge gleaned from other ancient Near Eastern Texts.[2] So far, however, very little use of resultant insights has been made in New Testament research, although this is one field where there is much common ground.[3] In a basic study K. Baltzer has demonstrated the persistence of a covenant scheme from the Old Testament into the Dead Sea Scrolls and early Christian literature, without a detailed endeavour to find it in the New Testament.[4] Preamble, historical prologue, stipulations, blessings and curses comprise the basic features of the scheme as represented in documents of the second millennium B.C. Baltzer identified parallels to these in sections of the Damascus Document and the Manual of Discipline from Qumran, and of the Didache, Barnabas and 2 Clement which he de-

---

[1] In his *Biblical Exegesis in the Qumran Texts* (Grand Rapids, Michigan, 1959, London, 1960); in *The Apostolic Defence of the Gospel* (London, 1959, reprinted, 1967); most notably in *This is That* (Exeter, 1968), and in such articles as those in *NTS* 2 (1955-56) pp. 176-90, *BJRL* 43 (1960-61), pp. 336-53.

[2] Surveys are available in K. A. Kitchen, *Ancient Orient and Old Testament* (London, 1966), pp. 92-96 and works noted there, and in D. J. McCarthy, *Der Gottesbund im Alten Testament* (Stuttgart, 1966, revised 1967).

[3] F. C. Fensham is an exception, see his studies "The Curse of the Cross and the Renewal of the Covenant" in *Biblical Essays* (Stellenbosch, 1966), pp. 219-26, "Die Offer en Maaltyd"; *Tydskrif vir Geesteswetensk* 5 (1965), pp. 77-85 (not accessible to me), and "Covenant, Promise and Expectation in the Bible" *ThZ* 23 (1967), pp. 305-22 with references. The essays by M. G. Kline in *WTJ* 27 (1964-5), pp. 1-20, 115-139, 28 (1965-6), pp. 1-37, should also be mentioned in this connexion.

[4] *Das Bundesformular* (Neukirchen-Vluyn, 1960), *cf.* A. Jaubert, *La Notion de l'Alliance dans le Judaïsme* (Paris, 1963). Since this paper was drafted J. Reumann's paper "Heilsgeschichte in Luke" has appeared (F. L. Cross ed. *Studia Evangelica* 4 [Berlin, 1968], pp. 86-115) where Baltzer's thesis is applied to the New Testament (pp. 108-15); my attention was kindly drawn to this by I. H. Marshall.

fined as dogmatic, ethical, blessings and curses. He located the preservation of the scheme in liturgical forms.

Now although it would be far-fetched to maintain that any New Testament book was constructed on this pattern, it would be surprising were the concept entirely absent from writings concerned with a new covenant. Hence it may be borne in mind when reading the Epistles that they were composed to explain various facets of the application of the New Covenant to those who professed to accept its requirements, though they are not themselves covenant texts. So it is likely that echoes of the ancient scheme will appear.

All covenants were largely concerned with the conduct of the subject party, and the Apostle Paul felt a need for the instruction of the Corinthians in their personal responsibility as adherents of the New Covenant. The covenant theme is patent in the terms of 1:2, violated by the attitudes condemned in 1:10 ff. Further, as subjects they should never engage in any activity contrary to their Suzerain's interests, seeking adjudication of disputes from another authority (6:1-8), or joining with vassals of another power in sensual pursuits (6:9-20; cf. 10:14-30), occupations for which there are numerous Old Testament parallels in political and moral spheres. In ancient times a vassal's persistent disloyalty might result in reprisals by the suzerain, culminating in exile, or in withdrawal of the suzerain's protection against hostile forces. Such a process is described in the long curses of Deuteronomy 28, vividly portrayed in Deuteronomy 29:18-28, and was partially activated in the days of the Judges, to take Israel as an example. A like effect is produced by the New Covenant: the Corinthians were weak, ill, and even dead through their misbehaviour (11:30). Here the Covenant provisions had taken force, as Paul emphasizes in chapter 11 by his juxtaposition of verses 26 and 27. Proclamation of the Lord's Death, which was the solemnizing of the New Covenant (verse 25), implies acceptance of its consequences. The judicial language apparent in the subsequent verses has been observed already;[1] we may look upon it as a reflection of the Old Testament's covenant lawsuits (*ríb*) where the Lord takes his people to court for their faithlessness.[2] Paul tries to prevent that shame overtaking the Corinthians by pointing to the effect of the Lord's Supper as proclaiming the inauguration of the New Covenant and their consequent blessing – proclaiming it, we understand, to those outside its circle who could be called upon in court, just as heaven and earth are summoned, being independent witnesses of the Old Covenant.[3] That Covenant told to the pagan nations and works of creation what God had done for Israel (cf. Dt. 29:22-28), at the same time as it was narrated for

---

[1] See C. F. D. Moule in W. D. Davies and D. Daube, eds., *The Background of the New Testament and Its Eschatology* (Cambridge, 1956), p. 470 and n. 3.
[2] References in K. A. Kitchen, *op. cit.*, p. 98, n. 44.
[3] Discussion by H. B. Huffmon, *JBL.* 78 (1959), pp. 290-93; the stone in Jos. 24:26, 27 is also comparable.

the benefit of the subsequent generation (Ex. 13:8). This proclamation may be considered primarily out-reaching to those who observe the life of the church, in the present context, angels (4:9; 11:10) and higher powers (as in Eph. 3:10; 6:12), and also to those who might be drawn by its message (like the "unbeliever" of 14:24).

As the actions against vassals provided for in ancient treaties were intended to be punitive and remedial, so is the hardship which might befall the Corinthians. Indeed, they were required to implement the discipline of offenders among themselves by the "handing over to Satan" (5:5). That so grave a move was not final condemnation is shown by 11:32, it was rather a chastening to bring repentance and restoration. Extruded from the Covenant's present benefits, the miscreant might be brought to realize his error, repent, and be received again. There is an obvious similarity with the machinery of the Old Testament covenant which delivered the disloyal nation to its enemies for a time, they acting as the, unwitting, agents of the Lord (so the Assyrians Is. 8:5 f, etc., Nebuchadrezzar Jer. 25:9 etc.).[1]

The Lord's Supper, we have seen, stressed the covenant-standing of the disciple of Jesus. Perhaps especial weight lies on the Judas-connotation of the words "in the night in which he was betrayed" (11:23)[2] in the light of the Corinthians' lax behaviour there and possible incurrence of guilt (11:27). In ancient times the obligated party laid his hand upon the sacrificial victim, identifying his fate with that of the animal should he break his oath, e.g. "This head is not a ram's head, it is Mati'-il's head . . . if Mati'-il [breaks] this treaty, as the head of this ram is cut off . . . so may the head of Mati'-il be cut off . . .".[3] While many major aspects of Jesus' death cannot be compared with the ancient covenant forms, this one may, and Paul undoubtedly had it in mind at this juncture, as commentators point out, referring principally to Exodus 24 and to the Passover.[4] In the account of the original Passover the precept is present in appropriate guise, "None of you shall go out of the door of his house (marked with the blood) until the morning" (Ex. 12:22). That is to say, any man who left the house repudiated the promised safety of the blood, and exposed himself to death of his own will. An analogous situation is envisaged in Joshua 2:18, 19: none of Rahab's family would be in danger unless they left the house marked by the scarlet strand, but anyone who did would be liable to the same fate as the other citizens of Jericho.

---

[1] On the themes of judgment and excommunication see C. F. D. Moule, *loc. cit.*, and G. W. H. Lampe in W. R. Farmer, C. F. D. Moule, R. R. Niebuhr, eds. *Christian History and Interpretation* (Cambridge, 1967), pp. 337–61.

[2] It would appear hard to avoid this association of ideas even if the primary sense is of God delivering Jesus to his enemies.

[3] Treaty of Ashur-nirari of Assyria with Mati'-il of Arpad, E. F. Weidner, *Archiv für Orientforschung* 8 (1932–33), pp. 17–27, col. i, 21 ff.; English translation in D. J. McCarthy, *Treaty and Covenant* (Rome, 1963), p. 195.

[4] See W. D. Davies, *Paul and Rabbinic Judaism*[2] (London, 1955), pp. 250 f., 365.

Each time the Corinthian Christians shared the Lord's Supper they purported to show their allegiance to the covenant it symbolized, and therefore could not but expect its provisions to be active upon them for good or for ill. This follows the ancient pattern in which the regular reiteration of the covenant terms by vassals was a condition; compare, for example, the formal requirements of Deuteronomy 16:1-12; 31:10-13 and the blessings and curses listed. Two purposes were accomplished by this prompting of memory: thanksgiving which involved renewal of loyalty to the gracious Suzerain, and recollection of the commitments undertaken in response (well illustrated in Jos. 24:16-18). To facilitate the repetition, copies of the covenant-terms were preserved in some sacred place – in the Ark in Israel, in various temples in other states – or engraved on "public" monuments as at Shechem (Dt. 27: 2 ff.) and Sefireh. Remembrance of the establishment of the covenant was, therefore, an integral feature of the pattern.

This similarity with the ancient covenant form is important for the interpretation of 11:24-25. We have seen the place of remembering the covenant among obligations placed upon a vassal, an obvious safeguard against human frailty, against the instinctive revolt at restraint. Yet J. Jeremias would understand these words as "This do, that God may remember me", arguing that "God remembers the Messiah in that he causes the kingdom to break in by the parousia" and "As often as the death of the Lord is proclaimed at the Lord's supper, and the maranatha rises upwards, God is reminded of the unfulfilled climax of the work of salvation until (the goal is reached, that) he comes".[1] He says of the command, "The usual interpretation, according to which it is the disciples who should remember, is strange. Was Jesus afraid that his disciples would forget him?"[2] Yet surely that *is* the point; because Jesus knew that the disciples might forget him and all that he signified, he instituted the meal of the New Covenant. Therein he was to be celebrated often as the Lord and the Lamb, providing the example recalled in exhortation to forgetful readers by Paul in Philippians 2 and by Peter in 1 Peter 2.

The usage of terms for remembrance in the Old Testament and in Jewish literature and inscriptions is a mainstay of Jeremias' view. Many references are collected, of which it is claimed, "for the most part they speak of God's remembrance".[3] However, scrutiny of the Old Testament texts gives reason to doubt the relevance of some and the force of others. At the time Jeremias completed the revision of the current edition of his book an exhaustive monograph on the Hebrew root ZKR "to remem-

---

[1] *The Eucharistic Words of Jesus*, ET of *Die Abendmahlsworte Jesu*[3] (Göttingen, 1960) revised to 1964 (London, 1966), pp. 252, 253.
[2] *Ibid.*, p. 251.
[3] *Ibid.*, p. 248. The following observations partly repeat the remarks of D. Jones, *JTS* N.S. 6 (1955), pp. 183-91, who deals with the LXX renderings of the O.T. passages.

ber" was published by W. Schottroff,[1] examining each occurrence and rendering unnecessary any detailed analysis here. What comes to notice when reading Jeremias' references is the careful precision of the Hebrew text when the subject of remembering is God, e.g. Exodus 28:29 *l^e-zikkārōn lip̄ne yhwh tāmîd̠*, "as a memorial before the Lord continually", cf. 28:12; Numbers 10:10 *w^ehāyû lāk̠em l^ezikkārôn lip̄nê '^elōhêk̠em*, "And they shall be a memorial of you before your God". In fact, whenever God is the subject, this is made clear either specifically, as in the passages just cited, or by the context of rituals in his sanctuary, as found several times in Ecclesiasticus 45.[2] On the other hand, the repetition of the Passover meal is to be simply *lāk̠em l^ezikkārôn*, "And this day shall be to you for a memorial, and you shall keep it as a feast to the Lord; throughout your generations you shall keep it, a feast ordained for ever" (Ex. 12:14). Therefore the phrase ἔμπροσθεν τοῦ θεοῦ is essential in Acts 10:4 if God is to do the remembering, and is not an optional addition to a firmly established formula.[3] (Accordingly Jeremias' related attempt to take Mark 14:9 as foretelling a remembrance by God is to be rejected.)

In the dedicatory or votive inscriptions recovered from early synagogues the unstated subject of the phrase *d^ek̠îr l^eṭab̠* may be understood as God with some degree of plausibility, "May God remember so-and-so with mercy".[4] Nevertheless, among scores of comparable Aramaic texts (Nabataean, Palmyrene, Hatrene) are many which add "in the presence of such-and-such a deity", suggesting that the remembering is carried out by human agents in invocation of the god.[5] Indeed, support for this view as a general interpretation can be found in the Jericho synagogue inscription quoted by Jeremias.[6] The structure was built at the instigation of a group of people whose names are not enumerated, perhaps because they were too many. But after the memorial formula stands the sentence "He who knows their names and those of their children and of their households shall write them in the Book of Life [beside] the Righteous", token of an assurance that they would not be forgotten by God, although men could not recall them by name. Certainly the intention of such texts is to bring the benefactor's name into the presence of God (the absence of a divine name or title may be explained by the context of the memorial, namely in the synagogue or its precinct, just as the pagan texts are found in the vicinity of a shrine and many of them lack a divine name[7]). Now a few Jewish

---

[1] *"Gedenken" im Alten Orient und im Alten Testament* (WMANT 15, Neukirchen-Vluyn, 1964).

[2] *Cf.* Schottroff's remarks, *op. cit.*, p. 313. The exegesis of Num. 5:15 and 1 Ki. 17:18 as bringing sin to God's memory (Jeremias, *op. cit.*, p. 248) is disputed by Schottroff, pp. 265–70.

[3] As Jeremias states, *op. cit.*, p. 248, n. 1.

[4] *Ibid.*, pp. 244, 245.

[5] Schotroff, *op. cit.*, pp. 73 f.

[6] *Op. cit.*, p. 245.

[7] Schottroff, *op. cit.*, pp. 74–77 on Nabataean practice. A. Negev, *IEJ* 17 (1967), pp. 253–5 proposes another explanation not yet substantiated.

dedications exhibit their authors' beliefs more clearly, expressing their sanctified bribery: "Remembered be for good Judan bar Ishmael who made this . . . As his reward may he have a share with the righteous" (Chorazin inscription, third century A.D.), and "May . . . be remembered for good whose acts of charity are constant everywhere and who have given five golden denarii. May the King of the Universe give his blessing in their undertakings" (Hammath-by-Gadara, early fifth century A.D.).[1] The remembrance formula can be understood as addressed to the reader, and his reaction can hardly be expected to take a form far different from that of Ecclesiasticus 45–50 (note especially 44:7–15), giving praise to God for the noble acts of "famous men and our fathers that begat us".

A similar explanation can be given for the common ejaculation *zikrônô librākā* "his memory for blessing" following the name of a dead person. While some require a visible structure (cf. Gen. 11:4; II Sam. 18:18), it is said of the righteous "their words are their monument" (Genesis Rabbah 82:10). Furthermore, the Ecclesiasticus passage suggests that an unblessed memory is almost equivalent to assignment to perdition, the lot of the wicked in Proverbs 10:7. Therefore the expressions *zikrônô librākā* "his memory for blessing", its fuller form *zikrônô librākā lᵉhayyê hā'ôlām habbā'* "his memory for blessing for life of the next world" *dᵉkîr lᵉṭab* "be remembered for good" and the like, can be applied to human remembrance as plausibly as to divine.

The result of this approach is to negate Jeremias' claim that in Palestinian Judaism formulae on the style of *dᵉkîr lᵉṭab* were "understood as a wish ('may the memory of the righteous be a blessing') relating to the merciful remembrance of God" as opposed to the interpretation of "hellenistic Judaism . . . referring to the good memories which the deceased left behind among his contemporaries".[2] Thus Paul's words mean that the Supper of the Lord was initiated to remind the disciples of the Lord of the work he had done.

Dissent from Jeremias' understanding of the remembrance does not preclude a prospective sense in that any covenant looks forward to the continuance of the suzerain's protection and to the obedience of the vassal. At all times the covenant-subjects are to be prepared against a visit from their lord (Gk. παρουσία as in Hellenistic Egypt[3]) or a summons to his presence, and their readiness is shown in the regular recollection of their promises and of his in a solemn repetition linking past, present, and future.

The ancient covenants provided for their physical preservation, principally through sanctions against any who might alter the manuscript or destroy it by some means. With a covenant like the New Covenant, not

---

[1] *Ibid.*, p. 86; E. L. Sukenik, *Ancient Synagogues in Palestine and Greece* (London, 1934), pp. 60, n. 2, 82.

[2] *Loc. cit.*, p. 246. J. J. Petuchowski, *JBL* 76 (1957), pp. 294–295 had argued against Jeremias' theory from the use of *zkr* "remember" in the Passover Haggadah.

[3] Arndt, p. 635, *s.v.*, 2b.

committed to writing in the first place but written on the hearts of its adherents (Jer. 31:33 etc.), the possibility of alteration is greater. Others of
Paul's letters demonstrate that fact, even among his own converts. For
those who destroyed the covenant documents divine annihilation was
promised, as much as for those who purposely contravened their terms.
Such apostates are condemned by Paul, also, "If any one has no love for the
Lord, let him be anathema", which is followed immediately by the cry of
the loyal vassal, "Our Lord, come!" (16:22) involving reward and punishment.[1] Meanwhile the memorial rite reiterating the basis of the covenant
is the most appropriate method of ensuring the faithful continuance of the
covenant people. Should the disciples of Jesus forget him, what man
would remember him as Lord (cf. Is. 53: 8 LXX = Acts 8:33)?

[1] Cf. C. F. D. Moule, NTS 6 (1960), pp. 307–10.

CHAPTER XVII

THE THEME OF ROMANS

LEON MORRIS

To the question "what is romans all about?" a variety of answers might be given, and, in fact, have been given. Most students see the Epistle as concerned basically with the salvation of man. Sometimes this is understood in general terms,[1] sometimes in terms of the gospel,[2] or perhaps with specific reference to justification.[3] The same essential point may be made by suggesting that Paul wished to put before the Roman church the essence of the gospel he preached.[4] Some see the Epistle as concerned basically with the problem of the Jew, regarding chapters 9–11 as the very core,[5] though others see these chapters as little more than a parenthesis. For some the letter is about the Christian life as a whole, and they pay special attention to the ethical exhortations which begin at chapter 12.[6] Others again are impressed by the tremendous scope of this

[1] This appears to be the meaning of W. Sanday and A. C. Headlam's view that "the main theme of the letter is the gathering in of the harvest, at once of the Church's history since the departure of its Master, and of the individual history of a single soul, that one soul which under God had had the most active share in making the course of external events what it was" (*A Critical and Exegetical Commentary on the Epistle to the Romans*, ICC [Edinburgh, 1907], p. xliv).

[2] Cf. Martin Luther's classic statement, "This Epistle represents the fundamental teachings of the New Testament and is the very purest Gospel" (*Luther's Preface to Romans*, trans. A. G. H. Kreiss [San Diego, 1937], p. 9). F. F. Bruce cites William Tyndale, "Forasmuch as this epistle is the principal and most excellent part of the New Testament, and the most pure Euangelion, that is to say glad tidings and that we call gospel . . ." (*The Epistle of Paul to the Romans*, TNTC [Grand Rapids, 1966], p. 9).

[3] Donald Grey Barnhouse gives as his reason for choosing to take Romans as the basis of a series of radio addresses that it "has the most complete diagnosis of the plague of man's sin, and the most glorious setting forth of the simple remedy of justification by faith apart from the works of the law" (*Man's Ruin* [Grand Rapids, 1952], pp. 1 f.).

[4] Cf. C. H. Dodd, "With this before them, the leaders of the church of Rome will be able to judge for themselves whether Paul is the dangerous innovator he was represented to be by his Jewish–Christian opponents, or a missionary whose work they can heartily support" (*The Epistle of Paul to the Romans*, MNTC [London, 1944], p. xxv). C. K. Barrett sees the Epistle as "Paul's exposition of 'his' Gospel to the Gentile churches which had come into existence independently of his efforts" (*A Commentary on the Epistle to the Romans*, BNTC [London, 1957], p. 7).

[5] F. J. Leenhardt emphasizes the importance of this section of the Epistle: "What we do about these three chapters is the touchstone of our interpretation of the entire work" (*The Epistle to the Romans* [London, 1961], p. 20). He sees in them support for his contention that the central theme of Romans is "the problem of the church", a view which he admits seems paradoxical (*op. cit.*, p. 19).

[6] Cf. V. P. Furnish, "God's righteousness, revealed in the event of Christ's coming, death, and resurrection, made real for the Christian in the event of his baptism into Christ, is also

Epistle and see it as in the nature of a compendium of Christian doctrine.[1] There is something to be said for each of these views. The variety of suggestions is noteworthy, but understandable in view of the complexity of the Epistle. And since this writing has shown a remarkable power to revitalize the Christian church, the subject is plainly well worth pursuing.[2]

I STATISTICS

An interesting point emerges if we approach the Epistle statistically. I am aware that Paul's is not a personality to be coldly dissected, nor his writings to be treated as if there were no problem that could not be solved by mathematics. His is a fiery spirit, and the unpredictable grammar of Romans is in itself a warning that we must not try to force its author into a mould. Yet for all that something can be learned by studying the words Paul uses and the way he uses them.

It comes as no surprise that the word he uses most frequently is some form or other of the definite article (1105x).[3] Nor that this is followed in order by καί (274x), ἐν (172x) and αὐτός (156x). These are all common words and are bound to occur frequently. But not everybody would expect that Paul's next most frequent word in this Epistle is θεός, "God", which is found no less than 153x. We may gauge something of the significance of this by noting that even some very common words do not occur as often. Thus δέ is found but 147x, the verb εἶναι in its various forms 113x, and the preposition εἰς 119x. When Paul uses "God" more often than such routine terms, then clearly God is very much in his mind. Apart from prepositions, pronouns and the like no word in Romans approaches the frequency of "God". The next most common word with what we might call theological significance is νόμος "law" (72x), after which come "Christ" (65x), ἁμαρτία, "sin" (48x), κύριος, "Lord" (43x), and πίστις "faith" (40x). It is clear that in Romans Paul speaks of God so often that no other subject comes even remotely near it.

[1] Thus Boyce W. Blackwelder says, "It is so profound in content and so systematic in presentation that it may be classified as a theological treatise", and again, "With but brief if any negative argument Romans is a positive presentation of the cardinal doctrines of the Christian message." He quotes approvingly A. M. Hunter's verdict: "In Romans we have the answer to the question, 'What is Christianity?' by the strongest thinker in the early church" (*Toward Understanding Romans* [Anderson, Ind.], 1962, pp. 37, 38).

[2] Cf. Anders Nygren, "The history of the Christian church is consequently witness to the fact that the Epistle to the Romans has in a peculiar way been able to supply the impulse for the renewal of Christianity. When man has slipped away from the gospel, a deep study of Romans has often been the means by which the lost has been recovered" (*Commentary on Romans* [Philadelphia, 1949], p. 3).

[3] I take this and the other statistics in this article from Robert Morgenthaler, *Statistik des Neutestamentlichen Wortschatzes* (Zürich, 1958).

revealed in the claim God makes for the believer's obedience. This obedience is expressed as man places himself at God's disposal, 'presents' himself for service. The exhortation of Rom. 12:1–2 and the specific appeals which are thus introduced summarize and focus the whole preceding argument" (*Theology and Ethics in Paul* [Nashville, 1968], p. 7).

The same essential point is made by another set of statistics. We may wonder whether Paul's emphasis on God is perhaps the typical New Testament position. The answer is that it is not. The word "God" occurs in Romans more often than in any other book in the New Testament except Acts where it is found 166x. Luke has it 122x and I Corinthians 105x, but no other book exceeds the century. As Acts is so much longer than Romans the word turns up more frequently in the latter. In Romans θεός occurs on an average once in every 46 words, in Acts once in 110. Romans occupies a volume of about 5 per cent of the total length of the New Testament, but it has about 11½ per cent of the occurrences of "God", more than twice the number we would expect from its size.

No other book in the New Testament has this same concentration on the God-theme. Thus of the Gospels Matthew refers to God 51x, but to Jesus 150x, while the figures for Mark are 48 and 81, for Luke 122 and 89, and for John 83 and 237. Luke is thus the only one to use "God" more than he does "Jesus". But here other factors are to be borne in mind. Thus he speaks of man exactly the same number of times as he does God (ἄνθρωπος 95x, ἀνήρ 27x), while verbs like εἰπεῖν "to say" (294x), and εἶναι "to be" (361x) are considerably in excess. There are no comparable phenomena in Romans. Perhaps we should point out here that while, as we have seen, Acts has θεός more often than any other book, and more often than any other theologically significant word, yet if we combine the totals for "apostle" (28x), and for two only of the apostles named, Paul (128x) and Peter (56x), we come to 212. In "The Acts of the Apostles" there is much about God, but, as the name of the book implies, more about God's apostles.

It is not otherwise in the Epistles generally. Sometimes these refer to God quite often. But usually they refer to Christ more often still. For example, Galatians, often thought to be very close to Romans in subject matter, uses "God" 31x, and "Christ" 37x, while for Ephesians the figures are 31x and 46x, and for Philippians 24x and 37x. Sometimes there is a greater emphasis on God, as in 1 Corinthians, but even here if we add "Lord" and "Jesus" to "Christ" we get a total of 155x as against 105x of "God". Hebrews appears to be an exception to this tendency, and, like Romans, it has a marked concentration on God, the term occurring 68x. But, while Hebrews does not use other theological terms as often as this, it employs θεός only once in 73 words, which does not approach the figure in Romans (once in 46 words, as we have already noted). Only 1 John uses θεός more often than Romans (once in 34 words). But here the shortness of the sample makes reliance on statistics a trifle more hazardous. It is also the case that in this Epistle ἡμεῖς is used nearly as often as in θεός, but there is nothing comparable in Romans.

When full allowance has been made for all this, it is clear that Paul's concentration on "God" in Romans is remarkable. No book in Scripture is as God-centred as is this. Fundamentally Romans is a book about God.

II THE NATURE OF GOD

What then does Paul tell us about this God on whom he concentrates so much? First, he says something about the kind of Being he is. He speaks of "the glory of the uncorrupt God" (1:23), and he tells us that there is but one God and that he is not a God of Jews only (3:29 f.). In the doxology[1] we find that God is eternal (16:26) and that he is wise (16:27; cf. "O the depths of the riches and wisdom and knowledge of God", 11:33).

Or again, Paul can speak of such attributes as the love of God (5:5, 8; 8:39[2]), or his faithfulness (3:3), or his truth (1:25; 3:7; 15:8; cf. "let God be true", 3:4). Sometimes such qualities are along the line of goodness (2:4; 11:22) or forbearance (2:4; 3:26), sometimes of severity (11:22) or wrath (1:18; 3:5; 9:22). God may be characterized as "the God of hope" (15:13), or "the God of peace" (15:33; 16:20).

III GOD SAVING MEN

But it is not with abstract qualities that this Epistle is primarily concerned. It is indeed a book about God, but it is about God in action, God saving men in Christ.[3] Here we should take notice of the fact that it speaks much of Christ. We have already noticed that this name occurs 65x, which is the highest total in any New Testament book. Next is 1 Corinthians with 62x, while the highest total in any non-Pauline book is 25x in Acts (though we should perhaps notice that the short 1 Peter has the word 22x). It is not in any way to belittle Paul's interest in Christ to say that these figures show there is not the same emphasis in Romans on Christ as on God.[4] No one in his right mind would wish to maintain that Paul is any other than deeply concerned about the Person and the work of Christ. But in this Epistle

[1] The authorship of the doxology is, of course, disputed. If it be rejected, then the point will not stand. But it is part of the text of the Epistle as we have it, and I have noticed it accordingly.

[2] Possibly we should add 8:35 with Aleph B Or, etc., but the better reading appears to be Χριστοῦ.

[3] Cf. F. Amiot, "Salvation, as we have seen, is always presented as the work of the Father and the Son in common, or rather as the work of the Father through the Son" (*The Key Concepts of St. Paul* [Edinburgh, 1962], p. 59).

[4] The point can be made that Romans, with 5 per cent of the volume of the New Testament yet has 12 per cent of the references to "Christ". But we should bear in mind that the Gospels greatly prefer the name "Jesus" whereas Paul prefers "Christ" (the Pauline corpus contains 379 out of the total of 529 New Testament references to Christ). If we combine the figures for "Jesus" with those for "Christ" as referring to the same Person, the percentage in Romans goes down to 7 per cent.

Paul's real emphasis is on God, on God working through Christ, it is true. But still God.[1]

The sphere in which God works is indicated by another batch of statistics. Paul has an interesting concentration, for example, on a series of words which deal with sin. Thus in Romans there occur 28 per cent of all the New Testament occurrences of the noun ἁμαρτία, and 16½ per cent of those of the corresponding verb ἁμαρτάνειν. This Epistle likewise contains 28 per cent of the occurrences of ἀδικία, 30 per cent of those of κακός, 47 per cent of those of παράπτωμα. With this we should take the death words, for Paul sees sin and death as linked in the closest of fashions ("the wages of sin is death", 6:23). He has the verb ἀποθνήσκειν in 20 per cent of its occurrences, the noun θάνατος in 18 per cent, and the adjective νεκρός in 12½ per cent. Paul is greatly concerned with the fact that men have sinned against God, and that this has resulted in death.

There is a similar concentration, perhaps we should say an answering concentration, on the righteousness words. Thus Romans has 36 per cent of the occurrences of the noun δικαιοσύνη, 38 per cent of the verb δικαιοῦν, and 50 per cent of the noun δικαίωμα. It similarly rates high with words like "condemnation", "judge", and "judgment". The salvation of which Paul writes takes account of these realities.

Especially noteworthy is his use of the term νόμος, "law". As we have already seen, he uses this word 72x, which is about 38 per cent of all its New Testament occurrences. We get some idea of the emphasis on this term from the fact that the next highest number in any New Testament writing is 32 in Galatians, followed by 17 in Acts. Paul employs the term in a bewildering variety of ways[2] and we have expressions like "the law of faith" (3:27), "the law of her husband" (7:2), "the law of my mind" (7:23), "the law of sin and death" (8:2). The most frequent use of the term, however, is for the law of Moses which appears to be in mind in more than 50 cases (there must remain an uncertainty on several occasions whether Paul is thinking of this law or of some wider application of the term). Paul, of course, regards this law as taking its origin in God. Sometimes he directly associates "law" with God, speaking of "the law of God" (7:22, 25; 8:7), though these passages do not necessarily refer to the Mosaic

---

[1] This is missed in such a work as M. Bouttier's, *Christianity according to Paul* (London, 1966). This is a valuable study, illuminating much, but it concentrates on Paul's view of Christ. It is true that in one short section of the work the author recognizes that "God is the ground of every action in Christ" (*op. cit.*, p. 50). But he does not give this anything like the emphasis it receives in Romans.

[2] D. E. H. Whiteley sees "four basic convictions" in the "substructure of the Apostle's thought about the Torah": "The first, shared with all Jews, was that the Law was God's gift and therefore good. The second, shared with many Jews, was that no one in fact obeyed the Law. The third, which a significant minority of the Jews also accepted, was that God's plan included the good of the Gentiles as well as that of Israel. The fourth, which cut him off from Judaism and made him a Christian, was that God had raised from the dead the Messiah of Israel, whom the rulers of the nation had given over to be crucified" (*The Theology of St. Paul* [Oxford, 1964], p. 79).

law. There can, however, be no doubt at all but that Paul regards God as
the originator of the Mosaic law. He repudiates the law when it is regarded
as a means of salvation, but he just as emphatically accepts it when it is seen
as part of God's gracious provision for the working out of his purpose
(7:12).[1]

IV RELATION TO GOD

It is clear that in this writing Paul is greatly concerned with sin and
righteousness and judgment. But in each case he is concerned with the
topic not for its own sake, but as it relates to God. Take, for example, his
treatment of sin. He does not speak of this simply as an ethical problem
or an ethical horror. It is an offence against God. Sinners are those who
dishonour God (2:23), they blaspheme the name of God (2:24). They are
men who do not seek after God (3:11), who have no fear of God (3:18).
Being under the control of "the mind of the flesh" they are at enmity with
God (8:7), indeed they cannot please him (8:8). The implication clearly is
that they ought to please him. But the tragedy of the fleshly life is that in
its very nature it is unable to do the things that please God. It is thus in that
state of hostility to God which can also be described as death (8:6).
Sinners have disobeyed God (11:30).

Or this may be expressed in terms of the knowledge of God. There is
dispute as to the extent of the revelation of God which Paul sees in nature
and the like. But it cannot be denied that he says that God has manifested
to men what can be known of him (1:19). The result is that there is a
sense in which men knew him (1:21). But the really significant thing is
that they refused to have God in knowledge (1:28), an unusual expression
which emphasizes that the crux of human sin is the alienation of the sinner
from real knowledge of God. This knowledge, moreover, is a knowledge
which the sinner refuses to have. It is not something which God with-
holds. Paul has already said plainly that God has made known what could
be made known. The God of whom he writes so movingly is not a God
who is trying to reject men. He is a God of hope (15:13; Romans has more
than 24% of the New Testament references to hope), and a God of perseverance and encouragement (15:5). Men are culpable when they reject
such a God and put the knowledge of God away from themselves. Paul
brings out something of the heinousness of all this by pointing out that it
means exchanging the glory of God for the likeness of created being
(1:23), or again exchanging the truth of God for the lie (1:25). So do
men degrade themselves when they reject God. But notice that throughout Paul is concerned with men's Godward relation. It is the glory *of
God* that men reject, the truth *of God* that they abandon. This general

[1] C. Hodge maintains that Paul sees the law as "the will of God revealed for our obedience;
commonly, however, with special reference to the revelation made in the Scriptures" (*Commentary on the Epistle to the Romans* [New York, 1896], p. 81).

attitude may be found even among the religious. Paul can speak of the men of his own nation as having a zeal for God, but a zeal which lacks knowledge. They do not know the righteousness of God nor submit to it (10:2 f.). Again there is a refusal to take God's way and the assertion of men's own ideas as the right way.

V PUNISHMENT AND GOD

Since men thus make the essence of their sin a wrong attitude to God, it is not surprising that their punishment is thought of as coming from God. In the very section of the Epistle in which Paul brings out the point that sinners refused the knowledge of God he has the solemn, thrice-repeated "God gave them up" to the consequences of their sin (1:24, 26, 28). He could have said that there is a natural process of cause and effect which works itself out. He could have said that to take up a position which rejects the knowledge of God means inevitably to live with all the implications of ignorance of God. But instead Paul prefers to stress that God is not inactive when the consequences follow. It is not that he pictures a vindictive God who reacts sharply to sin, lashing out against those who refuse to give him his due. It is rather that God pays men the compliment of taking their freedom seriously. He does not constrain them to serve him. But when they choose the wrong he sees to it that they go along with their choice and that they experience what that choice means.

Again, Paul can speak in terms of the wrath of God (1:18; 3:5; 9:22; about one third of all the New Testament occurrences of ὀργή are in this Epistle). C. H. Dodd and others have made much of the thought that this is an archaic idea[1] and that we should not take it too seriously in days like our own, when we have come to see that the love of God is such that wrath is excluded. But this is not grappling with either the teaching of Romans or the facts of life. Paul's words are not those of a man describing an impersonal process of cause and effect. As we have just seen, he goes out of his way to bring in the notion of the divine intervention in a situation where it would have been easy to say, "They exchanged the glory of the uncorrupt God for images of created being. And they suffered the inevitable consequences". But Paul is not talking about an absentee God who leaves his world to go on under natural laws without him. He is talking about a God who is very much involved. And this is a necessity for our thinking. If God created a moral universe then God is implicated when moral purposes and principles work out. It is difficult to see what meaning an

---

[1] Dodd expresses a preference for the translation "the Wrath of God" over Moffatt's "God's anger" on the grounds that "such an archaic phrase suits a thoroughly archaic idea" (*op. cit.* pp. 20 f.). He thinks that Paul retains the expression "not to describe the attitude of God to man, but to describe an inevitable process of cause and effect in a moral universe" (*op. cit.*, p. 23). I have elsewhere criticized this idea (*The Apostolic Preaching of the Cross*[3] [London, 1965], pp. 155 ff., 179 ff.).

impersonal process of cause and effect can have in a genuinely theistic universe.

VI GOD, RIGHTEOUSNESS, AND JUDGMENT

More important than the fact that sinners sin against God is that other fact that God takes action to bring men salvation.[1] Paul sees this as taking place because God set forth Christ as a propitiation (3:25). He sees the same process from another angle as redemption (3:24), or as reconciliation (5:10), or enjoying peace with God (5:1). It is connected with God's raising of Christ from the dead (10:9). It may not be out of place to notice that Christ is closely linked with the Father. He is at the right hand of God (8:34), and he is spoken of as "Son of God" (1:4), while there is also the disputed passage in which he may well be saluted as "God" and as "blessed for ever" (9:5).[2] When God works salvation through Christ he is not working through a lowly intermediary.

But in Romans the characteristic way of viewing God's saving work is through the righteousness terminology. It is a process of justification, of acquittal. This is sometimes dismissed as a concept of little account. Thus Albert Schweitzer long ago spoke of the doctrine of righteousness by faith as "a subsidiary crater, which has formed within the rim of the main crater – the mystical doctrine of redemption through the being-in-Christ".[3] This estimate, or something like it, has been made by many who prefer to concentrate on Paul's experience of fellowship with Christ. This is certainly not the way it is in Romans.[4] Here Paul has a good deal to say about judgment and the necessity for judgment, and about the way God saves men in agreement with judgment and not in defiance of it.[5]

[1] Cf. William Barclay, "As Paul saw so vividly, it was God who was behind the whole process of redemption. It is God's love, God's desire to save which dominates the whole scene. The initiative is the initiative of God. Behind every act of Jesus is God" (*The Mind of St Paul* [New York, 1958], p. 41).

[2] Barrett sees it as "grammatically easier" to take the words in the sense, "From them . . . springs the Christ himself, who is God over all, blessed for ever." The objection to this is theological: "Nowhere else in any epistle does Paul call Christ, God." He thinks, however, that perhaps "Paul wishes to say that Christ was in human terms a Jew, but in fact God." But in the end he has to leave it an open question whether the reference is to Christ or to the Father (*in loc.*).

[3] *The Mysticism of Paul the Apostle* (New York, 1931), p. 225. He also says that this doctrine "is something incomplete and unfitted to stand alone" (*op. cit.*, p. 226); and he has other similar statements.

[4] H. Conzelmann strongly asserts the centrality of justification for Paul (*Interp*, 22 [1968], pp. 171–86). V. P. Furnish holds that for Paul justification is not at the periphery. "Rather, because his concept of justification is related first of all to his affirmation of the righteousness and power of the covenant God who creates, upholds, and redeems, it stands at the very center of his gospel" (*op. cit.*, p. 146).

[5] Cf. Markus Barth, "Paul speaks of justification. By this he means an act of judgment – not a judgment which men might pass over themselves or over one another, but an act of God – by which God proves that our affairs are in his hands. By this act of judgment God sets right what has gone wrong because of good and evil human intentions and achievements" (*Interp*, 22 [1968], p. 148).

Paul is clear that all men will stand before God's judgment seat and he cites Scripture, his way of clinching an argument, to prove it (14:10 f; he is quoting Isa. 45:23). Every man will give an account of himself to God (14:12). None will escape (2:3) that even-handed judgment which will be "according to truth" (2:2), and again it will be a "righteous judgment (δικαιοκρισία)" (2:5). It will also be a thoroughgoing judgment for God will judge even men's "secret things" (2:16). Privilege will not count in that day, for it is not those who have heard the law, but those who have kept it who will be just before God (2:13). Paul has a very revealing passage when he is discussing God's wrath. He asks whether God is unrighteous (ἄδικος) when he brings on (ἐπιφέρων) the wrath. His answer is a vigorous repudiation, with the question, "Otherwise how would God judge the world?" (3:6). Judgment is not something which has to be established by reasoned argument. That God will judge the world is such a fixed point in Paul's horizon that he can take it for granted and argue from it.

The God Paul knows is a righteous God and final judgment is part of the way his righteousness works out. Paul can ask, "Is there unrighteousness (or injustice) with God?" (9:14), where the rhetorical question brings out the impossibility of our seeing God as anything other than completely righteous (or just). It is in line with this that he speaks several times of the righteousness (or justice) of God (1:17; 3: 5, 21, 22; 10:3, bis). When a God like this saves men, he does it in accordance with right. He does not ignore right in the way he saves. This has been missed by too many scholars. They appear to have been obsessed with the errors, as they saw them, of those in the reformed tradition who emphasized the penal theory of the atonement. It is possible to state this theory in a way which makes God less than loving. He appears then to be a stern judge, who insists that the law's penalty be inflicted, though apparently he is not too particular on whom. In trying to uphold a theory which stressed justice, those who put it forward in this way pictured a God who was far from just. They let Jesus Christ appear as the real Saviour, who intervened between the stern judge and hapless humanity. All this was so hopeless that men were glad to turn to such a theory as Aulén's view that on the cross all the forces of evil were defeated, and that this must be seen as a divine action.

But just as the penal view lends itself to the kind of caricature just outlined, so does that of Aulén to the charge that it proceeds from the basis that "Might is right". God saves men, on this view, not by upholding moral principles, but by overriding the opposition. We cannot do without Aulén's exultation in the victory. But we cannot do either without Paul's concern for the right. With all its bunglings the penal view at least sets out to give due recognition to what is clearly a basic fact for Paul, namely that God acts rightly. If he saves men, then he saves them in accordance with justice. No theory of the atonement will be ultimately satisfactory which fails to do justice to this aspect of the truth. God is righteous. If men are to be saved at all, it will be in a way which accords with this and not in a way which ignores it.

There is a well-known difficulty as to whether Paul means by "the right-eousness of God" righteousness as an ethical quality in God, or whether it signifies rather a righteousness which God gives to men. There seems no real doubt but that the answer must be "Both". The former meaning is clearly in mind when the Apostle speaks of our unrighteousness as comm-ending the righteousness of God (3:5). Or when he speaks of God's right-eousness as being shown in the cross (3:25, 26). But equally clearly it is the right standing which God gives to sinful men which is meant when Paul speaks of "a righteousness of God through faith in Jesus Christ" (3:22).[1] That the latter meaning must accord with the former should surely be obvious. God does indeed convey to men a righteousness they lack. But he does not do it in an unrighteous way. His righteousness is involved in the bringing of this salvation.

Because in his forbearance he had not in the past always punished sin-ners, there was the possibility that he might be thought not just (3:25 f.). But not now. In the light of the cross, God is seen to be both just and the justifier of the believer (3:26).[2] This does not mean that God saves men who are really righteous, for Paul says explicitly that he reckons men as right-eous quite apart from works (4:6), and even that he justifies impious men (4:5; "acquits the guilty"). But he has regard to the moral law in the means by which he saves them. Traditionally this has been taken to mean that Christ paid the penalty sinners had incurred. It seems to me that this is what Paul means. If, however, some prefer to reject this interpretation, let them remember that Paul is certainly saying that there is right, there is justice in the means whereby God brings about salvation. God does not push aside inconvenient moral considerations. He respects the moral law as he saves. This is an insight of Paul's that we cannot do without.

VII GOD IS IN OUR RESPONSE

It is, of course, important that men make the right response to this sav-ing deed of God in Christ. Paul does not envisage a divine activity which

---

[1] R. Bultmann stresses the divine activity: "The reason why 'righteousness' is called '*God's righteousness*' is just this: Its one and only foundation is God's grace – it is God-given, God-adjudicated righteousness." He quotes Rom. 10:3 and Phil. 3:9 and proceeds, "As 'their own' or 'my own' means the righteousness which man exerts himself to achieve by fulfilling the 'works of the Law,' so 'God's righteousness' means the righteousness from God which is con-ferred upon him as a gift by God's free grace alone" (*Theology of the New Testament* I [New York, 1951], p. 285).

[2] Cf. F. F. Bruce, "This, then, is the way in which God has demonstrated His righteousness – He has vindicated His own character and at the same time He bestows a righteous status on sinful men . . . this demonstration shows us how God remains perfectly righteous Himself while He pardons those who believe in Jesus and puts them in the right before His judgment bar" (*op. cit.*, p. 100).

operates completely apart from human response. We need only remember how naturally we follow "justification" with "by faith" to see how integral the response is. The Christian is characterized in the most natural way in terms of his faith (1:16; 3:22; 4:5, etc.). It should, perhaps, be stressed that it is always a faith directed to God (or God in Christ) that Paul thinks of. He is not interested in a general trustfulness, or a faith with no specific object. In the case of Abraham, for example, Paul more than once tells us that the patriarch believed God (4:3, 17). When he directs the strong brother to exercise his faith "before God" (14:22), the meaning is somewhat different. He is concerned with the outworking in daily life of the trust in God which is the basic Christian attitude. But for our purpose the important thing is the centrality of God. Important though the treatment of the weak brother is, even here Paul can find no better way of putting it than making the life of the strong God-centred. Faith in God is the significant saving attitude.

An interesting feature of this book about God is the way it continually sees God in the response to the saving act. Faith is never regarded, of course, as a meritorious work. It is a simple reliance on God. But even so, it is sometimes thought of not in purely human terms but as coming from God. He it is who divided to men their measure of faith (12:3).

This is implied in other expressions. Thus the saving message is called "the gospel of God" (1:1; 15:16). Grammatically this might mean "the gospel which tells us about God", but surely it must be taken in the sense "the gospel which comes from God", "the gospel of which God is the originator". The good news of salvation is not something which just "happened". God brought it about. The gospel is in fact "the power of God issuing in salvation" (1:16).[1] It is in line with this that God gives grace (15:15), and peace as well (1:7). Promise is an important concept – Romans has over 15 per cent of the New Testament occurrences of the noun. So also is mercy, for Romans has 28 per cent of those of the verb ἐλεεῖν. In all these ways Paul stresses that it is God who brings about salvation. This is the thought also when the saved are spoken of as God's "elect" (8:33). This thought stresses the divine initiative as does the cognate thought of "call" (1:7; 8:30, etc.). Men are not saved because they think it a good idea. They are saved because God chooses them and calls them.

This is brought out in an emphatic way in the sequence in which Paul tells us that "whom he foreknew he also predestined to be conformed to the likeness of his Son, so that he should be the firstborn among many brothers; and whom he predestined these he also called; and whom he called these he also justified; and whom he justified these he also glorified" (8:29 f.). The whole sweep of salvation is brought out in an eloquent

---

[1] Cf. William Baird, "The gospel is itself God's powerful act which brings about the very salvation which it proclaims" (*Paul's Message and Mission* [New York, 1960], p. 65).

rhetorical passage and at every stage the emphasis is on what God does. The salvation which means so much to Paul is a salvation brought about by God.

Repentance is an attitude which we most naturally think of as our part in the salvation process. But in Romans it is a response which takes place because God leads men to it (2:4). It is he who induces good dispositions in those who naturally are inclined to sin. So salvation is thought of as God reckoning righteousness (4:6). We could not attain righteousness by any "works of law" (3:20). The saved, even though weak brothers, are not to be regarded as other than "the work of God" (14:20).

This profound conviction of Paul's underlies the difficult discussion of the problem of Israel in chaps. 9–11. Indeed, it is only because Paul sees God as so central to all of life that the problem exists at all. If God had simply set before men the right way and left it to them to choose whether to walk in it or not, it would have been a matter for regret that Israel had not responded in the way they should, but there would be no real problem. Why should they not respond by rejecting God? What for Paul makes the situation so tremendously difficult is that he is talking about a God who works out his purposes and who called Israel to be his people. So he does not ask, "Did Israel reject God?" but rather, "Did God reject Israel?" (11:1). Not content to let the rhetorical question speak for itself, he goes on to say, "God did not thrust away his people whom he foreknew" (11:2). Israel's obduracy took place not because the people, freely choosing, rejected God. No. They "were hardened" (11:7). God gave them "a spirit of stupor" (or "numbness", 11:8). What happened can be put in the form "God did not spare the natural branches" (11.21), or "God shut them up to disobedience" (11:32). We should immediately add that Paul goes on in each case to see more than divine severity. In the former passage he notes that God is able to "graft them in again" (11:23), and in the latter that God's purpose is that he might "have mercy on all" (11:32). This latter thought leads Paul into a rhapsody as he exults in "the depth of the riches and wisdom and knowledge of God" (11:33 ff.). Notice that his theme is not the bliss of the redeemed or the wonder of restored Israel or the like, but the wonder of the excellence of God. It is God and not Israel that is his theme. Perhaps we should add the point that the God we see in Romans is interested in all mankind. Just as Paul wrestles with the problem of Israel, so does he with that of the Gentiles, and in Romans we find 18 per cent of all the New Testament occurrences of ἔθνος.

VIII GOD AT THE CENTRE OF LIFE

When he gets past the initial process whereby God makes a man a Christian into the way that man should live out his life, not surprisingly

Paul still sees God at the centre. Perhaps the simplest and most comprehensive way of putting it is that in which he implores his correspondents, "present your bodies a living sacrifice, holy, well-pleasing to God" (12:1; he puts "pleasing to God" ahead of "approved to men" in 14:18). He has a number of other expressions which emphasize the truth that the Christian must be utterly dedicated to God. He is to reckon himself as dead to sin, but "alive unto God" (6:11). Paul urges believers, "present yourselves to God as alive from the dead, and present your members to God as instruments of righteousness" (6:13). He uses strong language in speaking of them as "enslaved to God" (6:22). The verb δουλεύειν is another of the words found disproportionately frequently in Romans. In all 28 per cent of the verb's New Testament occurrences are found in this epistle as Paul brings out his point that the bondage to sin must be broken and has been broken by God. Now those thus set free must be wholly yielded, even "enslaved" to God. As he speaks of freedom from evil, Paul uses the verb to free, ἐλευθεροῦν, in this Epistle in four out of its seven New Testament occurrences. He looks for his readers to "bear fruit for God" (7:4). He distinguishes between "children of the flesh" and "children of God" (9:8), the implication being that believers display a character quite distinct from that of those whose horizon is bounded by this world. Elsewhere he uses the expression "children of God" again (τέκνα θεοῦ, 8:16, 21), and sometimes "sons of God" (υἱοὶ θεοῦ, 8:14, 19), and for emphasis, "sons of the living God" (9:26). Or again he may speak of "heirs of God" (8:17). The thought in this latter passage and probably also in some at least of the others, is that of privilege rather than responsibility. But this privilege is conceived in terms of relationship to God. It is this which matters right through Romans.

It is more usual to characterize Christians in terms of their faith in God than of their love to him, but the latter does occur when Paul speaks of them as "them that love God" (8:28). More characteristic perhaps is the reverse procedure whereby Christians are God's beloved ones (1:7)[1] In line with this God works out all things for good for them (8:28).

Arising from this is Paul's attitude to prayer. This must, of course, always be directed to God, but Paul goes out of his way three times to speak of "prayer to God" (10:1; 11:2; 15:30). Sometimes also he speaks of giving thanks to God (1:8; 6:17; 7:25; 14:6) or of making confession to God (14:11). Clearly God is at the centre of the life the Christian lives.

It is also true of secular life. It is no coincidence that it is in Romans that there occurs the passage in which Paul lays it down that there is no power

[1] In the face of those who set love and justice (which we have seen this Epistle to stress) in antithesis, we need Wolfhart Pannenberg's dictum: "Love is not opposed to justice, but rather constitutes the kernel of justice itself" (*Jesus – God and Man* [Philadelphia, 1968], p. 194). Without love there is no real justice. But, also, without justice love degenerates into sentimentality.

except under God (13:1) adding "the powers that be have been appointed by God."[1] He does not shrink from carrying this through to its logical conclusion. To resist authority is to resist a divine ordinance (13:2), and governmental authorities are God's servants. Paul can describe them as God's "ministers" (λειτουργοί, 13:6), and he speaks of the authority as God's "deacon" (διάκονος, 13:4). There must have been difficulties quite early in the church's history in relating this to the persecuting state, and again in modern times many have found the concept far from easy. But our concern is not with how we should interpret such passages in the light of the non-Christian character and actions of many states. It is rather with the fact that Paul had no hesitation in referring to a heathen state as owing its position and functions to God. The God of whom Paul writes in Romans is a God who is ceaselessly active and that in all of life. There is no "sacred" sphere to which he is confined or "secular" sphere from which he is absent.

This all-pervasive divine activity must be stressed over against the contention of some that Paul's overriding interest was the transforming experience that he experienced on the Damascus road or the like. Chester McCown can say, "Paul's mystical experiences were to him the very essence of his religion."[2] Paul does make some appeal to his own experience in Romans, but it is by way of showing his inadequacy to live a life pleasing to God. He does not dwell on what God has enabled him to do and be now that he has been converted. In fact throughout this Epistle he is not saying anything like, "On the Damascus road I had a tremendous experience. I saw Jesus Christ and my life was transformed. Come and share this experience." Rather he is saying, "God acted in Christ to bring men salvation." It is what God has done for the salvation of all men whoever they may be that is Paul's theme, with some concentration on this salvation viewed as justification. God's action, not man's experience, receives all the emphasis.

---

[1] A number of scholars, notably Oscar Cullmann, have put some emphasis on Paul's use of ἐξουσίαι to denote spirit forces. Thus, Dr Cullmann concludes his discussion this way: "The two-fold interpretation of the ἐξουσίαι of Rom. 13:1 as referring to the State and to the angel powers which stand behind it is thoroughly justified as an hypothesis, from the standpoint of philology, Judaistic concepts and the early Christian and Pauline theology" (*The State in the New Testament* [New York, 1956], p. 114; he adds that it is an hypothesis, not a final certainty). Clinton D. Morrison has discussed the question in some detail with copious references to the literature, citing authorities both pro and con. His own view is that there is a reference to spirit powers (*The Powers That Be* [London, 1960]). For our present purpose the resolution of the question is not important. Whatever the nature of the secular authorities they are subject to the God of whom Paul writes.

[2] *Contemporary Thinking about Paul*, Thomas S. Kepler ed. (New York, 1950), p. 114. It is perhaps significant that while some of the essays in the anthology have titles like "How Paul Thought of Christ", and "Paul and Jesus" (two have this title), none link Paul and God. There is an emphasis throughout on Christ. So also A. Schweitzer, "the Christ-mysticism is the centre of his thought" (*op. cit.*, p. 22); "Pauline personal religion is in its fundamental character mystical. It can no doubt find expression for its thought in the eschatological and juridical doctrines of salvation, but its own essential life lies in the mystical" (*op. cit.*, p. 25).

IX Conclusion

Thus throughout the Epistle there is a tremendous concentration on God. Sometimes Paul gives information about the kind of God God is, but mostly he is concerned with what God does. Paul's treatment of themes like justification or sanctification or predestination have so caught the imagination of scholars and others that they have tended to concentrate on them and to overlook the dominance of the God-theme. Partly, too, this has been helped by the fact that of necessity God is prominent throughout the New Testament. The whole Bible is a book about God. We tend to think that Romans in this respect is just like any book in scripture.

The point I have been concerned to make in this essay is that it is not. God comes more prominently before us in Romans than in any other part of the New Testament (with the possible exception of 1 John). Elsewhere Paul dwells on Christ and what Christ has done for men. This theme is not absent from Romans; but as long as we concentrate on it to the overlooking of the stress on God, we do not get quite what Paul is saying to us. Romans is a book about God and we must bear the fact in mind in all our interpretation of what it says. Otherwise we shall miss some of the wonderful things it says.

CHAPTER XVIII

FURTHER REFLEXIONS ON PHILIPPIANS 2:5-11

C. F. D. MOULE

A BARE LIST OF THE MAIN BOOKS AND ARTICLES ON THIS PASSAGE would occupy many pages – and, indeed, does so in R. P. Martin's excellent monograph[1] (and some more have appeared even in the short time since that was published[2]). It is none of my intention to go over the ground again. Instead, at the risk of seeming arrogant, I plunge straight in with a proposed interpretation which swims against the prevailing current of exegesis, although nearly, if not all, its suggestions have been anticipated. What I offer, therefore, constitutes an attempt to rehabilitate certain more or less neglected ideas, rather than anything original. It is offered respectfully to a colleague whose honesty and sterling scholarship have for many years been an incentive to me in my work; and, although it sets a question-mark against one small section of Dr Martin's book, it is offered with deep regard also to him, and in gratitude to him and his fellow-editor for inviting me to contribute to this volume.[3]

I

My proposal may be defined in six statements; but, for the sake of clarity, I prefix an explanatory paraphrase of the relevant parts of Phil. 2:5-11, exhibiting the results:

Adopt towards one another the same attitude which (was) also (found) in Christ Jesus, who, although in the form of God (and therefore, by worldly reckoning, one who might have been expected to help himself to whatever he wanted), did not reckon that equality with God consisted in snatching, but, instead, emptied himself and took the form of a slave (who does not even lay claim to his own self) . . . And that is why (i.e.

---

[1] *Carmen Christi: Phil. ii. 5–11 in Recent Interpretation and in the Setting of Early Christian Worship*, SNTS Monograph series ed. M. Black, Number 4 (Cambridge 1967).

[2] Among others, J. M. Furness has added another to the articles already cited by Martin: "Behind the Philippian Hymn", *ExpT* 79 (1968), pp. 178 ff. Dr R. P. Martin kindly draws my attention also to two recent writers who, he says, share (at least in part) the interpretation offered in this essay. They are R. Deichgräber, *Gotteshymnus und Christushymnus in der frühen Christenheit* (Göttingen, 1967) and I. H. Marshall in *Tyndale Bulletin* 19 (1968), pp. 104–27.

[3] I must also thank Dr E. Bammel at Cambridge, and many friends at Oxford, Basel, Zürich, Bern and Harvard, who saw or heard this paper at different stages of its evolution, and offered helpful criticisms and comments.

the fact that Jesus displayed the self-giving humility which is the essence of divinity is the reason why) God so greatly exalted him (in the resurrection and its sequel) and gave him the name (of his humanity – Jesus), which (because it epitomizes this divine self-giving) is in a position of (divine) supremacy over every name, so that at the name "Jesus" obeisance should be rendered such as is rendered only to God.

Now for my six statements:

(1) First, the elliptic phrase (verse 4) τοῦτο φρονεῖτε ἐν ὑμῖν ὃ καὶ ἐν Χριστῷ Ἰησοῦ (equally elliptic in the Vulgate: "Hoc enim sentite in vobis quod et in Christo Iesu") is not to be filled out, as is usual now, into τοῦτο φρονεῖτε ἐν ὑμῖν ὃ καὶ φρονεῖτε ἐν Χριστῷ Ἰησοῦ (meaning something like "adopt towards one another, in your mutual relations, the same attitude as you adopt towards Christ Jesus, in your union with him"). Rather, it should be expanded into τοῦτο τὸ φρόνημα φρονεῖτε ἐν ὑμῖν ὃ καὶ ἐν Χριστῷ Ἰησοῦ (i.e. "adopt towards one another, in your mutual relations, the same attitude which was found in Christ Jesus"). This rendering goes with the prevailing exegesis to the extent of rejecting what is almost certainly a mistake in the Authorised Version's "Let this mind be in you",[1] which represents, of course, the inferior reading φρονείσθω and which, when φρονεῖτε is read, can hardly be tolerated. It would make ἐν ὑμῖν mean "within each of you" (i.e. in your hearts), – at once an unlikely meaning for ὑμῖν and a redundant and unconvincing extension of φρονεῖτε (as though it were possible to think or adopt an attitude anywhere else but within oneself!). On the other hand, my rendering parts company with the present fashion by accepting the Authorised Version's "which was also in Christ Jesus"[2] – if that may be understood to mean "which (mind or attitude) was also found in (the case of) Christ Jesus".[3] The Authorised Version rendering is, according to F. W. Beare,[4] "impossible in itself, and leads to a total misunderstanding of the sense of the whole passage". But I submit that, on the contrary, in the modified form I suggest, it avoids two false assumptions of current exegesis. One of these is that ἐν Χριστῷ Ἰησοῦ is bound here to represent the "Pauline" incorporation in Christ, merely because it often does so in other contexts and because, taken so, it would form a closer parallel to the ἐν ὑμῖν. The other false assumption, springing from the first, is that Christians could be conceived of (whether by Paul or by someone whom he is

---

[1] So Luther: "ein jeglicher sei gesinnt".

[2] So Luther's "(sei gesinnt) wie Jesus Christus auch war", and the Zürcher Bibel's "[diese Gesinnung] die auch in Christus war".

[3] On the whole, this seems a more probable meaning than "which existed within Christ" – though even that, I think, is not impossible. While Φρονῶ ἐν ἐμαυτῷ might be a redundant phrase, τοῦτο φρόνημά ἐστιν ἐν ἐμοί is understandable. J. B. Lightfoot, in loc. (see note 10 below) reverts to the middle in his expansion of the sense: ὃ καὶ ἐφρονεῖτο. He adds, contrary to what I have said, that ἐφρόνει ἐν ἑαυτῷ would have been the regular construction.

[4] The Epistle to the Philippians, BNTC (London, 1959), p. 75.

quoting) as adopting one attitude in their mutual relations with one another, and another attitude as incorporated in Christ. A study of the Epistles suggests, rather, that the two relationships are one and inseparable, and that they must both be either right or wrong together.[1] No doubt it is possible for John Keble to wish that we might "live more nearly as we pray" – that is, live nearer to the Christian ideal. It is possible also for Paul to say (Gal. 5:25) that, if we owe our very life (our existence as Christians) to the Spirit, then we ought also to let our conduct be controlled by the Spirit. But neither of these phrases is comparable to saying that the outlook we have "in Christ Jesus" must be matched by the outlook we have in relation to each other. Such a phrase would imply a distinction between these two concentric (or, perhaps, even identical) spheres which would be most unlike New Testament thinking. In other words, in the phrase "Become what you are!" (which, though not in New Testament wording, undoubtedly expresses an authentically New Testament idea), the contrast is not between two spheres of existence but between an already given condition, on the one hand, and the implementing of it, on the other.[2] In terms of Pauline parallels, the given condition may be exemplified by Rom. 8:8, εἰ δὲ ἀπεθάνομεν σὺν Χριστῷ . . .; the implementing of it by verse 11, οὕτως καὶ ὑμεῖς λογίζεσθε ἑαυτοὺς εἶναι νεκροὺς μὲν τῇ ἁμαρτίᾳ . . . It is this latter note that I believe is struck by the τοῦτο φρονεῖτε of our passage; but a supposed ὃ καὶ φρονεῖτε ἐν Χριστῷ 'Ιησοῦ would not by any means correspond with the former. A very close parallel, on the other hand, to the sense which I am advocating for our passage is presented by Rom. 15:5: ὁ δὲ θεὸς . . . δῴη ὑμῖν τὸ αὐτὸ φρονεῖν ἐν ἀλλήλοις (=τοῦτο [φρόνημα] φρονεῖτε ἐν ὑμῖν) κατὰ Χριστὸν 'Ιησοῦν (=ὃ καὶ [ἦν] ἐν Χριστῷ 'Ιησοῦ). Even nearer at hand is Phil. 4:2, where Euodia and Syntyche are exhorted τὸ αὐτὸ φρονεῖν ἐν Κυρίῳ – which means, "to be harmonious with each other", not (which would be nonsense) "as they are harmonious in the Lord", but "as being in the Lord." I suspect that, in fact, this is the sort of thing that the advocates of the prevailing exegesis think they are making Phil 2:5 mean; but, if so, they are fatally ignoring the ὃ καί.

Having for many years maintained this exegesis, I was encouraged to find it supported by E. Larsson in his *Christus als Vorbild* (Uppsala, 1962), p. 233, and (tentatively, at least) by A. Schulz in his *Nachfolgen und Nachahmen* (München, 1962), p. 274.

(II) My second statement – and it is the heart of my contention – is that ἁρπαγμός in verse 6 is an abstract noun meaning "the act of snatching", and that οὐχ ἁρπαγμὸν ἡγήσατο τὸ εἶναι ἴσα θεῷ thus means "he did not regard equality with God as *consisting in* snatching".

This rendering, though proposed long ago, has been almost universally

---

[1] Cf. P. Ewald in the *Zahn Kommentar* (Leipzig, 1908), *in loc.*

[2] Cf. Ignatius *Smyrn.* 11, τέλειοι ὄντες τέλεια καὶ φρονεῖτε.

rejected in favour of some sense built up round one or other of the concrete meanings usually indicated, in Latin paraphrase, as either *res rapienda* – something that is to be snatched, something not yet possessed which is desirable and attractive; or *res rapta* – something already snatched, already in one's possession, which (it is assumed for the purposes of this context) is not to be let go of or surrendered. The former meaning is found in a large number of the patristic references in Wetstein *in loc.*,[1] and in J. B. Lightfoot's note on the phrase.[2] But as for the latter (*res rapta*), whatever appropriateness to the context it may have is derived from that last, quite arbitrary, addition to the meaning – namely, "not to be let go of". What is meant by the exegetes who adopt it is really not *res rapta* (which ἁρπαγμός might conceivably mean) but *res retinenda* – a desirable thing which is to be clung to; and it is questionable whether this sense of *retaining* inheres in ἁρπαγμός at all. In either case, as several writers have observed,[3] not ἁρπαγμός but ἅρπαγμα is the correct form to designate the concrete *res*; for, although it is perfectly true that a distinction in meaning is by no means always preserved between nouns ending in – μος and – μα, and it is possible to adduce other words in which these terminations seem to be virtually interchangeable, there appears to be no evidence that ἁρπαγμός, in particular, did, in fact, mean the same as ἅρπαγμα, except in those Christian Fathers who so interpreted it in the Philippians passage; and if their interpretation was due merely to a failure to understand the real meaning of the passage and a determination to make sense of it somehow, then the evidence for the equation is reduced to nil. In the only known places where this rare noun ἁρπαγμός is used outside Philippians 2 and Christian writers, who use it mostly in passages where Philippians 2 is explicitly discussed, it means (as W. Foerster admits) "die *Tätigkeit des* ἁρπάζειν".[4] The non-Christian passages are as follows.[5] Plutarch *Lib. Educ.* 15 (=11 F): καὶ τοὺς μὲν Θήβησι καὶ τοὺς ἐν "Ηλιδι (12A) φευκτέον ἔρωτας καὶ τὸν ἐν Κρήτῃ καλούμενον ἁρπαγμόν, τοὺς δ' 'Αθήνῃσι καὶ τοὺς ἐν Λακεδαίμονι ζηλωτέον. Before leaving Plutarch, note also the closely similar ἁρπασμός in *Quaest. Conv.* II:10:2 (= 644 A): οὐ γὰρ φιλικὸν οὐδὲ συμποτικὸν οἶμαι προοίμιον εὐωχίας ὑφόρασις καὶ ἁρπασμὸς καὶ χειρῶν ἅμιλλα καὶ διαγκωνισμός . . .). Pausanias I: 20:3: Διόνυσος, ἥκων ἐκ τῆς 'Αριάδνης τὴν ἁρπαγήν [v.l. τὸν ἁρπαγμόν]. Phrynichus *Ecl.* 302 (= Bekker's *Anecdota Graeca* I, p. 36): Δέσις ὁ δεσμός, ὡς ἅρπασις ὁ ἁρπαγμός, καὶ λόγισις ὁ λογισμός. Vettius Valens II. 38 p. 122: ἐὰν "Αρης κληρώσηται τὸν δαίμονα,

---

[1] J. J. Wetstein, *Novum Testamentum Graecum* etc., 2 (Amsterdam, 1752), pp. 268 ff.
[2] *Saint Paul's Epistle to the Philippians*[2] (London, 1888), pp. 133 ff.
[3] E.g., J. Ross, "ΑΡΠΑΓΜΟΣ (Phil. ii. 6)", *JTS* 10 (1909), pp. 573 f.; S. H. Hooke, *Alpha and Omega* (London, 1961), p. 258; F. E. Vokes, "'Αρπαγμός in Phil. 2:5–11", in *Studia Evangelica* 2 = *TU* 87 (1964), pp. 670–75 (pp. 671–3).
[4] *TWNT* 1, p. 472 (= *TDNT* 1, p. 473).
[5] See Foerster, *loc. cit.* and Bauer *s.v.* See additional note on p. 276.

Σελήνη δὲ τὸν γαμοστόλον, ἁρπαγμὸς ὁ γάμος ἔσται ... [In W. Kroll's edition (1908), there is a note: *"nempe ἁρπάγιμος".*] Of these, the Phrynichus passage seems to be concerned only with the comparative study of noun-formations, not with the meanings of the nouns in question. In all the others, ἁρπαγμός clearly means the act of snatching, or rape. It appears then, that, were it not for the Christian authors, we would have no reason whatever for imagining ἁρπαγμός to mean anything else. The considerably commoner noun ἁρπαγή can, indeed, mean both "snatching" and "booty snatched" (see, e.g., L. and S., *s.v.*),[1] but there is no secular evidence of the same for ἁρπαγμός. Stephanus' *Thesaurus* is thus strictly correct in its entry against ἁρπαγμός; *raptus, ipsa Rapiendi actio, Direptio: in qua signif. usitatius* 'Αρπαγὴ ... Is it arrogant, then, to suggest that the Greek Fathers have led us up the garden path? It would not, I think, be for the first time.[2]

To the interpretation of ἁρπαγμός we shall return. But, meanwhile, the rest of my position must be defined.

(III) My third suggestion is more speculative, and I would not lay any weight upon it, neither does my exegesis as a whole in any way depend upon it. I merely offer it for consideration. It is that the word δοῦλος is chosen, in verse 7, not primarily with reference to the Suffering Servant but mainly because slavery meant, in contemporary society, the extreme in respect of deprivation of rights. A slave, as property sold to another, scarcely belonged to himself. Pushed to its logical conclusion, slavery would deny a person the right to anything – even to his own life and person. This, indeed, far more than any actual maltreatment that a slave might or might not receive, is the essential gravamen against the institution of slavery, however little the rigorous logic of it may have, in fact, been pressed. So, if a human being, as such, possesses inherent rights, then slavery is, by definition intolerable; and the statement that Jesus so completely stripped himself of all rights and securities as to be comparable to a slave, constitutes a poignant description of his absolute and extreme self-emptying – even of basic human rights – and fits the context well. But I would not press the point. I mention it because it does not seem to have

---

[1] But in the LXX, even ἁρπαγή is abstract in eight of its nine occurrences, the one exception being Isa. 10:2 (= *šll*).

[2] The word used by the Peshitta in Phil. 2:6, *ḥṭuphya'*, often means the abstract "act of snatching" though it is also used of the concrete "booty" etc. The Reverend A. E. Goodman of Cambridge University (Lecturer in Aramaic) has very kindly surveyed the uses with Payne-Smith's *Thesaurus* and Brockelmann's *Lexicon* and concludes (in a letter to me): "There is then evidence of *ḥṭuphya'* used for both *raptus* and *res rapta* with by far the greater number of instances of *raptus*". His list is as follows: *abstract*: Ps. 62:10; Isa. 5:7; 61:8; Hab. 1:3, 9; 2:8, 17; (Pesh.) Matt. 23:25; Lk. 11:39; Heb. 10:34; Bar Hebr. *Chronicon* 457; *Liber Directionum* B.O. ii. 301; S. Isaac Antiochenus B.O. i. 226; S. Cyr. *Comm. in Lucam* 267:32; 298:15; Eus. Theoph. ii. 13:19; iii. 61:25; Titus of Bostra 127:14; 219:125. *Concrete*: Syr. Hex. 4 Kg. 21:14; Ezek. 25:7; Num. 14:3 (Pesh. has *bezta'*, "spoil", in each case). One certain case in O.T. – Isa. 3:14. Amos 3:10 is perhaps a borderline case, but the Heb. (*ḥmṣ*) suggests *abstract*.

been suggested by others.[1] In R. P. Martin's fine survey (*Carmen*, pp. 169–96) other suggestions are reviewed – that δοῦλος is a reference primarily to the Servant Songs, or to the righteous sufferer generally, or to servitude to astral powers; but this consideration of the essential implication of slavery does not figure.

(iv) Fourthly, regarding the word ὑπερύψωσεν in verse 9, I agree with those[2] who treat the ὑπέρ as simply elative, indicating not an additional exaltation to a status higher than before, but simply the highest possible exaltation. Nobody, as far as I know, has proposed that ὑπερνικῶμεν in Romans 8:37 should be laboriously and literalistically related to some previous victory on an inferior level. The Authorised Version is surely right in both places when it renders the one by "we are more than conquerors" and the other by "God also hath highly exalted him".[3]

(v) It follows from my first point – namely, the exegesis of the τοῦτο φρονεῖτε clause as "adopt in your relations with one another the same attitude which was found in Christ Jesus" – that I see the whole passage as an exhortation to follow the example of Christ. It must be emphasized that no attempt is here being made to determine the meaning of the passage in any independent existence it may have had before Paul used it. My concern – and it should surely be the first concern of any exegesis – is, if possible, to determine its meaning in its present setting and as used by Paul. E. Käsemann, among others, strenuously opposes this exemplary view, taking the passage as "kerygmatic", not exemplary.[4] But it is hard to deny that 2 Corinthians 8:9 constitutes evidence that Paul (at any rate) can appeal to the pattern of the incarnation as an example for Christians to follow: γινώσκετε γὰρ τὴν χάριν τοῦ Κυρίου 'Ιησοῦ Χριστοῦ, ὅτι δι' ὑμᾶς ἐπτώχευσεν πλούσιος ὤν. And ancient commentators certainly took it as a call to imitation. (See Wetstein's collection *in loc.*)[5]

To take this view is in no way to incur the charge of reducing the gospel to the humanistic level of imitating a fine example. All that is being suggested is that, *in this particular context*, Paul's primary concern is with the exemplary. Most certainly it must be said of Paul (if a parody may be permitted) that οὐ μίμησιν ἡγήσατο τὸ εἶναι ἐν Χριστῷ, ἀλλὰ καινὴν κτίσιν. Paul was never tired of stressing that it is a new nature that is required, not greater human effort; and that the gospel is not about good

---

[1] Since completing this essay, I have been told by the Reverend G. C. Thompson of Normanby Rectory, York, that he heard this idea put forward in lectures by Bishop T. Hannay, when he was Principal of the College of the Resurrection, Mirfield.

[2] See Martin, *op. cit.*, pp. 240 ff.

[3] Cf. Ps. 96 (MT 97): 9 and (with Martin, *op. cit.*, p. 242, n. 1) 1 Clem. 14:5, Dan. 3:65.

[4] "Kritische Analyse von Phil. 2:5-11", in *Exegetische Versuche und Besinnungen: erster Band* (Göttingen, 1960), pp. 51 ff.

[5] On this subject, see H. D. Betz, *Nachfolge und Nachahmung Jesu Christi im Neuen Testament* [*Beiträge zur historischen Theologie*, ed. G. Ebeling, 37] (Tübingen, 1967), pp. 163 ff. (p. 168). Cf. also E. J. Tinsley, *The Imitation of God in Christ* (London, 1960), pp. 134 ff.; and see the very carefully balanced estimate of E. Larsson, *Christus als Vorbild* (Uppsala, 1962), p. 263.

advice but about the gift of this new nature. But that need not have prevented him from using the gospel story of God's self-giving in Christ as a way of saying "Be generous and self-sacrificing towards one another, for this is the most God-like thing you can do; it is precisely here that we can recognise Christ's divinity".

(VI) Finally, there is one other proposal that I have to make. It is by no means necessary to the others and it may be treated as an addendum; but I do not think it is irrelevant. My proposal is that, after all, and despite all the weight of opinion to the contrary, verses 9–11 concern the name "Jesus", not the title "Lord". It is usual to interpret ἐν τῷ ὀνόματι 'Ιησοῦ in verse 9 to mean "at (or to) the name (which belongs to) Jesus", viz. the name "Lord" (see Martin, p. 250). But this is certainly not the most natural way of taking the words. In itself the phrase would most naturally mean "When the name 'Jesus' is uttered". I suggest, then, that "the name which is above every name", bestowed by God, is, after all, not the name "Lord" but the name "Jesus". God, in the incarnation, bestowed upon the one who is on an equality with him an earthly name which, because it accompanied that most God-like self-emptying, has come to be, in fact, the highest of names, because service and self-giving are themselves the highest of divine attributes. Because of the incarnation, the human name, "Jesus", is acclaimed as the highest name; and the Man Jesus thus comes to be acclaimed as Lord, to the glory of God the Father. This involves taking Χριστός, in the phrase Κύριος 'Ιησοῦς Χριστός, as simply an extension of the "earthly" name 'Ιησοῦς. This is, perhaps, slightly surprising, but does not seem to me impossible. 'Ιησοῦς Χριστός is very nearly (though, admittedly, not quite) a proper name in Paul.[1] Ephesians. 1:20 f., which presents, in some respects, a striking parallel, seems to be saying something similar of Χριστός as a name: God placed "Christ" far above every name that is named. On this showing, the Philippians passage becomes a Christian comment on the elevation of the name "Jesus" to a position such that it is no longer customary to call another human child by this formerly common name. On pp. 253 f., Martin alludes to the way in which Lohmeyer[2] and Käsemann[3] both emphasize the use of 'Ιησοῦς in this passage as carrying a reference to the Jesus of history; but my proposal would, I think (if I understand them rightly) go a step further than both these scholars. And it would constitute a return to my instinctive judgment, recorded in *An Idiom Book of New Testament Greek* (Cambridge,[1] 1953), p. 78, as against later doubts recorded in an addendum ([2] 1959, p. 205).

[1] Professor Gottfried W. Locher of Bern kindly communicated to me, in conversation, his own idea that (on the contrary) Χριστός here corresponds to the first part of the hymn, concerning the glorious *pre-existence*. On this showing, 'Ιησοῦς stands between Χριστός (representing the pre-existent glory) and Κύριος (representing the post-incarnational glory).

[2] E. Lohmeyer, *Der Brief an die Philipper,*[9] Meyer (Göttingen, 1952), p. 97.

[3] "Kritische Analyse", pp. 89 f.

II

We return now to my main point (II, pp. 266 ff.), that ἁρπαγμός means neither something not yet possessed but desirable (to be snatched at, *res rapienda*), nor something already possessed (*res rapta*) and to be clung to (*retinenda*), but rather the act of snatching (*raptus*). In spite of the evidence that, outside Christian writers, ἁρπαγμός was used in an abstract, not a concrete sense, the view that Christian writers were mistaken in taking it as concrete seems to have been adopted by comparatively few.[1] R. P. Martin (p. 135) cites only P. W. Schmidt,[2] P. Ewald,[3] J. Ross,[4] S. H. Hooke[5] and A. Feuillet,[6] and the last, as it seems to me does not, in fact, belong to this category, for (if I understand him rightly) his interpretation belongs rather to the *res rapienda* group. J. Ross might have been expected to have left, at least on English writers, more mark than he has. He formulates, as clearly as anyone, the view he represents. The phrase means, he argues, that Jesus "did not think that to be on an equality with God spelt rapacity, plundering, self-aggrandizement; that on the contrary He gave all away, did not set up as an earthly King, but was among His disciples 'as one that serveth', with all the infirmities of our mortality, submitting at last to the most shameful death. And here was St Paul exhorting them to imitate His mind" (pp. 573 f.) That Ross seems largely to have been forgotten, even by English writers, may be due to two or three causes. One is that the article has an amateurish air about it. It is very brief and very slenderly documented – so slenderly that, for instance, he refers vaguely to (p. 574) "the saying attributed to our Lord, Οὐκ ἐστὶν ἁρπαγμὸς ἡ τιμή", without even giving the reference. Presumably he was referring to the

---

[1] It should be said that, already among some of the early exegetes, especially the Latin Fathers, there was one mode of interpretation in which the noun could be taken as abstract. This was the interpretation which made the sentence mean, in effect, that Jesus, already in the form of God, did not see the being-on-an-equality-with-God *as an act of aggression*, for it was his right. Seeing that being-on-an-equality-with-God as his inherent right, not as an act of plunder, he nevertheless emptied himself. Lightfoot (*loc. cit.*) points out the syntactical difficulties of this. And, in any case, this interpretation does not require ἁρπαγμός to be abstract: it can still take it as *res rapienda* in the sense "something *requiring* to be snatched". The interpretation I am advocating is different. It takes ἁρπαγμός as abstract and without an expressed object.

[2] *Neutestamentliche Hyperkritik, an dem jüngsten Angriff gegen die Aechtheit des Philipperbriefes auf ihre Methode hin untersucht. Nebst einer Erklärung des Briefes* (Berlin, 1880). But, although Schmidt's footnote (p. 58 n. 3, on p. 59) seems to express this view ("Der ἁρπαγμός hat kein Objekt, er bedarf keines solchen. . . . . 'Ἁρπαγμός bedeutet, schon aus philologischen Gründen, nichts anderes als das Rauben . . . . . Die Philippischen Christen nun sind die ἁρπάζοντες . . . . ."), his paraphrase looks as though it adopted the *res rapienda* view: ". . . . . das Gottgleichsein nicht für ein Rauben hielt . . .".

[3] As in note 1, on p. 266 above, *ad loc.*

[4] As in note 3, on p. 267 above.

[5] As in note 3, on p. 267 above, pp. 257 f. ("Christ Jesus, who . . . did not think that likeness to God consisted in grasping for oneself. . . .")

[6] "L'homme-Dieu considéré dans sa condition terrestre (Phil. 2, 5 seq. et parall.)", *RB* 51 (1932) (=*Vivre et Penser*, second series), pp. 58 ff. (p. 64).

anonymous quotation (alluded to by Wetstein and J. B. Lightfoot, *in loc.*) in the *Catena Possini* (Rome, 1673) on Mark 10:42. But, if so, Ross was wrong in calling it a saying attributed to our Lord, for the words are: ὁ δὲ Σωτὴρ θεραπεύει αὐτοὺς . . . τῷ δεῖξαι, ὅτι οὐκ ἐστὶν ἁρπαγμὸς ἡ τιμή, τῶν ἐθνῶν γὰρ τὸ τοιοῦτον. Moreover, it is questionable how far the quotation is relevant to Ross' case, for, in the context it looks as though ἁρπαγμός has (as usual in the Christian interpreters) to mean *res rapienda* – or even needs to be emended to ἁρπάγιμος, "snatchable", as is suggested in the passage from Vettius Valens in Kroll's edition (see p. 268 above). The Latin version in the *Catena* goes: . . . *ostendo meritis obtineri legitimum honorem, non sorte aut raptu provenire.*[1]

Another reason for the neglect of Ross' article may be that he ties up his theory with rather implausible speculations about Jewish ideas of Messiahship, and about a prominent Jewish element in the Philippian church. But perhaps the most decisive reason for the neglect may be simply that Ross' point has not been fully taken – any more (on this showing) than that of the original passage in Philippians. Thus, R. P. Martin (*loc. cit.*) argues against it on the ground that, if ἁρπαγμός is taken in an active sense ("snatching"), there is no satisfactory answer to the question: What exactly was it that our Lord refused to plunder? The same problem leads W. Foerster, as Martin points out, to dismiss the proposal.[2] But to frame the problem in the form "If ἁρπαγμός is an 'active' noun, then what is its object?" is to miss the point. One might as well take the saying "It is more blessed to give than to receive" and puzzle over what it is that is given or received. ἁρπαγμός means simply "taking", "snatching", as opposed to "giving away".[3] It is a symptom of πλεονεξία, acquisitiveness. And the point of the passage (on this showing) is that, instead of imagining that equality with God meant *getting*, Jesus, on the contrary, *gave* – gave until he was "empty". It was a very common idea (and still is!) that God's almightiness means the ability to do what he likes: Godhead, like kingly power, has often been associated in popular thought with opulence and splendour. ἤδη κεκορεσμένοι ἐστέ, wrote Paul in one of his most sarcastic moments: ἤδη ἐπλουτήσατε· χωρὶς ἡμῶν ἐβασιλεύσατε (1 Cor. 4:8). That reflects the popular view of kingly power. Well, Philippians 2:7 is saying, Jesus thought otherwise: he thought of equality with God not as πλήρωσις but as κένωσις, not as ἁρπαγμός but as open-handed spending – even to death.[4]

---

[1] The *non sorte* (representing nothing in the Greek) is reminiscent of Greg. Naz. *Or.* IV, *in ulianum*, 98 (xlvi) (Migne, xxxv).

[2] *TWNT* I, p. 473 (= *TDNT* I, p. 474).

[3] So P. Ewald, *in loc.* (pp. 9f.): "Ebenso kann dabei das Objekt des ἁρπάζειν unbestimmt bleiben, indem aller Ton auf der Qualität des Verhaltens ruhrt ..."

[4] The remark of *Epistle to Diognetus* 10:5 is relevant: οὐ γὰρ τὸ καταδυναστεύειν τῶν πλησίον οὐδὲ τὸ πλέον ἔχειν βούλεσθαι τῶν ἀσθενεστέρων οὐδὲ τὸ πλουτεῖν καὶ βιάζεσθαι τοὺς ὑποδεεστέρους εὐδαιμονεῖν ἐστίν, οὐδὲ ἐν τούτοις δύναταί τις μιμήσασθαι θεόν, ἀλλὰ ταῦτα ἐκτὸς τῆς ἐκείνου μεγαλειότητος.

All this time, it has been tacitly assumed that ἁρπαγμὸν ἡγεῖσθαι can legitimately be interpreted to mean "reckon to be a matter of snatching", or (as Ross puts it) that Christ did not think that equality with God "spelt rapacity". But if there is any doubt on this score Ross can invoke some pertinent analogies from the New Testament. He appeals to such phrases as: ἐμοὶ γὰρ τὸ ζῆν Χριστὸς καὶ τὸ ἀποθανεῖν κέρδος (Phil. 1:21.); ἀλλὰ ἅτινα ἦν μοι κέρδη, ταῦτα ἥγημαι διὰ τὸν Χριστὸν ζημίαν (Phil. 3:7.); οὐ γάρ ἐστιν ἡ βασιλεία τοῦ θεοῦ βρῶσις καὶ πόσις, ἀλλὰ δικαιοσύνη κ.τ.λ. (Rom. 14:17); νομιζόντων πορισμὸν εἶναι τὴν εὐσέβειαν (1 Tim. 6:5 – this is a very close parallel in sense and syntax); τὴν τοῦ Κυρίου ἡμῶν μακροθυμίαν σωτηρίαν ἡγεῖσθε (2 Pet. 3:15). Ross also observes that, had the sense been *res rapienda*, it would have been more natural to use a gerund or gerundive such as ἁρπακτέον, or some phrase with δεῖ ἁρπάζεσθαι. Thus, Ross' position, when properly understood, is not lightly to be dismissed. Perhaps the most serious count against it is nothing to do with an "active" noun needing an expressed object, but rather that the pattern of Philippians 2:5–11 as a whole is undeniably that of a sequence – humiliation followed by exaltation, *descensus* followed by *ascensus*, loss followed by compensation; and this pattern, if pressed literally, does, of course, make nonsense of the identification and simultaneity of the two. A number of interpreters have accepted this pattern as basic to the sense. J. B. Lightfoot himself wrote of Jesus emptying himself of "the glories, the prerogatives, of Deity"![1] By contrast, the interpretation which I am urging (after Ross and others) is, in its essence, a "static" one, so to speak. Essentially, it is all at one time and on one level; there is no ultimate question of descent or ascent, of loss or compensation, because what is *styled* kenosis is, itself, the height of plerosis: the most divine thing is to give rather than to get. And that, admittedly, is not the pattern of the section as a whole; and it will not do, with K. Barth,[2] to try to get round the exaltation-climax in verses 9 ff. by denying that the διὸ καί ... denotes subsequent reward.

But the question is: Ought one to take this pattern literally? Or (to put a parallel question) is it impossible that Paul should combine a "static" simultaneity with an allusion to an historical sequence of birth, death and resurrection? We are familiar with the ironic ambivalence of the Johannine use of ὑψοῦν, by which the disgrace of lifting up on the cross is *identified* with that lifting up which is vindication and exaltation; but we forget, perhaps, that the very irony depends on its being possible to analyse and distinguish the two senses, although they are thus syncopated and superimposed. The force of such a *double entendre* always does depend upon the realisation that a curve has been forcibly squeezed out flat. But, if so,

---

[1] *Philippians* (as in n. 2, p. 267), p. 112.
[2] *Erklärung des Philipperbriefes* (Zürich, 1928), *in loc.*, quoted, and justly criticized, by Martin, *op. cit.*, p. 233.

S

then it follows that, even when the pattern is not syncopated but shown in sequence, we are still not necessarily debarred from recognizing that *essentially*, and *in the last analysis*, the two moments are one. God has "exalted" Christ "after" his "humiliation" precisely because, *essentially*, that humiliation *was* itself exaltation. And it has to be remembered that the much-lauded simultaneity of the Johannine irony is balanced by a deliberate use of successiveness in other passages, as, for instance, in John 13. Successiveness and simultaneity are not mutually contradictory, save to the most literal of literal-mindedness. In a word, the presentation of so-called "merit" and so-called "reward" in sequence is not to blind our eyes to the same writer's insight that, the two being identical, neither is an adequate term and both are only groping, picture-words.

III

If this is correct, then there is no intrinsic improbability in seeing the sentiment "Jesus did not reckon equality with God in terms of snatching" as embedded in the pictorial language of making costly sacrifices and, therefore and thereafter, receiving compensation. It only means that the sentiment constitutes a deeply Christian comment – a revolutionary comment – upon the world's values and its quantitative notions. And if it is objected that Paul does not, in fact, anywhere else express his conviction about Jesus in the "static", "simultaneous" way implied by the interpretation here adopted of οὐχ ἁρπαγμὸν ἡγήσατο, one may say that this is at least implied by his references to Christ's humility and self-giving as his essential characteristic. No encouragement is offered, in Paul's writings or anywhere else in the New Testament, to the pagan notion that Christ was temporarily forgoing honour and glory merely with a view to winning them back again. Whatever he did was in his divine love for men, not for gain. The glory that accrued was a revelation of the reality that was there already.

But given this interpretation of Philippians 2, Philippians 3 ceases to provide so close a parallel as has sometimes been suggested. F. C. Porter,[1] E. Käsemann,[2] and M. Bouttier[3] among others, have pointed to the parallel (see Martin, p. 145). And at first it does seem a striking parallel (not least because of the three-fold use of ἡγεῖσθαι). Paul had flung away what had formerly seemed precious, and, in exchange, had received something incomparably better:

ἅτινα ἦν μοι κέρδη,

ταῦτα ἥγημαι διὰ τὸν Χριστὸν ζημίαν.

But the passage in Ch. 2 would be an exact analogy to this only if Christ

[1] *The Mind of Christ in Paul* (New York, 1931), pp. 215 f.
[2] *Op. cit.*, p. 70, with acknowledgments to Bultmann for the suggestion.
[3] *La Condition chrétienne selon Saint Paul* (Geneva, 1964), Ch. I; English trans., *Christianity according to Paul* (London, 1966).

had been said to have deemed equality with God sheer loss and to have flung it away; and this, as we have seen, is not, after all, the most probable meaning of οὐχ ἁρπαγμὸν ἡγήσατο. . . . The most probable meaning, if my reasoning has been correct, is, rather, that the self-emptying was evidence of how Christ understood that equality with God which he possessed inalienably – indeed, that the self-emptying was an exhibition of that equality. St Paul's κέρδη might indeed be paraphrased by res retinendae; but that need only strengthen the contention that that is not the meaning of ἁρπαγμός.

For my first point, I was able to appeal, among more recent writers, to E. Larsson for support. For this second point, I have support in the 'sixties from the late S. H. Hooke, and, in some measure, from B. Reicke[1] and from F. E. Vokes (as in n. 3, p. 267 above). The latter spends some time establishing the case against identifying ἁρπαγμός with ἅρπαγμα. But he seems to me to miss the point when he goes on to take the passage to mean "that Jesus did not make his being on an equality with God *a means for self-aggrandisement, for seizing wealth or booty for himself*" (*op. cit.*, p. 624, my italics). In this he agrees with Meyer and Alford, alluded to by J. B. Lightfoot in his excursus on the passage in his commentary (see n. 2, p. 267 above); but, as will have been seen from my account of Ross' article, it is not correct to attribute this view to Ross, as Vokes does. To the unpublished lectures of F. C. Burkitt, which Vokes couples with Ross' article for this sense, I have not had access.

Since Vokes' article there has appeared an elaborate paper by the Danish philologist L. L. Hammerich: "An Ancient Misunderstanding (Phil. 2:6 'robbery')",[2] touched off in part by correspondence between him and me, in which I had expressed my views about the meaning of ἁρπαγμός. Following my hint, and examining the secular uses of ἁρπαγμός, Hammerich confirmed the meaning *raptus*, rather than *res rapienda* or *rapta*. But he gave a completely new turn to its meaning in the Philippians context by taking it to mean (ecstatic) rapture, and arguing that the point of the passage is that Jesus refused to use his divinity as an easy way of escape – refused to allow himself to be rapt away from all the tribulations of mortal life. Instead, he accepted the human lot and its pains and hazards. Hammerich conducts his exposition with learning and ingenuity, but, to my mind, it falls short of complete cogency. ἁρπαγμός certainly need not mean "rapture"; as we have seen, it clearly can mean "rape" or

---

[1] B. Reicke comes very near it, when he says ". . . le Christ n'a pas voulu utiliser son égalité avec Dieu pour tirer violemment à soi, pour harponner, les êtres de ce monde . . . La toutpuissance du Christ dans ce monde ne se base pas sur une aspiration de puissance mais sur la diaconie" ("Unité Chrétienne et Diaconie, Phil. ii. 1–11" in *Neotestamentica et Patristica*, Festschrift O. Cullmann (Leiden, 1962), pp. 203 ff. (p. 210)). But this, while duly giving ἁρπαγμός an abstract sense, for which the evidence is excellently summarised, nevertheless, in effect, paraphrases it as "*an occasion* for snatching".

[2] *Historisk-filosofiske Meddelelser udgivet af Det Kongelige Danske Videnskabernes Selskab* Bind 41, nr. 4, Copenhagen, 1966).

"snatching"; and it is this sense that, as it still seems to me, suits the context better. The passage requires that ἁρπαγμός be something that (by human judgments) might be expected of one who is already on an equality with God; and that it is a divine prerogative to help yourself to what you want is exactly what the popular mind imagined; whereas rapture belongs properly to a less than divine being who is caught away to some higher status.[1]

Thus, the case for interpreting ἁρπαγμός in our passage as *raptus* "snatching" or "acquisitiveness" seems to me to be a strong one. That deity means not, as is popularly supposed, getting, but, paradoxically, giving is, indeed, the heart of the revelation in Christ Jesus; and this insight can as intelligibly be embedded, as it is here, in the pattern of descent and ascent as it is – more tersely – in the ironic ambivalence of the Johannine use of ὑψοῦν. If so, the passage has nothing to do (as kenotic theories have) with the "how" of the incarnation, though it might be said to be about the "why" of it. It is a celebration, simply, of what Browning hailed in his now hackneyed lines about man's God-likeness:

> Rejoice we are allied
> To that which doth provide
> And not partake, effect and not receive!
> A spark disturbs our clod;
> Nearer we hold of God
> Who gives, than of His tribes that take, I must believe.

[1] P. Trudinger, "ἁρπαγμός and the Christological Significance of the Ascension", *ExpT* 79 (1968), p. 279, accepts Hammerich's view and applies it to the interpretation of the Ascension in the sense that this ultimate glorification was identical with the cross. But, for such an interpretation one only needs Ross' view.
Addendum to note 5, p. 267: I understand that there is further evidence in an unpublished Harvard thesis by R. W. Hoover. See his summary, "The term *ΑΡΠΑΓΜΟΣ* in Philippians 2:6 A Contribution to the study of the Sources of Early Christian Language and Theology", *H.T.R.* 61 (Oct. 1968), 640 f. I have unfortunately not been able, so far, to consult this thesis, which reaches a different conclusion from mine.

CHAPTER XIX

CAESAREA, ROME, AND THE CAPTIVITY EPISTLES

BO REICKE

Translated by Manfred Kwiran and W. Ward Gasque

STUDENTS OF THE HISTORY OF THE NEW TESTAMENT LITERATURE SHOULD not assume *a priori* that Paul's imprisonment presupposed by Phile-mon, Colossians, Ephesians, and Philippians refers to the same location. When the Book of Acts reports an imprisonment in Caesarea (ca. A.D. 58–60) and in Rome (ca. 60–62), the possibility that Philemon, Colossians, and Ephesians – whether "genuine" or not – may presuppose one loca-tion, and Philippians a different one, must be considered.

In point of fact, references contained in the two groups of letters which convey information concerning the sender and recipients are quite different. The assumption that we are here dealing with two different situations is, therefore, not unwarranted.

I

Certainly, as far as personalia are concerned, Philemon, Colossians, and Ephesians[1] form a group by themselves. The popular question concerning the Pauline or non-Pauline origin and contents of Colossians and Ephesians in no way influences this factor. We have as a starting-point the "genuine-ness" of Philemon, a fact which is recognized by contemporary scholar-ship in general. Whether Colossians and Ephesians are regarded as having been written by Paul or are believed to be forgeries, it is in any case neces-sary to find out what these related epistles tell us about the situation of the apostle, his fellow workers, and the correspondents. It is also noteworthy that Philemon and Colossians show no literary dependence on one another, and yet they contain similar personal references. Greetings are sent from practically the same people (Phm. 23; Col. 1:7; 4:12–19), and they were to be delivered (evidently at the same time) to the recipients by one Tychicus, who is accompanied by Onesimus (Phm. 2, 12; Col. 4:7–9). Ephesians, which is closely related to Colossians (regardless of the question whether it was written by Paul or by one of his disciples), also assumes that Tychicus was to bring this epistle (Eph. 6:21 ff.) to his fellow countrymen

---

[1] See literature cited in W. G. Kümmel, *Einleitung in das Neue Testament* (Heidelberg, 1963), pp. 241–64, 409 f., 412 [= ET, pp. 237–58, 389 f., 397].

in the province of Asia (Acts 20:4). Since this Tychicus can be assumed to be an Ephesian (after the analogy of his companion, Trophimus, in Acts 21:29), the readers who know him are to be sought first in Ephesus (so Eph. 1:1, majority reading). These references concerning the situation of the epistles, even if the situation was for some unknown reason invented, indicate that Tychicus first came to the Lycus River valley with the letters to Philemon and the Colossians and then went on to Ephesus through the Meander valley with the Ephesian letter (cf. 2 Tim. 4:12); or, alternatively, one could imagine the same route in reverse, depending on whether the letters originated in Caesarea or in Rome. At any rate, one has here a natural, uniform and straightforward description of the situation. Furthermore, the personal as well as the topographical circumstances clearly bind the three letters together; even on the assumption that Colossians and Ephesians are spurious, it would be necessary to take notice of the description of the situation.

On the other hand, Philippians[1] stands by itself. The only thing this epistle has in common with the others is the cooperation of Timothy (Phm. 1; Col. 1:1; Phil. 1:1). All the rest of the personalia are different. Epaphras and Epaphroditus are not to be identified: the former is in Colossae, while the latter is at home in Philippi. The suggestion that the prison epistles of Asia Minor and the epistle to the Philippians could have been dispatched in connexion with one another is made difficult by the geographical situation. In fact, however, there is no reason to assume that these three epistles were written during the same imprisonment of the apostle as Philippians. On the contrary, the differences between the two groups of letters suggest different occasions.[2]

II

First, the background of Philemon, Colossians, and Ephesians needs to be discussed. (The conclusion that only Caesarea fits the references in question may be mentioned at the start.)

Since the beginning of the present century, a number of authors have held the view that Ephesus was the place of origin for the prison epistles, even though the New Testament contains not the slightest reference to any such imprisonment for Paul. Paul mentions repeated arrests (2 Cor. 6:5; 11:23; Rom. 16:7), but he does not locate any of these in Ephesus. Luke gives the exact opposite impression: he tells how (ca. A.D. 56) the uproar of the silversmiths (Acts 19:23–34) was stopped by the officials (19:35–40; 21:1). Paul recalls the same dreadful encounter in 1 Corinthians 15:32 (ἐθηριομάχησα: to be understood figuratively; a real fight with

---

[1] See Kümmel (page 277, n. 1) for the literature, pp. 229–41, 409 [= ET, pp. 226–37, 389].

[2] The commentary which is still the most useful for introductory matters is J. B. Lightfoot, *St. Paul's Epistle to the Philippians* (London, 1868; many editions; most recently reprinted: Grand Rapids, Mich., 1963).

animals would have left other traces in the literature). The hypothetical imprisonment in Ephesus is conceivable as the occasion for the "Epistle to the Ephesians" only on the basis of the assumption that the epistle was a circular letter (since "in Ephesus" is omitted from some manuscripts); but the strong reading includes the words "in Ephesus". In the case of Philemon and Colossians, as well as Philippians, the theory of an Ephesian imprisonment is saddled with contradictions to the narrative of Acts. These three letters refer to Timothy as co-sender (Phlm. 1; Col. 1:1; Phil. 1;1); however, shortly prior to the riot in Ephesus, Timothy was to have gone to Macedonia (Acts 19:22). Mark and Luke are near the imprisoned Paul (Phm. 24; Col. 4:10, 14); yet Mark had not accompanied Paul to Asia Minor; and Luke, insofar as the "we"–references of Acts say anything about him, makes no mention of the arrest in Ephesus and was not there at that time. Thus the theory of an Ephesian imprisonment can neither be substantiated by any New Testament references, nor can it be brought into harmony with such.

On the other hand, the imprisonment of Paul in *Caesarea* at about A.D. 58–60 (Acts 23:33–26:32) fits quite well as background for the prison epistles addressed to Asia Minor.

As far as chronology is concerned, what Paul tells Philemon in Colossae about his situation (Phm. 9b) is extremely important: "I, Paul, [appeal to you] by the fact that I am such an old man, and now also a prisoner for Christ Jesus." According to the context (v. 8) Paul believes that he could claim his authority as an apostle. But he appeals rather to the sympathy of Philemon (ἀγάπη, 7:9a) and simply presents the following petition on behalf of Onesimus as an older man (πρεσβύτης, one who is over fifty years of age), and as a prisoner. There is no doubt that the wording "*now* also a prisoner" indicates that Paul has been arrested only shortly before, and that he considers his imprisonment to be a new situation and an honour. This fits only an imprisonment in Jerusalem and Caesarea (ca. A.D. 58–60). Therefore, in the case of Philemon an ideal possibility of dating and locating the origin of the letter has been suggested: Paul wrote the epistle most probably at ca. A.D. 59 in Caesarea.

In the case of Colossians and Ephesians, many experts are again concerned with the question of authenticity; it is doubted whether the theology and ecclesiology of these epistles make such an early date possible. However, one should also be critical enough to see the questionable nature of all systematized explanations concerning the stages of doctrinal development. In the religious world development does not run in one continuous line, but the thoughts flow rather differently according to the nature of the soil. On the personal and topographical level, Philemon, Colossians, and Ephesians demonstrate such complete agreement that they appear either to have originated in the same connexion or are the work of an editor who surreptitiously attempts to give the impression that they were written at the same time. In the latter case it would be useful to know how it occurred to later forgers to make use of some of the older names and dates contained in the brief letter to Philemon in order to legitimize Colossians or Ephesians, even when it must have been obvious to such forgers that the introduction of current problems and circumstances would have been more profitable than the search for such antiquities. This much is clear: the statements in Colossians and Ephesians agree with those of Philemon and indicate an origin at the same time, *viz.* A.D. 59 in Caesarea. Either rigid conceptions concerning the development of theology must be modified, or the present correspondence of personalia in the three letters have been deliberate.

On the geographical side, the simplest picture of the trips which are mentioned or presupposed is gained by assuming that the three epistles originated in Caesarea. Paul is accompanied by several Hellenistic Christians (Phm. 23 f.; Col. 1:7; 4:7–14). According to Luke, such Hellenistic-Jewish and Greek followers were present at Paul's return from the collection journey prior to Pentecost in A.D. 58 (Acts 20:16) and were the occasion (unjustly, according to Luke) for the tumultuous attack on Paul in Jerusalem (20:4; 16:28 f.; 24:19). Three persons who are mentioned in these epistles have a part in the account of this journey in Acts: Tychicus, Aristarchus, and Luke (the latter is included on the assumption that the "we"–passages include him [Acts 20:5, etc.]). It is possible that Tychicus, as well as his fellow countryman Trophimus, followed Paul to Jerusalem (Acts 21:29) and then also to Caesarea; however, he is no longer listed among the companions of Paul on his trip to Rome. The assumption that Tychicus, starting out on his trip from Caesarea, was to deliver the three letters to Asia (two to Colossae, one to Ephesus) leads to an uncomplicated and satisfying picture of the circumstances behind the sending of the letters. Moreover, Aristarchus conveys a greeting (Phm. 24) as a fellow prisoner of Paul (Col. 4:10) and as such takes part in the journey to Rome (Acts 27:2). Luke gives a similar greeting (Phm. 24; Col. 4:14) and the "we"–passages seem to indicate that he took part in the trip to Rome as well. It is possible to interpret these greetings from Aristarchus and Luke as coming either from Caesarea or from Rome; however, the numerous other names in the table of greetings encourages one to favour Caesarea as the place of origin, and it seems improbable that so many disciples of Paul shared his voyage by ship to Rome.

Epaphras (Phm. 23), who had recently arrived from Colossae (Col. 1:7f; 4:12), is among the other of Paul's fellow prisoners who send greetings. One can easily imagine him among the other Hellenistic companions of the apostle (some of whom were arrested in Palestine). Against the suggestion of his participation in Paul's trip to Rome is the fact that there is no evidence to suggest this; in addition, an arrest in Rome would not fit the description which Acts gives concerning the mild treatment which

Paul received there. Furthermore, the geographical circumstances allow for the assumption that the runaway slave, Onesimus of Colossae, had come to Palestine on foot, had asked for Paul's protection in Caesarea, and was sent back to Colossae with Tychicus (Phm. 12; Col. 4:7–9), again on foot. It is more difficult to imagine that this young slave journeyed to Rome by sea and then back again. In addition to providing a simpler explanation of the geographical data, the presence of the group of Hellenistic Christians, to whom attention has already been drawn, with Paul on his trip to Palestine following his third missionary journey may have prepared the way psychologically for Onesimus to confide in Paul.

It was especially during his imprisonment in Caesarea that Paul could have expected that he would be sent across Asia on his way to Rome, and thus he would be able to visit Colossae (Phm. 2). He might then go from Ephesus to Italy and eventually, having been acquitted, reach Spain (Rom. 15:3 f., 28). If, on the other hand, he wrote the three epistles in Rome, then the plans for a trip to Spain have to be dismissed as having been no more than a passing thought. However, in Rome, Paul would not have set his eyes on little Colossae as the goal for a trip following the journey to Spain.

Politically oriented concepts in Ephesians suggest that Caesarea fits best as the background for this letter (whether it was written by Paul or by a disciple). While in Jerusalem in A.D. 58, Paul himself experienced the animosity which the majority of the people there had for Greeks. The occasion was the claim that he had brought Greeks into the sanctuary (Acts 21:28 f.).[1] On the wall between the court of the Gentiles and the court of the women, where the so-called Holy Place started,[2] there were inscriptions containing restrictions which encouraged the division of mankind into Gentiles and Jews. A transgression of this line of demarcation by the uncircumcised meant the death penalty for the transgressor (Josephus, Bell. V.193 f.; Ant. XV. 417). Fragments of these inscriptions are today located in Istanbul and Jerusalem.[3]

Paul was taken in protective custody to Caesarea, to keep him safe from the Zealots and their hatred of foreigners. There the oral accusations

---

[1] Concerning the gates of the temple, cf. E. Stauffer, "Das Tor des Nikanor", *ZNTW* 44 (1952/53), pp. 44–66.

[2] The inner courts made up the "sanctuary" in the narrow sense of the word (τὸ ἱερόν: Acts 21:28; Josephus, *Ant.* XV. 419). Therefore, Luke's expression is not wrong (so H. Conzelmann, *Die Apostelgeschichte* (Tübingen, 1963), pp. 30 f., 123).

[3] C. Clermont-Ganneau, "Une stèle du temple de Jérusalem", *Revue archéologique*, nouv. ser. 23 (1872), pp. 214 ff.; W. Dittenberger, *Orientis graeci inscriptiones selectae* 2 (1905), Nr. 598; Strack-Billerbeck II (1924), pp. 761 f.; J. H. Iliffe, "The *Thanatos* Inscription from Herod's Temple. Fragment of a Second Copy", *The Quarterly of the Department of Antiquities in Palestine* 6 (1936), pp. 1–3; I. I. E. Hondius, *Supplementum epigraphicum graecum* 8, 1 (1937), Nr. 169; E. J. Bickermann, "The Warning Inscriptions of Herod's Temple", *JQR* 37 (1947), pp. 387 ff.; B. Reicke, "Hednigarnas begransade till Herodes' tempel", *Svenska Jerusalemsföreningens tidskrift* 46 (1947), pp. 116–24; J. Finegan, *Light from the Ancient Past* (Princeton, 1959), fig. 118 (following p. 282), also pp. 325–26; J. Frey, *Corpus inscriptionum judaicarum* 2 (1952), Nr. 1400.

of the Sanhedrin were brought forward (Acts 24:1–9). According to Josephus, at this particular time the animosity between Jews and Gentiles was even worse in Caesarea than in Jerusalem. Greeks (according to Josephus, they were Syrians) and Jews threw stones at one another. Each party denied the other the right of citizenship (ἰσοπολιτεία). The street battles spread even to Jerusalem after a new high priest by the name of Ishmael ben Phabi had come to power (in A.D. 59). The two parties in Caesarea appealed to the emperor; and, as one would expect, Burrus and Nero (in A.D. 61) declared the Greeks to be lawful citizens in Caesarea (Josephus, *Ant.* XX. 173–84). Similar riots in the year 66 in Caesarea ignited the Jewish War (Josephus, *Bell.* I. 284–92). During his imprisonment in Caesarea (A.D. 58–60) Paul would have had special reason to think about (a) the dividing wall in Jerusalem, (b) the animosity between Jews and Greeks, and (c) the disputation concerning the right of citizenship. It is no accident, therefore, that these topics of political concern influence the theological language of Ephesians: Paul speaks of (a) the ethnic dividing wall (Eph. 2:14 b), which has been removed in Christ, and the new temple (2:20); (b) the animosity between Jews and Gentiles (2:14 c, 16 b; cf. Col. 1:21), which has been changed into peace through Christ (2:15 b, 17); (c) the divine citizenship (2:19), which in Christ belongs also to the Gentiles (3:6), as well as the fact that every nationality (πατριὰ) on earth has its origin in God the Father (3:15; cf. Col. 3:11). These politically oriented terms in Ephesians fit the situation of Paul in Caesarea so exactly that this city alone is suitable as a background for the epistle. This would be true regardless of whether the epistle was written by Paul or by one of his co-workers. (If the epistle is a forgery, then the author had unusually accurate information to hand.) The reason that such political images are found useful in the case of Ephesians, but not so much in the case of Colossians, is due to the situation of the readers in Asia: in Ephesus, municipal citizenship had been granted to the Jews,[1] while in Colossae this privilege was not of immediate interest.

III

Other factors need to be considered in the attempt to locate the Pauline imprisonment lying behind the Philippian letter (cf. the reference to "chains", Phil. 1:7, 13, 14, 17).

The specific references in the epistle point towards Rome and thus to the years ca. A.D. 60–62 (Acts 28:16, 30), as it was generally assumed by the older criticism. It will be made clear by what follows that the attempts to locate the place of origin of this epistle in other places rest on unwarranted conclusions and partly on historical misinterpretations.

[1] B. Reicke, *Neutestamentliche Zeitgeschichte* (Berlin, 1964), p. 212 [= ET, *The New Testament Era* (Philadelphia, 1968), p. 287].

The total lack of evidence for a Pauline imprisonment in Ephesus speaks against this theory (cf. above). Some have interpreted the expression, "praetorium" (Phil. 1:13) as referring to the residence of the governor (as in the gospels). Paul states that his imprisonment is now common knowledge "to the entire praetorium and all the others". Here he thinks of a body of people and other individuals, not an official residence. At any rate, the word was not used for the personnel of a governor either in Greek or in Latin;[1] it is also noteworthy that the governor of Ephesus was not a propraetor, but rather a proconsul. Thus the use of the word "praetorium" in Philippians for a group of persons can only mean the imperial bodyguard which is designated by this loan-word from Latin in several Greek inscriptions (cf., among others, L. Huezey and H. Daumet, *Mission archéologique* [1876], Nr. 130–131; *Inscriptiones graecae* 14 [1890], Nr. 911; W. Dittenberger, *Orientis graeci inscriptiones* 2 [1905], Nr. 707); the term in Latin was the normal expression for the well-known guard (Pliny, *Hist.* XXV, 6:17; Suetonius, *Ner.* IX:2; Tacitus, *Hist.* 1:20, etc.).

Tiberius had placed this élite guard near the Porta Nomentana in Rome. During the first Christian centuries these praetorian cohorts remained stationed in the metropolis, although at times sections of the guard accompanied the emperor into the field of action. Inscriptions found in other areas (as the ones already mentioned) deal only with some veterans who previously had been praetorians. Representatives of the Ephesus theory believe, erroneously, that a few inscriptions found near a road close to Ephesus suggest that a local detachment of the imperial body was located there (*CIL*, 6085, 7135, and 7136). In fact, however, these inscriptions deal with a retired praetorian who after his service with the guard was assigned the position of gendarme (*stationarius*) on that highway. One can hardly create an entire force out of one policeman! The active praetorians had the responsibility of protecting the emperor and the capital city; the deployment of the group throughout the provinces during Paul's time would have been impossible militarily. Besides this, Asia was a senatorial province and was therefore ruled by civil authority; for this reason, no troops were stationed there.

The conclusion that the praetorium is to be understood as a body of persons also rules out Caesarea as the place of origin of Philippians. Auxiliary troops under the supervision of the procurator were stationed here, but none of the élite soldiers of the praetorium. Since the details of Philemon, Colossians, and Ephesians which have been discussed earlier in the present essay point to Caesarea, the very different statements of Philippians appear to suggest another locality. Only Rome, therefore, is entirely suitable as the location for the writing of Philippians.

[1] G. S. Duncan, *St. Paul's Ephesian Ministry* (London, 1929), p. 109: *Praetorium* "must be taken not of the place as a building but of the people who are associated with it". The negative remark is correct, but the positive conclusion does not fit the lexical finding.

As far as matters of chronology are concerned, it is to be observed that Paul no longer refers to his imprisonment as a new condition (as in Phm. 9). He no longer speaks emphatically concerning his sufferings as a prisoner in chains (Phm. 1, 9 f., 13; Col. 1:24; 4:18; Eph. 3:1, 13; 4;1; 6:20), but only makes vague references to "chains" (Phil. 1:7, 13 f., 17) in the sense of a limitation of his freedom. Furthermore, Paul no longer speaks of fellow prisoners (cf. Phm. 23; Col. 4:10), but only of fellow workers whom he is able to meet and send out at will (Phil. 2:19, 25, 28; 4:18). He is able to thank the recipients for sending a contribution for his support (2:25, 30; 4:10–18). This fits Paul's situation in Rome exactly. Here he was permitted to live in a rented room under the surveillance of a guard (Acts 28:16, 23, 30). In Philippians the apostle speaks of his legal standing (τὰ κατ᾽ ἐμέ, Col. 4:7; Eph. 6:21; Phil. 1:12) in an entirely new way: his defence of the gospel (Phil. 1:7, 16) has been effective (1:12), and he hopes that the legal procedures will soon be over (1:19–26; 2:24).

In terms of geography, the distance between Rome and Philippi causes no difficulty, even though some scholars consider it a problem because of the number of trips which are presupposed by the letter. Granted, the distance is about twice as long as the one between Ephesus and Philippi; but it is not as far as the one from Caesarea to the recipients. Moreover, the epistle presupposes only two journeys: (1) Epaphroditus has come from Philippi with a contribution for Paul (Phil. 4:18); and (2) a companion has reported to the people in Philippi concerning an illness which befell their envoy (Phil. 2:26, 30). Paul did not have to wait for confirmation of their having received this news, but rather counted on the speedy circulation of such news by faithful brethren. Neither did he wait for the return of Epaphroditus to Philippi before he wrote the epistle, but, rather, he had Epaphroditus take the completed letter along with him (2:25). Only a few months would be needed for Epaphroditus to make the journey, with the contribution from Philippi, to Rome and for Paul to send information to the Philippians by a companion. Good connections between Philippi and Rome existed in the Via Egnatia and the Via Appia. If the weather was not wholly unfavourable, a ship could make the passage from Greece to Italy in about a week (Pliny, *Hist.* XIX. 19:3 f. speaks of the stretch between Puteoli and Corinth as a record of five days and thereby gives us a picture of the possibilities).[1] Since Paul lived for two whole years in his rented room in Rome (Acts 28:30), there was ample time for the trips referred to in Philippians. The trip to Spain (Rom. 15:24, 28), which has been mentioned previously, is not in contradiction to his intended visit to Philippi (Phil. 1:26), if one locates the Epistle to the Philippians in Rome, since in the capital it would have been possible for Paul to think of a journey to the West and then hope for a new visit to the East, where Philippi was an important centre.

[1] E. Hilgert, "Schiffahrt", *BHH* 3 (1966), col. 1696.

It is of primary political importance that Philippi was a Roman colony settled by veterans (Acts 16:13). For those who had full privileges of citizenship in Philippi, military hierarchy and Roman citizenship were fundamental concepts of life. For this reason, it would also have been of interest to Paul to refer to the praetorium in the sense of the imperial bodyguard (Phil. 1:13). In Philippi, his readers knew Roman veterans, and the Roman praetorium was to them very well-known. This fact bolsters the apostle's report that practically the entire guard and others have come to realize that his imprisonment is the result of his proclamation of the gospel. Of course, Paul did not make a careful investigation in order to determine whether or not all the praetorians knew him; but he had the impression that in the barracks they spoke of him in a generally positive way.

A politically accused prisoner like Paul was guarded by a soldier (Acts 28:16) who was of the barracks of the praetorians. Josephus verifies this in his account of the arrest of Agrippa in Rome (*Ant.* XVIII.186–204). Of the two prefects of the bodyguard, one of them was responsible for the guarding of this kind of prisoner. During the Roman imprisonment of Paul and up to the year A.D. 62, the clever politician, Burrus, alone held this honour. Tacitus reports incidents at which Burrus used his guards as policemen, at times in opposition to Nero's cruel intentions (Tacitus, *Ann.* XIII. 48; XIV. 7–10; etc.). A prisoner who was accused of a foreign teaching could, occasionally, arouse the sympathy of the praetorian prefect. This, in fact, did occur between the oriental philosopher, Apollonius of Tyana, and the prefect, Aelianus (Philostratus, *Life of Apoll.* VII. 16–28). Although the account is highly imaginative, the dialogue between the philosopher and the prefect can clarify how the apostle was led to his optimistic report concerning the entire praetorium. Because of his discussions with the praetorians, he was convinced that the religious reason for his accusation was now known by the entire bodyguard.[1]

The Roman capital also provides the background for those images used by Paul in Philippians which refer to the political realm. This is true in the case of the exhortation to a worthy evangelical behaviour as a citizen (πολιτεύεσθε, Phil. 1:27), as well as of the reference concerning the true, heavenly commonwealth (πολίτευμα, 3:20).

It was impossible for the readers to misunderstand the reference to Rome and Nero's clients in the greeting from "those *of Caesar's household*" (Phil. 4:22). Clients and servants of the emperor lived in several places, but primarily in Rome. Here there also existed a Jewish synagogue of the Augustenses, the imperial freedmen (J. Frey, *Corpus inscriptionum judaicarum* 1 [Rome, 1936], p. LXXIII f.); and it was here also that Poppaea, in the year 62, protected the interests of the Jewish community Josephus, *Ant.* XX.195; *Vit.* 16). It is not surprising that the Christian proclamation

---

[1] Concerning the bodyguard, similarly F. F. Bruce, "Praetorium", *BHH* 3 (1966), col. 1482.

found at that time a hearing in the imperial court or with the imperial clients. Paul is happy to be able to extend greetings from clients of the imperial house to the readers in Philippi. This fine point is lost if one does not accept Rome as the place where Paul had such success in important circles (Phil. 1:12) and from where he writes to encourage the Philippian Christians to share in his joy (2:18, etc.).

CHAPTER XX

APOSTLES BEFORE AND DURING PAUL'S TIME

RUDOLF SCHNACKENBURG
English translation by Manfred Kwiran and W. Ward Gasque

IN SPITE OF THE STRENUOUS EFFORTS OF SCHOLARSHIP DURING THE PAST few decades,[1] the origin and early history of the apostolate remain still quite obscure. Yet there seems to be a consensus on some of the problems which would not have been self-evident a few decades ago. This is true, for example, in regard to the question whether the Lucan concept of "twelve apostles" is an early or late usage. Contrary to the opinion of the renowned English exegete, J. B. Lightfoot, who gave impetus to the critical debate with his excursus on the subject in his commentary on Galatians (1865), most critics today believe that Luke presents a relatively late idea which already assumes an entire history of the concept of apostleship. But concerning the question whether Luke created this idea, or whether he made it fit his theology in a special way, the most recent contributions to research are unable to agree.[2]

[1] Surveys of research: O. Linton, *Das Problem der Urkirche in der neuern Forschung* (Uppsala, 1932), pp. 69–101; E. M. Kredel, "Der Apostelbegriff in der neuern Exegese", *ZKT* 78 (1956), pp. 169–93, 257–305. – G. Klein, *Die zwölf Apostle* (Göttingen, 1961), pp. 22–65, gives an account of the present situation of the debate; J. Roloff, *Apostolat-Verkündigung-Kirche* (Gütersloh, 1965), pp. 9–37, presents the "main lines of the discussion concerning the apostolate" and attempts definite groupings. – For our examination, the following deserve special mention: K. H. Rengstorf in *TWNT* I (1933), pp. 406–48 [= *TDNT* I, pp. 407–47]; G. Sass, *Apostelamt und Kirche* (Munich, 1939); K. H. Rengstorf, "Der Apostel in der Didache", in *In Memoriam E. Lohmeyer* (Stuttgart, 1951), pp. 233–9; E. Käsemann, "Die Legitimität des Apostels", *ZNW* 41 (1942), pp. 33–71; A Fridrichsen, *The Apostle and His Message* (Uppsala, 1947); H. von Campenhausen, "Der urchristliche Apostelbegriff", *StTh* 1 (1947) pp. 96–130; H. Mosbech, "*Apostolos* in the New Testament", *StTh* 2 (1948), pp. 166–200; A. Verheul, "De moderne exegese over ἀπόστολος", *Sacris Erudiri* 1 (1948), pp. 380–96; J. Munck, "Paul, the Apostles and the Twelve", *StTh* 3 (1950), pp. 96–110; A. Wikenhauser, "Apostel", *RAC* I (1950), pp. 553–55; E. Lohse, "Ursprung und Prägung des christlichen Apostolates", *ThZ* 9 (1953), pp. 259–75; C. K. Barrett, "The Apostles in and after the New Testament", *Svensk Exegetisk Årsbok* 21 (1956), pp. 30–49; L. Cerfaux, "Pour l'histoire du titre Apostolos dans le Nouveau Testament", *RechSR* 48 (1960), pp. 78–92; W. Schmithals, *Das kirchliche Apostelamt* (Göttingen, 1961); P. Bläser, "Zum Problem der urchristlichen Apostelates", in *Unio Christianorum, Festschrift* for Archbishop L. Jaeger (Paderborn, 1962), pp. 92–107; B. Gerhardsson, "Die Boten Gottes und die Apostel Christi", *Sv. Ex. Arsbok* 27 (1962), pp. 89–131; G. Schille, *Die urchristliche Kollegialmission* (Zürich, 1967); A. Satake, "Apostolat und Gnade bei Paulus", *NTS* 15 (1968/69), pp. 96–107.

[2] It is G. Klein's main thesis that the apostleship of the twelve had its origin in the theology of Luke (*op. cit.*, pp. 202–10). In opposition to this, J. Roloff thinks that Luke has adopted existing traditions and made them serve his theology (*op. cit.*, pp. 232–5); likewise, H. von Campenhausen in *StTh* 1 (1948), pp. 117 f. Again different is W. Schmithals, who places Luke

There is no lack of literature on the subject of Paul's concept of an apostle. Most of the material pertaining thereto is readily available. Paul's own understanding of his ministry as an apostle stands in obvious tension with the Lucan concept of an apostle as a witness to the earthly life of Jesus. On the other hand, the question of how far Paul's conception of an apostle of Christ Jesus has influenced the development of the idea is debatable.[3] The biggest question is still, which concept of an apostle did Paul find present when he joined the church? In his epistles there are a number of passages where he mentions and recognizes those who were apostles before him and during his time. Since these references seem especially important in the task of trying to discover the original view of an apostle in the early church, perhaps even coming nearer to the origin of apostleship itself, they have received special attention in a number of recently published works. However, the incidental nature of the references to such apostles in the letters of Paul makes it quite difficult to understand. A renewed concern with these texts, which underlies the present discussion, need not be without value, although it cannot present the final word on the issue.

I

Some preliminary hermeneutical and methodological considerations are essential.

From the casual remarks of Paul, we cannot expect to derive a comprehensive view of the conception, or conceptions, of an apostle as held by the early Christian churches; his witness, therefore, remains of limited value. It would also be inappropriate to assume that later witnesses (e.g., the deutero-Paulines, the Apocalypse, or the Didache) would be entirely without value, since they may also, in spite of the fact that they were written at a later time, show clearer outlines and more distinct lines of development than the brief remarks of Paul. The uncertain factor in our investigation stems from the scanty knowledge which we possess of this early period, whether we view it from the point of view of the travelling missionaries in the Didache who, surprisingly, are called "apostles" (which seems to suggest a continuing concept of an apostle), or whether we start with the earliest witness and view those later appearances only as degenerate forms. Without denying the importance of later witnesses, I will limit

---

[3] Klein (*op. cit.*, p. 61), taking his cue from a remark by H. von Campenhausen, believes it to be a fact that Paul had nothing to do with the future development. This is true insofar as the idea of the "twelve apostles" is meant. It does not, however, exclude the idea that Paul in another respect had an indirect influence on the later image of an apostle. Cf. section VI of the present essay.

---

in a late tradition (he dates the Lucan writings as late as A.D. 120-30; *op. cit.*, pp. 243 f.) which developed in a branch of Hellenistic Christianity (*op. cit.*, pp. 233-8, 244-55).

myself primarily to the Pauline texts as the oldest documents available. For the historian these are, in any case, vital.[1]

With reference to the methodological treatment of the Pauline statements, the following points still need to be considered:

(a) Paul does not take us directly to the origin of the concept of apostleship. Even the oldest letter in which the term "apostle" appears (1 Thess. 2:7) was written about twenty years after the death of Jesus. During this time the idea of an apostle could have been already developed, changed, standardized, or even differentiated. Paul offers direct evidence only for the way in which the term was understood in his day, and he bears witness from his own perspective.

(b) It could also be, however, that Paul, by the use of a traditional formula, would become a witness of an earlier concept of an apostle, or even of one which he did not personally share. Of all the passages worth noting, only 1 Corinthians 15:7 deserves special attention in this connexion. The appearance of the resurrected Lord before "all the apostles" is mentioned. Whether or not Paul here formulated his own concept or made use of a traditional form is still debated by scholars. This we would like to examine.

(c) It would be incorrect and misleading to assume that Paul *must have* found a uniform concept of apostle in the early Christian churches. Even if he encountered divergent conceptions of an apostle, it is entirely possible that he had to fight for his own apostleship because, for various reasons, he was refused the recognition due to an apostle. D. Georgi deserves credit for being the one to point out that this is an often overlooked possibility. Since Paul in a dispute with his opponents never refers to a recognized characteristic of an apostle, Georgi attempts to win an *argumentum e silentio* by suggesting that at that time no such uniform designation of an apostle was in existence.[2] This argument needs to be examined and, if possible, supported by means of positive evidence.

(d) It is also important to note the place of origin and early Christian environment of the "apostles" mentioned by Paul, i.e. their connexion with certain congregations and areas. If it is possible that Paul came upon differing concepts of an apostle, it is worthwhile also to ask where these were recognized. The old interpretation of a "double" concept held by the church and the apostle, supported by K. Holl, the one typical of Jerusalem and the other of Paul, can be carried further by showing that it was not Paul who created a new concept, but that he found two or more differing interpretations already present.[3] *In concreto* this verification will

---

[1] Cf. the methodological observations of H. Greeven, "Propheten, Lehrer, Vorsteher bei Paulus," *ZNTW* 44 (1952/53), pp. 1–43, especially pp. 1 f. He consciously places the evidence for later developments to the side and tries to gain a picture of the organization of the church on the Pauline mission field solely from the most ancient sources.

[2] D. Georgi, *Die Gegner des Paulus im 2. Korintherbrief* (Neukirchen, 1964), pp. 42 f.

[3] K. Holl, "Der Kirchenbegriff des Paulus in seinem Verhältnis zu dem der Urgemeinde," *Gesammelte Aufsätze zur Kirchengeschichte* II (Tübingen, 1928), pp. 44–67. According to Holl,

be difficult, especially so for the opponents of Paul in 2 Corinthians, whose place of origin and self-image are highly disputed; yet this factor must be kept in mind.

II

Because the first appearance of the expression "apostle" in 1 Thessalonians 2:7 refers to Paul and probably also to his co-workers, Silvanus and Timothy (see below), we shall best start with Galatians 1:17–19. Paul, who in confrontation with his opponents insists that he does not owe his apostleship to men (1:1, 11 f.), did not after his call (on the road to Damascus) go immediately to Jerusalem to consult with those who were "apostles before him." That is to say, prior to Paul there were apostles in Jerusalem, and at least one of them is named – Cephas. When Paul, exactly three years afterwards, came to Jerusalem, he wanted to make the acquaintance of Cephas (ἱστορῆσαι), not just to meet him but also to discuss with this leader his future work (cf. 2:2).[1] "But I saw none of the other apostles, except James, the Lord's brother" (v. 19). Cephas is without question an "apostle"; but who are the others? Because the grammatical construction is vague, it is open to question whether Paul considered the Lord's brother, James, to be an apostle.[2] That the reference is to the "twelve" is also uncertain. At that time, long before the "apostolic council", they could still have been "in office"; it is only after the execution of James the son of Zebedee (Acts 12:1–2) that this group moves into the background. No new election takes place. But does Paul adapt himself to the language of Jerusalem? Or does he speak of the "apostles" from a later perspective? Since James, the brother of the Lord, did not belong to the twelve, and, according to our knowledge, did not do mission work, one has to ask whether he was even considered an "apostle". Yet we dare not dismiss it as a distinct possibility, not even after 1 Corinthians 15:7.[3] All that can be

---

[1] The verb means, first of all, "to visit for the purpose of coming to know someone" (Arndt, p. 383). It was chosen thoughtfully in order to avoid the impression that Paul received instruction from the authorities of Jerusalem (cf. H. Schlier, *Der Brief an die Galater*,[2] Meyer (Göttingen, 1962), p. 60. However, 2:2 shows that Paul valued the contact in Jerusalem at least for reasons of co-operation. J. Roloff, *op. cit.*, p. 86, believes that "the visit with Peter (Gal. 1:18) undoubtedly provided the opportunity for the exchange of παραδόσεις."

[2] W. Schmithals, *op. cit.*, pp. 54 f., supposes that the vagueness was intended by Paul: one could possibly include James among the apostles, though he does not care to do this himself. – In fact, it is quite conceivable that Paul himself was not sure who should be numbered among the "apostles" in Jerusalem. Concerning the difficult question of James, cf. P. Gaechter *Petrus und seine Zeit* (Innsbruck, 1958), pp. 258–310.

[3] J. Roloff, *op. cit.*, p. 64, n. 82, thinks that 1 Cor. 15:7 dispels every doubt concerning the apostleship of James, since a definite climax is implied in the order "James – all the apostles." However, this is not so certain, since the accent may also rest on the "apostles" (as a new reality); cf. next footnote.

Paul's concept of the church was in "extreme opposition" (p. 62) to the one represented by the early church in Jerusalem, and because of this the apostles also appear in a different perspective (p. 63). This contrast of Jerusalem *versus* Paul is still noticeable in much present-day research.

ascertained from this passage in Galatians is that three years after Paul's conversion there were apostles in Jerusalem, the majority of whom were not present during his visit.

Something more can be said, perhaps, if we compare 1 Corinthians 15:7 with this passage. The reference that Christ appeared to James and "then to all the apostles"[1] is obviously open to debate, because of the connexion with 15:5: "He appeared to Cephas, then to the twelve." Are there two parallel traditions present here? That is, was one tradition more interested in Cephas, and the other more in James, the Lord's brother? Does the phrase, "all the apostles", mean essentially the same group of individuals as "the twelve", perhaps only with the addition of James (as K. Holl has argued)? Or have the "apostles" no real connexion with the "twelve"? For methodological reasons (the investigation would lead too far and still remain unsolved) we must forget, for the time being at least, the question concerning the connexion between the "twelve" and the "apostles." Quite apart from the answer to this question, the following facts can be derived from 1 Corinthians 15:7:

(a) "Apostles" meant, at the time of Paul's writing, a cohesive group. This was recognized by K. Holl.[2] (b) This group could be situated in or near Jerusalem, since they are referred to in close connexion with James. (c) These "apostles" based their accreditation on the post-resurrection appearance of Jesus, or at least they valued it (otherwise this tradition could hardly have continued in the present form). This conclusion is supported if it is true that Paul has not formulated the definition but rather has received it by tradition. G. Klein's argument[3] seems quite probable: In the larger context (vv. 9 f.) Paul lays great stress upon the fact that he is an apostle, although, in the immediate context, it is the appearance of the risen Lord which receives attention. Why should he, on his own initiative, have stated that the risen Christ appeared to "all the apostles", a group in which he himself would not have been included? But if he had met this phrase, which apparently excluded his own apostleship, as a traditional formula, then one understands that he now wishes to point out his own apostleship. The appearance before all the apostles does not exclude the fact that he also, as last among those called to be witnesses,[4] was granted an appearance, that he too was an

---

[1] By placing πᾶς after the noun which has the article, the noun is emphasized; cf. Blass-Debrunner, sec. 275:5. Following the evidence of the papyri, E. Mayser thinks, however, that the linguistic sensitivity for such an emphasis was mostly gone (Grammatik der griechischen Papyri aus der Ptolemäerzeit II/2 (Berlin–Leipzig, 1934), pp. 97 f.

[2] Op. cit., p. 48; cf. also U. Wilckens, "Der Ursprung der Überlieferung der Erscheinungen des Auferstandenen," in Dogma und Denkstrukturen, Festschrift for E. Schlink (Göttingen, 1963), pp. 56–95, especially p. 65.

[3] Op. cit., pp. 40 f.; contra W. G. Kümmel, Kirchenbegriff und Geschichtsbewusstsein in der Urgemeinde und bei Jesus² (Göttingen, 1968), p. 7.

[4] Contra J. Roloff, op. cit., p. 51: πάντων in v. 8 includes πᾶσιν in v. 7 and carries it further. But then one would have the somewhat strange idea that the appearance to "all apostles" had not yet been concluded, i.e. that the risen Lord appeared successively to "all the apostles."

apostle. His own understanding of what an apostle was need not match the concept present in that formula.

If that is correct, then it does not follow that the appearances of the risen Lord created the apostleship; but it follows that in certain groups (in Jerusalem) an appearance of the Lord was evidently a qualifying, confirming, identifying, and perhaps also primarily an authorizing fact for an apostle. It is because of this that Paul stresses the fact that his Christophany is viewed as an appearance of the risen Lord with equal standing to the appearances to the "twelve", even if his was the "last" one. The expression which has just been mentioned also underscores the fact that Paul is interested in a chronological order of events without being able to guarantee them in detail – for ἔσχατον (in contrast to ἐλάχιστος (v. 9)) is surely meant to be chronological. On the other hand, it is this list which shows that the appearance of the risen Lord does not in itself make apostles out of those who were fortunate to have had the experience. That the "more than five hundred brethren" (v. 6) all became active as apostles and as such found recognition, is highly improbable; such an army of "apostles" would have left greater traces in the early Christian writings.

Another passage, 1 Corinthians 9:1, also records the fact that at least some of the early Christian apostles appealed to an appearance of the risen Lord and, on this basis, were recognized as "apostles" in certain circles. The context of the verse, however, is not altogether clear. According to his exposition concerning the partaking of meat offered to idols (ch. 8), Paul wishes to make clear by his own example that one can do without "authority" or freedom, and even under certain circumstances must forgo it (cf. 8:9–13). He himself does not make use of his right as an apostle to be supported by the church (9:12, 15, 18). But for this he was also apparently attacked. If he really knew himself to be an apostle, it may have been argued, he would not have forgone the support of the church. It is against this false conclusion that Paul wishes to defend himself (cf. v. 3), and he attempts, therefore, to substantiate his claim to apostleship. He asks, "Am I not an apostle?" It occurs to him that some deny him his right. It is for this reason that he continues to ask, "Did not I see the Lord?" Admittedly, it does not follow that an appearance of the Lord is an absolutely necessary qualification for an apostle;[1] but it is valuable to be able to claim it. In connexion with 1 Corinthians 15:7 it may be concluded that "to have seen the Lord" was understood, at least in certain circles, as the mark or confirmation of an apostle. As far as Paul is concerned, this is not enough to attest his apostleship; he adds still another argument: "Are you not my workmanship in the Lord?" That is to say, the congregation brought into existence through his preaching is also evidence of his apostleship. Paul

---

[1] This was seen already by A. von Harnack, *Die Mission und Ausbreitung des Christentums in den ersten drei Jahrhunderten*⁴ (Leipzig, 1924), I, p. 335, n. 5 [= ET, I, p. 322, n. 2]; cf. H. von Campenhausen in *StTh* 1, pp. 112 f.

underlines this point in the following sentence: "If to others I am not an apostle (i.e., if they reject me as an apostle), at least I am one to you; for you are the seal of my apostleship in the Lord" (v. 2). Who are the "others" who do not accept Paul as an apostle? It is probable that they are not any of the members of the church addressed by Paul, since he says they cannot doubt his apostleship. The indefinite expression allows for a number of possibilities: other missionaries, other congregations, perhaps also certain groups in Jerusalem. Here Paul is already conscious of opponents to his apostleship (as later more clearly – 2 Cor.) who could confuse the Corinthian congregation which he had founded (cf. 4:1–6), and he defends himself primarily against just such attacks. One may boast of an appearance of the risen Lord or claim successful missionary efforts; Paul was able to meet both requirements. It could very well be that the approaches of different groups lie behind the criteria mentioned above.

III

There are other passages in the Pauline epistles in which an appearance of the risen Lord as the qualification of an apostle is practically excluded. In the table of greetings in Romans 16, Andronicus and Junias are named. They are kinsmen (συγγενεῖς) of Paul and fellow prisoners, "men of note among the apostles", men who were Christians already before Paul. Their characteristics leave little doubt that they were Hellenistic (Diaspora) Jews who became heralds of Christ after their conversions. They shared with Paul an imprisonment (in Ephesus? or in Antioch?); or, as a less probable alternative, Paul calls them "fellow prisoners" because they too had once been in prison because of the gospel.[1] At any rate, they were active in the missionary churches. (For our purpose it makes little difference whether this list of greetings is from a letter addressed to Ephesus or to Rome. Because the early conversion of these men points towards the East, to Palestine or Syria, they could have come to Ephesus, or even to Rome, from there.)

Are Andronicus and Junias actually considered "apostles"? The phrase ἐπίσημοι ἐν τοῖς ἀποστόλοις allows also the translation: "well known among the group of apostles"; they themselves need not be apostles. But the supposition that they are characterized as exceptional apostles among other apostles is more likely.[2] Moreover, it is also possible that they belonged to the church at Antioch and that Paul had met them there.[3] However, since they are not mentioned among the leading men of

---

[1] So W. Sanday and A. C. Headlam, *The Epistle to the Romans,*[5] ICC (Edinburgh, 1954), cit. Cf. however, Col. 4:10 and Phil. 23.

[2] So also most recent commentaries; *contra* B. Weiss and T. Zahn.

[3] Cf. A. Schlatter, *Gottes Gerechtigkeit: Ein Kommentar zum Römerbrief*[2] (Stuttgart, 1952), p. 399. Schlatter thinks that they received the title "apostles" as emissaries of the church in Jerusalem, but there is no evidence for this. See following footnote.

Antioch, the "prophets and teachers" of Acts 13:1, it is also possible that they belonged to the "Hellenists" of Jerusalem, of which Acts 11:20 speaks. "But there were some of them, men of Cyprus and Cyrene, who on coming to Antioch spoke to the Greeks also, preaching the Lord Jesus." Even if we assign these early Christians, Andronicus and Junias, to the Jerusalem church, we must count them among the "Hellenists", as their names suggest and as their later activity as missionaries confirms. However, it seems highly improbable that they had seen the risen Lord. Luke deserves to be trusted in his account as far as the time when these Hellenistic Jews turned to faith in Christ, that is, a time when the appearances of Jesus were already past.

Andronicus and Junias, therefore, belonged to a group of "apostles" who were early and recognized heralds of the gospel, without being able to lay claim to an appearance of the risen Lord. Paul grants them the designation "apostle", certainly not just because of his own understanding of apostleship, but also because he had found this concept already present in the church. We may assume that this way of speaking of "apostles" was widespread among the Hellenistic Christian congregations, as also among the Jewish Christians of the Diaspora. Luke is of little help as far as Antioch is concerned, where one might suppose this way of speaking originated. This is not too surprising when one looks at Luke's concept of an apostle. Yet those who are sent out by the leading men of Antioch (i.e. Paul and Barnabas) are called apostles (Acts 13:1-3). It is worth noting that in Acts 14:4 and 14 Luke again uses the expression for Paul and Barnabas. However one may interpret this "inconsistency" (a problem which cannot be dealt with here), these passages are, nevertheless, witnesses for the fact that such recognized preachers of faith were designated "apostles."

The concept of an apostle which appears here can hardly be traced back to "emissaries of the church."[1] That is a special concept which rather reminds one of the Jewish institution of the šᵉlûhîm. Wherever such emissaries of the church are mentioned in the letters of Paul, they are clearly designated as such (2 Cor. 8:23: ἀπόστολοι ἐκκλησιῶν; Phil. 2:25: ἀπόστολος ὑμῶν). The "apostles" referred to in Romans 16:7, without further qualification, could hardly have been anything else but itinerant missionaries.

It is in this connexion also that the expression "apostles of Christ" (1 Thess. 2:7) takes on significance. It is only a slight exegetical possibility to understand the plural as referring to Paul alone.[2] If one compares this

---

[1] This is the main thesis of E. Lohse in his essay in *ThZ* 9 (1953). Against this view, cf. (among others) H. von Campenhausen, *art. cit.*, p. 103; W. Schmithals, *op. cit.*, p. 50; J. Roloff, *o.p cit.*, pp. 39 and 209.

[2] C. Masson, *Les deux Epîtres de Saint Paul aux Thessaloniciens* (Neuchâtel and Paris, 1957), *loc. cit.*, expresses some hesitation in connecting the title of apostle with these three passages, but only by reference to later passages which avoid using the title for Timothy. Against this view, cf. K. Staab, *RNT* (Regensburg, 1959), *loc. cit.*; E. M. Kredel, "Apostel", in *Handbuch theologischer Grundbegriffe*, ed. by H. Fries (Munich, 1962), I, pp. 61-67, especially p. 65.

with the words of Paul in 2 Corinthians 1:19, where the reference to the proclamation "through us" is expressly qualified by "Silvanus and Timothy and I," then it becomes clear that Paul in 1 Thessalonians 2:7 also includes his co-workers in the plural. In the address of the letter he refers to himself, Silvanus, and Timothy in one breath, although without the expression "apostle." "Apostle *of Christ*" Paul calls himself. But this need not be understood as a term coined by Paul. Rather, if Paul found the designation "apostle" already in existence, he could easily, in accordance with his personal understanding and manner of speech, refer also to the others as "apostles of Christ." Evidently, the "false apostles" whom Paul opposes in 2 Corinthians referred to themselves by that terminology (11:13). An appearance of the risen Lord to Silvanus, who already belonged to the church of Jerusalem (in Acts, he is called Silas: 15:22, 27, etc.), is not impossible; but for Timothy, it is out of the question. When Paul in 1 Thessalonians, then, calls himself and his fellow workers "apostles of Christ," this is an indication that this concept of apostle, i.e. as an early Christian preacher and missionary, was familiar to him. He probably knew it from the use which was made of the term in the church of the Hellenistic missionary region. When he later attaches the term "apostle of Jesus Christ" to himself and refrains from using it for his co-workers (cf. 1 Cor. 1:1; 2 Cor. 1:1; Gal. 1:1 f.), this could mean that by now his apostleship had been questioned from various sides and, as a result, he lays greater stress on his own qualifications as an apostle. He is a "called" apostle, "set apart for the gospel of God" (Rom. 1:1), authorized by Jesus Christ and God himself (Gal 1:1).

Even so, in his major epistles Paul is still very conscious of the fact that as an apostle he is also an active participant in the larger group of apostles. In 1 Corinthians 4:9 he brings the overbearing pneumatics of Corinth face to face with "the apostles", who, in their lowly existence, often faced with suffering and death, present a totally different picture from the one presented by those people who think of themselves as already "filled, having become rich, having reached the kingdom" (v. 8). The eyes of the Corinthians should have been opened by this comparison to see what the true Christian existence in this world is. It is clear that Paul here attaches himself to the apostolic band ("us the apostles"),[1] and according to the account which follows, and in view of his own hard apostolic life, one can scarcely doubt that he understands them to be preachers who labour in the Hellenistic missionary area. The apostles mentioned in this passage could hardly have had the experience of an appearance of the risen Lord; rather, they are recognized preachers. There is nothing to suggest that Paul was using a "wider" concept of apostle, since he includes himself in his specific under-

---

[1] Ἐσχάτους can hardly be connected as an attributive to τοὺς ἀποστόλους ("us, the last apostles"), and the plural can scarcely be understood as an editorial plural (so that Paul would be speaking only of himself). Cf. Harnack, *Mission und Ausbreitung* I, p. 334 (n. 3) [= ET, I, p. 321, n. 1], who suggests this.

standing of an apostle (1 Cor. 1:1; 9:1 f.). Therefore, a certain tension arises out of 1 Corinthians 15:7, 9; cf. 9:1, where Paul attaches importance to the appearance of the Lord to him. If one wishes to connect these observations, it might be suggested that Paul knows different "apostles" who are active in the early church, for whom there were no clear-cut and uniform criteria of recognition. In some circles, especially in the neighbourhood of Jerusalem, the experience of an appearance of the risen Lord was important; yet in other regions it did not matter. Which criteria were used outside of Palestine to give recognition to "apostles" remains an open question, in spite of the passages discussed.

It may be asked, to which group did the "other apostles" (1 Cor. 9:5) belong? Paul mentions them in connexion with his freedom as an apostle to request support from the churches. Verse 5 is probably to be taken with the following verse, where Paul asks whether Barnabas and he do not have the freedom to forget about manual work. That they might bring their wives along with them means that the congregations had to take care of them also.[1] In addition to the "other apostles," Paul also refers to "the brothers of the Lord and Cephas." These need not, however, be subsumed under the concept of an apostle. Yet according to the context Paul seems to think of them also as missionaries. The expression "apostle" is not, however, used with respect to them, nor is it in connexion with Barnabas. Thus the "other apostles" could mean "missionaries in the Hellenistic missionary area" (as 1 Cor. 4:9). This interpretation is supported by verse 12, where "others" who make use of their right to support from the church in Corinth are mentioned – surely, other itinerant preachers who had come into the church. Paul adds the "brothers of the Lord" and Cephas, because they were also known and respected in the church.

Alongside of Paul, those people whom he opposes in 2 Corinthians 10–13 have declared themselves to be apostles. The identification of these men, who so strongly irritated Paul with their missionary methods and presumptious claims, is a subject of dispute among scholars, and it is impossible to re-open the question in detail at this point.[2] Paul's opponents are of interest to us only insofar as they claim the position of apostles. From Paul's words, which are partly merely ironic and partly passionately serious, we understand that they themselves used the expression. Twice Paul asserts that he

---

[1] ἤ of v. 6 could correspond to μή of v. 5 (even though it could lead further; cf. 1 Cor. 1:13) cf. 9:8, 9; 11:22. Likewise most commentaries, among others: O. Kuss (1940), J. Moffatt (1938), H. Lietzmann-W. G. Kümmel (1949), J. Héring (1949), H.-D. Wendland (1954), J. Kürzinger (1968), H. Conzelmann (1969). – Contra J. B. Bauer, "Uxores circumducere (1. Cor. 9:5)", BZ 3 (1959), pp. 94–102.

[2] See especially E. Käsemann, art. cit.; R. Bultmann, "Exegetische Probleme des zweiten Korintherbriefes", SBU 9 (1947), pp. 20–30; J. Munck, Paulus und die Heilsgeschichte (Copenhagen, 1954), pp. 162–89. [E. T. Paul and the Salvation of Mankind (London, 1959), pp. 168–95]; G. Friedrich, "Die Gegner des Paulus im 2. Korintherbrief", in Abraham unser Vater, Festschrift for O. Michel (Leiden and Cologne, 1963), pp. 181–215; D. Georgi, Die Gegner des Paulus; J. Roloff, op. cit., pp. 75–82; W. G. Kümmel, Einleitung in das Neue Testament (Heidelberg, 1964), pp. 210 f. [= E.T., pp. 209 f.].

is in no way inferior to the "super-apostles" (11:5; 12:11), and once he speaks of the "false apostles" as disguising themselves as "apostles of Christ" (11:13). In an insistent manner the expression "apostle" was claimed by them, probably with the desire to push Paul to the side; it is for this reason that he calls them ironically "super-apostles."[1] Whether they called themselves "apostles of Christ", or whether Paul only uses the expression, cannot be clearly determined from 11:13; yet one must consider the first as a possibility, as though they consciously desired to compete with Paul.[2] It appears that Paul does not necessarily intend to question their use of the term "apostle"; what he is concerned about, rather, is the true function of an apostle. That is why he calls them "false apostles", a term which he coined especially for the occasion (hapax legomenon).[3]

In the course of the discussion there does not appear to be a recognized test of apostleship on either side. The opponents of Paul have registered their claim to still other titles besides the designation of apostles – "servants of Christ" (11:23; cf. also 11:15) and "workmen" (cf. 11:13). These expressions point in the same direction and permit the designation of "apostles" to be applied to them, because they considered themselves to be primarily heralds of Christ who pursue his cause in the churches with the aim of winning people and establishing churches. No matter whether they did this with impure motives in order to gain selfish honour and influence, were jealous of Paul (cf. Phil. 1:15, 17), were "deceitful" (2 Cor. 11:13), or were "bad" workers (cf. Phil. 3:2); in this activity they considered themselves to be "apostles". Only in this way can the reaction of Paul be explained: he does not attempt to deny their intended activity as apostles and servants of Christ, but he takes care to show that he is engaged in the same activity and has the qualities which they claim for themselves, only in a much higher degree. In a "jesting speech" Paul states: "Are they servants of Christ? I am a better one – I am talking like a madman!" (11:23). The difference lies for him in the understanding of the position of the herald: instead of self-honour, presumptuous behaviour, and proofs of power, there is labour and suffering, weakness and misery. Again, as in 1 Corinthians 9, he defends himself against the misinterpretation of his refusal to accept support from the Corinthians: it is just this which is proof of his correct understanding of the ministry of an apostle (11:7–12).

It is worthy of note that the question of an appearance of the risen Lord

---

[1] The conviction that ὑπερλίαν ἀπόστολοι cannot refer to the "first apostles" in Jerusalem, or to other men in the background there, but must be thought of in terms of the preachers who had come into the church is very prevalent in present-day research; cf. D. Georgi, op. cit., p. 39; J. Roloff, op. cit., p. 79, n. 129.

[2] Cf. D. Georgi, op. cit., p. 39: "Thus with the ἀπόστολους Χριστοῦ in 2 Cor. 11:13 a self-designation of the opponents is quoted. . . ."

[3] Cf. K. H. Rengstorf in TWNT I, pp. 446 f. [= TDNT I, p. 445.]

is not mentioned, either by the opponents or by the apostle. If those boastful messengers were Palestinians ("Hebrews" – 11:22), it is probable that they would have claimed the experience of an appearance of the risen Lord; of this, however, we hear nothing; it evidently does not belong to their claim. Paul makes one passing reference to the "signs of an apostle" (12:12); this was probably a shibboleth of the opponents, who understood thereby "signs and wonders and mighty works," as can be seen from what follows. Paul, who can also claim for himself such demonstrations of power, recognizes these as signs accompanying the spiritually effective proclamation (1 Cor. 2:4; cf. Rom. 15:19). Prior to that, however, he mentions the successful endurance of all difficulties (ἐν πάσῃ ὑπομονῇ, cf. 6:4),[1] which he evidently values as a greater "sign of an apostle" than wonders and mighty works.[2] This is the reason why he speaks with great hesitancy about the "visions and revelations" (12:1–5) which were granted to him. On the other hand, his opponents, it seems, used such things for their own boasting. Paul, by way of contrast, only wishes to boast about his weakness, by means of which he testifies to the power of Christ (12:9 f.).

Without going into the other possible claims of the opponents which marked their conception of an apostle, we can say that they considered a proclamation of Christ, produced by the Spirit and filled with power, as essential. Paul accepts this underlying conception of an apostle, but interprets the resulting image of an apostle in a very different manner. Christ himself must be proclaimed as crucified, and only in the second place as risen in the life of the one who proclaims (cf. 13:3 f.); or better, Christ wants to show his power of life to those who receive the gospel, primarily through the weakness of the herald.

The concept of an apostle, then, as a (charismatically effective) herald of Christ and itinerant missionary is confirmed through Paul's polemic against those people who caused trouble in Corinth. It is a concept which was in existence in the Hellenistic congregations of the Pauline missionary area.

V

Upon what did the apostles who were active in the Hellenistic mission alongside of Paul base their claim to apostleship? Here one must be careful in drawing upon the references to the "super-apostles" of Corinth, since not all "apostles" would have acted in a similar manner (cf. 1 Cor. 4:9 ff.).

---

[1] The similar passage, 2 Cor. 6:4 with the catalogue of sufferings which follows, shows that Paul does not mean simply "patience", but rather the conscious acceptance and endurance of the labours connected with the missionary task. Cf. H. Windisch, *Der zweite Korintherbrief*[9], Meyer (Göttingen, 1924), on 12:12: "The word is thus used for positive accomplishments and describes the perseverance and intensity of the productive activity. . . ."

[2] Accurately, E. Käsemann, *art. cit.*, p. 63: Paul gave miracles "only secondary importance".

According to 2 Corinthians 3:1-3 one may suppose that the opponents of Paul attempted to have their position certified by means of letters of recommendation; these cannot have been certificates of authorization from authorities in Jerusalem however, but rather recommendations from churches where these people had previously been active. Paul is here not only concerned with letters to the Corinthians, but also with those which had been written by them (3:1). Those messengers, in all probability, had the congregations give them letters attesting their "deeds"; this Paul had not done (cf. 12:11). For this reason, the letters of recommendation are no basis for assuming that these men had the official sanction of the Jerusalem church.[1] What Paul recognizes by his reference to "all the apostles," who are active alongside of him in his missionary area, and what he does not oppose in the "deceitful workmen" in Corinth, is the proclamation of Christ as such, which calls forth faith and establishes churches.

This observation throws light on 1 Corinthians 12:28. In dealing with the charismatic manifestations in Corinth, Paul, after he has stressed the diversity and the unity, the complementarity and the co-operation of the charismatic gifts, finally writes: "And God has appointed in the church first apostles, second prophets, third teachers, then workers of miracles, then healers. . . ." Are the ministries which Paul, for personal-subjective reasons, lists in the definite order of apostles, prophets, and teachers to be understood as charismatic offices which, like the gifts of the Spirit which immediately follow, are available to everyone who is baptized? Do we see here a charismatic constitution of the church, which consists only in gifts of the Spirit belonging to the church universal (i.e. above the congregational level) and localized only in individual churches where the gifts happen to be actually present?

In spite of the widespread acceptance of this hypothesis of Harnack, the reference to prophets and teachers should give one pause: these also had their place at first in local congregations. Certainly, at this point there appears a universal-church-oriented horizon, not with reference to the constitution of the church, but rather to the "principle of the life of the church" (J. Roloff) – that is, the principle that the body of Christ is made up of many members and every individual has his special task and service for the whole (cf. vv. 29 f.). Paul places "apostles, prophets, and teachers" at the head of the list as the holders of the three chronologically and essentially primary functions for the edification of the body of Christ."[2]

Is it possible to obtain still more detail concerning the office of an apostle from this passage? If one observes the special position of the three first mentioned ministries,[3] their arrangement and order of sequence in the

[1] Cf. D. Georgi, op. cit., pp. 241-6.
[2] J. Roloff, op. cit., p. 126.
[3] The special position is underlined by μέν, which is followed by no δέ. However, the activities introduced by ἔπειτα are clearly to be set apart from the triad at the beginning. δέ, which corresponds to μέν, is often dropped; cf. Arndt, p. 504, especially 2.c.

sentence, one may infer the following: (a) The enumeration is a traditional one, which existed before Paul, and therefore also implies a concept of an apostle which he had adopted. Thus it need not necessarily match his personal understanding of the meaning of the office of an apostle.

(b) In attempting to answer the question whether these are ministries which are tied to a specific congregation or extend beyond it, it is necessary to assume a downward progression from the apostles to the prophets and to the teachers. The teachers are by task and function[1] certainly members of a local congregation. The prophets, even though they also were residents in a fixed locality,[2] may have been more active beyond the individual congregation. However, the apostles are, according to the other passages which are similar to the present one (1 Thess. 2:7; 2 Cor. 9:5; 2 Cor. 11–12; Rom 16:7), itinerant missionaries. Thus one can understand that they head the list because of their "universal churchly" importance.

(c) But for this reason also the apostles receive priority; through their preaching churches were established and nourished. Thus there is also an anti-climax: their work is supported by the prophets (cf. also Eph. 2:20), while the teachers safeguard, deepen, and make fruitful the preaching and tradition within the churches.

(d) Whether or not the apostles are here a closed group is hard to say. In the case of the teachers, there is a steady development in the nature of this ministry, which is borne witness to directly by Ephesians 4:11, the Pastorals (where teaching is a task of the officials in whose charge is the instruction of the church), and in James 3:1. In the case of the prophets, one may suppose that there was a period of transition: it is possible that this charisma was given to all members of the church. But actually it appears that a limited and closed circle of prophets had come into being (cf. 1 Cor. 14:29 with Rev. 11:18; 16:6; 18:20, 24; 22:9). Is it also possible that the "apostles" had been at one time an "open" group, but later limited themselves more quickly to a closely knit circle of individuals? In Paul's time we find ourselves in a period of transition. In Ephesians 4:11 the distinction between apostles and "evangelists," who rank behind the prophets, is already drawn. In the area of the Hellenistic mission no clear-cut criteria for recognizing apostles could have existed in this time, although the situation might have been different in Jerusalem. Luke, in Acts 21:8, calls Philip, who was active in missionary work and who no doubt would have been recognized as an "apostle" in the Pauline mission field, only an "evangelist." Still, the designation might be simply Luke's.

(e) Apostleship is viewed as a charismatic ministry; otherwise the apostles could hardly be at the top of the list of charismatic gifts, named

---

[1] Cf. the careful presentation of H. Greeven in ZNTW 44 (1952/53), pp. 16–31. He understands the main task of the teachers to be the "presentation, transmission, and enrichment of the tradition" (p. 28).

[2] Cf. H. Greeven, art. cit., p. 9.

ahead of the prophets and teachers. But the manner in which God appointed the apostles and called them into the service of the body of Christ is not mentioned. The definite call to apostleship remains a problem here as well.

VI

What conclusions may we draw from these observations?

First, it has been confirmed that Paul did not know of a uniform concept of apostleship which had clear-cut criteria. Not once does he argue from such a basis, even though this must have been desirable in his case against those who opposed his apostleship. However, this *argumentum e silentio*, brought forward first by D. Georgi, can be supplemented by positive evidence. It has been observed that, on the one hand, Paul regarded the (last) appearance of the risen Lord in his Christophany on the road to Damascus as support for his claim to apostleship, and, on the other hand, that he places himself alongside of those apostles who, without these credentials, were active as itinerant missionaries and charismatic preachers. This can hardly be explained apart from the conclusion that he himself was confronted by different concepts of an apostle which did not show uniform criteria. He himself, in his claim to apostleship, being attacked from every side, tried to satisfy all the requirements which were placed before an apostle; and, beyond this, he attempted to prove that he was himself a true apostle of Jesus Christ by calling attention to his life of misery and suffering.[1]

A further conclusion which has been drawn is that in certain circles at Jerusalem it was expected, evidently, that an apostle should have experienced an appearance of the risen Lord, while in the Hellenistic mission field this requirement was not only waived but an emphasis was placed on successful missionary activity, which was possibly confirmed by "signs of an apostle," powerful preaching and proof of authority. In Corinth, which was a meeting point of the early Christian mission, the various interpretations came together. To this congregation, founded by Paul, came various messengers of Christ, especially itinerant missionaries who, upon their arrival, wanted to push Paul aside and who offered a different image of an apostle from the one the Corinthians had received from Paul. Also, at least some information had come to this church from the mother church in Jerusalem, and there had come into existence groups who guided themselves by the thoughts of those in Jerusalem and identified themselves with authorities there (cf. the Cephas-party of 1 Cor. 1:12; 3:22). How far those preachers who were active in the churches of Galatia and whose requirement that the Gentile Christians should also be circumcized and

---

[1] On this topic, see E. Güttgemanns, *Der leidende Apostel und sein Herr* (Göttingen, 1966), especially pp. 142–70.

follow the law had been rejected at the "apostolic council" in Jerusalem still depended on groups in Jerusalem and could call on them for support must remain finally undecided. But it is certain that they called Paul's apostleship into question. Paul does not recognize the opponents as "apostles", since they proclaim a gospel different in content from the true gospel and which is no longer the gospel of Jesus Christ (Gal 1:8 f.). As a positive proof of his apostleship Paul calls on his own Christophany, in which God himself revealed his Son to him, as well as the call to preach which was given simultaneously (1:15 f.). Also at this point, Paul safeguards himself in a basic way against the contesting of his apostleship, so that he lacks nothing by way of comparison with those who were "apostles before him." Nevertheless, it is not quite clear which criteria for judging the qualifications of an apostle one used in Jerusalem.

If one considers Paul's choice of words in 1 Thessalonians 2:7, 1 Corinthians 4:9; 12:28 f., and Romans 15:7, it appears that in the mission field he clearly associated himself more readily with the usage which regarded apostles as preachers and missionaries of Christ. To call this a "broader" concept of apostle would be misleading, since Paul himself does not make this distinction. It is only from our perspective that the "narrow" qualification of an apostle in Jerusalem sets itself over against the former usage. The "narrow" usage led to the limitation of the group of the apostles and to the guiding image of the "twelve apostles." Nevertheless, Paul's disputations with other preachers who appeared as doubtful "apostles" indicate that, in his mission field, reflection on the nature of apostleship became essential. As Paul himself pointed to his possession of the qualification of an apostle which had originated in Jerusalem and, at the same time, to his appointed mission through the Lord (on the Damascus road), he became, at least as far as his mission field is concerned, the model of an apostle. This is clearly shown by the Deuteropaulines (cf. Eph. 3:1, 7 f.) and the Pastorals. In this case he may have influenced the later development.[1]

It makes no sense to play the "charismatic" and "institutional" concepts of an apostle one against the other. Rather, the concept of an apostle, at the beginning, was not carefully defined. During this period Paul had to be active as an apostle and needed to succeed against those who contested

[1] The "ideal" image of the apostle which the pseudonymous epistles of Paul present should enable one to observe which features and functions of the prototype of an apostle are emphasized at any given time. In Eph. 3:1 ff. they are the (prophetic-apocalyptic) revelation of the mystery of Christ and the corresponding proclamation of the kingdom of Christ; in the Pastorals, Paul becomes the "herald and apostle" (1 Tim. 2:7; 2 Tim. 1:11), the guarantor of the tradition, of the correct teaching and the authority of the ecclesiastical official. The consciousness of the Pauline apostolic authority is at least reflected in these late writings. "They authorize the preaching and order of the church of the post-apostolic time by referring to the authority of the apostle," and they "turn the attention of the church for whom they have been written on Paul, and indeed exclusively on him" (N. Brox, *Die Pastoralbriefe* [Regensburg, 1969], p. 68). Cf. further J. Roloff, *op. cit.*, pp. 239–50; N. Brox, *op. cit.*, pp. 68–74.

his apostleship. He faced all the requirements, the ones which came from the "apostles before him" in Jerusalem, as well as those which were presented by "apostles during his time," and in this he clarified his own understanding of his ministry as an apostle. In a unique way he connects the consciousness of apostolic authority (cf. 1 Thess. 2:7; 2 Cor. 10:8; 13:10) and the charismatic preaching in which Christ makes himself known. By making this identification Paul made a major contribution to the clarification of the position of an apostle within the early church. Because he wished to become "all things to all men" (1 Cor. 9:22) and only desired to be a servant of Christ (2 Cor. 4:5) and "not to run in vain" (Gal. 2:2), he also helped to bridge the unexplained and diverging interpretations in the early church – as a true apostle of Jesus Christ and a promoter of unity and ecumenical co-operation.

CHAPTER XXI

THE ORIGIN OF PAULINE CHRISTOLOGY

MARGARET E. THRALL

IN THE ACQUISITION OF HIS CHRISTOLOGICAL BELIEFS PAUL WAS PERHAPS indebted to some extent to the circles of early Christians with whom he first made contact. Moreover, the Jewish habits of thought in which he had been reared assisted him to formulate and develop them. Nevertheless, it is very likely that the experience which converted him to Christianity had a profound initial effect on the formation of his thought about Christ. His own words suggest that this was so, since in Galatians 1 : 15–16 he speaks of the revelation of God's Son. His account of the event is very brief, but if the three longer accounts in Acts are taken into consideration as well, we have sufficient material to attempt to discover whether his basic beliefs about Christ can be derived from this experience. This is obviously not a new idea. Several Pauline scholars have previously made use of what information we possess about his conversion to elucidate some aspects of his Christology.[1] The previous treatment of the subject is in some respects unsatisfactory, however, and there are also some elements in Paul's experience which may possess a Christological significance which has not so far been recognized.

I

Before we begin to discuss the main themes of this essay there is one preliminary matter to be dealt with. To what extent is it legitimate to make use of the accounts of Paul's conversion in Acts? There are, after all, notorious discrepancies between the Acts record of the apostle's career and his own references to his past activities. Ought we to discount what Luke has to say about Paul's experience on the way to Damascus?

To do so, I suggest, would be to indulge in unnecessary scepticism. It is not at this point but at a later stage in Acts that the difficulties of correlation become really acute. Furthermore, it is possible to make out a positive case for the reliability of Acts in the matter of Paul's conversion, as Johannes Munck has shown.[2] He notes the following similarities between

---

[1] The work of the following scholars will be considered in this essay: O. Michel, "Die Entstehung der paulinischen Christologie", *ZNTW* 28 (1929), pp. 324–333; L. Cerfaux, *Le Christ dans la Théologie de saint Paul* (Paris, 1951), pp. 11–12; A. Feuillet, *Le Christ Sagesse de Dieu* (Paris, 1966), pp. 17–20, 35–36, 84, 160–61.

[2] Johannes Munck, *Paul and the Salvation of Mankind* (London, 1959), pp. 13–35.

Acts on the one hand and the references in Galatians and the First Epistle to the Corinthians on the other: the description of Paul as a persecutor of the Christians right up to the moment of his sudden conversion;[1] the strong element of compulsion he experienced;[2] the allusion to Old Testament texts from the Servant passages in Deutero-Isaiah and the call of Jeremiah;[3] lastly, the reticence about the manner in which Jesus appeared to Paul, coupled with the assertion that Paul did see him.[4] Munck concludes: "It is the apostle himself who shaped the story of his conversion and call as the churches were to hear it."[5]

If this defence of Acts is valid, then it would be permissible to use the accounts of the Damascus experience, provided that they are not contradicted by Paul himself and that they may be directly or indirectly substantiated by his own references.

II

Our main discussion divides into two parts. First, we shall consider some of the aspects of the Damascus experience which have previously received attention: the revelation of the risen Jesus as the Son of God and his appearance as a glorious heavenly being. Secondly, we shall discuss an element in the experience which does not immediately appear to possess Christological significance: its similarity to the calling of the Old Testament prophets.[6] It is possible that here we may have a clue to the origin of Paul's belief in the pre-existent Christ as the agent of creation.

Among comparatively recent writers on Paul, Cerfaux and Feuillet both agree that Paul's conviction that Christ was the Son of God derived from the moment of his conversion. He had seen Christ in divine glory, Cerfaux maintains, and the intuition came to him that this was God's Son, who was not a creature but belonged to a completely different order of reality, the divine order. The actual title Son of God was in all probability the content of the divine revelation.[7] Similarly, Feuillet claims that the Damascus experience convinced Paul "que le Christ est le Fils de Dieu au sens strict".[8] Both these scholars also equate the titles Son of God and Son of Man. Jesus revealed himself to Paul, Feuillet maintains, as the transcendent Son of Man, "un être céleste et glorieux qui s'est déjà manifesté de semblable manière à Étienne martyr".[9] This brings us to the more extensive treatment of the subject by Michel.[10] He claims that Paul's pre-Christian

---

[1] *Ibid.*, p. 13. See Gal. 1:13; Acts 9:1–2; 22:4–5; 26:9–11.
[2] *Ibid.*, pp. 20–24. See 1 Cor. 9:16; Acts 26:14.
[3] *Ibid.*, pp. 24–29. See Gal. 1:15 (cf. Isa. 49: 1–6; Jer. 1:4–5); Acts 26:12–18 (cf. Isa. 42: 6–7; Jer. 1:8).
[4] *Ibid.*, pp. 34–35. See 1 Cor. 9:1; 15:8; Acts 22:14; 26:16.
[5] *Ibid.*, p. 29.   [6] *Ibid.*, pp. 24–29.
[7] L. Cerfaux, *op. cit.*, p. 11.   [8] A. Feuillet, *op. cit.*, p. 19.
[9] *Ibid.*, p. 19; cf. Cerfaux *op. cit.*, pp. 330–31.
[10] O. Michel, *art. cit.*

U

concept of the Messiah was that of the transcendent Son of Man who was also the image of God, the reflection of God's being. It was this figure whom he believed to have appeared to him on the way to Damascus. The brilliant light in which he was revealed was that of God's own glory. Michel thus argues that Paul's vision actualized for him his previous concept of the heavenly Son of Man. He admits that the actual term Son of Man does not occur in Paul's letters. Nevertheless, he does refer to Christ as "the Man", which may be his own version of Son of Man. Moreover, in 1 Corinthians 15:27 he applies to Christ as the messianic King the words of Psalm 8:6, which in their context refer to "man" and "the son of man".

These discussions of the origins of Paul's beliefs about Christ might seem to provide us with a sufficient treatment of the significance of his conversion experience. In one way or another, the revelation of the divine Son, affirmed by Paul himself, is combined with one of the basic elements of the accounts in Acts, the bright light in which Jesus was revealed, and quite substantial conclusions are drawn from this evidence. Nevertheless, the views we have just described are less satisfactory than they might appear at first sight. Several questions arise for consideration. Did Paul really make use of a Son of Man Christology, as Cerfaux, Feuillet and Michel explicitly claim or implicitly assume? What conclusions should we arrive at if we were to take the themes of divine sonship and of divine glory separately and to develop each theme by itself instead of immediately combining them? And is there any important aspect of Paul's thought about Christ which remains to be explained once this has been done?

It is frequently claimed that Paul did think of Christ as the Son of Man.[1] But the arguments used to support the claim are not wholly convincing.[2] It is possible that his failure to use the actual term is due to its linguistic barbarity in Greek (although one wonders whether, as a title, he would not have found it acceptable enough linguistically[3]). But it has yet to be proved that he employs an obvious substitute. The term ὁ ἄνθρωπος might serve as such, but Paul does not use it. Michel is wrong here, and the verses he quotes fail to prove his point. In Romans 5:15 the phrase we have is: τοῦ ἑνὸς ἀνθρώπου Ἰησοῦ Χριστοῦ. Here ὁ ἄνθρωπος is qualified by the addition of εἷς, which bears the emphasis,[4] and the very phrase

---

[1] Reginald H. Fuller, *The Foundations of New Testament Christology* (London, 1965), p. 233, mentions the following scholars who have held this view: J. Weiss, W. Bousset, A. E. J. Rawlinson, J. Jeremias, O. Cullmann. (Fuller does not himself share it). Frederick W. Borsch, *The Son of Man in Myth and History* (London, 1967), p. 243, mentions William Manson and A. M. Hunter. (Borsch also thinks the theory a likely one.) We may add Alan Richardson, *An Introduction to the Theology of the New Testament* (London, 1958), pp. 138–39.

[2] For a recent refutation, see Anton Vögtle, "'Der Menschensohn' und die paulinische Christologie", *Studiorum Paulinorum Congressus Internationalis Catholicus 1961*, 1 (Rome, 1963), pp. 199–218.

[3] Vögtle, *art. cit.*, p. 205, points out that in Paul's generation it is hardly likely to have been misunderstood: it occurs in all the gospels, and even Luke uses it with no more hesitation than the other evangelists.

[4] Cf. Vögtle, *art. cit.*, pp. 208–09.

τοῦ ἑνὸς ἀνθρώπου is used in verse 19 of Adam, which shows that it is not as such a title of Christ. The other text quoted by Michel is 1 Corinthians 15:21: δι' ἀνθρώπου ἀνάστασις νεκρῶν. Here we do not even have the definite article to suggest that ἄνθρωπος might be a title. There is nothing to show that Paul meant anything more than "man".[1]

What, then, of the second argument employed by Michel and others? Does the application to Christ of Psalm 8:6 show that he is regarded as the Son of Man? R. H. Fuller would deny this, on the grounds that Paul only has in mind the actual words he quotes, and not the psalm as a whole.[2] But if he is thinking of the whole context, which does not seem improbable, then it is very likely that he saw the psalm as describing the glory of Adam before the Fall and so as a prediction of the glory of Christ, the last Adam. In other words, the psalm as a whole fits in very well with his Adamic Christology, which is well attested in the rest of 1 Corinthians 15, and we do not need to abstract the phrase "son of man" from verse 4 and regard it as evidence that Paul thought of Christ as the heavenly Son of Man.

At this point, of course, it will be claimed that Adam and the Son of Man are in reality one: the Adam myth is part of the Son of Man myth.[3] This is not so certain, however. It has been recently denied by Robin Scroggs, who argues against the view that Paul's Christology of the last Adam is really a Son of Man Christology.[4] The whole argument of his book shows that Jewish thought about Adam provides a sufficient framework for this aspect of Paul's thought, without bringing in the concept of the Son of Man.

If, then, there is really no evidence that Paul thought of Christ as the Son of Man, Michel's account of the significance of his conversion proves invalid, at least in this respect. And if there is no reason, as far as Paul is concerned, for equating the title Son of God with that of Son of Man (as Cerfaux and Feuillet do), it may be useful to look again at what he would understand by divine sonship at the time of his conversion. Similarly, if the radiant glory of his vision did not reveal Jesus to him as the heavenly Son of Man, then we need to ask what its significance was. In Feuillet's

---

[1] See D. E. H. Whiteley, *The Theology of St Paul* (Oxford, 1964), p. 117. Borsch, *op. cit.*, p. 241, thinks that while Paul avoided the title ὁ υἱὸς τοῦ ἀνθρώπου as linguistically unacceptable, he also avoided the mere ὁ ἄνθρωπος because this would lose some of the nuances suggested by Son of Man: "nuances of heirship, suggestions of the idea of relationship and being a counterpart". To convey the idea of Christ as Son of Man, and to pick up these nuances, he spoke of him as the *second* Man and the *last* Adam. It is much more likely, however, that if Paul wished to convey the notion of heirship in relation to Christ he would do so in terms of the title Son of God (see Rom. 8:14-17; Gal. 4:4-7). And the relationship he sees to exist between Christ and Adam is hardly that of the Son of Man to the Man in the mythical material which Borsch is dealing with.

[2] R. H. Fuller, *op. cit.*, p. 233.

[3] See Oscar Cullmann, *The Christology of the New Testament* (London, 1963), pp. 137-52, 166-81.

[4] Robin Scroggs, *The Last Adam* (Oxford, 1966), pp. xv-xvii, 102.

discussion, it seems to be the Son of Man concept which holds together the revelation of sonship and the revelation of glory. But if Paul did not see Christ as the Son of Man, then perhaps these two aspects of his experience may suggest two different lines of Christological development which should be considered separately.

We begin with the theme of sonship. Paul himself claims that God revealed to him his Son (Gal. 1:16). The same thing is implied in Acts 9:20, where we are told that immediately after his conversion Paul preached in the synagogues that Jesus was the Son of God.

But how would Paul have understood this? Would it immediately have suggested to him sonship in a strict or unique sense, as Cerfaux and Feuillet claim? It is very likely that, as a title for Christ, Son of God was pre-Pauline. Fuller maintains that it was derived from Jewish Davidic Messianology. It was current in the Palestinian church, where it referred to the status of Christ at the Parousia. In the Hellenistic Jewish Christian mission, the emphasis was shifted from the Parousia to belief in the present lordship of Jesus, and the term Son of God, along with other titles, was transferred to the exalted Christ.[1] In any case, it indicates the messianic status of Jesus, whether now or at the Parousia. Furthermore, it is likely that Paul, before his conversion, was aware not only of the messianic claims made for Jesus by the first Christians but also of this way of expressing them. There is a hint of this in Galatians 1:23, where the Christians of Judea are said to have heard: ʿO διώκων ἡμᾶς ποτε νῦν εὐαγγελίζεται τὴν πίστιν ἥν ποτε ἐπόρθει. A few verses previously he has suggested that the divine sonship of Jesus is the content of his preaching (Gal. 1:16). Thus, faith in Jesus as God's Son is the belief which once he had attempted to destroy.

If the title was pre-Pauline, and if Paul before his conversion was aware of its use in Christian circles, the revelation on the road to Damascus may simply have convinced him that the title was, after all, correctly applied. The crucified Jesus of Nazareth was the messianic Son of God. Certainly at this point we have gone somewhat beyond the notion of a human Davidic prince, since Jesus is in heaven, but it is not clear that we have arrived at the position described by Cerfaux, i.e. the belief that as God's Son Christ was not a creature but belonged to a completely different order of reality.[2] The Christ who is now in heaven is still the Jesus who was once on earth. Did he not have a creaturely origin, whatever his present exalted state? Admittedly Paul did come to believe in the sonship of Christ in a unique sense. But it is doubtful whether this conviction derived immediately from his Damascus experience.

The other theme that demands our attention at this point is that of glory. That Christ appeared to Paul as clothed in heavenly glory may be

---

[1] R. H. Fuller, op. cit., p. 187.
[2] L. Cerfaux, op. cit., p. 11.

deduced from the accounts in Acts, which speak of the brilliant light which
accompanied the vision:

Acts 9:3 αὐτὸν περιήστραψεν φῶς ἐκ τοῦ οὐρανοῦ
22:6 ἐκ τοῦ οὐρανοῦ περιαστράψαι φῶς ἱκανὸν περὶ ἐμέ
22:11 οὐκ ἐνέβλεπον ἀπὸ τῆς δόξης τοῦ φωτὸς ἐκείνου
26:13 εἶδον... οὐρανόθεν ὑπὲρ τὴν λαμπρότητα τοῦ ἡλίου περιλάμ-
ψαν με φῶς

It is generally agreed that this factor in Paul's experience is indirectly corroborated by his own remarks in 1 Corinthians 15. Christ appeared to him
as raised from the dead (1 Cor. 15:8). and this form of existence is characterized by glory (1 Cor. 15:43).

What was the Christological significance of this aspect of the vision?
Glory in origin belongs to God, according to biblical thought, and so one
might perhaps suppose that it indicated the divinity of Christ in the strictest
sense. This seems to be the conclusion drawn by E. W. Hunt in his recent
book on Paul. He claims: "As Paul depicts him, Jesus shared God's nature
completely." And one of the reasons given for this statement is that Paul
thinks of Christ as displaying the divine δόξα.[1]

But is this the conclusion that Paul himself would most readily have
drawn from what he believed himself to have seen? As we have already
remarked, he was convinced that the glorious being of his vision was *Jesus
raised from the dead*. This led him to see Christ as the model of eschatological humanity (1 Cor. 15:45-49), and here the theme of glory fits in very
well, if Paul's Jewish background is taken into account. In both the apocalyptic and the rabbinic traditions the hope for the restoration of human
nature in the eschaton is sometimes expressed through a description of the
exalted nature of Adam before the Fall. One aspect of the nature of Adam
was his endowment with divine glory, and the restoration of this glory
is promised at the end.[2] Paul, we may suppose, saw the risen Christ as the
fulfilment of this promise. The theme of glory, therefore, seems to offer an
explanation of his Adamic Christology, his belief in Christ as the pattern
and anticipation of eschatological humanity, rather than to show us how
he came to believe in Christ's divinity.

We have argued that the revelation of Jesus as God's Son led Paul to
believe in his messianic status, and that the revelation of his glory led to
the development of his Adamic Christology. In neither case is Christ
seen as divine in the strict sense, as a being who is other than a creature,
and so as the unique Son of God. The one who is revealed as exercising
messianic rule from heaven is precisely the Jesus who was once on earth.
The bearer of divine glory is the pattern of man's existence in the eschaton.
Similarly, we have no explanation as yet of Paul's belief in the pre-existent

---

[1] E. W. Hunt, *Portrait of Paul* (London, 1968), p. 188.
[2] See R. Scroggs, *op. cit.*, pp. 23-29, 46-58.

Christ as agent of creation. Messianic sonship and eschatological glory belong to the present and to the future. There is therefore an important area of Paul's Christological thought which our analysis of his Damascus experience has so far failed to elucidate.

III

The second half of this discussion will be chiefly concerned with the origin of Paul's conviction that Christ is the mediator of creation. We shall also consider how he came to regard Christ as the unique Son of God. Finally we shall discuss the question of the integration in Paul's mind of the various Christological themes which we have examined separately.

The origin of Paul's belief in Christ as the Lord through whom the entire universe came into existence (1 Cor. 8:6) has frequently been debated. Since our particular concern is with his Damascus experience, we shall mention only those theories which can be related in some way to his conversion.

A number of scholars have maintained that the belief arose through the identification of Christ with the figure of Wisdom.[1] Of these, both W. D. Davies and Feuillet offer suggestions which would provide some connexion with the Damascus experience.

According to W. D. Davies, the identification comes about because for Paul Jesus is the new Torah: "In a real sense conformity to Christ, His teaching and His life, has taken the place for Paul of conformity to the Jewish Torah. Jesus Himself – in word and deed or fact is a New Torah".[2] We should therefore expect that attributes ascribed to the Torah in rabbinic Judaism would be transferred by Paul to Christ. Now in Ecclesiasticus the figure of Wisdom is identified with the Torah (Sir. 24): here the Torah is regarded as the expression of the divine Wisdom. Davies claims that in Palestinian Judaism in Paul's day this identification had become commonplace. In this way the Torah was personified and brought into connexion with creation. Since for Paul Jesus was the new Torah, the way was open for him to identify Christ with Wisdom and so to ascribe to him pre-existence and creative activity.[3]

Now if this theory is correct, we should have an indirect link with Paul's conversion. It was this event which initially convinced him that the Law was superseded by Christ, and so might also have caused him to see Jesus as the new Torah.

The idea that he did see Christ in this way has, however, come in for

---

[1] See W. D. Davies, *Paul and Rabbinic Judaism* (London, 1962), pp. 147–76; A. Feuillet, *op. cit.,* p. 78; O. Michel, *art. cit.*; Eduard Schweizer, "Zur Herkunft der Präexistenz-vorstellung bei Paulus", *EvTh* 19 (1959), pp. 65–70, quoted by Ferdinand Hahn, *Christologische Hoheitstitel* (Göttingen, 1963), p. 315.

[2] W. D. Davies, *op. cit.,* p. 148.

[3] *Ibid.,* pp. 149–50, 168–76.

some criticism from Feuillet. The rabbinic examples cited to prove the identification of the Law and Wisdom are late, and cannot be used to show that these notions about the Torah were current in the New Testament period. Moreover, the assimilation of Wisdom and the Torah in Ecclesiasticus is only partial. The Law is simply one of the means through which Wisdom finds expression. To Wisdom alone belong pre-existence and participation in creation. And is Christ a new Law? Is he not rather the antithesis of the Law? According to Feuillet, therefore, it is doubtful whether Paul sees Christ as the new Torah. But even if he does, this would by no means lead to the identification of Christ with Wisdom, and his endowment with Wisdom's attributes.[1]

There seems to be some force in these criticisms. Feuillet himself offers a different explanation of Paul's identification of Christ and Wisdom, and does directly relate it to his vision on the way to Damascus. In the moment of his conversion he realized that Christ was Son of God in the strictest sense. He was therefore immediately able to identify him with the divine Wisdom who was said to have been *brought forth* by Yahweh before the mountains and the hills were formed (Prov. 8. 24–25).[2]

How convincing is this? There are two possible objections to Feuillet's theory. First, we have seen that the revelation of Jesus as Son of God was originally of messianic significance, and that the emphasis lay on his present exaltation and future dignity. This would not immediately suggest identification with a pre-existent figure related to creation in the past. Secondly, more simply, the figure of Wisdom is feminine. It is therefore doubtful whether the apprehension of Christ's divine sonship would lead to the adoption of Wisdom as a congruous and explanatory image.

So far we do not appear to have a satisfactory explanation of the identification of Christ with Wisdom. We have been working on the assumption that the identification was made first, and that as a consequence Paul came to ascribe cosmic functions to Christ. But it is very possible that the reverse process took place. It could have happened that the apostle first came to believe in Christ as the mediator of creation and then consequently adopted Wisdom terminology as a means of expressing this belief.

This brings us to the work of Oscar Cullmann. In the course of his discussion of the title κύριος he suggests a different explanation of the origin of belief in Christ's pre-existence as the agent of creation. He thinks that the early Christians were led to associate Christ with creation as a result of their belief in his present lordship. He maintains that "a backward glance from faith in the present Lord of all creation leads inevitably to the assumption that he was destined for this lordship from the very beginning, and that therefore from the very beginning he was closely related to

[1] A. Feuillet, *op. cit.*, pp. 192–93.
[2] *Ibid.*, p. 84.

creation".[1] He also thinks that this process was assisted by the application to Christ of passages in the Old Testament which speak of God as κύριος and refer to his creative functions. He calls attention to the quotation of Psalm 102: 25 in Hebrews 1:10.[2]

If Cullmann's theory may be validly applied to Paul, we should have a close connexion with his conversion. According to the narratives in Acts, κύριος was the title appropriate to the glorious being of his vision (Acts 9:5; 22:8; 26:15). And Paul himself uses the title when he alludes to it (1 Cor. 9:1). If the apprehension of Christ as Lord inevitably carried with it a backward reference to creation, then we may directly derive Paul's belief in Christ as the agent of creation from his experience on the way to Damascus.

This explanation seems to come nearer the truth of the matter than the other theories we have considered. In support of it we may also point out that in Paul as well as in Hebrews we have some instances of the application to Christ, as Lord, of verses in the Old Testament which have in mind God as creator. In 1 Corinthians 10:26 we have a quotation from Psalm 24:1 (LXX Ps. 23:1): $τοῦ$ $κυρίου$ $[γὰρ]$ $ἡ$ $γῆ$ $καὶ$ $τὸ$ $πλήρωμα$ $αὐτῆς$. The term κύριος here in all probability refers to Christ, since it certainly does so in the preceding verses 21–22. And in the psalm the following verse clearly alludes to God's creative activity: $Αὐτὸς$ $ἐπὶ$ $θαλασσῶν$ $ἐθεμελίωσεν$ $αὐτήν$. Similarly, in 1 Corinthians 2:16 we have a quotation of Isaiah 40:13: $τίς$ $γὰρ$ $ἔγνω$ $νοῦν$ $κυρίου$. The conclusion of the verse suggests the equivalence of Christ with the κύριος of the quotation. And again, the verse in Deutero–Isaiah is associated with the idea of God as creator, if it is seen in the context of the chapter as a whole (see vv. 22 and 28).

Nevertheless, it is not certain that we have here a sufficient explanation of the origin of the Pauline doctrine we are considering. As we shall see, it is in all probability connected with the idea of Christ as Lord rather than with the identification of him with Wisdom, and to that extent Cullmann sets us on the right lines. But his theory as it stands is not entirely convincing. The primary reference of the title κύριος is to the present exaltation of Christ. It is no doubt capable of extension backwards in time, but does it necessarily demand it? And did the application of Old Testament texts to Christ help to produce fundamental Christological concepts, or only to substantiate them? In what follows, it will be suggested that one aspect of Paul's conversion experience contained a more necessary and intrinsic backward reference than is contained in the apprehension of Christ as κύριος taken by itself. It was this aspect of the event which provided the impetus for the development of his belief in Christ as the pre-existent agent of creation.

[1] O. Cullmann, op. cit., p. 218.
[2] Ibid., p. 234.

IV

This intrinsic backward reference is derived from the fact that Paul's experience is seen to be analogous to that of the prophets of the Old Testament. The similarities are examined at some length by Johannes Munck.[1] He notes the parallelism between the train of thought in Galatians 1:15–16 and that of Jeremiah 1:4–5, both of which passages speak of God's choice of his human instrument prior to birth. It is also characteristic of the apostle and the prophets that their call was something for which they were entirely unprepared. Furthermore, there was, as we have seen,[2] a strong element of compulsion in Paul's experience, and to this we have parallels in Amos and Jeremiah:

> The lion has roared;
>   who will not fear?
> The Lord God has spoken;
>   who can but prophesy?
> (Amos 3:8)

> If I say, "I will not mention him,
>   or speak any more in his name",
> there is in my heart as it were a
>   burning fire
> shut up in my bones,
> and I am weary with holding it in,
>   and I cannot.
> (Jer. 20:9)

Now in the case of the prophets, it is of course God who calls them and compels them to prophesy. Similarly, in Galatians 1:15–16 it is God who has called Paul, separated him, revealed to him his Son, and entrusted him with the mission to the Gentiles. The backward reference of Paul's conversion appears to point us to the work of God, and not to the function of Christ, which is our main concern. In the accounts in Acts, however, it is Christ who speaks and reveals himself, and all three accounts designate Christ as the author of the commission to preach to the Gentiles (see especially Acts 26:17). What are we to make of this? Does Acts here plainly contradict Paul? Are the narratives in Acts in this respect unreliable? By no means. They complement, rather than contradict, Paul, and fit in very well with his general Christological position. It is characteristic of his theology to assign identical functions or attributes to God and to Christ. In Romans 8:9 the Spirit is at the same time the Spirit of God and the

---

[1] J. Munck, *op. cit.,* pp. 24–30.
[2] See above, p. 305.

Spirit of Christ; and whereas in Romans 14;10[1] it is God's tribunal before which Christians are to appear, in 2 Corinthians 5:10 the tribunal belongs to Christ. Let us therefore suppose that the account of Paul's experience in Acts is correct, and that in his vision it did seem to him that he was being addressed by Christ. It would be entirely congruous with his general position that he should speak of the whole experience as due to the initiative of God.[2]

If, then, it appeared to be Christ who spoke to Paul and commissioned him, and if at the same time this call and the overwhelming compulsion which it exerted seemed to be the call and the compulsion experienced by the prophets, then we do have here an intrinsic backward reference to some prior function exercised by Christ within the old dispensation. If to Paul the form of his vocation corresponded with that of the prophets, then, conversely, their calling must have followed the same pattern as his. If it was Christ who spoke to him and summoned him to the apostolic mission, then was it not also Christ who had addressed and summoned the prophets? In other words, was not the heavenly being revealed to him as κύριος on the way to Damascus perhaps to be identified in some sense with the Lord who was the author of the prophetic revelation?

A. T. Hanson has suggested that when Paul saw some situation in the Old Testament as parallel to an event in the life of Jesus or of the church, he believed that the pre-existent Christ was at work there, and so identified the κύριος of the Septuagint with Jesus.[3] If this is so, then the first few verses describing the call of Jeremiah may have acquired for him this sort of significance: καὶ ἐγένετο λόγος κυρίου πρὸς αὐτόν, πρὸ τοῦ με πλάσαι σε ἐν κοιλίᾳ ἐπίσταμαί σε καὶ πρὸ τοῦ σε ἐξελθεῖν ἐκ μήτρας ἡγίακά σε, προφήτην εἰς ἔθνη τέθεικά σε (Jer. 1:4–5).

We have already remarked on the general parallelism between these verses and Galatians 1:15–16:[4] this situation in the Old Testament is reproduced in the call of the apostle to the Gentiles. In this instance, then, the Lord whose word came to Jeremiah may be identified with Christ.

It is therefore possible to argue that Paul's Damascus experience led to his identifying Christ, on some occasions at least, as the Lord who spoke to the prophets. If so, we have a clear connexion with the belief in Christ as mediator of creation. For according to the Old Testament, the word of the Lord which came to the prophets is also the divine word which called creation into existence: τῷ λόγῳ τοῦ κυρίου οἱ οὐρανοὶ ἐστερεώθησαν (Ps. 33:6; LXX Ps. 32:6). If the Lord who speaks in the

---

[1] There is a textual variant here: Χριστοῦ for Θεοῦ. But Θεοῦ has the better MSS. attestation, and Χριστοῦ is fairly obviously an assimilation to 2 Cor. 5:10.

[2] If Phil. 3:12 is a reference to his conversion, we have here the complementary reference to the action of Christ. See G. J. Inglis, "St. Paul's Conversion in His Epistles", *Theology* 34 (1937), pp. 214–28. [See J. Dupont's essay in the present volume, pp. 179 ff. Edd.]

[3] A. T. Hanson, *Jesus Christ in the Old Testament* (London, 1965), p. 162.

[4] See above, p. 313.

prophetic literature can sometimes be identified with Christ, then Christ can also be identified with the Lord by whose word the heavens were established: εἷς κύριος Ἰησοῦς Χριστός, δὶ οὗ τὰ πάντα (1 Cor. 8:6). And so, for Paul, the Christ through whom God spoke on the way to Damascus may have come to be identified with the one through whom God had spoken when he created the universe.

There is no direct confirmation of this process of thought which we have attributed to Paul. It does, however, provide an explanation of his adoption of Wisdom terminology as a means of expressing his belief in the pre-existence of Christ. For Wisdom is not only God's assistant in creation but also the medium of prophetic inspiration:

> in every generation she passes into holy souls and makes them friends of God and prophets.
>
> (Wis. 7:27)

If Paul's belief in Christ's pre-existence originated in a conviction that he was in some way connected with the prophets, the Wisdom concept may have commended itself as applicable in this respect, in addition to its suitability for expressing his consequent conviction that Christ was the agent of creation.

V

We have seen that several major elements in Paul's Christology may be derived ultimately from his conversion experience: belief in Christ as last Adam, as messianic Son of God, and as the pre-existent Lord through whom the universe came into being. But we have not yet precisely accounted for his belief in the unique divine sonship of Christ as this is implied, for example, in Romans 8:32. It is possible that belief in this further dimension of sonship may have evolved in Paul's mind through the assimilation of the υἱός concept to that of the divine κύριος. It is as the Son that Christ is represented as exercising his messianic rule in 1 Corinthians 15. 25–28. But the title κύριος would be equally appropriate as an expression of the exercise of dominion by Christ, and is so used in Philippians 2:9–11. As we have seen, κύριος is also used to describe Christ as the pre-existent agent of creation, the one who participates in the activity of God himself. The title υἱός may come to share this significance, and so may become a description of Christ as divine in the strict sense. In turn, it may then help to explain the pre-existent relationship between God and Christ.

A final question we might ask is whether Paul had coherently integrated in his own mind his belief in the divinity of Christ and his conception of him as the pattern of eschatological humanity. That this process of integration had in fact taken place is perhaps suggested by two adjacent texts in the Epistle to the Romans. In Romans 8:32 we have a reference to the unique divine sonship of Christ: ὅς γε τοῦ ἰδίου υἱοῦ οὐκ ἐφείσατο. In Romans 8:29, however, Paul speaks of Christ as the model for the future existence of believers: οὓς προέγνω, καὶ προώρισεν συμμόρφους τῆς εἰκόνος τοῦ υἱοῦ αὐτοῦ. It is as the Son of God that Christ provides the pattern of eschatological humanity. Thus, his divinity and his humanity are integrated in the concept of sonship.

What does this mean? So far we have spoken of the sonship of Christ in terms of his supremacy over creation. But the reverse side of the coin is his obedience to God, mentioned in 1 Corinthians 15:27-28 as the continuous background and ultimate outcome of his messianic rule. It is a truism to say that in Jewish thought the ideas of sonship and obedience were very closely linked. We might equally well say, then, that for Paul it is the idea of obedience which unites belief in the divine and in the human aspects of Christ's nature. He believes Christ to be wholly obedient to God, and therefore both to participate in a unique relationship to God as his Son and also to become the model of eschatological humanity. That he does believe Christ to be supremely obedient is evidenced in Romans 5:19 and Philippians 2:8. That this quality makes possible his exercise of divine functions is not expressly stated, but it seems very likely that the element of subordinationism in Paul's Christology provides him with a means of asserting Christ's divinity without appearing to deny his faith in the one God. And it is clear that Christ is seen as the last Adam because he reverses the disobedience of the first Adam.

It follows that Paul did not suppose that when Christ became man he took on some wholly different role, as though he were an actor playing several parts. He played himself, though on a different stage. Paul does not explicitly define the nature of man. But several related passages in the Epistle to the Romans imply that the essence of genuine human existence, the form of being for which man was created, is not so much some eschatological state of glory considered in and by itself as the enjoyment of eternal life in relationship with God and in obedience to God (Rom. 5:19, 21; 6:1-11). The essence of personality is not the σῶμα by itself – whether genetically or eschatologically determined – but the human self existing with God and living for God as God's obedient son. If this is a fair representation of the implications of Paul's thought, for him Christ as man is fundamentally Christ as himself. Paul could not be accused of holding a crudely supernatural view of incarnation. Christ is not God dressed up as man. In some sense he is God, but he does not need to dress up and to assume an alien role. He is the revelation within time and space of God's eternal humanity.

PART III

CHAPTER XXII

THE CHI-RHO SIGN – CHRISTOGRAM AND/OR STAUROGRAM?

MATTHEW BLACK

NEXT TO THE UBIQUITOUS IHS, THE *CHI-RHO* SIGN HAS ESTABLISHED itself in Christian tradition as perhaps the most popular of all Christian monograms. Its widespread use in the Church Catholic is usually attributed to its employment by the Emperor Constantine in the banner or *Labarum* – a word of still unexplained origin – which the first Christian Emperor commissioned for himself and his armies after his conquest of Rome and adoption of Christianity as the official ¬eligion of the Empire.

The monogram is found in Christian art and tradition in two variant forms. The more familiar form is ☧, with the Chi superimposed on the Rho, the traditional explanation of the sign as a monogram for *ΧΡιστός* being obvious at a glance. The alternative form is that of a plain cross, the perpendicular stroke forming a *Rho*, thus ⳨, the *Chi* letter apparently having been turned round to form out of what we now call a St. Andrew's cross, a traditional upright cross.

It is now certain that both forms of the "sign" are pre-Constantinian. Constantine may have popularized the monogram, in particular in the *Chi-Rho* formation; but he did not invent the sign; the discovery of both forms in pre-Constantinian graffiti in the Vatican[1] and of the perpendicular form in the Bodmer papyri (*ca.* A.D. 250) provide incontrovertible proof of their use long before the age of Constantine. Moreover, in the papyri, the perpendicular form is found as a contraction for *Tau Rho* in the Greek word σταυρός 'Cross', written, ⳨ρος[2] and this latter discovery raises a number of new problems in connexion with the traditional sign.

Was it originally a sign for the Cross and not a *Chi-Rho* contraction for *Χριστός*, i.e., a *staurogram* rather than a *christogram*? Which of the two forms was the earlier? Was the staurogram sign original and later turned into a christogram, the *Chi-Rho* – *Χριστός* monogram being the result of an aetiological explanation of the sign after its original meaning as a staurogram had been forgotten? Or are there other explanations? What is known about the origins and history of these "signs"?

[1] Margherita Guarducci, *The Tomb of St. Peter* (London, 1960), p. 111.
[2] See below. p. 327.

The purpose of this essay is to look for some possible answers to these new questions raised by the recent discoveries.

I

Before the new discoveries the fundamental work on the subject was that of Max Sulzberger.[1] In substantial agreement with the views of his predecessor, J. B. de Rossi, Sulzberger concluded that that most ancient monogram of Christ appeared in the form ✳ in Asia Minor and in Rome about the year A.D. 270: the traditional Christian monogram ☧ was not attested before the time of Constantine. Another form of the monogram, combining the christogram with the Cross, was simplified as ☦, and appeared a little before the middle of the fourth century A.D. at the same time as the first simple crosses ($+$), i.e., the ☦ form was also post-Constantine. A serious difficulty in Sulzberger's theory, of which he himself was fully aware, was the existence of a Christian inscription from Egypt, dated in the third century (on the grounds of script), where the form ☦ was preceded by an A and followed by an Ω[2]. Sulzberger argued that this particular sign had been added to the inscription at a later date. In line with a popular form of explanation in earlier theories, Sulzberger also maintained: "Les monogrammes de Jésus sont de simples abréviations, empruntées à l'écriture païenne, qui peu à peu sont devenus des symboles assimilés à la croix" (p. 447).

The next significant contribution to the subject was made, almost incidentally, in a notice by Jean de Savignac of the Bodmer Papyri XIV (Luke) and XV (John):[3] Savignac drew attention to the abbreviation ⳨ which is uniquely employed at Luke 9:23 and 14:27 in P⁷⁵ in the writing of σρον (σταυρόν) and σρωθηναι (σταυρωθῆναι), the latter also occurring in Bodmer II, P66. "Il faut en conclure que le monogramme ☦, date, en Egypte tout au moins, du IIe s. et qu'il est en realite le plus ancient de tous".[4] The monogram in this form, therefore, must have belonged to the third-century Egyptian inscription under which it had been inscribed and cannot have been (as Sulzberger argued) a later addition. This particular form of abbreviation was evidently chosen – Savignac thinks – because it was shaped like a cross (it is still apparently assumed that it is with a christogram, i.e., an abbreviation for 'Christ' with which we have to do). At the same time Savignac also continues the theory of pagan borrowing, and considers that resemblance of ☦ with the Egyptian hieroglyph ☥ read as *ankh* and meaning 'life', has also contributed to the choice of this particular shape: the historical development of the Christ monogram is reconstructed in

---

[1] "Le Symbole de la croix et les monogrammes de Jésus chez les premiers chrétiens" in *Byzantion* t. II (1925), pp. 337–448.
[2] See further below.
[3] P⁷⁵, "Les Papyrus XIV et XV" in *Scriptorium* XVII (1963), Chronique, pp. 50 ff.
[4] *Op. cit.*, p.51.

the following order: ✷ ⳨ ⳨ ✷.[1] Scriptural precedent or support for the connexion is sought at 1 Corinthians 1:18: ὁ λόγος τοῦ σταυροῦ δύναμις θεοῦ ἐστιν, Colossians 3:4, ὅταν ὁ Χριστὸς φανερωθῇ, ἡ ζωὴ ἡμῶν, and in Johannine passages which make a similar connexion of Christ and life, e.g., 3:14, 7:28, 12:32, 33. Savignac admits a difficulty in the acceptance of a pagan symbol by a religion born out of Judaism. Gnostic Christianity, however, had no such scruples, and provided the channel for the introduction of the "pagan" symbol. Valentinus, who gives a central place to the Cross in his thought, has already associated it with the Tree of Life, as does also the gospel of Truth (f. IX, p. 18, X, p. 20). At f.X, p. 20, line 27 in the latter, the same contraction is found as in P75, P66, viz., CPOC, and Savignac maintains that the Egyptian *Ankh* sign is found on the last page of the Codex Jung.

The next significant contribution to the discussion was made by Professor K. Aland.[2] Whereas Savignac had confined himself to a few observations of the contracted form ⳨ in P75 and P66, Aland investigated all occurrences of both noun and verb and, extending his inquiries to other papyrus texts of the New Testament. The contraction occurs frequently in both P75 and P66, in both noun and verb. It seems to have established itself more securely in P66, but it is also attested in other Papyrus texts. The evidence is more than sufficient to prove that the contraction was a regular one at this early period (mid-third century).

Aland argues that the new Papyrus data give us "not only the oldest form of the christogram, but also the possibility of explaining this much discussed sign" (p. 174). He suggests that in this form of the sign, we have an "Urform" or "Vorform" of the christogram, itself originally not a christogram at all, but a *staurogram*, i.e., a symbol of the Cross. He cites in support Lactantius' account of the vision of Constantine: 'commonitus est in quiete Constantinus, ut caeleste signum dei notaret in scutis atque ita proelium committeret. facit ut iussus est et transversa X littera, summo capite circumflexo, Christum in scutis notat' (*de mort. pers.* 44:5): this is interpreted by Aland: 'Transversa X littera, d.h. doch wohl: er lässt das X senkrecht stellen und biegt den nun senkrechten einen Balken zu einem P um, so dass sich genau das Zeichen ergibt, das wir in P66 "und seinen Nachfolgern finden:⳨.'

The Lactantius passage is one on which there have been wide differences of interpretation. Since Lactantius evidently understands the heavenly "sign" to be the christogram (*Christum in scutis notat*), the text has been emended to give this result, the most widely accepted conjecture being that

---

[1] Savignac cites G. Lefèvre, *Recueil*, No. 423, and recently Maria Crammer, *Das Altägyptische Lebenszeichen in christlichen (koptischen) Aegypten* (Wiesbaden, 1955), pp. 8, 9, fig. 7 (1)

[2] "Bemerkungen zum Alter und zur Entstehung des Christogrammes anhand von Beobachtungen bei P66 und P75", in *Studien zur Überlieferung des neuen Testaments und seines Textes* (Berlin, 1967), pp. 173 ff. Cf. his "Neue neutestamentliche Papyri" in *NTS* 10 (1963), pp. 62–79 and 11 (1964), pp. 1–3.

of Gregoire, to supply the capital letter I, viz., *transversa X littera* ⟨I⟩, "the letter X being crossed by I with the head bent into a circle", (i.e., ⟨R⟩ , the regular christogram).[1] This "emendation" of Lactantius does not seem to have been entirely unconnected with the desire to find a *Chi-Rho* symbol in the text. Aland's translation seems the most natural one ("the letter X having been turned round (transversa), its top having been given a loop"). The objection of Sulzberger that the latter sign was unknown before the middle of the fourth century is no longer valid, with the new discoveries. The "heavenly sign" which Lactantius so describes was a *staurogram*; and this fully accords with his universal use of the expression *caeleste signum* as the sign of the Cross.[2] We are then obliged, however, to assume that, in his interpretation of the *staurogram*, Lactantius has explained it as a christogram or confused it with a christogram (*Christum in scutis notat*). With this explanation there is no need to indulge in doubtful interpretations of the verb *notat* as meaning "inscrire le nom de Dieu au moyen d'un signe, d'un monogramme'.[3]

II

The new discoveries shed fresh light on Eusebius's account of the vision of Constantine and its sequel. The story is told in Eusebius's *Life of Constantine* (i:26–31). When the Emperor was seeking divine help against Maxentius, he and his army saw "the *tropaion* of the Cross" (σταυροῦ τρόπαιον) illumined in the heavens with a written message attached to it: 'By this conquer' (τούτῳ νικᾷ). On the following night Christ appeared to the Emperor in a dream "with the same sign that had appeared in heaven" (σὺν τῷ φανέντι κατ᾽ οὐρανὸν σημείῳ) and commanded him to make a copy of it. This he did, placing a transverse bar on a long spear encased in gold to form a Cross. At the top of this cruciform standard there was fastened a wreath woven of precious stones and gold in which

---

[1] Cf. J. Moreau, ed. *Lactance*, "De la Mort des Persécuteurs" in *Sources chrétiennes*, no. 39 (Paris), p. 435.

[2] *Institut*, IV. 26, 42; 27:2; 27:8; de Mort. X. 2, etc.

[3] Cf. Moreau, *op. cit.*, p. 433: "*Caeleste signum*, employé seul, ne peut, en effet, signifier *monogramma Dei* (Fr Altheim, *Literatur u. Gesellschaft im ausgehenden Altertum*, I [Halle, 1948], p. 145, n. 13). Mais le verbe *notare* a un sens très particulier: il signifie 'exprimer un mot, une idée, au moyen d'une abréviation, en une ou deux lettres' (Altheim, o.l., pp. 145–6); *notare signum*, c'est *significare nota* (cf. *Christum notat* et Serv., ad *Aen.*, III, 44: la Sibylle fait connaître ses prophéties par des *signa*, ce qui veut, dire *notis litterarum – significet aliquid*). Fr Altheim, dans le travail cité, remarque justement que la différence entre *signum* et *nota* n'est pas nette. Il a tort cependant de croire que *caeleste signum Dei* ne peut être autre chose que le signe de la croix; il oublie le caractère unique de l'expression chez Lactance. Dans tous les textes de cet auteur que nous avons cités, il s'agit ou bien de *signum* employé sans détermination, ou de symbole de la passion. Mais dans le cas qui nous occupe, *signum* est déterminé par *Dieu*, et *signum Dei notare* signifie *Deum nota significare*, 'inscrire le nom de Dieu au moyen d'un signe, d'un monogramme'. Il est dès lors inutile de supposer que le signe adopté devait nécessairement être cruciforme, et de lui donner la forme ⇉. Cette croix monogrammatique n'apparaît guère avant le milieu du IVe siècle." (sic!)

was the symbol of the Saviour's epithet (lit., the 'saving epithet'), two letters signifying the name of Christ in which the Rho in the middle was crossed by a X.

ὑψηλὸν δόρυ χρυσῷ κατημφιεσμένῳ κέρας εἶχεν ἐγκάρσιον σταυρου σχήματι πεποιημένον. ἄνω δὲ πρὸς ἄκρῳ τοῦ παντὸς στέφανος ἐκ λίθων πολυτελῶν καὶ χρυσοῦ συμπεπληγμένος κατεστήρικτο, καθ' οὗ τῆς σωτηρίου ἐπηγορίας τὸ σύμβολον, δύο στοιχεῖα τὸ Χριστοῦ ὄνομα παραδηλοῦντα . . . χιαζομένου τοῦ ῥῶ κατὰ τὸ μεσαίτατον.

Below this was a portrait of Constantine and his children, and from the cross-bar there hung a banner, the standard known as the Labarum.

From coins of the period[1] it is clear that the basic design of the cruciform, gold-encased lance with the "crown" or "wreath" was ☧. What is of special interest is that the 'cross-structure' with the Chi–Rho sign at the top has the *staurogram* foundation, with a christogram surmounting it. The report in the legend that it was an illumined *Cross* which Constantine saw and that it was the "trophy of the Cross" he modelled is substantially correct: the "sign" by which he conquered was the sign of the cross, a *staurogram*, but at the same time this was ingeniously combined with the *christogram* symbol in the artistic reproduction of the "divine sign".

This combination of both forms of this early Christian symbol in the Constantinian banner suggests that they both come out of pre-Constantinian tradition. Archaeological discoveries, as well as the Papyrus evidence, support the pre-Constantinian origin of both forms: as noted above,[2] particularly rich inscriptional material in this connexion has been discovered in the graffiti in the Vatican excavations.

III

Savignac's theory of a pagan origin for these symbols, mediated by Gnosticism, e.g., the tracing of the *staurogram* form to Valentinus, is regarded as doubtful by Aland;[3] more convincing evidence would require to be produced. Certainly, as Aland points out, the alleged presence of an *Ankh* symbol on the last folio of the Jung Codex does not appear to be borne out by the actual evidence: what is found, as the editors have noted, is the phrase ὁ ☧ ἅγιος, i.e., Le Christ saint. On the other hand, Margherita Guarducci reports the presence of the *Ankh* sign among the Vatican graffiti,[4] and it has been found elsewhere in Christian inscriptions.[5]

[1] See, e.g. the reproduction in George Pitt-Rivers, *The Riddle of the Labarum and the origin of Christian Symbols* (London, 1966), p. 19, fig. (c).
[2] P. 319.
[3] *Op. cit.*, p. 179.
[4] *Op. cit.*, p. 141.
[5] E.g. on an amulet with the inscription Θεὸς ὁ μόνος Θεὸς Ιης. See E. Peterson, *EIS THEOS* (Göttingen, 1926), p. 310, reproduced in E. Stauffer, *Theologie des Neuen Testaments* (Stuttgart, 1947), Abh. 51 (p. 352).

Whether this may have in any way influenced the *staurogram* is a debatable question; it may conceivably be an independent sign for ζωὴ αἰώνιος which entered Christian tradition, through Gnosticism, from Egyptian sources.

F.-J. Dölger[1] and E. Dinkler[2] have sought to trace the origins of the staurogram/christogram symbols in the Hebrew–Jewish tradition rather than in Egyptian pagan sources. Impressive evidence from inscriptions on tombs and ossuaries has been produced to show that the cross sign was already used in pre-Christian Hebrew tradition, in both the perpendicular and Chi-form ($+$ X): in every case examined "Die Fundstelle oder der Text der Inschrift machen die jüdische Herkunft teils zweifellos, teils wahrscheinlich" (Dinkler, p. 161). Both forms of the cross represent the North Semitic, but also the old Hebraic, Phoenician and Aramaic letter for the Hebrew *Tau* (ת), the last letter in the Hebrew alphabet, which has not only the meaning "sign", but also "sign of a cross" (Dinkler, p. 163 ff.) and is used with the meaning of a "saving sign" or talisman at Ezekiel 9:4 ff.

Dinkler rightly attaches great importance to the Ezekiel passage for the subsequent development of the *Tau* symbolism. In the context of Ezekiel's first Temple vision, Jahweh says to the "man clothed in linen, with a writing case at his side": "Go through the city, through Jerusalem, and put a mark (Tau, $+$ or X) upon the foreheads of the men who sigh and groan over all the abominations that are committed in it. And to the others he said in my hearing. 'Pass through the city after him, and smite; your eye shall not spare, and you shall show no pity; slay old men outright, young men and maidens, little children and women, but touch no one upon whom is the mark.' "[3] G. A. Cooke comments (ICC Ezekiel, *in loc.*):"The form of the *mark* is suggested by the word used, *tau*, the last letter of the Heb. alphabet, written $+$ in the ancient script; the simplest of signs to make, and as such it served to attest a document among both Hebrews (Job 31:35) and Babylonians ..." In Ezekiel the "sign" is a kind of sacred "seal" allotted to those "who sigh and groan", i.e., show evidence of repentance by disassociating themselves from the evil in the world and adhering to the Torah of Jahweh. The "sign" is a "protective" sign (*Schutzzeichen*), here closely associated with the thought of repentance: those who repent are so marked out that they may be spared on the coming day of judgment. There is also quite certainly (as the commentaries note) a connexion with the "sign" or "mark" of ownership, the branding of slaves or cattle. The sign marks out those who belong to Jahweh and, therefore, are under his protection. The "sign" on the lintels of the doors in the Exodus story (Exod. 12:22 ff.) is to be similarly understood.

As B. Stade[4] pointed out, this idea of being the "property" of deity is

[1] *Jahrbuch für Antike und Christentum*: Beiträge zur Geschichte des Kreuzzeichens, 1958–61.
[2] "Zur Geschichte des Kreuzsymbols" *ZThK* 48 (1951), pp. 148–72.
[3] Ezek. 9:4–6.
[4] "Beiträge zue Pentateuchkritik I: Das Kainszeichen", *ZATW* 14 (1894), pp. 250 ff.

more widely attested in the Old Testament than might at first appear; and the assumption of a widespread custom of religious marking or "sealing" is also supported in many passages, if it is not always easy or possible to distinguish cases of literal "cult-marks" from metaphorical language. The context of Genesis 4:15 the "mark of Cain" makes it clear that this was originally also a *protective* mark and not a mark of shame: it is called *'oth*, "a sign", and was no doubt envisaged as a sign on the forehead. Stade argued further that it is to be regarded as a "tribal sign"; Cain is branded not as an individual but as a representative of his tribe. Ezekiel 9:4, however, tells against this view, for here it is a mark on a selected few out of Israel, a saved Remnant. But the "sign of Cain" is no doubt Jahweh's "sign": cf. Isaiah 44:5: "This one will say, 'I am the Lord's', another will call himself by the name of Jacob, and another will write on his hands 'The Lord's' and so name himself by the name of Israel." This last verse seems to imply, at any rate for exilic times, the practice of physical marking, on the forehead or the hand of the sign of Jahweh – possibly the Tau sign ($+$ or X). Leviticus 19:28, 21:5 ff. and Deuteronomy 14:1 are also relevant: the prohibition of "tattooing" only serves to show how prevalent the custom was. I Kings 20:41 is interpreted by Stade as meaning that the removal of the bandage from the prophet's eyes meant the revealing to the king of Jahweh's "mark" on his forehead.

What more natural than to mark one's flesh indelibly – forehead or palm especially – with the sign of the deity to whom one belonged and whose protection and help one sought.

Dinkler goes on to show that the idea of an "Eigentums- and Schutzzeichen" of Jahweh does not cease in post-exilic times. He cites *Psalms of Solomon* 15:6–9.

> For the mark of God ($\tau\grave{o}\ \sigma\eta\mu\epsilon\hat{\iota}ov\ \tauo\hat{v}\ \theta\epsilono\hat{v}$)˙
> is upon the righteous that they may be saved.
> Famine and sword and pestilence (shall be) far from the righteous, . . .
>
> And they that do lawlessness shall not escape the judgment of God; . . .
> For the mark of destruction ($\tau\grave{o}\ \sigma\eta\mu\epsilon\hat{\iota}ov\ \tau\hat{\eta}s\ \dot{\alpha}\pi\omega\lambda\epsilon\acute{\iota}as$)
> is upon their forehead.

The imagery is the same as in Ezekiel 9:4 and Exodus 12:22 f. Specially important for the New Testament is the Damascus Document (CD ix.10–12B).

> "These [the 'poor of the flock', i.e., the Qumran community] shall escape during the period of visitation, but the rest shall be handed over to the sword when the Messiah comes from Aaron and Israel. Just as it was during the period of the first visitation, concerning which He spake through Ezekiel *'to set a mark upon the foreheads'* of them that sigh and cry, but the rest were delivered to 'the sword that avengeth with the vengeance of the covenant'" (Trans. Charles).

These passages show not only that the "sign of Jahweh" survived in certain circles as a kind of talisman and sign of divine ownership, but that it received a special emphasis in Jewish eschatology as a "messianic" sign with the same connotation.[1] Moreover, it can scarcely be coincidence that the imagery in the New Testament and early Christian literature of the "signing" or "sealing" of the faithful are most numerous where a Jewish background or Jewish sources are most in evidence. Bousset surmised that the frequent mention in such passages of the "sealing" implied "dass auch bei Christen zur Zeit der Apokalypse es noch hier und da Brauch war, sich durch der Haut einigeritzte Namen (Gottes oder Jesu) gegen allerlei Gefahren zu schützen".[2] As Dinkler remarks, the marking of the names of the Lamb or the Father, on the one hand, on the foreheads of those who were thus "sealed" as δοῦλοι τοῦ θεοῦ (Rev. 7:3 f.; 9:4; 14:1; 22:4) and, on the other, those who bore the χάραγμα τοῦ θηρίου on head or forehead (Rev. 13:6 f.; 14:9; 16:2; 20:4) has its basis and inspiration in the Old Testament imagery, especially the ideas of Ezekiel 9:4 and *Psalms of Solomon* 15:6-9.

IV

The contribution of archaeology and the Papyri to our knowledge of such customs and practices is evident. If we can be confident – and the evidence from Jewish ossuaries and inscriptions seems conclusive – that the σημείωσις τοῦ ταῦ in the double form +, X was familiar in Judaism, then the origin of the double form of the Christian symbol ⳨ and ⳩ may be explicable as deriving from such Jewish "signs of Jahweh". The Chi (X) alone is attested in inscriptions for Christ;[3] it occasionally is written ✸✸[4]. The vertical stroke may have been simply a means of distinguishing the Christian symbol from the Hebrew–Jewish Tau. In the Letter of Barnabas (9:8) the Greek Tau has already become a symbol of the Cross.[5]

The evidence of the Papyri seems to point to the ⳨ sign as the more primitive. The Vatican inscriptions, however, which have both, reveal that the *Chi–Rho* sign was also a pre-Constantinian one. Since both forms of the Hebrew Tau, + and X, are found together, it is attractive to conjecture that the addition of the loop or the *Rho* was originally intended to indicate the word Χριστός, *the first two letters* of the name (as in most

---

[1] Cf. Dinkler, op. cit., p. 147. Dinkler is inclined to believe that the "Stigmatisierung" in a physical sense (a tattooing on the head or palm of the Tau in the Old Hebrew script) also survived.

[2] *Die Offenbarung Johannes* (Göttingen, 1906), p. 281.

[3] Guarducci, op. cit., p. 111.

[4] Cf. above, p. 320.

[5] Aland, op. cit., p. 177.

abbreviations). The Tau-Rho contraction seems secondary and aetiological, for the use of the contraction ℞ for σταυρός, from the second and fourth letters, seems a little artificial. It seems to me probable, however, that the original sign, whether its base was a *Chi* or a *Tau*, symbolized a Cross, and that the addition of the loop or the *Rho* giving the contraction for Χριστός, not only identified the sign as a Christian talisman, *but turned it into a christo-staurogram*, i.e., it was, as Eusebius and Lactantius respectively describe it, σωτήριον σημεῖον, τοῦ σωτηρίου τροπαῖον πάθους (*Hist. Ecc.* ix. 9, 10; *de vita Constant.* 1,40, 2; 41); a *signum veri et divini sanguinis, signum passionis, signum immortale (Instit.* IV, 26, 42; 27:2; 27:8; *Epit.* 46, 6–7; *de Mort.* X.2).

In his rhetorical description of the Banner of Constantine with its mysterious Labarum, Gibbon[1] (drawing on the *Vita Const.*, but interpreting it freely) understood the symbolism of the *Chi–Rho* monogram in just such a manner (italics mine): " . . . the principal standard which displayed the triumph of the cross was styled the LABARUM, an obscure, though celebrated, name, which has been variously derived from all the languages of the world. It is described (Eusebius in *Vita Constantine.*, I.i.c. 30, 31) as a long pike intersected by a transversal beam. The silken veil which hung down from the beam was curiously inwrought with the images of the reigning monarch and his children. The summit of the pike supported a crown of gold, which enclosed the mysterious monogram, *at once expressive of the figure of the Cross and the initial letters of the name of Christ.*"

V

There are two possible answers to the questions this essay raised on the meaning, relationships and origins of the two traditional forms of the "*Chi–Rho*" sign. (1) The original Christian sign was ℞ , a *staurogram*, and this was aetiologically explained as a *Chi–Rho*, and turned into a *christogram*, a monogram of Christ. (2) In the light of the antiquity of the two forms of the Hebrew letter ת , + and X, as a sign for Jahweh in Hebrew and Jewish tradition, especially in its messianic and eschatological connotation, the addition of a loop in the first form, + becoming ℞ , and a *Rho* in the second, X becoming ⳨, turned this Jewish "Eigentums und Schutzzeichens Jahweh" into a Christian *tropaion*, a victory-sign of the Passion, designating not simply Christus, but *Christus crucifixus.*

[1] Chapter xx (*The Decline and Fall of the Roman Empire* by Edward Gibbon [New York, 1899 edit.] vol. ii, pp. 260, 261).

CHAPTER XXIII

ACTS AND EPISTLES IN APOCRYPHAL WRITINGS

DONALD GUTHRIE

THE LARGE AMOUNT OF PSEUDEPIGRAPHICAL LITERATURE WHICH circulated during the early period of the history of the church serves one useful function. It provides a most effective contrast with the canonical New Testament books, which cannot fail to stamp the latter as productions of a different kind. It has always been recognized that imitation is a form of flattery which often leads to a greater appreciation of the real thing. It is with this end in view that the present study will look at some of the apocryphal Acts and Epistles. A study of the structure and methods of compilation of apocryphal books will throw light on certain problems which arise out of the canonical models.

I

There were several apocryphal Acts but only the four earliest will be examined. These are the Acts of John, of Paul, of Peter and of Andrew.[1] The most significant will be the Acts of Paul, because it alone of these books was highly regarded in some quarters within the orthodox church, as for instance at Alexandria. Moreover, of the production of this book some details are known because Tertullian referred to the matter and to the attitude of the Asiatic church towards it.

(a) The Acts of John

This was considered by M. R. James[2] to be the earliest of the apocryphal Acts, and was dated mid-second century. According to Photius (A.D. 890) this Acts, together with the other major pseudo-Acts (Paul, Peter, Andrew and Thomas), was the work of Leucius Charinus, who was supposed to have been a disciple of John[3], but M. R. James restricts this author's activity to the Acts of John alone.[4]

---

[1] Cf. Lipsius-Bonnet, *Acta Apostolorum Apocrypha* II (1898), for the texts. C. Schmidt published some important works on the apocryphal acts, of which the most notable for our purpose are *Die alten Petrusakten, TU* n.f. ix 1 (1905) and two on *Acta Pauli*, one on the Heidelberg coptic text in 1904 and the other on the Hamburg text in 1936.

[2] *The Apocryphal New Testament* (Oxford, 1924), p. 228.

[3] According to Epiphanius; cf. P. Carrington, *The Early Christian Church* II (Cambridge, 1957), p. 354.

[4] In his *Apocrypha Anecdota* II (Cambridge, 1897), M. R. James pointed out the appropriateness of the choice of the name Leucius by a writer of a book of Acts, because of its resemblance

In the strictest sense the Acts of John is not pseudepigraphical, for the story is told generally in the third person except where speeches are attributed to John and to other speakers. It is therefore rather a religious romance published under an apostolic name. But two tendencies which it displays are significant for our purpose since they furnish useful background material. (i) There is a very definite desire to enhance the honour of the apostle by the description of numerous miracles, especially the raising of the dead. And (ii) there is a decidedly dogmatic motive in propagating what appear to be Valentinian ideas.[1]

The details of John mentioned in this book are based on traditional material. The scenes are set in Ephesus and mention is made of the adjoining cities of Miletus and Smyrna.[2] Numerous people are named in the book, but only three of the names bear any resemblance to names found in the canonical writings, Andronicus (31, cf. Rom. 16:7), Tertullus (59, Acts 24.1, 2) and the latter's wife called Aristobula, which might be an echo of Aristobulus (Rom. 16:10). But the other fifteen names are quite unknown in canonical tradition.[3] In this respect the Acts of John differs from the Acts of Paul, where more of the names are culled from such a source.

The exceptions to the third person style are curious. In 60 a "we-section" abruptly appears, while in the next section the first person singular is used ("But when the day was now dawning I arose first"); but the "I" is sharply distinguished from John, who is then said to be still asleep (61). The plural "we" is continued to the end of section 62, not to be resumed again until sections 72 and 73. It occurs again only in the Latin account of John's death (or assumption). This supplies an interesting parallel with the canonical Acts, where "we-sections" again appear and disappear. In the Acts of John, it may well be a direct imitation of Luke's style which would show an early awareness of this characteristic. Clearly the author of this book does not intend to use John as a pseudonym, but is making himself out to be an associate of the apostle.

In a speech attributed to John there are clear marks of identification to show which John is intended. "For when he had chosen Peter and Andrew which were brethren he comes to me and James my brother" (88). John

[1] Carrington op. cit., p. 355, illustrates from the background of the Gnostic threefold division of mankind. J. Quasten, Patrology (Utrecht-Antwerp, 1950), p. 136, considers that the speeches of this book "evince unmistakably Docetic tendencies".

[2] Cf. Acts of John 18, 35, 55.

[3] The following are mentioned: Damonicus, Aristodemus, Cleobius Marcellus (18), Lycomeded, Cleopatra, Callippus (19), Verus (30), Drusiana, Aristippus, Xenophon (59), Craton (xiv), Stacteus (xvii), Atticus and Eugenius (xviii). [References follow James, op. cit.]

to Luke (pp. xi-xii). On the connexion of the Acts of John with those of Paul and Peter, cf. M. Blumenthal, Formen und Motive in den apokryphen Apostelgeschichten, TU XLVIII (Leipzig, 1933), pp. 161-6. By form-critical methods he concluded that these were not directly dependent upon each other; Thomas was derived from Paul and John, and Andrew was indebted to all the others. But some recent writers would dispute this view of Andrew (see note 1, p. 336).

connects himself with James and Peter on the mount of transfiguration (90), and in the same incident he claims special privilege "because he (i.e. the Lord) loved me". Since the only mention of John in the canonical Acts is in company with Peter, the imitative process is again apparent. Again he says "all we his disciples were at Gennesaret" (92), and in the next section "sometimes when I would lay hold on him". The conscious attempt to achieve verisimilitude is here unmistakable. Moreover, the author's high estimate of John is clear from the descriptions he uses, e.g. "apostle of Christ" (26, 55), "servant of God" (19, 74), "holy apostle" (62, XVIII). But all these terms are found within the canonical books, and would be quite natural in describing one of the apostolic circle. A similar high estimate of John is found in one passage (92), where it is said that all the other disciples slept, but John watched, an obvious mark of his super-iority. This tendency to exalt one apostle beyond the others was a feature of Gnostic writers.

According to A. F. Findlay[1] this author was a man of great literary gifts and deep religious feeling. Yet although the book may shine among its pseudepigraphical fellows, it is considerably inferior to the canonical Acts, both in literary form and spiritual purpose.

(b)   The Acts of Paul

This book is more important for our study because it appears to be an orthodox work and because we happen to possess a comment upon the author's production by Tertullian, who records the strong disapproval of the church against it. The book is sometimes dated ca.A.D. 160, although recent studies have tended towards a date nearer A.D. 200.[2] It is an impor-tant witness to the approach to pseudepigraphy at a time when the New Testament canon was gaining increasing fixation.

The first important consideration is the relationship of this book to the canonical Acts. There is no doubt about the author's close acquaintance with the latter book, but there are differences in his treatment of the his-torical facts. The main framework seems to be Paul's first missionary journey,[3] as is evident from the mention of Antioch, Iconium and Myra, particularly in connection with the martyrdom of Thecla. Yet whereas in the canonical account Barnabas was with him, in this account he is alone. Moreover, there is no mention of the sea voyage. On the other hand, there are further journeys mentioned which differ from the canonical account;

[1] *Byways in Early Christian Literature* (Edinburgh, 1923), p. 210. Findlay was of the opinion that the "we-sections" in this book were suggested by the "we-sections" in Acts, and if this is true it shows the strong imitative impulse. Cf. also G. Schimmelpfang, "Johannesakten", in Hennecke's *Neutestamentliche Apokryphen* (Tübingen, 1904), p. 431, on his literary charac-teristics.

[2] So C. Schmidt, *op. cit.*, on the strength of the Hamburg text and G. Quispel *VC* 10 (1956), p. 147, on the basis of its use of the Acts of Andrew.

[3] But cf. M. R. James' suggestion that the *Acta Pauli* may have been intended as a continua-tion of the canonical Acts, *JTS* 6 (1905), pp. 244-6.

for from Myra Paul goes to Sidon, Tyre and probably Jerusalem in the reverse order from his final journey to Rome (Acts 27. 3, 5), although the author may have had the details of Acts 21 : 3, 5 here in mind. At least, some confusion seems to have occurred in Acts of Paul 4, where, after describing the departure of Paul from Myra, the narrative mentions him in company with two Christian couples, eating bread under a tree, which is not easy to reconcile with the sea journey which the narrative requires. The author appears to be little concerned about the way his narrative fits into the Acts story, provided some impression of a connection is created by the use of parallel names.[1] Leon Vouaux considered the choice of names to be quite arbitrary.[2]

These observations are sufficient to establish the nature of this book as a pious romance; because it also displays certain tendencies which appear to be germane to the question of pseudepigraphy in general, it is worthwhile to make further comment on it. 3 *Corinthians* (This is an apocryphal epistle 1 & 2 Cor. are canonical = in N.T.) Corinthians will be considered separately when apocryphal epistles are examined.

Of the fifty-six names of persons mentioned, few are taken from the New Testament and even those that are appear in a different role. Titus appears as Paul's precursor at Iconium and Rome,[3] which is not out of keeping with canonical references to him as Paul's special representative (cf. 2 Cor. 2:13; 7:13 ff.; 8:7). Onesiphorus (cf. 2 Tim. 1:16; 4:19) has his residence at Iconium instead of Ephesus, although it is not impossible that this man originated in Iconium and that a correct tradition is here preserved.[4] Demas (cf. 2 Tim. 4:10) and Hermogenes (cf. 2 Tim. 1:15) become leading heretics,[5] while in the Corinthian correspondence names are mentioned of which one only appears in the canonical Corinthian epistles, i.e. Stephanus (1 Cor. 16:17), although Eubulus is mentioned in 2 Tim. 4:21 in a different context, and Theophilus in the preface to the canonical Acts (Acts 1:1). Eutychus (Acts 20:9), a young man of Troas, becomes a deacon at Corinth (spelt Eutyches). Luke is said to have come to Rome from Galatia and Titus from Dalmatia,[6] and here there seems to be a reminiscence of 2 Timothy 4:10 with Luke substituted for Crescens. Another curious transposition is the appearance of Barsabas Justus, the losing candidate for apostolic office in Acts 1:23, as one of Caesar's chief men.[7] But the great

[1] Cf. J. Gwynn, article on "Thecla", in *Dictionary of Christian Biography*, edited Smith and Wace (London, 1887), IV.

[2] *Les Actes de Paul et ses lettres apocryphes* (Paris, 1913), p. 115, "On saisit facilement le procédé; l'auteur n'emprunte en somme à la source authentique que des noms de villes, unis par un lien plus ou moins lâche, ou même complètement séparés, et il fait de ces noms l'usage arbitraire qui lui convient".

[3] *Acts of Paul* in James, *The Apocryphal New Testament*, pp. 272, 29.

[4] Cf. E. B. Redlich, *St. Paul and his Companions* (London, 1913), pp. 258 f.

[5] James, *op. cit.*, p. 272.

[6] Cf. James, *op. cit.*, p. 293. Cf. also M. Dibelius, *Die Pastoralbriefe*[3] (Tübingen, 1955), p. 97.

[7] Cf. James, *op. cit.*, p. 294.

majority of names bear no resemblance at all to canonical personalia. Moreover, there are some mistakes of an historical kind, as for instance in the reference to the Roman Governor at Iconium.[1] In face of these facts some reserve must be exercised before assuming that the Acts of Paul is a typical example of the use of personalia in pseudepigrapha to add verisimilitude. If that was the author's purpose he badly bungled the attempt, and the work would have possessed an appearance of greater veracity had the personalia been omitted.[2] Strangely enough there are no personalia in the incorporated 3 Corinthians, which achieved some success in separate circulation in spite of, or perhaps even because of this. The fact that among the canonical names used one only, Stephanus, does not occur in the canonical Acts or 2 Timothy, suggests that these two books were the author's chief sources, and may further indicate that this book is intended as a continuation of the canonical Acts.

Another aspect which deserves mention is the use of traditional and other material unconnected with canonical sources. Apart from Nero only one personage known in secular history is introduced and that is Queen Tryphaena, a great niece of the Emperor Claudius.[3] This fact, together with the royal route chosen from Antioch to Iconium which was not usual in the second century, suggested to Sir William Ramsay[4] that the author used an earlier traditional source; but his views on this are not widely accepted. Various opinions are held regarding the Thecla story,[5] making it difficult to reach any conclusion over the extent of the author's inventiveness. But that a major portion of his romance is his own fiction pure and simple can hardly be challenged. His portrait of Paul is an interesting study[6] for it is not exactly flattering, although it is clear that the author held the apostle in high esteem. Some think that this latter fact makes it improbable that he invented the portrait, but perhaps it is no more than a portrait of a representative Jew. There is certainly a touch of realism about it which speaks much for the artistic imagination of the author if it is his own invention.

When the purpose of this fiction is considered, tradition helpfully supplies one answer; Tertullian[7] reports that the author, a presbyter of Asia,

---

[1] Cf. C. H. Turner, *Studies in Early Church History* (Oxford, 1912), p. 181, who also drew attention to the confusion over the two Antiochs.

[2] It is on this score that A. F. Findlay rejected Schmidt's opinion that the author was a deliberate forger, who, he argued, could not have shown less skill, *op. cit.*, p. 270.

[3] Cf. James, *op. cit.*, pp. 272, 278.

[4] *The Church in the Roman Empire before A.D. 170*[4] (Edinburgh, 1905), pp. 375–428.

[5] M. Goguel, *Introduction au Nouveau Testament,* Tome IV, Les Epîtres pauliniennes (Paris, 1925), p. 77, admits the possibility of the existence of such a person as Thecla but denies the possibility of reconstructing her history. He mentions Harnack, Rolffs, Clemen and Vouaux as holding a similar opinion. Ramsay and Zahn were more certain of her real existence, while Rey, Schmidt and Kruger regarded her as an invention. J. Gwynn, *op. cit.*, gives a full discussion of the historicity of Thecla. On the romance-motive behind the story, cf. Blumenthal, *op. cit.*, p. 157.

[6] Cf. James, *op. cit.*, p. 273.   [7] *De Baptismo,* xvii.

did it for love of Paul (*amore Pauli*). But this statement does not tell us what he hoped to achieve by this means, unless it was to enhance the reputation of Paul.[1] But if so it was not a success among many of his own contemporaries, for his fiction was apparently soon discovered and unhesitatingly condemned. One further comment may be made on Tertullian's statement.[2] He was evidently aware that some people were using this book to support the right of women to teach; and if the author intended to support such a cause, his purpose would be definitely dogmatic. But although his approach to women teachers in the church was novel, his doctrine appears to have been orthodox.

The place of this book in the early church is of great importance because it throws considerable light on the orthodox attitude towards such fictions. That the second century church took a strong line is evident from the fact that the presbyter-author was unfrocked (*loco decessisse*). But there has been some dispute over the precise reason for such action. Did the church deprive the presbyter of his office on account of his fiction, or on account of his teaching?[3]

Tertullian himself condemns no particular doctrine in the book, and we have no reason to suppose that the Asiatic church did either. At least, had Tertullian been aware of any error advanced in the book it is hard to believe that he would have restrained himself from attacking it, in view of his attacks on so many heretical notions. It seems reasonably conclusive that the presbyter was not condemned on account of unorthodox views, but on account of his fiction. Indeed, Tertullian reports that the condemnation followed the author's own confession of being author of the book.[4] There is no room here for the theory that the church in Asia might regard the work as a legitimate convention, and certainly Tertullian lends no support to this view. To him the work falsely (*perperam*) bears Paul's name and was fabricated as if by Paul's authority (*construxit quasi titulo Pauli*). The fact that the author claims to have done it *amore Pauli*

---

[1] In discussing the author's purpose, A. F. Findlay, *op. cit.*, pp. 269–70, suggests that he "was an enthusiastic hero-worshipper, and he wrote a tale to glorify his hero of the kind that he knew would be eagerly read. In doing so, he made him the mouthpiece of his own thoughts and convictions, believing that he was doing the apostle honour; and his purpose was served when these were lodged in men's minds with the vividness of appeal which a fascinating story can commend." Findlay excuses the author on the grounds that he possessed a different "conscience for historical veracity from our own" (*op. cit.*, p. 271).

[2] Tertullian, *op. cit.*, "Quod si qui Paulo perperam inscripta legunt exemplum Theclae ad licentiam mulierum docendi tingendique defendunt, scint in Asia prebyterum, qui eam scripturam construxit, quasi titulo Pauli de suo cumulans, convictum atque confessum id se amore Pauli fecisse, loco decessisse." A. Souter, "The Acta Pauli" etc., in Tertullian, *JTS* 25 (1924), p. 292, mentioned a different text which reads "quodsi que *acta pauli* que perperam scripta sunt. . . ."

[3] R. A. Lipsius, *Die apokryphen Apostelgeschichten* (1887) II, pt. 1, pp. 448 ff., maintained that our present work is a catholic recension of a Gnostic original.

[4] J. Gwynn, *art. cit.*, p. 869, strongly maintained that the presbyter was punished for fraud.

apparently made no difference.[1] Neither the church in Asia nor the African Tertullian seems to have been moved by such methods of hero-worship. It should, moreover, be noted that the people whom Tertullian is informing were evidently appealing to the Acts of Paul as if it set forth the genuine Pauline approach to the position of women. They were apparently unaware that the work was unauthentic and Tertullian sees no necessity to do more than draw their attention to the fact.

Yet this book achieved some popularity among orthodox Christians. Origen cited it and regarded it as optional whether his readers chose to receive it.[2] But it is not mentioned again until the fourth century. The Claromontanus list contains it but distinguishes it from canonical books, as does Eusebius,[3] although he does not place it among the heretical books (*notha*) but among the disputed books. Methodius referred to Thecla, while Ephraem[4] actually wrote a commentary on 3 Corinthians. To Aphraates this spurious epistle appears to have been on a par with the canonical books. In the West both Jerome and Augustine rejected it. The history of the book, while it shows some popularity in some quarters, makes clear that this book was never considered as apostolic with any serious claim to canonicity.[5] This happened only to 3 Corinthians in Eastern regions.

(c) *The Acts of Peter.* According to M. R. James[6] this book was probably written by an author from Asia Minor not later than A.D. 200. He has drawn much from the Acts of John, but his theological approach is less unorthodox. The book is an instructive example of the propagation of a literary device through imitation, and is a pointer to the way in which such devices might have become conventional. This is further supported by the fact that the author was apparently also well acquainted with the

---

[1] A strange feature of this claim to have written *amore Pauli* is the lack of understanding of Paul shown in the book. As Gwynn remarked, "with a large and verbally exact knowledge (characteristic of one who had a "love of Paul") of the parts of the New Testament whence a knowledge of Paul's life and teaching is to be gathered – his Epistles and the Acts – the author combines an utter want of faculty to appreciate or reproduce their spirit", *ibid.,* p. 890. The author shows some attempted ingenuity by including here and there a Pauline phrase as, for instance, in the beatitudes in Paul's speech in Onesiphorus' house.

[2] In *De principiis* I. 2. 3. In his commentary on Jn. 20:12, Origen says, "If it pleases anyone to receive what is written in the Acts of Paul. . . ."

[3] *Ecclesiastical History* III. iii. 5.

[4] Ephraem did not suspect the unauthenticity of this work for, as Vouaux (*op. cit.,* p. 34) has pointed out, he condemned the practice of the Bardesanites for having written some Acts of the Apostles under the forged names of apostles.

[5] J. Gwynn, *art. cit.,* p. 894, comments on this book as follows, "Thus the contents of these Acts of Paul and Thecla serve indirectly to confirm the authenticity of the canonical Acts by showing how difficult, it may safely be said how impossible it would be for a *falsarius*, even if writing at no great distance in place or time from the scene and date of his fictitious narrative, to avoid betraying himself by mistakes such as the author of our Acts has fallen into. And the history of the reception of his work proves further that such attempt to palm off pseudo-apostolic documents for genuine was not difficult of exposure, nor passed over as a light offence."

[6] *Op. cit.,* p. 300.

Acts of Paul. Indeed the first three chapters of the Vercelli Acts of Peter relate to Paul and not to Peter, leading some scholars to attach them to the Acts of Paul, but M. R. James[1] was not inclined to favour this. In any case the Acts of Paul, unlike this book, is not heretical.

While the major part of this work is a fictitious invention, there are a few points where it touches historical tradition. Paul's visit to Spain is mentioned (IV), and Peter's contest with Simon in Judea is recalled (V, XVII, XVIII), but a new feature is Peter's second clash with Simon in Rome and the latter's manner of death (XXIII ff). There may be some earlier tradition behind this, but it is difficult to be certain.[2] The account of Peter's martyrdom, in which Peter himself is made to request to be crucified upside down, is probably based on the allusion in John 21:18; but the whole account is tinged with Gnosticizing tendencies, resembling in this the *Acts of John*. This Petrine romance steers clear of the framework of Acts, and is clearly intended to be supplementary to the canonical account to satisfy curiosity regarding the later history of Peter.

As a literary production this book does not shine, nor does its doctrine inspire. There are ascetic characteristics, as for instance in the stress on the continence of women (cf. Acts of Paul). There is also a marked love of the extraordinary. Some are raised from the dead (cf. XXV ff, where three youths are raised in succession), a dog speaks with a man's voice (IX) as does an infant (XV), while on two occasions Simon the sorcerer is said to fly (IV, XXXII); but the most unusual act of Peter the wonder-worker is the resurrection of the dead herring (XIII), which as Carrington[3] suggests may have been poking fun at the type of miracle attributed to Simon. Another instance of the heightening of the miraculous is the restoration of a statue smashed to pieces (XI). The writer is not lacking in imagination, but his production is poor in quality when compared with the canonical Acts. It is no wonder that in spite of its circulation in many quarters it never even approached being considered as canonical. Its unauthentic character must have been too obvious to the more discerning minds of the church, while its late appearance would naturally create almost insuperable suspicions.

While not strictly pseudepigraphic in form, it nevertheless contains many samples of Petrine speeches in the first person; and the author's method in these speeches is worth noting. Peter is made to refer to his denial, although the allusion is quite vague (VII): he is reminded of his faithlessness when doubting in the waters (X); he speaks of being "with the sons of Zebedee" at the Transfiguration (XX), but the account of this bears only the faintest resemblance to the canonical accounts. He also

---

[1] *Ibid.*, p. 306.
[2] P. Carrington, *The Early Christian Church* (Cambridge, 1959), II, p. 358, thinks that "the readers of the tale would look for the points which were familiar to them, and the writer would use these points to provide a semblance of historical outline for his inventions."
[3] *Ibid.*, p. 357.

recalls Simon's homage to him (and to Paul!) in Judea (XXIII). These details may rightly be regarded as personalia introduced to add an appearance of verisimilitude to the narrative. Many names are included which are unknown from biblical sources (such as Theon, Eubula [also in the Acts of Paul], Italicus, Autulus, Agrippinus, Nicostratus, Chryse and many others).

The mentality of the author towards his literary device must be assessed against the fact that he represents deceit as a device of the devil, exemplified in his representative Simon (cf. XVII). "God who is full of all truth" is the God he worships, while he makes Peter confess from the cross that truth and falsehood issue from his tongue (XXXIX). It is difficult to believe that a man so conscious of the nature of deceit would have considered that his own work fell under this category.

(d) *The Acts of Andrew*. Until recently it had been maintained that this book was a third century product; but with the discovery of a Coptic fragment of the book it is now suggested that it was produced during the last quarter of the second century.[1] It probably influenced the production of later Acts associated with Andrew's name, although little direct relationship can be established. The book is a defence of Gnostic theology and therefore had a distinctly dogmatic purpose. It is significant because the whole narrative centres upon the importance of Andrew, about whom so little is recorded in the canonical Gospels. It is practically certain that no historical importance can be attached to the legends included in this book. Andrew appears to have been chosen as a symbol for propaganda purposes. Since no hint is given in the canonical Acts about Andrew's missionary activities, it was an easy matter to resort to imagination to fill in the lacunae. The Gnostic Acts of Andrew set those activities in Asia Minor and Greece, while the later Acts of Andrew and Matthias placed them in Scythia. The location is not a matter of great importance, but the arbitrary character of the selection throws some light on the mental processes by which this series of apocryphal books were produced. In the same vein is the creation of a number of speeches in which Andrew verbosely addresses various people and even things (as for instance his cross). Historical probability was not a high priority for this author.

The book is of interest because of its connection with the other early apocryphal Acts. Indeed, G. Quispel[2] has dated this book before the Acts of Paul, in certain scenes of which he thinks an imitation of the Acts of Andrew can be found. In this case an orthodox apocryphal Acts is seen to have imitated a Gnosticizing one.

[1] Cf. P. M. Peterson's study, *Andrew, Brother of Simon Peter* (1963). Cf. also G. Quispel, *VC* 10 (1956), pp. 129–48; and J. Barns, *JTS* ns 11 (1960), pp. 63–70.

[2] *Op. cit.*, p. 147.

General Considerations on these Acts

These samples of apocryphal Acts were the prelude of a mass of literary productions of a similar kind. With the Acts of Thomas they were formed into a corpus by the Manichaeans and substituted for the canonical Acts.[1] In addition to these, the numerous minor Acts, produced during the later period, are testimony to the fertile although often dull imagination of Christian romancers. They show the ease with which the mental atmosphere, which was peculiarly adapted to foster the spread of fictitious stories about the apostles and the use of pseudepigraphy, could and did develop. The main features of the earlier works may be summarized as follows:

(i) They are mainly associated with the major apostles, although there was a strong tendency at a later period to develop narratives to satisfy the curiosity of Christians regarding the subsequent history of other apostles and even of their disciples.[2]

(ii) They were undoubtedly modelled on the canonical Acts as far as their narrative form, but the parallels are often very loose. In narratives about the apostles other than Peter or Paul, the pseudepigraphic authors had no canonical precedent and could therefore give free play to their imagination.

(iii) As in the case of the apocryphal gospels there is a heightening of the miraculous and a glossing over of the human weakness of the apostolic wonder-workers.[3]

(iv) In some of these Acts no dogmatic purpose is clear, but in the majority it is dominant. Even where no heretical tendencies can be traced, as in the Acts of Paul, certain practices of an unorthodox kind may be discerned (e.g baptism by women).

(v) The pseudonymous device is confined mostly to speeches attributed in the first person to the apostolic hero. But this has been accounted for by the conventions of ancient historiography.

(vi) Some of the extra-canonical material may reflect genuine tradition, although it is seldom possible to indicate its extent. The portrait of Paul in the Acts of Paul furnishes an example of this.

(vii) Fictitious names are freely introduced, but they are mostly unconnected with the canonical personalia. Where persons known from

---

[1] M. R. James, *op. cit.,* p. 228.

[2] A. F. Findlay, *op. cit.,* p. 186, well expressed this point, "The writers of the apostolic romances had little conscience for the facts of history – history, indeed, was not their concern – and their audience, whose appetite was whetted for any tales bearing on the heroic age of the faith, was not disposed to be critical". L. Duchesne, *The Early History of the Church,* I (London, 1909), p. 370, commented, "The curiosity of the little world of Christians led them to give too ready a welcome to Gospels which were not officially recognized and especially to the pious romances about the apostles which claimed to be genuine."

[3] J. Geffcken, *Christliche Apokryphen* (Tübingen, 1908), pp. 25, 26. On the other hand, A. Walker, *Apocryphal Gospels, Acts and Revelations* (Edinburgh, 1870), p. xiii, maintained a distinction on this score, with the Acts containing less of miracle. He explained the difference on the grounds that the Gospels were suited to the *vilis plebecula* and the Acts to the *Academia.* For the "Wundermotive" in the Apocryphal Acts, cf. Blumenthal, *op. cit.,* pp. 144 ff.

Y

canonical sources are mentioned, there are often differences which suggest that the authors did not place much store by "personalia" to achieve acceptance for their works.

II

Pseudepigraphic Epistles. The study of extra-canonical examples of apocryphal epistles has greater importance than that of any other apocryphal Christian writings because of the number of canonical epistles and the number of hypotheses which involve the assumption that pseudepigraphy was a commonly accepted device. And yet, paradoxically, pseudepigraphic letters are fewer in number than the other types, a factor which immediately demands explanation. M. R. James comments, "This form did not find much favour with the makers of apocrypha..... It does appear that the epistle was on the whole too serious an effort for the forger, more liable to detection, perhaps, as a fraud, and not so likely to gain the desired popularity as a narrative or an Apocalypse. Certain it is that our apocryphal epistles are few and not impressive".[1] Those which James includes number six: the Letters of Christ and Abgarus, the Letter of Lentulus, the Epistle to the Laodiceans, the Correspondence between Paul and Seneca, the Epistle of the Apostles and 3 Corinthians (included in the Acts of Paul). Of these only the two Pauline letters and the Epistle of the Apostles merit consideration for our purpose, for these alone with any probability are sufficiently early to warrant examination. Besides being later, the others make little attempt to conform to the accepted epistolary form, which may suggest that later pseudepigraphists were more interested in the pseudonymous ascription than the literary form. The correspondence between Paul and Seneca is notable in this respect, for the letters are not shaped according to the pattern we should expect, and there is not the remotest similarity between the literary style of either men and these poorly produced counterfeits. Their later popularity is but the measure of popular credulity, although it should not be forgotten that even Jerome included Seneca in his catalogue of Christian authors, presumably on the strength of this correspondence.

(a) *Third Corinthians.* This spurious epistle is being examined apart from its original context in the Acts of Paul because of its later separate circulation in the Syriac-speaking church, where it even appears to have achieved some sort of canonicity for a time. It has recently been suggested by M. Testuz,[2] who has published the Bodmer Greek text of the Corinthian correspondence that 3 Corinthians had an independent history and was later incorporated into the Acts of Paul. If this theory were correct, it would provide an example of an orthodox anti-heretical pseudepigraphical

[1] *Op. cit.*, p. 476.
[2] M. Testuz, *Papyrus Bodmer* X (1959).

epistle. But it is more probable that the author of the Acts of Paul was himself the creator of this correspondence. Ephraem commented on it and placed it on a level with the other Pauline epistles. It is therefore an example of a definite pseudepigraphon which not only possessed a popular appeal, but also received the favour of a notable Eastern Father. Yet the fact that it was placed among the Pauline Epistles suggests that its pseudepigraphical character was not suspected and its Pauline claims treated as genuine.

In this epistle the author's motive for producing it is transparent. It is placed in an historical setting in the Acts of Paul, which sufficiently accounts for its appearance. Paul is represented as at Philippi when he received a letter from the Corinthian church, which is troubled about two false teachers, one of whom is significantly named Simon (no doubt an allusion to Simon Magus, reputed father of all Christian heresies). This introductory letter lists six erroneous doctrines being propagated. (i) The prophets must not be used, (ii) God is not Almighty, (iii) There shall be no resurrection of the flesh, (iv) Man is not made by God, (v) Christ is not come in the flesh, nor was born of Mary, and (vi) The world is not born of God but of the angels.[1] It is not difficult to recognize in this description the tenets of certain Gnostic sects, and the spurious Pauline epistle is clearly designed to answer these false assertions. It looks as if the author is transferring to the Corinthians the problems of his own age and is purporting to give the answer that he imagines Paul would have given. If this is a true account of the author's purpose, it would supply a valuable support for the theory that certain New Testament epistles were produced with a similar aim (e.g. the Pastorals). But the author's methods as well as his motives must be taken into account.

The most important consideration is to discover the extent to which the author attempts to approximate to Pauline literary style and teaching. He begins well; the opening phrase ("Paul, a prisoner of Jesus Christ") is identical with Philemon 1 (cf. also Eph. 3:1), while the addressees are described in words parallel to Colossians 1:2 ("the brethren in Corinth"). But the use of $X\alpha\iota\rho\epsilon\iota\nu$[2] in the opening salutation shows that the author's imitative purpose is not strong, for this does not occur in Paul's epistles at all. After this the epistle shows little direct contact with Paul's epistles until towards the end, although there are many phrases which may be mental echoes of the author's acquaintance with these epistles. For instance, "in the midst of many tribulations" might echo 2 Corinthians 1:4 ($\epsilon\pi\grave{\iota}$ $\pi\acute{\alpha}\sigma\eta$ $\tau\hat{\eta}$ $\theta\lambda\acute{\iota}\psi\epsilon\iota$ $\acute{\eta}\mu\hat{\omega}\nu$) or 6:4 ($\grave{\epsilon}\nu$ $\theta\lambda\acute{\iota}\psi\epsilon\sigma\iota\nu$, $\grave{\epsilon}\nu$ $\grave{\alpha}\nu\acute{\alpha}\gamma\kappa\alpha\iota\varsigma$, $\grave{\epsilon}\nu$ $\sigma\tau\epsilon\nu\upsilon\chi\omega\rho\acute{\iota}\alpha\iota\varsigma$) or perhaps an even closer parallel in 2 Corinthians 2:4, where Paul says that he wrote to the Corinthians $\grave{\epsilon}\kappa$ $\pi\upsilon\lambda\lambda\hat{\eta}\varsigma$ $\theta\lambda\acute{\iota}\psi\epsilon\omega\varsigma$. If 2

---

[1] Cf. M. R. James, *op. cit.*, p. 289.
[2] Cited from Harnack's reconstructed Greek text in Kleine Texte, *Apokrypha IV, Die apokryphen Briefe des Paulus an die Laodicener und Korinther* (Bonn, 1905), p. 13.

Corinthians 2:4 was in the author's mind, he may be providing a lost epistle; but this must remain conjectural, since we do not know his interpretation of this verse. It is unlikely that he had unravelled the complicated Corinthian problem or was even aware of its existence. He may well have thought it proper to make some allusion to θλίψις in a Pauline letter. Other echoes from Paul's epistles are: – "The teachings of the evil one" (cf. 1 Tim. 4:1): "them that falsify his words" (3) (cf. 2 Cor. 2:17, 4:2): "for I delivered to you in the beginning the things which I received (4) (cf. 1 Cor. 15:3, almost verbatim); "of the seed of David according to the flesh" (5) (cf. Rom. 1:3); "that he might come down into this world and redeem all flesh by his flesh" (6) (cf. 1 Tim. 1:15, Tit. 2:14, Gal. 1:4); "quickened by adoption" (8) (cf. Rom. 8:11, 15, 23, Gal. 4:4, 5); "the temple of righteousness in his body" (17) (cf. 1 Cor. 3:17, Eph. 2:21); "children of wrath" (19) (cf. Eph. 2:3); "flee from their doctrine" (21) (cf. Eph. 2:5, 6; Col 3:6); these are all phrases which may well have formed part of the author's stock phraseology, culled subconsciously from Paul's epistles but revealing no sustained effort at verbal or stylistic imitation. It is rather different in the long passage from 24–33, where direct indebtedness to 1 Corinthians 15 seems unmistakable. In 24 the author speaks of those who say there is no resurrection of the flesh (cf. 1 Cor. 15:12); in 26 he uses the analogy of seeds (cf. 1 Cor. 15:35 ff), while in 33 the phrase occurs "at the sound of the trumpet, in the twinkling of an eye" (cf. 1 Cor. 15:52). In this passage Matthew's gospel is also echoed in the citing of the incident of Jonah (29, 30) (cf. Matt. 12:40) and in the expression, "How much more, O you of little faith" (31, 32) (cf. Matt. 6:30). In the concluding section, 34–40, a few echoes of Pauline phrases occur, the most notable being in 35, "for I bear these bonds that I may win Christ, and I therefore bear his marks in my body that I might attain to the resurrection of the dead", which is clearly a conflation of Philippians 3:8, 11 and Galatians 6:17. The same passage in Galatians may have provided the idea of "rule" in 36 (cf. Gal. 6:16) and the expression "let no man trouble me" in 34 (cf. Gal. 6:17). The idea of God as witness in 34 may be compared with Romans 1:9, and I Thessalonians 2:5.[1]

This survey of Pauline parallels has brought to light some interesting data about this early pseudo-Paulinist's method of compilation. The influence of the genuine Corinthian epistles is, as we should expect, stronger than that of any other epistles. Whereas isolated echoes from several others are probable, the author does not show a deep acquaintance with them. Moreover, he does not model the form of his letter on any canonical example. It is surprising, for instance, that he does not approximate more closely to 1 and 2 Corinthians, although the differences between those two

---

[1] It is significant that the author does not make Paul speak in the first person except in phrases which seem to be directly echoed from his epistles. The only possible exception is that in which he makes Paul say, "I marvel not if the teachings of the evil one run abroad apace" (2).

epistles would provide some safeguard against the detection of obvious deviations. Apart from the introductory statement about Paul being a prisoner and an allusion to his tribulations, there are no conscious attempts to maintain his identity. In this case, no doubt, the author would hardly have considered it necessary since the narrative in the Acts of Paul itself supplies the setting, unless the epistle was produced independent of and prior to the narrative.

If the expected Pauline phraseology is largely lacking, the same is true of the characteristic Pauline teaching. It is not merely a lack of some of the great Pauline concepts, which need not be imported into every letter that Paul wrote, but the poverty of the ideas which are attributed to him. Although the Corinthians' own letter raises issues of fundamental importance, there is only the most meagre attempt at a doctrinal answer. Indeed, there is no real conception of how Paul would have tackled the problem. Each point raised by the Corinthians is touched upon but there is no grappling with essential issues as we should expect from Paul. The whole attempt reveals the author's pathetic lack of spiritual stature. Even in that part which shows closest acquaintance with Paul, i.e. the part dealing with the resurrection, the author has weakened the apostle's incomparable argument with an allusion to Jonah. It is not without justification that P. Wendland[1] called this epistle, together with that to the Laodiceans, "paltry and clumsy"; and there are few who would dispute this opinion. The majority of early Christians were not deceived by its pseudo-apostolicity, and even its Syrian "canonicity" was certainly short-lived since soon after the time of Ephraem the Syrian church rejected it.[2]

(b) *The Epistle to the Laodiceans.* In the Muratorian Fragment a statement occurs regarding two works spuriously attributed to Paul, which is full of significance for our present purpose. "Fertur etiam ad Laudicenses, alia ad Alexandrinos Pauli nomine finctae ad heresem Marcionis et alia plura quae in catholica ecclesia recipi non potest".[3] ("For there is also one to the Laodiceans, another to the Alexandrians, forged in the name of Paul for Marcion's heresy and several others which cannot be received in the Catholic church"). It is therefore certain that pseudepigraphic Pauline epistles were circulating during the second century A.D., although none of these have been preserved. Nothing is known of the letter to the Alexandrians, but differences of opinion exist regarding that to the Laodiceans. It can hardly be the epistle still extant under that name, for that epistle was not forged in the interests of Marcionism. It contains nothing which would have advanced Marcion's cause; and had the anonymous author of the fragment

---

[1] *Die urchristlichen Literaturformen* (Tübingen, 1912), p. 301, "dürftig und ungeschickt".
[2] It found no place in the Peshitta.
[3] Cited from Souter's text, *The Text and Canon of the New Testament* (2nd edit., C. S. C. Williams, 1954), p. 192. For the Latin text and English translation conveniently set side by side, cf. D. Theron's *Evidence of Tradition* (London, 1957), pp. 107 ff.

been acquainted with this colourless Pauline pseudepigraphon he could not have added, "fel enim cum melle misceri non congruit" (for gall ought not to be mixed with honey). There seems to be a distinct cleavage between the Marcionite and Catholic approaches to the pseudonymous device. "Pauli nomine finctae" makes it clear that the church which the Fragment represents (no doubt Rome) could never accept forgeries and was far from regarding the practice of pseudepigraphy as a literary convention. The incongruity of gall and honey no doubt reflects the orthodox attitude towards Marcion's heresy, but the fact remains that literary methods were being used which could never command the respect of the Roman church. An important factor in the present case is the full recognition of the spurious character of the epistles under review. The Fragment tells us nothing about any epistles unwittingly regarded as genuine although really pseudepigraphic, but it clearly suggests that the church was acutely sensitive to forgery (finctae).

Some comments are necessary on the extant epistle to the Laodiceans, as it is occasionally appealed to as a parallel to suggested canonical pseudepigrapha.[1] Harnack[2] dated it most probably before the middle of the third century. M. R. James[3] suggested that the word "finctae" might have been singular in the original text and would then apply only to the Epistle to the Alexandrians, in which case it would be possible to link the other reference with our extant epistle to the Laodiceans and date it during the second century. Harnack's[4] opinion of it as the most worthless document which has come to us from the ancient church will be shared by most, although it is mystifying why it commanded such respect in the western church (particularly in England) for a period of more than a thousand years. It is more important as a testimony to the gullibility of the medieval church than for its own sake.

Although its earliest attestation is from the pseudo-Augustinian Speculum, there is evidence that in the time of Jerome, "certain persons read also an Epistle to the Laodiceans but it is rejected by all".[5] In spite of this emphatic rejection, interest in the epistle did not die; and a great variety of Latin MSS representing all the great nations of the West – Italy, Spain, France, Ireland, England, Germany and Switzerland – placed this epistle among the canonical books. With the Renaissance its spuriousness was again fully recognized. The main interest for our present purpose is whether the epistle throws any light on the ingredients of a successful pseudepigraphon.

The motive for the writing is clear enough. The tantalizing reference to

---

[1] Cf. e.g. C. L. Mitton, The Epistle to the Ephesians (Oxford, 1951), p. 116.
[2] Der Laodicenerbrief in Kleine Texte, pp. 2, 3.
[3] Op. cit., p. 478.
[4] Op. cit., p. 3.
[5] Cited by J. B. Lightfoot, The Epistle to the Colossians and to Philemon (London, 1900), p. 291, from Vir. III. 5, "Legunt quidam et ad Laodicenses, sed ab omnibus exploditur."

such an epistle in Colossians 4:16 offered a tempting invitation to would-be pseudonymous authors, and it is easy to see that this extant epistle would supply the missing writing.[1] To some minds a lost epistle by an inspired author is unthinkable, and to supply the lack would be regarded as a real service. Unlike most pseudepigrapha there is no dogmatic motive and the author appears to have been quite artless. M. R. James[2] justly commented that "it is not easy to imagine a more feebly constructed cento of Pauline phrases". This feebleness in the production shows the character of the imitator.[3]

Similarly the author's method of working is clear. He used the genuine Philippian letter as a framework for his own composition, reproducing phrases from it in practically the same order as in the original. These extracts are made from all four chapters of Philippians, interspersed with occasional phrases from other epistles (Galatians, Colossians, the Pastoral epistles).[4] The conclusion is inescapable that the author wrote with a copy of Philippians before him, and that the echoes of other epistles are from memory and arise from a feeble attempt to introduce some variation from his model. This epistle is not strictly an imitation of Paul; it is sheer plagiarism.[5] But the fact that it constitutes so close a reproduction of Pauline phrases was no doubt responsible for its long period of assumed canonicity. It suggests that the closer a pseudepigraphon is to the style and language of its putative author the more successful it is likely to be. This pseudonymous author, dull and uninspired as he was, possessed enough psychological insight to recognize this. But his insight does not appear to have been shared by the general run of pseudepigraphists.

(c) *The Epistle of the Apostles.* In spite of the title of this book it is not strictly epistolary. Quasten[6] calls it an apocalypse. It purports to be a revelation granted by Christ to his disciples; and, except for a brief opening statement (in the Ethiopic text) in the third person, the first plural is used throughout. The authors are named in section two where eleven apostolic names are cited. A peculiarity is the inclusion of both Peter and Cephas (which appear to be used of the same person in canonical sources) and Nathaniel (who is not included in any canonical lists). Moreover, John, not Peter, heads the list.

The author is not well-informed historically, for he couples Archelaus with Pilate as being responsible for the crucifixion. This Archelaus may not be the one mentioned in Matthew 2:22, but the son-in-law of Agrippa I.[7] Even so the chronology is at variance with the Gospel records. The

---

[1] Cf. M. Goguel, *Introduction au Nouveau Testament* IV (Paris, 1925), ii, p. 50 n.

[2] *Op. cit.,* p. 479.

[3] Cf. Goguel, *op. cit.,* p. 438. He calls it "un pur exercise de rhétorique".

[4] For these parallels see Lightfoot, *op. cit.,* pp. 291, 292, and Harnack, *op. cit.,* pp. 4–6.

[5] It should be noted that, as in the case of 3 Corinthians, the only use of the first person occurs in direct echoes of Pauline phrases.

[6] *Patrology,* p. 151.

[7] Cf. J. de Zwaan's article in *Amicitae Corolla* (edited H. G. Wood, 1933), p. 349.

author certainly makes use of the four gospels, especially John. He also appears to have used some non-canonical books, notably the Apocalypse of Peter. It is perhaps noteworthy in this connection that he couples both Peter and Andrew with Thomas as the doubters after the resurrection (section two). Could it be that he was no lover of Peter? It may be that the epistle is an eastern protest against Roman ecclesiastical domination, as de Zwaan[1] maintained.

Paul is brought into the picture with commendation: the Lord is made to foretell not only his future influence, but also his heavenly revelation, (a fact which throws doubt on M. Rist's[2] contention that this passage was designed to refute Marcion's view that Paul's revelation was superior to others). Indeed, Rist maintained that the whole book was intended to combat Marcionism, but Goodspeed[3] regarded it as a kind of apostolic summary for the whole world. For our present study the main importance of the book is that it provides an orthodox example of a group pseudonym which was imitated later by Gnostics.[4]

III

General considerations on pseudepigraphic epistles

It is an important question why the epistolary form was so little favoured in apocryphal works. M. R. James' opinion has already been cited and his threefold suggestion that the epistles were (a) too serious, (b) too easily detected, and (c) less popular than narrative or apocalypses is worthy of further comment.

The first point is probable enough. Epistles give less rein to the author's imagination and restrict him to a too rigid situation. The modern novelist does not often choose the epistolary form, although this has at times been used quite effectively.[5] A continuous narrative of a fictitious kind makes far less demands than an exacting letter, which must bear some similarity to what the putative author might be expected to write. The greater ease of detection may also be readily admitted, for generally speaking there are genuine models with which to compare and where this is true the pseudepigraphist would need to proceed with more ingenuity than most possessed. From the readers' point of view, more scope would be offered for narratives and kindred literature; and the absence of epistolary forms serves to remind us of the type of reading public for whom the pseudepi-

---

[1] *Ibid.*, p. 354.

[2] *Journal of Religion* 22 (1942), p. 45. It should be noted that Simon and Cerinthus are twice mentioned (sections 1, 7): were these symbolic of Marcion and his followers? It is not self-evident.

[3] *A History of Early Christian Literature* (Chicago, 1942), p. 35.

[4] Hennecke-Wilson mention several Gospels attributed to the Twelve, all of which were of Gnostic origin, *New Testament Apocrypha* I (1963), pp. 263 ff.

[5] An example of its use for didactic religious purposes may be seen in C. S. Lewis' *Screwtape Letters*.

grapha were mainly designed, i.e. the less serious and therefore more easily gullible type. Although some other forms of pseudepigrapha may have become literary conventions among Jews and Christians, there is a striking lack of evidence for such a convention in the use of epistles. Against the background of the wide popularity of this form in the Graeco–Roman secular world, its almost complete absence from Jewish and Christian literature is remarkable, and cannot fail to be highly significant in the examination of pseudepigraphic epistolary hypotheses in New Testament criticism.

CHAPTER XXIV

THE FIRST CHAPTER OF THE EPISTLE TO THE ROMANS AND THE MODERN MISSIONARY MOVEMENT

A. F. WALLS

I

There is no telling what may happen when people begin to read the Epistle to the Romans. What happened to Augustine, Luther, Wesley and Barth launched great spiritual movements which have left their mark in world history. But similar things have happened, much more frequently, to very ordinary people as the words of this Epistle came home to them with power.[1]

The explosive effect of the Epistle to the Romans has been as marked in the missionary movement as anywhere else. The number of nineteenth century missionary sermons and appeals based on Romans 10:14 f. alone is beyond calculation. A district secretary of the Church Missionary Society at the middle of the century[2] sees this section as the climax of the epistle. The opening has proved that Jews and Gentiles are equally guilty in God's sight, and thus in equal need of salvation; Paul goes on to state the method of salvation, justification by faith; and then to prove the importance and propriety of its publication to the Gentiles; and by the section 10:11–15, "binds all who have the gospel to send it to them".[3] Half a century later, A. T. Pierson, one of the formative influences on the movement of the 80's and 90's which transformed the size and nature of the European and American missionary forces, was characteristically speaking of Romans 10 as "The unparalleled missionary chapter of the Bible" and, equally characteristically, dividing its content alliteratively as The Market for Missions, the Message of Missions, the Methods of Missions and the Motive for Missions.[4]

Another theme beloved of nineteenth-century preachers was that of Romans 3:29 "Is he not the God of the Gentiles also?" – or, as W. Y. Fullerton insisted, "God is the God of the heathen also".[5] But this affirma-

[1] F. F. Bruce, *The Epistle of Paul to the Romans* TNTC (London, 1963), p. 60.
[2] John Johnson, *Sermons* I (London, 1850), pp. 113 ff.
[3] *Ibid.*, p. 115.
[4] A. T. Pierson, "The Market for Missions" reproduced in *Missionary Sermons: a selection from the discourses delivered on behalf of the Baptist Missionary Society on various occasions* (London, 1925), pp. 185 ff. The sermon was originally delivered in 1903.
[5] W. Y. Fullerton, "The God of the Heathen Also", *ibid.*, pp. 299–310. The sermon was delivered in 1909.

tion proceeds directly from the argument of 1:18 f. about the universality of God's wrath,[1] and the section, especially that which refers specifically to the pagan world (1:18–32) has not unnaturally had a history of its own in missionary thought.

The Christian view of non-Christian religions reflects traditions of thought which have come to be denominated respectively those of "continuity" and "discontinuity",[2] the one stressing God's activity in the world outside the sphere of Scripture or church, recognizing or seeking points of contact between the Biblical revelation and that other activity, as certainly God's own; the other stressing the radical difference between God's redeeming actions in saving history and any system whatever of human thought or life, seeing religion in itself under the judgment of God, sometimes denying any affinity between that revelation and "religion" at all.[3] Both traditions are very ancient, going back to the earliest Christian centuries, arguably both to the New Testament.[4] The representatives of each, with their favourite Scripture passages, have ever claimed to represent the mind of the New Testament; and, further, have supported their views with a wealth of empirical evidence about non-Christian religious thought and life.

II

Romans 1:18 ff., save for the modern debate about the nature and extent of the knowledge of God implied in 1:20, has not been an exegetical battlefield between the traditions in the way provided, for instance, by the missionary content of the Iconium and Areopagus addresses in Acts.[5] Its special place in the missionary movement is due to the fact that at various times people saw there, or thought they saw there, the non-Christian world that they themselves knew; and at other times, assuming these verses to give the origin of non-Christian religion, they were puzzled to account for other features of non-Christian religion which did not apparently accord with such a picture. That Paul's intention in the section as a whole is to show the whole world under judgment has hardly been in

[1] It is inappropriate to argue here the old question (for Calvin discussed a form of it) whether 1:18 – 3:20 is in fact a digression. See C. K. Barrett, *The Epistle to the Romans, BNTC* (London, 1957), p. 33.

[2] These terms were popularized through the discussions at the International Missionary Council Meeting at Tambaram, Madras, in 1938: see especially *The Authority of the Faith* (Tambaram Series I) (London, 1939). Behind the discussions lay Hendrik Kraemer's preparatory volume, *The Christian Message in a Non-Christian World* (London, 1938). See also C. F. Hallencreutz, *Kraemer towards Tambaram: a study in Hendrik Kraemer's Missionary Approach* (Uppsala, 1966).

[3] Cf. on this whole question K. Barth, *Kirchliche Dogmatik* I/2, especially c. 17 (= *Church Dogmatics I: The Doctrine of the Word of God*, part 2 [Edinburgh, 1956], pp. 280–361); A. Th. van. Leeuwen, *Christianity in World History* (London, 1964).

[4] P. Beyerhaus, "Religionen und Evangelium, Kontinuität oder Diskontinuität?" *Evang. Missions Magazin* 3 (1967), pp. 118–135.

[5] Cf. B. Gärtner, *The Areopagus Speech and Natural Revelation* (Uppsala, 1955).

doubt; that the specific details of 1:22–27 reflect a view of contemporary Graeco-Roman society in decadence has usually also been recognized. But what is the relation of these particulars to the general principle? Is Paul simply describing how the seamier side of contemporary pagan society came into being? Or is he describing the origin of all non-Christian religions – perhaps even of religion itself? Does he assume the wilful rejection of an universal primitive monotheism? And – given an answer to any of these – how are the phenomena of non-Christian religion actually in view at the time to be accommodated to it? It is such questions as these, or rather, the assumed answers to them, which underlie much of the debate arising from Christian evangelization.

For the early Christian missionary thinkers, it was not Romans 1 which expressed the most important Christian contact with the non-Christian world. For them pagan society and pagan popular religion was at least broadly similar to that which Paul knew; and the most liberal of them had no desire to declare affinity with it. Justin, who is quite prepared to believe that Socrates and anyone else who spoke according to *logos*, and inasfar as they did so, were Christians before Christ,[1] is also certain that the gods of the street corner are demonic parodies, the direct result of wicked impositions by evil spirits.[2] Such thinkers were much more concerned to maintain their affinity with the philosophical tradition, which for them represented the glory of their inheritance, and which rejected popular religion as strenuously as they did; in fact, it was a mark of the Logos at work in Socrates that he defied popular religion and, like the Christians, was branded an atheist for doing so.[3] Justin, in fact, has reached a place where many another missionary was to come over the next eighteen centuries: he has concluded that there is more than one type of non-Christian tradition. There is that which is palpably devilish; there is that which is compatible with the Gospel and strenuously opposed to what it opposes.

The long period during which Western Europe was almost insulated from the non-Christian world meant that, apart from Jews, the only non-Christian peoples of whom most Christians, at least in the countries which became Protestant, knew much were those same Greeks and Romans, brought to life again by the new learning. Paul's catalogue of loathsomeness could be amply documented from other sources ("Of these abominations thou hast with Lactantius, Eusebius and Augustine", says Calvin).[4] Other sources also revealed that some pagans stood aloof from these abominations: Calvin's first major work, after all, was a commentary on Seneca. But with no regular living contact with a self-consciously non-Christian society, it was easy for Reformed Christians to separate, as the early apologists did, the philosophic from the religious tradition of

[1] *Apology* I. 46.
[2] *Ibid.*, I. 5.
[3] *Ibid.*, I. 6.
[4] In Rom. 1:23.

classical paganism. Romans 1:18 ff. indicated how "idolatry" – i.e., all religion outside Israel and the church – took its origin.

III

When, in North America, contact with a non-Christian people was resumed, there was little reason to question this judgment. As the colonists looked upon the Indians – often with a desire for their salvation[1] – they saw the darkened heart changing the glory of the uncorruptible God into an image, the bodies given up to lust and dishonour plainly enough.[2] There was not even a Seneca. The connexion between ancient and modern heathenism was also apparent:

> Let us inquire into the records of *antiquity*, let us consult the experience of all ages, and we shall find, that those who had no guide but the light of nature, no instructor but unassisted reason, have wandered in perpetual uncertainty, darkness, and error. Or let us take a view of the *present* state of those countries that have not been illuminated by the gospel; and we shall see, that notwithstanding the improvements of near six thousand years, they remain to this day covered with the grossest darkness, and abandoned to the most immoral and vicious practices.[3]

Despite the clear manifestation of the "invisible things of God" some ancient heathen denied his existence, while the rest worshipped His creatures, and "even the most despicable beings in the order of nature".

> This was the state of the Gentile nations when the light of the gospel appeared to scatter the darkness that overspread the face of the earth. And this has been the case, so far as has yet appeared, of all the nations ever since, upon whom the Sun of righteousness has not arisen with healing in his wings. Every new discovered country opens a new scene of astonishing ignorance and barbarity; and gives us fresh evidence of the universal corruption of human nature.[4]

For the preacher of missionary ordination sermons, viewing the Amerindians from without, this was no doubt enough. But those who penetrated more closely into Indian society, while unequivocal in their affirmation of human depravity, saw other factors also. So early a missionary as John Eliot (1604–1690), a man living close to the Indians and learning their language, is struck by the fact that this people, although idolatrous

---

[1] R. Pierce Beaver, *Church, State and the American Indians* (St. Louis, 1966); "American missionary motivation before the Revolution", *Church History* 31 (1962), pp. 216–26.

[2] Joseph Sewall, *Christ Victorious over the powers of darkness ... preached ... at the ordination of the Reverend Mr. Stephen Parker* (Boston, 1733). Reprinted in R. Pierce Beaver, *Pioneers in Mission: the early missionary ordination sermons, charges, and instructions* (Grand Rapids, 1966), pp. 41–64 (see p. 47).

[3] Ebenezer Pemberton, *A Sermon preached in Newark, June 12, 1744 at the ordination of Mr. David Brainerd*. An edition published in New Haven in 1822 has been reprinted in R. Pierce Beaver, *Pioneers in Mission*, pp. 111–24 (see p. 113).

[4] Pemberton, *op. cit.* in *Pioneers in Mission*, p. 114.

and immoral, did believe, despite first appearances, in the Deity; that they believed also in the immortality of the soul, and an eternity of happiness or misery – they even had a tradition of one man who had actually seen God. Eliot, like several of his Puritan colleagues, came to the conclusion that the Indians were a remnant of the ten lost tribes of Israel. This would also explain their food taboos and purification rites, and their story of a general deluge. Over the years an idea with breathtaking implications grew in him: might not the Amerindians be only a fragment of the Semitic peoples who had broken away from the rest? Might not the peoples of India, of China, of Japan also be descended from the ten tribes? Alas then, why do they not all talk Hebrew? Eliot can speak only for his own language, but at least its grammatical frame is nearer to Hebrew than to Latin or Greek. Perhaps Chinese, Japanese, the Indian languages, are all degenerate forms of Hebrew. Perhaps – far more important – the conversion of the Indians, of which his own labours were a pledge, is but the sign that God is going to break eastward for the conversion of Israel, the ten tribes as well as the two?[1]

It is easy to laugh at the enthusiasms of this lonely missionary; but he is grasping at a rationalization of a fact of experience. On a simple reading of Romans 1:18 ff., Indian religion ought to be unrelievedly idolatrous. The presence of other elements can be explained as survivals in debased form of part of the Jewish revelation. Not only so, but in other parts of the world – India, China, Japan – traces of the same redemptive revelation may be found. By elimination, only in Africa, and among other Hamitic peoples, will Romans 1 apply in all its rigour as a picture of religion.[2]

At a later period, Jonathan Edwards, a warm supporter of missions and no stranger to the Indians himself, again finds the truth of Romans 1:18ff. confirmed by his own observations:

> The doctrine of St. Paul, concerning the blindness into which the Gentiles fell, is so confirmed by the state of religion in Africa, America, and even China, where, to this day no advances towards the true religion have been made, that we can no longer be at a loss to judge of the insufficiency of unassisted reason to dissipate the prejudices of the Heathen world, and open their eyes to religious truths.[3]

Whence, then, come such approximations to "religious truths" as any of these may have? Edwards answers, from outside. Heathenism since the fall has been so dark that such a custom as sacrifice for sin could not

---

[1] This aspect of Eliot's thought is well documented by S. H. Rooy, *The Theology of Missions in the Puritan Tradition* (Delft, 1965), pp. 230 ff.

[2] Eliot, however, did not base his missionary work upon this theory, or advocate or practise any restriction of evangelization to his supposed "Semites". The call to preach Christ took precedence over all speculations as to how He would bring in His kingdom. Cf. Rooy, *op. cit.*, p. 235.

[3] Jonathan Edwards, *Works* (1817 edition) VIII, p. 193.

have originated there. It *must* have been derived from the Jews. In the paganism of the old world, Plato, though a lesser philosopher than Socrates, yet knew more than he about true religion. The reason is that Socrates, unlike Plato, never left Greece, and was thus less open to outside influences.[1]

On such an explanation of those elements in non-Christian religion which cannot be ascribed to wilful blindness, it would be, of course, in the devil's interest to isolate peoples as far as possible from infectious contact with revealed religion. And Edwards argues that this actually happened: America was first peopled by the direct action of the devil. Satan, alarmed at the success of the gospel in the first three Christian centuries, surprised by the fall of the heathen Empire in the time of Constantine and fearing that his kingdom might be completely overthrown, led the Indians away into America so that he could keep them for himself.[2]

IV

Meanwhile, in contemporary Europe, far away from the real heathen, the genteel debate about "natural theology" was going forward. The argument of the *consensus gentium* acquired fresh importance. "No nation without belief in God", said the theologian; and the sceptic made answer, "How do you know?"

The evidence of the Jesuit missionaries from China became an absorbing interest. On the face of it, it represented a triumph for orthodoxy, and for the presence of "natural" religion; for here was a people which had allegedly preserved the knowledge of God and obeyed a pure morality for more than two thousand years. Leibnitz, whom we do not usually think of as a herald of the missionary movement, wanted Protestant missionaries to teach revealed religion to the Chinese who had preserved natural religion so effectively. In the end, of course, the other orders defeated the Jesuits on the interpretation of the Chinese texts, and this particular source of evidence for natural theology (which was in any case inconveniently proving too much) passed out of view – though attention was always available for accounts by travellers of the beliefs of non-Christian societies.[3]

Only a small part of the debate about China was concerned with the exegesis of Romans or any other apostolic book; nor, despite the undoubtedly sincere plea of Leibnitz for a Protestant mission, was it really conducted with any idea of doing anything. The Chinese, like the Tahitians later, were being called in to help solve a European problem. By contrast,

[1] Works VIII, 188 ff. Cf. Rooy, *op. cit.*, p. 299.
[2] Rooy, *op. cit.*, p. 300 f.
[3] On views of paganism, cf. F. E. Manuel, *The Eighteenth Century confronts the Gods* (Cambridge, Mass. 1959); on the European debate on the Jesuit evidence, cf. E. L. Allen, "Missions and Theology in the Eighteenth Century," *HJ* 56 (1958), pp. 113–22.

the members and agents of the missionary societies which began to form by the end of the century, were desperately concerned with action: action for the salvation of the souls of those to whom they went. The terms in which men spoke of non-Christian religions were transformed as a result. For one thing, the Evangelical Revival, which underlay the new movement, had brought a more radical view and more vivid sense of the nature of sin; for another, earnest men were transmitting accounts of what they actually saw.

And what they saw was not usually a grave, distant, polite people preserving over thousands of years the knowledge of God and pure morality – the terms of the earlier eighteenth-century debate – but human sacrifice, the immolation of widows, the pictorial representations of *lingam* and *yonni*, cult prostitution, the victims crushed beneath the car of Jagannath. The picture of Romans 1:18 ff., in fact, emerged again, less from a theory of religion than from the effect of observation; and the words and phrases of Romans 1:18 ff. ring out time and again as missionaries view the religion of non-Christian peoples.[1] Further, just as the early apologists shared with the philosophical tradition much of the polemic against popular religion, so the missionaries in India had allies – liberal intellectuals with burning desire for religious reformation, like Rajah Ram Mohan Roy, and angry young men like some of Duff's early converts, rebelling against the traditional practices.[2]

Africa likewise recalled Romans 1 for many observers. David Jonathan East, one of a small host of writers on West Africa in the 1840's, produces an imposing account (based on travellers' tales) of African slavery, drunkenness, immorality and lack of commercial probity. He then quotes Romans 1:28–31. "What an awful comment upon this affecting portion of Holy Writ are the humiliating facts which these and the preceding chapters record."[3] In another place, however, East recognizes that African paganism, though reprehensible, is in one respect different from that of Romans 1. Though African peoples have images, they do not make images of the Supreme God: they simply ignore him for the subordinate divinities and spirits.

[1] Some representative works describing Indian religion may be cited: William Ward, *An account of the Writings, Religion and Manners of the Hindoos*, 4 vols. (Serampore, 1811), 2 vols. (London, 1817) ("It is probable, indeed, that no heathen nation has made a single idol in honour of 'the living and true God', and that direct worship to Him was never offered by any heathen", I, p. xiv); Claudius Buchanan, *Christian Researches in Asia* (London, 1811), and *An Apology for promoting Christianity in India* (London, 1813); A. Duff, *India and Indian Missions, including sketches of the Gigantic System of Hinduism* (Edinburgh, 1839). On the attack on idolatry, cf. K. Ingham, *Reformers in India, 1793–1833* (Cambridge, 1956), pp. 33–54.

[2] George Smith, *The Life of Alexander Duff* (London, 1881), chapters 5–6. For the view of Hinduism of an Indian convert, cf. e.g. K. M. Banerjee, *Dialogues on the Hindu Philosophy* (1861); Nehemiah Goreh, *Rational Refutation of the Hindu Philosophical Systems* (Calcutta, 1862; repr. Madras, 1897).

[3] D. J. East, *Western Africa; its condition and Christianity the means of its recovery* (London, 1844), p. 71. The work is based on a collation of earlier writings.

Thus it appears, that if they have not "changed the glory of the incorruptible God into an image, made like to corruptible man, and to birds, and to four-footed beasts and creeping things – they have, in their view, excluded him from the government of his world, and substituted in his room the wild creatures of their own imaginations, identifying these professedly spiritual existences with what is material, and oft times grossly absurd.[1]

African paganism thus demonstrates the principles of Romans 1:18 ff., but identity in detail is not demanded.[2]

V

As the nineteenth century proceeded, such missionary views came into contact, and sometimes collision, with new patterns of thought. There was the new interest, itself partly a result of the missionary movement,[3] in the literature of Eastern religions. There was the regnant hypothesis, held with all the intensity of a new found faith, of the evolution of religion. There was the whole new science, with evolution as its basis, of anthropology, and The Golden Bough to link them all together.

There were many points of conflict. The missionary affirmation of the idea of a supreme God was immediately suspect; for animistic peoples who had not reached the appropriate stage, such a conception could only be a missionary invention. The charge was quite unjustified, for, on the reading of Romans 1 which most early missionaries had, there was no need to invent a High God in any non-Christian religion. They found the High God in African religion because he was there, not because their theology demanded his presence.

As the evolutionist doctrine gained repute, the rival doctrine of a primitive monotheism, from which all non-Biblical religions were descended, was more clearly enunciated, and Romans 1:20 ff. was its prime source. Sir Monier Monier Williams, an influential Sanskrit scholar and himself a devout Evangelical, argued that, just because of the original monotheism behind all religions, one could expect to find fragments of truth.[4] No longer was it necessary to presuppose borrowing from Jewish sources to explain every acceptable element in non-Christian religion. At

---

[1] East, op. cit., p. 148.

[2] The existence of a conception of a Supreme God in African traditional religion, spoken of but not regularly worshipped, was frequently recognized by early nineteenth-century observers. Cf. J. Beecham, Ashantee and the Gold Coast (London, 1841), chapter 7.

[3] The greatest name is, of course, that of Friedrich Max Müller, certainly no pillar of evangelical orthodoxy or pattern of missionary zeal; but Sir Monier Monier Williams, Professor of Sanskrit at Oxford from 1860, was closely associated with the missionary movement, and James Legge, Professor of Chinese there from 1875 had been a missionary with the London Missionary Society in China. Missionary reports, studies and researches were un-doubtedly a major contributory factor to the discovery by the West of Eastern religious literature.

[4] M. Monier Williams, Indian Wisdom, or Examples of the religious, philosophical and ethical doctrines of the Hindus (London, 1875), pp. 143 f. (4th edn., p. 132 n.).

Z

one point he went further, and declared that some of the essential doctrines of Christianity were present in germ in all religions, awaiting the
development and fulfilment which only Christianity could bring.[1]

It was possible, however, to affirm a primitive monotheism without
drawing all these conclusions. Principal (later Bishop) Moule, a deep
influence on scores of the new type of missionary who went out in such
numbers in the 1880's, gave exegetical backing to such a view.[2] The great
Johannes Warneck was among those who observed in paganism a memory
tenuous and not understood, of the primeval revelation:

> Dispassionate study of heathen religions confirms Paul's view that heathenism
> is a fall from a better knowledge of God.

In early days humanity had a greater treasure of spiritual goods, but neglected its knowledge and renounced its dependence until nothing remained
but a dim presentiment.[3] Not that all saw anything as formalized as a
primitive monotheism in Romans 1. A. E. Garvie, a formative influence
on several important missionary writers of the twentieth century, argued
that the essence of Paul's argument had nothing to do with the origin of
religions at all but simply with the "close connexion between false views of
God and wrong standards of duty", and that the Roman society of which
Paul was primarily speaking had, to common knowledge, suffered a decline.[4]

In fact, one arm at least of the missionary movement began to develop
the line of argument indicated, though later repudiated, by Monier
Williams. Long years of study of the classics of Eastern religions indicated
that Christianity was in fact their fulfilment – the "crown", to use the
expression of the outstanding protagonist of this school, John Nicol
Farquhar.[5] To pass from Duff's description of e.g. Hinduism to Farquhar's is to move to a different world. Yet each is describing exactly what
he saw. Of course, time had brought changes – some of what Duff had

---

[1] M. Monier Williams, *Modern India and the Indians* (London, 1887), p. 234. For this position,
which Williams eventually rejected, cf. E. J. Sharpe, *Not to Destroy but to Fulfil* (Uppsala,
1965), pp. 50 ff.

[2] "The believer in the holy Scriptures . . . will receive this view of the primeval history of
Theism as a true report of God's account of it. Remembering that it concerns an otherwise
unknown moment of human spiritual history, he will not be disturbed by alleged evidence
against it from lower down the stream." H. C. G. Moule, *The Epistle of Paul to the Romans*
(Expositor's Bible) (London, 1893), p. 45. Cf. also his Cambridge Bible commentary (1879) on
Rom. 1:21.

[3] Quoted by S. M. Zwemer, *The Influence of Animism on Islam* (London, 1920). Cf. J.
Warneck, *The Living Forces of the Gospel* (E.T. Edinburgh, n.d.), p. 98: "The heart of the
heathen is like a palimpsest, the original writing of which is written over and become unseen.
No one knows anything of the words of wisdom covered over there." Andrew Lang's theory
of the High Gods, developed in opposition to the nature-myth school, took its origin from
missionary reports. See W. Schmidt, *The Origin and Growth of Religion* (E.T. London, 1935),
pp. 172 ff.

[4] A. E. Garvie, *Romans,* Century Bible, *ad loc.*

[5] J. N. Farquhar, *The Crown of Hinduism* (Oxford, 1913). See E. J. Sharpe, *op. cit., passim.*

seen had gone for ever. But the main difference lies in the fact that Far-quhar had, as it were, met Seneca.

Farquhar's series "The Religious Quest" (the singular is significant) reveals the sources of change. Sydney Cave is thoroughly representative of the contributors when he declares that the first missionaries were dis-qualified from seeing the best in the non-Christian world because the sacred books were closed to them. When one looks at, for instance, the Saivite Temple in Tanjore one can understand the violent reactions of the pioneers; but the Hinduism we now face (1919) is very different from that of a century ago. "We are concerned with the 'Higher Hinduism'. Idol-atry is doomed."[1]

Such judgments and such a viewpoint on Hinduism was the fruit of the study of its literature. It is thus hardly surprising that when the World Missionary Conference of 1910 came to discuss "points of contact" and "preparation for Christianity" in the religions, it was on Animism, which has no literature, that there was most hesitation.[2]

As we have seen, Monier Williams came to retract his idea of a develop-ment of religions with Christianity as the crown; his last position stressed that a gulf – "not a mere rift across which the Christian and non-Christian may shake hands and interchange similar ideas in regard to essential truths" – lay between the Bible and the "so-called Sacred Books of the East".

> Be fair, be charitable, be Christ-like, but let there be no mistake. Let it be made absolutely clear that Christianity cannot, must not be watered down to suit the palate of either Hindu, Parsee, Confucianist, Buddhist, or Mohammedan, and that whosoever wishes to pass from the false religion to the true can never hope to do so by the rickety planks of compromise . . .[3]

He spoke to the depths. For many missionaries the practical way of expressing an attitude to the religions came to be that, while elements of good remained, the *systems* stood condemned.

VI

It would be inappropriate here to take the story through Tambaram and beyond, though the Epistle to the Romans has always been in

---

[1] S. Cave, *Redemption, Hindu and Christian* (Oxford, 1919).

[2] *World Missionary Conference, Edinburgh 1910: Report of Commission IV. The Missionary Message in Relation to Non-Christian Religions.* See especially ch. 2: "Some deny the existence of any point of contact, or preparation for Christianity in any of the beliefs and rites of Animism – it may be noted that these witnesses find practically no religious content in Animism. . . ." Cf. Warneck, *op. cit.,* pp. 85 ff. On the other hand, in 1900 an African Christian, the Rev. (later Bishop) James Johnson was telling missionary-minded students that Africa "is conscious of the existence of God, believes in that existence, believes in divine providence, believes that every good and perfect gift comes from above, from Him who is the Father of us all. . . . Africa desires and intends to worship Him, but she knows not how to do it." (In *Students and the Missionary Problem* [London, 1900], pp. 74 f.).

[3] E. Stock, *History of the Church Missionary Society* III (London, 1899), p. 304.

the background, and occasionally, as in the controversy over 1:20, right in its forefront. The traditions of continuity and discontinuity will, no doubt, continue to lock horns in the missionary debate, and the Epistle to the Romans will continue to challenge, quicken and rebuke those who desire to declare the righteousness of God. As one reviews the place which the first chapter has hitherto had in the thought of the missionary movement, some features stand out which indicate its continuing relevance.

Christian evangelists have found themselves addressing men in societies with coherent patterns of thought – within systems of belief and activity. It has been convenient to provide names like "Buddhism" and "Hinduism" to cover numbers of these systems. The validity of this process is not a theme to discuss here; but at least we should not talk as if Paul used them himself. Perhaps too much of the debate about continuity or discontinuity has been concerned with systems. As a result, we have men, each genuinely describing what he saw, producing such different interpretations of "Hinduism" as those of Duff and Farquhar. When this is introduced into the context of Romans 1, we have one party inviting all to recognize that these non-Christian religions lie manifestly under the wrath of God for their manifest deeds, and another pointing to particular persons, books or doctrines, and saying in effect (as Bishop Ryle said of the necessity of baptism by immersion for Eskimos), Let those believe it who can.

Argument about which is the correct, or the more correct, picture of "Hinduism" is beside the point in the light of Romans 1:18 ff., for Paul's concern here is not with systems at all, but with men. It is *men* who hold down the truth in unrighteousness, who do not honour God, who are given up to dishonourable passions. It is upon men, who commit ungodly and wicked deeds, that the wrath of God is revealed.

As systems, and ultimately the collective labels for systems which we call the world religions, have slipped into the place of ungodly men in the interpretation of Romans 1, so Christianity, also conceived as a system, has sometimes slipped into the place of the righteousness of God. The true system has been opposed to false systems condemned there. It has sometimes, but not always, been realized that "Christianity" is a term formally identical with the other labels; that it certainly covers as wide a range of phenomena as most of them; that, if the principalities and powers work within human systems, they can and do work within this one. Man-in-Christianity lies under the wrath of God just as much, and for the same reasons, as Man-in-Hinduism. It was the realization of this which saved the earliest generations of the modern missionary movement from the worst sort of paternalism. Man was vile everywhere, not only in Ceylon. The Christian preacher had the same message of *repentance* and faith for the non-Christian world as he had been preaching in the Christian world;[1] for it was not Christianity that saves, but Christ.

This in turn relates to another point: the close connexion of Romans 2 with Romans 1. The "diatribe" form of Romans 1–2 has often been remarked, as has the indebtedness of the language to Wisdom 13–14 and its closeness to the normal, accepted Jewish polemic against idolatry.[2] The thrust of Romans 1 lies in Romans 2; not in the origin of paganism but in the hopelessness of the virtuous. And, before going on to show the free acceptance of men of all kinds through faith in Christ, Paul offers (Rom. 2:17 ff.) a satirical commentary on Diaspora Judaism's understanding of its mission. Here was a busy, missionizing people: a guide to the blind, a light to those that sit in darkness, a corrector of the foolish, a teacher of children – the Wisdom of the opening chapters of Proverbs and the Servant of Isaiah 42 rolled into one – who yet for all their exaltation of the Decalogue, stole, committed adultery and sacrilege, and, as the Scripture said about the Jews of an earlier time, caused the heathen to blaspheme the name of God because of what they saw in his people. Some sharp things have been said from time to time to missionaries. Some of them are in the New Testament.

[1] Cf. e.g. Sewell's sermon in Beaver, *op. cit.*, quoted above. The missionary preacher's task is identical with that of the congregational minister.

[2] Cf. Bruce, *op. cit.*, p. 86, on 21:16: "We can almost envisage him as he dictates his letter to Tertius, suddenly picking out the complacent individual who has been enjoying the exposure of these sins he 'has no mind to', and telling him that he is no better than anyone else".

INDEXES

INDEX OF MAIN SUBJECTS TREATED

INDEX OF MODERN AUTHORS

INDEX OF REFERENCES TO HOLY SCRIPTURE AND TO OTHER ANCIENT WRITINGS

A. THE OLD TESTAMENT

B. THE APOCRYPHA AND PSEUDEPIGRAPHA OF THE OLD TESTAMENT

C. THE NEW TESTAMENT

AA